POSTCARDS

FROM

ARIZONA

Marble Canyon and the Colorado River, viewed from the less explored North Rim of the Grand Canyon. See chapter 6. © David Muench/Tony Stone Images.

The Desert Botanical Garden in Phoenix is exclusively devoted to cacti and other desert plants. See chapter 4. © John Elk III Photography.

Horseback riding in the Superstition Mountains, which, according to legend, harbor a lost gold mine. See chapter 4. © John Elk III Photography.

The Organ Pipe Cactus is a national monument in one of Arizona's least visited and most remote areas. See chapter 10. © Tom Bean/Tony Stone Images.

Arizona draws countless visitors for its golfing alone. See chapter 1 for our favorite courses.
© *Richard Maack/Adstock Photos.*

Biking in Oak Creek Canyon, near Sedona. Sedona offers some of the best outdoor access of any city in the Southwest. See chapter 5. © Michael Shedlock/New England Stock.

A mile deep, 277 miles long, and up to 18 miles wide, the Grand Canyon is Arizona's number one attraction—and it never fails to inspire. See chapter 6. Opposite: Mule riders descend to the bottom. © Tom Bean/Tony Stone Images. Top: Whitewater rafting on the Colorado River. © Dewitt Jones Productions. Bottom: A magnificent view of the canyon from Cape Solitude on the South Rim. © Chuck Lawsen/Adstock Photos.

Native American crafts are ubiquitous in the Four Corners region. See chapter 7 for a primer. Top photo: Navajo rugs, like these at the famous Hubbell Trading Post, take hundreds of hours to make. © John Elk III Photography. Bottom photo: Navajo turquoise jewelry. © Dave Bartruff Photography.

A Hopi Kachina doll, used to bring rain and ensure health, happiness, long life, and harmony in the universe. See chapter 7. © John Elk III Photography.

The dramatic landscape of Monument Valley is a favorite backdrop for Hollywood and television directors. See chapter 7. © John Elk III Photography.

The 37-mile-long Paria Canyon trailhead follows the meandering route of a narrow slot canyon for much of its length. See chapter 7. © James Kay/Adstock Photos.

Betatakin, an Anasazi cliff dwelling, is part of the Navajo National Monument. See chapter 7.
© Dewitt Jones Productions.

The popular Lake Powell, created by the damming of the Colorado River at Glen Canyon,
is a strange oasis in the middle of hundreds of miles of parched desert land. See chapter 7.
© Nik Wheeler Photography.

Trout fishing in the Black River, near Alpine—the Alps of Arizona. See chapter 8.
© *Richard Maack/Adstock Photos.*

A spiral petroglyph in Saguaro National Park, near Tucson. See chapter 9. © David Muench/ Tony Stone Images.

The desert provides the perfect environment for hot-air ballooning—cool, still air and wide-open spaces. See chapters 4, 5, and 9 for ballooning companies in Phoenix, Sedona, and Tucson. © Michael R. Stoklos/Adstock Photos.

The Petrified Forest was once a vast, humid swamp. See chapter 7. © *Phil Degginger/Tony Stone Images.*

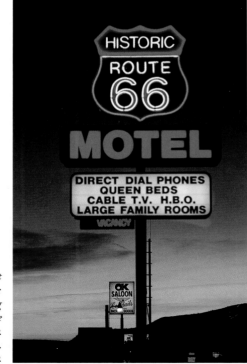

Legendary Route 66 symbolizes a lost America. See chapters 7 and 11. Above: The Wigwam Motel has been causing double takes along Route 66 since the 1940s. © John Elk III Photography. Right: A self-conscious motel sign. © Nik Wheeler Photography.

When should I travel to get the best airfare?
Where do I go for answers to my travel questions?
What's the best and easiest way to plan and book my trip?

frommers.travelocity.com

Frommer's, the travel guide leader, has teamed up with **Travelocity.com**, the leader in online travel, to bring you an in-depth, easy-to-use resource designed to help you plan and book your trip online.

At **frommers.travelocity.com**, you'll find free online updates about your destination from the experts at Frommer's plus the outstanding travel planning and purchasing features of Travelocity.com. Travelocity.com provides reservations capabilities for 95 percent of all airline seats sold, more than 47,000 hotels, and over 50 car rental companies. In addition, Travelocity.com offers more than 2,000 exciting vacation and cruise packages. Travelocity.com puts you in complete control of your travel planning with these and other great features:

    Expert travel guidance from Frommer's - over 150 writers reporting from around the world!

    Best Fare Finder - an interactive calendar tells you when to travel to get the best airfare

    Fare Watcher - we'll track airfare changes to your favorite destinations

    Dream Maps - a mapping feature that suggests travel opportunities based on your budget

    Shop Safe Guarantee - 24 hours a day / 7 days a week live customer service, and more!

Whether traveling on a tight budget, looking for a quick weekend getaway, or planning the trip of a lifetime, Frommer's guides and Travelocity.com will make your travel dreams a reality. You've bought the book, now book the trip!

Frommer's®

Arizona
2001

by Karl Samson

with Jane Aukshunas

IDG Books Worldwide, Inc.
An International Data Group Company
Foster City, CA • Chicago, IL • Indianapolis, IN • New York, NY

ABOUT THE AUTHORS

Karl Samson and **Jane Aukshunas,** husband-and-wife travel-writing team, find that the sunny winter skies of the Arizona desert are the perfect antidote to the dreary winters of their Pacific Northwest home. Each winter they flee the rain to explore Arizona's deserts, mountains, cities, and small towns. It is the state's unique regional style, Native American cultures, abundance of contemporary art, and, of course, the boundless landscapes that keep the duo fascinated by Arizona. Summers find the team researching their other books, including *Frommer's Washington, Frommer's Oregon,* and *Frommer's Seattle & Portland.*

IDG BOOKS WORLDWIDE, INC.

An International Data Group Company
909 Third Avenue
New York, NY 10022

Find us online at **www.frommers.com**

ISBN 0-7645-6115-4
ISSN 1053-2471

Editor: Myka Carroll
Production Editor: Donna Wright
Photo Editor: Richard Fox
Design by Michele Laseau
Staff Cartographers: John Decamillis, Roberta Stockwell, Elizabeth Puhl
Production by IDG Books Indianapolis Production Department

SPECIAL SALES

For general information on IDG Books Worldwide's books in the U.S., please call our Consumer Customer Service department at 1-800-762-2974. For reseller information, including discounts, bulk sales, customized editions, and premium sales, please call our Reseller Customer Service department at 1-800-434-3422.

Manufactured in the United States of America

5   4   3   2   1

Contents

List of Maps

An Invitation to the Reader

In researching this book, we discovered many wonderful places—hotels, restaurants, shops, and more. We're sure you'll find others. Please tell us about them, so we can share the information with your fellow travelers in upcoming editions. If you were disappointed with a recommendation, we'd love to know that, too. Please write to:

Frommer's Arizona 2001
IDG Books Worldwide, Inc.
909 Third Avenue
New York, NY 10022

An Additional Note

Please be advised that travel information is subject to change at any time—and this is especially true of prices. We therefore suggest that you write or call ahead for confirmation when making your travel plans. The authors, editors, and publisher cannot be held responsible for the experiences of readers while traveling. Your safety is important to us, however, so we encourage you to stay alert and be aware of your surroundings. Keep a close eye on cameras, purses, and wallets, all favorite targets of thieves and pickpockets.

What the Symbols Mean

✪ **Frommer's Favorites**

Our favorite places and experiences—outstanding for quality, value, or both.

The following abbreviations are used for credit cards:

AE	American Express	EURO	Eurocard
CB	Carte Blanche	JCB	Japan Credit Bank
DC	Diners Club	MC	MasterCard
DISC	Discover	V	Visa
ER	EnRoute		

Find Frommer's Online

www.frommers.com offers up-to-the-minute listings on almost 200 cities around the globe—including the latest bargains and candid, personal articles updated daily by Arthur Frommer himself. No other Web site offers such comprehensive and timely coverage of the world of travel.

The Best of Arizona

Planning a trip to a state as large and diverse as Arizona involves a lot of decision-making (other than which golf clubs to take), so in this chapter we've tried to give you some direction. Below we've chosen what we feel is the very best the state has to offer—the places and experiences you won't want to miss. Although places and activities listed here are written up in more detail elsewhere in this book, this chapter should give you an overview of Arizona's highlights and get you started planning your trip.

1 The Best Scenic Drives

- **Apache Trail** (east of Phoenix): Much of this winding road, which passes just north of the Superstition Mountains, is unpaved and follows a rugged route once ridden by Apaches. This is some of the most remote country you'll find in the Phoenix area, with far-reaching desert vistas and lots to see and do along the way. See chapter 4.
- **Oak Creek Canyon** (Sedona): Slicing down from the pine country outside Flagstaff to the red rocks of Sedona, Oak Creek Canyon is a cool oasis. From the scenic overlook at the top of the canyon to the swimming holes and hiking trails at the bottom, this canyon road provides a rapid change in climate and landscape. See chapter 5.
- **Canyon de Chelly National Monument** (Chinle): This fascinating complex of canyons on the Navajo Indian Reservation has only limited public access because it is still home to numerous Navajo families. However, there are two roads that parallel the north and south rims of the canyon providing lots of scenic overlooks. See chapter 7.
- **Through Monument Valley** (north of Kayenta): This valley of sandstone buttes and mesas is one of the most photographed spots in America and is familiar to people all over the world from the countless movies, TV shows, and commercials that have been shot here. A 17-mile dirt road winds through the park, giving visitors close-ups of such landmarks as Elephant Butte, the Mittens, and Totem Pole. See chapter 7.
- **Up Mount Lemmon** (Tucson): Sure, the views of Tucson from the city's northern foothills are great, but the views from Mount Lemmon are even better. With a ski area at its summit, Mount

Arizona

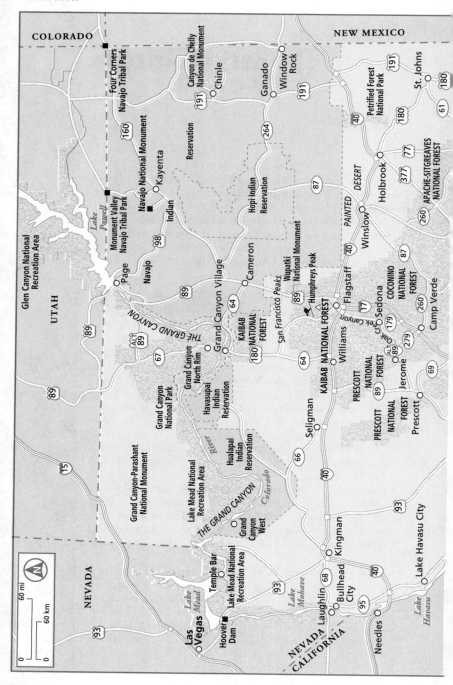

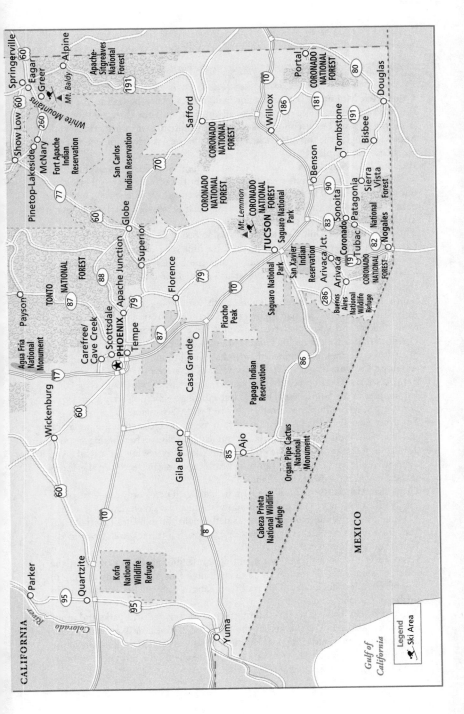

Lemmon rises up from the desert like an island rising from the sea. Along the way the road climbs from cactus country to cool pine forests. See chapter 9.

2 The Best Day Hikes & Nature Walks

- **Camelback Mountain** (Phoenix): For many Phoenicians the trail to the top of Camelback Mountain is a ritual, a Phoenix institution. Sure, there are those who make this a casual but strenuous hike, but many more turn it into a serious workout by jogging to the top and back. We prefer a more leisurely approach to enjoy the views. See chapter 4.
- **Picacho Peak State Park** (south of Casa Grande): The hike up this central Arizona landmark is short but strenuous, and from the top there are superb views out over the desert. The best time of year to make the hike is in spring, when the peak comes alive with wildflowers. Picacho Peak is between Casa Grande and Tucson just off I-10. See chapter 4.
- **The West Fork of Oak Creek Trail** (outside Sedona): The West Fork of Oak Creek is a tiny stream that meanders for miles in a narrow steep-walled canyon. This is classic canyon country, and the hardest part of a hike here is having to turn around without seeing what's around the next bend up ahead. See chapter 5.
- **South Kaibab Trail** (Grand Canyon South Rim): Forget the popular Bright Angel Trail, which is a human highway near the top. This trail offers better views to day hikers and is the preferred downhill route for anyone heading down to Phantom Ranch for the night. This is a strenuous hike even if you go only a mile or so down the trail. Remember, the trip back is all uphill. See chapter 6.
- **Antelope Canyon** (Page): More a slow walk of reverence than a hike, this trail lets you see the amazing beauty that can be created when water and rock battle one another in the Southwest. The trail leads through a picture-perfect sandstone slot canyon, which in places is only a few feet wide. See chapter 7.
- **The Keet Seel Trail** (Navajo National Monument): There is something magical and mystical about arriving at an ancient cliff dwelling after hiking 8 miles through a desert canyon. At the end of your hike, after resting for a while, you can explore the ruins. There's a campsite nearby, so you can sleep with the ghosts of the Anasazi for a night. See chapter 7.
- **The White House Ruins Trail** (Canyon de Chelly): There's only one Canyon de Chelly hike that the general public can do without a Navajo guide, and that's the $2^{1}/_{2}$-mile trail to White House Ruins, a small Anasazi pueblo site. The trail leads from the canyon rim across bare sandstone, through a tunnel, and down to the floor of the canyon. See chapter 7.
- **Seven Falls** (Tucson): There is something irresistible about waterfalls in the desert, and on this trail you get more than enough falls to satisfy any craving to cool off on a hot desert day. This trail is in Sabino Canyon Recreation Area in northeast Tucson. See chapter 9.
- **Heart of Rocks Trail** (Cochise County): While the big national parks and monuments in northern Arizona get all the publicity, Chiricahua National Monument, down in the southeast corner of the state, quietly lays claim to some of the most spectacular scenery in Arizona. On this trail you'll hike through a wonderland of rocks. See chapter 10.

3 The Best Places to Commune with Cacti

- **Boyce Thompson Southwestern Arboretum** (east of Phoenix): Located just outside the town of Superior, this was the nation's first botanical garden established in a desert environment. It's set in a small canyon framed by cliffs, with desert plantings from all over the world—a fascinating place for an educational stroll in the desert. See chapter 4.
- **Desert Botanical Garden** (Phoenix): There's no better place in the state to learn about the plants of Arizona's Sonoran Desert and the many other deserts of the world. Displays at this Phoenix botanical garden explain plant adaptations and how indigenous tribes once used many of this region's wild plants. See chapter 4.
- **Arizona–Sonora Desert Museum** (Tucson): The name is misleading—this is actually more of a zoo and botanical garden than a museum. Naturalistic settings house dozens of species of desert animals, including a number of critters you wouldn't want to meet in the wild (rattlesnakes, tarantulas, scorpions, black widows, and Gila monsters). See chapter 9.
- **Saguaro National Park** (Tucson): Lying both east and west of Tucson, this park preserves "forests" of saguaro cacti and is the very essence of the desert as so many people imagine it. You can hike it, bike it, or drive it. See chapter 9.
- **Tohono Chul Park** (Tucson): Although this park is not all that large, it packs a lot of desert scenery into its modest space. Impressive plantings of cacti are the star attractions here, but there are also good wildflower displays in the spring. See chapter 9.
- **Organ Pipe Cactus National Monument** (west of Tucson): The organ pipe cactus is a smaller, multitrunked relative of the giant saguaro and lives only along the Mexican border about 100 miles west of Tucson. This remote national monument has hiking trails, scenic drives, even a large natural spring. See chapter 10.

4 The Best Golf Courses

- **The Boulders South Course** (Carefree, near Phoenix; ☎ 800/553-1717 or 480/488-9009): If you've ever seen a photo of someone teeing off beside a massive balancing rock and longed to play that same hole, then you've dreamed about playing The Boulders South Course. The South Course, a desert-style design by Jay Morrish, plays around and through the jumble of massive boulders for which the resort is named. See chapter 4.
- **Gold Canyon Golf Resort** (at Gold Canyon Ranch, Apache Junction, near Phoenix; ☎ 480/982-9449): Located east of Phoenix, Gold Canyon offers superb golfing at the foot of the Superstition Mountains. The second, third, and fourth holes on the Dinosaur Mountain Course are the truly memorable ones. They play across the foot of Dinosaur Mountain and are rated among the tops in the state. See chapter 4.
- **The Tournament Players Club (TPC) of Scottsdale** (Scottsdale; ☎ 480/585-3600 or 480/585-3939): If you've always dreamed of playing where the pros play, then you may want to schedule a visit to the Scottsdale Princess and book a tee time on the Stadium Course, which is the site of the PGA Tour's Phoenix Open. See chapter 4.
- **Troon North Golf Club** (Scottsdale; ☎ 480/585-5300): Designed by Tom Weiskopf and Jay Morrish, this semiprivate desert-style course in north Scottsdale is named for the famous Scottish links that overlook both the Firth of Forth

and the Firth of Clyde—but that's where the similarities end. Troon North has two 18-hole courses, but the original, known as the Monument Course, is still the favorite. See chapter 4.

- **The Wigwam Gold Course** (Litchfield Park, near Phoenix; ☎ 623/935-3811): If you're a traditionalist who eschews those cactus- and rattlesnake-filled desert target courses, you'll want to beg, borrow, or steal a tee time on the Wigwam Resort's Gold Course. This 7,100-yard resort course west of Phoenix has long been an Arizona legend. See chapter 4.

- **Sedona Golf Resort** (Sedona; ☎ 520/284-9355): It's easy to think that all of Arizona's best courses are in the Phoenix and Tucson areas, but it just isn't so. Up in the red-rock country, at the mouth of Oak Creek Canyon, lies the Sedona Golf Resort, a traditional course that's among the best in the state. See chapter 5.

- **Omni Tucson National Golf Resort and Spa** (Tucson; ☎ 520/575-7540): With its wide expanses of grass, this traditional course, site of the PGA Tour's Tucson Open, is both challenging and forgiving. The 18th hole of the Orange and Gold courses is considered one of the toughest finishing holes on the tour. See chapter 9.

- **Starr Pass Golf Club** (Tucson; ☎ 520/670-0400): Where once stagecoaches rumbled through the desert, golfers now swing their clubs on a course designed by Robert Cupp and Craig Stadler. Built along an old stagecoach route just west of downtown, the Starr Pass course seduces players with its deceptively difficult 15th hole, which plays through a narrow pass. See chapter 9.

- **Ventana Canyon Golf and Racquet Club** (Tucson; ☎ 520/577-1400): Two Tom Fazio–designed courses, the Canyon Course and the Mountain Course, are shared by two of the city's finest resorts. Both desert-style courses play through some of the most stunning scenery anywhere in the state. If we had to choose between the two, we'd go for the Canyon Course. See chapter 9.

- **Emerald Canyon Golf Course** (Parker; ☎ 520/667-3366): Canyons, cliffs, and ravines are the hazards you'll be avoiding on this very interesting municipal course way out on the bank of the Colorado River. While it may not be the best in the state, it plays through some astounding scenery and is a good value. See chapter 11.

5 The Best Bird Watching

- **Madera Canyon:** The mountain canyons of southern Arizona tend to attract a variety of bird life, from species common in the lowland deserts to those that prefer thick forest settings. Madera is a good place to experience this variety. See chapter 9.

- **Buenos Aires National Wildlife Refuge:** Gray hawks and masked bobwhite quails are among the refuge's rarer birds, but a wetland (cienaga), lake, and stream attract plenty of others. See chapter 10.

- **Cave Creek Canyon:** Although there are other rare birds to be seen in this remote canyon, most people come in hopes of spotting the elegant trogon, which reaches the northernmost limit of its range here. See chapter 10.

- **Patagonia:** With a year-round stream and a Nature Conservancy preserve on the edge of town, Patagonia is one of the best spots in the state for sighting various flycatcher species. See chapter 10.

- **Ramsey Canyon Preserve:** Nearly 200 species of birds, including 14 species of hummingbirds, frequent this canyon, making it one of the top birding spots in the country. See chapter 10.

- **San Pedro Riparian National Conservation Area:** Water is a scarce commodity in the desert, so it isn't surprising that the San Pedro River attracts a lot of animal life, including more than 300 bird species. This is a life-list bonanza spot. See chapter 10.
- **Willcox Ponds:** Wading birds in the middle of the desert? You'll find them at the Willcox sewage-treatment ponds south of town. Avocets, sandhill cranes, and a variety of waterfowl all frequent these shallow bodies of water. See chapter 10.

6 The Best Offbeat Travel Experiences

- **Taking a Vortex Tour in Sedona:** Crystals and pyramids are nothing compared to the power of the Sedona vortexes, which just happen to be in the middle of some very beautiful scenery. Organized tours shuttle believers from one vortex to the next. If you offer it, they will come. See chapter 5.
- **Gazing at the Stars:** Insomniacs and stargazers will find plenty to keep them sleepless in the desert as they peer at the stars through telescopes at Lowell Observatory in Flagstaff or Kitt Peak National Observatory near Tucson. In the town of Benson, you can even stay at a B&B that doubles as an astronomical observatory. See chapters 6 and 9.
- **Sleeping in a Wigwam:** Back in the heyday of Route 66, the Wigwam Motel in Holbrook lured passing motorists with its unusual architecture: concrete wigwam-shaped cabins. Today this little motel is still a great place for anyone who appreciates retro style. See chapter 7.
- **Touring Walpi Village:** Of the Hopi villages that stand atop the mesas of northeastern Arizona, only Walpi, one of the oldest, offers guided tours. The Hopi guides share information on the history of the village and the Hopi culture. See chapter 7.
- **Digging for Artifacts at Raven Site Ruin:** Looking at Anasazi ruins is all well and good, but how would you like to get your hands dirty digging for ancient artifacts? At the White Mountain Archaeological Center near St. Johns, you can (for a fee) participate in an ongoing archaeological dig. See chapter 8.
- **A Visit to Biosphere 2:** This giant terrarium, in which humans were the residents, is a research center for understanding how the earth's ecosystems operate. The giant greenhouses in the middle of the desert are straight out of post-apocalyptic sci-fi. See chapter 9.
- **Walking Across the London Bridge:** The famous bridge was falling down until a farsighted (and perhaps slightly daft) developer transported it to the middle of the Arizona desert. You'll find the bridge in Lake Havasu City, and if it's not too blazingly hot, you can stroll across it and admire all the surrounding pseudo-Tudor architecture. See chapter 11.

7 The Best Family Experiences

- **Pioneer Arizona Living History Museum** (north of Phoenix): This museum features old buildings and costumed interpreters who show and tell what life was like for Arizona pioneers a century ago. See chapter 4.
- **Wild West Restaurants:** No family should visit Arizona without spending an evening at a "genuine" cowboy steak house. With gunslingers and gimmicks (one place cuts off your necktie, another has a slide from the bar to the dining room), cowboy bands, and false-fronted buildings, these Arizona eateries are all entertainment and loads of fun. See chapters 4 and 9.

- **Riding the Grand Canyon Railway:** Not only is this train excursion a fun way to get to the Grand Canyon, but it also lets you avoid the parking problems and congestion that can prove so wearisome. Shoot-outs and train robberies are to be expected in this corner of the Wild West. See chapter 6.
- **A Week on a Houseboat:** Renting a floating vacation home on lakes Powell, Mead, Mohave, or Havasu is a summer tradition for many Arizona families. With a houseboat, you aren't tied to one spot and can cruise from one scenic beach to the next. See chapters 6 and 11.
- **Arizona–Sonora Desert Museum** (Tucson): This is actually a zoo featuring the animals of the Sonoran Desert. There are rooms full of snakes, a prairie dog town, bighorn sheep, mountain lions, and an aviary full of hummingbirds. Kids and adults love this place. See chapter 9.
- **Shoot-Outs at the O.K. Corral:** Tombstone may be "the town too tough to die," but poor Ike Clanton and his buddies the McLaury boys have to die over and over again at the frequent reenactments of the famous gunfight. See chapter 10.

8 The Best Museums

- **Heard Museum** (Phoenix): This is one of the nation's premier museums and is devoted to Native American cultures. In addition to historical exhibits, a huge kachina collection, and an excellent museum store, there are annual exhibits of contemporary Native American art as well as dance performances and demonstrations of traditional skills. See chapter 4.
- **Phoenix Art Museum** (Phoenix): This large art museum has acres of wall space and houses an outstanding collection of contemporary art as well as a fascinating exhibit of miniature rooms. See chapter 4.
- **Scottsdale Museum of Contemporary Art** (Scottsdale): This is the Phoenix area's newest museum and is noteworthy as much for its bold contemporary architecture as for its wide variety of exhibits. Unlike the majority of area art galleries, this museum eschews cowboy art. See chapter 4.
- **Museum of Northern Arizona** (Flagstaff): The geology, ethnography, and archaeology of this region are all explored in fascinating detail at this Flagstaff museum. Throughout the year there are excellent special exhibits and festivals focusing on the region's different tribes. See chapter 6.
- **University of Arizona Museum of Art** (Tucson): This collection ranges from the Renaissance to the present, with a set of 15th-century Spanish religious panels the focus of the collection. Georgia O'Keeffe and Pablo Picasso are among the artists whose works are on display here. See chapter 9.
- **Amerind Foundation Museum** (west of Willcox): Although located in the remote southeastern corner of the state near Willcox, this museum and research center houses a superb collection of Native American artifacts. Displays focus on tribes of the Southwest, but other tribes are also represented. See chapter 10.

9 The Best Places to Discover the Old West

- **Rodeos:** Any rodeo, and this state has plenty, will give you a glimpse of the Old West, but Arizona has two that claim title to being the oldest in the country. Whether you head for the rodeo in Prescott or the one in Payson, you'll see plenty of bronco busting, bull riding, and beer drinking. See chapters 5 and 8.

- **Guest Ranches:** The Old West lives on at guest ranches all over the state, where rugged wranglers lead city slickers on horseback rides through desert scrub and mountain meadows. Campfires, cookouts, and cattle are all part of the experience. See chapters 5, 9, and 10.
- **Monument Valley** (north of Kayenta): John Ford made it the hallmark of his Western movies, and today the starkly beautiful and fantastically shaped buttes and mesas of this valley are the quintessential Western landscape. You'll recognize it the moment you see it. See chapter 7.
- **Old Tucson Studios** (Tucson): Although many of the original movie sets burned in a 1995 fire, this combination back lot and amusement park provides visitors with a glimpse of the most familiar Old West—the Hollywood West. Sure, the shoot-outs and cancan reviews are silly, but it's all in good fun, and everyone gets a thrill out of seeing the occasional film crew in action. See chapter 9.
- **Tombstone:** This is the real Old West—Tombstone is a real town, unlike Old Tucson. However, "the town too tough to die" was reincarnated long ago as a major tourist attraction with gunslingers in the streets, stagecoach rides, and shoot-outs at the O.K. Corral. See chapter 10.

10 The Best Places to See Native American Ruins

- **Besh-Ba-Gowah Archaeological Park** (Globe): These reconstructed ruins have been set up to look the way they might have appeared 700 years ago, providing a bit more cultural context than other ruins in the state. See chapter 4.
- **Casa Grande Ruins National Monument** (west of Florence): Unlike most of the other ruins in the state, this large and unusual structure is built of packed desert soil. Inscrutable and perplexing, Casa Grande seems to rise from nowhere. See chapter 4.
- **Tonto National Monument** (east of Phoenix): Located east of Phoenix on the Apache Trail, this is one of the only easily accessible cliff dwellings in Arizona that you can still visit; you don't have to just observe from a distance. See chapter 4.
- **Montezuma Castle National Monument** (north of Camp Verde): Located just off I-17, this is the most easily accessible cliff dwelling in Arizona, although it cannot be entered. Nearby Montezuma's Well also has some small ruins. See chapter 5.
- **Wupatki National Monument** (north of Flagstaff): Not nearly as well known as the region's Anasazi cliff dwellings, these ruins are set on a wide plain. A ball court similar to those found in Central America hints at cultural ties with the Aztecs. See chapter 6.
- **Canyon de Chelly National Monument:** Small cliff dwellings up and down the length of Canyon de Chelly can be seen from overlooks, and a trip into the canyon itself offers a chance to see some of these ruins up close up. See chapter 7.
- **Navajo National Monument** (west of Kayenta): Although both Keet Seel and Betatakin ruins are at the end of long hikes, their size and state of preservation make them among the finest examples of Anasazi cliff dwellings. See chapter 7.

11 The Best Luxury Hotels & Resorts

- **Arizona Biltmore Resort & Spa** (Phoenix; ☎ **800/950-0086** or 602/955-6600): Combining discreet service and the architectural styling of Frank Lloyd Wright, the Arizona Biltmore has long been one of the most popular resorts in the state. Recent renovations have done much to improve the quality of the rooms, and a new pool is a big hit with families. See chapter 4.

- **The Boulders** (Carefree; ☎ **800/553-1717** or 480/488-9009): Taking its name from the massive blocks of eroded granite scattered about the grounds of the resort, the Boulders is among the most exclusive and expensive resorts in the state. Pueblo architecture fits seamlessly with the landscape, and the golf course is the most breathtaking in Arizona. See chapter 4.

- **The Fairmont Scottsdale Princess** (Scottsdale; ☎ **800/344-4758** or 480/585-4848): The Moorish styling and numerous fountains and waterfalls of this Scottsdale resort create a setting made for romance. Two superb restaurants—one serving Spanish cuisine and one serving gourmet Mexican fare—top it off. See chapter 4.

- **Four Seasons Resort Scottsdale at Troon North** (Scottsdale; ☎ **800/332-3442** or 480/515-5700): This new resort in north Scottsdale takes aim at the Valley's top-end luxury resorts and clearly hits the mark. The setting is dramatic, the accommodations are spacious and luxurious, and the next-door neighbor is one of Arizona's top golf courses. The only drawback is the out-of-the-way location. See chapter 4.

- **Hyatt Regency Scottsdale** (Scottsdale; ☎ **800/55-HYATT** or 480/991-3388): Contemporary desert architecture, dramatic landscaping, a water playground with its own beach, a staff that's always at the ready to assist you, several good restaurants that aren't overpriced, and even gondola rides—it all adds up to a lot of fun at one of the most smoothly run resorts in Arizona. See chapter 4.

- **Marriott's Camelback Inn** (Scottsdale; ☎ **800/24-CAMEL** or 480/948-1700): This is one of the few Scottsdale resorts that retains an old Arizona atmosphere without sacrificing comfort or modern conveniences. A full-service spa caters to those who crave pampering, while two golf courses (one recently renovated) provide plenty of challenging fairways and greens. See chapter 4.

- **The Phoenician** (Scottsdale; ☎ **800/888-8234** or 480/941-8200): This Xanadu of the resort world is brimming with marble, crystal, and works of art, and with staff seemingly around every corner, the hotel offers its guests impeccable service. Two of the resort's dining rooms are among the finest restaurants in the city, and the views are hard to beat. See chapter 4.

- **Royal Palms Hotel and Casitas** (Phoenix; ☎ **800/672-6011** or 602/840-3610): With its Mediterranean styling and towering royal palms, this resort seems far removed from the glitz that prevails at most area resorts. The Royal Palms is a classic, perfect for romantic getaways, and the 14 designer showcase rooms are among the most dramatically styled rooms in the valley. See chapter 4.

- **Enchantment Resort** (Sedona; ☎ **800/826-4180** or 520/282-2900): A dramatic setting in a red-rock canyon outside Sedona makes this the most stunningly situated resort in the state. Guest rooms are for the most part quite large and constructed in a pueblo architectural style. If you want to feel as though you're vacationing in the desert, this place fills the bill. See chapter 5.

- **Loews Ventana Canyon Resort** (Tucson; ☎ **800/23-LOEWS** or 520/299-2020): With the Santa Catalina Mountains rising up in the backyard of this resort and an almost-natural waterfall only steps away from the lobby, this is Tucson's most dramatic resort. Contemporary styling throughout makes constant reference to the desert setting. See chapter 9.

12 The Best Historic Inns & Hotels

- **Hassayampa Inn** (Prescott; ☎ **800/322-1927** or 520/778-9434): Built as a luxury hotel in 1927, the Hassayampa is Prescott's premier historic inn and sits only a block off Courthouse Plaza. Many of the rooms, which vary considerably in size, have original furnishings, and one is said to be haunted. See chapter 5.
- **El Tovar Hotel** (Grand Canyon Village; ☎ **303/297-2757**): This classic log-and-stone mountain lodge stands in Grand Canyon Village only feet from the south rim of the Grand Canyon. Although the lobby is small, it's decorated with the requisite trophy animal heads and has a stone fireplace. See chapter 6.
- **Grand Canyon Lodge** (Grand Canyon North Rim; ☎ **303/297-2757**): This, the Grand Canyon's other grand lodge, sits right on the north rim of the canyon. Rooms are primarily in cabins, which aren't quite as impressive as the main lodge building, but guests tend to spend a lot of time sitting on the lodge's two viewing terraces or in the sunroom. See chapter 6.
- **La Posada** (Winslow; ☎ **520/289-4366**): Designed by Mary Elizabeth Jane Colter, who also designed many of the buildings on the South Rim of the Grand Canyon, La Posada opened in 1930 and was the last of the great railroad hotels. Today the hotel is in the process of being restored to its former glory. See chapter 7.
- **Arizona Inn** (Tucson; ☎ **800/933-1093** or 520/325-1541): With its pink stucco walls and colorful, fragrant gardens, this small Tucson resort dates from Arizona's earliest days as a vacation destination and epitomizes slower times, when guests came for the entire winter, not for a quick weekend getaway. See chapter 9.

13 The Best B&Bs

- **Briar Patch Inn** (Sedona; ☎ **888/809-3030** or 520/282-2342): Oak Creek Canyon, near Sedona, where this collection of luxurious cottages is located, is an oasis in the desert. Few experiences are more restorative than breakfast on the shady banks of the creek. See chapter 5.
- **Canyon Villa** (Sedona; ☎ **800/453-1166** or 520/284-1226): Located in the Village of Oak Creek only a block away from another of the state's top B&Bs, this inn provides luxurious accommodations and fabulous views of the red rocks. There's also a pool. See chapter 5.
- **The Graham Bed & Breakfast Inn & Adobe Village** (Sedona; ☎ **800/228-1425** or 520/284-1425): With its little "village" of luxury suites, this B&B is among the most elegant in the state. Everything about the inn's casita suites is calculated to pamper and put you in a mood for a romantic getaway. Forget about the red rocks; these rooms are reason enough for a visit to Sedona. See chapter 5.
- **The Inn on Oak Creek** (Sedona; ☎ **800/499-7896** or 520/282-7896): Built right out over Sedona's Oak Creek, with shade trees all around and the Tlaque-paque Shopping Plaza only a block away, this inn offers a wide array of luxurious and interestingly decorated rooms, most of which have creek or red-rock views. See chapter 5.
- **Rocamadour** (Prescott; ☎ **888/771-1933** or 520/771-1933): Set amid the rounded boulders of the Granite Dells just north of Prescott, this inn combines a spectacular setting with French antiques and very luxurious accommodations. You won't find a more memorable setting anywhere in the state. See chapter 5.

- **The Inn at 410** (Flagstaff; ☎ **800/774-2008** or 520/774-0088): This restored 1907 bungalow offers a convenient location in downtown Flagstaff, pleasant surroundings, comfortable rooms, and delicious breakfasts. Rooms all feature different, distinctive themes, and eight of them have their own fireplaces. See chapter 6.
- **Paisley Corner Bed & Breakfast** (Eagar; ☎ **520/333-4665**): Although this inn is not nearly as luxurious as others on this list, it is noteworthy for its authenticity of interior design. Victorian antiques fill the house, including the kitchen. There's even a vintage soda fountain in one of the parlors. See chapter 8.
- **Red Setter Inn & Cottage** (Greer; ☎ **888/99-GREER** or 520/735-7441): This large, new log home in the quaint mountain village of Greer is one of Arizona's most enjoyable and romantic B&Bs. It's set on the bank of the Little Colorado River in the shade of large ponderosa pine trees. The inn is also a great place for ski vacations. See chapter 8.
- **"Across The Creek" at Aravaipa Farms** (Winkelman; ☎ **520/357-6901**): If you're looking for the quintessential desert B&B experience, this is it, though it isn't exactly for everyone. To reach this inn, you have to drive through Aravaipa Creek (or have the innkeeper shuttle you across). Exploring the nearby wilderness area is the main activity in this remote area. See chapter 9.
- **The Royal Elizabethan** (Tucson; ☎ **877/670-9022** or 520/670-9022): Located in downtown Tucson half a block from the Temple of Music and Art, this territorial-style historic home is filled with beautiful Victorian antiques and lots of architectural details. Guest rooms also have lots of touches not often seen in historic B&Bs, including "vintage" phones, TVs, small refrigerators, and safes. See chapter 9.

14 The Best Swimming Pools

- **Hyatt Regency Scottsdale** (Scottsdale; ☎ **800/55-HYATT** or 480/991-3388): This Scottsdale resort boasts a 10-pool, $2^1/_2$-acre water playground complete with sand beach, waterfalls, sports pool, lap pool, adult pool, three-story waterslide, large whirlpool, and lots of waterfalls. See chapter 4.
- **The Phoenician** (Scottsdale; ☎ **800/888-8234** or 480/941-8200): This system of seven pools is as impressive as the Hyatt's but has a much more sophisticated air about it. Waterfalls, a waterslide, play pools, a lap pool, and the crown jewel, a mother-of-pearl pool (actually opalescent tile), all add up to plenty of aquatic fun. See chapter 4.
- **Pointe Hilton Squaw Peak Resort** (Phoenix; ☎ **800/876-4683** or 602/997-2626): They don't just have a pool here; they have a River Ranch, with an artificial tubing river, a waterslide, and a waterfall pouring into the large, freeform main pool. See chapter 4.
- **Pointe Hilton Tapatio Cliffs Resort** (Phoenix; ☎ **800/876-4683** or 602/866-7500): The Falls, a slightly more adult-oriented pool complex than that at sister property Pointe Hilton Squaw Peak Resort, includes two lagoon pools, a 40-foot waterfall, a 130-foot waterslide, and rental cabanas. See chapter 4.
- **Wyndham Buttes Resort** (Tempe; ☎ **800/WYNDHAM** or 602/225-9000): A lush stream cascading over desert rocks seems to feed this freeform pool, a desert oasis fantasy world unmatched in the state. A narrow canal connects the two halves of the pool, and tucked in among the rocks are several whirlpools. See chapter 4.

- **Arizona Inn** (Tucson; ☎ **800/933-1093** or 520/325-1541): Although the pool at this historic lodge isn't very large, it more than makes up for its size with its pleasant setting in a garden filled with fragrant flowering vines and citrus trees. See chapter 9.
- **Westin La Paloma** (Tucson; ☎ **800/WESTIN-1** or 520/742-6000): With a 170-foot waterslide and enough poolside lounge chairs to put a cruise ship to shame, the pool at this Tucson foothills resort is a fabulous place to while away an afternoon. There's an adults-only pool, too. See chapter 9.

15 The Best Restaurants

- **Marquesa** (Scottsdale; ☎ **480/585-4848**): Located amid the Moorish architecture of the Scottsdale Princess resort, this Spanish restaurant specializes in Catalonian dishes. To dine here is to be totally immersed in a Mediterranean experience. See chapter 4.
- **Mary Elaine's** (Scottsdale; ☎ **480/423-2530**): Located in Scottsdale's posh Phoenician resort, Mary Elaine's is where the elite dine in the Valley of the Sun. The menu focuses primarily on modern French flavors, although the chef doesn't limit himself. See chapter 4.
- **T. Cook's** (Phoenix; ☎ **602/808-0766**): Located within the Mediterranean cloisters of the Royal Palms Resort, T. Cook's is the most romantic restaurant in Phoenix. No other restaurant (with the possible exception of Marquesa) so thoroughly transports you to another place with both its decor and its cuisine. See chapter 4.
- **Vincent Guerithault on Camelback** (Phoenix; ☎ **602/224-0225**): The bold flavors of the Southwest are the focus of this ever-popular Phoenix restaurant, where presentation is every bit as important as taste. Even if you aren't a fan of chilies, you'll find plenty of unusual flavor combinations to tempt your palate. See chapter 4.
- **The Heartline Cafe** (Sedona; ☎ **520/282-0785**): Combining the zesty flavors of the Southwest with the best of the rest of the world, Sedona's Heartline Cafe frequently comes up with surefire winners guaranteed to please jaded palates. See chapter 5.
- **Café Poca Cosa** (Tucson; ☎ **520/622-6400**): It's small, it's hip, and it's very reasonably priced. Located in the Clarion Hotel & Suites Santa Rita, the Cafe Poca Cosa serves some of the most creative and complex Mexican food since *Like Water for Chocolate*. See chapter 9.
- **Janos/J Bar** (Tucson; ☎ **520/615-6100**): Serving a combination of regional and Southwestern dishes, Janos has for many years been one of Tucson's premiere restaurants. The restaurant is located just outside the front door of the Westin La Paloma resort, and is as formal a place as you'll find in Tucson. J Bar is Janos's less formal bar and grill. See chapter 9.
- **The Tack Room** (Tucson; ☎ **520/722-2800**): Superb service, creative Southwestern dishes, and an authentic Arizona atmosphere make Tucson's Tack Room one of the finest restaurants in the West. Although the steaks are the traditional favorite, other dishes are well worth consideration. See chapter 9.
- **Cose Buone** (Patagonia; ☎ **520/394-2366**): Fine dining and a Laundromat side by side? Yes, it's true. Very reasonably priced four-course Italian dinners are served in this casual spot in eclectic Patagonia, a small town on the edge of Arizona's wine country. See chapter 10.

- **Café Roka** (Bisbee; ☎ **520/432-5153**): As fun a town as Bisbee is, if not for this restaurant it probably wouldn't be nearly as popular a weekend getaway as it is. For many years now this has been *the* place to eat in town. Café Roka could easily hold its own in Tucson or Scottsdale, but then, it wouldn't have nearly as much character. See chapter 10.

Planning a Trip to Arizona: The Basics

Whether you're headed to Arizona to raft the Grand Canyon or to play golf in Phoenix, you'll find all the advance-planning answers you need at your fingertips in this chapter—everything from when to go to how to get there.

1 The Regions in Brief

The Valley of the Sun This name refers to the sprawling metropolitan Phoenix area, which covers more than 400 square miles and includes more than 20 cities and communities surrounded by several distinct mountain ranges. It's the economic and population center of the state.

The Sonoran Desert Extending from the state of Sonora, Mexico, in the south to central Arizona in the north, the Sonoran Desert is surprisingly green and characterized by the massive saguaro cactus. It's in the Sonoran Desert that most of Arizona's cities are found.

The Four Corners The point where Arizona, Utah, Colorado, and New Mexico come together is the only place in the United States where four states share a common boundary. The Four Corners region of Arizona is almost entirely Hopi and Navajo reservation land. This high-plateau region of spectacular canyons and towering mesas and buttes includes Canyon de Chelly, the Painted Desert, the Petrified Forest, and Monument Valley.

The White Mountains Located in eastern Arizona, the White Mountains are laced with trout streams, covered by a huge pine forest, and home to far more wildlife than people. Arizona's largest and most popular ski area is located here on the White Mountain Apache Indian Reservation near the town of McNary. Cooler temperatures make this region a very popular summer-vacation destination.

Arizona's West Coast Although Arizona is a landlocked state, its western region is referred to as the West Coast because of the hundreds of miles of lakeshore created by the damming of the Colorado River. The low-lying stretches of the Colorado River are the hottest places in Arizona.

Canyon Country From the Grand Canyon in the north to Oak Creek Canyon in the south, the rugged north-central part of the state alternates high, forested mountains with deep canyons. The 2,000-foot-high Mogollon Rim cuts through this region.

The Arizona Strip   Located north of the Grand Canyon and bordering on southern Utah, this is the most remote and untraveled region of Arizona. The Grand Canyon acts as a natural boundary between this region and the rest of the state, and the lack of paved roads or towns keeps away all but the most dedicated explorers. The newly designated Grand Canyon-Parashant National Monument lies at the western end of the Arizona Strip.

Southeastern Arizona   Mile-high elevations give this region one of the most temperate climates in the world. Tucson is at the northern edge of this region (and not so temperate), but otherwise there are few towns of any size. Mountain "islands" that rise out of the desert are home to more than 200 species of birds, and the wide grassy valleys make this a ranching region.

2 Visitor Information & Money

VISITOR INFORMATION

If you have more questions than we can answer in this book, there are a number of places that may have the answers for you. For statewide travel information, contact the **Arizona Office of Tourism,** 2702 N. Third St., Suite 4015, Phoenix, AZ 85004 (☎ **800/842-8257** or 602/230-7733). The Arizona Office of Tourism's Web site is **www.arizonaguide.com**. For additional Arizona information on the Internet, see "Planning Your Trip: An Online Directory" after this chapter. And keep in mind that every city and town in Arizona has either a tourism office or a chamber of commerce that can give you information. See the individual chapters for addresses of these sources.

If you're a member of the **American Automobile Association (AAA),** remember that you can get a map and guidebook covering Arizona and New Mexico. You can also request the club's free *Southwestern CampBook,* which includes campgrounds in Arizona, Utah, Colorado, and New Mexico, by calling your local AAA chapter.

MONEY

What will a vacation in Arizona cost? That depends on your comfort needs. If you drive a RV or carry a tent, you can get by very inexpensively and find a place to stay almost anywhere in the state. If you don't mind staying in motels that date from the Great Depression and can sleep on a sagging mattress, you can stay for less money in Arizona than almost anyplace else in the United States (under $30 a night for a double). On the other hand, you can easily spend several hundred dollars a day on a room at one of the state's world-class resorts. If you're looking to stay in clean, modern motels at interstate highway off-ramps, expect to pay $45 to $65 a night for a double room in most places.

It's never a problem to find an ATM when you're on the road. Throughout the state, the Star, Cirrus, and Plus networks are widely available, so you can get cash through these networks as well as with a major credit card as you travel. If you should have trouble finding an ATM, you can call ☎ **800/424-7787** for Cirrus locations or ☎ **800/843-7587** for Plus locations. Expect to pay a $1.50 service fee at most ATMs in the state.

But some people still prefer the security of traveler's checks, which are accepted at hotels, motels, restaurants, and most stores. Call American Express (☎ **800/221-7282**) for more information.

Arizona is a year-round destination, although people head to different parts of the state at different times of year. In Phoenix, Tucson, and other parts of the desert, the high season runs from October to mid-May, with the highest hotel rates in effect during January and February. However, up at the Grand Canyon the busy season is during the summer; that's when hotel rates are the highest, and crowds are the largest.

The all-around best times to visit are in spring and autumn, when temperatures are cool in the mountains and warm in the desert, but without extremes (although you shouldn't be surprised to get a bit of snow as late as Memorial Day in the mountains and thunderstorms in the desert in August and September). These are also good times to save money because summer rates are in effect at the desert resorts, and the crowds aren't as dense at the Grand Canyon. This period sometimes coincides with the spring wildflower season, which begins in midspring and extends until April and May, when the tops of saguaro cacti become covered with waxy white blooms.

If for some reason you happen to be visiting the desert in July or August, be prepared for sudden thunderstorms. These storms often cause flash floods that make many roads in the state briefly impassable. Road signs warning motorists not to enter low areas when flooded are meant to be taken very seriously.

Also, don't even think about venturing into narrow slot canyons, such as Antelope Canyon near Page or the West Fork of Oak Creek Canyon, if there's any chance of a storm anywhere in the region. Rain falling miles away can send flash floods roaring down narrow canyons with no warning. In 1997, several hikers died when they were caught in a flash flood in Antelope Canyon.

One more thing to keep in mind: Sedona is just high enough that it actually gets cold in the winter—sometimes it even snows. So if you're looking for sunshine and time by the pool, you'll be more likely to head home happy if you book your Sedona vacation some time other than in the winter.

CLIMATE

The first thing you should know is that the desert can be cold as well as hot. Although winter is the prime tourist season in Phoenix and Tucson, night temperatures can be below freezing and days can even be too cold for sunning or swimming. However, on the whole, winters in Arizona are positively delightful.

In the winter, sunseekers flock to the deserts, where temperatures average in the high 60s by day. In the summer, when desert temperatures top 110°F, the mountains of eastern and northern Arizona are pleasantly warm, with daytime averages in the low 80s. Yuma is one of the desert communities where winter temperatures are the highest in the state, and Prescott and Sierra Vista, in the 4,000- to 6,000-foot elevation range, claim two of the most temperate climates in the world.

The accompanying climate charts will give you an idea of the state's climatic diversity.

Phoenix's Average Temperatures (°F) & Days of Rain

	Jan	Feb	Mar	Apr	May	June	July	Aug	Sept	Oct	Nov	Dec
Avg. High	65	69	75	84	93	102	105	102	98	88	75	66
Avg. Low	38	41	45	52	60	68	78	76	69	57	45	39
Days of Rain	4	4	3	2	1	1	4	5	3	3	2	4

Money-Saving Tips

Planning a winter vacation in Arizona can easily induce sticker shock. However, there are a few sun-country options for vacationers on a tight budget.

- If you don't absolutely have to have all the amenities of a big resort, there are endless chain motel options in the Phoenix and Tucson areas. However, even these accommodations are often overpriced for what you get. Still, you'll be in the sun, and you'll likely have a pool for cooling off. Alternatively, you can get a bit more for your money if you leave the cities and head to such smaller towns as Wickenburg, Bullhead City, Lake Havasu City, and Yuma. All four of these towns are usually plenty warm in the winter and offer better accommodation values than the cities do.

- You can save a substantial amount on hotel rates by joining the American Automobile Association (AAA). The savings on just a few nights' lodging can cover the cost of the annual AAA membership.

- To avoid ATM fees, use your card as a debit card at a grocery store and get cash back from your purchase.

- Have lunch at an expensive restaurant, and you'll be able savor the ambience at a fraction of the cost of dinner. Often the lunch menu includes some items from the dinner menu at much lower prices.

- Ask when hotel room rates drop for the summer and schedule your trip for right after the rates go down (or just before they go back up in the fall). Many resorts also have a short discounted season just before Christmas. Travel then and you can save hundreds of dollars over a visit in January.

- Pick up rental cars somewhere other than the Phoenix or Tucson airports. Rental car companies operating inside the airport charge 20% or more in taxes and service fees. Taxes and service charges outside the airport are about half as much.

Flagstaff's Average Temperatures (°F) & Days of Rain

	Jan	Feb	Mar	Apr	May	June	July	Aug	Sept	Oct	Nov	Dec
Avg. High	41	44	48	57	67	76	81	78	74	63	51	43
Avg. Low	14	17	20	27	34	40	50	49	41	31	22	16
Days of Rain	7	6	8	6	3	3	12	11	6	5	5	6

Arizona Calendar of Events

January

- **Fiesta Bowl Classic,** Sun Devil Stadium, Tempe. College football classic. For information, call ☎ **800/635-5748** or 480/350-0900. January 1 or 2.

- **Phoenix Open Golf Tournament,** Scottsdale. Prestigious PGA golf tournament at the Tournament Players Club. Phone ☎ **602/870-0163** for details. Mid- to late January.

- **Wings Over Willcox,** Willcox. Birding tours, workshops, and, of course, watching the sandhill cranes at the Willcox sewage recycling ponds. Call ☎ **520/384-2272** for details. Third weekend in January.

February

- **Parada del Sol Parade and Rodeo,** Scottsdale. The state's longest horse-drawn parade, plus a street dance and rodeo. For more information, call ☎ **480/502-1880.** Early February.
- **World Championship Hoop Dance,** Phoenix. Native American dancers from around the nation take part in this colorful competition held at the Heard Museum. Call ☎ **602/252-8840** for details. Early February.
- **Tubac Festival of the Arts,** Tubac. Exhibits by North American artists and craftspeople. For more information, call ☎ **520/398-2371.** Early to mid-February.
- **Gem, Mineral & Fossil Showcase of Tucson.** Dealers from all over the world converge at more than two dozen locations around Tucson selling everything from precious stones to dinosaur eggs; although some sell only wholesale, many offer goods to the public as well. Call ☎ **520/624-1817.** First two weeks of February.
- **Tucson Gem and Mineral Society Show.** This huge show at the Tucson Convention Center offers seminars, museum displays from around the world, and dealers selling just about any kind of rock you can imagine. For details, call ☎ **520/322-5773** or 520/624-1817. Mid-February.
- **Arizona Renaissance Festival,** Apache Junction. This 16th-century English country fair has costumed participants and includes tournament jousting. Phone ☎ **520/463-2700** for details. Weekends from early February to March.
- **O'odham Tash,** Casa Grande. One of the largest annual Native American festivals in the country, attracting dozens of tribes that participate in rodeos, arts-and-crafts exhibits, and dance performances. Call ☎ **520/836-4723.** Mid-February.
- **All-Arabian Horse Show,** Scottsdale's Westworld. A celebration of the Arabian horse. For additional information, call ☎ **480/515-1500** or 480/312-6802. Mid- to late February.
- **Tucson Open.** A major stop on the golf tour, held at the Omni Tucson National Golf Resort and Spa. Call ☎ **800/882-7660** or 520/571-0400 for information. Mid- to late February.
- **La Fiesta de los Vaqueros,** Tucson. Cowboy festival and rodeo at the Tucson Rodeo Grounds, including the Tucson Rodeo Parade, the world's largest nonmotorized parade. Call ☎ **520/741-2233** for details. Late February.
- **Flagstaff Winterfest.** Snowshoeing and cross-country ski tours, sleigh rides, music, and family snow games. For details, call ☎ **800/842-7293** or 520/774-4505. Month of February.

March

- **Heard Museum Guild Indian Fair,** Phoenix. Indian cultural and dance presentations and one of the greatest selections of Native American crafts in the Southwest make this a fascinating festival. Plus, with the festival entrance fee you get admission to the Heard Museum. Go early to avoid the crowds. Call ☎ **602/252-8840** for details. First weekend in March.
- **Sedona International Film Festival,** Sedona. View various new indie features, documentaries, and animations before they (hopefully) get

picked up for wider distribution. Phone ☎ **800/780-ARTS** or 520/203-4TIX. First weekend in March.

- **Franklin Templeton Tennis Classic,** Scottsdale. Top names in men's professional tennis, such as Andre Agassi and Pete Sampras, compete in this tournament at the Scottsdale Princess hotel. For information, call ☎ **480/922-0222.** Early March.
- **Wiener Dog Nationals,** Phoenix. How 'bout those dachshunds? Watch this great low-ridin' action at the Phoenix Greyhound Park. You'll see the greyhounds run, too. Call ☎ **602/273-7181.** Early March.
- **Chandler Ostrich Festival,** Chandler. Give the carnival a miss and head straight for the ostrich races. Although brief, these unusual races are something you've got to see at least once in your life. For more details, call ☎ **480/963-4571.** Early to mid-March.
- **Scottsdale Arts Festival,** Scottsdale Mall. This visual and performing arts festival has free concerts, an art show, and children's events. For more information, phone ☎ **480/994-ARTS.** Second weekend in March.
- **Wak Pow Wow,** Tucson. Tohono O'odham celebration at Mission San Xavier del Bac, featuring many Southwestern Native American groups. Call ☎ **520/294-5727** for more information. Mid-March.
- **Yaqui Easter Lenten Ceremony,** Tucson. Religious ceremonies at Old Pasqua Village blending Christian and Yaqui Native American beliefs. For further information, phone ☎ **520/791-4609.** Holy Week.
- **Territorial Days,** Tombstone. Tombstone's birthday celebration. For more information, call ☎ **800/457-3423.** Late March.
- **Welcome Back Buzzards,** Superior. A flock of turkey buzzards arrives annually at the Boyce Thompson Arboretum to roost in the eucalyptus trees, and this festival celebrates their arrival. For details, call ☎ **520/689-2723.** Late March.
- **The Tradition,** Scottsdale. This Senior PGA tournament at Cochise Course at Desert Mountain hosts the big names. Call ☎ **480/595-4070** for more information. Late March to early April.

April

- **Tucson International Mariachi Conference.** Mariachi bands from all over the world come to compete before standing-room only crowds. Call ☎ **520/884-9920,** ext. 243, for more information. Mid- to late April.
- **Allstate Golf & Celebrity Tennis Tournament,** Tucson. One of the largest celebrity tennis events in the United States, held at the Randolph Tennis Center and Starr Pass. Phone ☎ **520/623-6165** for more information. Mid- to late April.
- **Waila Festival,** Tucson. A festival celebrating the social dances of the Tohono O'odham nation, featuring "chicken scratch" music—a kind of polka—and native foods. Call ☎ **520/628-5774** for more information. Late April.
- **Maricopa County Fair,** Phoenix. The Arizona State Fairgrounds hosts a midway, agricultural and livestock exhibits, and entertainment. For details, phone ☎ **602/252-0717.** Late April to early May.
- **Plaza Suite,** Tucson. Open-air jazz concerts at St. Philip's Plaza. For details, call the Tucson Jazz Society at ☎ **520/743-3399.** Sundays in April and May.

May

- **Cinco de Mayo,** Tucson, Phoenix, and other cities. Celebration of the Mexican victory over the French in a famous 1862 battle, complete with food, music, and dancing. Call ☎ **602/262-5025** for details on the festivities in Phoenix; call ☎ **520/292-9326** for more information on the celebration in Tucson's Kennedy Park. Around May 5.

- **Phippen Western Art Show and Sale,** Prescott. This is the premier Western art sale. For more information, call ☎ **520/778-1385.** Memorial Day weekend.
- **Wyatt Earp Days,** Tombstone. Gunfight reenactments in memory of the shoot-out at the O.K. Corral. Call ☎ **800/457-3423** for further details. Late May.
- **Sedona Chamber Music Festival,** Sedona. Chamber music is performed by companies from around the world at various venues. Phone ☎ **520/204-2415** for details. May.
- **Enduring Creations: Masterworks of Native American Art,** Flagstaff. The finest Hopi, Zuni, Navajo, and Pai art and craft work is offered for sale in changing exhibits at the Museum of Northern Arizona. For details, phone ☎ **520/774-5213.** Ongoing event from late May to mid-September.

June

- **Juneteenth Festival,** Tucson. Festival in Kennedy Park celebrating African American Independence Day, including food, a fashion show, and a craft marketplace. Call ☎ **520/791-4355.** Third weekend in June.

July

- **Independence Day.** For information about fireworks displays in Phoenix, call ☎ **602/534-FEST;** in Tucson, phone ☎ **520/791-4860.** July 4.
- **Annual Hopi Artists Exhibition,** Flagstaff. Exhibition and sale at the Museum of Northern Arizona, including cultural events. Call ☎ **520/774-5213** for more details. Fourth of July weekend.
- **Prescott Frontier Days,** Prescott. This is the oldest rodeo in the United States. Phone ☎ **800/266-7534** or 520/445-3103 for details. First week of July.
- **Annual Navajo Artists Exhibition,** Flagstaff. Exhibition and sale at the Museum of Northern Arizona, including cultural events. For details, call ☎ **520/774-5213.** Last weekend in July or first weekend in August.

August

- **Payson Rodeo,** Payson. The second of Arizona's rodeos claiming to be the world's oldest. For details, call ☎ **800/672-9766** or 520/474-4515. Mid-August.
- **Southwest Wings Birding Festival,** Sierra Vista. Spotting hummingbirds and looking for owls and bats keep participants busy. Includes lectures and field trips. For more information, phone ☎ **800/288-3861** or 520/459-EVNT. Mid-August.
- **Arizona Cowboy Poets' Gathering,** Prescott. Not just traditional and contemporary poetry, but yodeling and storytelling that focuses on the cowboy lifestyle. For more information, call ☎ **520/445-3122.** Third weekend in August.
- **La Fiesta de San Agustín,** Tucson. Celebration to honor the patron saint of Tucson, with a Mexican fiesta theme. For more information, phone ☎ **520/628-5774.** Late August.

September

- **Navajo Nation Fair,** Window Rock. A very large fair featuring traditional music and dancing by North American tribes. Call ☎ **520/ 871-6478** for more information. Early September.
- **State Championship Old Time Fiddler's Contest,** Payson. Fiddlers from around Arizona try their best to out-fiddle each other, along with clogging and buck dancing. For details, call ☎ **800/6PAYSON** or 520/474-4515. Late September.
- **Scottsdale Center for the Arts Annual Gala.** Jazz, ballet, music, art exhibits, and special events. Phone ☎ **480/994-2787** for further information. Late September.
- **Jazz on the Rocks,** Sedona. Open-air jazz festival held in the red rocks. For details, call ☎ **520/282-1985.** Late September.

October

- **Sedona Arts Festival,** Sedona. One of the better arts festivals in the state. For additional information, phone ☎ **800/288-7336** or 520/204-9456. Mid-October.
- **Coors Rodeo Showdown,** Phoenix. Top rodeo stars compete in this world finals rodeo at the America West Arena. For details, call ☎ **800/ 946-9711.** Mid- to late October.
- **Fiesta de los Chiles,** Tucson. Lots of hot chiles, served in dishes from around the world, along with crafts and music. For more information, call ☎ **520/326-9686.** Mid- to late October.
- **Helldorado Days,** Tombstone. Fashion show of 1880s clothing, tribal dancers, and street entertainment. Call ☎ **800/457-3423** for details. Third weekend of October.
- **Arizona State Fair,** Phoenix. This shindig at the Arizona State Fairgrounds features rodeos, top-name entertainment, and ethnic food. Phone ☎ **602/252-6771** for more information. Late October to early November.
- **Annual Cowboy Artists of America Exhibition,** Phoenix. The Phoenix Art Museum hosts the most prestigious and best-known Western art show in the region. For details, call ☎ **602/257-1222.** Late October.

November

- **Thunderbird Balloon Classic,** Scottsdale. More than 150 hot-air balloons fill the Arizona sky. Call ☎ **602/978-7330** or 602/978-7208 for details. Early November.
- **Western Music Festival,** Tucson. Concerts and workshops by Western music performers. Phone ☎ **520/743-9794** for details. Mid-November.
- **Festival of Lights,** Sedona. Thousands of luminárias are lit at dusk at the Tlaquepaque Arts and Crafts Village on Thanksgiving eve, and stay up until early January. For details, call ☎ **800/288-7336.**

December

- **Old Town Fall Festival of the Arts,** Tempe. Hundreds of artists and artisans, featuring free entertainment and plenty of food, set up along Mill Avenue. For additional information, call ☎ **480/967-4877.** Early December.
- **Luminária Nights,** Tucson. A glowing display of holiday lights at the Botanical Gardens. For details, call ☎ **520/326-9255.** First weekend in December.
- **Fourth Avenue Street Fair,** Tucson. Outdoor arts-and-crafts festival. Phone ☎ **520/624-5004** for more information. Early December.

- **Fiesta Bowl Parade,** Phoenix area. Huge, nationally televised parade, featuring floats and marching bands. Phone ☎ **800/635-5748** or 480/350-0900 for more information. December 31.

4 The Active Vacation Planner

Arizona is known the world over for active, adventure-oriented vacations for the sole reason that the state is home to the Grand Canyon—the most widely known white-water-rafting spot in the world. For others, Arizona is synonymous with winter golf and tennis. Whichever category of active vacationer you fall into, you'll find information below to help you arrange your trip to Arizona.

BIKING   With its wide range of climates, Arizona offers good biking somewhere in the state every month of the year. In the winter there's good road biking around Phoenix and Tucson, while from spring through fall, the southeastern corner of the state offers some good routes. In the summer the White Mountains in the eastern part of the state and Kaibab National Forest between Flagstaff and Grand Canyon National Park offer good mountain biking. There is also excellent mountain biking at several Phoenix parks, and Tucson is one of the most bicycle-friendly cities in the country. **Backroads,** 801 Cedar St., Berkeley, CA 94710-1800 (☎ **800/462-2848** or 510/527-1555), offers a 6-day, inn-to-inn mountain-bike trip through the red-rock country of central Arizona.

BIRD WATCHING   Arizona is a birder's bonanza. Down in the southeastern corner of the state, many species found primarily south of the border reach the northern limits of their territories. Combine this with several mountains that rise like islands from the desert and provide an appropriate habitat for hundreds of species, and you have some of the best bird watching in the country. Birding hot spots include Ramsey Canyon Preserve (known for its many species of hummingbirds), Cave Creek Canyon (nesting site for elegant trogons), Patagonia-Sonoita Creek Sanctuary (home to 22 species of flycatchers, kingbirds, and phoebes, as well as Montezuma quails), Madera Canyon (another "mountain island" that attracts many of the same species seen at Ramsey Canyon and Sonoita Creek), Buenos Aires National Wildlife Refuge (home to masked bobwhite quail and gray hawks), and the sewage ponds outside the town of Willcox (known for its avocets and sandhill cranes). To find out which rare birds have been spotted lately, call the **Tucson Audubon Society's Rare Bird Hotline** (☎ **520/698-1005**).

Serious birders who want to be sure of adding lots of rare birds to their life lists may want to visit southeastern Arizona on a guided tour. These are available through **High Lonesome Ecotours** (☎ **800/743-2668;** www.hilonesome. com), which charges about $850 to $1,050 per person for a 4-day birding trip.

CANOEING/KAYAKING   OK, so maybe these sports don't jump to mind when you think of the desert, but yes there are rivers in the desert (and they happen to be some of the best places to see wildlife). Contact **Permagrin River Adventures,** 6331 S. College St., Tempe, AZ 85283 (☎ **480/755-1924;** www.go-permagrin.com); Permagrin also offers various canoeing and kayaking courses.

There are also a couple of companies that rent canoes on the Colorado River south of Lake Mead. See chapter 11 for details.

FISHING   The fishing scene in Arizona is as diverse as the landscape. Large and small lakes around the state offer excellent fishing for warm-water game fish such as largemouth, smallmouth, and striped bass. Good trout fishing can be found up on the Mogollon Rim and in the White Mountains there, as well as in the Grand Canyon, and the more easily accessible sections of the free-running Colorado River between Glen Canyon Dam and Lees Ferry.

Fishing licenses for nonresidents are available for 1 day, 5 days, 4 months, and 1 year. Various special stamps and licenses may also apply. Nonresident fishing-license prices range from $8 for a 1-day license to $38 for a 1-year license ($10 additional for a trout stamp). Also keep in mind that if you're heading for an Indian reservation, you'll have to get a special permit for that reservation. For more information, contact the **Arizona Game and Fish Department,** 2222 W. Greenway Rd., Phoenix, AZ 85021 (☎ **602/942-3000**).

GOLF   For many of Arizona's winter visitors, golf is the main reason to visit the state. The state's hundreds of golf courses range from easy public courses to PGA championship links that have challenged the best.

In Phoenix and Tucson, greens fees, like room rates, are seasonal. In the popular winter months, fees at resort courses range from about $70 to $185 for 18 holes, although this usually includes a mandatory golf-cart rental. In the summer months, fees often drop to less than half this amount. Almost all resorts also offer special golf packages as well.

For information on some of the state's top courses, see "Hot Links," the special golf feature in this chapter. For more information on golfing in Arizona, contact the **Arizona Golf Association,** 7226 N. 16th St., Suite 200, Phoenix, AZ 85020 (☎ **800/458-8484** within Arizona or 602/944-3035; www. azgolf.org), which publishes a directory ($5) listing all the courses in the state. You can also contact *Golf Arizona,* 16446 Tombstone Dr., Fountain Hills, AZ 85268 (☎ **800/942-5444**), which publishes a guide to where to play golf in Arizona. You can also pick up a copy of the *Tucson and Southern Arizona* or *Greater Phoenix Golf Guide* at visitors bureaus, golf courses, and many hotels and resorts.

HIKING/BACKPACKING   Despite its reputation as a desert state, a large percentage of Arizona is forestland, and within these forests are wilderness areas and countless miles of hiking trails. In northern Arizona, there are good day hikes in Grand Canyon National Park, in the San Francisco Peaks north of Flagstaff, outside Page (near Lake Powell), and in Navajo National Monument. In the Phoenix area, popular day hikes include the trails up Camelback Mountain and Squaw Peak and the many trails in South Mountain Park. In the Tucson area, there are good hikes on Mount Lemmon and in Saguaro National Park, Sabino Canyon, and Catalina State Park. In the southern part of the state, there are good day hikes in Chiricahua National Monument, Coronado National Forest, in the Nature Conservancy's Ramsey Canyon Preserve and Patagonia-Sonoita Creek Sanctuary, in Cochise Stronghold, and in Organ Pipe National Monument. See the individual chapters for details on these areas.

The state's two most popular overnight backpack trips are the hike down to Phantom Ranch and the hike into Havasu Canyon, a side canyon of the Grand Canyon. Another popular multiday backpack trip is through Paria Canyon, beginning in Utah and ending in Arizona at Lees Ferry. There are also backpacking opportunities in the San Francisco Peaks north of Flagstaff and in the White Mountains of eastern Arizona.

Guided backpacking trips of different durations and levels of difficulty are offered by the **Grand Canyon Field Institute,** P.O. Box 399, Grand Canyon, AZ 86023 (☎ **520/638-2485;** www.grandcanyon.org/fieldinstitute). Backpacking trips into the Grand Canyon are also offered by **Grand Canyon Trail Guides,** P.O. Box 87, Grand Canyon, AZ 86023 (☎ **888/283-3194** or 520/638-3194; http://grandcanyontrailguides.com). **Backroads,** 801 Cedar St., Berkeley, CA 94710-1800 (☎ **800/462-2848** or 510/527-1555), better known for its bike trips, also offers a 6-day walking/hiking trip in Arizona. **Wilderness Adventures,** 4211 E. Elwood St., Suite 1, Phoenix, AZ 85040 (☎ **602/438-1800;** www.wildernessadventures.com), which specializes in team building and rock climbing, has a variety of guided backpacking trips, including trips along various sections of the Arizona Trail and a trip down into Havasu Canyon. This company also offers trips exploring some little-known Arizona canyons. These trips combine hiking and rock climbing.

HORSEBACK RIDING/WESTERN ADVENTURES   All over Arizona there are stables where you can saddle up for short rides. Among the more scenic spots for riding are the Grand Canyon, Monument Valley Navajo Tribal Park, Canyon de Chelly National Monument, the red-rock country around Sedona, Phoenix's South Mountain Park, at the foot of the Superstition Mountains east of Phoenix, and at the foot of the Santa Catalina Mountains outside Tucson. See the individual chapters for listings of riding stables; see below for information on overnight guided horseback rides.

Among the most popular guided adventures in Arizona are the mule rides down into the Grand Canyon. These trips vary in length from 1 to 3 days; for reservations and more information, call **Amfac Parks & Resorts** (☎ **303/297-2757**). Be advised, however, that you'll need to make mule ride reservations many months in advance. If at the last minute (5 days or less from the day you want to ride) you decide you want to go on a mule trip into the Grand Canyon, contact **Grand Canyon National Park Lodges** (☎ **520/638-2631**), on the off chance there might be space available.

It's also possible to do overnight horseback rides and cattle drives. For more information, contact **Don Donnelly Stables,** 6010 Kings Ranch Rd., Gold Canyon (☎ **800/346-4403** or 480/982-7822; www.dondonnelly.com), which does overnight horseback trips in Monument Valley, the White Mountains, and the Superstition Mountains, among other places, or **Arizona Trail Tours** (☎ **520/394-2701**), which offers a 4-day trip through Coronado National Forest in southern Arizona.

HOT-AIR BALLOONING   For much of the year the desert has the perfect environment for hot-air ballooning—cool, still air and wide-open spaces. Consequently, there are dozens of hot-air balloon companies operating across the state. Most are in the Phoenix and Tucson areas, but several others operate near Sedona, which is by far the most picturesque spot in the state for a balloon ride. See the individual chapters for specific information.

HOUSEBOATING   With the Colorado River turned into a long string of lakes, houseboat vacations are a natural in Arizona. Although this doesn't have to be an active vacation, fishing, hiking, and swimming are usually part of a houseboat stay. Rentals are available on Lake Powell, Lake Mead, Lake Mohave, and Lake Havasu. However, the canyon lands scenery of Lake Powell makes it the hands-down best spot for a houseboat vacation—reserve well in advance for a summer trip. No prior experience (or license) is necessary, and plenty of hands-on instruction is provided before you leave the marina. See chapters 7 and 11 for more information on houseboat rentals.

Hot Links

You don't have to be a hotshot golfer to get all heated up over the prospect of a few rounds of golf in Arizona. Combine near-perfect golf weather most of the year with great views and some very unique challenges, and you've got all the makings of a great game. Phoenix and Tucson are well known as winter golf destinations, but the state also offers golf throughout the year at higher-altitude courses in such places as Prescott, Flagstaff, and the White Mountains.

State legislation aimed at conserving water limits the acreage that Arizona golf courses can irrigate, which has given the state some of the most distinctive and difficult courses in the country. These desert or "target" courses are characterized by minimal fairways surrounded by natural desert landscapes. You might find yourself teeing off over the tops of cacti or searching for your ball amid boulders and mesquite. If your ball comes to rest in the desert, you can play the ball where it lies or, with a one-stroke penalty, drop it within two club lengths of the nearest point of grass (but no nearer the hole).

Keep in mind that resort courses and daily fee public courses are not cheap. For most of the year, greens fees, which include golf-cart rentals, range from around $90 to $150 or more. Municipal courses usually have greens fees of less than $40 for 18 holes, with golf-cart rental costing extra (usually less than $20).

It might not seem so initially, but summer is really a good time to visit many of Arizona's golf resorts. No, they don't have air-conditioned golf carts or indoor courses, but in summer, greens fees can be less than half what they are in winter. How does $38 for a round on the famous Gold Course at the Wigwam Golf and Country Club sound?

The Phoenix/Scottsdale area, known as the Valley of the Sun, has the greatest concentration of golf courses in the state. Whether you're looking to play one of the area's challenging top-rated resort courses or an economical-but-fun municipal course, you'll find plenty of choices.

For spectacular scenery at a resort course, it's just plain impossible to beat **The Boulders** (☎ **480/488-9009**), located north of Scottsdale in the town of Carefree. Elevated tee boxes beside giant balanced boulders are enough to distract anyone's concentration. Way over on the east side of the valley in Apache Junction, the **Gold Canyon Golf Resort** (☎ **480/982-9449**) has what have been rated as three of the best holes in the state: the second, third, and fourth holes on the Dinosaur Mountain course. Jumping over to Litchfield Park, on the far west side of the valley, you'll find the **Wigwam Golf and Country Club** (☎ **623/935-3811**) and its three 18-hole courses; the Gold Course here is legendary. Other noteworthy resort courses in the area include the links at **The Phoenician** (☎ **480/423-2449**), which mix traditional and desert-style holes. The **Gainey Ranch Golf Club,** at the Hyatt Regency Scottsdale Resort at Gainey Ranch (☎ **480/951-0022**), offers three decidedly different 9-hole courses: the Dunes, the Arroyo, and the Lakes courses, each with its own set of challenges, however, you must be a guest of the resort to play here. The semiprivate **Troon North Golf Club** (☎ 480/585-5300), a course that seems only barely carved out of raw desert, garners the most local accolades (and charges some of the highest greens fees in the state). If you want to swing where the pros do, beg, borrow, or steal a tee time on the Stadium Course at the **Tournament Players Club of Scottsdale** (☎ 480/585-3600. The area's favorite municipal course is the **Papago Golf Course** (☎ 602/275-8428), which has a killer 17th hole.

In recent years, Tucson has been giving the Valley of the Sun plenty of competition when it comes to great golf courses. Among the city's resort courses, the Mountain Course at the **Ventana Canyon Golf and Racquet Club** (☎ 520/577-1400) is legendary, especially the spectacular 107-yard par-3 third hole. Likewise, the eighth hole on the Sunrise Course at **El Conquistador Country Club** (☎ 520/544-1800) is among the most memorable par-3 holes in Tucson. If you want to play where the pros do, book a room at the **Omni Tucson National Golf Resort and Spa** (☎ 520/575-7540), home of the Tucson Open. For a little history with your fairways, try the **Starr Pass Golf Club** (☎ 520/670-0400). The 15th hole here plays through a narrow pass once used by stagecoaches. **Randolph North** (☎ 520/325-2811), Tucson's best municipal course, is the site of the city's annual LPGA tournament. The **Silverbell Municipal Course** (☎ 520/743-7284) boasts a bear of a par-5 17th hole.

Courses worth trying in other parts of the state include the 18-hole course at **Rancho de los Caballeros** (☎ 520/684-2704), a luxury ranch resort outside Wickenburg. *Golf Digest* has rated its course one of Arizona's top 10. For concentration-taxing scenery, few courses compare with the **Sedona Golf Resort** (☎ 520/284-9355), which has good views of the red rocks; try it at sunset. In mile-high Prescott, the **Antelope Hills Golf Club** (☎ 520/776-7888) offers two 18-hole courses that provide a respite from the summer heat in the lowlands. Even higher and cooler in summer, the **Alpine Country Club** (☎ 520/339-4944), in the White Mountains, is one of the highest elevation golf courses in the country. South of Tucson near Nogales, the **Rio Rico Resort and Country Club** (☎ 520/281-8567) offers a challenging back nine. Over along the Colorado River, there are a couple of memorable courses. Lake Havasu City's **London Bridge Golf Club** (☎ 520/855-2719) offers a view of, you guessed it, the London Bridge. For more dramatic views, check out the **Emerald Canyon Golf Course** (☎ 520/667-3366), a municipal course in Parker that plays up and down small canyons and offers the sort of scenery usually associated only with the most expensive desert resort courses.

One last tip: If your ball should happen to land in the coils of a rattlesnake, consider it lost and take your penalty. Rattlesnakes make lousy tees.

The Arizona Trail

While it sounds as though it could have been a movie starring John Wayne, the Arizona Trail is actually an ambitious plan to build a border-to-border trail across the state of Arizona from Utah to Mexico. The trail, which will be 750 miles long and link many existing trails, will be open for nonmotorized travel only. Hikers, mountain bikers, horseback riders, and cross-country skiers will all be able to enjoy various sections of the trail, which will at times cross through designated wilderness areas (closed to mountain bikes).

Connecting alpine meadows and desert arroyos, free-flowing rivers and man-made reservoirs, ponderosa pine forests and stands of saguaros, the trail will cross through the seven life zones and many landscapes that make up Arizona. As it meanders across the state, the trail takes in some of the most spectacular scenery in the Southwest, including the Grand Canyon, the San Francisco Peaks, the Mogollon Rim, and the Santa Catalina Mountains. For more information, contact the **Arizona Trail Association,** P.O. Box 36736, Phoenix, AZ 85067-6736 (☎ **602/252-4794;** www.aztrail.org).

SKIING   Although Arizona is better known as a desert state, it does have plenty of mountains and even a few ski areas. The two biggest and most popular ski areas are **Arizona Snowbowl** (☎ **520/779-1951**) outside Flagstaff and **Sunrise Park** (☎ **520/735-7518** or 520/735-7600) on the Apache Reservation outside the town of McNary in the White Mountains. Snowbowl is the more popular because of the ease of the drive from Phoenix and its proximity to good lodging and dining options in Flagstaff. Although Arizona Snowbowl has more vertical feet of skiing, Sunrise offers almost twice as many runs and the same snow conditions. Both of these ski areas offer ski rentals and lessons. When it's a good snow year, Tucsonians head up to **Mount Lemmon Ski Valley** (☎ **520/576-1321**), the southernmost ski area in the United States. Snows here aren't as reliable as they are farther north.

In a good snow year, cross-country skiers can find plenty of snow-covered forest roads to ski outside Flagstaff (there's also a Nordic center at Arizona Snowbowl), at Sunrise Park outside the town of McNary, at the South Rim of the Grand Canyon, in the White Mountains around Greer and Alpine, outside Payson on the Mogollon Rim, and on Mount Lemmon outside Flagstaff.

TENNIS   Resorts all over Arizona have tennis courts; after golf, this is the most popular winter sport in the desert. Many resorts require you to wear traditional tennis attire and don't include court time in the room rates. Although there may be better courts in the state, none can match the views you'll have from the courts at Enchantment Resort outside Sedona. Just don't let the scenery ruin your game.

WHITE-WATER RAFTING   The desert doesn't support a lot of roaring rivers, but with the white water in the Grand Canyon you don't need too many other choices. Rafting the Grand Canyon is the dream of nearly every white-water enthusiast, and if rafting the canyon is one of your dreams, plan ahead. Companies and trips are limited, and they tend to fill up early. For a discussion and list of companies that run trips down the canyon, see chapter 6.

For 1-day rafting trips on the Colorado below the Grand Canyon, contact **Hualapai River Runners,** P.O. Box 246, Peach Springs, AZ 86434 (☎ **800/622-4409** or 520/769-2210; www.hualapaitours.com). Two-day trips, which spend the night camped by the river and cover the same distance (only more slowly), can also be chartered if you have eight people in your group. For a half- or full-day float on the Colorado above the Grand Canyon, contact **Wilderness River Adventures,** P.O. Box 717, Page, AZ 86040 (☎ **800/528-6154** or 520/645-3279), which runs trips from the Glen Canyon Dam to Lees Ferry.

Daylong and multiday rafting trips are also available on the upper Salt River east of Phoenix. **Far Flung Adventures** (☎ **800/231-7238** or 520/425-7272; www.farflung.com), **Sun Country Rafting** (☎ **800/272-3353** or 602/493-9011), and **Mild to Wild Rafting** (☎ **800/567-6745**) all run trips of varying lengths down this river (conditions permitted).

5 Educational & Volunteer Vacations

Arizona has a number of opportunities for those wanting to combine a vacation with an educational or volunteer experience.

If you'd like to turn a trip to the Grand Canyon into an educational vacation, contact the **Grand Canyon Field Institute,** P.O. Box 399, Grand Canyon, AZ 86023 (☎ **520/638-2485**), which offers a variety of programs from rim-based day hikes to backpacking to indoor classes. Programs are offered from early spring to late fall and include photography and drawing classes, backpacking trips for women, a llama trek, an archaeology trip, and plenty of guided hikes and backpacking trips with a natural history or ecological slant.

Learning Expeditions, a program run by the **Arizona State Museum,** occasionally offers scholar-led archaeological tours, including a trip to Navajo and Hopi country. For more information, call the marketing department at the Arizona State Museum (☎ **520/626-8381;** www.statemuseum.arizona.edu), P.O. Box 210026, Tucson, AZ 85721. The **Museum of Northern Arizona** offers educational backpacking, river rafting, and van tours primarily in the Colorado Plateau in Northern Arizona in a program called Ventures. Trips range from several days to more than a week. For details, contact the Museum of Northern Arizona, 3101 N. Fort Valley Rd., Flagstaff, AZ 86001 (☎ **520/774-5211, ext 220;** www.musnaz.org).

The Nature Conservancy, 300 E. University Blvd., Suite 230, Tucson, AZ 85705 (☎ **520/622-3861;** www.tnc.org), is a nonprofit organization dedicated to the global preservation of natural diversity. The Conservancy accomplishes this goal by identifying and purchasing land that is home to rare plants, animals, and natural communities. The organization has several preserves in Arizona, seven of which are open to the public for hiking, bird watching, and nature study and to which they operate educational field trips of 1 to 4 days. Trips are listed in the Conservancy's Arizona chapter newsletter; information about overnight accommodations, trips, and membership is available by phone or on its Web site.

If you enjoy the wilderness and want to get more involved in its preservation, consider a Sierra Club Service Trip. These trips are for the purpose of building, restoring, and maintaining hiking trails in wilderness areas. It's a lot of work, but a lot of fun as well. For more information on Sierra Club trips, contact the **Sierra Club Outing Department,** 85 Second St., Second Floor, San Francisco, CA 94105 (☎ **415/977-5630**). The Sierra Club also offers hiking, camping, and other sorts of adventure trips to various destinations in Arizona.

You can also join a work crew organized by the **Arizona Trail Association** (☎ **602/252-4794;** www.aztrail.org). These crews spend 1 to 2 days building and maintaining various stretches of the Arizona Trail, which will eventually stretch from the Utah state line to the Mexico border.

Another sort of service trip is being offered by the National Park Service. It accepts volunteers to pick up garbage left by thoughtless visitors to Glen Canyon National Recreation Area. In exchange for picking up trash, you'll get to spend 5 days on a houseboat called the Trash Tracker, cruising through the gorgeous canyon lands of Lake Powell. Volunteers must be at least 18 years old and must provide their own food, sleeping bag, and transportation to the marina. For more information, contact **Glen Canyon National Recreation Area,** P.O. Box 1507, Page, AZ 86040 (☎ **520/608-6404**).

If you'd like to lend a hand at an archaeological dig, contact the **White Mountain Archaeological Center and Raven Site Ruin,** H.C. 30, Box 30, St. Johns, AZ 85936 (☎ **520/333-5857**), which is near Springerville on the edge of the White Mountains.

Finally, if you are interested in architecture or the ecology of urban design, you may be interested in helping out on the continued construction of **Arcosanti,** the slow realization of architect Paolo Soleri's dream of a city that merges architecture and ecology. Located 70 miles north of Phoenix, Arcosanti offers 5-week learning-by-doing workshops. For an application, contact the Cosanti Foundation, Arcosanti, HC 74, Box 4136, Mayer, AZ 86333 (☎ **520/632-7135;** www.arcosanti.org).

6 Health & Insurance

STAYING HEALTHY   If you've never been to the desert before, you should be sure to prepare yourself for this harsh environment. No matter what time of year it is, the desert sun is strong and bright. Use sunscreen when you're outdoors—particularly if you're up in the mountains, where the altitude makes sunburn more likely. The bright sun also makes sunglasses a necessity.

Even if you don't feel hot in the desert, the dry air steals moisture from your body, so drink plenty of fluids. You may want to use a body lotion as well. Skin dries out quickly in the desert air.

It's not only the sun that makes the desert a harsh environment. There are poisonous creatures out there, too, but with a little common sense and some precautions you can avoid them. Rattlesnakes are very common in the desert, but your chances of meeting one are slight (except during the mating season in April and May) because they tend not to come out in the heat of the day. However, never stick your hand into holes among the rocks in the desert and look to see where you're going to step before putting your foot down.

Arizona also has a large poisonous lizard called the Gila monster. These black-and-orange lizards are far less common than rattlesnakes, and your chances of meeting one are slight.

Although the tarantula has developed a nasty reputation, the tiny black widow is more likely to cause illness. Scorpions are another insect danger of the desert. Be extra careful when turning over rocks or logs that might harbor either black widows or scorpions.

INSURANCE   Before going out and spending money on various sorts of travel insurance, check your existing policies to see if they'll cover you while you're traveling. Make sure your health insurance covers you when you're away from home. Some credit and charge cards offer automatic flight insurance when you buy an airline ticket with that card. These policies insure against death or dismemberment in the case of an airplane crash. Also, check your cards to see if any of them pick up the loss-damage waiver (LDW) when you rent a car. The LDW can run as much as $17 a day and can add 50% or more to the cost of renting a car. Check your automobile insurance policy; it, too, may cover the LDW. If you own a home or have renter's insurance, see if that policy covers off-premises theft and loss wherever it occurs. If you're traveling on a tour or have prepaid a large chunk of your travel expenses, you might want to ask your travel agent about trip-cancellation insurance.

If, after checking all your existing insurance policies, you decide that you need additional insurance, reputable issuers of travel insurance include **Travel Guard International,** 1145 Clark St., Stevens Point, WI 54481 (☎ **800/ 826-1300**), and **Travelex Insurance Services,** P.O. Box 9408, Garden City, NY 11530-9408 (☎ **800/228-9792**). Both companies offer medical, baggage, trip cancellation or interruption insurance, and flight insurance against death or dismemberment.

7 Tips for Travelers with Special Needs

FOR TRAVELERS WITH DISABILITIES   When making airline reservations, always mention your disability. Airline policies differ regarding wheelchairs and guide dogs. Most hotels now offer wheelchair-accessible accommodations, and some of the larger and more expensive resorts also offer TDD telephones and other amenities for the hearing and sight impaired.

A World of Options, a book of resources for travelers with disabilities, covers everything from biking trips to scuba outfitters. It costs $35 ($30 for members) and is available from **Mobility International USA,** P.O. Box 10767, Eugene, OR, 97440 (☎ **541/343-1284,** voice and TDD; www.miusa.org). Annual membership for Mobility International is $35, which includes its biannual newsletter, *Over the Rainbow.*

Travelin' Talk Network, P.O. Box 1796, Wheat Ridge, CO 80034 (☎ **303/232-2979;** www.travelintalk.net), operates a Web site for travelers with disabilities, and each month e-mails a newsletter ($19.95 per year) with information about discounts, accessible hotels, trip companions, and other traveling tips. Those without Internet access can also subscribe and receive the newsletter by mail every other month. Another online newsletter and database, **www.access-able.com**, is operated by the same company and supplies information about trip planning, accessible cruise ships, and travel agents that specialize in trips for people with disabilities.

Many of the major car-rental companies now offer hand-controlled cars for drivers with disabilities. Avis can provide such a vehicle at any of its locations in the United States with 48-hour advance notice; Hertz requires between 24 and 72 hours of advance reservation at most of its locations. **Wheelchair Getaways** (☎ **800/642-2042;** www.wheelchair-getaways.com) rents specialized vans with wheelchair lifts and other features for travelers with disabilities in about 38 cities across the United States.

Travelers with disabilities might also want to consider joining a tour that caters specifically to them. **Accessible Journeys** (☎ **800/TINGLES** or 610/521-0339), for slow walkers and wheelchair travelers, offers excursions to the Tucson and the Phoenix areas. **Wilderness Inquiry** (☎ 800/728-0719 or 612/379-3858) offers trips to the Grand Canyon for persons of all abilities.

If you plan to visit many of Arizona's national parks or monuments, you can avail yourself of the **Golden Access Passport,** which is available at any national park or monument that charges admission. This lifetime pass permits free entry into most national parks and monuments, and is issued free to any U.S. citizen or permanent resident who has been medically certified as disabled or blind. In addition, the pass provides discounts on certain camping and other fees.

FOR GAY MEN & LESBIANS   To get in touch with the Phoenix gay community, you can contact the **Gay and Lesbian Community Center,** 24 W. Camelback Rd., Suite C (☎ 602/265-7283). At the community center and at gay bars around Phoenix, you can pick up various community publications, including *Echo* and *Heat Stroke.* **Wingspan,** Tucson's lesbian, gay, and bisexual community center, is at 300 E. Sixth St. (☎ 520/624-1779). *Observer* (☎ 520/622-7176) is a local Tucson gay newspaper available at Wingspan and Antigone Bookstore, 411 N. Fourth Ave. (☎ 520/792-3715).

FOR SENIORS   When making airline reservations, always mention that you're a senior citizen—many airlines offer discounts. You should also carry some sort of photo ID card (driver's license, passport, and so on) to avail yourself of senior-citizen discounts on attractions, hotels, motels, and public transportation, as well as one of the best deals in Arizona for senior citizens: the **Golden Age Passport,** which is available for $10 to U.S. citizens and permanent residents age 62 and older. This federal government pass allows lifetime entrance privileges at most national parks and monuments, and a 50% reduction on federal use fees such as camping. You can apply in person for this passport at a national park, national forest, or other location where it's honored, and you must show reasonable proof of age.

If you aren't a member of the **American Association of Retired Persons (AARP),** 601 E St. NW, Washington, DC 20049 (☎ 800/424-3410 or 202/424-3410), you should consider joining. This association provides discounts for many lodgings, car rentals, airfares, and attractions throughout

---

❷ Did You Know?

- Arizona has more mountainous regions than Switzerland (nearly 20,000 square miles) and more forestland than Minnesota (nearly 20,000,000 acres).
- Arizona was the last territory in the continental United States to become a state.
- The Grand Canyon is one of the seven natural wonders of the world.
- The Hopi village of Oraibi is one of the two oldest continuously inhabited settlements in the United States (Acoma, New Mexico, is the other).
- The Spanish were in Arizona a quarter century before St. Augustine, Florida, was founded and 70 years before the British founded Jamestown, Virginia.
- The bolo tie is the official state neckwear of Arizona.
- Arizonan Sandra Day O'Connor was the first woman appointed to the United States Supreme Court.

Arizona, although you can sometimes get a similar discount simply by showing your ID.

The Mature Traveler, a monthly 12-page newsletter on senior citizen travel, is a valuable resource. It is available by subscription ($32 a year) from GEM Publishing Group, Box 50400, Reno, NV 89513-0400. GEM also publishes *The Book of Deals,* a collection of more than 1,000 senior discounts on airlines, lodging, tours, and attractions around the country; it's available for $9.90 by calling ☎ **800/460-6676.**

Grand Circle Travel is another of the literally hundreds of travel agencies specializing in vacations for seniors (347 Congress St., Boston, MA 02210 (☎ **800/221-2610** or 617/350-7500). *But beware:* Many of them are of the tour-bus variety, with free trips thrown in for those who organize groups of 20 or more. Seniors seeking more independent travel should probably consult a regular travel agent. **SAGA International Holidays,** 222 Berkeley St., Boston, MA 02116 (☎ **800/343-0273**), offers inclusive tours and cruises for those 50 and older. SAGA also sponsors the more substantial "Road Scholar Tours," which are fun-loving but with an educational bent, and is an agent for Smithsonian Institution tours.

If you'd like to do a bit of studying on vacation in the company of like-minded older travelers, consider looking into **Elderhostel,** 75 Federal St., Boston, MA 02110 (☎ **877/426-8056;** www.elderhostel.org).

8 Getting There

BY PLANE

Arizona is served by many airlines flying to both Phoenix and Tucson from around the United States. Dozens of car-rental companies are located both at Sky Harbor International Airport in Phoenix and at Tucson International Airport.

Phoenix and Tucson are both served by the following airlines: **Aero México** (☎ 800/237-6639), **America West** (☎ 800/235-9292), **American** (☎ 800/433-7300), **Continental** (☎ 800/525-0280), **Delta** (☎ 800/221-1212), **Northwest/KLM** (☎ 800/225-2525), **Shuttle by United** (☎ 800/748-8853, **Southwest** (☎ 800/435-9792), and **United** (☎ 800/241-6522). The following airlines serve Phoenix but not Tucson: **Alaska Airlines** (☎ 800/426-0333), **Frontier Airlines** (☎ 800/432-1359), **TWA** (☎ 800/221-2000), and **US Airways** (☎ 800/428-4322).

Consolidators, also known as bucket shops, are a good place to find low fares. Consolidators buy seats in bulk from the airlines and then sell them back to the public at prices below even the airlines' discounted rates. Their small boxed ads usually run in the Sunday travel section of newspapers at the bottom of the page. Before you pay, however, ask for a confirmation number from the consolidator and then call the airline itself to confirm your seat. Be prepared to book your ticket with a different consolidator—there are many to choose from—if the airline can't confirm your reservation. Also be aware that bucket shop tickets are usually nonrefundable or rigged with stiff cancellation penalties, often as high as 50% to 75% of the ticket price. And when an airline runs a special deal, you won't always do better with a consolidator.

For discount and last-minute bookings, contact **McCord Consumer Direct** (☎ 800/FLY-ASAP or 800/454-7700; www.better1.com), which can often get you tickets at significantly less than full fare. **1-800-airfare** (www.1800airfare.com) was formerly owned by TWA but now offers the deepest discounts on many other airlines and can sometimes provide a next-day ticket. There are also "rebators," such as **Travel Avenue** (☎ **800/333-3335** or 312/876-1116), which rebate part of their commissions to you.

BY CAR

The distance to Phoenix from Los Angeles is approximately 369 miles; from San Francisco, 778 miles; from Albuquerque, 455 miles; from Salt Lake City, 660 miles; from Las Vegas, 287 miles; and from Santa Fe, 516 miles.

If you're planning to drive through northern Arizona anytime in the winter, bring chains.

BY TRAIN

Flagstaff and Phoenix have **Amtrak** (☎ **800/872-7245** in the United States and Canada for information and reservations; www.amtrak.com) service from Los Angeles to the west and Albuquerque, Santa Fe, Kansas City, and Chicago to the east aboard the Southwest Chief. The Sunset Limited connects Orlando, New Orleans, Houston, San Antonio, El Paso, and Los Angeles with Tucson and Phoenix. The train stops in Flagstaff or Tucson, and passengers must take a shuttle bus to Phoenix. At press time, the fare from Los Angeles to Phoenix was between $37 and $104 one-way and $74 to $208 round-trip. This trip, including shuttle bus, can take between 12 and 19 hours, depending on the schedule. Earlier bookings secure lower fares.

PACKAGE TOURS

If you prefer to let someone else do all your travel preparations, then a package tour might be for you—whether you just want to lie by the pool at a resort for a week or see the whole state in 2 weeks. The best way to find out about package tours to Arizona is to visit a travel agent, who will likely have several booklets about different tours and airfare/hotel-room packages offered by different airlines.

Gray Line of Phoenix, P.O. Box 21126, Phoenix, AZ 85036 (☎ **800/732-0327** or 602/495-9100), offers Arizona excursions lasting from 1 to 3 days. Tours include the Grand Canyon by way of Sedona and Oak Creek Canyon.

Maupintour, 1421 Research Park Dr., Suite 300, Lawrence, KS 66049-3858 (☎ **800/255-4266** or 785/331-1000), one of the largest tour operators in the world, offers several Arizona itineraries that cover the Grand Canyon, the Four Corners region, Phoenix, and Scottsdale.

SPECIALTY TOURS If you have an interest in the Native American cultures of Arizona, you might want to consider doing a tour with **Discovery Passages,** 1161 Elk Trail, Box 630, Prescott, AZ 86303 (☎ **520/717-0519**), which has tours that visit the Hopi, Navajo, Apache, Tohono O'odham, Hualapai, Yavapai, and Havasupai reservations. **Crossing Worlds,** P.O. Box 623, Sedona, AZ 86339 (☎ **800/350-2693** or 520/649-3060), also offers 1-day and multiday tours throughout the Four Corners region. Tours go to the Hopi mesas, as well as to backcountry ruins on the Navajo Reservation to view cliff dwellings and rock art.

Women's World Adventure, 215 Disney Lane, Sedona, AZ 86336 (☎ **800/664-8922;** www.womensadv.com), offers weeklong tours of the Four Corners region for women only. These tours visit Canyon de Chelly, Lake Powell, the Grand Canyon, and Havasu Canyon. The cost is $1,595 per person.

If you'd like to add a tour into Mexico to your Arizona visit, contact **Ajo Stage Line,** 1041 Solana Rd., Ajo, AZ 85321 (☎ **800/942-1981** or

520/387-6467). Owner Will Nelson leads 1-day and multiday trips to the Gulf of California at Puerto Peñasco, to the rugged El Pinacate region of the Sonoran Desert, to the north rim of the Grand Canyon, and to Kartchner Cavern. Prices range from about $75 to $795.

If you're an experienced motorcycle rider looking for a new way to tour Arizona and the Southwest, consider a guided motorcycle tour with **Ride-Away World Adventures** (☎ **480/488-0080;** www.rideaway.com), which offers tours of 1 to 10 days and can arrange motorcycle rentals as well. Some tours use the Phoenix/Scottsdale area as a base for extended day trips, while other tours head out across the state. Shorter tours are around $165 per day; prices vary on the 10-day tours from about $2,300 to $3,900.

9 Getting Around

BY CAR

Because Phoenix and Tucson are major resort destinations, they both have dozens of **car-rental agencies.** Prices at rental agencies elsewhere in the state tend to be higher, so if at all possible, try to rent your car in either Phoenix or Tucson. Major rental-car companies with offices in Arizona include **Alamo** (☎ 800/327-9633), **Avis** (☎ 800/331-1212), **Budget** (☎ 800/527-0700), **Dollar** (☎ 800/800-4000), **Enterprise** (☎ 800/736-8222), **Hertz** (☎ 800/654-3131), **National** (☎ 800/227-7368), **Payless** (☎ 800/237-2804), and **Thrifty** (☎ 800/367-2277).

Rates for rental cars vary considerably between companies and with the model you want to rent, the dates you rent, and your pickup and drop-off points. If you call the same company three times and ask about renting the same model car, you may get three different quotes, depending on current availability of vehicles. It pays to start shopping early and ask lots of questions—rental agents don't always volunteer information about how to save, so you have to experiment with all the parameters. At press time, Budget was charging $136 per week for a compact car with unlimited mileage in Tucson.

If you're a member of a frequent-flyer program, check to see which rental-car companies participate in your program. Also, when making a reservation, be sure to mention any discount you might be eligible for, such as corporate, military, or AAA, or any specials offered. Beware of coupons offering discounts on rental-car rates—they often discount the highest rates only. It's always cheaper to rent by the week, so even if you don't need a car for 7 days, you might find that it's still cheaper than renting for 4 days only.

Taxes on car rentals vary between 10% and 24% or more and are always at the high end at both the Phoenix and Tucson airports. You can save up to 10% (the airport concession fee recoupment charge) by renting your car at an office outside the airport. Be sure to ask about the tax and the loss-damage waiver (LDW) if you want to know what your total rental cost will be before making a reservation.

A right turn on a red light is permitted after a complete stop. Seat belts are required for the driver and for all passengers; children 4 years and younger, or who weigh 40 pounds or less, must be in a children's car seat. General speed limits are 25 to 35 m.p.h. in towns and cities, 15 m.p.h. in school zones, and 55 m.p.h. on two-lane highways, except rural interstate highways, where the speed limit ranges from 65 to 75 m.p.h.

Always be sure to keep your gas tank topped off. It's not unusual to drive 60 miles without seeing a gas station in many parts of Arizona. *Note:* A breakdown in the desert can be more than just an inconvenience—it can be dangerous. Always carry drinking water with you while driving through the desert, and if you plan to head off on back roads, it's a good idea to carry extra water for the car as well.

The best road maps of Arizona are produced by the American Automobile Association (you have to be a member to get them). Other maps are available from tourist information offices in Phoenix and Tucson. You can also pick up state road maps at almost any gas station.

BY PLANE

Arizona is a big state (the sixth largest), so if your time is short, you might want to consider flying between cities. Several small commuter airlines offer service within the state. They include **America West Airlines** and **America West Express** (☎ 800/235-9292), **Mesa Airlines** (☎ 800/637-2247), **Sunrise Airlines** (☎ 888/394-1851), **Skywest** (☎ 800/453-9417), and **United Express** (☎ 800/241-6522). Cities and towns served by these airlines include Phoenix, Tucson, Flagstaff, the Grand Canyon, Kingman, Prescott, Show Low, Bullhead City (Laughlin, Nevada), Lake Havasu City, and Yuma.

BY TRAIN

The train is not really a viable way of getting around much of Arizona because there is no north-south Amtrak train service between Grand Canyon/Flagstaff and Phoenix or between Tucson and Phoenix. However, Amtrak will sell you a ticket to Phoenix, which includes a shuttle-bus ride from Flagstaff or Tucson. Additionally, you can now get to the town of Williams, 30 miles west of Flagstaff, on Amtrak, and in Williams transfer to the Grand Canyon Railway excursion train, which runs to Grand Canyon Village at the South Rim of the Grand Canyon (see chapter 6 for details). Be aware, however, that the Williams stop is on the outskirts of town; you'll have to arrange to be picked up before you board the train.

Fast Facts: Arizona

American Express   There are offices or representatives in Phoenix and Scottsdale. For more information, call American Express at ☎ **800/528-4800.**

Banks & ATM Networks   ATMs in Arizona generally use the following systems: Star, Cirrus, Plus, American Express, MasterCard, and Visa.

Bed-and-Breakfasts   **Advance Reservations Inn Arizona/Mi Casa-Su Casa Bed & Breakfast Reservation Service,** P.O. Box 950, Tempe, AZ 85280-0950 (☎ **800/456-0682** or 480/990-0682; www.azres.com), can book you into more than 65 homes in the Valley of the Sun (and a total of 280 throughout the state), as can **Arizona Trails Bed & Breakfast Reservation Service,** P.O. Box 18998, Fountain Hills, AZ 85269-8998 (☎ **888/799-4284** or 480/837-4284; fax 480/816-4224; www.arizonatrails.com), which also books tour and hotel reservations. For a list of some of the best B&Bs in the state, contact, the **Arizona Association of Bed and Breakfast Inns,** P.O. Box 22086, Flagstaff, AZ 86002-2086 (☎ **800/284-2589;** www.arizona-bed-breakfast.com).

Business Hours   The following are general open hours; specific establishments may vary. **Banks:** Monday through Friday from 9am to 5pm (some are also open on Saturday from 9am to noon). **Stores:** Monday through Saturday from 10am to 6pm and on Sunday from noon to 5pm (malls usually stay open until 9pm Monday through Saturday). **Bars:** Although they generally open around 11am, bars in Arizona are legally allowed to be open Monday through Saturday from 6am to 1am and on Sunday from 10am to 1am.

Camera/Film   Because the sun is almost always shining in Arizona, you can use a slower film—that is, one with a lower ASA number. This will give you sharper pictures. If your camera accepts different filters, and especially if you plan to travel in the higher altitudes of the northern part of the state, you'd do well to invest in a polarizer, which reduces contrast, deepens colors, and eliminates glare. Also, be sure to protect your camera and film from heat. Never leave your camera or film in a car parked in the sun—temperatures inside the car can climb to more than 130°F, which is hot enough to damage sensitive film.

Car Rentals   See "Getting Around," earlier in this chapter.

Climate   See "When to Go," earlier in this chapter.

Driving Rules   See "Getting Around," earlier in this chapter.

Emergencies   In most places in Arizona, ☎ **911** is the number to call in case of a fire, police, or medical emergency. A few small towns have not adopted this emergency phone number, so if 911 doesn't work, dial 0 (zero) for the operator and state the type of emergency.

Information   See "Visitor Information & Money," above, and individual city chapters and sections for local information offices.

Legal Aid   If you're in need of legal aid, first look in the White Pages of the local telephone book under Legal Aid. You may also want to contact the Travelers Aid Society. In Phoenix the phone number for Community Legal Services is ☎ **602/258-3434.** In Tucson the number for Southern Arizona Legal Aid is ☎ **800/234-7252** or 520/623-9461, and for Travelers Aid of Tucson, it's ☎ **520/622-8900.**

Liquor Laws   The legal age for buying or consuming alcoholic beverages is 21. You cannot purchase any alcoholic drinks from 1 to 6am Monday through Saturday and from 1 to 10am on Sunday.

Pets   If you plan to travel with a pet, it's always best to check when making hotel reservations. At Grand Canyon Village, there's a kennel where you can board your pet while you hike down into the canyon.

Police   In most places in Arizona, phone ☎ **911.** A few small towns have not adopted this emergency phone number, so if 911 doesn't work, dial 0 (zero) for the operator and state the type of emergency.

Safety   When driving long distances, always carry plenty of drinking water, and if you're heading off onto dirt roads, extra water for your car's radiator is also a good idea. When hiking or walking in the desert, keep an eye out for rattlesnakes; these poisonous snakes are not normally aggressive unless provoked, so give them a wide berth, and they'll leave you alone. Black widow spiders and scorpions are also desert denizens that can be dangerous, although the better-known tarantula is actually much less of a threat. If you go turning over rocks or logs, you're likely to encounter one of Arizona's poisonous residents.

Taxes   There's a state sales tax of 5.5% (local communities levy additional taxes), car-rental taxes ranging from around 10% to more than 20%, and hotel room taxes from around 6% to around 14%.

Time Zone   Arizona is in the mountain time zone. However, the state does not observe daylight saving time, so time differences between Arizona and the rest of the country vary with the time of year. From the last Sunday in October until the first Sunday in April, Arizona is 1 hour later than the West Coast and 2 hours earlier than the East Coast. The rest of the year Arizona is on the same time as the West Coast and is 3 hours earlier than the East Coast. There is an exception, however—the Navajo Reservation observes daylight saving time. However, the Hopi Reservation, which is completely surrounded by the Navajo Reservation, does not.

Weather   For current weather information, call ☎ **602/265-5550.**

Planning Your Trip: An Online Directory

by Lynne Bairstow

Lynne Bairstow is the co-author of *Frommer's Mexico* and the
editorial director of *e-com* magazine.

Day by day, the Internet becomes more integrated into our lives—
including the way we plan and book our travel. By early 2000, one in
every 10 trips was being booked online, a trend that's sure to accelerate.

The Internet not only provides a wealth of destination information,
but also gives you the chance to compare experiences with fellow travelers, ask experts for pre-trip advice, seek out discounted fares once
accessible only to travel-industry insiders, and stay in touch via e-mail
while you're away. The instant communication and storehouse of
information have revolutionized the way travel is researched, reserved,
and realized.

The Frommer's Online Directory will help you take better advantage of the planning information available online, and it's best used in
conjunction with this book. Part 1 lists general Internet resources that
can make any trip easier, such as sites for finding the best possible
prices on airline tickets. In Part 2, you'll find some top online guides
for Arizona.

Please keep in mind that this is not a comprehensive list, but rather
a discriminating selection to get you started. Recognition is given to
sites based on their content value and ease of use, and are not paid
for—unlike some Web-site rankings, which are based on payment.
Finally, remember this is a press-time snapshot of leading Web sites—
some undoubtedly will have evolved, changed, or moved by the time
you read this.

1 Top Travel-Planning Web Sites

While the Internet was once a conglomerate of sites for researching
places to visit, several key companies have emerged that offer comprehensive travel planning and booking. In addition to Frommer's Online
(see above), we list the other top online travel agencies below, along
with some more specialized services.

WHY BOOK ONLINE?

Online agencies have come a long way over the past few years, now
providing tips for finding the best fare as well as giving you suggested
dates or times to travel that yield the lowest price if your plans are at
all flexible. Other sites even allow you to establish the price you're willing to pay, and then check the airlines' willingness to accept it. However, in some cases, these sites may not always yield the best price.

Editor's Note: What You'll Find at the Frommer's Site

We highly recommend **Arthur Frommer's Budget Travel Online (www.frommers.com)** as an excellent travel planning resource. Of course, we're a little biased, but you'll find indispensable travel tips, reviews, monthly vacation giveaways, and online booking. Among the most popular features of this site is the regular "Ask the Expert" bulletin boards, which feature one of the Frommer's authors answering your questions via online postings.

Subscribe to Arthur Frommer's Daily Newsletter (**www.frommers. com/newsletters**) to receive the latest travel bargains and insider travel secrets in your e-mailbox every day. You'll read daily headlines and articles from the dean of travel himself, highlighting last-minute deals on airfares, accommodations, cruises, and package vacations. You'll also find great travel advice by checking our "Tip of the Day" or "Hot Spot of the Month."

Search our Destinations archive (**www.frommers.com/destinations**) of more than 200 domestic and international destinations for great places to stay, tips for traveling there, and what to do while you're there. Once you've researched your trip, the online reservations system (**www. frommers.com/booktravelnow**) takes you to Frommer's favorite sites for booking your vacation at affordable prices.

Unlike a travel agent, for example, they might not have access to charter flights offered by wholesalers.

Online booking sites aren't the only places to reserve airline tickets—all major airlines have their own Web sites and often offer incentives—bonus frequent flyer miles or Net-only discounts, for example—when you buy online or buy an e-ticket.

The new trend is toward conglomerated booking sites. A consortium of U.S.- and European-based airlines are planning to launch an as-yet-unnamed Web site that will offer fares lower than those available through travel agents. United, Delta, Northwest, and Continental have initiated this effort, based on their success at selling airline seats at their own online sites.

The best of the travel-planning sites are now highly personalized; they store your seating preferences, meal preferences, tentative itineraries, and credit-card information, allowing you to quickly plan trips or check agendas.

In many cases, booking your trip online can be better than working with a travel agent. It gives you the widest variety of choices, control, and the 24-hour convenience of planning your trip when you choose. All you need is some time—and often a little patience—and you're likely to find the fun of online travel research will greatly enhance your trip.

WHO SHOULD BOOK ONLINE?

Online booking is best for travelers who want to know as much as possible about their travel options, for those who have flexibility in their travel dates and are looking for the best price, and for bargain hunters driven by a good value, who are open-minded about where they travel.

One of the biggest successes in online travel for both passengers and airlines is the offer of last-minute specials, such as American Airlines' weekend deals or other Internet-only fares that must be purchased online. Another advantage is that you can cash in on incentives for booking online, such as rebates or bonus frequent flyer miles.

Business and other frequent travelers also have found numerous benefits in online booking, as the advances in mobile technology provide them with the ability to check flight status, change plans, or get specific directions from handheld computing devices, mobile phones, and pagers. Some sites will even e-mail or page passengers if their flight is delayed.

Online booking is increasingly able to accommodate complex itineraries, even for international travel. The pace of evolution on the Net is rapid, so you'll probably find additional features and advancements by the time you visit these sites. What the future holds for online travelers is ever-increasing personalization and customization.

TRAVEL-PLANNING & BOOKING SITES

Below are listings for the top sites for planning and booking travel. The following sites offer domestic and international flight, hotel, and rental-car bookings, plus news, destination information, and deals on cruises and vacation packages. Free (one-time) registration is required for booking.

Travelocity (incorporates Preview Travel). www.travelocity.com; www.previewtravel.com; www.frommers.travelocity.com

Travelocity is Frommer's online travel-planning and booking partner. Travelocity uses the SABRE system to offer reservations and tickets for more than 400 airlines, plus reservations and purchase capabilities for more than 45,000 hotels and 50 car-rental companies. An exclusive feature of the SABRE system is its **Low Fare Search Engine,** which automatically searches for the three lowest-priced itineraries based on a traveler's criteria. Last-minute deals and consolidator fares are included in the search. If you book with Travelocity, you can select specific seats for your flights with online seat maps, and also view diagrams of the most popular commercial aircraft. Its hotel finder rovides street-level location maps and photos of selected hotels. With the **Fare Watcher** e-mail feature, you can select up to five routes and receive e-mail notices when the fare changes by $25 or more.

Travelocity's **Destination Guide** includes updated information on some 260 destinations worldwide-supplied by Frommer's.

Note to AOL Users: You can book flights, hotels, rental cars, and cruises on AOL at keyword: Travel. The booking software is provided by Travelocity/Preview Travel and is similar to the Internet site. Use the AOL "Travelers Advantage" program to earn a 5% rebate on flights, hotel rooms, and car rentals.

Staying Secure

More people still look online than book online, partly due to fear of putting their credit-card numbers out on the Net. Secure encryption has removed this fear for most travelers. In some cases, however, it's simply easier to buy from a local travel agent who can deliver your tickets to your door (especially if your travel is last-minute or if you have special requests). You can find a flight online and then book it by calling a toll-free number or contacting your travel agent, though this is somewhat less efficient. To be sure you're in secure mode when you book online, look for a little icon of a key or a padlock at the bottom of your Web browser.

✪ Expedia. expedia.com

Expedia is Travelocity's major competitor. It offers several ways of obtaining the best possible fares: **Flight Price Matcher** service allows your preferred airline to match an available fare with a competitor; a comprehensive **Fare Compare** area shows the differences in fare categories and airlines; and **Fare Calendar** helps you plan your trip around the best possible fares. Its main limitation is that like many online databases, Expedia focuses on the major airlines and hotel chains, so don't expect to find too many budget airlines or one-of-a-kind B&Bs here.

TRIP.com. www.trip.com

TRIP.com began as a site geared toward business travelers, but its innovative features and highly personalized approach have broadened its appeal to leisure travelers as well. It is the leading travel site for those using mobile devices to access Internet travel information.

TRIP.com includes a trip-planning function that provides the average and lowest fare for the route requested, in addition to the current available fare. Among its most popular features are Flight TRACKER and intelliTRIP. **Flight TRACKER** allows users to track any commercial flight en route to its destination anywhere in the United States, while accessing real-time FAA-based flight monitoring data. **intelliTRIP** is a travel search tool that allows users to identify the best airline, hotel, and rental-car rates in less than 90 seconds.

In addition, the site offers e-mail notification of flight delays, plus city resource guides, currency converters, and a weekly e-mail newsletter of fare updates, travel tips, and traveler forums.

Yahoo! Travel. www.travel.yahoo.com

Yahoo! is currently the most popular of the Internet information portals, and its travel site is a comprehensive mix of online booking, daily travel news, and destination information. The **Best Fares** area offers what it promises, plus provides feedback on refining your search if you have flexibility in travel dates or times. There is also an active section of Message Boards for discussions on travel in general and specific destinations.

SPECIALTY TRAVEL SITES

Although the sites listed above provide the most comprehensive services, some travelers have specialized needs that are best met by a site that caters specifically to them.

For adventure travelers, **iExplore (www.iexplore.com)** is a great source for finding information on and booking adventure and experiential travel. The site combines secure Internet booking functions with hands-on expertise and 24-hour live customer support by seasoned adventure travelers, catering to those interested in trips off the beaten path. The company is a supporting member of the Ecotourism Society, and is committed to environmentally responsible travel worldwide.

Another excellent site for adventure travelers is **Away.com (www.away. com),** which features unique vacations for challenging the body, mind, and spirit. Trips may include cycling in the Loire Valley, going on an African Safari, or assisting in the excavation of a Mayan ruin. For those without the time for such an extended, exotic trip, offbeat weekend getaways are also available. Trips are listed according to cultural, adventure, and green-travel categories.

GORP (Great Outdoor Recreation Pages; **www.gorp.com**) has been a standard for adventure travelers since its founding in 1995 by outdoor enthusiasts

Diane and Bill Greer. Tapping their own experiences, they created this Web site that offers unique travel destinations and encourages active participation by fellow GORP visitors through the sophisticated menu of online forums, contests, and discussions.

For travelers who prefer more unique accommodations, **InnSite (www. innsite.com)** offers listings for inns and B&Bs in all 50 U.S. states and dozens of countries around the globe. Find an inn at your destination, have a look at images of the rooms, check prices and availability, and then send e-mail to the innkeeper if you have further questions. This is an extensive directory of bed-and-breakfast inns, but includes a listing only if the proprietor submitted one (*Note:* it's free to get an inn listed).

Another good resource for mostly one-of-a-kind places in the United States and abroad is **Places to Stay (www.placestostay.com),** which focuses on resort accommodations.

"Have Kids, Still Travel!" is the motto of the **Family Travel Forum** (FTF; **www.familytravelforum.com**), a site dedicated to the promotion and support of travel with children. FTF is supported by memberships, which are available in flexible prices ranging from a $2.95 monthly fee to a heftier annual fee for more comprehensive services. Since no advertising is accepted, FTF provides its members with honest, unbiased information, informed advice, and practical tips designed to make traveling with children a healthier, safer, hassle-free experience, not to mention a better value.

LAST-MINUTE DEALS & OTHER ONLINE BARGAINS

There's nothing airlines hate more than flying with lots of empty seats. The Net has enabled airlines to offer last-minute bargains to entice travelers to fill those seats. Most of these are announced on Tuesday or Wednesday and are valid for travel the following weekend, but some can be booked weeks or months in advance. You can sign up for weekly e-mail alerts at the airlines' sites or check sites that compile lists of these bargains, such as **Smarter Living** or **WebFlyer** (see below). To make it easier, visit a site that will round up all the deals and send them in one convenient weekly e-mail. But last-minute deals aren't the only online bargains; other sites can help you find value even if you haven't waited until the eleventh hour. Increasingly popular are travel auction sites and services that let you name the price you're willing to pay for an air seat or vacation package.

⭐ **1travel.com. www.1travel.com**
Here you'll find deals on domestic and international flights, cruises, hotels, and all-inclusive resorts such as Club Med. 1travel.com's **Saving Alert** compiles last-minute air deals so you don't have to scroll through multiple e-mail alerts. A feature called **Farebeater** searches a database that includes published fares, consolidator bargains, and special deals exclusive to 1travel.com. *Note:* The travel agencies listed by 1travel.com have paid for placement.

Cheap Tickets. www.cheaptickets.com
Cheap Tickets has exclusive deals that aren't available through more mainstream channels. One caveat about the Cheap Tickets site is that it will offer fare quotes for a route, then later show this fare is not valid for your dates of travel—most other Web sites, such as Expedia, consider your dates of travel before showing what fares are available. Despite its problems, Cheap Tickets can be worth the effort because its fares can be lower than those offered by its competitors.

LastMinuteTravel.com. www.lastminutetravel.com

Suppliers with excess inventory come to this online agency to distribute unsold airline seats, hotel rooms, cruises, and vacation packages. It's got great deals, but you have to put up with an excess of advertisements and slow-loading graphics.

✪ **Priceline.com. http://travel.priceline.com**

Even people who aren't familiar with many Web sites have heard about Priceline.com. Launched in 1998 with a $10-million ad campaign featuring William Shatner, Priceline lets you "name your price" for domestic and international airline tickets and hotel rooms. In other words, you select a route and dates, guarantee with a credit card, and make a bid for what you're willing to pay. If one of the airlines in Priceline's database has a fare lower than your bid, your credit card will automatically be charged for a ticket.

But you can't say when you want to fly—you have to accept any flight leaving between 6am and 10pm on the dates you selected, and you may have to make a stopover. No frequent flyer miles are awarded, and tickets are non-refundable and can't be exchanged for another flight. So if your plans change, you're out of luck. Priceline can be good for travelers who have to take off on short notice (and who are thus unable to qualify for advance-purchase discounts). But be sure to shop around first, because if you overbid, you'll be required to purchase the ticket—and Priceline will pocket the difference between what it paid for the ticket and what you bid.

Priceline says that over 35% of all reasonable offers for domestic flights are being filled on the first try, with much higher fill rates on popular routes (New York to San Francisco, for example). It defines "reasonable" as not more than 30% below the lowest generally available advance-purchase fare for the same route.

Smarter Living. www.smarterliving.com

Best known for its e-mail dispatch of weekend deals on 20 airlines, Smarter Living also keeps you posted about last-minute bargains on everything from Windjammer Cruises to flights to Iceland.

Travelzoo.com. www.travelzoo.com

At this Internet portal, over 150 travel companies post special deals. It features a Top 20 list of the best deals on the site, selected by its editorial staff each Wednesday night. This list is also available via an e-mail list, free to those who sign up.

WebFlyer. www.webflyer.com

WebFlyer is a comprehensive online resource for frequent flyers and also has an excellent listing of last-minute air deals. Click on "Deal Watch" for a roundup of weekend deals on flights, hotels, and rental cars from domestic and international suppliers.

Know When the Sales Start

While most people learn about last-minute weekend deals from e-mail dispatches, it can pay to check the airline sites to find out precisely when they post their special fares. Because deals are limited, they can vanish within hours, sometimes minutes—often before you even read your e-mail. An example: Southwest's specials are posted at 12:01am Tuesdays (Central time). So if you're looking for a cheap flight, stay up late and check Southwest's site to grab the best new deals.

ONLINE TRAVELER'S TOOLBOX

Veteran travelers usually carry some essential items to make their trips easier. Following is a selection of online tools to smooth your journey.

Visa ATM Locator. www.visa.com/pd/atm/
MasterCard ATM Locator. www.mastercard.com/atm
Find ATMs in hundreds of cities in the United States and around the world. Both include maps for some locations and both list airport ATM locations. *Tip:* You'll usually get a better exchange rate using ATMs than exchanging traveler's checks at banks, but check in advance to see what kind of fees your bank will assess for using an overseas ATM.

Intellicast. www.intellicast.com
Weather forecasts for all 50 states and cities around the world. Note that temperatures are in Celsius for many international destinations, so don't think you'll need that winter coat for your next trip to Athens.

✪ Mapquest. www.mapquest.com
The best of the mapping sites that lets you choose a specific address or destination; in seconds, it will return a map and detailed directions. It really is easier than calling, asking, and writing down directions. The site also links to special travel deals and helpful sites.

Net Café Guide. www.netcafeguide.com/mapindex.htm
Locate Internet cafes at hundreds of locations around the globe. Catch up on your e-mail, log on to the Web, and stay in touch with the home front, usually for just a few dollars per hour.

Web Travel Secrets. www.web-travel-secrets.com
If this list leaves you yearning for more travel-oriented sites, Web Travel Secrets offers one of the best compilations around. One section offers advice and tips on how to find the lowest prices for airlines, hotels, and cruises. The other section provides a comprehensive listing of Web travel links for airfare deals, airlines, booking engines, cars, cruise lines, discount travel and best deals, general travel resources, hotels and hotel discounters, search engines, and travel magazines and newsletters.

2 The Top Web Sites for Arizona

GENERAL SITES FOR ARIZONA

Access Arizona. www.accessarizona.com
An online news magazine devoted to the state, Access Arizona provides local news as well as a steady stream of entertainment, dining, and event listings.

✪ Arizona Central. www.azcentral.com
The online home of the *Arizona Republic,* this site isn't just a good online entertainment listing—it's a good online newspaper. It has music, movie, and restaurant reviews, as well as a complete rundown of local sports.

✪ Arizona Guide. www.arizonaguide.com
Produced by the Arizona Office of Tourism and Arizona Central (the online home of the *Arizona Republic* newspaper), Arizona Guide is a must-visit site for anyone planning a vacation here.

Arizona History Traveler. www.azhistorytraveler.org
A look at Arizona tourism from a historical perspective. The site offers summaries, by region, of about 15 monuments, museums, and landmarks that

Online Directory

Check E-Mail at Internet Cafes While Traveling

Until a few years ago, most travelers who checked their e-mail while traveling carried a laptop—an expensive and often technologically troublesome option. Thankfully, Web-based free e-mail programs have made it much easier to check your mail.

Just open an account at any one of the numerous "freemail" providers—the original leaders continue to be **Hotmail** (hotmail.com), **Excite** (www.excite.com), and **Yahoo! Mail** (mail.yahoo.com), although many are available. AOL users should check out **AOL Netmail,** and **USA.NET** (www.usa.net) comes highly recommended for functionality and security. You can find hints, tips, and a mile-long list of freemail providers at **www.emailaddresses.com.**

Then all you'll need to check your mail is a Web connection, easily available at Net cafes and copy shops around the world. After logging on, just call up your freemail's Internet address, enter your user name and password, and you'll have access to your mail. From these sites, you can download all your e-mail—even from office accounts—or your local or national Internet Service Provider address. There will be a section generally called "check other mail" that allows you to add the names of other e-mail servers.

The downside is that most Web-based e-mail sites allow a maximum of only 3MB capacity per mail account, which can fill up quickly. Also, message sending and receiving is not immediate; some messages may be delayed by several hours or even days.

Internet cafes have become ubiquitous, so for a few dollars an hour you'll be able to check your mail and send messages from virtually anywhere in the world. Interestingly, Internet cafes tend to be more common in very remote areas, where they may offer the best form of access for an entire community, especially if phone lines are difficult to obtain.

help define where the state has been in its 87-year history. It also includes contact information for nearly 100 historic parks, museums, and cultural centers around the state.

Arizona Reporter. www.azreporter.com
Provides a travel section with regular articles highlighting destinations around the state, as well as events calendars and entertainment listings.

Arizona Tourist Bureau. www.arizonatourism.com/index.html
This site offers information not only on tourist destinations, but on car rentals and RV parks. It lets you book hotel reservations online and take a photo tour.

AZ US Web Works. azuswebworks.com/az/index.html
US Web Works offers a virtually text-free breakdown of the entire state, offering extensive links to cities, monuments, colleges, and museums, as well as trails, maps, and travel information.

PHOENIX
ONLINE GUIDES & ENTERTAINMENT SITES

✪ **CitySearch: Phoenix. www.phoenix.citysearch.com**
Movie, concert, and restaurant reviews, and a month-by-month list of recommended events make finding an evening's entertainment easier than ever. A

visitors' guide breaks down the city's essentials, and links to maps and directions prove invaluable for those trying to find their way around town.

Greater Phoenix Convention & Visitors Bureau.
www.arizonaguide.com/cities/phoenix
Everything the professional traveler to Phoenix needs, from accommodation information to meeting planners. And don't miss the golf course guide.

Phoenix Area Guide. http://phoenix.areaguides.net
This guide offers Yellow Pages, White Pages, maps, classifieds, and more. A travel guide section includes things to see and do, as well as local history and a breakdown of cities in the area.

Phoenix Downtown. www.downtownphx.org
This site offers contact information for a huge number of downtown businesses, including events, restaurants, bars and clubs, and shopping.

TUCSON
ONLINE GUIDES & ENTERTAINMENT SITES

✪ Best of Tucson. **www.desert.net/tw/bot/index.htm**
Produced by the *Tucson Weekly,* this is an essential site for visitors. Offering best-of lists for everything from fine dining to fried pickles, the site covers food, shopping, outdoors, bars, cafes, and city life.

✪ Tucson Area Guide. **http://tucson.areaguides.net**
A well-rounded look at Tucson, offering advice on everything from food to lodging to weather reports. This site is very well organized and a great starting point for first-time visitors.

Tucson Citizen. www.tucsoncitizen.com
The local newspaper offers current listings of arts, entertainment, and sports, as well as weather conditions and updated news reports.

✪ Tucson Hikes. **www.azstarnet.com/~aflach/index.htm**
A thorough list of hikes in and around Tucson, cross-indexed by difficulty, season, and region. Each listing offers trail length, estimated time, difficulty, a description of the trail, and directions on how to get there. If you're a hiker, don't miss this site.

The Ultimate Arizona Vacation Guide.
www.webcreationsetc.com/Azguide/Tucson
Everything a visitor to Tucson could need, including maps, facts, attractions, and discounted hotel and car rentals. For those who want to explore, the guide covers not only Tucson, but all of Southern Arizona.

GRAND CANYON

✪ The American Experience: Lost in the Grand Canyon.
www.pbs.org/wgbh/pages/amex/canyon
If it's Grand Canyon history you're looking for, look no farther. This beautiful Web site accompanies PBS's documentary film about John Wesley Powell's 1869 expedition down the Colorado River into the last uncharted territory in the United States. Find your way around via timeline navigation, a People & Events section, or historical maps.

Gateway to the Grand Canyon. www.thegrandcanyon.com
Having recently undergone site reconstruction for easier navigation, the Grand Canyon Gateway offers nuts and bolts, including park information, attractions and tours, festivals and events, camping and lodging, and where to eat.

✪ **Grand Canyon Explorer.** **www.kaibab.org**
There are slicker sites on the Web, but the amount of information in the Grand Canyon Explorer is staggering. Dozens of articles offer news about what's going on, and links cover everything from how to get there to how the canyon got there, with maps, suggested hikes and trips, weather, and lodging. A virtual tour leads armchair travelers through the Canyon.

Grand Canyon Information Site. **www.thecanyon.com**
The information site of the National Park Service is just that—a place to find any and all information you need before you travel to the Canyon. Whether obtaining backcountry or river permits, looking for camping or lodging information, figuring out the logistics of your trip, or simply looking for news or a bit of history, this is a good place to start.

✪ **National Park Service Site.** **www.nps.gov/grca**
A straightforward overview of the information visitors require: phone numbers, operating hours, transportation information, driving directions, fees, and recommended activities.

OTHER ARIZONA PARKS & RECREATION AREAS

Canyon Country. **www.canyon-country.com**
Maps, tours, and lodging information for Lake Powell, Lake Mead, the Grand Canyon, and Monument Valley. Short articles, recommendations, and online travel packages provide helpful information, but this site is best used for getting straight facts about Arizona's great outdoors.

Ghost Town of the Month. **www.inficad.com/~ghosttown/ghost.html**
Step into the desert and visit the West's haunting past. This site provides a surprisingly deep directory of the ghost towns of Arizona, with photos, town histories, and recommended times for visiting.

Glen Canyon. **www.nps.gov/glca/home.htm**
The Glen Canyon site offers the straight facts: phone numbers, operating hours, transportation information, driving directions, fees, events, and recommended activities.

Lake Mead National Recreation Area. **www.nps.gov/lame**
Another in the National Park Service series, this site on Lake Mead offers the visitor all the essential information, including a sizable section on recommended activities.

Monuments. **www.azuswebworks.com/az/monuments.html**
Links to national monuments around the state, directing visitors to official government sites, unofficial sites put together by outdoor lovers, and quality commercial sites. If you're curious about a specific park, this is a great place to start.

Petrified Forest National Park. **www.nps.gov/pefo**
This National Park Service site provides all the basic information a visitor needs, including a list of program activities and camping facilities available in the park.

Saguaro National Park. **www.saguaro.national-park.com**
This independent site offers an array of informative links, including an activities calendar, camping, hiking and lodging guides, maps, weather forecasts, and even a chat room for nature lovers.

GETTING AROUND

Arizona Department of Transportation Trailmaster. **www.azfms.com**
All the information a traveler could need about road conditions, closures, and weather patterns. Nearly 50 freeway cameras help the prepared driver avoid congestion. You can even find parking information for locations around the state.

Arizona Rail Passenger Association. **www.psn.net/~azrail**
This community organization promotes rail travel, featuring stories of interest on its site, as well as a deep array of information on train stations, schedules, rail maps, and background on the trains themselves.

Phoenix Sky Harbor International Airport. **www.phxskyharbor.com**
All the basics for Phoenix Sky Harbor Airport, including flight schedules and site map.

Tucson International Airport. **www.tucsonairport.org**
This site has become a "time-saving tool for worldwide flight scheduling." Flight schedules, site maps, airline information, and directions to the airport are provided.

Sun Tran. **www.suntran.com**
Tucson's public transportation system, Sun Tran, has a Web site that offers schedules, maps, and lists of services.

Online Directory

3 For Foreign Visitors

The American West is well known and well loved in many countries. Arizona's images are familiar from Western novels, movies, television shows, and advertisements. And, of course, the Grand Canyon is one of the wonders of the world. However, despite Arizona being the Wild West, you are likely to encounter typically American situations in Arizona, and this chapter should help you prepare for your trip.

1 Preparing for Your Trip

ENTRY REQUIREMENTS

Immigration law is a hot political issue in the United States these days, and the following requirements may have changed somewhat by the time you plan your trip. Check at any U.S. embassy or consulate for current information and requirements. You can also plug into the **U.S. State Department's** Internet site at **www.state.gov**.

VISAS The U.S. State Department has a **Visa Waiver Pilot Program** allowing citizens of certain countries to enter the United States without a visa for stays of up to 90 days. At press time, these countries included Andorra, Argentina, Australia, Austria, Belgium, Brunei, Denmark, Finland, France, Germany, Iceland, Ireland, Italy, Japan, Liechtenstein, Luxembourg, Monaco, the Netherlands, New Zealand, Norway, San Marino, Slovenia, Spain, Sweden, Switzerland, and the United Kingdom. Citizens of these countries need only a valid passport and a round-trip air or cruise ticket in their possession upon arrival. If they first enter the United States, they may also visit Mexico, Canada, Bermuda, and/or the Caribbean islands and return to the United States without a visa. Further information is available from any U.S. embassy or consulate. Canadian citizens may enter the United States without visas; they need only proof of residence.

Citizens of all other countries must have (1) a valid passport that expires at least 6 months later than the scheduled end of their visit to the United States, and (2) a tourist visa, which can be obtained without charge from any U.S. consulate.

OBTAINING A VISA To get a visa, the traveler must submit a completed application form (either in person or by mail) with a $1^1/_2$-inch-square photo, and must demonstrate binding ties to a residence abroad. Usually you can get a visa at once or within 24 hours, but it may take longer during the summer rush from June through August. If you cannot go in person, contact the nearest U.S. embassy or consulate for directions on applying by mail. Your travel agent or airline office may also be able to supply you with visa applications and instructions. The U.S. consulate or embassy that issues your visa determines whether you will be issued a multiple- or single-entry visa and any restrictions on the length of your stay.

British subjects can get up-to-date passport and visa information by calling the **U.S. Embassy Visa Information Line** (☎ **0891/200-290**) or the **London Passport Office** (☎ **020/7271-3000** for recorded information).

MEDICAL REQUIREMENTS   Unless you're arriving from an area known to be suffering from an epidemic (particularly cholera or yellow fever), inoculations or vaccinations are not required for entry into the United States. If you have a disease that requires treatment with narcotics or syringe-administered medications, carry a valid signed prescription from your physician to allay any suspicions that you may be smuggling narcotics (a serious offense that carries severe penalties in the United States).

DRIVER'S LICENSES   Foreign driver's licenses are mostly recognized in the United States, although you may want to get an international driver's license if your home license is not written in English.

CUSTOMS REQUIREMENTS   Every visitor over 21 years of age may bring in, free of duty, the following: (1) 1 liter of wine or hard liquor; (2) 200 cigarettes, 100 cigars (but not from Cuba), or 3 pounds of smoking tobacco; and (3) $100 worth of gifts. These exemptions are offered to travelers who spend at least 72 hours in the United States and who have not claimed them within the preceding 6 months. It is altogether forbidden to bring into the country foodstuffs (particularly fruit, cooked meats, and canned goods) and plants (vegetables, seeds, tropical plants, and the like). Foreign tourists may bring in or take out up to $10,000 in U.S. or foreign currency with no formalities; larger sums must be declared to U.S. Customs on entering or leaving, which includes filing form CM 4790. For more specific information regarding U.S. Customs, call your nearest U.S. embassy or consulate, or contact the **U.S. Customs** office at ☎ **202/927-1770** or www.customs.gov/travel/travel.htm.

INSURANCE

Although it's not required of travelers, health insurance is highly recommended. Unlike many European countries, the United States does not usually offer free or low-cost medical care to its citizens or visitors. Doctors and hospitals are expensive, and in most cases require advance payment or proof of coverage before they render their services. Other policies can cover everything from the loss or theft of your baggage and trip cancellation to the guarantee of bail in case you're arrested. Good policies also cover the costs of an accident, repatriation, or death. See "Health & Insurance" in chapter 2, "Planning a Trip to Arizona: The Basics," for more information. Packages such as **Europ Assistance** in Europe are sold by automobile clubs and travel agencies at attractive rates. **Worldwide Assistance Services** (☎ **800/821-2828**) is the agent for Europ Assistance in the United States.

Although lack of health insurance may prevent you from being admitted to a hospital in non-emergencies, don't worry about being left on a street corner to die: The American way is to fix you now and bill the living daylights out of you later.

MONEY

CURRENCY   The U.S. monetary system has a decimal base: one American **dollar** ($1) = 100 **cents** (100¢).

Dollar bills commonly come in $1 (a "buck"), $5, $10, $20, $50, and $100 denominations (the last two are not welcome when paying for small purchases and are not accepted in taxis). There are also $2 bills (seldom encountered).

There are six denominations of coins: 1¢ (1 cent, or a "penny"), 5¢ (5 cents, or a "nickel"), 10¢ (10 cents, or a "dime"), 25¢ (25 cents, or a "quarter"), 50¢ (50 cents, or a "half dollar"), and $1 coins, of which there are three types in circulation (the older, large Eisenhower dollar, the smaller Susan B. Anthony dollar, and the new golden Sacagawea dollar. Note that U.S. coins are not stamped with their numeric value.

The foreign-exchange bureaus so common in Europe are rare even at airports in the United States, and nonexistent outside major cities. Try to avoid having to change foreign money or traveler's checks not denominated in U.S. dollars at a small-town bank or even a branch bank in a big city. In fact, leave any currency other than U.S. dollars at home—it could prove more nuisance to you than it's worth.

TRAVELER'S CHECKS Traveler's checks *denominated in U.S. dollars* are readily accepted at most hotels, motels, restaurants, and large stores, but might not be accepted at small stores or for small purchases. The best place to change traveler's checks is at a bank. Do not bring traveler's checks denominated in other currencies. The three traveler's checks that are most widely recognized are **Visa, American Express,** and **Thomas Cook.**

CREDIT CARDS & ATMS Credit cards are the most widely used form of payment in the United States: **Visa** (BarclayCard in Britain), **MasterCard** (Eurocard in Europe, Access in Britain, Chargex in Canada), **American Express, Diners Club, Discover,** and **Carte Blanche.** You must have a credit or charge card to rent a car. There are, however, a handful of stores and restaurants that do not take credit cards, so be sure to ask in advance. Most businesses display a sticker near their entrance to let you know which cards they accept. (*Note:* Often businesses require a minimum purchase price, usually around $10, to use a credit card.)

It is strongly recommended that you bring at least one major credit card. Hotels, car-rental companies, and airlines usually require a credit-card imprint as a deposit against expenses, and in an emergency a credit card can be priceless.

You'll find automated-teller machines (ATMs) on just about every block in larger cities. Some ATMs allow you to draw U.S. currency against your bank and credit cards. Check with your bank before leaving home, and remember that you need your personal identification number (PIN) to do so. Most accept Visa, MasterCard, and American Express, as well as ATM cards from other U.S. banks. Expect to be charged up to $3 per transaction, however. One way around these fees is to ask for cash back at grocery stores that accept ATM cards and don't charge usage fees. Of course, you'll have to purchase something first.

SAFETY

GENERAL SAFETY SUGGESTIONS While tourist areas are generally safe, U.S. urban areas tend to be less safe than those in Europe or Japan. You should always stay alert. It is wise to ask your hotel front desk staff or the city or area's tourist office if you're in doubt about which neighborhoods are safe. Avoid deserted areas, especially at night, and don't go into public parks at night unless there's a concert or similar occasion that will attract a crowd.

Avoid carrying valuables with you on the street, and don't display expensive cameras or electronic equipment. If you are using a map, consult it inconspicuously—or

Travel Tip

Be sure to keep a copy of all your travel papers separate from your wallet or purse, and leave a copy with someone at home should you need it faxed in an emergency.

better yet, try to study it before you leave your room. Hold onto your pocketbook, and place your billfold in an inside pocket. In public places, keep your possessions in sight.

Remember also that hotels are open to the public, and in a large hotel, security may not be able to screen everyone entering. Always lock your room door—don't assume that once inside your hotel you are automatically safe.

DRIVING   Safety while driving is particularly important. Ask your rental agency about personal safety or request a brochure of traveler safety tips when you pick up your car. Get written directions or a map with the route marked in red from the agency to show you how to get to your destination. If possible, arrive and depart during daylight hours.

Recently more and more crime has involved cars and drivers. If you drive off a highway into a questionable neighborhood, leave the area as quickly as possible. If you have an accident, even on the highway, stay in your car with the doors locked until you assess the situation or until the police arrive. If you are bumped from behind on the street or are involved in a minor accident with no injuries, and the situation appears to be suspicious, motion to the other driver to follow you to the nearest police precinct, gas station, or open store. *Never* get out of your car in such situations.

Park in well-lit, well-traveled areas if possible. Always keep your car doors locked, whether the vehicle is attended or unattended. Look around you before you get out of your car and never leave any packages or valuables in sight. If someone attempts to rob you or steal your car, do *not* try to resist the thief/carjacker—report the incident to the police department immediately by calling ☎ **911.**

Also, make sure you have enough gasoline in your tank to reach your intended destination so that you're not forced to look for a service station in an unfamiliar and possibly unsafe neighborhood—especially at night.

2 Getting to the U.S.

Airlines with direct or connecting service from London to Phoenix (along with their phone numbers in Great Britain) include **American** (☎ 0345/567-567; www. americanair.com), **British Airways** (☎ 0345/222-111; www.british-airways.com), **Continental** (☎ 0800/776-464; www.flycontinental.com), **Delta** (☎ 0800/414-767; www.delta-air.com), **TWA** (☎ 020/8814-0707 in London, or 0800/221-2000; www.twa.com), **United** (☎ 020/8990-9900 in London, or 0800/888-555 outside London; www.ual.com), and **US Airways** (☎ 0800/783-5556; www.usairways.com). American, Delta, and United fly into Tucson.

From Canada there are flights to Phoenix from Toronto on **Air Canada** (☎ 888/247-2262; www.aircanada.ca), **American** (☎ 800/433-7300; www. americanair.com), **Delta** (☎ 800/221-1212; www.delta-air.com), **Northwest** (☎ 800/ 225-2525; www.nwa.com), **TWA** (☎ 800/221-2000; www.twa.com), **United** (☎ 800/241-6522; www.ual.com), and **US Airways** (☎ 800/428-4322; usairways.com), and from Vancouver on **Alaska Airlines** (☎ 800/426-0333; www.alaskaair.com), **America West** (☎ 800/235-9292; www.americawest.com), **Canadian Airlines** (☎ 800/426-7000; www.cdnair.ca), **Northwest,** and **United.**

There are flights to Tucson from Toronto on **American, Continental** (☎ 800/ 525-0280; www.continental.com), **Delta, Northwest,** and **United,** and from Vancouver on **American, America West, Canadian Airlines,** and **United.**

From New Zealand and Australia, there are flights to Los Angeles on **Qantas** (☎ 13 13 13; www.qantas.com.au) and **Air New Zealand** (☎ 0800/737-000 in Auckland; www.airnewzealand.co.nz). Continue on to Phoenix or Tucson on a regional airline such as **America West** (☎ 800/235-9292; www.americawest.com) or **Southwest** (☎ 800/435-9792; www.southwest.com). If you're heading to the Grand Canyon, it's easier to take a flight from Los Angeles to Las Vegas.

AIRLINE DISCOUNTS   Travelers from overseas can take advantage of the **advance-purchase excursion (APEX)** fares offered by the major U.S. and European carriers. For more money-saving airline advice, see "Getting There," in chapter 2.

IMMIGRATION & CUSTOMS CLEARANCE   The visitor arriving by air, no matter what the port of entry, should cultivate patience before setting foot on U.S. soil. Getting through Immigration Control might take as long as 2 hours on some days, especially summer weekends. Add the time it takes to clear Customs, and you'll see that you should make a very generous allowance for delay in planning connections between international and domestic flights—an average of 2 to 3 hours at least.

In contrast, travelers arriving by car or by rail from Canada will find border-crossing formalities streamlined practically to the vanishing point. And air travelers from Canada, Bermuda, and some places in the Caribbean can sometimes go through Customs and Immigration at the point of departure, which is much quicker.

3 Getting Around the U.S.

For specific information on traveling to and around Arizona, see "Getting There" and "Getting Around" in chapter 2.

BY PLANE   Some large airlines (for example, United and Delta) offer travelers on their transatlantic or transpacific flights special discount tickets under the name **Visit USA,** allowing mostly one-way travel from one U.S. destination to another at very low prices. These discount tickets are not on sale in the United States and must be purchased abroad in conjunction with your international ticket. This system is the best, easiest, and fastest way to see the United States at low cost. You should get information well in advance from your travel agent or the office of the airline concerned, since the conditions attached to these discount tickets can be changed without advance notice.

BY CAR   The United States is a car culture through and through. Driving is the most cost-effective, convenient, and comfortable way to travel through the West. The interstate highway system connects cities and towns all over the country, and in addition to these high-speed, limited-access roadways, there's an extensive network of federal, state, and local highways and roads. Driving will give you a lot of flexibility in making, and altering, your itinerary and in allowing you to see some off-the-beaten-path destinations that cannot be reached easily by public transportation. You'll also have easy access to inexpensive motels at interstate highway off-ramps.

BY TRAIN   International visitors can also buy a **USA Railpass,** good for 15 or 30 days of unlimited travel on **Amtrak** (☎ 800/USA-RAIL). The pass is available through many foreign travel agents. Prices in 2000 for a 15-day pass are $295 off-peak, $440 peak; a 30-day pass costs $385 off-peak, $550 peak. (With a foreign passport, you can also buy passes at some Amtrak offices in the United States, including locations in San Francisco, Los Angeles, Chicago, New York, Miami, Boston, and Washington, D.C.) Reservations are generally required and should be made for each part of your trip as early as possible. Amtrak also offers an **Air/Rail Travel Plan** that allows you to travel by both train and plane; for information call ☎ **800/440-8202.**

BY BUS   Although bus travel is often the most economical form of public transit for short hops between U.S. cities, it can also be slow and uncomfortable—certainly not an option for everyone (particularly when Amtrak, which is far more luxurious, offers similar rates). **Greyhound/Trailways** (☎ **800/231-2222**), the sole nationwide bus line, offers an **Ameripass** for unlimited travel for 7 days at $169, 15 days at $249, 30 days at $349, and 60 days at $479. Passes must be purchased at a Greyhound terminal. Special rates are available for senior citizens and students.

Fast Facts: For the Foreign Traveler

Automobile Organizations   Auto clubs can supply maps, suggested routes, guidebooks, accident and bail-bond insurance, and emergency road service. The **American Automobile Association (AAA)** is the major auto club in the United States. If you belong to an auto club in your home country, inquire about AAA reciprocity before you leave. You may be able to join AAA even if you're not a member of a reciprocal club; to inquire, call **AAA** (☎ **800/222-4357**). AAA is actually an organization of regional auto clubs; so look under "AAA Automobile Club" in the White Pages of the telephone directory. AAA has a nationwide **emergency road service** telephone number (☎ **800/AAA-HELP**).

Business Hours   See "Fast Facts: Arizona" in chapter 2.

Climate   See "When to Go" in chapter 2.

Currency   See "Money" under "Preparing for Your Trip," earlier in this chapter.

Currency Exchange   You'll find currency-exchange services in major international airports. There's a **Thomas Cook** office (☎ **800/287-7362**) at Sky Harbor Airport in Phoenix, but not at Tucson International Airport. Elsewhere, they may be quite difficult to come by. In Phoenix, **Bank of America**, at 101 N. First Ave. (☎ **602/594-2371** or 888/279-3264), will exchange money, as will any of the bank's other branches. Also, ask at your hotel desk; some hotels might be able to change major currencies for you.

Drinking Laws   The legal age for purchase and consumption of alcoholic beverages is 21; proof of age is required and often requested at bars, nightclubs, and restaurants, so it's always a good idea to bring ID when you go out. Beer and wine can often be purchased in supermarkets, but liquor laws vary from state to state.

Do not carry open containers of alcohol in your car or any public area that isn't zoned for alcohol consumption. The police can, and probably will, fine you on the spot. And nothing will ruin your trip faster than getting a citation for DUI ("driving under the influence"), so don't even think about driving while intoxicated.

Electricity   Like Canada, the United States uses 110 to 120 volts AC (60 cycles), compared to 220 to 240 volts AC (50 cycles) in most of Europe, Australia, and New Zealand. If your small appliances use 220 to 240 volts, you'll need a 110-volt transformer and a plug adapter with two flat parallel pins to operate them here. Downward converters that change 220 to 240 volts to 110 to 120 volts are difficult to find in the United States, so bring one with you.

Embassies & Consulates   All embassies are located in Washington, D.C. Some consulates are located in major U.S. cities, and most nations have a mission to the United Nations in New York City. If your country isn't listed below, call **directory information** in Washington, D.C. (☎ **202/555-1212**) for the number of your national embassy.

The embassy of **Australia** is at 1601 Massachusetts Ave. NW, Washington, DC 20036 (☎ **202/797-3000;** www.austemb.org). There is no consulate in Arizona; the nearest is at Century Plaza Towers, 19th Floor, 2049 Century Park East, Los Angeles, CA 90067 (☎ **310/229-4800**). There are also consulates in Atlanta, New York, Honolulu, and San Francisco.

The embassy of **Canada** is at 501 Pennsylvania Ave. NW, Washington, DC 20001 (☎ **202/682-1740;** www.canadianembassy.org). There is no consulate in Arizona; the nearest is at 550 S. Hope St., 9th Floor, Los Angeles, CA 90071 (☎ **213/346-2700**). Other Canadian consulates are in Buffalo (NY), Detroit, New York, and Seattle.

The embassy of **Ireland** is at 2234 Massachusetts Ave. NW, Washington, DC 20008 (☎ **202/462-3939;** www.irelandemb.org). There is no consulate in Arizona; the nearest is at 44 Montgomery St., Suite 3830, San Francisco, CA 94104 (☎ **415/392-4214**). Other Irish consulates are in Boston, Chicago, and New York.

The embassy of **New Zealand** is at 37 Observatory Circle NW, Washington, DC 20008 (☎ **202/328-4800;** www.nzemb.org). There is no consulate in Arizona; the nearest is in Los Angeles at 12400 Wilshire Blvd., Suite 1150, Los Angeles, CA 90025 (☎ **310/207-1605**). Other New Zealand consulates are in Salt Lake City, San Francisco, and Seattle.

The embassy of the **United Kingdom** is at 3100 Massachusetts Ave. NW, Washington, DC 20008 (☎ **202/462-1340;** www.britain-info.org). There is no consulate in Arizona; the nearest is in Los Angeles at 11766 Wilshire Blvd., Suite 400, Los Angeles, CA 90025 (☎ **310/477-3322**). Other British consulates are in Atlanta, Boston, Chicago, Dallas, Houston, Miami, New York, San Francisco, and Seattle.

Emergencies   Call ☎ **911** to report a fire, call the police, or get an ambulance. This is a toll-free call (no coins are required at a public telephone).

If you encounter problems, check the local telephone directory to find an office of the **Traveler's Aid Society,** a nationwide nonprofit social-service organization geared to helping travelers in difficult straits. The society's services might include reuniting families separated while traveling, providing food and/or shelter to people stranded without cash, or even emotional counseling. If you're in trouble, seek it out.

Gasoline (Petrol)   Petrol is known as gasoline (or simply "gas") in the United States, and petrol stations are known as both gas stations and service stations. Gasoline costs less here than it does in Europe, and taxes are already included in the printed price. One U.S. gallon equals 3.8 liters or .85 Imperial gallons.

Holidays   Banks, government offices, post offices, and many stores, restaurants, and museums are closed on the following legal national holidays: January 1 (New Year's Day), the third Monday in January (Martin Luther King, Jr. Day), the third Monday in February (Presidents' Day, Washington's Birthday), the last Monday in May (Memorial Day), July 4 (Independence Day), the first Monday in September (Labor Day), the second Monday in October (Columbus Day), November 11 (Veterans' Day/Armistice Day), the fourth Thursday in November (Thanksgiving Day), and December 25 (Christmas). Also, the Tuesday following the first Monday in November is Election Day and is a federal government holiday in presidential-election years (held every 4 years, and next in 2004).

Internet Access   Checking the Yellow Pages under Internet Access may turn up a few cybercafes. Alternatively, many copy shops (Kinko's is one large national chain) provide Internet access. See "Planning Your Trip: An Online Directory" for more information. Also, if you are traveling with your laptop computer, note that many hotels, especially those frequented by business travelers, have telephones with data ports and dual phone lines in guest rooms.

Legal Aid   The foreign tourist will probably never become involved with the American legal system. If you are "pulled over" for a minor infraction (for example, of the highway code, such as speeding), never attempt to pay the fine directly to a police officer; this could be construed as attempted bribery, a much more serious crime. Pay fines by mail or directly into the hands of the clerk of the court. If accused of a more serious offense, say and do nothing before consulting a lawyer. Here the burden is on the state to prove a person's guilt beyond a reasonable doubt, and everyone has the right to remain silent, whether he or she is suspected of a crime or actually arrested. Once arrested, a person can make one telephone call to a party of his or her choice. Call your embassy or consulate.

Mail   Generally found at intersections, mailboxes are blue with a red-and-white stripe and carry the inscription U.S. MAIL. If your mail is addressed to a U.S. destination, don't forget to add the five-digit postal code (or ZIP code), after the two-letter abbreviation of the state to which the mail is addressed.

   At press time, domestic postage rates were 20¢ for a postcard and 33¢ for a letter. For international mail, a first-class letter of up to one-half ounce costs 60¢ (48¢ to Canada and 40¢ to Mexico), a first-class postcard costs 55¢ (45¢ to Canada and 40¢ Mexico), and a preprinted postal aerogramme costs 60¢.

Medical Emergencies   To call an ambulance, dial ☎ **911** from any phone. No coins are needed.

Newspapers & Magazines   National newspapers include *The New York Times, USA Today,* and *The Wall Street Journal.* National news weeklies include *Newsweek, Time,* and *U.S. News & World Report.* In large cities most newsstands offer a small selection of the most popular foreign periodicals and newspapers, such as *The Economist, Le Monde,* and *Der Spiegel.* For information on local publications, see the "Fast Facts" sections for Phoenix and Tucson (chapters 4 and 9).

Safety   See "Safety" in "Preparing for Your Trip," earlier in this chapter.

Taxes   The United States does not have a value-added tax (VAT) or other indirect tax at a national level. Every state, and each county and city in it, is allowed to levy its own local tax on purchases. Taxes are already included in the price of certain services, such as public transportation, cab fares, telephone calls, and gasoline.

   In Arizona the state sales tax is 5.5%, but communities can add local sales tax on top of this. Expect to pay around 20% tax on car rentals at either the Tucson or Phoenix airport (considerably less if you rent outside these airports). Hotel room taxes range from around 6% to 14%. Travelers on a budget should keep both car-rental and hotel-room taxes in mind when planning a trip.

Telephone & Fax   The telephone system in the United States is run by private corporations, so rates, especially for long-distance service and operator-assisted calls, can vary widely. Generally, hotel surcharges on long-distance and local calls are astronomical, so you're usually better off using a **public pay telephone,** which you'll find clearly marked in most public buildings and private establishments as well as on the street. Convenience grocery stores and gas stations always have them. Many convenience groceries and packaging services sell **prepaid calling cards** in denominations up to $50; these cards can be the least expensive way to call home. Many public phones at airports now accept American Express, MasterCard, and Visa credit cards. **Local calls** made from public pay phones in most locales cost either 25¢ or 35¢. Pay phones do not accept pennies, and few take anything larger than a quarter.

Most long-distance and international calls can be dialed directly from any phone. **For calls within the United States and to Canada,** dial 1 followed by the area code and the seven-digit number. **For other international calls,** dial 011 followed by the country code, city code, and telephone number of the person you are calling.

Calls to area codes **800, 888,** and **877** are toll-free. However, calls to numbers in area codes **700** and **900** (chat lines, bulletin boards, "dating" services, and so on) can be very expensive—usually a charge of 95¢ to $3 or more per minute, and they sometimes have minimum charges that can run as high as $15 or more.

For **reversed-charge or collect calls,** and for **person-to-person calls,** dial 0 (zero, not the letter *O*) followed by the area code and number you want; an operator then comes on the line, and you should specify that you are calling collect, or person-to-person, or both. If your operator-assisted call is international, ask for the overseas operator.

For **local directory assistance** ("information"), dial 411; for long-distance information, dial 1 and then the appropriate area code and 555-1212.

Most hotels have **fax machines** available for guest use (be sure to ask about the charge to use it). A less expensive way to send and receive faxes may be at stores such as Mail Boxes Etc., a national chain of packing service shops (look in the Yellow Pages directory under "Packing Services").

There are two kinds of telephone directories in the United States. The **White Pages** list private households and business subscribers in alphabetical order. The inside front cover lists emergency numbers for police, fire, ambulance, the Coast Guard, poison-control center, crime-victims hotline, and so on. The first few pages tell you how to make long-distance and international calls, complete with country codes and area codes. Government numbers are usually printed on blue paper within the White Pages. Printed on yellow paper, the **Yellow Pages** list all local services, businesses, industries, and houses of worship according to activity, with an index at the front or back. (Drugstores/pharmacies and restaurants are also listed by geographic location.) The Yellow Pages include city plans or detailed area maps, postal ZIP codes, and public transportation routes.

Time   The United States is divided into six time zones. From east to west, they are eastern standard time (EST), central standard time (CST), mountain standard time (MST), Pacific standard time (PST), Alaska standard time (AST), and Hawaii standard time (HST). Always keep the changing time zones in mind if you are traveling (or even telephoning) long distances in the United States. For example, noon in New York City (EST) is 11am in Chicago (CST), 10am in Phoenix (MST), 9am in Los Angeles (PST), 8am in Anchorage (AST), and 7am in Honolulu (HST).

Arizona is in the mountain time zone, but it does *not* observe daylight saving time (summertime). Consequently, from the first Sunday in April until the last Sunday in October, there is no time difference between Arizona and California and other states on the West Coast. However, there is a 2-hour difference to Chicago and 3 hours to New York.

Tipping   Tipping is so ingrained in the American way of life that the annual income tax of tip-earning service personnel is based on how much they should have received in light of their employers' gross revenues. Accordingly, they may have to pay tax on a tip you didn't actually give them. Here are some rules of thumb:

In hotels, tip **bellhops** at least $1 per bag ($2 to $3 if you have a lot of luggage) and tip the **chamber staff** $1 to $2 per day (more if you've left a disaster area to clean up, or if you're traveling with kids and/or pets). Tip the **doorman** or **concierge** only if he or she has provided you with some specific service (for example, calling a cab for you or obtaining difficult-to-get theater tickets). Tip the **valet parking attendant** $1 every time you get your car.

In restaurants, bars, and nightclubs, tip **service staff** 15% to 20% of the check, tip **bartenders** 10% to 15%, tip **checkroom attendants** $1 per garment, and tip **valet parking attendants** $1 per vehicle. Tip the **doorman** only if he has provided you with some specific service (such as calling a cab for you). Tipping is not expected in cafeterias and fast-food restaurants.

Tip **cab drivers** 15% of the fare.

As for other service personnel, tip **skycaps** (luggage carriers) at airports at least $1 per bag ($2 to $3 if you have a lot of luggage) and tip **hairdressers** and **barbers** 15% to 20%.

Toilets   You won't find public toilets or "rest rooms" on the streets in most U.S. cities, but they can be found in hotel lobbies, bars, restaurants, museums, department stores, railway and bus stations, or service stations. Note, however, that restaurants and bars in resorts or heavily visited areas may reserve their rest rooms for the use of their patrons. Some establishments display a notice that toilets are for the use of patrons only. You can ignore this sign or, better yet, avoid arguments by paying for a cup of coffee or a soft drink, which will qualify you as a patron. Large hotels and fast-food restaurants are probably the best bet for good, clean facilities.

4 Phoenix, Scottsdale & the Valley of the Sun

Time and again Phoenix, a city named by an early settler from Britain, has lived up to its name. Like the phoenix of ancient mythology, Arizona's capital city rose from its own ashes—in this case, the ruins of an ancient Indian village. While it took nearly a century for this Phoenix to take flight, the city has risen from the dust of the desert to become one of the largest metropolitan areas in the country.

Although the city has had its economic ups and downs, the Phoenix metropolitan area, often referred to as the Valley of the Sun, is currently booming. The Camelback Corridor, which leads through north-central Phoenix, has become the corporate heartland of the city, and shiny glass office towers keep pushing up toward the desert sky. This burgeoning stretch of road has also become a corridor of upscale restaurants and shopping plazas, anchored by the Biltmore Fashion Park, the city's temple of high-end consumerism, and today Phoenicians flock to this area both for work and play.

Even downtown Phoenix, long abandoned as simply a place to work, has taken on an entirely new look in the past few years and has positioned itself as the sports and events district for the Valley of the Sun. First came the America West Arena. Then more recently, the Arizona Diamondbacks baseball team took up residence in the Bank One Ballpark (BOB), one of the nation's only baseball stadiums with a retractable roof. So, on days when there are games or concerts scheduled at either of these venues, you can bet that downtown Phoenix will be a lively place. Additionally, the downtown area offers quite a few interesting attractions, including the world-class Arizona Science Center, the Phoenix Museum of History, historic Heritage Square (downtown's only remaining historic block), the Phoenix Museum of Art, and the Heard Museum.

In Scottsdale, luxury resorts sprawl across the landscape, convertibles and SUVs clog the streets, and new golf courses, luxury housing developments, and upscale shopping centers keep springing up like wildflowers after a rainstorm. This city until recently billed itself as the West's most Western town, but Scottsdale today is more of a Beverly Hills of the desert. The city has also now sprawled all the way north to Carefree, and it is here, in north Scottsdale, that the valley's newest golf courses and resorts are to be found.

Throughout the metropolitan area the population is growing at such a rapid pace that an alarm has been raised: Slow down before we become another Los Angeles! Why the phenomenal growth? In large part it's due to the climate. More than 300 days of sunshine a year is a powerful attraction, and although summers are blisteringly hot, the mountains—and cooler temperatures—are only 2 hours away. However, in winter the Valley of the Sun truly shines. While most of the country is frozen solid, the valley is sunny and warm. This great winter climate has helped make this area the resort capital of the United States. However, with stiff competition from resorts in the Caribbean, Mexico, and Hawaii, Valley of the Sun resorts have had to do a lot of keeping up with the Joneses in recent years. Bigger and splashier pools have been added, and nearly every resort in the valley has added a full-service health spa.

Golf, tennis, and lounging by the pool are only the tip of the iceberg (so to speak) when it comes to winter activities in the Valley of the Sun. With the cooler winter weather comes the cultural season, and between Phoenix and the neighboring cities of Scottsdale, Tempe, and Mesa, there's an impressive array of music, dance, and theater to be enjoyed. Scottsdale is also well known as a center of the visual arts, ranking only behind New York and Santa Fe in its concentration of art galleries.

Over the years, Phoenix has both enjoyed the benefits and suffered the problems of rapid urban growth. It has gone from tiny agricultural village to sprawling cosmopolitan metropolis in little more than a century. Along the way it has lost its past amid urban sprawl and unchecked development; at the same time, it has forged a city that's quintessentially 20th-century American. Shopping malls, the gathering places of America, are raised to an art form in Phoenix. Luxurious resorts create fantasy worlds of waterfalls and swimming pools. Perhaps it's this willingness to create a new world on top of an old one that attracts people to Phoenix. Then again, maybe it's just all that sunshine.

1 Orientation

ARRIVING

BY PLANE   Centrally located 3 miles from downtown Phoenix, **Sky Harbor Airport** has three terminals, and in these three terminals you'll find car-rental desks, information desks, hotel-reservation centers with direct lines to various valley hotels, and a food court. There's a free 24-hour shuttle bus operating every 5 to 10 minutes between the three terminals (less frequently during the night). For general airport information, call ☎ **602/273-3300;** for airport paging, call **602/273-3456;** for lost and found, call **602/273-3307.**

Getting to & from the Airport   There are two entrances to the airport. The west entrance can be accessed from either the Squaw Peak Parkway (Ariz. 51) or 24th Street, and the east entrance can be accessed from the Hohokam Expressway (Ariz. 143), which is an extension of 44th Street. If you're headed to downtown Phoenix, leave by way of the 24th Street exit and continue west on Washington Street. If you're headed to Scottsdale, take the 24th Street exit, go north on the Squaw Peak Parkway to the Indian School Road or Lincoln Drive exit, and then drive east, or get on the 202 east loop to 101 north. For Tempe or Mesa, take the 44th Street exit.

If you want to come and go in style, you can arrange to have a stretch limo pick you up and take you back to the airport (or anywhere else in town, for that matter). **Transtyle** (☎ **800/410-5479** or 480/948-6131) charges a flat fee of $120 between the airport and most Phoenix and Scottsdale resorts.

SuperShuttle (☎ **800/BLUE-VAN** or 602/244-9000) offers 24-hour door-to-door van service between Sky Harbor Airport and resorts, hotels, and homes throughout the valley. Fares average about $7 to $10 to the downtown and Tempe area (about $6 for each additional person), and about $14 to $28 per person to Scottsdale

> *As the mythical phoenix rose reborn from its ashes, so shall a great civilization rise here on the ashes of a past civilization. I name thee Phoenix.*
>   —"Lord" Bryan Philip Darrel Duppa, the British settler who named Phoenix

and the northern area of the city. When heading back to the airport for a departure, call in advance (☎ 602/244-9000).

Taxis can also be found waiting outside all three airport terminals, or you can call **Yellow Cab** (☎ 602/252-5252) or **Checker Cab** (☎ 602/257-1818).

Valley Metro provides **public bus service** throughout the valley with the Red Line (R) operating between the airport and downtown Phoenix, Tempe, and Mesa. The Red Line operates daily between about 5am and 10pm. You can pick up a copy of *The Bus Book,* a guide and route map for the Valley Metro bus system, at Central Station, at the corner of Central Avenue and Van Buren Street.

BY CAR   Phoenix is connected to Los Angeles and Tucson by I-10 and to Flagstaff via I-17. If you're headed to Scottsdale, the easiest route is to take the Red Mountain Freeway (Ariz. 202) east to U.S. 101 north. U.S. 101 will eventually loop all the way around the north side of the valley. The Superstition Freeway (U.S. 60) leads to Tempe, Mesa, and Chandler.

BY TRAIN   There is no direct passenger rail service to Phoenix. However, Amtrak's Southwest Chief connects Phoenix (via a bus connection from Flagstaff) with Los Angeles to the west and Albuquerque, Santa Fe, Kansas City, and Chicago to the east. Amtrak's Sunset Limited connects Phoenix (via a bus from Tucson) with Orlando, New Orleans, Houston, San Antonio, El Paso, and Los Angeles. Amtrak connector buses arrive and depart from the old Phoenix **Amtrak railroad terminal,** 401 W. Harrison St. (☎ 800/872-7245 or 602/253-0121; www.amtrak.com).

VISITOR INFORMATION

You'll find **tourist information desks** in the baggage claim areas of all three terminals at Sky Harbor Airport. However, the city's main visitor information center is the **Greater Phoenix Convention and Visitors Bureau,** 50 N. Second St. (☎ 877/225-5749 or 602/254-6500; www.phoenixcvb.com), on the corner of Adams Street in downtown Phoenix. The city also operates a small visitor center at the Biltmore Fashion Park shopping center at the corner of Camelback Road and 24th Street (☎ 602/955-1963).

The **Visitor Information Line** (☎ 602/252-5588) has recorded information about current events in Phoenix.

If you're staying in Scottsdale, you may want to contact or drop by the **Scottsdale Chamber of Commerce and Visitors Center,** 7343 Scottsdale Mall, Scottsdale, AZ 85251-4498 (☎ 800/877-1117 or 480/945-8481; www.scottsdalecvb.com).

CITY LAYOUT

MAIN ARTERIES & STREETS   Over the past decade, the Phoenix area has seen the construction of numerous new freeways. It is now possible to drive from the airport to Scottsdale by freeway rather than having to deal with stoplights and local traffic. U.S. 101, which currently exists only in two unconnected sections (one between Tempe and Scottsdale and the other between north Phoenix and Peoria on the east side of the valley) will eventually form a loop around the east, north, and west sides of the valley, providing freeway access to Scottsdale from I-17 on the north side of Phoenix and from U.S. 60 in Tempe.

I-17 (Black Canyon Freeway), which connects Phoenix with Flagstaff, is the city's main north-south freeway. This freeway curves to the east just south of downtown (where it is renamed the **Maricopa Freeway** and merges with I-10). **I-10,** which connects Phoenix with Los Angeles and Tucson, is called the **Papago Freeway** on the west side of the valley and as it passes north of downtown; as it curves around to pass south of the airport, it merges with I-17 and is renamed the Maricopa Freeway. At Tempe, this freeway curves around to the south and heads out of the valley.

North of the airport, **Arizona 202 (Red Mountain Freeway)** heads east from I-10 and passes along the north side of Tempe, providing access to downtown Tempe, Arizona State University, Mesa, and Scottsdale (via U.S. 101). On the east side of the airport, **Arizona 143 (Hohokam Expressway)** connects Arizona 202 with I-10.

At the interchange of I-10 and Arizona 202, northwest of Sky Harbor Airport, **Arizona 51 (Squaw Peak Freeway)** heads north through the center of Phoenix and is the best north-south route in the city. This freeway is currently being extended north from Bell Road and will eventually link up with the U.S. 101 loop.

Just south of the airport, **U.S. 60 (Superstition Freeway)** heads east to Tempe, Chandler, Mesa, and Gilbert. **U.S. 101** leads north from U.S. 60 (and Ariz. 202) toward Scottsdale. This freeway is currently being extended north from Shea Boulevard and now provides the best route from the airport to the Scottsdale resorts.

Secondary highways in the valley include the **Beeline Highway (Ariz. 87),** which starts out as Country Club Drive in Mesa and leads to Payson, and **Grand Avenue (U.S. 60),** which starts downtown and leads to Sun City and Wickenburg.

Phoenix and the surrounding cities of Mesa, Tempe, Scottsdale, and Chandler, and even those cities farther out in the valley, are laid out in a grid pattern with major avenues and roads about every mile. For traveling east to west across Phoenix, your best choices (other than the above-mentioned freeways) are Camelback Road, Indian School Road, and McDowell Road. For traveling north and south, 44th Street, 24th Street, and Central Avenue are good choices. Hayden Road is a north-south alternative to Scottsdale Road, which gets jammed at rush hours.

FINDING AN ADDRESS   Central Avenue, which runs north to south through downtown Phoenix, is the starting point for all east and west street numbering. **Washington Street** is the starting point for north and south numbering. North-to-south numbered *streets* are to be found on the east side of the city, while north-to-south numbered *avenues* will be found on the west. For the most part, street numbers change by 100 with each block. Odd-numbered addresses are on the south and east sides of streets, while even-numbered addresses are on north and west sides of streets.

For example, if you're looking for 4454 East Camelback Rd., you'll find it 44 blocks east of Central Avenue between 44th and 45th streets on the north side of the street. If you're looking for 2905 North 35th Ave., you'll find it 35 blocks west of Central Avenue and 29 blocks north of Washington Street on the east side of the street. Just for general reference, Camelback marks the 5000 block north.

STREET MAPS   The street maps handed out by rental-car companies are almost useless for finding anything in Phoenix, so, as soon as you can, stop in at a minimart and buy a Phoenix map. Unfortunately, you'll probably also have to buy a separate Scottsdale map. You can also get a simple map at either one of the airport tourist information desks or at the downtown visitor information center.

Phoenix, Scottsdale & the Valley of the Sun

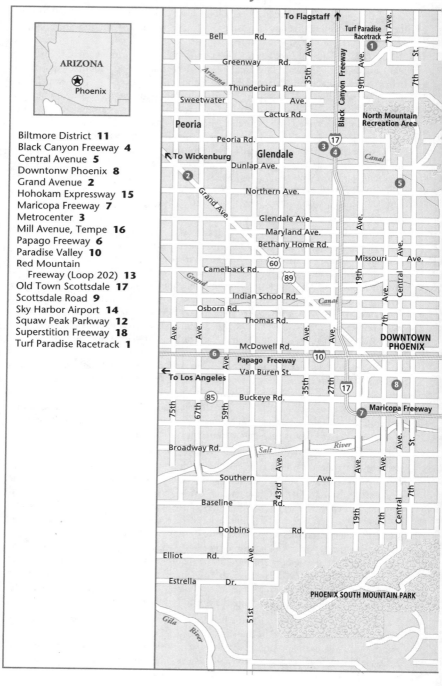

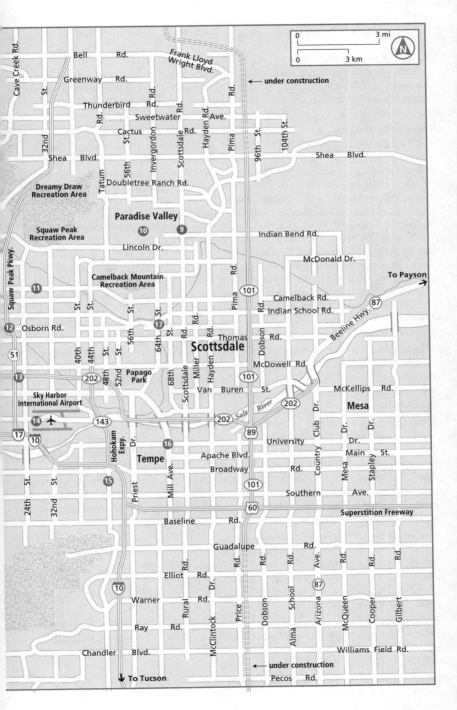

Neighborhoods in Brief

Because of urban sprawl, Phoenix has yielded its importance to the Valley of the Sun, an area encompassing Phoenix and its metropolitan area of more than 20 cities. Consequently, neighborhoods, per se, have lost much of their significance as outlying cities have taken on regional importance. However, this said, there are some neighborhoods worth noting.

Downtown Phoenix   Roughly bordered by Thomas Road on the north, Buckeye Road on the south, 19th Avenue on the west, and Seventh Street on the east, downtown is primarily a business, financial, and government district, where both the city hall and state capitol are located. However, in the past few years, downtown Phoenix has been rising from the ashes of neglect and positioning itself as the valley's prime sports, entertainment, and museum district. The Arizona Diamondbacks play big-league baseball in the **Bank-One Ballpark (BOB),** while the Phoenix Suns shoot hoops at the **America West Arena.** There are three major performing arts venues—the historic **Orpheum Theatre, Phoenix Symphony Hall,** and the **Herberger Theater Center.** At the Arizona Center shopping and entertainment plaza, there is a huge multiplex movie theater. Downtown museums include the **Phoenix Museum of History** and the **Arizona Science Center,** both of which are located in Heritage and Science Park. Other attractions in the downtown area include **Heritage Square** (historic homes), the **Arizona State Capitol Museum,** and **the Arizona Mining & Mineral Museum.** On the northern edge of downtown are the **Heard Museum,** the **Phoenix Central Library** (an architectural gem), and the **Phoenix Art Museum.**

Biltmore District   The Biltmore District, also known as the **Camelback Corridor,** centers along Camelback Road between 24th and 44th streets and is Phoenix's upscale shopping, residential, and business district. The area is characterized by modern office buildings and is anchored by the Arizona Biltmore Hotel and Biltmore Fashion Park shopping mall.

Scottsdale   A separate city of more than 200,000 people, Scottsdale extends from Tempe in the south to Carefree in the north, a distance of more than 20 miles. Scottsdale Road between Indian School Road and Shea Boulevard has long been known as **"Resort Row"** and is home to more than a dozen major resorts. However, as Scottsdale has sprawled ever northward, so, too, have resorts been opening in north Scottsdale. **Old Scottsdale** capitalizes on its cowboy heritage and has become the valley's main shopping district, with boutiques, jewelers, Native American crafts stores, souvenir shops, and numerous restaurants.

Tempe   Tempe is the home of Arizona State University and has all the trappings of a university town. Nightclubs and bars abound here. The center of activity, both day and night, is **Mill Avenue,** which has dozens of interesting shops along a stretch of about 4 blocks. This is one of the few areas in the valley where locals actually walk the streets and hang out at sidewalk cafes (Old Town Scottsdale often has people on its streets, but few are locals).

Paradise Valley   If Scottsdale is Phoenix's Beverly Hills, then Paradise Valley is its Bel-Air. The most exclusive neighborhood in the valley is almost entirely residential, but you won't see too many of the more lavish homes because they're set on large tracts of land.

Mesa   This eastern suburb of Phoenix is the Valley's main high-tech area. Large shopping malls, many inexpensive motels, and a couple of small museums attract both locals and visitors to Mesa.

Glendale   Located west of Phoenix proper, Glendale has numerous historic buildings in its downtown and has, with its dozens of antiques stores, become the antiques capital of the valley.

Carefree & Cave Creek   Located about 20 miles north of Old Scottsdale, these two communities represent the Old West and the New West. Carefree is a planned community and is home to the prestigious Boulders resort and El Pedregal shopping center. Cave Creek plays up its Western heritage in its architecture and preponderance of bars, steakhouses, and shops selling Western crafts and other gifts.

2 Getting Around

BY CAR

Phoenix and the surrounding cities that together make up the Valley of the Sun sprawl over more than 400 square miles, so if you want to make the best use of your time, it's essential to have a car. Outside downtown Phoenix, there's almost always plenty of free parking wherever you go (although finding a parking space can be time consuming in Old Scottsdale and at some of the more popular malls and shopping plazas).

RENTALS   All the major rental-car companies have offices in Phoenix, with desks inside the airline terminals at Sky Harbor Airport, and because this is a major tourist destination, there are often excellent rates. However, taxes on car rentals at Sky Harbor airport run about 24%. The best rates are those reserved at least a week in advance, but car-rental companies change rates frequently as demand goes up and down. If you book far enough in advance, you might get a compact car for less than $165 per week. See also chapter 2, "Planning a Trip to Arizona: The Basics," for general tips on car rentals.

All the major rental-car companies have offices at Sky Harbor Airport as well as other locations in the Phoenix area. Among them are the following: **Alamo** (☎ 800/327-9633, 602/273-9690 or 602/244-0897); **Avis** (☎ 800/331-1212 or 602/273-3222); **Budget** (☎ 800/527-0700 or 602/267-4000); **Dollar** (☎ 800/800-4000 or 602/275-7588); **Enterprise** (☎ 800/736-8222 or 602/225-0588); **Hertz** (☎ 800/654-3131 or 602/267-8822); **National** (☎ 800/227-7368 or 602/275-4771); and **Thrifty** (☎ 800/367-2277 or 602/244-0311).

If you'd like a bit more style while you cruise from resort to golf course to nightclub to wherever, how about a Corvette? **Rent-a-Vette,** 1215 N. Scottsdale Rd., Tempe (☎ **480/941-3001**), can put you behind the wheel of a car that will get you a bit more respect from valet parking attendants at area restaurants. A Corvette will run you $149 to $249 a day. Rent-a-Vette also rents Porsche Boxters, Mustang GTs, Jaguars XKAs, and Plymouth Prowlers, with rates at $249 a day for a Prowler.

At the rugged end of the car-rental spectrum is **Arizona Jeep & Hummer,** 7677 N. 16th St., Phoenix (☎ **602/674-8469**), which rents Jeep Wranglers for $99 to $129 for a half day or $149 to $169 for a full day and Hummers for $199 for a half day and $299 for a full day. Rates go down the more days you rent, and special lower rates are sometimes available. Along with your rental, you can get a trail book and directions for various trails into the desert. For two or more people, this is an economical alternative to doing a Jeep tour.

If a Jeep still doesn't offer enough excitement and wind in your hair, how about a motorcycle? **Western States Motorcycle Tours,** 9401 N. Seventh Ave. (☎ **602/943-9030**), rents Harley-Davidson, BMW, and Suzuki motorcycles for between $70 and $175 per day ($400 to $750 per week). You must have a valid motorcycle driver's license to rent one of these bikes. In Arizona you don't have to wear a helmet, so you really can ride with the wind in your hair.

BY PUBLIC TRANSPORTATION

Unfortunately, **Valley Metro** (☎ 602/253-5000), the Phoenix public bus system, is not very useful to tourists. It's primarily meant to be used by commuters, and most routes stop running before 9pm. For the most part, there's no bus service on Sunday, and some buses don't run on Saturday either. But if you decide you want to take the bus, pick up a copy of *The Bus Book* at one of the tourist information desks in the airport (where it's sometimes available), at Central Station at the corner of Central Avenue and Van Buren Street, or any Frys or Safeway supermarkets. There are both local and express buses. Local bus fare is $1.25, and express bus fare is $1.75. A 10-ride ticket book, all-day passes, and monthly passes are available.

Of slightly more value to visitors is the free **Downtown Area Shuttle (DASH),** which provides bus service within the downtown area. These buses operate Monday through Friday between 6:30am and 5:30pm. The buses stop at regular bus stops every 6 to 12 minutes. This shuttle is primarily for downtown workers, but attractions along the route include the state capitol, Heritage Square, and the Arizona Center shopping mall. In Tempe, **Free Local Area Shuttle (FLASH)** buses provide a similar service on a loop around Arizona State University. The route includes Mill Avenue and Sun Devil Stadium, and as the name implies, these buses are free. For information on both DASH and FLASH, phone ☎ 602/253-5000.

In Scottsdale you can ride the **Scottsdale Round Up** (☎ 480/312-7696) shuttle buses between Scottsdale Fashion Square and Old Town Scottsdale. These buses operate Monday through Saturday.

BY TAXI

Because distances in Phoenix are so great, the price of an average taxi ride can be quite high. However, if you don't have your own wheels and the bus isn't running because it's late at night or the weekend, you won't have any choice but to call a cab. **Yellow Cab** (☎ 602/252-5252) charges $3 for the first mile and $1.50 per mile after that. **Scottsdale Cab** (☎ 480/994-1616) charges $2 per mile, with a $5 minimum.

Fast Facts: Phoenix

American Express   There are American Express offices at 2508 E. Camelback Rd. (☎ 602/468-1199), open Monday through Saturday 10am to 6pm, and at 6900 E. Camelback Rd., Scottsdale (☎ 480/949-7000), open Monday through Friday 9:30am to 5:30pm and Saturday 9:30am to 3pm.

Airport   See "Orientation," earlier in this chapter.

Baby-Sitters   If your hotel can't recommend or provide a sitter, contact the **Granny Company** (☎ 602/956-4040). For **baby equipment rentals,** such as a crib or stroller, contact Baby Boom Rentals (☎ 602/331-8881).

Car Rentals   See "Getting Around," earlier in this chapter.

Climate   See "When to Go," in chapter 2.

Dentist   Call **800-DENTIST** for a referral.

Doctor   Call the **Maricopa County Medical Society** (☎ 602/252-2844) or the **Physician Referral and Resource Line** (☎ 602/230-2273) for doctor referrals.

Emergencies   For police, fire, or medical emergency, phone ☎ **911.**

Eyeglass Repair   The **Nationwide Vision Center** has more than 10 locations around the valley, including 5130 N. 19th Ave. (☎ **602/242-5293**); 3202 E. Greenway, Paradise Valley (☎ **602/788-8413**); 4615 E. Thomas Rd. (☎ **602/952-8667**); and 933 E. University Dr., Tempe (☎ **480/966-4992**).

Hospitals   The **Good Samaritan Regional Medical Center,** 1111 E. McDowell Rd. (☎ **602/239-2000**), is one of the largest hospitals in the valley.

Hotlines   The **Visitor Information Line** (☎ **602/252-5588**) has recorded tourist information on Phoenix and the Valley of the Sun. **Pressline** (☎ **602/271-5656**) provides access to daily news, the correct time, weather, and other topics.

Information   See "Visitor Information" under "Orientation," earlier in this chapter.

Internet Access   If your hotel doesn't provide Internet access, your next best bet is to visit one of the **Kinko's** in the area. There are Kinko's locations in downtown Phoenix at 259 N. First Ave. (☎ **602/252-4055**), off the Camelback corridor at 4801 N. Central Ave. (☎ **602/241-9440**), and in Scottsdale at 4150 N. Civic Center Blvd. (☎ **480/946-0500**), and at a couple of other locations.

Lost Property   If you lose something in the airport, call ☎ **602/273-3307;** on a bus, call ☎ **602/253-5000.**

Maps   See "City Layout" under "Orientation," earlier in this chapter.

Newspapers & Magazines   *The Arizona Republic* is Phoenix's daily newspaper. The Thursday paper has a special section (called "The Rep") with schedules of the upcoming week's movie, music, and cultural performances. *New Times* is a free weekly news and arts journal with comprehensive listings of cultural events, film, and rock-music club and concert schedules. The best place to find *New Times* is at corner newspaper dispensers in downtown Phoenix, Scottsdale, or Tempe.

Pharmacies   Call ☎ **800/WALGREENS** for the Walgreens pharmacy that's nearest you; some are open 24 hours a day.

Police   For police emergencies, phone ☎ **911.**

Post Office   The **Phoenix Main Post Office** is at 4949 E. Van Buren St. (☎ **800/275-8777**), open Monday through Friday 8am to 5pm .

Safety   Don't leave valuables in view in your car, especially when parking in downtown Phoenix. Put anything of value in the trunk, or under the seat if you're driving a hatchback. Take extra precautions after dark in the south-central Phoenix area and downtown. Violent acts of road rage are all too common in Phoenix, so it's a good idea to be polite when driving. Aggressive drivers should be given plenty of room.

Many hotels now provide in-room safes, for which there's sometimes a daily charge. Others will be glad to store your valuables in a safety-deposit box at the front office.

Taxes   State sales tax is about 5% (plus variable local taxes). Hotel room taxes vary considerably by city but are mostly between 10.25% and 10.625%. However, it is in renting a car that you really get pounded. Expect to pay taxes in excess of 20% when renting a car at Sky Harbor Airport. Add to this an additional $2.50 Cactus League charge, and you end up with a considerable amount on top of the rental fee. You can save up to 10% (the airport concession fee recoupment charge) by renting your car at an office outside the airport.

Taxis See "Getting Around," earlier in this chapter.

Transit Information For **Phoenix Transit System** public bus information, call ☎ **602/253-5000.**

Weather The phone number for weather information is ☎ **602/271-5656, ext. 1010.**

3 Where to Stay

Because the Phoenix area has long been popular as a winter refuge from cold and snow, it now has the greatest concentration of resorts in the continental United States. However, even with all the hotel rooms here, sunshine and spring training combine to make it hard to find a room on short notice between February and April (the busiest time of year in the valley). If you're planning to visit during these months, make your reservations as far in advance as possible. Also keep in mind that during the winter, the Phoenix metro area has some of the highest room rates in the country. Sure, the city has plenty of moderately priced motels, but even these places tend to jack up their prices in winter. Hotels are increasingly turning to the airline model: Rates go up and down with demand, so you never know what they might be charging on a given date. Also, don't forget that it's often possible to get a lower room rate simply by asking. If a hotel isn't full and isn't expected to be, you should be able to get a lower rate. Unfortunately, the reverse also holds true.

With the exception of valet parking services and parking garages at downtown convention hotels, parking is free at most Phoenix hotels. If there is a parking charge, we have noted it. You'll find that all hotels have no-smoking rooms and all but the cheapest have wheelchair-accessible rooms.

Also, keep in mind that most resorts offer a variety of weekend, golf, and tennis packages, as well as special off-season discounts and corporate rates (which you can often get just by asking). We've given only the official "rack rates," or walk-in rates, below, but it always pays to ask if there's any kind of special discount or package available. Don't forget your ACCOMMODATIONS or AARP discounts if you belong to these organizations. (If you aren't already a member, it's worth joining just to get the discounts.) Also keep in mind that business hotels downtown and near the airport often lower their rates on weekends.

If you're looking to save some money, consider traveling during the shoulder seasons of late spring and late summer. Temperatures are not at their midsummer peak nor are room rates at their midwinter highs. (And if you can stand the heat of summer, you can often save more than 50% on room rates.) If you'll be traveling with children, always ask whether your child will be able to stay for free in your room, and whether there's a limit to the number of children who can stay for free.

Request a room with a view of the mountains whenever possible. You can overlook a swimming pool anywhere, but some of the main selling points of Phoenix and Scottsdale hotels are the views of Mummy Mountain, Camelback Mountain, and Squaw Peak.

BED & BREAKFAST INNS While most people dreaming of an Arizona winter vacation have visions of luxury resorts dancing in their heads, there are also plenty of bed-and-breakfast inns around the valley. **Advance Reservations Inn Arizona/Mi Casa-Su Casa Bed & Breakfast Reservation Service,** P.O. Box 950, Tempe, AZ 85280-0950 (☎ **800/456-0682** or 480/990-0682; www.azres.com), can book you into more than 65 homes in the Valley of the Sun (and a total of 280 throughout the state), as can **Arizona Trails Bed & Breakfast Reservation Service,** P.O. Box 18998,

Fountain Hills, AZ 85269-8998 (☎ **888/799-4284** or 480/837-4284; fax 480/816-4224; www.arizonatrails.com), which also books tour and hotel reservations.

PRICE CATEGORIES   Because it is such a popular winter resort destination, the Valley of the Sun is one of the more expensive places in the United States for a vacation. If you've been thinking of saving money by skipping the Caribbean or Hawaii this year, think again. When a standard room at a top resort goes for well over $250 and a Super 8 Motel charges close to $100, price categories become very subjective. Consequently, we have categorized accommodations based on their relative cost when compared with other Valley of the Sun accommodations.

SCOTTSDALE
VERY EXPENSIVE

✪ **Hyatt Regency Scottsdale.** 7500 E. Doubletree Ranch Rd., Scottsdale, AZ 85258. ☎ **800/55-HYATT** or 480/991-3388. Fax 480/483-5550. www.hyatt.com. 493 units. A/C MINIBAR TV TEL. Jan–late May $375–$500 double, from $900 suites and casitas; late May–early Sept $155–$305 double, from $250 suites and casitas; early Sept–Dec $330–$460 double, from $500 suites and casitas. AE, CB, DC, DISC, JCB, MC, V.

From the colonnades of palm trees to the lobby walls that slide away, this luxurious resort is designed to astonish. Future archaeologists excavating the site would probably think it was a temple. Surrounded by a lake, gardens, fountains, and fishponds, the 2¹/₂-acre water playground is the resort's focal point. This extravagant complex of 10 swimming pools includes a waterslide, a sand beach, a water-volleyball pool, waterfalls, and a huge whirlpool spa. (You'd never know this was the desert.) The resort's Hopi Learning Center, staffed by Hopi interpreters, provides a glimpse into Native American culture.

The grounds are planted with hundreds of tall palm trees that frame the gorgeous views of the distant McDowell Mountains; closer at hand, original works of art have been placed throughout the resort. Guest rooms are luxurious and very comfortable and reflect the desert location. Robes, hair dryers, and scales are all standard.

Dining/Diversions: The Golden Swan, serving regional American cuisine, includes a popular waterside terrace dining area (see "Where to Dine" in this chapter). There's also a casual Southwestern restaurant and an Italian cafe that offers after-dinner gondola rides. A lobby bar features live music nightly. There are also two bars and a grill near the pool.

Amenities: Twenty-seven outstanding holes of golf (with lots of water hazards), 10 pools, eight tennis courts, a croquet court, jogging and bicycling trails, and a full-service health spa with exercise equipment, aerobics classes, saunas, and body and beauty treatments. A concierge, 24-hour room service, valet/laundry service, and children's programs are available.

✪ **Marriott's Camelback Inn.** 5402 E. Lincoln Dr., Scottsdale, AZ 85253. ☎ **800/ 24-CAMEL** or 480/948-1700. Fax 480/951-8469. www.camelbackinn.com. 453 units. A/C MINIBAR TV TEL. Jan to mid-May $329–$419 double, $515–$2,050 suite; mid-May to early Sept $159–$295 double, $215–$1,525 suite; early Sept–Dec $255–$329 double, $395–$1,550 suite. AE, CB, DC, DISC, EURO, JCB, MC, V. Small pets accepted.

Set at the foot of Mummy Mountain and overlooking Camelback Mountain, the Camelback Inn, which opened in 1936, is one of the grande dames of the Phoenix hotel scene. Over the past few years it has undergone $35 million worth of renovations, yet the resort still retains its traditional Southwestern character and solid sense of place. Although the two 18-hole golf courses are the main attractions for many guests here, the spa is among the finest in the state, and there's an extensive pool

Phoenix, Scottsdale & the Valley of the Sun Accommodation

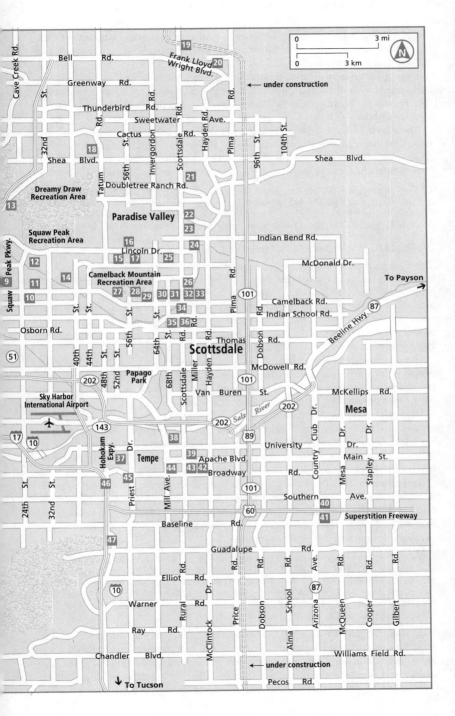

complex that appeals to families. The guest rooms, which are spread out over the sloping grounds, are decorated with contemporary Southwestern furnishings and art, and all have balconies or patios.

Dining/Diversions: The Chaparral serves new American cuisine in a relaxed atmosphere, while the Navajo Room is more casual. Healthy meals are served at the spa's restaurant. There are also two snack bars, a lounge for cocktails, and a cafe for espresso and pastries.

Amenities: Two outstanding 18-hole golf courses, a pitch-and-putt course, six tennis courts, three pools, three whirlpools, a playground, basketball and volleyball courts, one of the best full-service health spas in the valley, concierge, room service, baby-sitting, children's programs, valet/laundry service, car-rental desk.

✪ **The Phoenician.** 6000 E. Camelback Rd., Scottsdale, AZ 85251. ☎ **800/888-8234** or 480/941-8200. Fax 480/947-4311. www.thephoenician.com. 654 units. A/C MINIBAR TV TEL. Late Dec to mid-May $525–$655 double, $1,350–$5,500 suite; mid-May to early June $435–$485 double, $1,224–$5,500 suite; early June to mid-Sept $195–$245 double, $500–$5,300 suite; mid-Sept to late Dec $435–$485 double, $1,225–$5,500 suite. AE, CB, DC, DISC, MC, V. Valet parking $18. Pets under 25 lbs. accepted.

The Phoenician consistently ranks among the finest resorts in the world, and no expense was spared in the construction of the palatial resort, which is situated on 250 acres at the foot of Camelback Mountain. Polished marble and sparkling crystal abound in the lobby, but the view of the valley through a long wall of glass is what commands most guests' attention. Service here is second to none, and the pool complex is one of the finest in the state. The resort's spa offers all the pampering anyone could ever need, and there are also 27 challenging holes of golf.

Guest rooms are as elaborate as the public areas and include sunken bathtubs for two, Berber carpets, three phones, large patios, terry robes, bathroom scales, hair dryers, and wall safes. And that's just the *standard* room. The separate Canyon Building has its own private pool complete with rental cabanas.

Dining/Diversions: Mary Elaine's, Phoenix's ultimate special-occasion restaurant, features modern French cuisine and great views. The Terrace Dining Room serves Italian and is less formal, while Windows on the Green features Southwestern cuisine with a golf course view. There are also poolside snack bars. Afternoon tea in the lobby is also very popular and posh.

Amenities: In addition to the golf course and full-service spa, there are nine pools (including one lined with opalescent tiles), a waterslide, a putting green, 11 tennis courts, a whirlpool, lawn games, rental bikes, and a shopping arcade. Also available are a car-rental desk, business center, concierge, 24-hour room service, valet/laundry service, baby-sitting, and children's programs.

Regal McCormick Ranch Resort & Villas. 7401 N. Scottsdale Rd., Scottsdale, AZ 85253-3548. ☎ **800/222-8888** or 480/948-5050. Fax 480/991-5572. www.regal-hotels.com. 179 units. A/C MINIBAR TV TEL. Jan 1–Apr 30 $219–$299 double, from $360 suite or villa; May 1–May 31 $149–$199 double, from $274 suite or villa; June 1 to mid-Sept $109–$149 double, from $224 suite or villa; mid-Sept to Dec 31 $169–$219 double, from $294 suite or villa. AE, CB, DC, DISC, MC, V.

Surrounded by green lawns, a golf course, and a lake, this relatively small resort strives to convince you that you're not in the desert. The lake (complete with sailboats for guests) is the focal point, but more traditional resort activities are available at the two 18-hole golf courses and on the three tennis courts. The guest rooms all have their own private balconies or patios, and more than half the rooms overlook the lake. If you're here with your family, consider the spacious villas. So if you like the heat but not the desert, this resort, with its lakefront setting, is a good bet.

Dining/Diversions: The resort's restaurant serves good Southwestern fare, and there is an adjacent bar and grill. Both have views of the lake.

Amenities: Two 18-hole golf courses, outdoor pool overlooking lake, three lighted tennis courts (and pro shop, lessons, and clinics), whirlpool, walking/jogging paths, concierge, room service, valet/laundry service.

Renaissance Scottsdale Resort. 6160 N. Scottsdale Rd., Scottsdale, AZ 85253. ☎ **800/ HOTELS-1** or 480/991-1414. Fax 480/951-3350. www.renaissancehotels.com. 171 units. A/C MINIBAR TV TEL. Jan to mid-May $210–$229 double, $259–$325 suite; Mid-May to early Sept $75 double, $99–$105 suite; early Sept–Dec $75–189 double, $99–$285 suite. AE, DC, DISC, MC, V. Pets under 25 lbs. accepted ($50 deposit).

Located behind the upscale Borgata shopping center (which is designed to resemble an Italian village), the Renaissance Scottsdale Resort is an unpretentious-yet-luxurious boutique resort. Set amid shady lawns, the resort consists of spacious suites designed for those who need plenty of room and comfort. More than 100 of the suites have their own private hot tubs on private patios, and all the suites are done in Southwestern style. Several excellent restaurants are within walking distance, which makes this a good choice for gourmands who don't want to spend their vacation fighting rush-hour traffic on Scottsdale Road.

Dining/Diversions: The resort's restaurant and lounge are in a separate building (in front of the Borgata). There's also a poolside bar.

Amenities: Around the resort's spacious grounds you'll find two swimming pools, two hot tubs, four tennis courts, a jogging trail, putting green, and a croquet lawn. There are also bicycles for guests and access to a nearby health club (for an additional charge). A concierge, room service, and valet service are all available.

☺ The Sunburst Resort. 4925 N. Scottsdale Rd., Scottsdale, AZ 85251. ☎ **800/ 528-7867** or 480/945-7666. Fax 480/946-4056. www.sunburstresort.com. 210 units. A/C MINIBAR TV TEL. Jan to mid-Apr $235–$285 double, $635–$950 suite; mid-Apr to mid-May $215–$255 double; $575–$850 suite; late May to mid-Sept $95–$135 double, $300–$450 suite; mid-Sept to Dec $185–$225 double, $500–$750 suite. AE, CB, DC, DISC, MC, V.

An exceptional location in the heart of the Scottsdale shopping district, a dramatic Southwestern styling, and a small but well-designed pool area are the primary appeals of this resort. The focal point of the lobby is a massive sandstone fireplace; in the resort's lushly planted courtyard is a small lagoon-style pool complete with sand beach, short waterslide, and flame-topped columnar waterfalls. An artificial stream, waterfalls, and fake sandstone ruins all add up to a fun desert fantasy landscape (although not on the grand scale to be found at some area resorts).

Guest rooms are comfortable and decorated in new "Old West" styling, with cowhide prints and peeled log furnishings. Bathrooms have double vanities, and French doors open onto patios.

Dining/Diversions: The resort's dining room features a mix of Mediterranean and Southwestern flavors. There's also a lobby bar.

Amenities: Pools, whirlpool, fitness room, concierge, room service, valet/laundry. There's no golf course, but tee times can be arranged at nearby courses.

EXPENSIVE

Doubletree La Posada Resort. 4949 E. Lincoln Dr., Scottsdale, AZ 85253. ☎ **800/ 222-TREE** or 602/952-0420. Fax 602/840-8576. www.laposadaresort.com. 262 units. A/C MINIBAR TV TEL. Mid-Sept to mid-May $140–$200 double, $400–$550 suite; mid-May to mid-Sept $79–$112 double; $400–$550 suite. AE, CB, DC, DISC, MC, V.

If you prefer to spend your time by the pool rather than on the fairways, La Posada is a great choice, especially if you have the kids along. The pool here, which has a view of Camelback Mountain, covers half an acre and features its own two-story waterfall that cascades over artificial boulders. Connecting the two halves of the pool is a swim-through grotto complete with bar/cafe (and fitness room).

Mission-revival architecture prevails throughout the resort. The guest rooms are larger than average and have tiled bathrooms with a double vanity.

Dining/Diversions: The Garden Terrace restaurant has a nice view of Camelback Mountain and offers somewhat pricey Southwestern cuisine (although Sunday brunch is a great deal by Phoenix standards). There's also an adjacent lounge, as well as a poolside grill.

Amenities: In addition to facilities mentioned above, there are tennis and racquetball courts, two putting greens, four whirlpools, a fitness room, a volleyball court, and a tennis pro shop. A car-rental desk, concierge, room service, and laundry/valet service are also available.

✪ **Doubletree Paradise Valley Resort.** 5401 N. Scottsdale Rd., Scottsdale, AZ 85250. ☎ **800/222-TREE** or 480/947-5400. Fax 480/481-0209. www.doubletreehotels.com. 387 units. A/C MINIBAR TV TEL. Sept–May $175–$335 double, from $300 suite; May–Aug $85–$145 double, from $189 suite. AE, CB, DC, DISC, MC, V.

This resort gives a bow to the pioneering architectural style of Frank Lloyd Wright, and thus stands out from other comparable Scottsdale resorts. Built around several courtyards containing swimming pools, bubbling fountains, and desert gardens, the resort has much the look and feel of the Hyatt Regency (although on a less grandiose scale). Mature palm trees lend a sort of Moorish feel to the grounds and cast fanciful shadows in the gardens.

Guest rooms have a very contemporary feel, with lots of blond wood, and, in some cases, high ceilings that make the rooms feel particularly spacious. There are also large closets and separate dressing rooms and bathrooms, and coffeemakers, hair dryers, and irons/ironing boards are standard.

Dining/Diversions: A skylit dining room serves Southwestern dishes, while grilled meals are available on an adjacent patio. A lobby lounge serves drinks and light meals, often to the accompaniment of live music. There's also a poolside bar.

Amenities: Two outdoor pools (set in palm-shaded courtyards and with small waterfalls), tennis and racquetball courts, a fitness center, putting green, saunas, whirlpools, business center, valet/laundry service, car-rental desk, concierge, room service, valet/laundry service, baby-sitting.

Embassy Suites Paradise Valley at Stonecreek Golf Club. 4415 E. Paradise Village Pkwy. S., Paradise Valley, AZ 85032. ☎ **800/EMBASSY** or 602/569-0888. Fax 602/569-1308. www.embassysuitesaz.com. 270 units. A/C TV TEL. Oct–Apr $159–$199 double; May–June $129–$169 double; July–Sept $109–$149 double. Rates include full breakfast. AE, CB, DC, DISC, JCB, MC, V.

While cities from New York to San Francisco are busy opening chic and stylishly contemporary hotels as fast as they can, the Valley of the Sun has nearly missed the boat completely. That is, until this Embassy Suites opened in 2000. As soon as you see the dyed concrete floor and unusual wall sculpture in the lobby, you'll know that this is not your standard business hotel. However, it might be difficult to take your eyes off the views across Stonecreek Golf Course to Camelback Mountain, Mummy Mountain, and Squaw Peak, and those views just get better the higher up you go in the hotel (be sure to ask for a room on the south side of an upper floor). Keep in mind that this is an all-suite property, and the two-room accommodations are very spacious and have galley kitchens.

Dining/Diversions: The hotel's dining room overlooks the driving range and serves contemporary American dishes. There's also an adjacent lounge and a nightly complimentary cocktail reception.

Amenities: Pool, whirlpool, fitness room, room service, concierge, valet/laundry service.

Marriott's Mountain Shadows Resort & Golf Club. 5641 E. Lincoln Dr., Scottsdale, AZ 85253. ☎ **800/228-9290** or 480/948-7111. Fax 480/951-5430. 337 units. A/C MINIBAR TV TEL. Jan to mid-May $179–$199 double, $305–$700 suite; mid-May to early Sept $69–$149 double, $135–$415 suite; early Sept–Dec $149–$199 double, $265–$650 suite. AE, CB, DC, DISC, JCB, MC, V. Small pets accepted.

Located across the road from Marriott's Camelback Inn, Mountain Shadows offers better views of Camelback Mountain and an entirely different ambience. Mountain Shadows, built in the late 1950s and architecturally dated, is, however, well maintained and will appeal to anyone looking for an informal atmosphere. An 18-hole executive course keeps most guests happy, but guests can also use the Camelback Inn's courses (and its superb spa).

Standard rooms are large and have high ceilings, wet bars, king-size beds, and balconies. The rooms around the main pool, although large, can be a bit noisy. Those rooms in the Palm section offer the best views of the mountain.

Dining/Diversions: There's a seafood restaurant and a more casual Southwest-style cafe, as well as a bar and grill, a country club dining room, and a poolside snack bar.

Amenities: In addition to the golf course, there are eight tennis courts, three pools (one of which is quite large), two whirlpools, a fitness center, a volleyball court, pro shops, a business center, concierge, room service, valet/laundry service, car-rental desk, baby-sitting, children's programs, and guided mountain hikes.

Radisson Resort Scottsdale. 7171 N. Scottsdale Rd., Scottsdale, AZ 85253. ☎ **800/333-3333** or 480/991-3800. Fax 480/948-1381. www.radisson.com/scottsdaleaz. 318 units. A/C TV TEL. Mid-Jan to late May $139–$299 double, $359–$1,500 suite; late May–late June $175–$199 double, $295–$1,500 suite; late June to mid-Sept $125–$149 double, $199–$1,500 suite; mid-Sept to mid-Jan $220–$245 double, $325–$1,500 suite. AE, CB, DC, DISC, JCB, MC, V.

With all its green lawns and big trees, this resort feels far more Midwestern than southwestern, but if you want greenery and a conservative atmosphere, this is a good bet. Most guests are attracted by the resort's 21 tennis courts or two 18-hole golf courses. A large Japanese-style health spa rounds out the resort amenities here. Most rooms are large and have comfortable chairs and private patios, but the golf-course rooms, with their views of the McDowell Mountains, are our favorites.

Dining/Diversions: There's a rather formal dining room serving new American fare, a spa restaurant, a pub, a poolside snack bar, and even a tiny patisserie.

Amenities: In addition to the golf, tennis, and spa facilities, you'll find a pro shop, three pools, whirlpool, a health club ($15 charge), a concierge, room service, valet/laundry service, a car-rental desk.

MODERATE

Holiday Inn Hotel & Conference Center. 7353 E. Indian School Rd., Scottsdale, AZ 85251. ☎ **800/695-6995** or 480/994-9203. Fax 480/941-2567. www.holidayinnscottsdale.com. 206 units. A/C TV TEL. Mid-Jan to mid-Apr $105–$165 double, from $250 suite; mid-Apr to late May $89–$129 double, from $189 suite; late May–early Sept $50–$90 double, from $145 suite; early Sept–Dec 31 $89–$129 double, from $189 suite. AE, CB, DC, DISC, JCB, MC, V. Pets accepted.

Guest rooms at this low-rise hotel in Old Town Scottsdale are fairly small (as are the bathrooms), but the location right on the beautifully landscaped Scottsdale Civic

Center Mall (a park, not a shopping center) is very appealing. You're only a block off Scottsdale's famous shopping and gallery neighborhood, and the Scottsdale Center for the Arts is just across the mall. The best rooms are those opening onto the mall—be sure to request one. The hotel's dining room is a very economical steakhouse overlooking the park. There's also a lively lounge, small outdoor pool, tennis court, whirlpool, putting, baby-sitting, room service, and shopping shuttle.

☉ Holiday Inn SunSpree Resort. 7601 E. Indian Bend Rd., Scottsdale, AZ 85250. ☎ **800/852-5205** or 480/991-2400. Fax 480/998-2261. www.holiday-inn.com/scottsdale-rst. 200 units. A/C TV TEL. Oct–late Apr $119–$190 double; late Apr–late May $99–$170 double; late May–Sept $59–$100 double. AE, CB, DC, DISC, JCB, MC, V.

During the winter and spring, it's almost impossible to find a reasonably priced resort in Scottsdale, but this attractive and economical hotel fits the bill. Situated on 16 acres amid wide expanses of lawn, the SunSpree Resort certainly is not as luxurious as most other area resorts, but with its relatively low rates and policy of allowing kids under 12 to eat free in the resort's main restaurants, this is a good choice for families (the adjacent McCormick-Stillman Railroad Park is also a big hit with kids). Guest rooms have a plush feel that belies the economical rates. Ask for a mountain view or lakeside room with a patio. There's a restaurant overlooking the lake, as well as a lobby lounge and poolside bar, and room service is available. In addition to a swimming pool and whirlpool, the resort has a fitness room, tennis, volleyball, croquet, and horseshoes.

La Hacienda Resort. 7320 E. Camelback Rd., Scottsdale, AZ 85251. ☎ **480/994-4170.** www.suitedreamsaz.com. 22 units. Mid-Nov to late May $99–$149 double, $159–$279 suite; mid-May to Dec 31 $79–$89 double, $109–$179 suite. AE, MC, V. Pets accepted.

Don't be taken in by the name; this little place is hardly a resort, but it is a well-placed and well-priced getaway spot with the look and feel of an updated 1960s apartment court. Funky and hip are the watchwords here, although the hipness is mostly in the tiny lobby, which has decoupaged walls, faux-painted floors, and an espresso machine. The inn's grassy little courtyard, which has a small pool and a hot tub, is set off from busy Camelback Road by a brick wall that gives the complex a private, residential feel. Rooms are fairly well maintained and range from big to huge. Although the bathrooms are small, most rooms have full kitchens. Within just a few blocks are lots of nightclubs, great restaurants, and excellent shopping. This hotel is a good choice for younger travelers.

INEXPENSIVE

Despite the high-priced real estate, Scottsdale does have a few relatively inexpensive chain motels, although during the winter season prices are higher than you'd expect. The rates given here are for the high season. The **Days Inn—Scottsdale/Fashion Square Resort,** 4710 N. Scottsdale Rd. (☎ **480/947-5411**), charging $79 to $130 double; **Motel 6—Scottsdale,** 6848 E. Camelback Rd. (☎ **480/946-2280**), charging $72 double; and **Rodeway Inn—Phoenix/Scottsdale,** 7110 E. Indian School Rd. (☎ **480/946-3456**), charging $63 to $120 double.

Econo Lodge-Scottsdale Riverwalk. 6935 Fifth Ave., Scottsdale, AZ 85251. ☎ **800/55-ECONO** or 480/994-9461. Fax 480/947-1695. www.choicehotels.com. 92 units. A/C TV TEL. Oct 1 to mid-Apr $69–$109 double; mid-Apr to June 30 $59–$99 double; July 1–Sept 30 $49–$89 double. Rates include continental breakfast. AE, CB, DC, DISC, JCB, MC, V.

For convenience and price, this motel can't be beat (at least not in Scottsdale). Located at the west end of the Fifth Avenue shopping district, this motel is within walking distance of some of the best shopping and dining in Scottsdale. The guest rooms are large and have been recently renovated. The three-story building is arranged around a central courtyard where you'll find the pool. Local phone calls are free, and there's a fitness room.

NORTH SCOTTSDALE, CAREFREE & CAVE CREEK
VERY EXPENSIVE

✪ **The Boulders.** 34631 N. Tom Darlington Dr. (P.O. Box 2090), Carefree, AZ 85377. ☎ **800/553-1717,** 888/472-6229, or 480/488-9009. Fax 480/488-4118. www.grandbay. com. 160 casitas. A/C MINIBAR TV TEL. Mid-Jan to late Apr $565 double, from $765 villa; early to mid-Jan, late Apr–late May, and early Sept to early Dec $450 double, from $625 villa; late May–early June and mid-Dec $265 double, from $425 villa; mid-June to early Sept $185 double, from $415 villa (all rates plus $20 to $24 nightly service charge). AE, CB, DC, DISC, MC, V. Pets accepted ($100 refundable deposit).

Set amid a jumble of giant boulders 45 minutes north of Scottsdale, this resort epito-mizes the Southwest aesthetic and is the state's premier golf resort. Adobe buildings blend unobtrusively into the desert, as do the two noted golf courses, which feature the most breathtaking tee boxes in Arizona. If you can tear yourself away from the fair-ways, you can relax around either of two pools, play tennis (no boulders on the courts), or take advantage of the full-service spa. The distance from Scottsdale is this resort's only real shortcoming.

The lobby is an organic adobe structure with tree-trunk pillars, a flagstone floor, and a collection of Native American artifacts on display. The guest rooms continue the adobe styling with stucco walls, beehive fireplaces, and beamed ceilings. The bath-rooms are large and luxuriously appointed with tubs for two, separate showers, double vanities, and hair dryers. The best views are from second-floor rooms.

Dining/Diversions: The Latilla Room, the resort's premier restaurant, serves innovative American cuisine. The Palo Verde Room is a more casual spot serving Southwestern dishes. There's also a country club dining room, and, in the resort's El Pedregal Marketplace, several other dining options. A comfortable lounge features live jazz in the evenings.

Amenities: Two 18-hole golf courses, full-service spa, fitness center, six tennis courts, three pools, jogging and hiking trails, pro shop, rental bikes, concierge, room service, valet/laundry service, baby-sitting, children's programs (holidays only), rock-climbing program.

The Fairmont Scottsdale Princess. 7575 E. Princess Dr., Scottsdale, AZ 85255. ☎ **800/344-4758** or 480/585-4848. Fax 480/585-0086. www.fairmont.com. 650 units. A/C MINI-BAR TV TEL. $149–$539 double; $309–$3,500 suite. AE, CB, DC, DISC, MC, V.

With its royal palms, tiled fountains, waterfalls, and classical art and antiques, the Princess is a modern rendition of a Moorish palace and offers a truly exotic atmos-phere unmatched by any other valley resort. It's also home to the Phoenix Open golf tournament and the city's top tennis tournament, which means the two golf courses here are superb and the courts are top-notch. For those not tempted by golf or tennis, there's a full-service spa and fitness center. This resort, which is located a 20-minute drive north of Old Scottsdale, will delight anyone in search of a romantic hideaway.

The guest room decor is elegant Southwestern, and all the rooms have private bal-conies. The spacious bathrooms have double vanities and a separate shower and tub. For more space, there's a wide variety of suites available.

Dining/Diversions: The Marquesa serves superb (and expensive) Spanish cuisine, while upscale Mexican and strolling mariachis are the specialties at La Hacienda. See "Where to Dine," below, for more information on these two restaurants. There are a couple of casual restaurants and, at the golf course, a steakhouse. For drinks you'll find a quiet lounge and a rowdy Wild West saloon.

Amenities: In addition to the two 18-hole golf courses, there are seven tennis courts; three pools; whirlpools; racquetball, squash, and basketball courts; a fitness trail; a complete spa and fitness center; boutiques; tennis and golf pro shops; and a business center. There's even a fishing pond here (which kids love). A concierge, 24-hour room service, valet/laundry service, baby-sitting, and shopping shuttle are also available.

Four Seasons Resort Scottsdale at Troon North. 10600 E. Crescent Moon Dr., Scottsdale, AZ 85255. ☎ **800/332-3442** or 480/515-5700. Fax 480/515-5599. www.fourseasons.com. 210 units. A/C MINIBAR TV TEL. Mid-Dec to mid-May $475–625 double, $850–$3,500 suite; mid-May to mid-June and mid-Sept to mid-Dec $395–$495 double, $850–$3,500 suite; mid-June to mid-Sept $250–$300 double, $475–$3,500 suite. AE, DC, DISC, JCB, MC, V. Pets accepted.

With the late 1999 opening of this Four Seasons Resort, the valley resort scene got cranked up yet another notch on the luxury accommodations scale. Located in the foothills of north Scottsdale and adjacent to the Troon North golf course (one of the state's most highly acclaimed courses), the Four Seasons is working hard to knock The Boulders from its pinnacle. With casita accommodations scattered across a boulder-strewn hillside, the Four Seasons can certainly boast one of the most dramatic settings in the valley. Likewise, the guest rooms and suites are among the most spacious and luxurious you'll find in Arizona. If you can afford it, opt for one of the suites with an outdoor shower (a luxury usually found only in tropical resorts) and private plunge pool.

Dining/Diversions: With three restaurants on the premises, it's easy to forget how far out of the Scottsdale mainstream you are up here. There's a formal dining room serving new American fare, a more casual bistro serving Italian and California-style dishes, and a poolside bar/cafe serving lighter fare. There's also a lobby lounge.

Amenities: Large two-level pool, whirlpool, children's pool, four tennis courts, large fitness center (instructors available), full-service health spa, 24-hour room service, concierge, valet/laundry service, overnight shoeshine, children's programs.

EXPENSIVE

Scottsdale Marriott at McDowell Mountains. 16770 N. Perimeter Dr., Scottsdale, AZ 85260. ☎ **800/228-9290** or 480/502-3836. Fax 480/502-0653. www.marriottscottsdale. com. 270 units. A/C TV TEL. Jan to mid-May $229–$289 double; mid-May to mid-Sept $99–$209 double; mid-Sept to Dec $189–$209 double. AE, DC, DISC, JCB, MC, V.

This new all-suite resort, not far from the Scottsdale Princess, overlooks the Tournament Players Club (TPC) Desert Course. While this may not be the TPC's main course, it still manages to give this hotel a very resort-like feel. Suites provide lots of space and have luxurious bathrooms done in marble and granite. Some suites have balconies, and those overlooking the golf course are worth requesting, although there are also good views of the McDowell Mountains from some rooms.

Dining/Diversions: The hotel's Zambra Grille serves Mediterranean food, and there's also a lounge serving tapas. Poolside, there's a bar and grill.

Amenities: Pool, whirlpool, sauna, fitness room, room service, concierge, guest laundry, valet service.

CENTRAL PHOENIX & THE CAMELBACK CORRIDOR
VERY EXPENSIVE

♻ **Arizona Biltmore Resort & Spa.** 24th St. and Missouri Ave., Phoenix, AZ 85016. ☎ **800/950-0086** or 602/955-6600. Fax 602/954-2571. www.arizonabiltmore.com. 730 units. A/C TV TEL. Early Sept–Dec and early May to mid-June $295–$420 double, from $420 suite; Jan 1–early May $330–$495 double, from $650 suite; mid-June to early Sept, $165–$245 double, from $340 suite (all rates plus $12 daily service fee). AE, CB, DC, DISC, EURO, JCB, MC, V. Pets under 15 lbs. accepted in cottage rooms with $250 deposit, $50 nonrefundable.

For timeless elegance, a prime location, and historic character, no other resort in the valley can touch the Arizona Biltmore. For decades this has been the favored Phoenix address of celebrities and politicians, and the distinctive cast-cement blocks designed by Frank Lloyd Wright make it one of the valley's architectural gems. What this all means is that the Biltmore is *the* Phoenix address for those who can afford to stay where they want. While the two golf courses are the main draws for many guests, the children's activities center makes it a popular choice for families. Biltmore Fashion Park shopping center is also nearby.

Of the several different styles of accommodations, the "resort rooms" are the largest and most comfortable and have balconies or patios. The rooms in the Arizona Wing, added in 1999, are also good choices. The villa suites are the Biltmore's most spacious and luxurious accommodations.

Dining/Diversions: Wright's offers a formal setting and serves excellent new American cuisine amid the handiwork of Frank Lloyd Wright. The Biltmore Grill serves meals with a touch of the Southwest both in flavors and decor. There's a quiet lobby/terrace bar and a poolside bar/restaurant. Afternoon tea, a Phoenix institution, is served in the lobby.

Amenities: Two 18-hole golf courses, 18-hole putting course, a full-service spa, five swimming pools (including one with a waterslide and one with rental cabanas), two whirlpool spas, seven lighted tennis courts, fitness center, sauna, steam room, jogging paths, rental bicycles, lawn games, business center, shops, concierge, room service, courtesy car, valet/laundry service, car-rental service.

Hermosa Inn. 5532 N. Palo Cristi Rd., Paradise Valley, AZ 85253. ☎ **800/241-1210** or 602/955-8614. Fax 602/955-8299. www.hermosainn.com. 35 units. A/C TV TEL. Early Jan–early May $260–$330 double, $435–$635 suite; early May–late May $170–$210 double, $435–$520 suite; late May to mid-Sept $95–$140 double, $300–$450 suite; early Sept–early Jan $220–$275 double, $400–$550 suite. Rates include continental breakfast. AE, CB, DC, DISC, MC, V. Pets under 20 lbs. accepted with $250 deposit, $50 nonrefundable. Take 32nd St. north from Camelback Rd., turn right on Stanford Rd., and then turn left on N. Palo Cristi Rd. From Lincoln Dr., turn south on N. Palo Christi Rd. (east of 32nd St.).

This luxurious boutique hotel, once a guest ranch, is now one of the only hotels in the Phoenix area to offer a bit of Old Arizona atmosphere. Originally built in 1930 as the home of Western artist Lon Megargee, the inn is situated in a quiet residential neighborhood on more than 6 acres of neatly landscaped gardens. If you don't like the crowds of big resorts, but do enjoy the luxury, this is the spot for you.

Rooms here vary from cozy to spacious and are individually decorated in tastefully contemporary Western and Southwestern decor that would look at home on the pages of any interior design magazine. The largest suites, which have more Southwestern flavor than just about any other rooms in the area, incorporate a mixture of contemporary and antique Southwestern furnishings and accent pieces.

Dining/Diversions: Lon's, the hotel's dining room, is named for the hotel's original owner and is located in the original adobe home. Excellent new American and Southwestern cuisine is served in the rustic, upscale setting. See "Where to Dine," below, for more information.

Amenities: Small outdoor pool, two whirlpools, three tennis courts, concierge.

The Ritz-Carlton Phoenix. 2401 E. Camelback Rd., Phoenix, AZ 85016. ☎ **800/241-3333** or 602/468-0700. Fax 602/468-9883. 281 units. A/C MINIBAR TV TEL. Early Sept to mid-May $325–$375 double, $375–$425 suite; mid-May to early Sept $199–$249 double, $249–$299 suite. AE, CB, DC, DISC, MC, V. Valet parking $18.

Located directly across the street from the Biltmore Fashion Park shopping center in the heart of the Camelback Corridor business and shopping district, the Ritz-Carlton is the city's finest nonresort hotel, known for providing impeccable service. The public areas are filled with European antiques, and although this decor might seem a bit out of place in Phoenix, it's still utterly sophisticated. In the guest rooms, you'll find reproductions of antique furniture and marble bathrooms with ornate fixtures.

Dining/Diversions: Bistro 24 is a casual and lively French bistro. The elegant lobby lounge serves afternoon tea as well as cocktails, while in The Club, fine cigars and premium spirits are the order of the day.

Amenities: Small outdoor pool, fitness center, saunas, concierge, 24-hour room service, valet/laundry service, baby-sitting.

○ **Royal Palms Hotel and Casitas.** 5200 E. Camelback Rd., Phoenix, AZ 85018. ☎ **800/ 672-6011** or 602/840-3610. Fax 602/840-6927. www.royalpalmshotel.com. 116 units. A/C TV TEL. Jan 1–early June $345–$495 double, $385–$3,500 suite; early June–early Sept $175–$295 double, $200–$2,500 suite; early Sept–Dec $295–$425 double, $335–$3,500 suite (all rates plus $16 daily service fee). AE, CB, DC, DISC, MC, V.

The Royal Palms, midway between Scottsdale and Biltmore Fashion Park, reopened in 1997 after a complete renovation and is now one of the finest, most romantic resorts in the valley. The main building, constructed more than 50 years ago, was built by Cunard Steamship executive Delos Cooke in the Spanish mission style and is filled with European antiques that once belonged to Cooke. Antique water fountains and lush walled gardens give the property the tranquil feel of a Mediterranean monastery cloister.

The most memorable rooms at the resort are the individually designed deluxe casitas. Each of these rooms has a distinctive decor (ranging from opulent contemporary to classic European). These rooms also have completely private back patios and front patios that can be enclosed by heavy curtains. Other rooms are luxuriously appointed, although not quite so opulent.

Dining/Diversions: T. Cook's serves Mediterranean cuisine amid European antiques and is one of the city's most romantic restaurants (see "Where to Dine," below). An adjacent bar/lounge conjures up a Spanish villa setting. There's also a poolside bar and grill.

Amenities: Swimming pool with cabanas, whirlpool, tennis court, large exercise room, concierge, 24-hour room service, valet/laundry service.

EXPENSIVE

Embassy Suites Biltmore. 2630 E. Camelback Rd., Phoenix, AZ 85016. ☎ **800/ EMBASSY** or 602/955-3992. Fax 602/955-6479. 232 units. A/C TV TEL. Jan–Apr $239 double, May and Sept–Dec $179–$199 double, June–Aug $109–$119 double. Rates include full breakfast. AE, CB, DC, DISC, MC, V.

Located across the parking lot from the Biltmore Fashion Park (Phoenix's most upscale shopping center), this atrium hotel makes a great base if you want to be within walking distance of half a dozen good restaurants. The huge atrium is filled with interesting tile work and other artistic Southwestern touches, as well as tropical greenery, waterfalls, and ponds filled with koi (Japanese carp).

Unfortunately, the rooms, all suites, are dated and a bit of a let-down after passing through the atrium greenhouse, but they're certainly large. All have a microwave and refrigerator.

Dining/Diversions: The hotel's atrium houses the breakfast area and a romantic lounge with huge banquettes shaded by palm trees. Just off the atrium is a very contemporary high-end steakhouse. There's also a complimentary evening cocktail hour.

Amenities: Large outdoor pool, whirlpool, fitness room, concierge, room service, valet/laundry, courtesy car.

MODERATE

Hacienda Alta. 5750 E. Camelback Rd., Phoenix, AZ 85018. ☎ **480/945-8525.** 3 units. A/C TV. $100–$125 double; $150 suite. Rates include full breakfast. No credit cards.

Located adjacent to The Phoenician, yet very much in its own separate world surrounded by a desert landscape, this home offers a very convenient location, reasonable rates, and a chance to feel away from it all in the middle of the city. Don't expect the fussiness of most other B&Bs; owners Margaret and Ed Newhall make this casual, eclectic place a fun home away from home. The inn is housed in a 1920s territorial-style adobe home, and in the old gardens you'll find orange and grapefruit trees, which often provide juice for breakfast. There's also a large suite with a sleeping loft, whirlpool tub, fireplace, and balcony overlooking the Phoenician's golf course.

Maricopa Manor. 15 W. Pasadena Ave., Phoenix, AZ 85013. ☎ **800/292-6403** or 602/274-6302. Fax 602/266-3904. www.maricopamanor.com. 6 suites. A/C TV TEL. Sept–May $149–$229 double; June–Aug $89–$129 double. Rates include continental breakfast. AE, DC, DISC, MC, V.

Centrally located between downtown Phoenix and Scottsdale, this B&B is just a block off busy Camelback Road and for many years has been one of Phoenix's only official B&Bs. The inn's main home, designed to resemble a Spanish manor house, was built in 1928 and the many orange trees, palms, and large yard all lend a country air. All the guest rooms are large suites, and although the furnishings seem a bit dated, the rooms are quite comfortable. One suite has a sunroom and kitchen, and another has two separate sleeping areas. There are tables in the garden where you can eat your breakfast, which is delivered to your door. The inn also has a pool and hot tub.

Sierra Suites. 5235 N. 16th St., Phoenix, AZ 85016. ☎ **800/4-SIERRA** or 602/265-6800. Fax 602/265-1114. 113 units. A/C TV TEL. Oct–Apr $119–$139; May–Sept $49–$59. AE, DISC, MC, V.

Billing itself as a temporary residence and offering discounts for stays of 5 days or more, this hotel consists of studio-style apartments and is located just north of Camelback Road and not far from Biltmore Fashion Park. Although designed primarily for corporate business travelers on temporary assignment in the area, this hotel makes a good choice for families as well. All rooms have full kitchens, big closets and bathrooms, and separate sitting areas. Facilities include an exercise room, a pool, and a whirlpool. Local phone calls are free.

NORTH PHOENIX
VERY EXPENSIVE

☉ **Pointe Hilton Squaw Peak Resort.** 7677 N. 16th St., Phoenix, AZ 85020-9832. ☎ **800/876-4683** or 602/997-2626. Fax 602/997-2391. www.pointehilton.com. 564 units. A/C MINIBAR TV TEL. Jan–late Apr $239–$329 double, $839 grande suite; late Apr–late May and early Sept–Dec $189–$249 double, $729 grande suite; late May–early Sept $99–$149 double, $449 grande suite (all rates plus $8 daily resort fee). AE, CB, DC, DISC, EURO, JCB, MC, V.

Located at the foot of Squaw Peak, this lushly landscaped resort in north Phoenix makes a big splash with its Hole-in-the-Wall River Ranch, a 9-acre aquatic playground that features a tubing "river," waterslide, waterfall, sports pool, and lagoon pool. An 18-hole putting course, game room, and children's activity center also help make it a great family vacation spot. The resort is done in the Spanish villa style, and most of the guest rooms are large, two-room suites outfitted with a mix of contemporary and Spanish colonial–style furnishings.

ⓘ Family-Friendly Hotels

Hyatt Regency Scottsdale *(see p. 71)*   Not only is there a totally awesome water playground complete with sand beach and waterslide, but the Kamp Hyatt Kachina program provides supervised structured activities.

The Phoenician *(see p. 74)*   Kids absolutely love the waterslide here, and kids and parents both appreciate the Funicians Club, a supervised activities program for children ages 5 to 12. A putting green and croquet court offer further diversions.

Doubletree La Posada Resort *(see p. 75)*   If you're a kid, it's hard to imagine a cooler pool than the one here. It's got a two-story waterfall, a swim-through cave, and big artificial boulders. There are also horseshoe pits, a volleyball court, and a pitch-and-putt green.

Pointe Hilton Squaw Peak Resort *(see p. 83)*   A waterslide, a tubing river, a waterfall, water volleyball, a miniature golf course, a video games room, and a kids' program guarantee that your kids will be exhausted by the end of the day.

Holiday Inn SunSpree Resort *(see p. 78)*   Economical rates, a good Scottsdale location adjacent to the McCormick-Stillman Railroad Park, lots of grass for running around on, and free meals for kids under 12 make this one of the valley's best choice for families on a budget.

Dining/Diversions: The resort has a Mexican restaurant in an 1880 adobe building plus a Western-theme restaurant. There's also a more upscale dining room that serves contemporary American and Southwestern dishes.

Amenities: In addition to the River Ranch pools, there are four other pools, several whirlpools, a full-service spa (with racquetball courts, fitness room, lap pool, sauna, steam room, and aerobics classes), an 18-hole golf course (4 miles away), four tennis courts, jogging trails, rental bikes, shops, business center, concierge, room service, valet/laundry service, rental-car desk, baby-sitting, and children's programs.

Pointe Hilton Tapatio Cliffs Resort. 11111 N. Seventh St., Phoenix, AZ 85020. ☎ **800/ 876-4683** or 602/866-7500. Fax 602/993-0276. www.pointhilton.com. 585 units. A/C MINIBAR TV TEL. Jan–late Apr $239–$329 double, $909 grande suite; late Apr–late May and early Sept–Dec $189–$249 double, $739 grande suite; late May–early Sept $99–$149 double, $549 grande suite (all rates plus $8 daily resort fee). AE, CB, DC, DISC, EURO, JCB, MC, V.

If you love to lounge by the pool, then this resort is a great choice. The Falls, a 3-acre water playground, includes two lagoon pools, a 138-foot waterslide, 40-foot-high cascades, a whirlpool tucked into an artificial grotto, and poolside rental cabanas for that extra dash of luxury. Hikers will enjoy the easy access to trails in the adjacent North Mountain Recreation Area, while golfers can avail themselves of the resort's golf course. There's also a small full-service health spa. All rooms are spacious suites with Southwest furnishings, and the corner rooms, with their extra windows, are particularly bright. Situated on the shoulder of North Mountain, Tapatio Cliffs offers the steepest grounds of Phoenix's three Pointe resorts (get your heart and brakes checked).

Dining/Diversions: Different Pointe of View offers stupendous hilltop views, an expensive international menu, and an extensive wine cellar (see "Where to Dine," below). There's also a casual steakhouse and a more formal, club-like dining room. There are two poolside cafes.

Amenities: In addition to facilities mentioned above, there are 12 tennis courts, five other pools, whirlpools, a fitness center with steam room and sauna, rental bikes, a golf and tennis shop, a business center, a concierge, room service, rental-car desk, free shuttle between Pointe Hilton properties, horseback riding, and baby-sitting.

Sheraton Crescent Hotel. 2620 W. Dunlap Ave., Phoenix, AZ 85021. ☎ **800/423-4126** or 602/943-8200. Fax 602/371-2856. www.arizonaguide.com/sheratoncrescent. 342 units. A/C TV TEL. Jan to mid-Apr $250–$280 double, from $400 suite; mid-Apr to late May and mid-Sept to Dec $130–$230, from $230 suite; late May to mid-Sept $59–$135 double, from $230 suite. AE, CB, DC, DISC, MC, V. Small pets accepted.

Located in Phoenix's north-central business district and across I-17 from the Metro-center mall, this business hotel is a sister property to The Phoenician and displays much the same decorative style (with lots of marble), albeit on a more subdued level. Although situated away from downtown and the Camelback Corridor business districts, this is still one of the city's better choices for business travelers, especially if you appreciate an abundance of athletic facilities. Guest rooms are designed with business travelers in mind, and provide plenty of space, comfort, and convenience. The king rooms with balconies are worth asking for.

Dining/Diversions: The hotel's big, casual restaurant serves new American cuisine. There's also a small lounge.

Amenities: The hotel's small main pool is in a lush garden setting and has a long waterslide that's a hit with kids. Other facilities include a large fitness center, whirlpool, sauna, two tennis courts, two squash courts, and volleyball and basketball courts. Concierge, room service, and valet/laundry service are available.

EXPENSIVE

Embassy Suites—Phoenix North. 2577 W. Greenway Rd., Phoenix, AZ 85023-4222. ☎ **800/EMBASSY** or 602/375-1777. Fax 602/375-4012. www.embassy-suites.com. 314 units. A/C TV TEL. Nov–Apr $129–$159 double; May–Oct $89–$109 double. Rates include full breakfast. AE, CB, DC, DISC, MC, V.

This resort-like hotel in north Phoenix is right off I-17 and well away from the rest of the valley's resorts (and good restaurants), but if you happen to have relatives in Sun City or are planning a trip north to Sedona or the Grand Canyon, it's a good choice. The lobby of the Mission-style, all-suite hotel has the feel of a Spanish church interior, but instead of a cloister off the lobby, there is a garden courtyard with a huge swimming pool and lots of palm trees. The guest rooms are all suites, although furnishings are fairly basic, and bathrooms are small.

Dining/Diversions: The casual restaurant in the lobby serves moderately priced meals. There's also a piano lounge and poolside bar. Complimentary evening cocktails.

Amenities: Large pool, two tennis courts, exercise room, whirlpool, sauna, sand volleyball court, two racquetball courts, room service, valet/laundry service.

MODERATE/INEXPENSIVE

Among the better moderately priced chain motels in north Phoenix are the **Best Western InnSuites Hotel Phoenix,** 1615 E. Northern Ave. at 16th Street (☎ **602/ 997-6285**), charging $99 to $129 double; and the **Best Western Bell Motel,** 17211 N. Black Canyon Hwy. (☎ **602/993-8300**), charging $89 to $109 double. Rates are for the high season; for toll-free phone numbers.

Among the better budget chain motels in the north Phoenix area are the **Motel 6— Sweetwater,** 2735 W. Sweetwater Ave. (☎ **602/942-5030**), charging $50 to $56 double; and **Super 8—Phoenix Metro/Central,** 4021 N. 27th Ave. (☎ **602/ 248-8880**), charging $50 to $56 double. Rates are for the high season.

DOWNTOWN PHOENIX
VERY EXPENSIVE

Crowne Plaza—Phoenix Downtown. 100 N. First St., Phoenix, AZ 85004. ☎ **800/ 2CROWNE** or 602/333-0000. Fax 602/333-5181. 532 units. A/C TV TEL. Oct–Apr $239–$279 double; June–Sept $139–$179 double. AE, DC, DISC, JCB, MC, V. Valet parking $10.

This 19-story business and convention hotel is your best choice in downtown, although with the crowds of conventioneers, individual travelers are likely to feel overlooked. A Mediterranean villa theme has been adopted throughout the public areas with slate flooring and walls painted to resemble cracked stucco. Guest rooms continue the Mediterranean feel and are designed with the business traveler in mind.

Dining/Diversions: There's a cafe for breakfast and a bar and grill with a bit of character (but very standard fare).

Amenities: Fitness room, swimming pool, whirlpool spa, room service, concierge, massages, valet/laundry service, business center.

EXPENSIVE

Hyatt Regency Phoenix. 122 N. 2nd St., Phoenix, AZ 85004. ☎ **800/233-1234** or 602/252-1234. Fax 602/254-9472. www.phoenix.hyatt.com. 712 units. A/C TV TEL. $134–$274 double; $450–$1,550 suite. AE, CB, DC, DISC, JCB, MC, V. Valet parking $17; self-parking $12.

Located directly across the street from the Phoenix Civic Plaza, this high-rise Hyatt is almost always packed with conventioneers. Whether full or empty, the hotel always seems somewhat understaffed, so don't expect top-notch service if you're stuck here on a convention. However, the attractive lobby certainly provides plenty of space for lounging. The rooms are fairly standard, although comfortably furnished. Ask for a room above the eighth floor to take advantage of the views from the glass elevators.

Dining/Diversions: The Compass Room is Arizona's only rotating rooftop restaurant and serves Southwestern dishes. The food is usually decent, and the views are interesting. There's also the more casual and inexpensive Terrace Café in the hotel's atrium and a contemporary restaurant/bar at street level.

Amenities: Small outdoor pool, exercise room, whirlpool, tennis courts, shopping arcade, concierge, room service, valet/laundry service.

MODERATE

○ **Hotel San Carlos.** 202 N. Central Ave., Phoenix, AZ 85004. ☎ **602/253-4121.** Fax 602/253-6668. www.hotelsancarlos.com. 132 units. A/C TV TEL. Jan–Apr $139 double, $185 suite; May–Sept $89 double, $125 suite; Oct–Dec $105 double, $169 suite. Rates include continental breakfast. AE, CB, DC, DISC, MC, V. Valet and self-parking $15. Pets allowed, $25.

If you don't mind staying in downtown Phoenix with the convention crowds, you'll get a good value at this historic hotel. Built in 1928 and listed on the National Register of Historic Places, the San Carlos is a small hotel that provides that touch of elegance and charm missing from the other downtown hotels. Unfortunately, rooms are rather small by today's standards and the decor needs updating. There's an Italian restaurant in the lobby, an adjacent espresso bar, and an Irish pub. The hotel also features valet/laundry service and a rooftop pool.

TEMPE, MESA, SOUTH PHOENIX & THE AIRPORT AREA
VERY EXPENSIVE

The Pointe Hilton South Mountain Resort. 7777 S. Pointe Pkwy., Phoenix, AZ 85044. ☎ **800/876-4683** or 602/438-9000. Fax 602/431-6535. www.pointehilton.com. 638 units. A/C MINIBAR TV TEL. Jan–late Apr $239–$329 double, $869 grande suite; late Apr–late May and early Sept–Dec $189–$249 double, $729 grande suite; late May–early Sept $99–$149 double, $539 grande suite (all rates plus $8 daily resort fee). AE, CB, DC, DISC, EURO, JCB, MC, V.

On the south side of the valley, this Pointe Hilton resort abuts the 17,000-acre South Mountain Park, and although the grand scale of the resort seems designed primarily to accommodate convention crowds, individual travelers, especially active ones, will find plenty to keep them busy here. Golfers get great views from the greens, urban cowboys can ride right into the sunset on South Mountain, and if it's abs and pecs you want to work on, the 40,000-square-foot fitness center should keep you pumped up.

The guest rooms here are all suites and feature contemporary Southwestern furnishings. Mountainside suites offer the best views of the golf course and South Mountain.

Dining/Diversions: Rustler's Rooste is a Western-themed restaurant featuring cowboy bands and rattlesnake appetizers (see "Where to Dine," below). A second restaurant features continental cuisine and a more sedate atmosphere. There's also a casual Mexican restaurant and a place for healthful meals at the fitness center.

Amenities: Two 18-hole golf courses, 10 tennis courts, four racquetball courts, six swimming pools, volleyball courts, riding stables, pro shop, health club, concierge, room service, valet/laundry service, massages, rental-car desk, baby-sitting.

✪ **Wyndham Buttes Resort.** 2000 Westcourt Way, Tempe, AZ 85282. ☎ **800/ WYNDHAM** or 602/225-9000. Fax 602/438-8622. www.wyndham.com. 353 units. A/C MINIBAR TV TEL. Labor Day–late May $215–$294 double, from $475 suite; late May–Labor Day $99–$159 double, from $375 suite. AE, CB, DC, DISC, MC, V.

This spectacular resort, only 3 miles from Sky Harbor Airport, makes the utmost of its craggy hilltop location (although some people complain that the freeway in the foreground ruins the view). Few other valley resorts have as much of a sense of place; the rocky setting and desert landscaping leave no doubt you're in the Southwest. From the cactus garden, stream, and waterfall in the lobby to the circular restaurant and the freeform swimming pools, every inch of this resort is calculated to take your breath away. The pools (complete with waterfalls) and four whirlpools (one is the most romantic in the valley) are the best reasons to stay here.

Guest rooms are stylishly elegant, and many have views across the valley (marred slightly by the adjacent freeway). The highway-view rooms are a bit larger than the pool-view rooms, but second floor pool-view rooms have patios. Unfortunately for fans of long soaks, most bathrooms have only ³/₄-size tubs (but there are great whirlpool spas around the grounds).

Dining/Diversions: The Top of the Rock restaurant snags the best view around, and sunset dinners are memorable (see "Where to Dine," below). An informal dining room, complete with waterfall and fish pond, is located below the lobby. There are bars below Top of the Rock (with only a partial view), in the lobby, and by the pool.

Amenities: Four tennis courts, a fitness center, concierge, room service, valet/laundry service, a business center.

EXPENSIVE

✪ **Fiesta Inn.** 2100 S. Priest Dr., Tempe, AZ 85282. ☎ **800/528-6481** or 480/967-1441. Fax 480/967-0224. 270 units. A/C TV TEL. Jan 1–late Apr $155 double; late Apr–May $119 double; June–Sept $85 double; Oct–Dec $139 double. AE, CB, DC, DISC, MC, V. Pets accepted.

Reasonable rates, shady grounds, extensive recreational facilities (three tennis courts, putting green, driving range, pool, and fitness room), and a location close to the airport, ASU, and Tempe's Mill Avenue make this older, casual resort one of the best deals in the valley. OK, so it isn't as fancy as the resorts in Scottsdale, but you can't argue with the rates. Guest rooms are large, with refrigerators, coffeemakers, and hair dryers, and local phone calls are free.

Dining/Diversions: The restaurant serves reliable American fare, and there's also a lounge.

Amenities: Room service, concierge, complimentary airport shuttle, valet/laundry service.

Tempe Mission Palms Hotel. 60 E. 5th St., Tempe, AZ 85281. ☎ **800/547-8705** or 480/894-1400. Fax 480/968-7677. www.missionpalms.com. 303 units. A/C TV TEL. Jan–May $179–$279 double; $229–$299 suite; June–Aug $99–$159 double, $129–$179 suite; Sept–Dec $169–$239 double, $199–$259 suite. AE, CB, DC, DISC, JCB, MC, V.

College students, their families, and anyone else who wants to be close to Tempe's nightlife will find this an ideal, although somewhat overpriced, location right in the heart of the Mill Avenue shopping, restaurant, and nightlife district. When you've had enough of the hustle and bustle on Mill Avenue, you can retreat to the hotel's rooftop pool. For the most part, guest rooms are quite comfortable and boast lots of wood, marble, and granite.

Dining/Diversions: The hotel's restaurant serves Southwestern meals at reasonable prices. You'll also find a lounge off the lobby and a poolside bar.

Amenities: Medium-size outdoor pool, tennis court, fitness center, whirlpool, sauna, business center, room service, complimentary airport shuttle, valet/laundry service.

Twin Palms Hotel. 225 E. Apache Blvd., Tempe, AZ 85281. ☎ **800/367-0835** or 480/967-9431. Fax 480/968-1877. 140 units. A/C TV TEL. Jan–Apr $159 double; May–Sept $79 double; Oct–Dec $129 double. $170–$350 suite year-round. AE, CB, DC, DISC, MC, V.

Although the rooms at this midrise hotel just off the ASU campus are just standard rooms (with coffeemakers), the Twin Palms is a great choice for fitness fanatics. Hotel guests have full access to the nearby ASU Student Recreation Complex, which covers 135,000 square feet and includes a huge weight-training room; Olympic pool; and racquetball, tennis, and basketball courts. When you stay here, you're also close to Sun Devil Stadium, the ASU-Karsten Golf Course, and busy Mill Avenue.

Diversions: There's a small bar off the lobby.

Amenities: In addition to fitness center access, there's a complimentary airport shuttle, and local phone calls are free.

MODERATE/INEXPENSIVE

Apache Boulevard in Tempe becomes Main Street in Mesa, and along this stretch of road there are numerous old motels charging some of the lowest rates in the valley. However, these motels are very hit-or-miss. If you're used to staying at nonchain motels, you might want to cruise this strip and check out a few places. Otherwise, try the chain motels mentioned below (which tend to charge $20 to $40 more per night than nonchain motels).

Chain motel options in the Tempe area include the **Days Inn—Tempe,** 1221 E. Apache Blvd. (☎ **480/968-7793**), charging $69 to $124 double; **Super 8— Tempe/Scottsdale,** 1020 E. Apache Blvd. (☎ **480/967-8891**), charging $67 to $81 double; and **Travelodge—Tempe,** 1005 E. Apache Blvd. (☎ **480/968-7871**), charging $59 to $99 double.

Chain motel options in the Mesa area include the **Days Inn—Mesa,** 333 W. Juanita Ave. (☎ **480/844-8900**), charging $86 to $106 double; **Motel 6—Mesa North,** 336 W. Hampton Ave. (☎ **480/844-8899**), charging $54 double; and **Super 8—Mesa,** 6733 E. Main St. (☎ **480/981-6181**), charging $67 to $69 double.

Chain motels in the airport area include the **Best Western Airport Inn,** 2425 S. 24th St. (☎ **602/273-7251**), charging $90 to $120 double, and **Rodeway Inn Airport East,** 1550 S. 52nd St. (☎ **480/967-3000**), charging $80 to $110 double. Rates are for the high season.

OUTLYING RESORTS

Gold Canyon Golf Resort. 6100 S. Kings Ranch Rd., Gold Canyon, AZ 85219. ☎ **800/624-6445** or 480/982-9090. Fax 480/983-9554. www.gcgr.com. 101 units. A/C TV TEL. Mid-Jan to mid-Apr $200–$230 double; mid-Apr to Sept $125–$155 double; Oct to mid-Jan $175–$205 double. AE, DC, DISC, MC, V.

Located way out on the east side of the valley near Apache Junction, Gold Canyon is a favorite of devoted golfers who come to play some of the most scenic holes in the state (the Superstition Mountains provide the backdrop). Although nongolfers will appreciate the scenery here, the small pool makes it clear that golfers, not swimmers, take the fore here. The guest rooms, housed in blindingly white pueblo-inspired buildings, are large, and some have fireplaces while others have whirlpools.

Dining/Diversions: The main dining room serves Southwestern and new American fare, and there's a bar and grill serving simple meals.

Amenities: Two gorgeous 18-hole golf courses, two tennis courts, a pool, a whirlpool, horseback riding, rental bikes, room service.

The Wigwam Resort. 300 Wigwam Blvd., Litchfield Park, AZ 85340. ☎ **800/327-0396** or 623/935-3811. Fax 623/935-3737. www.wigwamresort.com. 331 units. A/C MINIBAR TV TEL. Early Jan–early May $330–$390 double, $390–$525 suite; early May–late June $245–$295 double, $295–$380 suite; late June–early Sept $145–$185 double, $185–$275 suite; early Sept–early Jan $245–$295 double, $295–$430 suite. AE, CB, DC, DISC, MC, V. Pets under 20 lbs. accepted ($50 deposit, $25 nonrefundable).

Located 20 minutes west of downtown Phoenix and twice as far from Scottsdale, this resort opened its doors to the public in 1929 and remains one of the nation's premier golf resorts. Three challenging golf courses and superb service are the reasons most people choose this resort, which, although elegant, is set amid flat lands that lack the stunning desert scenery of the Scottsdale area.

Most of the guest rooms are in Santa Fe–style buildings, surrounded by green lawns and colorful gardens. All rooms are spacious and feature contemporary Southwestern furniture. Some rooms have fireplaces, but the most popular rooms are those along the golf course.

Dining/Diversions: The resort's Terrace Dining Room serves continental cuisine, and the Arizona Kitchen serves acclaimed Southwestern fare. There's also a clubhouse restaurant and a poolside bar and grill. Afternoon tea and evening cocktails are served in a lobby lounge, and there's also a sports bar.

Amenities: Three golf courses, putting green, golf lessons, nine tennis courts, tennis lessons, pro shop, two pools, bicycles, volleyball, croquet, trap and skeet shooting, exercise room, sauna, holiday and summer children's programs, concierge, room service, valet/laundry service, massages.

4 Where to Dine

Just as the Valley of the Sun boasts some terrific resorts, it is also full of excellent restaurants, and Scottsdale and the Biltmore Corridor are home to most of the city's best dining establishments. If you have only one expensive meal while you're here, I'd suggest a resort restaurant that offers a view of the city lights. Other meals not to be missed are the cowboy dinners served amid Wild West decor at such places as Pinnacle Peak and Rustler's Rooste.

Phoenix, Scottsdale & the Valley of the Sun Dining

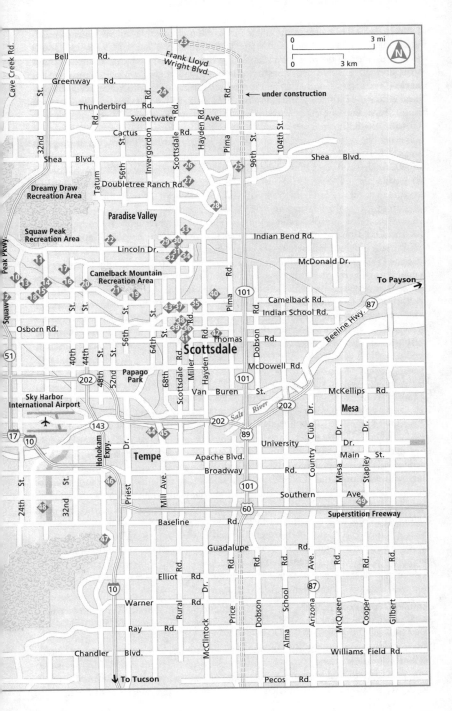

Bell Rd.

Greenway Rd.

Frank Lloyd Wright Blvd.

← under construction

Thunderbird Rd.

Sweetwater

Cactus

Shea Blvd.

Dreamy Draw
Recreation Area

Squaw Peak
Recreation Area

Paradise Valley

Lincoln Dr.

Camelback Mountain
Recreation Area

Osborn Rd.

Scottsdale

Papago
Park

Sky Harbor
International Airport

Tempe

Indian Bend Rd.

McDonald Dr.

To Payson

Camelback Rd.

Indian School Rd.

Thomas Rd.

McDowell Rd.

Van Buren St.

Salt River

Mesa

McKellips Rd.

University Dr.

Apache Blvd.

Broadway Rd.

Main St.

Southern Ave.

Superstition Freeway

Baseline Rd.

Guadalupe Rd.

Elliot Rd.

Warner Rd.

Ray Rd.

Chandler Blvd.

↓ To Tucson

Pecos Rd.

Williams Field Rd.

Shea Blvd.

To Payson

Beeline Hwy.

Cave Creek Rd.

32nd St.

Tatum

56th St.

Invergordon

Scottsdale Rd.

Hayden Rd.

Pima

96th St.

104th St.

Squaw Peak Pkwy.

40th St.

44th St.

48th St.

52nd St.

56th St.

64th St.

68th St.

Scottsdale Rd.

Miller Rd.

Hayden Rd.

Pima Rd.

Dobson Rd.

Country Club Dr.

Mesa Dr.

Stapley Dr.

24th St.

32nd St.

Priest Dr.

Mill Ave.

Rural Rd.

McClintock Dr.

Price

Dobson Rd.

School Rd.

Alma

Arizona Ave.

McQueen Rd.

Cooper Rd.

Gilbert Rd.

91

Phoenix also has plenty of those big and familiar chains that you've heard so much about. There's a **Hard Rock Cafe,** 2621 E. Camelback Rd. (☎ **602/956-3669**) where you can toss down a burger and then buy that all-important T-shirt to prove you've been here. As Phoenix has become more and more Arizona's version of Los Angeles, it has also acquired all the important California chains, such as **California Pizza Kitchen,** 2400 E. Camelback Rd. (☎ **602/553-8382**), located in Biltmore Fashion Park, and also in Scottsdale at 10100 Scottsdale Rd. at Gold Dust Avenue (☎ **480/596-8300**).

The big chain steakhouses are also duking it out here in Phoenix. You'll find two **Ruth's Chris** steakhouses: in the Biltmore district at 2201 E. Camelback Rd. (☎ **602/957-9600**) and in the Scottsdale Seville shopping plaza, 7001 N. Scottsdale Rd., Scottsdale (☎ **480/991-5988**). You'll find **Morton's Steakhouses** in the Biltmore district at 2501 E. Camelback Rd. (☎ **602/955-9577**) and in north Scottsdale across from the Scottsdale airport, 15233 N. Kierland Blvd. (☎ **480/951-4440**).

Good places to go trolling for a place to eat include the trendy Biltmore Fashion Park and Old Town Scottsdale. At the former, which by the way is a shopping mall, not a park, you'll find the above mentioned chain restaurant California Pizza Kitchen—as well as nearly a dozen other excellent restaurants. In Old Town Scottsdale, within an area of roughly 4 square blocks, you'll find about a dozen good restaurants. A few of our favorites in both places are listed here.

Phoenix is a sprawling city, and it can be a real pain to have to drive around in search of a good lunch spot. If you happen to be visiting the Phoenix Art Museum, the Heard Museum, or the Desert Botanical Gardens anytime around lunch, stay put for your noon meal. All three of these attractions have cafes serving decent, if limited, menus.

SCOTTSDALE
EXPENSIVE

The Chaparral. At Marriott's Camelback Inn, 5402 E. Lincoln Dr. ☎ **480/948-1700,** ext. 7888. Reservations highly recommended. Main courses $22–$34. AE, CB, DC, DISC, MC, V. Daily 6–10pm. NEW AMERICAN.

They've changed the decor and the menu, but rest assured that Camelback Mountain is still the view out the window. No longer does the menu feature the timeless continental classics it once did. These days you'll start off with herb-laced focaccia, potato rolls, and salted rosemary lavosh—all incredibly tempting. The rich lobster bisque—covered with puff pastry and served with a spoonful of caviar crème fraîche—is a holdover from the old menu; it's an elegant dining experience not to be missed. Some dishes are more successful than others. Hits include a moist and flavorful sea bass crusted with tomato and parsley, and, for garlic lovers, lobster tail with aïoli (garlic mayonnaise). Service is as attentive as you would expect, and some wines are even fairly moderately priced. It's not as formal an environment as it once was—you can now get away with dressing "comfortably casual" here.

El Chorro Lodge. 5550 E. Lincoln Dr. ☎ **480/948-5170.** Reservations recommended. Lunch $8–$17; full dinner $12–$63. AE, CB, DC, DISC, MC, V. Mon–Fri 11am–3pm and 5:30–11pm; Sat–Sun 5:30–11pm. CONTINENTAL.

Built in 1934 as a school for girls and converted to a lodge and restaurant 3 years later, El Chorro Lodge is a valley landmark set on its own 22 acres of desert. It's one of the area's last old traditional restaurants. At night, lights twinkle on the saguaro cactus, and the restaurant takes on a timeless tranquility, even if the interior is a little dowdy.

The adobe building houses several dining rooms, but the patio is the place to sit, either in the daytime or on a chilly night near the crackling fireplace. The traditional decor and menu that features such classic dishes as chateaubriand and rack of lamb are popular with both old-timers and families. In addition to the favorites, there are several dishes low in salt and fat, as well as seafood dishes. Save room for the legendary sticky buns.

Golden Swan. At the Hyatt Regency Scottsdale Resort, 7500 E. Doubletree Ranch Rd. ☎ **480/991-3388.** Reservations recommended. Main courses $27.50–$36; Sun brunch $34. AE, DC, DISC, MC, V. Daily 6–10pm; Sun brunch 9:30am–2pm. REGIONAL AMERICAN.

At this restaurant within the Hyatt Regency Scottsdale Resort, a combination of cuisine and setting make for very special meals. Dramatically spotlit royal palms, geometric architecture, and the sound of fountains and waterfalls set the tone; the food is just as pleasurable, beautifully presented with plenty of attention to details. Artistically arranged entrees generally offer several distinctive flavors, some subtle, some bold— for example, orange-honey barbecued salmon on a truffle oil–risotto cake or a grilled lamb chop with jalapeño-honey mustard crusted with toasted pistachios and served with a cheddar cheese hominy timbale. Save room for one of the Golden Swan's decadent desserts—perhaps a silky chocolate mousse cake with fresh berries soaked in zinfandel sauce accented by bright green crushed pistachios. Before or after dinner, the open-air lounge at the resort is a romantic place to have a drink and listen to live music.

Mancuso's. At the Borgata, 6166 N. Scottsdale Rd. ☎ **480/948-9988.** Reservations recommended. Main courses $18–$29; pastas $17–$24. AE, CB, DC, DISC, MC, V. Daily 5–10:30pm. NORTHERN ITALIAN/CONTINENTAL.

With its ramparts, towers, stone walls, and narrow, uneven alleyways leading through the complex, the Borgata is built in the style of a medieval Italian village, so it seems only fitting that Mancuso's would affect the look of an elaborate baronial banquet hall. A cathedral ceiling, arched windows, and huge roof beams set the stage for the gourmet continental cuisine; and a pianist playing soft jazz sets the mood. If you lack the means to start your meal with the beluga caviar, perhaps *carpaccio di manzo*— sliced raw beef with mustard sauce and capers—will do. Veal is a specialty, but it is always difficult just to get past the pasta offerings. Lately, more fish and daily seafood specials have been added to the menu. The professional service will have you feeling like royalty by the time you finish your dessert and coffee.

✪ **Mary Elaine's.** At The Phoenician, 6000 E. Camelback Rd., Scottsdale. ☎ **480/ 423-2530.** Reservations highly recommended. Jacket required for men. Main courses $37–$45; 6-course seasonal tasting menu $110 (matched wines are an additional $55). AE, CB, DC, DISC, MC, V. Mon–Thurs 6–10pm; Fri–Sat 6–11pm. FRENCH/MEDITERRANEAN.

Located on the top floor of The Phoenician's main building, Mary Elaine's is one of the finest restaurants in the valley and boasts one of the best views as well. The restaurant is the height of elegance and sophistication (Austrian crystal, French Ercuis silver, and Wedgwood china), although those seeking a more casual, alfresco setting can dine on the patio most of the year.

The chef focuses on the flavors of the modern French kitchen, which are usually dictated by the changing seasons. A recent menu included seared foie gras with 100-year-old balsamic vinegar, John Dory fish with fennel, artichokes, and pearl onions, and red currant–glazed rack of venison. Mary Elaine's will go out of its way to accommodate a vegetarian—call beforehand to make a request. The very extensive wine list has won numerous awards.

Windows on the Green. At The Phoenician, 6000 E. Camelback Rd., Scottsdale. ☎ **480/423-2530.** Reservations recommended. Main courses $18.50–$42; regional tasting menu $59. AE, CB, DC, DISC, MC, V. Wed–Mon 6–10pm. SOUTHWESTERN.

Slightly more casual than The Phoenician's premier restaurant, Mary Elaine's, but no less elegant, Windows on the Green has a sweeping view of the resort's golf course. Chef Michael Snoke turns the familiar into the extraordinary when serving up such dishes as quail stuffed with jalapeño cheddar grits, blue cornmeal–crusted trout, and prickly pear sorbet. While the flavors on the menu here are predominantly Southwestern, not every dish is doused with chili peppers. Diners with sensitive palates will find plenty to choose from. The wine list is chosen to complement these regional flavors. All in all, a good but somewhat pricey introduction to Southwestern cuisine.

MODERATE

Another area restaurant worth trying is **Sam's Cafe,** North Scottsdale Road and Shea Boulevard (☎ **480/368-2800**), which has other branches around the valley. For more information on Sam's Cafe, see the "Downtown Phoenix" section later in this chapter.

6th Avenue Bistrot. 7150 E. 6th Ave. ☎ **480/947-6022.** Reservations recommended. Main courses $7.25–$12.50 at lunch, $15–$22 at dinner. AE, MC, V. Sun–Mon 5–9pm; Tues–Thurs 11am–2pm and 5–9pm; Fri–Sat 11am–2pm and 5–10pm. CLASSIC FRENCH.

Who says French has to be fussy? This little bistro less than a block off Scottsdale Road is as casual as a French restaurant gets (although it's a bit more formal in the evening). The draw here is a simple menu of reliable dishes at fairly reasonable prices: a bit of country pâté, tenderloin of pork with port-wine sauce, a hearty Beaujolais, all topped off with *mousse au chocolat,* and you have a perfect French dinner. Lunch here is a great deal, and wines by the glass are reasonably priced.

✪ **Café Terra Cotta.** At the Borgata, 6166 N. Scottsdale Rd., Suite 100. ☎ **480/948-8100.** Reservations recommended for dinner. Main courses $8–$22. AE, DC, DISC, MC, V. Daily 11:30am–9:30pm. SOUTHWESTERN.

Café Terra Cotta started out in Tucson, where it invented the concept of trendy foods, and they haven't stopped cookin' since. The list of Southwestern choices at this casually sophisticated and low-key restaurant is long, including wood-oven pizzas, sandwiches, and smaller meals as well as full-size main courses. Imaginative combinations are the rule, so you'll want to take your time with the menu before ordering. For example, roll this over your imaginary taste buds: chili-roasted duck breast with chipotle sauce on a potato-horseradish pancake and carrot-jicama salad. Don't miss the garlic custard with warm salsa vinaigrette, which goes great with a glass of wine chosen from the well-rounded wine list.

Cowboy Ciao Wine Bar & Grill. 7133 E. Stetson Dr. (corner 6th Ave.). ☎ **480/WINE-111.** Reservations recommended. Main courses $7–$11 at lunch, $12–$24 at dinner. AE, DC, DISC, MC, V. Tues–Sat 11:30am–2pm and 5–10pm; Sun 5–10pm. SOUTHWESTERN/ITALIAN.

Delicious food, low prices, and a fun and trendy atmosphere furnished in "cowboy chic"—that sums up what makes Cowboy Ciao a great place for a meal. Located in fashionable downtown Scottsdale, this place attracts a diverse group of people who like to dive into the likes of cocoa-dusted scallops with peanut sauce or grilled halibut with a lemon-pepper couscous. Large, fresh salads get two thumbs up. Cowboy Ciao is also notable for its wine list and bar, where customers can order a flight (tasting assortment) of wines. We wouldn't miss the chocolate lottery dessert, consisting of a double chocolate and espresso torte plus an Arizona state lottery ticket.

❸ Franco's Trattoria. 8120 N. Hayden Rd. ☎ **480/948-6655.** Reservations recommended. Main courses lunch $7–$11, dinner $12.50–$26. AE, MC, V. Tues–Fri 11:30am–2pm and 5:15–10pm; Sat 5:15–10pm. Open Mon for both lunch and dinner Oct–Mar. Closed July. TUSCAN ITALIAN.

Dining at Franco's Trattoria is like taking a trip to Tuscany. Franco bustles around shaving hard cheeses, which arrive on the table accompanied by bread and olive oil, and chats with his regulars in an atmosphere that's both congenial and romantic. For starters, the *insalata capricciosa,* a salad of fennel, goat cheese, sun-dried tomatoes, beans, arugula, radicchio, and red onion, fairly bursts with flavor, as do the homemade raviolis and risottos. If you want something spicy (you are in the Southwest), try the *spezzatino di vitello dolce forte,* veal with tomato, rosemary, raisins, vinegar and hot pepper. Lots of places claim to make the world's best tiramisu, but Franco's, made from his grandmother's recipe, truly takes the cake. It's the best you'll ever have, and it packs a wallop with its brandy, amaretto, and espresso–infused ladyfingers. Wines are very reasonably priced, and the service is knowledgeable and personable.

L'Ecole. At the Scottsdale Culinary Institute, 8100 E. Camelback Rd. (just east of Hayden Rd.). ☎ **480/990-7639.** Reservations highly recommended several days in advance. 3 courses $9.25–$13 at lunch, 5 courses $25 at dinner. DISC, MC, V. Mon–Fri 11:30am–1pm and 6–7:30pm. Closed every 3rd Monday. CONTINENTAL/INTERNATIONAL.

This culinary opportunity is a well-kept local secret—there aren't many places where you can get a three-course lunch for under $10 or a five-course dinner for $25. In spite of the fact that you don't have to bring a lot of money here, you do have to have a lot of patience—the cooking and serving is done by students, and it's all a learning experience for them. For an appetizer, you might try the wild raspberry salad; for an entree, sole français is nice, followed by crème brûlée or pecan pie. There is a respectable selection of wines and liquors to accompany the meal. This is such a good deal that people drive from all over the valley to eat here.

Pepin. 7363 Scottsdale Mall. ☎ **480/990-9026.** Reservations recommended. Main courses $13–$25; tapas $5–$9. AE, CB, DC, DISC, MC, V. Tues–Thurs 11:30am–3pm and 4:30–10pm; Fri–Sat 11:30am–3pm and 4:30–11pm; Sun 5–10pm. Happy hour, Tues–Fri 4:30–6:30pm. SPANISH.

For traditional Spanish fare and plenty of lively entertainment, you won't do better than Pepin. Located on the Scottsdale Mall, this small Spanish restaurant offers such a wide selection of tapas that you can easily have dinner without ever glancing at the main-course list. However, there are also several styles of paella, most of which are seafood extravaganzas. Thursday through Saturday evenings, there are live flamenco performances, and Friday and Saturday evenings, there's also salsa dancing. Call for times.

Rancho Pinot. 6208 N. Scottsdale Rd. (south of Lincoln Dr.). ☎ **602/468-9463.** Reservations recommended. Main courses $17–$26. AE, DISC, MC, V. Tues–Sat 5:30–10pm. Summer hours subject to change. CONTEMPORARY AMERICAN.

Rancho Pinot, in a shopping center adjacent to the Borgata, combines a "homey" cowboy chic decor with nonthreatening contemporary American cuisine and has long been a favorite with Scottsdale and Phoenix residents. The menu here changes regularly and tends to emphasize well-cooked meats served with vegetables allowed to express their own distinctiveness rather than wallowing in heavy sauces. Look elsewhere if you're craving wildly creative flavor combinations, but if you like simple, well-prepared food, Rancho Pinot may be the place. You might start with grilled squid salad with preserved lemon and then move on to a house specialty, Nonni's chicken, braised with white wine, mushrooms, and herbs, or a handmade pasta. There's a short but well-chosen list of beers and wines by the glass, and for dessert, delectably rich homemade ice cream. The staff is friendly and tends to treat you as though you were a regular even if it's your first visit.

Razz's Restaurant and Bar. 10321 N. Scottsdale Rd. (in the Windmill Plaza) ☎ **480/905-1308.** Reservations recommended. Main courses $17–$24. AE, DC, MC, V. Tues–Sat 5–10pm. INTERNATIONAL.

Razz Kamnitzer, a native Venezuelan, is one in a line of seven chefs in his family. No wonder his restaurant is such a hit. Located in a nondescript shopping mall on the southeast corner of Shea Boulevard and Scottsdale Road, the restaurant is chic, but not stuffy, crowded, and lively. Razz has been on the Phoenix restaurant scene for some years and is known for his cuisine, which includes edible flowers, herbs, and exotic vegetable and fruits. On a recent night, the menu included such wide-ranging dishes as twice-roasted duck breast with berry-orange sauce; an Indonesian-style noodle dish with chicken, shrimp, pork, and vegetables; and grilled rack of lamb with tamarind and garlic marinade.

✪ **Restaurant Hapa.** 6204 N. Scottsdale Rd. (behind Trader Joes). ☎ **480/998-8220.** Reservations recommended. Main courses $16–$29; small plates $6–$16. AE, MC, V. Mon–Sat 5:30–10pm. PAN ASIAN.

This small and somewhat intimate space is popular with all ages and features a Zen decor, with huge mirrors covering one wall. They have a way with a grill here that really brings out the flavor of shrimp and fish and also turns out some excellent grilled vegetables. From the depths of the wood-burning oven come such dishes as game hen and deftly prepared fish with roasted vegetables. We like the strong flavor combinations on the small plates a lot: spicy squid salad in a chili-lemongrass sauce; shrimp, quail, and chicken satay with three sauces; and pork and ginger potstickers with curried mustard sauce. To round out this Asian-American eating experience, try a delicious dessert such as warm chocolate mango cake with lemongrass ice cream and mango fruit sauce, a melting mélange of contrasting flavors. An adjoining sushi lounge is open during the same hours as the restaurant.

✪ **Roaring Fork.** 7243 E. Camelback Rd. ☎ **480/947-0795.** Reservations highly recommended. Main courses $14–$25. AE, MC, V. Mon–Sat 5:30–10pm. SOUTHWESTERN.

This trendy and very Southwestern restaurant, near the intersection of Camelback and Scottsdale roads, is the creation of chef Robert McGrath, formerly of The Phoenician's Windows on the Green. With its stone walls, mélange of Mexican hacienda and Italian villa architectural styles, and impeccably upscale Southwestern interior, Roaring Fork is a much more casual space than Windows on the Green, yet the cuisine is just as creative. Just be sure you try the sugar-chile glazed duck breast with green chile macaroni (a house specialty). Filled with herb-infused rolls and corn muffins accompanied by honey-chile butter, the bread basket alone is enough to make you weep with joy. There may not be any chilies in the desserts, but they're still worth saving room for. If you can't get a table, it's no disappointment to dine at the bar, since the rebar lariats there hold bowls of bar munchies, including pieces of spicy jerky. And don't miss the huckleberry margaritas. Robert McGrath takes a very hands-on approach with his restaurant—you might see him waiting tables and checking with diners to be sure they're enjoying their meals.

✪ **Roy's of Scottsdale.** 7001 N. Scottsdale Rd, at the Scottsdale Seville. ☎ **480/905-1155.** Reservations recommended. Main courses $16.50–$27; smaller plates $7–$11. AE, MC, V. Sun–Thurs 5–10pm; Fri–Sat 5–11pm. EURO-ASIAN.

So you decided to go to Arizona instead of Hawaii this year, but you really prefer pan-Asian flavors to those of the Southwest. Don't worry—even in Scottsdale you can now get Hawaiian chef Roy Yamaguchi's patented pan-Asian cuisine. Brilliant combinations and flamboyant presentations are the hallmark here, and despite lively atmosphere, service usually runs like clockwork. The menu includes nightly specials such as an unusual fried spicy tuna roll or wood-fired tiger shrimp and bacon pizza. Signature entrees include blackened ahi tuna with a hot soy-mustard sauce and meat loaf with wild-mushroom gravy. If you can't get a reservation, you can usually get seats at the counter, which provides a great floor show of cooks preparing food at lightning speed. From the counter, you can also see what's being made and order dishes that look tempting. Desserts are both delicious and beautifully sculpted.

There's another Roy's at 24th Street and Camelback Road in the Camelback Esplanade (☎ **602/381-1155**).

Sushi Ko. 9301 E. Shea Blvd. #126 (in the Mercado del Rancho shopping plaza) ☎ **480/860-2960.** Reservations recommended for dinner. Main courses lunch $5–$10, dinner $7–$19. AE, DC, DISC, MC, V. Mon–Fri 11:30am–2pm and 5:30–10pm; Sat–Sun 5:30–10pm. JAPANESE.

Recommended by those who know good sushi and popular with the Japanese community, Sushi Ko is a little restaurant in a shopping plaza not far from both the Fairmont Scottsdale Princess and the Hyatt Regency Scottsdale Resort. What makes this place stand out, in addition to the fresh and well-prepared sushi, are the unusual items that appear on the sushi menu—fresh sardine sushi, monk fish pâté, *Edamame* (steamed and salted soybeans that you pop from the shell and eat), and dynamite green mussels (mussels baked with mushrooms and mayonnaise; sounds strange but tastes great). Table-side cooking is a specialty here, and you can get *shabu-shabu,* a hot-pot dish of thinly sliced beef and vegetables served with ponzu sauce.

Veneto Trattoria Italiana. 6137 N. Scottsdale Rd. (in Hilton Village). ☎ **480/948-9928.** Reservations recommended. Main courses $8–$22. AE, CB, DC, DISC, MC, V. Mon–Sat 11:30am–2:30pm and 5–10pm. VENETIAN ITALIAN.

This casual and pleasantly low-key bistro, specializing in the cuisine of Venice, serves simple and satisfying "peasant food" (surprising, since the owner formerly ran the restaurant at the Giorgio Armani boutique in Beverly Hills). A salad of thinly sliced smoked beef, shaved parmesan, and arugula greens, or tender calamari rings served over spinach and savoy cabbage make great starters, followed by *luganega con verzette e polenta,* a lightly spiced sausage with perfectly prepared polenta. *Baccala mantecato* (creamy fish mousse on grilled polenta, made with dried salt cod soaked in milk overnight) may sound unusual, but it's heavenly—for this alone we would recommend the restaurant. For a finale, the *semifreddo con frutta secca,* a partially frozen meringue with dry fruits in a pool of raspberry sauce, has an intoxicating texture. There's outdoor seating on the patio (you can almost forget you're in a shopping mall) and a welcoming bistro ambience inside.

INEXPENSIVE

✪ **Bandera.** 3821 N. Scottsdale Rd., Scottsdale. ☎ **480/994-3524.** Reservations not accepted. Main courses $10–$23. AE, DISC, MC, V. Sun–Thurs 4:30–10pm; Fri–Sat 4:30–11pm. AMERICAN.

If you spent all day wandering in and out of Scottsdale galleries without buying a single bronze statue, you just might be a frugal traveler. If so, you'll want to know about Bandera. Actually, if you've been craving barbecue or grilled chicken for a few hours, chances are it's because you've been smelling the wood-roasted chickens turning on the rotisseries in Bandera's back-of-the-building, open-air stone oven. What an aroma!

The succulent spit-roasted chicken is served with the ultimate comfort food, a mountain of creamy mashed potatoes flecked with green onion and black pepper. Sure, you could order prime rib, clams, or leg of lamb, but you'd be a fool if you did. Stick with the chicken or maybe the honey-barbecued ribs, and you won't go wrong. The succulent smoked salmon appetizer is also a hit. This place may be a California chain, but, hey, Californians know good food.

Carlsbad Tavern. 3313 N. Hayden Rd., Scottsdale (south of Osborn). ☎ **480/970-8164.** Reservations recommended at dinner. Main courses $7–$19. AE, DC, DISC, MC, V. Mon–Sat 11am–1am; Sun 1pm–1am; limited menu available from 10 or 11pm until 1am. NEW MEXICAN.

Carlsbad Tavern blends the fiery tastes of New Mexican cuisine with a hip and humorous atmosphere featuring bats (a reference to Carlsbad Caverns). On the menu you'll find traditional New Mexican dishes, such as lamb *pierna* and *carne adovada,* simmered in a fiery red chili sauce. Nouvelle Southwestern specialties include a spicy peppercorn cream–sauced pasta with grilled chicken, andouille sausage, and pine nuts, and a robust chorizo meatloaf sandwich. Cool off your taste buds with a margarita made with fresh-squeezed juice. A lagoon makes this place feel like a beach bar, and a big patio fireplace is really cozy on a cold night.

El Guapo's Taco Shop & Salsa Bar. 3015 N. Scottsdale Rd., Scottsdale (in Plaza 777). ☎ **480/423-8385.** Main dishes $2–$8. No credit cards. Mon–Sat 10:30am–8pm. MEXICAN.

El Guapo means "handsome," which certainly doesn't refer to this little hole-in-the-wall taco shop, but might be referring to Danny, the proprietor. The tacos—among them mahi-mahi, *carne asada,* or marinated pork—are prepared without the standard lettuce and tomatoes so that you can build your own by liberally dousing your order with salsa and vegetable toppings from the salsa cart. It takes two or three tacos to make a meal, so you can try a few different types. El Guapo has homemade-style cheese crisps, burritos, and nachos, too. Try the armadillo eggs—jalapeño peppers stuffed with cheese and deep-fried. There are only half a dozen tables here, and the salsa bar takes up a good part of the shop.

El Paso Barbeque Company. 8220 N. Hayden Rd. ☎ **480/998-2626.** Main courses $6–$17. AE, DISC, MC, V. Sun–Thurs 11am–10pm; Fri–Sat 11am–11pm. BARBECUE.

This is barbecue Scottsdale style, with an upscale cowboy decor and a bar with two noisy TVs that can make for difficult conversation. But hey, if you're not in a romantic mood, this place is worth the trip for some lip-smacking barbecue, which runs the gamut from ribs to smoked chicken to more uptown barbecued salmon and prime rib. The pulled pork with a smoky sauce and fresh coleslaw is scrumptious. There's also a wide variety of sandwiches, which makes this a good lunch spot or place to get carry-out. Want to dine on the lighter side? Order the smoked salmon salad.

Oregano's Pizza Bistro. 3622 N. Scottsdale Rd. (south of Indian School Rd.). ☎ **480/ 970-1860.** Reservations not accepted. Main courses $5–$17. AE, DC, DISC, MC, V. Mon–Thurs 11am–10pm; Fri–Sat 11am–11pm; Sun noon–10pm. PIZZA/PASTA.

With very reasonable prices and a location convenient to the many shops and galleries of Old Scottsdale, this sprawling pizza joint (two buildings and the courtyard/parking lot between) is a big hit with the area's young crowd. Both the thin-crust pizzas—topped with barbecue chicken and feta cheese (and, by the way, too much for one person)—and the Chicago stuffed pizza are all the good things pizza should be. In addition to pizza, the menu includes artichoke lasagna, barbecued wings, a variety of salads, and even a pizza cookie for dessert. Because this is such a popular spot, expect a wait at dinner.

Other locations: in Phoenix, 130 E. Washington St. (☎ **602/253-9577**), and in Tempe, 523 W. University Dr. (☎ **480/858-0501**).

NORTH SCOTTSDALE, CAREFREE, & CAVE CREEK
EXPENSIVE

La Hacienda. At the Fairmont Scottsdale Princess resort, 7575 E. Princess Dr. (about 12 miles north of downtown Scottsdale). ☎ **480/585-4848.** Reservations recommended. Main courses $22–$30. AE, CB, DC, DISC, MC, V. Daily 6–10pm. GOURMET MEXICAN.

As you might have guessed by the price range above, this is not your average taco stand. La Hacienda serves gourmet Mexican cuisine in an upscale, glamorous-but-rustic setting reminiscent of an early 1900s Mexican ranch house (stone tiled floor, Mexican glassware and crockery, a beehive fireplace). Gourmet Mexican means such dishes as the signature suckling pig stuffed with chorizo sausage, or rack of lamb unlike any you may have had before—with a pumpkin seed crust and chili-plum sauce. Live music nightly adds to the lively atmosphere at this place.

✪ **Marquesa.** At the Fairmont Scottsdale Princess resort, 7575 E. Princess Dr. (about 12 miles north of downtown Scottsdale). ☎ **480/585-4848.** Reservations recommended. Main courses $29–$41; champagne brunch $47. AE, CB, DC, DISC, MC, V. Tues–Thurs 6–10pm; Fri–Sat 6–11pm; Sun brunch 10:30am–2:30pm. MEDITERRANEAN/CATALAN.

The Marquesa is as romantic a restaurant as you're likely to find in the valley: High-backed chairs, chandeliers, muted lighting, and large classical Spanish paintings create an ambience reminiscent of an 18th-century Spanish villa. The menu is a contemporary interpretation of Catalonian (regional Spanish) with Italian, French, Greek, and Moroccan influences. Lobster cakes with a morel mushroom fondue make for a robustly flavored starter. *Paella Valenciana,* which is the restaurant's signature dish and includes such ingredients as lobster, frog legs, mussels, shrimp, cockles, and fragrant saffron rice, should not be missed. Among the caloric works of art called dessert you might find a crème fraîche flan with roasted pears. The Sunday "market-style" brunch here is one of the best in the valley.

Michael's. 8700 E. Pinnacle Peak Rd. (at the Citadel). ☎ **480/515-2575.** Reservations recommended. Main courses $18–$26. AE, DC, MC, V. Mon–Sat 11am–2:30pm and 6–10pm; Sun 10am–2:30pm (brunch) and 6–10pm. CONTEMPORARY AMERICAN/INTERNATIONAL.

Located in the Citadel shopping/business plaza in north Scottsdale, Michael's was once a remote culinary outpost. However, as Scottsdale's upscale suburbs have marched ever northward, the city has bulldozed its way to Michael's doorstep. Push through the restaurant's front door, and you'll find out exactly why foodies are willing to make the drive out here. The setting is simple yet elegant, which allows the drama of food presentation to take the fore. Picture dishes such as mushroom strudel with poached prawns in a red pepper sauce; bacon-wrapped pork médaillons on baked Asian pears with lemongrass demi-glace; or grilled loin of lamb on a goat cheese and potato tart. Don't miss the "silver spoons" hors d'oeuvres—tablespoons each containing three or four ingredients that burst with flavors. Throughout the year, Chef Michael partners with other local chefs to present special themed lunches and dinners. Call ☎ **480/515-3550** for information.

Restaurant Oceana. 8900 E. Pinnacle Peak Rd. (at Pima Rd.), La Mirada shopping center. ☎ **480/515-2277.** Reservations recommended. Main courses $19–$36. AE, DC, DISC, MC, V. Mon–Thurs 5:30–9pm; Fri–Sat 5:30–10pm. Also open for dinner Sun during winter. SEAFOOD.

North Scottsdale seems to be where the action is these days when it comes to new resorts, golf courses, posh suburbs, and restaurants. Among the best of the latter is a rather small seafood restaurant in an attractive shopping center that has no less than four upscale restaurants. As the name implies, Oceana specializes in all things finny, plus plenty of crustaceans; everything is as fresh as it can be here in the middle of the desert. A wood oven and a sushi bar guarantee that the restaurant will appeal to a wide variety of palates. However, standouts well worth trying include the wood-oven baked mussels, the house smoked salmon, the grilled rare ahi tuna, and the Dungeness crab cakes. When it comes time for dessert, be sure to order a sampler plate.

CENTRAL PHOENIX & THE CAMELBACK CORRIDOR
EXPENSIVE

Christopher's Fermier Brasserie and Paola's Wine Bar. 2584 E. Camelback Rd. (in Biltmore Fashion Park). ☎ **602/522-2344.** Reservations recommended. Main courses $9–$11 at lunch, $17–$30 at dinner. AE, DISC, MC, V. Mon–Thurs 11am–3pm and 5–10pm; Fri 11am–3pm and 5–11pm; Sat noon–3pm and 5–11pm; Sun noon–3pm and 5–10pm. RUSTIC FRENCH.

Christopher Gross's venue in Biltmore Fashion Park covers many bases. There's a wine bar, a brewery, a cigar room, and a restaurant. Tasty standouts in the restaurant include a velvety roasted–red bellpepper soup with truffle essence and the house-smoked salmon, both holdovers from Gross's previous restaurant. Duck cassoulet with Merguez sausage was remarkably uninteresting. The brewery produces a wide range of beer styles; to give them all a try, order a flight. We prefer the darker ones. A wine bar menu is served from 3 to 5pm, when you can nibble on such things as smoked chicken pizza, French and California cheeses with wine, or Gross's signature dessert, a chocolate mousse tower.

Coup des Tartes. 4626 N. 16th St. ☎ **602/212-1082.** Reservations recommended. Main courses $14–$19. AE, DISC, MC, V. Tues–Sat 5:30–9:30pm. FRENCH.

Chain restaurants, theme restaurants, restaurants that are all style and little substance. Sometimes in Phoenix it seems impossible to find a genuinely homey little hole in the wall restaurant that serves good food. Coupe des Tartes, only 2 blocks off Camelback Road yet easy to miss, is just such a hole in the wall. With barely a dozen tables and no liquor license (bring your own wine), Coupe des Tartes is about as removed from the standard Phoenix glitz as you can get without getting on a plane and leaving town. The food is primarily rustic French to go with the casual atmosphere. Start your meal with pate de campagne or brie brûlée, which is covered with caramelized apples. The entree menu is always quite short, but you might opt for a lemon-herb encrusted pork tenderloin with chèvre mashed potatoes or filet mignon with a prosciutto-mushroom sauce. For desert, don't miss the banana brûlée tart.

Eddie Matney's. 2398 E. Camelback Rd. ☎ **602/957-3214.** Reservations recommended. Main courses lunch $9–$14, dinner $15–$25. AE, DISC, MC, V. Mon–Thurs 11:30am–2:30pm and 5–10:30pm; Fri 11:30am–2:30pm and 5–11:30pm; Sat 5–11:30pm; Sun 5–10:30pm. CONTEMPORARY AMERICAN.

Eddie Matney has been on the Phoenix restaurant scene for quite a few years now and continues to keep local foodies happy with his mix of creativity and comfort. This current restaurant is an upscale bistro in a glass office tower at Camelback Road's most upscale corner, which means it is a popular power lunch and business dinner spot but also works well for a romantic evening out. The menu ranges far and wide for inspiration and features everything from Eddie's famous meatloaf to trout wrapped in grape leaves and topped with four-onion marmalade. There are plenty of southwestern and Mediterranean influences on the menu here, and the lunch menu is almost as creative as the dinner menu (but at lower prices).

Harris'. 3101 E. Camelback Rd. ☎ **602/508-8888.** Reservations highly recommended. Main courses $8–$19 at lunch, $17–$32 at dinner. AE, DC, DISC, MC, V. Mon–Fri 11:30am–2pm and 5:30–10pm; Sat 5:30–10pm. STEAKS.

If you haven't noticed yet, beef is back in a big way. Enormous slabs of steak, perfectly cooked and allowed to express their inner beefiness unsullied by silly sauces are de rigueur from Manhattan to Marin County these days, and no longer is it necessary to visit some steakhouse that has aged longer than the meat it serves. Today steaks are being served in settings once reserved for various incarnations of nouvelle cuisine. Harris', smack in the middle of the bustling big-money Camelback Corridor, is one of Phoenix's biggest contemporary steakhouses and popular with wealthy retirees. With a Southwestern pueblo-modern styling, valet parking attendants, and prime rib a specialty of the house, this impressive restaurant leaves no doubt that this is where you'll find your beef. Make sure you've got plenty of space left on your credit card—a meal here will definitely set you back some bucks. At lunch (when prices are lower), the New York steak salad with bleu cheese and candied pecans fairly snaps with flavor—ask for it if you don't see it on the menu.

✪ **Lon's.** At the Hermosa Inn, 5532 N. Palo Cristi Rd. ☎ **602/955-7878.** Reservations recommended late in the week. Main courses $8–$13 at lunch, $18–$27 at dinner. AE, CB, DISC, MC, V. Mon–Fri 11:30am–2pm and 6–10pm; Sat 6–10pm; Sun 10am–2pm (brunch) and 6–10pm. AMERICAN REGIONAL.

What we like most about this place is the setting. It's one of the most "Arizonan" places in the Phoenix area—a Mexican-style hacienda with tile roof and gardens all around. The hacienda once belonged to Lon Megargee, a cowboy artist whose paintings decorate the interior of the restaurant. At midday this place is popular with both retirees and the power-lunching set, and at dinner the place really bustles with a wide mix of people, including smart young things. Begin with rosemary-infused sourdough rolls and a large platter of fried sweet potatoes and red onion rings, which are delicious—salty-sweet and crispy. Dinner entrees are beautifully presented works of art, blending subtle flavors such as grilled salmon with fennel and leeks or pan-seared tiger prawns with watercress sauce. There's a great selection of wines by the glass, a little on the pricey side, and an emphasis on after-dinner drinks. The little bar is cozy and romantic, and the patio offers beautiful views of Camelback Mountain.

Roxsand. 2594 E. Camelback Rd. ☎ **602/381-0444.** Reservations recommended. Main courses $9–$13 at lunch, $19–$26 at dinner. AE, DC, DISC, MC, V. Mon–Thurs 11am–3pm and 5–10pm; Fri–Sat 11am–3pm and 5–11pm; Sun noon–3pm and 5–9:30pm. NEW AMERICAN/FUSION.

Located on the second floor of the exclusive Biltmore Fashion Park shopping mall, Roxsand is a place of urban sophistication, a restaurant at which to see and be seen. Here you'll find fusion cuisine, a creative combination of international influences. We attempted to choose among Moroccan *b'stilla* (braised chicken in phyllo with roasted-eggplant puree), African spicy shrimp salad, and curried lamb tamale. And those were just the appetizers. Sauces sometimes lack complexity, but we can recommend the air-dried duck with pistachio onion marmalade, buckwheat crêpes, and three sauces: Szechuan black-bean sauce, evil jungle prince sauce, and plum sauce. After dinner, get some exercise and amble over to the awesome dessert case; your choice will be served to you on a dinner plate adorned with additional cookies and perhaps a dollop of sorbet.

✪ **T. Cook's.** In the Royal Palms Resort, 5200 E. Camelback Rd. ☎ **602/808-0766.** Reservations highly recommended. Main courses lunch $12–$16, dinner $19–$29. AE, DC, DISC, MC, V. Mon–Sat 6am–2pm and 5:30–10pm; Sun 10am–2pm (brunch) and 5:30–10pm. MEDITERRANEAN.

Simply put, there is no restaurant in the Valley of the Sun more romantic than T. Cook's. Located within the walls of the Mediterranean-inspired Royal Palms resort, this restaurant is surrounded by decades-old gardens and even has palm trees growing right through the roof of the dining room. The focal point of T. Cook's open kitchen is a wood-fired oven that produces dishes such as spit-roasted chicken and rosemary pork loin with fig-apple chutney and garlic mashed potatoes. However, dishes that don't originate in the wood oven, such as the sautéed lobster with fresh tortellini and asparagus are also worth considering. T. Cook's continues to make big impressions right through to the dessert course. If you happen to be a chocoholic, you'll find nirvana in the chocolate sampler, a collection of confectionery sculptures guaranteed to dazzle the eye as well as satisfy the primordial need for chocolate. Although this is one of the most popular upper-end restaurants in Phoenix these days, it luckily manages to avoid pretentiousness.

✪ **Vincent Guerithault on Camelback.** 3930 E. Camelback Rd. ☎ **602/224-0225.** Reservations highly recommended. Main courses $8.75–$12.50 at lunch, $16–$29 at dinner. AE, DC, MC, V. Mon–Fri 11:30am–2:30pm and 6–10pm; Sat 5:30–10pm. SOUTHWESTERN.

Vincent Guerithault has long been a local restaurant celebrity, and his restaurant has an intimate, unpretentious French country atmosphere. Despite the continental decor, the cuisine is solidly Southwestern, with chilies appearing in numerous guises. For a starter, it's hard to beat the aggressive flavors of a smoked-salmon quesadilla with dill and horseradish cream. Moving on to the main course, grilled meats and seafood are the specialty here and might come accompanied by a cilantro salsa or by habañero pasta. The extensive wine list has both Californian and French wines. There's a parking attendant at the door, and the number of luxury cars here should tip you off that this is one of Phoenix's top restaurants. At lunch, the menu is basically the same as at dinner (only with smaller portions). With nearly all items at about $10, lunchtime is a great opportunity to taste the food if you're on a budget.

MODERATE

Altos. 5029 N. 44th St. (at the NE corner of 44th St. and Camelback). ☎ **602/808-0890.** Reservations recommended. Main courses $19–$23; tapas $8–$12. AE, MC, V. Sun–Thurs 5:30–10pm; Fri–Sat 5:30–11pm. CONTEMPORARY SPANISH.

Well hidden in the back of a Camelback Road shopping plaza, Altos is a little difficult to find, but it's definitely worth searching out. It's a casually chic place to enjoy a light meal of *tapas* (small dishes) and sangria, although more substantial dishes are also quite good. Contemporary and classic treatments of Spanish food are the specialty here, including tapas such as mussels in sherry sauce or sautéed shrimp with almonds. Paella with seafood, chicken, Basque sausage, and saffron rice is a complex melding of flavors, while some dishes are more straightforward, such as the *pinchitos* (kebabs). Brandy bread pudding or espresso crème brûlée rounds out the experience, along with live flamenco guitar on weekends. There's also salsa dancing now on Wednesday nights in the restaurant's little loft bar.

C-Fu Fine Asian Dining. 3113 E. Lincoln Dr. (in the Biltmore area) ☎ **602/808-9899.** Reservations recommended on weekends. Dishes $9–$20. AE, DC, DISC, MC, V. Mon–Thurs 11am–3pm and 5–10pm; Fri 11am–3pm and 5–11pm; Sat noon–3pm and 5–11pm; Sun 5–10pm. CHINESE/JAPANESE.

For years the valley has loved C-Fu; the only problem was that the restaurant was way out in Chandler. Now C-Fu is also in Phoenix, less than a mile from the Arizona Biltmore, and with the new location has come a more up-to-date spin on Chinese food. Dishes here are creative and interesting, blending Chinese cuisine with a bit of contemporary American. There's also a sushi bar thrown in for good measure. Considerable *feng shui* went into the designing of the stylishly contemporary interior, which is quite serene. There are also huge fish tanks showcasing both decorative and edible fish. Tasty standouts on the Chinese menu include a sublime shrimp and mango platter, crab meat in cream sauce over snow pea leaves, and grilled pork tenderloin Beijing style. For dessert, we like the banana *lumpia,* banana wrapped up like an egg roll and fried.

Richardson's. 1582 E. Bethany Home Rd. ☎ **602/265-5886** or 602/230-8718. Reservations accepted only for parties of 4 or more. Main courses $9–$22. AE, CB, DC, MC, V. Mon–Fri 11am–midnight; Sat–Sun 10am–midnight. NEW MEXICAN.

Tucked into an older corner shopping center with far too few parking spaces, Richardson's is almost invisible amid the glaring lights and flashing neon of this otherwise unmemorable neighborhood. This place isn't touristy or trendy, although it's generally a mob scene at dinner; however, if you enjoy creative, spicy cooking at good prices, it's worth the wait. Have a margarita while you're at it. If you're in the mood for a light meal, try one of the skewers—chicken, beef, shrimp, and sausage grilled over pecan wood. A more substantial appetite may be assuaged by a New Mexican platter containing a tamale, a chile relleno, a burrito, rice and beans, and green chile. The pecan-wood pizza oven is always fired up to cook delicious pizzas, and for dessert, prickly pear–syrup flan is as creamy as a good crème brûlée. Richardson's also serves Southwestern-style breakfasts daily from 10 or 11am until 4pm.

INEXPENSIVE

5 & Diner. 5220 N. 16th St. ☎ **602/264-5220.** Sandwiches/plates $5–8. AE, MC, V. Daily 24 hours. AMERICAN.

If it's 2am and you just have to have a big burger and a side of fries after a night of dancing, head for the 24-hour 5 & Diner. You can't miss it; it's the classic streamlined diner that looks as though it just materialized from New Jersey.

There's another location in Paradise Valley at 12802 N. Tatum Blvd. (☎ **602/996-0033**) and one in Scottsdale at Scottsdale Pavilions, 9069 E. Indian Bend Rd. (☎ **480/949-1957**).

Blue Burrito Grille. In the Biltmore Plaza, 3118 E. Camelback Rd. ☎ **602/955-9596.** Reservations not accepted. Main courses $4.50–$7. AE, MC, V. Daily 11am–11pm. MEXICAN.

Located in a shopping plaza that also houses the most exclusive and expensive jewelry store in the valley, this is obviously not your usual greasy-tortilla Mexican joint. Catering to a health-conscious affluent community, the Blue Burrito specializes in healthful Mexican food (with no lard and plenty of vegetarian offerings). OK, so the deep-fried chimichanga isn't good for you, but the chicken fajita burritos, fish tacos, enchiladas rancheras, and tamales Mexicanos certainly are. If you want to blow the healthfulness of your meal, have it with a mango margarita. This is a great place for fast, cheap, healthy food smack in the middle of the Camelback Corridor shopping district. Also in Phoenix at 3815 N. Central Ave. (☎ **602/234-3293**), 7318 E. Shea Blvd. in Scottsdale (☎ **480/951-3151**), and 420 S. Mill St., Tempe (☎ **480/921-1332**).

Ed Debevic's Short Orders Deluxe. 2102 E. Highland Ave. ☎ **602/956-2760.** Reservations not accepted. Sandwiches and blue-plate specials $4.25–$9. AE, DC, DISC, MC, V. Sun–Thurs 11am–9pm; Fri–Sat 11am–10pm. AMERICAN.

Hidden away behind the Smitty's supermarket in the Town and Country Shopping Center, Ed's is a classic 1950s diner right down to the little jukeboxes in the booths. Not only does it make its own burgers, chili, and bread, but Ed Debevic's serves the best malteds in Phoenix. The sign in the front window that reads WAITRESSES WANTED, PEOPLE SKILLS NOT NECESSARY should give you a clue that service here is unique.

This place stays busy, and the waitresses are overworked (although they do break into song now and again), so don't be surprised if your waitress sits down in the booth with you to wait for your order. That's just the kind of place Ed runs, and as Ed says, "If you don't like the way I do things—buy me out."

Vintage Market. 24th St. and Camelback Rd. (Biltmore Fashion Park). ☎ **602/955-4444.** Reservations not necessary. Salads/sandwiches $7. AE, DC, MC, V. Mon–Wed 10am–7pm; Thurs–Sat 10am–9pm; Sun 11am–6pm. UPSCALE DELI.

This is a prime people-watching spot and a great place for European-style sandwiches, accompanied by strong coffee in demitasse cups or a glass of wine chosen from a long list. There's also a wine bar. Prices here are lower than at practically any other place in Biltmore Fashion Park, and you can get the likes of a Mediterranean focaccia or Asian vegetable and shrimp salad. Also in Scottsdale at The Borgata, 6166 N. Scottsdale Rd. (☎ **480/315-8199**).

DOWNTOWN PHOENIX
MODERATE

✪ **Sam's Cafe.** In the Arizona Center, 455 N. 3rd St. ☎ **602/252-3545.** Reservations recommended. Main courses $8–$19. AE, CB, DISC, MC, V. Mon–Thurs 11am–10pm; Fri–Sat 11am–11pm; Sun 11am–9pm. SOUTHWESTERN.

Sam's Cafe, one of only a handful of decent downtown restaurants, serves food that's every bit as imaginative, but not nearly as expensive, as that served at other (often overrated) Southwestern restaurants in Phoenix. Breadsticks served with picante-flavored cream cheese, grilled vegetable tacos, and angel-hair pasta in a spicy jalapeño sauce with shrimp and mushrooms all have a nice balance of flavors and are just spicy enough. Salads and dipping sauces are complex and interesting. The downtown Sam's has a large patio that stays packed with the lunchtime, after-work, and convention crowds and overlooks a fountain and palm garden.

Other Sam's restaurants are located in the Biltmore Fashion Park at 2566 E. Camelback Rd. (☎ **602/954-7100**) and in Scottsdale at North Scottsdale Road and Shea Boulevard (☎ **480/368-2800**).

INEXPENSIVE

Alice Cooper'stown. 101 E. Jackson St. ☎ **602/253-7337.** Reservations not accepted. Sandwiches/barbecue $6–$19. AE, MC, V. Daily 11am–11pm. BARBECUE.

Another venue comes to the realm of eat-o-tainment with the opening of Alice Cooper's sports-and-rock theme restaurant located between the Bank One Ballpark and America West Arena. Sixteen video screens are the centerpiece of the restaurant (and most likely they'll be showing sports), but there is also an abundance of memorabilia on the walls, from Alice Cooper's platinum records to guitars from Fleetwood Mac and Eric Clapton to plenty of celebrity photographs. Barbecue occurs in various permutations, from a huge and pretty tasty sandwich to a BBQ Feast platter. There are plenty of other choices too, such as a 2-foot-long hot dog, ribs, and "Megadeth" meatloaf. The waitstaff even wears Alice Cooper makeup.

Honey Bear's BBQ. 2824 N. Central Ave. ☎ **602/279-7911.** Sandwiches and dinners $3.70–$12.50. AE, CB, DC, MC, V. Mon–Sat 10am–10pm; Sun 10am–9:30pm. BARBECUE.

We can definitely say that Honey Bear's has a dud-free menu, and it couldn't be simpler—pork barbecue, beef barbecue, or chicken barbecue. Accompanied maybe by some coleslaw to stick on top of a sandwich or sweet potato pie for dessert. This fast food joint has another location at 5012 E. Van Buren St. (☎ **602/273-9148**).

① Family-Friendly Restaurants

Ed Debevic's Short Orders Deluxe *(see p. 103)*   This classic 1950s diner is full of cool stuff, including little jukeboxes in the booths. You can tell your kids about hanging out in places like this when you were a teenager.

Pinnacle Peak Patio *(see p. 107)*   Way out in north Scottsdale, this restaurant is a Wild West steakhouse complete with cowboys, shoot-outs, hayrides, and live Western music nightly.

Rawhide Western Town & Steakhouse *(see p. 107)*   Kids love dancing to the country music and pretending they're in a real Old West town, which isn't difficult, since Rawhide, with its big wide street, looks pretty authentic. Did you know they cook up 50 *tons* of beans here annually?

Rustler's Rooste *(see p. 108)*   Similar to Pinnacle Peak, but closer to the city center, Rustler's Rooste has a slide from the lounge to the main dining room, a big patio, and live cowboy bands nightly. See if you can get your kids to try the rattlesnake appetizer—it tastes like chicken.

✪ **MacAlpine's Nostalgic Soda Fountain & Coffee Shoppe.** 2303 N. 7th St. ☎ **602/252-7282.** Sandwiches/specials $3.25–$6. AE, MC, V. Mon–Thurs 7am–3pm; Fri–Sat 7am–11pm; Sun 11am–5pm. AMERICAN.

This very authentic place hasn't changed much since its beginnings in 1928—in fact, it's the oldest operating soda fountain in the Southwest. The atmosphere is laid back, and wooden booths and worn countertops show the patina of time. They'll be glad to fix you up a breakfast egg on a bagel or a big hamburger or tuna sandwich on good bread. To wash it down, order a chocolate phosphate, raspberry iced tea, or huge iced mocha.

✪ **Pizzeria Bianco.** In Heritage Square, 623 E. Adams St. ☎ **602/258-8300.** Reservations accepted for 6 or more. Pizzas $8–$11. MC, V. Tues–Sat 5–10pm; Sun 5–9pm. ITALIAN.

Even though this historic brick building is located smack dab in the center of downtown Phoenix, the atmosphere is so friendly and cozy it feels like your neighborhood local. The wood-burning oven turns out deliciously rustic, chewy-crusted pizzas, such as one with red onion, Parmesan, rosemary, and crushed pistachio. Pizzeria Bianco makes its own fresh mozzarella cheese, which can be ordered as an appetizer or on a pizza. We also liked the roasted vegetables and the salad with fennel, dandelion greens, and orange, drizzled with olive oil.

TEMPE, MESA, SOUTH PHOENIX & THE AIRPORT AREA
MODERATE

✪ **House of Tricks.** 114 E. 7th St., Tempe. ☎ **480/968-1114.** Reservations recommended. Main courses $13–$22. AE, CB, DC, DISC, MC, V. Mon–Sat 11am–10pm. Closed first 2 weeks of Aug. NEW AMERICAN.

Because this restaurant is housed in a pair of Craftsman bungalows surrounded by an attractive garden of shady trees, it has a completely different feel from Mill Avenue, Tempe's main drag, which is only 2 blocks away. This is where Arizona State University students take their parents when they come to visit, but it's also a nice spot for a romantic evening and a good place to try innovative cuisine without blowing your vacation budget. The grape arbor–covered patio, where there's also a shady bar, is the preferred seating area. The dinner menu changes regularly and consists of a single page of tempting salads, appetizers, and main dishes. The garlic-inspired Caesar salad and the house-smoked salmon with avocado, capers, and lemon cream are good bets for starters. Among the entrees, look for the pork rack with jalapeño marmalade.

Monti's La Casa Vieja. 1 W. Rio Salado Parkway (at the corner of Mill Ave.), Tempe. ☎ **480/967-7594.** Reservations recommended for dinner. Main courses $5–$27. AE, CB, DC, DISC, MC, V. Sun–Thurs 11am–10pm; Fri–Sat 11am–midnight. AMERICAN.

If you're tired of the glitz and glamour of the Valley of the Sun and are looking for Old Arizona, head down to Tempe to Monti's La Casa Vieja. The adobe building was constructed in 1873 (*casa vieja* means "old house" in Spanish) on the site of the Salt River ferry in the days when the Salt River flowed year-round and Tempe was nothing more than a ferry crossing. Today local families who have been in Phoenix for generations know Monti's well and rely on the restaurant for solid meals and low prices—you can get a filet mignon for under $11. The dining rooms are dark and filled with memorabilia of the Old West.

INEXPENSIVE

✪ **The Farm at South Mountain.** 6106 S. 32nd St. ☎ **602/276-6360.** Sandwiches and salads $8.50. AE, DC, MC, V. Tues–Sun 8am–3pm (if weather is inclement, call to be sure it's open). Take Exit 151A off I-10 and go south on 32nd St. SANDWICHES & SALADS.

If being in the desert has you dreaming of shady trees and green grass, you'll enjoy this little oasis reminiscent of a New England orchard or Midwestern farm. A rustic outbuilding surrounded by potted flowers has been converted to a stand-in-line restaurant where you can order a mesquite grilled eggplant sandwich or have a choice of fresh salads such as a pecan turkey Waldorf with sour cream and dried apricot dressing. Breakfast choices are baked goods such as muffins and scones, teas, and juices. The grassy lawn is ideal for a picnic on a blanket under the pecan trees.

Friday and Saturday nights, seven-course gourmet dinners ($55 per person) using garden produce are served at the old farmhouse. Reservations are a necessity; in fact, it's best to call as far ahead as possible. For more information, call **Quiescence** at ☎ 602/305-8192.

Organ Stop Pizza. 1149 E. Southern Ave., Mesa (southwest corner of Southern Ave. and Stapley Dr.). ☎ **480/813-5700.** Pizza and pastas $4.50–$14. Credit cards not accepted. Sun–Thurs 4–9pm; Fri–Sat 4–10pm. PIZZA.

The pizza here may not be the best in town, but the Mighty Würlitzer theater organ, the largest in the world, sure is memorable. The massive instrument contains over 5,500 pipes, and four turbine blowers provide the wind to create the sound. Forty-foot ceilings make for great acoustics. Performances begin at 4:30pm and continue throughout the evening. As you marvel at skill of the organist, who performs songs ranging from "Livin' la Vida Loca" to "The Phantom of the Opera," you can enjoy simple pizzas, pastas, or snack foods such as nachos or onion rings.

DINING WITH A VIEW

Different Pointe of View. At the Pointe Hilton Tapatio Cliffs Resort, 11111 N. 7th St. ☎ **602/863-0912.** Reservations highly recommended. Main courses $26–$36. AE, CB, DC, DISC, MC, V. Mon–Thurs 5:30–9:30pm; Fri–Sat 5:30–10pm (lounge open later); Sun 5:30–9:30pm. REGIONAL AMERICAN.

Built right into a mountaintop, this restaurant takes in dramatic, sweeping vistas of the city, mountains, and desert through its curving walls of glass. Come early, and you can enjoy views to the north from the lounge before heading into the south-facing dining room. The menu changes regularly but is always dependable (herb-crusted rack of lamb with sweet potato fries; sautéed shrimp and sea scallops with lobster sherry sauce). However, despite the excellent food, award-winning wine list, and live jazz Wednesday through Saturday, the view steals the show.

○ **Top of the Rock.** At Wyndham Buttes Resort, 2000 Westcourt Way, Tempe. ☎ **602/ 225-9000.** Reservations recommended. Main courses $21–$30; Sun brunch $35. AE, CB, DC, DISC, MC, V. Sun–Thurs 5–10pm; Fri–Sat 5–11pm; Sun 10am–2pm (brunch) and 5–10pm. CONTEMPORARY AMERICAN/SOUTHWESTERN.

All the best views in Phoenix are from resorts and their restaurants, so if you want to dine with a view of the valley, you're going to have to pay the price. Luckily, quality accompanies the high prices here at the Top of the Rock, which is built into a rocky hillside and has a dramatic desert setting above Tempe. In addition to the stunning, romantic setting, you can enjoy some very creative cuisine. On the appetizer list, the lobster Napoleon (lobster layered with wonton and Boursin cheese in a white-wine–chervil butter sauce) should not be missed. Sauces on the entree menu offer a good range of flavors from mellow to bold. The ambience is a little on the formal side, so dress up for this dining experience. You won't go wrong ordering any dessert made with chocolate.

COWBOY STEAKHOUSES
Although Arizona doesn't claim to have invented the steakhouse or cow towns, the state certainly has cornered the market on combining the two. Wild West theme restaurants abound here in the Phoenix area. These family restaurants generally provide big portions of grilled steaks and barbecued ribs, outdoor and "saloon" dining, live country music, and various sorts of entertainment, including stagecoach rides and shoot-outs in the street.

Pinnacle Peak Patio. 10426 E. Jomax Rd., Scottsdale. ☎ **480/585-1599.** Reservations recommended on weekends. Main courses $12.50–$25 (children's menu $3–$6). DC, DISC, MC, V. Mon–Thurs 4–10pm; Fri–Sat 4–11pm; Sun noon–10pm. Take Scottsdale Rd. north to Pinnacle Peak Rd., turn right and continue to Pima Rd., turn left and follow the signs. STEAK.

Businessmen beware! Wear a tie into this restaurant, and you'll have it cut off and hung from the rafters (there's somewhere around a quarter million ties hangin' up there). Although you can indulge in mesquite-broiled steaks (they even have a 2-lb. porterhouse monster) with all the traditional trimmings, a meal here is more an event than just an opportunity to put on the feedbag. The real draw is all the free Wild West entertainment—gunfights, cowboy bands, two-stepping, and cookouts. Also of interest are the museum-like displays of interesting collections such as can openers, police badges, and license plates. Although Pinnacle Peak Patio is strictly Hollywood Western, it is now surrounded by the valley's poshest suburbs.

○ **Rawhide Western Town & Steakhouse.** 23023 N. Scottsdale Rd. (4 miles north of Bell Rd.), Scottsdale. ☎ **480/502-5600.** Reservations accepted for parties of 9 or more. Main courses lunch $8–$12, dinner $12–$23. AE, CB, DC, DISC, MC, V. Oct–May Mon–Thurs 5–10pm, Fri–Sun 11:30am–3pm 5–10pm; Apr daily 11:30am–3pm and 5–10pm; May–Sept daily 5–10pm. Lunch served Oct–Mar Fri–Sun 11:30am–3pm and Apr daily 11:30am–3pm. STEAKS.

Sure it's a tourist trap, but Rawhide is so much fun and such a quintessentially Phoenician experience that it's one of our favorite valley restaurants. There's plenty of entertainment, including country-music bands, shoot-outs, stagecoach rides, a petting zoo, and a resident magician. Kids love pretending they're in a real old Western town, which isn't difficult since Rawhide, with its big wide street, looks pretty authentic.

Along with mesquite-broiled steaks, including not only beef but buffalo as well, you'll find a few barbecue items and fruit pie à la mode. They get a lot of visitors here, as evidenced by the fact the kitchen cooks up about 200,000 pounds of steak and 50 tons of beans annually.

Rustler's Rooste. At the Pointe Hilton on South Mountain, 7777 S. Pointe Hwy., Phoenix. ☎ **602/431-6474.** Reservations recommended. Main courses $13–$32. AE, CB, DC, DISC, MC, V. Sun–Thurs 5–10pm; Fri–Sat 5–11pm. STEAKS.

This location doesn't exactly seem like cowboy country. However, up at the top of the hill you'll find a fun Western-theme restaurant where you can slide from the bar down to the main dining room. The view north across Phoenix is entertainment enough for most people, but there are also Western bands playing for those who like to kick up their heels. If you've ever been bitten by a snake, you can exact your revenge here by ordering the rattlesnake appetizer. Follow that (if you've got the appetite of a hard-working cowpoke) with the enormous cowboy "stuff" platter consisting of, among other things, broiled sirloin, barbecued ribs, cowboy beans, fried shrimp, barbecued chicken, and swordfish kebabs.

BREAKFAST, BRUNCH & QUICK BITES

Most of Phoenix's best Sunday brunches are to be had at restaurants in major hotels and resorts. Among the finest are those served at ✪ **Marquesa** (in the Scottsdale Princess), at the **Golden Swan** (in the Hyatt Regency Scottsdale Resort), at **Wright's** (in the Arizona Biltmore Resort & Spa), at the **Terrace Dining Room** (in The Phoenician), and at the **Garden Terrace Restaurant** (in the Doubletree La Posada). For information on the two former restaurants, see the "Scottsdale" section of "Where to Dine." For information on the latter three restaurants, see "Where to Stay." The **Desert Botanical Garden,** 1201 N. Galvin Pkwy. (☎ **480/941-1225**), in Papago Park, serves brunch with its Music in the Garden concerts held on Sundays between September and March. Tickets are $13.50 and include admission to the gardens. Sunday brunch is served for an additional charge.

If your idea of the perfect breakfast is a French pastry and a good cup of coffee, try **Pierre's Pastry Café,** 7119 E. Shea Blvd., Scottsdale (☎ **480/443-2510**), where the croissants and brioche have a luxurious, buttery texture (desserts here are also irresistible). Along Camelback Road, in the Biltmore Plaza shopping center, try **La Madeleine,** 3102 E. Camelback Rd. (☎ **602/952-0349**), which is *the* place for a luscious and leisurely French breakfast amid antique French farm implements. The bakery here also does great breads, if you happen to be thinking about a picnic. There's another La Madeleine at Fashion Square Mall, 7014 E. Camelback Rd. (☎ **480/945-1663**) in Scottsdale, and one at Tatum and Shea Boulevards in Paradise Valley (☎ **480/483-0730**).

For fruit smoothies and muffins and healthy things, try **Wild Oats Community Market,** which has stores at 3933 E. Camelback Rd. (☎ **602/954-0584**), in North Phoenix at 13823 N. Tatum Blvd. (☎ **602/953-7546**), and in Scottsdale at 7129 E. Shea Blvd. (☎ **480/905-1441**) at the corner of Scottsdale Road. Almost three dozen different kinds of bagels, plus large, inexpensive delicatessen-style breakfasts can be had at **Chompie's,** 3202 E. Greenway Rd. (☎ **602/971-8010**), 9301 E. Shea Blvd. in the Mercado del Rancho Centre, Scottsdale (☎ **480/860-0475**), and at 1160 E. University Dr., Tempe (☎ **480/557-0700**).

For a quick bite when in downtown Phoenix, the **Gardenside Food Court** at the Arizona Center offers several options.

CAFES & COFFEE

If you've got a serious coffee habit and want some of the best espresso in the valley, then search out **The Village Coffee Roastery,** 8120 N. Hayden Rd., E104 (☎ **480/905-0881**), in Scottsdale near Franco's Trattoria. The coffee's freshly roasted, and there are lots of shade-grown and organic beans. In Old Town Scottsdale, try **The Author's Café,** 4014 N. Goldwater Blvd. (☎ **480/481-3998**), a stylish little cafe next door to The Poisoned Pen, a mystery bookstore.

5 Seeing the Sights

DISCOVERING THE DESERT & ITS NATIVE CULTURES

Deer Valley Rock Art Center. 3711 W. Deer Valley Rd. ☎ **623/582-8007.** Admission $4 adults, $2 seniors, $1 children 6–12, free for children 5 and under. Oct–Apr Tues–Sat 9am–5pm, Sun noon–5pm; May–Sept Tues–Fri 8am–2pm, Sat 9am–5pm, Sun noon–5pm. Closed major holidays. Take Deer Valley Rd. exit off I-17 on the north side of Phoenix and go west to just past 35th Ave.

Located in the Hedgepeth Hills in the northwest corner of the Valley of the Sun, the Deer Valley Rock Art Center preserves an amazing concentration of Native American petroglyphs, some of which date back 5,000 years. Although these petroglyphs may not at first seem as impressive as more famous images that have been reproduced ad nauseam in recent years, the sheer numbers make this a fascinating spot. The drawings, which range from simple spirals to much more complex renderings of herds of deer, are on volcanic boulders along a $^1/_4$-mile trail. An interpretive center provides background information on this site and on rock art in general.

✪ **Desert Botanical Garden.** Papago Park, 1201 N. Galvin Pkwy. ☎ **480/941-1225.** www.dbg.org. Admission $7.50 adults, $6.50 seniors, $4 students 13–18, $1.50 children 5–12, children under 5 free. Oct–Apr daily 8am–8pm; May–Sept daily 7am–8pm. Closed Dec 25. Bus: 3.

Located adjacent to the Phoenix Zoo and devoted exclusively to cacti and other desert plants, this botanic garden displays more than 20,000 plants from all over the world. The Plants and People of the Sonoran Desert trail is the state's best introduction to ethnobotany (human use of plants) in the Southwest. Along the trail are interactive displays that demonstrate how Native Americans once used wild and cultivated plants. You can make a yucca-fiber brush and practice grinding corn and mesquite beans. At the garden's Center for Desert Living, there are demonstration gardens and an energy- and water-conservation research house. If you come late in the day, you can stay until after dark and see night-blooming flowers and dramatically lit cacti. A cafe on the grounds serves surprisingly good food. In the spring and fall, there are concerts in the garden. The Christmas season sees the gardens illuminated by *luminárias* (candles inside small bags) at night. A new wildflower trail is scheduled to open in early 2001.

✪ **Heard Museum.** 2301 N. Central Ave. ☎ **602/252-8848.** Admission $7 adults, $6 seniors, $3 children 4–12. Daily 9:30am–5pm. Closed major holidays. Bus: Blue (B), Red (R), O.

The Heard Museum is one of the nation's finest museums dealing exclusively with Native American cultures, and as such, it is an ideal introduction to the indigenous cultures of Arizona. **Native Peoples of the Southwest** is an extensive exhibit that examines the culture of each of the major tribes of the region. Included in the exhibit are a Navajo hogan, an Apache wickiup, and a Hopi corn-grinding display. In the large Katsina Doll Gallery you'll get an idea of the number of different kachina spirits that populate the Hopi and Zuni religions. The museum's Crossroads Gallery

Phoenix, Scottsdale & the Valley of the Sun Attractions

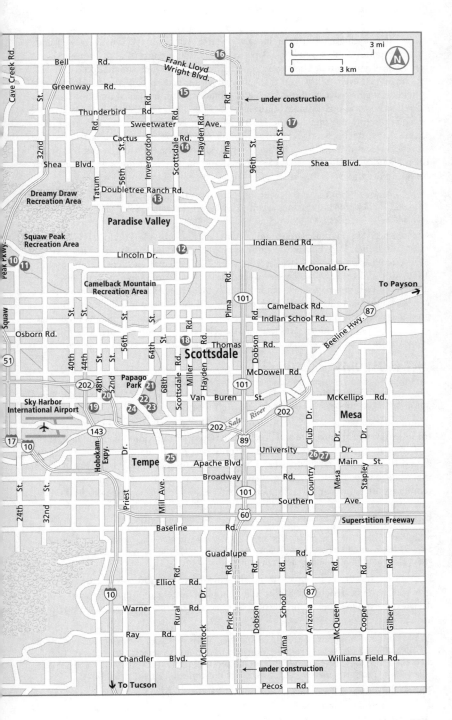

offers a fascinating look at contemporary Native American art. On many weekends there are performances by Native American singers and dancers, and throughout the week artists demonstrate their work. Guided tours of the museum are offered daily.

The biggest event of the year is the annual spring **Indian Fair and Market,** which is held on the first weekend in March and includes performances of traditional dances as well as arts and crafts demonstrations and sales.

The museum also operates the **Heard Museum North,** El Pedregal Festival Marketplace, 34505 N. Scottsdale Rd. (☎ **480/488-9817**), which is adjacent to The Boulders resort in Carefree. This fairly large gallery features changing exhibits and is open Monday to Saturday 10am to 5:30pm and Sunday noon to 5pm. Admission is $2 for adults and $1 for children ages 4 to 12.

Pueblo Grande Museum & Cultural Park. 4619 E. Washington St. (between 44th St. and 48th St.). ☎ **602/495-0901.** Admission $2 adults, $1.50 seniors, $1 children 6–17; free on Sun. Mon–Sat 9am–4:45pm; Sun 1–4:45pm. Closed major holidays. Bus: Yellow (Y).

Located near Sky Harbor Airport and downtown Phoenix, the Pueblo Grande Museum and Cultural Park houses the ruins of an ancient Hohokam village. This was one of several villages along the Salt River between A.D. 300 and 1400. Sometime around 1450, this and other villages were mysteriously abandoned. One speculation is that drought and a buildup of salts from irrigation water reduced the fertility of the soil and forced the people to leave their homes and seek more fertile lands. Before touring the grounds to view the partially excavated ruins, you can walk through the small museum, which displays many of the artifacts that have been dug up on the site. The museum sponsors interesting workshops, demonstrations, and tours throughout the year.

ART MUSEUMS

Arizona State University Art Museum. In the Nelson Fine Arts Center, 10th St. and Mill Ave., Tempe. ☎ **480/965-2787.** Free admission. Tues 10am–9pm; Wed–Sat 10am–5pm; Sun 1–5pm. Closed major holidays. Bus: Red (R), Yellow (Y), 66, or 72.

Although it isn't very large, the Arizona State University Art Museum is memorable for its innovative architecture and excellent temporary exhibitions. The building, stark and angular, captures the colors of sunset on desert mountains with its purplish gray stucco facade and pyramidal shape. The museum entrance is down a flight of stairs that leads to a cool underground garden area. Inside are galleries for crafts, prints, contemporary art, Latin American art, a temporary exhibition gallery, two outdoor sculpture courts, and a gift shop. The museum's collection of American art includes works by Georgia O'Keeffe, Edward Hopper, and Frederic Remington.

Fleischer Museum. Perimeter Center, 17207 N. Perimeter Dr., Scottsdale. ☎ **480/585-3108.** Free admission. Daily 10am–4pm. Closed major holidays. Located just north of Frank Lloyd Wright Blvd and east of Hayden Rd.

Located in a modern office park in north Scottsdale, this museum was the country's first gallery dedicated to the California School of American Impressionism, which drew extensively on French Impressionist styles and holds a quiet place in American art history.

✪ **Phoenix Art Museum.** 1625 N. Central Ave. (at the northeast corner of McDowell Rd.). ☎ **602/257-1222.** www.phxart.org. Admission $7 adults, $5 seniors and students, $2 children 6–18, free for children under 6; no admission charge on Thurs. Tues–Wed and Sat–Sun 10am–5pm; Thurs–Fri 10am–9pm. Closed major holidays. Bus: Blue (B), Red (R), O.

This is the largest art museum in the Southwest, and acres of wall space enable it to display canvases of a size rarely seen in museums. Little exhibit halls tucked into out-of-the-way corners, dead-end hallways hung with art, and the museum's two buildings (connected by an enclosed stainless-steel pedestrian bridge) make this a place to spend plenty of time exploring. If you're the linear type, it's easy to completely miss entire exhibit areas here.

Housed within this labyrinth, you'll find a very respectable collection that spans the major artistic movements from the Renaissance to the present. The collection of modern and contemporary art is particularly good, with works by Diego Rivera, Frida Kahlo, Pablo Picasso, Karel Appel, Mark Rothko, Alexander Calder, Henry Moore, Georgia O'Keeffe, Henri Rousseau, and Auguste Rodin.

The large first-floor gallery is used for special exhibits including major touring retrospectives. The Thorne Miniature Collection is one of the museum's most popular exhibits and consists of tiny rooms on a scale of 1 inch to 1 foot. The rooms are exquisitely detailed, right down to the leaded-glass windows of an English lodge kitchen. Other exhibits include decorative arts, historic fashions, Asian art, Spanish colonial furnishings and religious art, and, of course, a Western American exhibit featuring works by members of the Cowboy Artists of America

✪ **Scottsdale Museum of Contemporary Art.** 7380 E. Second St., Scottsdale. ☎ **480/ 994-ARTS.** Admission $5 adults, $3 students, free for children under 15; no admission charge on Thurs. Tues–Wed and Fri–Sat 10am–5pm; Thurs 10am–9pm; Sun noon–5pm. Bus: 41, 50, 72. Also accessible on Scottsdale Round Up shuttle bus.

Scottsdale may be obsessed with art featuring lonesome cowboys and solemn Indians, but this boldly designed museum makes it clear that patrons of contemporary art are also welcome here. Cutting-edge art, from the abstract to the absurd, fills the galleries here, with exhibits rotating every few months. Shows scheduled in 2001 will feature the work of James Turrell, Donald Sultan, Mary Bates, and Wolfgang Laib. In addition to the galleries in the main museum building, there are several more galleries in the adjacent Scottsdale Center for the Arts, which also has a pair of Dale Chihuly art-glass installations. There is an excellent museum shop.

HISTORY MUSEUMS & HISTORIC LANDMARKS

Arizona Historical Society Museum in Papago Park. 1300 N. College Ave. (just off Curry Rd.), Tempe. ☎ **480/929-0292.** Free admission. Mon–Sat 10am–4pm; Sun noon–4pm. Bus: 66.

This museum, at the headquarters of the Arizona Historical Society, focuses its modern, well-designed exhibits on the history of central Arizona over the past century. Temporary exhibits on the lives and works of the people who helped shape this region are always highlights of a visit here. One of the more interesting permanent exhibits features life-size statues of everyday people from Arizona's past (a Mexican miner, a Chinese laborer, and so on). Quotes relate their individual stories, and props reveal what items they might have traveled with during their days in the desert.

✪ **Arizona State Capitol Museum.** 1700 W. Washington St. ☎ **602/542-4581.** Free admission. Mon–Fri 8am–5pm; Sat 10am–3pm. Closed state holidays. Bus: Yellow (Y).

In the years before Arizona became a state, the territorial capital moved from Prescott to Tucson, then back to Prescott, and finally settled in Phoenix. In 1898, a stately territorial capitol building was erected (with a copper roof to remind the local citizenry of the importance of that metal in the Arizona economy). Atop this copper roof was placed the statue *Winged Victory,* which still graces the old capitol building today. This building no longer serves as the actual state capitol, but has been restored to the way it appeared in 1912, the year Arizona became a state. Among the rooms on view are the senate and house chambers, as well as the governor's office. Excellent historical exhibits provide interesting perspectives on early Arizona events and lifestyles.

Historic Heritage Square. 115 N. 6th St., at Monroe. ☎ **602/262-5029** or 602/262-5071. Rosson House tours, $4 adults, $3 seniors, $1 children 6–12, free for children under 6. Hours vary for each building; call for information. Bus: Red (R), Yellow (Y), 0.

Although the city of Phoenix was founded as recently as 1870, much of its history has been obliterated. Heritage Square is a collection of some of the few remaining houses in Phoenix that date from the 19th century and the original Phoenix town site. All the buildings are listed on the National Register of Historic Places, and most display Victorian architectural styles popular just before the turn of the century. Today they house museums, restaurants, and gift shops. The Eastlake Victorian Rosson House, furnished with period antiques, is open for tours. The Silva House, a neoclassical revival-style home, houses historical exhibits on turn-of-the-century life in the Valley of the Sun. In the Stevens-Haustgen House, you'll find a gift shop, and in the Stevens House is the Arizona Doll and Toy Museum. The Burgess Carriage House contains a gift shop and ticket window for the Rosson House tours. The Teeter House, an 1899 bungalow, is a Victorian tearoom. The old Baird Machine Shop contains Pizzeria Bianco.

Phoenix Museum of History. 105 N. 6th St. ☎ **602/253-2734.** Admission $5 adults; $3.50 seniors, ACCOMMODATIONS, and students; $2.50 children 6–12; free for children under 6. Mon–Sat 10am–5pm; Sun noon–5pm. Closed major holidays. Bus: Red (R) or Yellow (Y).

Located adjacent to Heritage Square in downtown Phoenix, this state-of-the-art museum is one of the anchors of the city's downtown revitalization plan. It presents an interesting look at the history of a city that, to the casual visitor, might not seem to *have* any history. Interactive exhibits get visitors involved in the displays, and unusual exhibits make this place much more interesting than your average local history museum. A beer-bottle sidewalk shows how one saloon-keeper solved the problem of the muddy streets that once plagued the city; another exhibit shows how "lungers" (tuberculosis sufferers) inadvertently helped originate the tourism industry in Arizona.

SCIENCE & INDUSTRY MUSEUMS

✪ **Arizona Science Center.** 600 E. Washington St. ☎ **602/716-2000.** www.azscience. org. Admission $8 adults, $6 seniors and children 3–12, free for children under 4. Planetarium and film combination tickets also available. Daily 10am–5pm. Closed Thanksgiving and Christmas. Bus: Red (R), Yellow (Y), 0.

Aimed primarily at children but also loads of fun for adults, the Arizona Science Center, a hands-on facility, is one of the anchors of Phoenix's ongoing renewal of the city's downtown. In this large facility you'll find state-of-the-art interactive exhibits covering a variety of topics from the human body to coping with living in the desert. However, it is not the topics so much as the individual displays that make this museum fun. There's a huge ant farm, a virtual reality game that puts you inside a video game, a massive truck tire weighing almost 4 tons, a flight simulator, and a cloud maker. The ever-popular soap-bubble play area is housed on a terrace on the museum's roof, as is a star-gazing area. In addition to the many exhibits, the science center includes a planetarium (night sky and laser shows) and a large-screen theater, both of which carry additional charges. There are also plenty of fun temporary exhibits.

Mesa Southwest Museum. 53 N. MacDonald St. (at the corner of 1st St.), Mesa. ☎ **480/644-2230.** Admission $4 adults, $3.50 seniors, $2 children 3–12, free for children under 3. Tues–Sat 10am–5pm; Sun 1–5pm. Closed major holidays. Bus: Red (R).

Located in downtown Mesa, this museum appeals mostly to children, but its exhibits on prehistoric indigenous cultures in the region will likely interest adults as well. Exhibits cover Mesoamerican art and Spanish mission life. Kids will love the fossils (including a complete mammoth skeleton) and animated dinosaurs. The mine and jail (this really was the old jail) displays are also a lot of fun for kids. There are usually a

⭐ Frommer's Favorite Phoenix Experiences

Hiking up Camelback Mountain or Squaw Peak. Hiking the trails up these two mountains is a favorite activity among the city's more active residents. Both trails are steep climbs, but the views from up top are superb. Bring water and start early in the morning if it's going to be a hot day.

Having Dinner with a View. There's something bewitching about gazing down at the twinkling lights of the city while enjoying a delicious meal at one of the area's few hillside restaurants.

Lounging by the Pool. Nothing is more relaxing than lounging by one of the spectacular pools and gazing up at the desert mountains from a world-class Valley of the Sun resort.

Taking the Scottsdale Art Walk. Thursday evenings from October to May, both dilettantes and connoisseurs turn out to visit the nearly 60 art galleries in downtown Scottsdale, many of which have artists on hand and provide complimentary refreshments.

Attending a Spring Training Baseball Game. Get a head start on all your fellow baseball fans by going to a spring-training game while you're in Phoenix. Just be sure to book your hotel well in advance; these games are the biggest thing going in the valley each spring.

Mountain Biking in South Mountain or Papago Park. The trails of these two desert parks are ideal for mountain biking, and whether you're a novice making your first foray onto the dirt or a budding downhill racer, you'll find miles of riding that are just your speed.

Spending the Day at a Spa. When it comes to stress relief, there's nothing like a massage or an herbal wrap. The chance to lie back and do nothing at all is something few of us take the time for anymore, so a day at the spa just might be the best thing you can do for yourself on an Arizona vacation.

Catching a Performance by Estéban. Scottsdale's best and most popular lounge act is a Spanish guitarist who goes by the name of Estéban. The high-energy music pulls in huge crowds, and the lounge walls are usually thrown open to the night air. Order a cocktail or some dessert and you've got a great, relatively cheap night out.

couple of different temporary exhibits at any given time that may include displays of contemporary art or regional history. The museum has recently expanded and in 2000 will have doubled its display space.

The museum also operates the nearby **Sirrine House Historic Home Museum,** 160 N. Center St., which is filled with period antiques from the late 19th and early 20th centuries. This historic home is open on weekends during the winter.

A MUSEUM MISCELLANY: PLANES, FLAMES & MORE.

Arizona Mining & Mineral Museum. 1502 W. Washington St. ☎ **602/255-3795.** Free admission. Mon–Fri 8am–5pm; Sat 11am–4pm. Closed state holidays. Bus: Yellow (Y).

Arizonans have been romancing the stones for more than a century at colorfully named mines, such as the Copper Queen, the Sleeping Beauty, the No-Name Creek, the Lucky Boy, and the Bluebird. Out of such mines have come countless tons of copper, silver, and gold, as well as beautiful minerals with tongue-twisting names. Azurite, chalcanthite, chalcoaluminate, malachite, and chrysocolla are just some of the richly colored and fascinatingly textured minerals on display at this small downtown museum dedicated to the state's mining industry. Rather than playing up the historical or profit-making side of the industry, exhibits focus on the amazing variety and beauty of Arizona minerals.

Buffalo Museum of America. 10261 N. Scottsdale Rd. (at the southeast corner of Shea Blvd.), Scottsdale. ☎ **480/951-1022.** Admission $3 adults, $2.50 seniors, $2 children 6–17, free for children under 6. Mon–Fri 9am–5pm. Closed major holidays. Bus: 72 or 106.

Scottsdale may not be the home where the buffalo roam, but it does have a fascination with the Old West, so it seems appropriate to find here a museum dedicated to these fabled behemoths of the plains. This small museum is the culmination of one man's infatuation with the American bison, which is commonly known as the buffalo. The museum houses stuffed buffaloes, bronze buffaloes, buffalo paintings, and all manner of buffalo memorabilia, including a rifle that once belonged to Buffalo Bill Cody.

Champlin Fighter Aircraft Museum. 4636 Fighter Aces Dr., Mesa (at Falcon Field Airport off McKellips Rd.). ☎ **480/830-4540.** Admission $6.50 adults, $3 children 5–12, free for children under 5. Daily 10am–5pm. From U.S. 60, take the Greenfield exit, go north to McKellips Blvd., and follow the green signs.

This aeronautical museum, dedicated exclusively to fighter planes and the fighter aces who flew them, houses aircraft from World Wars I and II, the Korean War, and the Vietnam War, with a strong emphasis on the wood-and-fabric biplanes and triplanes of World War I (several Sopwiths and Fokkers). From World War II, there's a Spitfire, a Messerschmitt, and a Goodyear Corsair. Jet fighters from more recent battles include a MiG-15, a MiG-17, and an F4 Phantom. In total, there are 33 flyable fighters here.

Hall of Flame Firefighting Museum. Papago Park, 6101 E. Van Buren St. ☎ **602/275-3473.** Admission $5 adults, $4 seniors, $3 students 6–17, $1.50 children 3–5, free for children under 3. Mon–Sat 9am–5pm; Sun noon–4pm. Closed Jan 1, Thanksgiving, and Dec 25. Bus: 3.

The world's largest firefighting museum houses a fascinating collection of vintage fire trucks. The displays date from a 1725 English hand pumper to several classic fire engines from this century. All are beautifully restored and, of course, fire-engine red (mostly). In all, there are more than 90 vehicles on display.

ARCHITECTURAL HIGHLIGHTS

In addition to the architectural landmarks listed below, there are a couple of other buildings of which Phoenix is justly proud.

The **Arizona Biltmore,** 24th Street and Missouri Avenue (☎ **602/955-6600**), although not designed by Frank Lloyd Wright, shows the famed architect's hand in its distinctive cast-cement blocks and also displays sculptures, furniture, and stained glass designed by Wright. The best way to soak up the ambience of this exclusive resort (if you aren't staying here) is over dinner, a cocktail, or tea. If you'd like to spend the day by the pool, you can even rent a cabana.

On a hilltop adjacent to the Arizona Biltmore, you can see the famed **Wrigley Mansion,** 2501 E. Telawa Trail. (☎ **602/955-4079**), a classically elegant mansion that was built by chewing-gum magnate William Wrigley Jr. between 1929 and 1931 as a present for his wife, Ada. Built with Italianate styling, the many levels and red-tile roofs make it seem like an entire village. Today the mansion is a National Historic Landmark with the interior restored to its original elegance. Tours are offered Tuesday and Thursday at 10am and 3pm and cost $10. Although this is currently a private club, lunch is open to the public.

Tovrea Castle, 5041 E. Van Buren St. (☎ 602/262-6412), another architectural confection of the Phoenix landscape, has been likened to a giant wedding cake and is currently under renovation. However, it is scheduled to open to the public some time in mid-2001. Call for information.

Among the more recent buildings to garner architectural praise in Phoenix are the **new City Hall** and restored **Orpheum Theatre,** which sit back to back on Third Avenue between Washington and Adams streets. The new City Hall is a bold contemporary construction as intriguing as the main library, while the Orpheum is a classically elegant historic building. The two styles clash in a manner that typifies old and new Phoenix.

Opened in 1995, the **Burton Barr Library,** 1221 N. Central Ave. (☎ 602/262-4636), is among the most daring pieces of public architecture in the city. No fan of futuristic art or science fiction should miss a visit. The five-story cube is partially clad in ribbed copper sheeting, enough copper to produce roughly 17,500,000 pennies (it took a lot of overdue books to pay for that feature). The building's design makes use of the desert's plentiful sunshine to provide light for reading, but also incorporates computer-controlled louvers and shade sails to reduce heat and glare.

Cosanti. 6433 Doubletree Ranch Rd., Scottsdale. ☎ **480/948-6145.** www.cosanti.com. Admission by donation; guided tours: minimum 5 people, $5 per person. Daily 9am–5pm. Closed major holidays. Drive 1 mile west of Scottsdale Rd. on Doubletree Ranch Rd.

This complex of cast-concrete structures served as a prototype and learning project for architect Paolo Soleri's much grander Arcosanti project currently under construction north of Phoenix (see "En Route to Northern Arizona," below, for details). It's here at Cosanti that Soleri's famous bells are cast, and most weekday mornings, you can see the foundry in action.

Mystery Castle. 800 E. Mineral Rd. ☎ **602/268-1581.** Admission $5 adults, $4 seniors, $2 children 5–14. Thurs–Sun 11am–4pm. Closed July–Sept. Take Central Ave. south to Mineral Rd. (2 miles south of Baseline Rd.) and turn east.

Built for a daughter who longed for a castle more permanent than those built in sand at the beach, Mystery Castle is a wondrous work of folk-art architecture. Boyce Luther Gulley, who had come to Arizona in hopes of curing his tuberculosis, constructed the castle during the 1930s and early 1940s using stones from the property. The resulting 18-room fantasy has 13 fireplaces, a wedding chapel, parapets, and many other unusual touches. This castle is a must for fans of folk-art constructions, and tours are usually led by the daughter for whom the castle was built.

✪ **Taliesin West.** 12621 Frank Lloyd Wright Blvd. (at 114th St.), Scottsdale. ☎ **480/860-2700.** Basic tours, Oct 1–May 31 $14.50 adults, $12 seniors and students, $3 children 4–12, free for children 3 and under; June 1–Sept 30 $10 adults, $8 students and seniors, $3 children 4–12, free for children 3 and under. Oct 1–May 31 daily 10am–4pm; June 1–Sept 30 daily 8am–3pm. Closed Easter, Thanksgiving, Christmas, New Year's Day, and occasional special events. From Scottsdale Rd., go east on Shea Blvd. to 114th St., then north 1 mile to the entrance road.

Architect Frank Lloyd Wright fell in love with the Arizona desert and in 1937 opened a winter camp here that served as his office and school. Today Taliesin West is the headquarters of the Frank Lloyd Wright Foundation and School of Architecture.

Tours explain the buildings of this campus and include a general background introduction to Wright and his theories of architecture. Wright believed in using local materials in his designs, and this shows up at Taliesin West where local stone was used for building foundations. He developed a number of innovative methods for dealing with the extremes of the desert climate, such as sliding wall panels to let in varying amounts of air and light.

Architecture students, and anyone interested in the work of Wright, will enjoy browsing through the excellent books in the gift shop. Expanded basic tours called Insight Tours ($20 adults, $16 seniors, students, and children), behind-the-scenes tours ($35 per person), and guided desert hikes ($20 per person) are also available at certain times of year. Call ahead and check the schedule to be sure you can get the tour you want at the time you want.

ZOOS & PARKS

The newest and perhaps most unusual park in the Phoenix metro area centers on the new **Tempe Town Lake,** created in 1999 by damming the Salt River with inflatable dams. With the construction of Tempe Town Lake, Tempe now has a 2-mile-long lake on which to go boating, and lining the north and south shores of the lake are bike paths and parks. The best lake access is at Tempe Town Beach, at the foot of the Mill Avenue Bridge. Here you can rent kayaks ($11.25 to $16.50 per hour) and other small boats. Tempe Town Lake is the focus of a grand development plan known as the Rio Salado Project, which will eventually include a hotel and other commercial facilities.

Among the city's most popular parks are its natural areas and preserves. These include South Mountain Park, Papago Park, Phoenix Mountains Preserve (site of Squaw Peak), North Mountain Preserve, North Mountain Recreation Area, and Camelback Mountain–Echo Canyon Recreation Area. For more information on these parks, see "Hiking," "Bicycling," and "Horseback Riding" under "Outdoor Pursuits," later in this chapter.

Out of Africa Wildlife Park. Fort McDowell Rd., Fountain Springs. ☎ **480/837-7779.** Admission $13.95 adults, $12.95 seniors, $4.95 children ages 3–12, free for children under 3. Oct 1–Memorial Day Tues–Sun 9:30am–5pm; Memorial Day–Sept Wed–Fri 4–9:30pm, Sat 9:30am–9:30pm, Sun 9:30am–5pm. Take Ariz. 87 northeast from Mesa and 2 miles past Shea Blvd., turn right on Fort McDowell Rd.

Lions and tigers and bears, oh my! That's what you'll see at this small wildlife park northeast of Scottsdale, and all these animals will be putting on shows for you rather than just lazying in the shade as they do at most zoos. The most popular performances are those in the park's swimming pool. You've probably never seen tigers, wolves, and bears having so much fun in the water.

The Phoenix Zoo. Papago Park, 455 N. Galvin Pkwy. ☎ **602/273-1341.** www.phoenixzoo. org. Admission $8.50 adults, $7.50 seniors, $4.25 children 3–12, free for children under 3. Labor Day–Apr daily 9am–5pm; May 1–Labor Day daily 7:30am–4pm. Closed Dec 25. Bus: 3.

Home to more than 1,300 animals, the Phoenix Zoo is known for its mixed-species, 4-acre African veldt exhibit and its baboon colony. The Southwestern animal exhibits are also of particular interest, as are the giant Galapagos tortoises. All the animals in the zoo are kept in naturalistic enclosures and what with all the palm trees and tropical vegetation, it's easy to forget that this is the desert, especially when you wander through the rainforest exhibit. Kids will enjoy Harmony Farm, a hands-on farm area.

ESPECIALLY FOR KIDS

In addition to the children's activities suggested below, kids are also likely to enjoy the Arizona Science Center, the Mesa Southwest Museum, the Hall of Flame Firefighting Museum, the Phoenix Zoo, and Out of Africa Wildlife Park—all described in detail above.

Arizona Doll & Toy Museum. In Heritage Square, 602 E. Adams St. ☎ **602/253-9337.** Admission $2.50 adults, $1 children. Tues–Sat 10am–4pm; Sun noon–4pm. Closed Aug. Bus: Red (R), Yellow (Y), 0.

Located in the Stevens House on Heritage Square in downtown Phoenix, the Arizona Doll and Toy Museum is as interesting to adults as it is to kids. "Class E. Dresser

You Paid What?

47,000 hotels, 700 airlines, 50 rental car companies. And a few million ways to save money.

Travelocity.com

A Sabre Company

Go Virtually Anywhere.

AOL Keyword: Travel

Will you have enough stories to tell your grandchildren

Yahoo! Travel

Ladies Shop" and "Hattie's Millinery and Dry Goods" miniature shop from the Mott Collection (which were originally at Knotts Berry Farm in Los Angeles) are on display.

Arizona Museum for Youth. 35 N. Robson St. (between Main and 1st sts.), Mesa. ☎ **480/644-2467.** www.ci.mesa.az.us/amfy. Admission $2.50, free for children under 2. Fall–spring Sun and Tues–Fri 1–5pm, Sat 10am–5pm; summer Tues–Sat 9am–5pm, Sun 1–5pm. Closed for 2 weeks between exhibits. Bus: R.

Using both traditional displays and participatory activities, this museum allows children to explore the fine arts and their own creativity. The museum is housed in a refurbished grocery store, which has for past exhibits been transformed into a zoo, a ranch, and a foreign country. Exhibits are geared mainly to toddlers through 12-year-olds, but all ages can work together to make an object or experience the activities.

Castles & Coasters. 9445 N. Metro Pkwy. E. ☎ **602/997-7575.** Ride and game prices vary. Open daily (hours change seasonally; call ahead). Bus: Red (R) or 27.

Located adjacent to Metrocenter, one of Arizona's largest shopping malls, this small amusement park boasts a very impressive rollercoaster and plenty of tamer rides. There are also four 18-hole miniature-golf courses and a huge pavilion full of video games.

CrackerJax Family Fun & Sports Park. 16001 N. Scottsdale Rd. (¹⁄₄ mile south of Bell Rd.), Scottsdale. ☎ **480/998-2800.** Activity prices vary. Open daily (hours change seasonally; call ahead). Bus: 72.

Three miniature-golf courses are the main attraction here, but you'll also find a bilevel driving range, batting cages, go-cart tracks, sand volleyball courts, and a video-game arcade.

McCormick-Stillman Railroad Park. 7301 E. Indian Bend Rd., Scottsdale. ☎ **480/ 312-2312.** Train and carousel rides $1, train museum $1 ages 13 and up. Hours vary with the season, call for schedule. Bus: 72.

If you or your kids happen to like trains, then you won't want to miss this Scottsdale park dedicated to railroading. Within the park are a 5/12-scale model railroad that takes visitors around the park, restored cars and engines, two old railway depots, and model railroad layouts operated by a local club. There's also a 1929 carousel and a general store. You'll find the park on the corner of Scottsdale Road and Indian Bend Road.

6 Organized Tours & Excursions

The Valley of the Sun is a sprawling, often congested, place, and if you are unfamiliar with the area, you may be surprised at how great the distances are. If map reading and urban navigation are not your strong points, you may want to consider taking a guided tour. There are numerous companies offering tours of both the Valley of the Sun and the rest of Arizona. However, tours of the valley tend to include only brief stops at highlights.

BUS TOURS   Gray Line of Phoenix (☎ 800/732-0327 or 602/495-9100) is one of the largest tour companies in the valley. It offers a 3¹⁄₂-hour tour of Phoenix and the Valley of the Sun for $30 per adult. The tour points out such local landmarks as the state capitol, Heritage Square, Arizona State University, and Old Town Scottsdale.

GLIDER RIDES   The thermals that form above the mountains in the Phoenix area are ideal for sailplane (glider) soaring. On the south side of the valley, **Arizona Soaring** (☎ 800/861-2318 in Arizona or 520/568-2318; 480/821-2903 for information), in the community of Maricopa, offers sailplane rides as well as instruction. A basic 20-minute flight is $69.95, and for $99.95 you can take an aerobatic flight with loops, rolls, and inverted flying. To reach the airstrip, take I-10 east to exit 164

Vacationing in the Fast Lane

Want to learn how to drive like a grand-prix racer? At the **Bob Bondurant School of High Performance Driving** (☎ **800/842-7223** or 520/796-1111; www. bondurant.com), you can do just that. For more than 30 years this school has been training drivers in how to handle cars the way the pros do. A 2¹/₂-hour Lap the Oval course (offered only twice a year) will run you $325 to $350, while a 4-day Grand Prix road racing course will set you back $3,275. Make reservations at least 3 months in advance.

(Maricopa Road), go 15 miles, turn west on Arizona 238 and continue for 6¹/₂ miles more. On the north side of the valley, there's **Turf Soaring School,** 8700 W. Carefree Hwy., Peoria (☎ **602/439-3621**), which charges $75 for a basic flight and $110 for an aerobatic flight. This outfit also offers flights for two people ($125), although your combined weight can't exceed 300 pounds.

HOT-AIR BALLOON RIDES The still morning air of the Valley of the Sun is perfect for hot-air ballooning, and because of the stiff competition, prices are among the lowest in the country—between $90 and $140 per person for a 1- to 1¹/₂-hour ride. Companies to try include **A Aerozona Adventure** (☎ **888/ 991-4260** or 480/991-4260), **Adventures Out West** (☎ **800/755-0935** or 602/ 996-6100), and **Unicorn Balloon Company** (☎ **800/468-2478** or 480/ 991-3666; www.unicornballoon.com).

JEEP TOURS Want to get off the pavement and do a little four-wheeling? Jeep tours through the desert are offered by a dozen or more companies around the valley. Most hotels and resorts have particular companies they work with, so if you want to do a Jeep tour, try contacting the concierge at your hotel. Alternatively, you can contact one of the following companies. Most will pick you up at your hotel, take you off through the desert, give you lots of information on this corner of the West, and maybe even let you try shooting a six-gun while you're out in the desert. Tour prices are around $65 to $100 for a 4-hour tour. Companies to try include **Western Events** (☎ **800/567-3619** or 480/860-1777), **Arizona Bound Tours** (☎ **480/994-0580**), and **Rawhide Land & Cattle** (☎ **800/294-JEEP** or 480/488-0023). The last company operates out of the popular Rawhide Wild West town/restaurant. For slightly more unique tours, try **Desert Storm Hummer Tours** (☎ **480/922-0020**), which uses those ultimate sport utility vehicles, or **Arizona Unique Buggy Adventures** (☎ **480/488-2466**), which uses unusual open-sided off-road buggies for its tours.

Some Jeep tour companies also offer the chance to do some gold panning. If this interests you, contact **Western Events** (☎ **800/567-3619** or 480/860-1777), which also does ghost-town excursions, or **Arrowhead Desert Tours** (☎ **800/514-9063** or 602/942-3361).

SCENIC FLIGHTS If you're short on time but still want to at least see the Grand Canyon, you can book an air tour in a small plane. **Westwind Tours** (☎ **888/ 869-0866** or 480/991-5557) charges $240 to $295 for its Grand Canyon tours and offers a trip for $415 that takes in Monument Valley as well. This company flies out of both the Scottsdale Airport and the Deer Valley Airport in the northwest part of the valley.

7 Outdoor Pursuits

BICYCLING   Although the Valley of the Sun is a sprawling place, it's mostly flat, which makes bicycling a breeze as long as it isn't windy or in the heat of summer. **Wheels 'n Gear,** 7607 E. McDowell Rd., Scottsdale (☎ **480/945-2881**), in the Plaza Del Rio Shopping Center, rents mountain bikes for between $24 and $40 per day and has off-road trail maps available. Among the best mountain-biking spots in the city are South Mountain Park (use the entrance off 48th Street), Papago Park (at Van Buren Street and Galvin Parkway), and North Mountain Recreation Area (off Seventh Street between Dunlap Avenue and Thunderbird Road).

If you'd rather have someone show you some of the desert's best mountain biking, contact **Desert Biking Adventures** (☎ **888/249-BIKE** or 602/320-4602), which leads 2-, 3-, and 4-hour mountain-bike tours through the desert (and specializes in downhill rides). Tour prices range from $55 to $100.

If you'd rather confine your cycling to a paved surface, there's no better route than Scottsdale's **Indian Bend Wash greenbelt,** a paved multiuse path that extends for more than 15 miles along Hayden Road (from north of Shea Boulevard to Tempe). The Indian Bend Wash pathway can be accessed at many points along Hayden Road.

GOLF   With nearly 200 courses in the Valley of the Sun, golf is just about the most popular sport in Phoenix and one of the main reasons people flock here during the winter months. Sunshine, spectacular views, and coyotes, quail, and doves for company make playing a round of golf in the valley a truly memorable experience.

However, despite the number of courses, it can still be difficult to get a tee time on any of the more popular courses (especially during the busy months of February through April). If you are staying at a resort with a golf course, be sure to make your tee-time reservations at the same time you make your room reservations. If you aren't staying at a resort, you might still be able to play a round on a resort course if you can get a last-minute tee time. Try one of the tee-time reservation services below.

The only thing harder than getting a winter or spring tee time in the Valley of the Sun is facing the bill at the end of your 18 holes. Greens fees at most public and resort courses range from around $90 to $125, with the top courses at the most expensive resorts often charging around $180 (or even more). Municipal courses, on the other hand, charge less than $30. You can save money on many courses by opting for twilight play, which usually begins at 1, 2, or 3pm. We've listed high- and low-season greens fees below; you'll find that spring and fall fees fall somewhere in-between.

You can get more information on Valley of the Sun golf courses from the **Greater Phoenix Convention & Visitors Bureau,** 50 N. Second St., Phoenix, AZ 85004 (☎ **877/225-5749** or 602/254-6500). You can also pick up a copy of the *Greater Phoenix Golf Guide* at the Visitors Bureau, golf courses, and many hotels and resorts.

To make sure you get to play those courses you've been dreaming about, it's a good idea to make reservations well in advance. Many companies around the valley will save you the hassle of booking tee times by making reservations for you. One of these companies, **Golf Xpress** (☎ **800/878-8580** or 602/404-GOLF), can make reservations farther in advance than you could if you called the golf course direct. This company also makes hotel reservations, rents golf clubs, and provides other assistance to golfers visiting the valley. **Par-Tee-Time Golf** (☎ **800/827-2223** or 602/230-7223) is another company that makes advance reservations. For last-minute reservations, call **Stand-by Golf** (☎ **480/874-3133**).

The valley's many resort courses are, of course, the favored fairways of valley visitors. For spectacular scenery, the two Jay Morrish–designed 18-hole courses at ✪ **The Boulders,** 34631 N. Tom Darlington Dr., Carefree (☎ **800/553-1717** or 480/488-9028), just can't be beat. Given the option, play the South Course and watch out as you approach the tee box on the seventh hole—it's a real heart-stopper. Tee times for non-resort guests are very limited in the winter and spring, and you'll pay $225 for a round. However, in summer you can play here for only $75 (just be sure you get the earliest possible tee time and bring plenty of water).

Jumping over to Litchfield Park, on the far west side of the valley, you'll find **The Wigwam Golf and Country Club,** 300 Wigwam Blvd. (☎ 623/935-3811), and, count 'em, three championship 18-hole courses. ✪ **The Gold Course** here is legendary, but even the Blue and Red courses are worth playing. These are traditional courses for purists who want vast expanses of green instead of cactus and boulders. In the high season, greens fees are $130 for the Gold Course and $100 ($55 twilight) for the Blue and Red courses (in summer, $38). High-season reservations for non-guests can be made no more than 5 days in advance.

Way over on the east side of the valley at the foot of the Superstition Mountains is the ✪ **Gold Canyon Golf Resort,** 6100 S. Kings Ranch Rd., Gold Canyon (☎ **480/982-9449**), which has been rated one of the best public courses in the state and has what have been rated as three of the best holes in the state—the second, third, and fourth holes on the Dinosaur Mountain course, a visually breathtaking desert-style course. Greens fees on this course range from $95 to $110 in winter and $50 to $60 in summer. The resort's second course, the Sidewinder, is a more traditional course and is less dramatic, but is much more economical. Greens fees in winter range from $45 to $65 and from $35 to $55 in summer. Make reservations a week in advance. It's well worth the drive.

If you want to swing where the pros do, beg, borrow, or steal a tee time on the Tom Weiskopf and Jay Morrish–designed Stadium Course at the ✪ **Tournament Players Club (TPC) of Scottsdale,** 17020 N. Hayden Rd. (☎ **480/585-3600** or 480/585-3939), which annually hosts the Phoenix Open. The 18th hole here has standing room for 40,000 spectators, but it is hoped there won't be that many around (or any TV cameras) the day you double bogey on this hole. The TPC's second 18, the Desert Course, is actually a municipal course, thanks to an agreement with the landowner, the Bureau of Land Management. Stadium course greens fees are $181 in the winter/spring and $81 in the summer. Desert Course greens fees range from $38 to $48.

At the **Gainey Ranch Golf Club,** at the Hyatt Regency Scottsdale Resort at Gainey Ranch, 7600 E. Gainey Club Dr. (☎ **480/951-0022**), you'll find three decidedly different 9-hole courses (the Dunes, the Arroyo, and the Lakes courses), each with its own set of challenges. However, these courses are open only to guests of the resort.

If a traditional course that has been played by presidents and celebrities alike interests you, then try to get a tee time at one of the two 18-hole courses at the **Arizona Biltmore Country Club,** 24th Street and Missouri Avenue (☎ 602/955-9655). The two courses here are more relaxing than challenging, good to play if you're not yet up to par. Greens fees are $150 in the winter/spring and $48 in summer. Reservations can be made 30 days in advance. There's also a championship 18-hole putting course at the hotel.

The two courses at the **Camelback Golf Club,** 7847 N. Mockingbird Lane (☎ **480/596-7050**), offer distinctly different experiences. However, the Resort course has recently undergone a complete redesign, with new water features, among other changes. The Indian Bend course is a links-style course with great mountain views and lots of water hazards. Greens fees are $105 to $185 in winter/spring and $30 to $75 in summer. Make reservations up to 30 days in advance.

Set at the base of Camelback Mountain, **The Phoenician Golf Club,** 6000 E. Camelback Rd. (☎ **800/888-8234** or 480/423-2449), at the valley's most glamorous resort, has 27 holes that mix traditional and desert styles. Greens fees if you aren't staying at the resort are $180 in winter/spring and $90 in summer.

Of the valley's many daily-fee courses, it is the two 18-hole courses at ✪ **Troon North Golf Club,** 10320 E. Dynamite Blvd., Scottsdale (☎ **480/585-5300**), seemingly just barely carved out of raw desert, that garner the most local accolades. Greens fees are $240 in winter/spring and $75 to $90 through the summer. Reservations are taken up to 30 days in advance (and fill up quickly in winter).

However, the Pete Dye–designed **ASU-Karsten Golf Course,** 1125 E. Rio Salado Pkwy., Tempe (☎ **480/921-8070**), part of Arizona State University, is also highly praised and a very challenging training ground for top collegiate golfers. Greens fees are $65 to $88 in the winter and $25 in the summer. Make reservations at least 5 days in advance in the winter.

If you haven't yet gotten your handicap down, but want to try a desert-style course, then head to **Tatum Ranch Golf Club,** 29888 N. Tatum Ranch Dr., Cave Creek (☎ **480/585-2399**), which is regarded as a forgiving course with a desert sensibility. However, this course is in the process of going private and may no longer be accepting outside play by the time you read this. Greens fees are $60 to $110 in the winter and somewhere around $40 to $60 in the summer.

Other worthwhile daily-fee courses include **Kokopelli Golf Resort,** 1800 W. Guadalupe Rd., Gilbert (☎ **480/926-3589** or 480/962-GOLF), with greens fees of $75 in winter and $39 in summer, and **The Legend at Arrowhead,** 21027 N. 67th Ave., Glendale (☎ **623/561-1902** or 480/962-GOLF), with greens fees of $60 to $80 in winter and $25 to $35 in summer. The **Kierland Golf Club,** 15636 Clubgate Dr., Scottsdale (☎ **480/922-9283**), which was designed by Scott Miller and consists of three 9-hole courses that can be played in combination, is another much-talked-about local daily-fee course. Greens fees are $125 to $145 in winter and $50 to $65 in summer.

Of the municipal courses in Phoenix, **Papago Golf Course,** 5595 E. Moreland St. (☎ **602/275-8428**), at the foot of the red sandstone Papago Buttes, offers fine views and economical rates ($18 to $28 in high season) and has a killer 17th hole. **Encanto Golf Course,** 2775 N. 15th Ave. (☎ **602/253-3963**), is equally inexpensive for a round of golf ($18 to $28 in the high season). Keep in mind that these rates don't include a golf cart, which is another $18 or so.

HIKING   Several mountains around Phoenix, including Camelback Mountain and Squaw Peak, have been set aside as parks and nature preserves, and these natural areas are among the city's most popular hiking spots. The city's largest nature preserve, **Phoenix South Mountain Park,** said to be the largest city park in the world, contains miles of hiking, mountain-biking, and horseback-riding trails, and the views of Phoenix from here are spectacular, especially at sunset. To reach the park, simply drive south on Central Avenue or 48th Street.

Perhaps the most popular hiking trail in the city is the trail to the top of ✪ **Camelback Mountain,** which is near the boundary between Phoenix and Scottsdale. This is the highest mountain in Phoenix, and the 1.2-mile trail to the summit is very steep. Don't attempt this one in the heat of the day, and take at least a quart of water with you. The reward for your effort is the city's finest view. To reach the trailhead for Camelback Mountain, drive up 44th Street until it becomes McDonald Drive, then turn right on East Echo Canyon Drive, and continue up the hill until the road ends at a large parking lot.

At the east end of Camelback Mountain you'll find the Cholla Trail, which is longer than the trail at the west end and sees far fewer hikers. The only parking for this trail is along Invergordon Road at Chaparral Road, just north of Camelback Road (along the east boundary of The Phoenician resort). Be sure to park in a legal parking space and watch the hours that parking is allowed. This trail starts out fairly easy and then toward the top gets steep, rocky, and quite difficult. However, there are great views down onto the fairways of The Phoenician's golf course.

Squaw Peak in the Phoenix Mountains Preserve offers another aerobic workout of a hike and has views almost as spectacular as those from Camelback Mountain. Squaw Peak is reached from Squaw Peak Drive off Lincoln Drive between 22nd and 23rd streets.

For much less vigorous hiking, try the North Mountain Recreation Area in North Mountain Preserve. This natural area, located on either side of Seventh Street between Dunlap Avenue and Thunderbird Road, has more flat hiking than Camelback Mountain or Squaw Peak.

Farther afield are numerous hiking opportunities in the Superstition Mountains to the east and the McDowell Mountains to the north.

HORSEBACK RIDING   Even in the urban confines of the Phoenix metro area, people like to play at being cowboys, and if you get the urge to saddle up, there are plenty of places around the valley to go for a horseback ride. Keep in mind that most stables require or prefer reservations.

On the south side of the city, try **Ponderosa Stables,** 10215 S. Central Ave. (☎ **602/268-1261**), or **South Mountain Stables,** 10005 S. Central Ave. (☎ **602/276-8131**), both of which lead rides into South Mountain Park and charge $17 per hour. In the Scottsdale area, try **MacDonald's Ranch,** 26540 N. Scottsdale Rd. (☎ **480/585-0239**), which charges $24 for a 1-hour ride and $36 for a 2-hour ride.

On the east side of the Valley, you'll find several riding stables in the foothills of the Superstition Mountains. **Trail Horse Adventures,** 2151 N. Warner Rd., Apache Junction (☎ **800/SADDLEUP** or 480/982-6353), which offers rides ranging in length from 2 hours to all day ($33 to $135) or longer. The company arranges riding lessons, overnight pack trips, picnics, and hayrides. Over in Gold Canyon, you'll find one of the most famous names in Arizona horseback riding. **Don Donnelly Stables,** 6010 Kings Ranch Rd., Gold Canyon (☎ **800/346-4403** or 480/982-7822), offers 2-hour sunset rides for $36 per person. These stables also do overnight rides, cookouts, and hayrides.

IN-LINE SKATING   In the Scottsdale area, you can rent in-line skates, including all protective equipment, at **Scottsdale Bladez,** 14692 Frank Lloyd Wright Blvd. (☎ **480/391-1139**), for $4 per hour or $12 per day. You can also rent equipment at **Wheels 'n Gear,** 7607 E. McDowell Rd. (☎ **480/945-2881**), which is in the Plaza Del Rio Shopping Center (adjacent to the popular Indian Bend Wash greenbelt trail) and charges $6 for 2 hours or $12 per day.

The folks at these shops can point you toward nearby spots that are good for skating. One of the best places to skate is the **Indian Bend Wash greenbelt,** a paved multiuse path that extends for around 15 miles. It runs parallel to Hayden Road in Scottsdale from north of Shea Boulevard to Washington Street. The Indian Bend Wash pathway can be accessed at many points along Hayden Road.

TENNIS   Most major hotels in the area have one or more tennis courts, and there are several tennis resorts around the valley. If you're staying someplace without a tennis court, try the **Scottsdale Ranch Park,** 10400 E. Via Linda, Scottsdale (☎ **480/312-7774**). Court fees range from $3 to $5 for 1^{1}/$_{2}$ hours of singles play.

WATER PARKS   At **Waterworld Safari Water Park,** 4243 W. Pinnacle Peak Rd., Glendale (☎ **623/581-1947**), you can free-fall 6½ stories down the Avalanche speed waterslide or catch a gnarly wave in the wave pool. Other waterslides offer tamer times. **Mesa Golfland-Sunsplash,** 155 W. Hampton, Mesa (☎ **480/834-8319**), has a wave pool and a tunnel called "the Black Hole." **Big Surf,** 1500 N. McClintock Rd. (☎ **480/947-7873**), has a wave pool, underground tube slides, and more.

All three of these parks charge about $16 for adults and $13 for children 4 to 11 (prices tend to go down after 3 or 4pm). All are open from approximately Memorial Day to Labor Day, Monday to Saturday 10am to about 8 or 9pm (Big Surf until 6pm only) and Sunday 11am to 7pm.

WHITE-WATER RAFTING & TUBING ON THE SALT RIVER   The desert may not seem like the place for white-water rafting, but up in the mountains to the northeast of Phoenix, the ✪ **Upper Salt River** still flows wild and free and offers some exciting rafting. Most years from about late February to late May, snowmelt from the White Mountains turns the river into a Class III and IV river filled with exciting rapids (however, some years there just isn't enough water). Companies operating full-day, overnight, and multiday rafting trips on the upper Salt River (conditions permitting) include **Far Flung Adventures** (☎ **800/231-7238** or 520/425-7272; www.farflung.com), **Sun Country Rafting** (☎ **800/272-3353** or 602/493-9011), and **Mild to Wild Rafting** (☎ **800/567-6745**). Prices range from around $80 to $100 for a day trip up to around $650 for a multiday trip. Mild to Wild also offers 2- and 4-day float trips on the Verde River.

Tamer river trips can be had from **Salt River Recreation** (☎ **480/984-3305**), which has its headquarters 20 miles northeast of Phoenix on the Bush Highway (Power Road) at the intersection of Usery Pass Road in the Tonto National Forest. For $10 the company will rent you a large inner tube and shuttle you by bus upriver for the float down. The inner-tubing season runs from May through September.

8 Spectator Sports

Phoenix has gone nuts over pro sports and is now one of the few cities in the country with all four of the major sports teams (baseball, basketball, football, and hockey). Add to this baseball's spring training, a second ice hockey team, professional women's basketball, three major golf tournaments, the annual Fiesta Bowl college football classic, and ASU football, basketball, and baseball, and you have enough action to keep even the most rabid sports fans happy. For sports fans, the best month to visit is probably March, when you could feasibly catch spring baseball training, the Suns, the Coyotes, and ASU basketball and baseball, as well as the Franklin Templeton Tennis Classic, The Tradition, and the Standard Register PING LPGA Tournament.

Call **ETM/Dillard's Box Office** (☎ **800/638-4253** or 480/503-5555) or **Ticketmaster** (☎ **480/784-4444;** www.ticketmaster.com) for tickets to most of the events below. For tickets to sold-out events, try **Tickets Unlimited** (☎ **800/289-8497** or 602/840-2340) or **Ticket Exchange** (☎ **800/800-9811** or 602/254-4444).

AUTO RACING   At the **Phoenix International Raceway,** 7602 S. 115th Ave. (at Baseline Road), Avondale (☎ **602/252-2227**), there is NASCAR and Indy car racing on the world's fastest 1-mile oval. Tickets range from $10 to $40.

BASEBALL   The **Arizona Diamondbacks** (☎ **602/514-8400**) play in downtown Phoenix at the Bank One Ballpark (BOB), a state-of-the-art stadium with a retractable roof that allows for comfortable play during Phoenix's blistering summer temperatures. The retractable roof makes this one of the only enclosed baseball stadiums with natural grass. Tickets ($4 to $55) are available at the Bank One Ballpark ticket office and through ETM/Dillard's Box Office outlets (☎ **800/638-4253** or 480/503-5555; www.etm.com).

For decades, however, it has been spring training that has given Phoenix its annual shot of baseball, and don't think that the Cactus League's preseason exhibition games will be any less popular just because the Diamondbacks are in town. Spring-training games may rank second only to golf in popularity with winter visitors to the valley. Seven major league baseball teams have spring-training camps around the valley during March and April, and exhibition games are scheduled at six different stadiums. Ticket prices range from $3 to $19. Tickets for the Diamondbacks, Cubs, and Athletics are sold through ETM/Dillard's Box Office outlets (☎ **800/638-4253** or 480/503-5555), tickets for the Padres, Mariners, Brewers, and Angels are sold through Ticketmaster (☎ **480/784-4444**), and tickets for the Giants are sold through Bass Tickets (☎ **800/225-2277**). Get a schedule of games from the convention and visitors bureau or an ETM/Dillard's Box Office outlet, or check the *Arizona Republic* while you're in town. Games often sell out, especially on weekends, so be sure to order tickets in advance if you're a serious fan.

Teams training in the valley include the **San Francisco Giants,** Scottsdale Stadium, 7408 E. Osborn Rd., Scottsdale (☎ 800/225-2277 or 480/312-2580); the **Oakland A's,** Phoenix Municipal Stadium, 5999 E. Van Buren St., Phoenix (☎ 602/392-0217); the **Anaheim Angels,** Tempe Diablo Stadium, 2200 W. Alameda Dr., Tempe (☎ 480/438-9300); the **Chicago Cubs,** HoHoKam Park, 1235 N. Center St., Mesa (☎ 480/964-4467), the **San Diego Padres,** Peoria Sports Complex, 16101 N. 83rd Ave., Peoria (☎ 800/409-1511 or 623/878-4337), the **Seattle Mariners,** Peoria Sports Complex, 16101 N. 83rd Ave., Peoria (☎ 800/409-1511 or 623/878-4337), and the **Milwaukee Brewers,** Maryvale Baseball Park, 3508 N. 53rd Ave., Phoenix (☎ 623/245-5500).

BASKETBALL   The NBA's **Phoenix Suns** play at the America West Arena, 201 E. Jefferson St. (☎ **602/379-SUNS**). Tickets are $10 to $80 and are available at the America West Arena box office and through ETM/Dillard's Box Office outlets (see above). Suns tickets are hard to come by. If you want good seats, you really have to buy your tickets on the day they go on sale (usually in mid-September). If you forget to plan ahead, try contacting the box office the day before or the day of a game to see if tickets have been returned. Otherwise, you'll have to try a ticket agency and pay the premium.

Phoenix also has a Women's National Basketball Association (WNBA) team, the **Phoenix Mercury** (☎ **602/252-WNBA** or 602/379-7800), which plays at the America West Arena, 201 E. Jefferson St., between mid-June and mid-August. Ticket prices range from $8 to $36.

FOOTBALL   The **Arizona Cardinals** (☎ **800/999-1402** or 602/379-0102) play at Arizona State University's Sun Devil Stadium, which is also home to the Fiesta Bowl Football Classic. Tickets are $30 to $125. Except for a few specific games each season, it is generally possible to get Cardinals tickets.

While the Cardinals get to use Sun Devil Stadium, this field really belongs to Arizona State University's **Sun Devils** (☎ **480/965-2381**). Tickets are $16 and are sold through ETM/Dillard's Box Office outlets (see above).

Despite the desert heat and presence of a baseball team, Phoenicians don't give up football just because it's summer. The **Arizona Rattlers** arena football team

(☎ 602/514-8383) plays 50-yard indoor football at the America West Arena, 201 E. Jefferson St. Tickets are $9 to $37 and are available at the America West Arena box office.

GOLF TOURNAMENTS   It's not surprising that, with nearly 200 golf courses and ideal golfing weather throughout the winter and spring, the Valley of the Sun hosts three major PGA tournaments each year. Tickets for all three tournaments are available through ETM/Dillard's Box Office outlets (see above).

The **Phoenix Open Golf Tournament** (☎ 602/870-0163; www.phoenixopen. com) in January is the largest. Held at the Tournament Players Club (TPC) of Scottsdale, this tournament attracts more spectators than any other golf tournament in the world (nearly 400,000 each year). The 18th hole of the TPC has standing room for 40,000. Tickets usually go on sale in June with prices starting around $20.

Each March, the **Standard Register PING LPGA Tournament** (☎ 602/495-4653), held in the year 2000 at the Legacy Golf Resort, lures nearly 150 of the top women golfers from around the world. Daily ticket prices are $15, and weekly tickets are around $50.

The Tradition (☎ 480/595-4070), a Senior PGA Tour event held each April at the Desert Mountain golf course, has a loyal following of fans who would rather watch the likes of Jack Nicklaus and Lee Trevino than see Tiger Woods win yet another tournament. Daily tickets are $40, and they usually go on sale in January.

Now even amateurs can get in on some tournament action at the **Phoenix Amateur Golf Championship** (☎ 877/988-GOLF), which is held in mid-July (partly to prove that it's possible to play golf in the summer in Phoenix).

HOCKEY   Ice hockey in the desert? It may not make sense, but even Phoenicians are crazy about ice hockey (maybe it's all those northern transplants). The NHL's **Phoenix Coyotes** (☎ 888/255-PUCK or 480/563-PUCK) play at America West Arena, 201 E. Jefferson St. Tickets range from $10.50 to $80. Tickets are sold through ETM/Dillard's Box Office outlets (see above).

HORSE/GREYHOUND RACING   The **Phoenix Greyhound Park,** 3801 E. Washington St. (☎ 602/273-7181), is a large, fully enclosed, and air-conditioned facility offering seating in various grandstands, lounges, and restaurants. There's racing throughout the year, and tickets are $1.50 to $3.

Turf Paradise, 1501 W. Bell Rd. (☎ 602/942-1101), is Phoenix's horse-racing track. The season runs from October to May, with post time at 12:30pm Friday through Tuesday. Admission ranges from $1 to $5.

RODEOS, POLO & HORSE SHOWS   Cowboys, cowgirls, and other horsey types will find plenty of the four-legged critters going through their paces most weeks at **Westworld Equestrian Center,** 16601 N. Pima Rd., Scottsdale (☎ 480/312-6802). With its 500 stables, 11 equestrian arenas, and a polo field, this 400-acre complex provides an amazing variety of entertainment and sporting events. There are rodeos, polo matches, an Arabian horse show, horse rentals, and horseback-riding instruction. Ticket prices vary with the event.

TENNIS TOURNAMENTS   Each March, top international men's tennis players compete at the **Franklin Templeton Tennis Classic** (☎ 480/922-0222), which is held at the Scottsdale Princess Resort, 7575 E. Princess Dr., Scottsdale. Tickets run about $10 to $55 and are available through ETM/Dillard's Box Office outlets (see above).

9 Day Spas

Ever since the first "lungers" showed up in the Phoenix area hoping to cure their tuberculosis, the desert has been a magnet for those looking to get healthy. In the first half of the 20th century, health spas were all the rage in Phoenix, and with the health-and-fitness trend continuing to gather steam, it comes as no surprise that health spas are now immensely popular in the Valley of the Sun. In the past few years, several of the area's top resorts have added new full-service health spas or expanded existing ones to cater to guest's increasing requests for services such as massages, body wraps, mud masks, and salt glows.

If you can't or don't want to spend the money to stay at a top resort and avail yourself of the spa, you may still be able to indulge. Most of the valley's resorts open the doors of their spas to the public, and, for the cost of a body treatment or massage, you can spend the day at the spa, taking classes, working out in a fitness room, lounging by the pool, and otherwise living the life of the rich and famous. Barring this indulgence, you can slip into a day spa, of which there are many scattered around the valley, and take a stress-reduction break the way other people take a latte break.

The new hot and happening place to be pampered is ✪ **The Gainey Village Health Club and Spa,** 7477 E. Doubletree Ranch Rd., Scottsdale (☎ 480/609-6980), a state-of-the-art spa and exercise facility near the Hyatt Regency Scottsdale resort. Specialized treatments include massage in a hydrotherapy tub or with water pressure and a couples massage (complete with champagne and chocolate truffles) in a VIP room with a waterfall shower. Of course, spa treatments include just about anything else you can think of, from mineral skin glows to pumpkin peels to purifying facials. With any hour-long treatment here (average price $75 to $95), you can use the extensive exercise facilities or take a class.

Located high on the flanks of Mummy Mountain with a nice view over the valley, **The Spa at Camelback Inn,** 5402 E. Lincoln Dr., Scottsdale (☎ 480/596-7020), is a great place to spend the day being pampered. For the cost of a single 1-hour treatment—between $95 and $105—you can use all the facilities. Among the treatments available are a para-joba body moisturizer that will leave your skin feeling like silk. Multiple-treatment packages range in price from $150 to $275.

The **Centre for Well Being,** at The Phoenician, 6000 E. Camelback Rd., Scottsdale (☎ 800/843-2392 or 480/423-2452), is the valley's most prestigious day spa, the place to head if you want to be pampered with the rich and famous. For anywhere from $95 to $355, you can spend the day at the spa receiving one or more treatments and using the spa's many facilities. A single treatment (say a thermal moor mud wrap or a Turkish body scrub) entitles you to use the facilities for the rest of the day.

If you want a truly spectacular setting for your day at the spa, head north to Carefree and the **Sonoran Spa at The Boulders,** 34631 N. Tom Darlington Dr. (☎ 480/488-9009). Here individual treatments cost $99 to $135, and day-packages run about $285. Included with any treatment is use of the extensive facilities and lap pool. At press time, there were plans to build a Golden Door health spa in 2001. When completed, this should become one of the valley's top spas.

The historic setting and convenient location of the **Arizona Biltmore Spa,** 24th Street and Missouri Avenue (☎ 800/950-0086 or 602/955-6600), make this 20,000-square-foot facility an excellent choice if you're spending time along the Camelback Corridor. The spa menu is extensive and includes the likes of balneotherapy, water goddess Sedona mud purification treatment, lymphatic massages, and bindi herbal body treatments. If you aren't staying at the resort, you can use the facilities for

$25; body and beauty treatments range from $60 to $175. Use of the facilities is free with a 60-minute treatment.

The Mist Spa, at the Radisson Resort & Spa Scottsdale, 7171 N. Scottsdale Rd., Scottsdale (☎ **877/MIST-SPA** or 480/905-2882), allows non-resort guests use of the facilities for $25 per day (fee is waived with purchase of a 50-minute spa treatment). The 20,000-square-foot spa has a Japanese design, complete with Japanese-style massage rooms and a tranquil rock garden in a central covered courtyard. Spa treatments, which include the likes of collagen facials, honey steam wraps, Dead Sea mud wraps, and green tea detoxifying wraps, cost between $70 and $115.

10 Shopping

For the most part, shopping in the valley means malls. They're everywhere, and they're air-conditioned, which, we're sure you'll agree, makes shopping in the desert far more enjoyable when it's 110°F outside.

Scottsdale and the Biltmore District of Phoenix (along Camelback Road) are the valley's main upscale shopping areas, while Old Scottsdale (one of the few outdoor shopping areas) plays host to hundreds of boutiques, galleries, jewelry stores, and Native American crafts stores. The Western atmosphere of Old Scottsdale is partly real and partly a figment of the local merchants' imaginations, but nevertheless it's the most popular tourist shopping area in the valley. It also happens to be the heart of the valley's art market, with dozens of art galleries along Main Street.

Shopping hours are usually Monday through Saturday 10am to 6pm and Sunday noon to 5pm, and malls usually stay open until 9pm Monday to Saturday.

ANTIQUES

Downtown Glendale (located west of Phoenix) is the valley's main antiques district. Four times a year, the Phoenix Antique Market (☎ **800/678-9987** or 602/943-1766) stages Arizona's largest collectors' shows at the Arizona State Fairgrounds, 19th Avenue and McDowell Road. In the year 2000, dates are the third weekend of January, May, September, and November. Otherwise, call for dates.

Antiques Super-Mall. 1900 N. Scottsdale Rd., Scottsdale. ☎ **480/874-2900.**

If you make only one antiques stop, make it here. This is one of the biggest antiques malls in the valley and within a block are two others: the **Antique Centre,** 2012 N. Scottsdale Rd. (☎ **480/675-9500**), and the **Antique Trove,** 2020 N. Scottsdale Rd. (☎ **480/947-6074**).

Arizona West Galleries. 7149 E. Main St., Scottsdale. ☎ **480/994-3752.**

Nowhere else in Scottsdale will you find such an amazing collection of cowboy collectibles and Western antiques. There are antique saddles and chaps, old rifles and six-shooters, sheriff's badges, spurs, and the like.

Bishop Gallery for Art & Antiques. 7164 Main St., Scottsdale. ☎ **480/949-9062.**

This cramped shop is wonderfully eclectic, featuring everything from Asian antiques to unusual original art. Definitely worth a browse.

ART

In the Southwest, only Santa Fe is a more important art market than Scottsdale, and along the streets of Old Scottsdale you'll find dozens of ✪ **art galleries** selling everything from monumental bronzes to contemporary art created from found objects. On Main Street, you'll find primarily cowboy art, both traditional and contemporary, while on North Marshall Way, you'll find much more imaginative and daring contemporary art.

Art One. 4120 N. Marshall Way, Scottsdale. ☎ **480/946-5076.**

If you want to see the possible directions that area artists will be heading in the next few years, stop in at this Marshall Way gallery that specializes in works by art students and other area cutting-edge artists. The works here can be surprisingly good, and the prices are very reasonable.

gallerymateria. 4222 N. Marshall Way, Scottsdale. ☎ **480/949-1262.**

It's difficult to classify this fascinating boutique, which answers the question, "Is it useful, or is it art?" with clothing and household items that could double as art (with prices to match). You'll also find jewelry that looks like miniature sculptures, and crafts at the cutting edge of style using new materials or traditional materials in innovative ways. There are two parts to the boutique, and in between there's a sculpture courtyard.

✪ **Lisa Sette Gallery.** 4142 N. Marshall Way, Scottsdale. ☎ **480/990-7342.**

If you aren't a fan of cowboy or Native American art, you may feel left out of the Scottsdale art scene. Don't despair. Instead, drop by this gallery, which represents premier glass-artist William Morris as well as many others. International, national, and local artists share wall space here, with a wide mix of media represented.

Meyer Gallery. 7173 E. Main St., Scottsdale. ☎ **480/947-6372.**

This gallery is most notable for its selection of Old West, landscape, and mood paintings by living impressionists. The proprietor also has a cute Jack Russell terrier that likes to chase tennis balls.

Overland Gallery. 7155 Main St., Scottsdale. ☎ **480/947-1934.**

Traditional Western paintings and a collection of Russian Impressionist paintings form the backbone of this gallery's fine collection. These are museum-quality works (prices sometimes approach $100,000) and definitely worth a look.

Roberts Gallery. In El Pedregal Festival Marketplace, 34505 N. Scottsdale Rd., Carefree. ☎ **480/488-1088.**

The feathered masks and sculptures of Virgil Walker are the highlights at this gallery, and if you have an appreciation for fine detail work, you'll likely be fascinated by these pieces. Walker creates fantasy figures, every inch of which are covered with feathers.

BOOKS

Major chain bookstores in the Phoenix and Scottsdale area include **Borders Books Music & Café** at 2402 E. Camelback Rd., Phoenix (☎ **602/957-6660**), and **Barnes & Noble Booksellers** at 10235 N. Metro Parkway East, Phoenix (☎ **602/678-0088**), 4847 E. Ray Rd., Phoenix (☎ **480/940-7136**), and 10500 N. 90th St., Scottsdale (☎ **480/391-0048**).

T. A. Swinford. 7134 W. Main St., Scottsdale. ☎ **480/946-0022.**

Rare and out-of-print books about the American West are the specialty here. If you're looking for the likes of *Triggernometry, A Gallery of Gunfighters* (1934) or *Range Murder: How the Red-Sash Gang Dry-Gulched Deputy United States Marshal George Wellman* (1955), you'll find it here.

A CHOCOLATERIE

✪ **Chocolaterie Bernard C.** In Hilton Village, 6137 N. Scottsdale Rd. ☎ **480/483-3139.**

If you have *ever* had a genuine Belgian praline (chocolate, not one of those puffy cookies), then you will not want to leave Scottsdale without paying a visit to this chocolate shop. If you have *never* had a Belgian chocolate, you won't want to miss this shop either. The exquisite chocolate confections here will make you forget all about Godiva.

FASHION

See also "Western Wear," below.

WOMEN'S WEAR

In addition to the shops mentioned below, there are many excellent shops in malls all over the city. Favorite spots for upscale fashions include Biltmore Fashion Park, the Borgata of Scottsdale, El Pedregal Festival Marketplace, and Scottsdale Fashion Square. See "Malls & Shopping Centers" below for details on these malls and shopping plazas.

Carol Dolighan. At the Borgata, 6166 N. Scottsdale Rd., Scottsdale. ☎ **480/922-0616.**

The hand-painted, handwoven, and handmade dresses, skirts, and blouses here abound in rich colors. Each is unique. There's another Carol Dolighan store in El Pedregal Festival Marketplace, 34505 N. Scottsdale Rd. (☎ **480/488-4505**) in Carefree.

Objects. 7051 Fifth Ave., Scottsdale. ☎ **480/994-4720.**

This eclectic shop carries hand-painted, wearable art both casual and dressy, unique artist-made jewelry, African masks and Indian art, books, and all kinds of delightful and unusual things.

Uh Oh. In Hilton Village, 6137 N. Scottsdale Rd., Scottsdale. ☎ **480/991-1618.**

You'll find simple, tasteful, and oh-so-elegant fashions, footwear, jewelry, and accessories. The Southwestern contemporary styling makes this a great place to pick up something to be seen in. A second store is in La Mirada shopping plaza, 8900 E. Pinnacle Peak Rd., Scottsdale (☎ **480/515-0203**).

GIFTS & SOUVENIRS

One of the best places to shop for souvenirs is the Arizona Center mall in downtown Phoenix. See "Malls & Shopping Centers" below for details.

✪ **Bischoff's Shades of the West.** 7247 Main St., Scottsdale. ☎ **480/945-3289.**

This is one-stop shopping for all things Southwestern. From T-shirts to regional foodstuffs, this sprawling store has it all. It's got a good selection of candles, chile garlands (*ristras*), and wrought-iron cabinet hardware that can give your kitchen a Western look, and Mexican crafts that all fit in with a Southwest interior decor.

A GOLF SHOP

✪ **In Celebration of Golf.** 7001 N. Scottsdale Rd., Suite 172, Scottsdale. ☎ **480/951-4444.**

Sort of a supermarket for golfers (with a touch of Disneyland thrown in), this amazing store sells everything from clubs and golf shoes to golf art and golf antiques. There are even unique golf cars on display in case you want to take to the greens in a custom car. A golf simulation room allows you to test out new clubs and get in a bit of video golfing at the same time. An old club-maker's workbench, complete with talking mannequin, makes a visit to this shop educational as well as a lot of fun.

Ten Fun Ways to Blow $100 (More or Less) in the Valley of the Sun

With greens fees for 18 holes of golf as high as $240, it is obvious that the Valley of the Sun is not exactly a cheap place for a vacation. Still, if you've budgeted plenty of money for your vacation or simply want to splurge on a memorable experience, there are quite a few great ways to blow 100 bucks while in town. Here are some of our favorites.

1. **Spend a day at a spa.** It's not often you can blow 100 bucks and come away feeling good about it, but for between $90 and $105, you can spend the day at one of the valley's resort spas getting pampered and de-stressed. You can also spend quite a bit more than $100 in a day, but can you really put a price on well being? See "Day Spas," above.

2. **Rent a Vette** (☎ **480/941-3001**). Sometimes you just have to go over budget. For $149 a day, you can rent a new Corvette from Rent-a-Vette and head out for a high-speed spin in the desert or just cruise around Scottsdale looking like you belong.

3. **Hire a stretch limo for a couple of hours.** For $110 (plus a mandatory 20% gratuity for the driver) you can rent a six-passenger stretch limo from Arizona Limousines (☎ **800/678-0033** or 602/267-7097) for 2 hours. Just ride around, or maybe have the limo take you to a resort for a cocktail. Unfortunately, there's a 3-hour minimum on weekends, which would cost you $165 plus tip.

4. **Play a round of golf on an Arizona legend.** If you can get a tee time, $100 will get you a twilight round of golf on the Gold Course at the Wigwam Resort (☎ **623/935-3811**) out west in Litchfield Park. This is one of the oldest and most famous courses in the valley.

5. **Rent a cabana at the Pointe Hilton Tapatio Cliffs Resort** (☎ **602/866-7500**). If you've got a Motel 6 vacation budget but long for the resort life,

JEWELRY

Jewelry by Gauthier. 4211 N. Marshall Way, Scottsdale. ☎ **888/411-3232** or 480/941-1707.

This store sells the designs of the phenomenally talented jewelry designer Scott Gauthier. Very stylish, modern designs using precious stones make every piece of jewelry in this shop a miniature work of art. This is the only place you'll see Gauthier's work for sale in the United States. The elegant shop features a lit-from-below green onyx floor.

Molina Fine Jewelers. 3134 E. Camelback Rd. ☎ **800/257-2695** or 602/955-2055.

While you don't have to have an appointment to shop at this very exclusive jewelry store, it's highly recommended. With an appointment, you'll get personalized service as you peruse the Tiffany exclusives and high-end European jewelry. If you can spend as much on a necklace as you can on a Mercedes, this is where to shop for your baubles.

why not rent a poolside cabana at this north Phoenix resort? The cabanas go for $95 a day and are located in the resort's aquatic playground known as The Falls. Sure it would be cheaper to go to Big Surf, but the experience just wouldn't be the same.

6. **Take a hot-air balloon ride.** There is no better way to see the desert than drifting above it at dawn in a hot-air balloon, and there's just about no cheaper way in the country to take to the air than in the oldest form of flying machine. For $90 to $140 you can get airborne. See "Organized Tours & Excursions," above.

7. **Take a hummer of a back-roads tour.** Why ride in a Jeep when you can ride in a Hummer, the ultimate off-road vehicle? For $90 to $100, Desert Storm Hummer Tours (☎ **480/922-0020**) will give you a ride to remember, and you'll get an up-close and personal look at the Arizona desert.

8. **Order the seasonal tasting menu at Mary Elaine's (☎ 480/423-2530).** If you've never had a $100 dinner, maybe now is the time to indulge. How else will you ever be able to call yourself a true gourmand? This six-course dinner will set you back $110 (not including tax, tip, wine, or the cost of proper dining attire).

9. **Go on a C-note shopping spree at Biltmore Fashion Park.** Maybe $100 won't buy much at this boutique-filled upscale shopping plaza, but the fun of it can be trying to find the best $100 buy in the mall. Now there's a challenge to keep a shopaholic busy for the afternoon.

10. **Take a glider ride.** Sure, it sounds tame (there isn't even an engine), but opt for an aerobatic flight ($110) at Turf Soaring School (☎ **602/439-3621**) and you'll get a good idea of what it's like to be top gun. Loops and inverted flying make it clear that getting high in Arizona is a load of fun.

MALLS & SHOPPING CENTERS

Arizona Center. Van Buren St. and Third St. ☎ **480/949-4FUN.**

With its gardens and fountains, this modern downtown shopping center is both a peaceful oasis amid downtown's asphalt and a great place to shop for Arizona souvenirs (check out the Arizona Highways Gift Shop). Arizona Center is also home to several nightclubs and some of downtown's best restaurants.

Biltmore Fashion Park. E. Camelback Rd. and 24th St. ☎ **602/955-8400.**

With its garden courtyards and upscale boutiques, this open-air shopping plaza is *the* place to be if shopping is your obsession and you keep your wallet full of platinum cards. Shops bear the names of international designers and exclusive boutiques such as Polo, Gucci, Laura Ashley, and Cole-Haan. Saks Fifth Avenue and Macy's are the two anchors. There are also more than a dozen moderately priced restaurants here, and valet parking is available.

✪ **The Borgata of Scottsdale.** 6166 N. Scottsdale Rd. ☎ **480/998-1822.**

Designed to resemble a medieval Italian village complete with turrets, stone walls, and ramparts, the Borgata is far and away the most architecturally interesting shopping mall in the valley. There are about 50 upscale boutiques, art galleries, and restaurants here.

✪ **El Pedregal Festival Marketplace.** 34505 N. Scottsdale Rd., Carefree. ☎ **480/488-1072.**

Located adjacent to The Boulders resort 30 minutes north of Old Scottsdale, El Pedregal is the most self-consciously Southwestern shopping center in the valley. It's worth the long drive out here just to see the neo–Santa Fe architecture and colorful accents. The shops offer high-end merchandise, fashions, and art. The Heard Museum also has a branch here.

Scottsdale Fashion Square. 7014–590 E. Camelback Rd. (at Scottsdale Rd.), Scottsdale. ☎ **480/941-2140.**

Scottsdale has long been the valley's shopping Mecca, and for years this huge mall has been the reason why. It now houses five major department stores—Nordstrom, Dillard's, Neiman Marcus, Robinsons-May, and Sears—and smaller stores such as Eddie Bauer, J. Crew, and Louis Vuitton.

NATIVE AMERICAN ARTS, CRAFTS & JEWELRY

✪ **Bischoff's Shades of the West.** 3925 N. Brown St., Scottsdale. ☎ **480/946-6155.**

This museum-like store and gallery is affiliated with another nearby Bischoff's (see above under "Gifts & Souvenirs"). However, here you'll find higher-end jewelry, Western-style home furnishings and clothing, ceramics, books and music with a regional theme, and contemporary paintings.

Faust Gallery. 7103 E. Main St., Scottsdale. ☎ **480/946-6345.**

Old Native American baskets and pottery, as well as old and new Navajo rugs are the specialties at this interesting shop. The gallery also sells Native American and Southwest art, including ceramics, colorful paintings, bronzes, home furnishings, and unusual sculptures.

Gilbert Ortega Museum Gallery. 3925 N. Scottsdale Rd. ☎ **480/990-1808.**

You'll find Gilbert Ortega shops all over the valley (including several in Old Scottsdale), but this is the biggest and best. As the name implies, there are museum displays throughout the store. Cases full of jewelry are the main attraction here, but there are also baskets, sculptures, pottery, rugs, paintings, and kachinas. Other branches are located at 7237 E. Main St., Scottsdale (☎ **480/481-0788**); at Koshari I in the Borgata, 6166 N. Scottsdale Rd., Scottsdale (☎ **480/998-9699**); at the Hyatt Regency Hotel, 122 N. Second St., Phoenix (☎ **602/265-9923**), and at Scottsdale Fashion Square (☎ **480/423-5818**.

✪ **Heard Museum Gift Shop.** In the Heard Museum, 2301 N. Central Ave. ☎ **602/252-8344.**

The Heard Museum (see "Seeing the Sights," above) has an awesome collection of very aesthetic, extremely well-crafted, and very expensive Native American jewelry, art, and crafts of all kinds. Fortunately, because the store doesn't have to charge sales tax, you'll save a bit of money. This is the best place in the valley to shop for Native American arts and crafts; you can be absolutely assured of the quality.

⭐ **John C. Hill Antique Indian Art.** 6962 E. First Ave., Scottsdale. ☎ **480/946-2910.**

This store is for collectors and has one of the finest selections of Navajo rugs in the valley, including quite a few older ones. There are also kachinas, superb Navajo and Zuni silver-and-turquoise jewelry, baskets, and pottery. This shop sells only the highest quality items, so you can familiarize yourself with what the best looks like.

Old Territorial Shop. 7220 E. Main St., Scottsdale. ☎ **480/945-5432.**

This is the oldest Indian arts-and-crafts store on Main Street and offers good values on a large selection of jewelry, sand paintings, concha belts, kachinas, fetishes, pottery, and Navajo rugs.

OUTLET MALLS & DISCOUNT SHOPPING

Arizona Mills. 5000 Arizona Mills Circle, Tempe. ☎ **480/491-9700.** From I-10, take the Baseline Rd. east exit. From AZ 60, exit Priest Dr. south.

This huge shopping mall in Tempe is on the cutting edge when it comes to shop-o-tainment. Not only will you find lots of name-brand outlets, but you'll also find a big video arcade and an IMAX theater. With nearly ³/₄ mile of sensory bombardment, it might be a good idea to bring earplugs and walking shoes.

Last Chance. 1919 E. Camelback Rd. ☎ **602/248-2843.**

This is it, the last chance for men's and women's clothes and shoes. If it doesn't sell here, it's headed south of the border where they sell clothes by the pound. If ever there were such a thing as combat shopping, you'd find it here. The clothes are unbelievably cheap, but are often damaged goods (returns and such), so be sure to inspect every article closely before committing.

My Sister's Closet. 6206 N. Scottsdale Rd., Scottsdale (near Trader Joes). ☎ **480/443-4575.**

This is where the crème de la crème of Scottsdale's used clothing comes to be resold. You'll find such labels as Armani, Donna Karan, and Calvin Klein. Prices are pretty reasonable, too. Also at **Town & Country** shopping plaza at 20th Street and Camelback Road, Phoenix (☎ **602/954-6080**).

Wigwam Outlet Stores. 1400 N. Litchfield Rd. ☎ **623/935-9730.** Take the Litchfield Rd. exit off I-10.

If you're headed west from Phoenix and need a shopping break, you'll likely find some good deals at this outlet mall near the famous Wigwam resort. Bass, Bugle Boy, Harry & David, Mikasa, and Levi's are just some of the many stores.

WESTERN WEAR

Az-Tex Hat Company. 3903 N. Scottsdale Rd., Scottsdale. ☎ **800/972-2116** or 480/481-9900.

If you're looking to bring home a cowboy hat from your trip to Arizona, this is a good place to get it. The small shop in Old Scottsdale offers custom shaping and fitting of both felt and woven hats. There's a second store at 15044 N. Cave Creek Rd., Phoenix (☎ **602/971-9090**).

Out West. In El Pedregal Festival Marketplace, 34505 N. Scottsdale Rd., Carefree. ☎ **888/454-WEST** or 480/488-0180.

If the revival of 1950s cowboy fashions and interior decor has hit your nostalgia button, then you'll want to hightail it up to this eclectic shop. All things Western are available, and the fashions are both beautiful and fun (although fancy and pricey). They've even got home furnishings.

Saba's Western Stores. 7254 Main St., Scottsdale. ☎ **480/949-7404.**

Since 1927, this store has been outfitting Scottsdale's cowboys and cowgirls, visiting dude ranchers, and anyone else who wants to adopt the look of the Wild West. Call for other locations around Phoenix.

✪ **Sheplers Western Wear.** 9201 N. 29th Ave. ☎ **602/870-8085.**

Although it isn't the largest Western-wear store in the valley, Sheplers is still sort of a department store of cowboy duds. If you can't find it here, it just ain't available in these parts. Other locations include 8979 E. Indian Bend Rd., Scottsdale (☎ **480/ 948-1933**); 2643 E. Broadway Rd., Mesa (☎ **480/827-8244**); and 2700 W. Baseline Rd., Tempe (☎ **602/438-7400**).

Stockman's Cowboy & Southwestern Wear. 23587 N. Scottsdale Rd. (at the corner of Pinnacle Peak Rd.), Scottsdale. ☎ **480/585-6142.**

This is one of the oldest Western-wear businesses in the valley, although the store is now housed in a modern shopping plaza. You'll find swirly skirts for cowboy dancing, denim jackets, suede coats, and flashy cowboy shirts. Prices are reasonable and quality is high.

11 Phoenix After Dark

If you're looking for nightlife in the Valley of the Sun, you won't have to look hard, but you may have to drive quite a ways. Although much of the valley's nightlife scene is centered on Old Scottsdale, Tempe's Mill Avenue, and downtown Phoenix, you'll find things going on all over.

The best place to look for nightlife listings is in the *Phoenix New Times,* a weekly newspaper that tends to have the most comprehensive listings. This is also the publication to check for club listings and schedules of rock concerts at various concert halls. *The Rep Entertainment Guide,* published by *The Arizona Republic,* is another good place to look for listings of upcoming events and performances, although you won't find as many club listings as in the *New Times. The Rep* is included in the Thursday edition of the paper but is also distributed free of charge from designated newspaper boxes on sidewalks around the Valley. *Get Out,* published by the *Tribune,* is another similar tabloid format arts-and-entertainment publication that is available free and can be found around Scottsdale and Tempe. Other publications to check for abbreviated listings are *Valley Guide Quarterly, Key to the Valley, Where Phoenix/Scottsdale,* and *Quick Guide Arizona,* all of which are free and can usually be found at hotels and resorts.

Tickets to many concerts, theater performances, and sporting events are available through **Ticketmaster** (☎ **480/784-4444;** www.ticketmaster.com), which has outlets at Wherehouse Records, Tower Records, and Robinsons-May department stores. Tickets are also available at all **ETM/Dillard's** department store box offices (☎ **800/ 638-4253** or 480/503-5555).

THE CLUB & MUSIC SCENE

The Valley of the Sun has a very diverse club and music scene that's spread out across the length and breadth of the valley. However, there are a few concentrations of clubs and bars (downtown Scottsdale, Tempe's Mill Avenue, downtown Phoenix).

With at least three sports bars, as many regular bars, a massive multiplex movie theater, and half a dozen restaurants, downtown Phoenix's **Arizona Center** is a veritable entertainment mecca. Within a few blocks of this mega-entertainment complex, you'll also find Phoenix Symphony Hall, the Herberger Theater Center, and several sports bars. However, much of the action revolves around games and concerts at the America West Arena and the Bank One Ballpark (BOB).

Another place to wander around until you hear your favorite type of music is **Mill Avenue** in Tempe. Because Tempe is a college town, there are plenty of clubs and bars on this short stretch of road.

In **Scottsdale,** you'll find an eclectic array of clubs in the neighborhoods surrounding the corner of Camelback Road and Scottsdale Road (especially along Stetson Drive, which is divided into two sections east and west of Scottsdale Road). This is where the wealthy (and the wannabes) come to party, and you'll see lots of limos pulling up in front of the hot spot of the moment (currently Axis/Radius).

As we're sure you know if you're a denizen of any urban club scene, nightclubs come and go. If you're interested in finding out what's hot, check the *New Times* for ads of places that play your kind of music. Many dance clubs in the Phoenix area are open only on weekends, so be sure to check what night the doors will be open. Bars and clubs are allowed to serve alcohol until 1am.

COUNTRY

✪ Handlebar-J. 7116 E. Becker Lane, Scottsdale. ☎ **480/948-0110.** No cover–$3.

We're not saying that this Scottsdale landmark is a genuine cowboy bar, but cowpokes do make this one of their stops when they come in from the ranch. You'll hear live git-down two-steppin' 7 nights a week and free dance lessons Wednesday, Thursday, and Sunday.

The Rockin' Horse Saloon. 7316 E. Stetson Dr., Scottsdale. ☎ **480/949-0992.** Cover varies from $5 to $50.

Located in the heart of Scottsdale, the Rockin' Horse is an ever-popular bar that books the best of local and national country acts.

Rusty Spur Saloon. 7245 E. Main St. (Old Scottsdale). ☎ **480/941-2628.**

A small, rowdy, drinkin' and dancin' place frequented by tourists, this bar is a lot of fun, with peanut shells all over the floor, dollar bills stapled to the walls, and the occasional live act in the afternoon or evening.

ROCK & R&B

The Bash on Ash. 230 W. 5th St., Tempe. ☎ **480/966-8200** or 480/966-5600. Cover $2–$21.

Located in downtown Tempe, this small club is the Valley's main swing-dance club. There are lessons and live bands several nights a week.

✪ Cajun House. 7117 E. 3rd Ave., Scottsdale. ☎ **480/945-5150.** Cover $5–$13.50.

The interior of this cavernous dance club is done up as a New Orleans street scene with doors opening into various bars, dining rooms, and lounges. Lots of fun and well worth checking out.

BLUES

Char's Has the Blues. 4631 N. 7th Ave. ☎ **602/230-0205.** No cover–$6.

Yes, indeed, Char's does have those mean-and-dirty, lowdown blues, and if you want them too, this is where you head in Phoenix. All the best blues brothers and sisters from around the city and around the country make the scene. You'll find this club 4 blocks south of Camelback Road.

The Rhythm Room. 1019 E. Indian School Rd. ☎ **602/265-4842.** No cover–$15.

This blues club, long the valley's most popular, books quite a few national acts as well as the best of the local scene, and has a dance floor if you want to move to the beat.

JAZZ

Orbit Restaurant & Jazz Club. In Uptown Plaza, Central Ave. and Camelback Rd. ☎ **602/265-2354.** No cover (2-drink minimum if you're not having dinner).

Big and trendy, this space has a very urban feel to it, which is surprising considering its shopping plaza location. Orbit is one of the most popular jazz clubs in the valley, although the music line-up sometimes includes blues and Motown.

✪ **Timothy's.** 6335 N. 16th St. ☎ **602/277-7634.** No cover.

This is the valley's top upscale jazz spot and attracts a well-off crowd. There's live jazz nightly, performed by the house band or touring combos. Timothy's is hard to beat when you're looking for an elegant, romantic evening of dining and listening to lively jazz.

COMEDY & CABARET

The Tempe Improv. 930 E. University Dr., Tempe. ☎ **480/921-9877.** Cover $12–$15 plus 2-item minimum.

With the best of the national comedy circuit harassing the crowds and rattling off one-liners, the Improv is the valley's most popular comedy club. Dinner is served and reservations are advised.

DANCE CLUBS & DISCOS

✪ **Axis/Radius Nightclubs.** 7340 E. Indian Plaza, Scottsdale. ☎ **480/970-1112.** Cover $5–$10.

If you're looking to do a bit of celebrity spotting, Axis is the place. Currently Scottsdale's hottest dance club and liveliest singles scene, this two-story glass box is a boldly contemporary space with an awesome sound system. You'll find this bar 2 blocks east of Scottsdale Road and 1 block south of Camelback.

Buzz Original Funbar. Southeast corner of Scottsdale Rd. and Shea Blvd. ☎ **480/991-FUNN.** No cover–$7.

In Scottsdale, folks like to think big. The resorts are big, the houses are big, the cars are big, the restaurants are big, and the nightclubs are big. Buzz boasts three different theme areas, including the Rat Pack Lounge, the Rhino Room (with a zebra-striped dance floor), and a patio up on the roof.

Club Rio. 430 N. Scottsdale Rd., Tempe. ☎ **480/894-0533.** Cover $5.

Popular primarily with students from ASU, which is just across the Tempe Town Lake, this club has a dance floor big enough for football practice. Music is primarily Top 40, alternative, and retro music, and there are also plenty of live shows.

Pepin. 7363 Scottsdale Mall, Scottsdale. ☎ **480/990-9026.** Cover $8.

A DJ plays Latin dance music from 10pm on Friday and Saturday at this small Spanish restaurant located on the Scottsdale Mall. Thursday through Saturday evenings, there are live flamenco performances.

Phoenix Live! at Arizona Center. 455 N. 3rd St. ☎ **602/252-2502.** No cover–$5.

Located on the second floor of the Arizona Center shopping center in downtown Phoenix, this trio of clubs (a piano bar, a dance club, and a sports bar) provides enough options to keep almost any group of bar hoppers happy. Also in Arizona Center, you'll find Moondoggie's, a beach-theme bar.

Sanctuary. 7340 E. Shoeman Lane, Scottsdale. ☎ **480/970-5000.** Cover $5–$10.

As the newest hot club in downtown Scottsdale, Sanctuary has raised the bar for high-end dance clubs. As with other area mega-clubs, there are different theme rooms, including a Moroccan room. Plenty of great martinis.

THE BAR, LOUNGE & PUB SCENE

AZ88. 7353 Scottsdale Mall, Scottsdale. ☎ **480/994-5576.**

Located across the park from the Scottsdale Center for the Arts, this sophisticated bar/restaurant has a cool ambience that's just right for a martini before or after a performance. There's also a great patio area.

Bandersnatch Brew Pub. 125 E. 5th St., Tempe. ☎ **480/966-4438.**

With good house brews and a big patio in back, Bandersnatch is a favorite of those unusual ASU students who prefer quality to quantity when it's beer-drinking time. There's live music Wednesday (Celtic music) through Saturday nights.

Durant's. 2611 N. Central Ave. ☎ **602/264-5967.**

In business for decades, Durant's has long been downtown Phoenix's favorite after-work watering hole. Through wine coolers, light beers, and microbrews, Durant's has remained true to the martini and other classic cocktails.

The Famous Door. 7419 Indian Plaza, Scottsdale. ☎ **480/970-1945.**

Scottsdale's ultimate cigar bar, The Famous Door affects a Rat Pack aesthetic and treats cigars with reverence. Plenty of different martinis are available for accompaniment.

Hops! Bistro & Brewery. Scottsdale Fashion Square, 7014 E. Camelback Rd. ☎ **480/946-1272.**

Take a down-home idea—brewing your own beer—and mix it up with a bit of Phoenix chic (by way of San Diego) and you get Hops!, a huge, upscale brew pub with a boldly contemporary dining room that serves creative American cuisine.

✪ **Hyatt Regency Scottsdale Lobby Bar.** 7500 E. Doubletree Ranch Rd., Scottsdale. ☎ **480/991-3388.**

The open-air lounge just below the main lobby of this posh Scottsdale resort sets a romantic stage for nightly live music (often by Spanish guitarist Estéban). Wood fires burn in patio fire pits, and the terraced gardens offer plenty of dark spots for a bit of romance.

The Squaw Peak Bar. In the Arizona Biltmore Resort & Spa, 24th St. and Missouri Ave. ☎ **602/955-6600.**

Even if you can't afford the lap of luxury, at least you can pull up a comfortable chair in the lounge of the luxurious Arizona Biltmore. Sink into a seat next to the one you love and watch the sunset test its color palate on Squaw Peak. Alternatively, you can slide into a seat near the piano and let the waves of mellow jazz wash over you

T. Cook's. 5200 E. Camelback Rd. ☎ **602/808-0766.**

Even if you aren't planning on having dinner at this opulent Mediterranean restaurant, you'll certainly enjoy lounging in the bar. With its mix of Spanish colonial and '50s tropical furnishings, this is as romantic a lounge as you'll find anywhere in the valley. For even more romance, snuggle up out on the patio by the fireplace

Thirsty Camel. At The Phoenician, 6000 E. Camelback Rd. ☎ **480/423-2530.**

Whether you've made your millions or are still working your way up the corporate ladder, you owe it to yourself to spend a little time in lounging in the lap of luxury. You may never drink in more ostentatious surroundings than here at Charles Keating's Xanadu. The view's pretty good, too.

COCKTAILS WITH A VIEW

The Valley of the Sun has more than its fair share of spectacular views. Unfortunately, most of them are from expensive restaurants. All these restaurants have lounges, though, where for the price of a drink (and perhaps valet parking) you can sit back and ogle a crimson sunset and the purple mountains' majesty.

Your choices include **Different Pointe of View** at the Pointe Hilton Tapatio Cliffs Resort, **Rustler's Rooste** at the Pointe Hilton on South Mountain, and **Top of the Rock** at The Buttes. All these restaurants can be found in the "Where to Dine" section of this chapter.

SPORTS BARS

Alice Cooper'stown. 101 E. Jackson St. ☎ **602/253-7337.** Most nights no cover; special shows up to $25.

Sports and rock mix it up at this downtown restaurant/bar run by, you guessed it, Alice Cooper. Lots of TVs (including an impressive wall of monitors) and lots of signed sports and rock memorabilia. The Bank One Ballpark is only a block away.

America's Original Sports Bar. 455 N. 3rd St. ☎ **602/252-2502.** No cover–$5.

Located in the Arizona Center, this huge sports bar (nearly an acre) is a sort of fun center for grown-ups. There's a huge back deck and innumerable TVs (a half dozen of which are giant-screen). There's even a Phoenix Sports Hall of Fame.

Majerle's Sports Grill. 24 N. 2nd St. ☎ **602/253-9004.**

If you're a Phoenix Suns fan, you won't want to miss this sports bar only a couple of blocks from the America West Arena where the Suns play. Suns memorabilia covers the walls.

McDuffy's. 230 W. 5th St., Tempe. ☎ **480/966-5600.**

With more than 60 TVs and nearly two dozen beers on tap, this sports bar is a favorite of Sun Devils fans.

GAY & LESBIAN BARS & DANCE CLUBS

✪ **Ain't Nobody's Business.** 3031 E. Indian School Rd. ☎ **602/224-9977.**

Located in a small shopping plaza, this is the city's most popular lesbian bar, with pool tables and a nonsmoking lounge. On weekends the dance floor is usually packed.

Amsterdam. 718 N. Central Ave. ☎ **602/258-6122.**

Just a few doors away from Crowbar, Amsterdam draws a crowd that prefers sipping martinis to tossing down beers. There's no sign outside—you just have to look carefully for the number.

Crowbar. 702 N. Central Ave. ☎ **602/258-8343.** Cover $8.

This downtown Phoenix club stays packed with sweaty bodies on weekends. The decor is sort of industrial Gothic, with lots of big candles dripping wax down faux stone pillars. The after-hours scene pulls in the underagers and goes on until 4am. Open Thursday through Sunday.

THE PERFORMING ARTS

The performing-arts scene in the Valley of the Sun grows more robust with each passing year. Major performing-arts venues are scattered across the valley, so no matter where you happen to be staying, you're likely to find performances being held somewhere nearby. Downtown Phoenix claims the valley's greatest concentration of performance halls, including the Phoenix Symphony Hall, the Orpheum Theatre, and the Herberger Theater Center. You'll also find large performance halls in Scottsdale, Mesa, Tempe, Chandler, and Sun City.

Calling these venues home are the valley's major performance companies—the Phoenix Symphony, Scottsdale Symphony Orchestra, the Arizona Opera Company, Ballet Arizona, Center Dance Ensemble, Actors Theatre of Phoenix, and Arizona Theatre Company. Adding to the performances held by these companies are the wide variety of touring companies that make stops in the valley throughout the year. These national and international acts give the valley just the diversity of performers you would expect to find in a city of this size.

While you'll find box office phone numbers listed below, you can also purchase most performing-arts tickets through **Ticketmaster** (☎ 480/784-4444) or **ETM/Dillard's Box Office** outlets (☎ 800/638-4253 or 480/503-5555), found in Dillard's department stores around the city. For tickets to sold-out shows, check with your hotel concierge if you are staying at a hotel that has a concierge. Or try **Western States Ticket Service** (☎ 602/254-3300) or **Tickets Unlimited** (☎ 800/289-8497 or 602/840-2340).

MAJOR PERFORMING-ARTS CENTERS

Phoenix's premier performance venue is the **Phoenix Symphony Hall,** 225 E. Adams St. (☎ 602/262-7272), which is home to the Phoenix Symphony and the Arizona Opera Company and also hosts other classical music performances, Broadway touring shows, and various other concerts and theatrical productions

The **Orpheum Theatre,** 203 W. Adams Street (☎ 602/262-7272), a historic Spanish colonial baroque theater, was built in 1929 and at the time was considered the most luxurious theater west of the Mississippi. Today its ornately carved sandstone facade stands in striking contrast to the glass-and-steel City Hall building with which the theater shares a common wall. Today, the Orpheum is once again the most elegant performance hall in the valley, and if you have time for only one show while in town, try to make it here.

In Scottsdale, the **Scottsdale Center for the Arts,** 7380 E. Second St., Scottsdale (☎ 480/994-ARTS; www.ScottsdaleArts.org), hosts a wide variety of performances and series ranging from alternative dance to classical music. This center seems to get the best of the touring performers who come through the valley.

The Frank Lloyd Wright–designed **Grady Gammage Memorial Auditorium,** Mill Avenue and Apache Boulevard, Tempe (☎ 480/965-3434), on the Arizona State University campus, is at once massive and graceful. This 3,000-seat hall hosts everything from barbershop quartets to touring Broadway shows.

In Scottsdale, near the Borgata shopping center, you'll find **ASU's Kerr Cultural Center,** 6110 N. Scottsdale Rd. (☎ 480/965-5377), a tiny venue in a historic home. This center offers up an eclectic season that includes music from around the world.

OUTDOOR VENUES

Given the weather, it should come as no surprise that Phoenicians like to go to performances under the stars.

The city's top outdoor venue is the **Blockbuster Desert Sky Pavilion** (☎ 602/254-7200), located ½ mile north of I-10 between 79th and 83rd avenues. This

20,000-seat amphitheater is open year-round and hosts everything from Broadway musicals to rock concerts; tickets run about $10 to $70.

The **Mesa Amphitheater,** at the corner of University Drive and Center Road in Mesa (☎ **480/644-2567**), is a much smaller amphitheater that holds rock concerts throughout the summer and occasionally other times.

Throughout the year, the **Scottsdale Center for the Arts** (☎ **480/994-ARTS**) stages performances outdoors in the adjacent Scottsdale Amphitheater on the Scotts-dale Civic Center Mall.

Outdoor concerts are also held at various parks and plazas around the valley during the warmer months of the year. Check local papers for listings of such events.

Two perennial favorites of valley residents take place in particularly attractive sur-roundings. The Music in the Garden concerts at the **Desert Botanical Garden,** 1201 N. Galvin Pkwy. (☎ **480/941-1225**), in Papago Park, are held on Sundays between September and March. The season always includes an eclectic array of musical styles. Tickets are $13.50 and include admission to the gardens. Sunday brunch is served for an additional charge. Way up in Carefree, the **El Pedregal Festival Marketplace** (☎ **480/488-1072**) stages jazz, blues, and rock concerts on Thursday evenings (7 to 9:30pm) from April through June and the month of September. Tickets are $5 to $10.

CLASSICAL MUSIC, OPERA & DANCE

The **Phoenix Symphony** (☎ **800/776-9080** or 602/495-1999), the Southwest's leading symphony orchestra, performs at the Phoenix Symphony Hall (tickets run $19 to $43), while the **Scottsdale Symphony Orchestra** (☎ **480/945-8071**) performs at the Scottsdale Center for the Arts (tickets go for $15 to $20).

Opera buffs may want to see what the **Arizona Opera Company** (☎ **602/266-7464; www.azopera.com**) has scheduled. This company stages up to five operas, both familiar and more obscure, each year and splits its time between Phoenix and Tucson (tickets cost $20 to $70). Performances are held in Phoenix Symphony Hall.

Ballet Arizona (☎ **602/381-1096**) performs at the Symphony Hall, the Orpheum, and the Herberger Theater Center and stages both classical and contem-porary ballets (tickets run $16 to $48). The **Center Dance Ensemble** (☎ **602/252-8497**), the city's contemporary dance company, stages several productions a year (one during the Christmas holidays) at the Herberger Theater Center (tickets go for $18). Between September and March each year, **Southwest Arts & Entertainment** (☎ **602/482-6410**) brings acclaimed dance companies and music acts from around the world to Phoenix, with performances staged at various area venues (tickets range from about $7 to $45).

THEATER

With nearly a dozen professional companies and the same number of nonprofessional companies taking to the boards throughout the year, there is always some play being staged somewhere in the valley. So if you're a fan of live theater, check around. You're likely to find something to pique your interest.

The **Herberger Theater Center,** 222 E. Monroe St. (☎ **602/252-8497**), which is located downtown and vaguely resembles a Spanish colonial church, is the city's main hall for live theater. Its two Broadway-style theaters together host hundreds of perfor-mances each year, including productions by the **Actors Theatre of Phoenix (ATP)** and the **Arizona Theatre Company (ATC).** ATP tends to stage smaller, lesser-known off-Broadway–type works, with musicals, dramas, and comedies equally represented; tickets go for $19 to $33. ATC is the state theater company of Arizona and splits its performances between Phoenix and Tucson. Founded in 1967, the ATC is the major force on the Arizona thespian scene. Productions range from world premieres to recent Tony award-winners to classics. Tickets run $22 to $34. Also performing at the Herberger is the **Arizona Jewish Theatre Co.,** which stages plays by Jewish playwrights and with Jewish themes. Tickets range from $24.50 to $26.50.

The **Phoenix Theatre,** 100 E. McDowell Rd. (☎ **602/258-1974** or 602/254-2151), has been around for almost 80 years and stages a wide variety of productions; tickets are $25 to $27. If your interest lies in Broadway plays, see what the **Valley Broadway Series** (☎ **480/965-3434**) has scheduled. The series, focusing mostly on comedies and musicals, is held at the Gammage Auditorium in Tempe; tickets cost about $29 to $49. The **Theater League** (☎ **602/952-2881**) is another series that brings in Broadway musicals. Performances are held in the Orpheum Theatre, and tickets cost about $33 to $40. Scottsdale's small **Stagebrush Theatre,** 7020 E. Second St. (☎ **480/990-7405**), is a community theater that stages tried-and-true comedies and musicals, with the occasional drama thrown in. Tickets are about $12 to $17. For more daring new works and children's theater, check the schedule at **PlayWright's Theatre,** 1121 N. First St. (☎ **602/253-5151**). Tickets are about $12.

CASINOS

Casino Arizona. U.S. 101 and Indian Bend Rd. and U.S. 101 and McKellips Rd. ☎ **480/850-7777.**

This pair of casinos are the newest and most conveniently located casinos in the area. They're both located just off U.S. 101 on the east side of Scottsdale and offer plenty of slot machines, cards, and other games of chance.

Fort McDowell Casino. On Fort McDowell Rd. off Ariz. 87, 2 miles northeast of Shea Blvd., Fountain Hills. ☎ **800/THE-FORT.**

Phoenicians, once among the mainstay clientele of casinos in Nevada, now need not even leave the valley to throw their hard-earned dollars at the slot machines and videopoker games.

Gila River Casino. Exit 162 off I-10 south of Phoenix. ☎ **800/WIN-GILA.**

With two separate casino buildings at the same exit off I-10, the Gila River Casino wants to make sure it snags some business from passing motorists. Keno, bingo, and slots machines are available.

Harrah's Phoenix Ak-Chin Casino. 15406 Maricopa Rd., Maricopa. ☎ **800/HARRAHS.**

Located 25 miles south of Phoenix and just south of the town of Maricopa, this glitzy casino on the Ak-Chin Indian Reservation brings Las Vegas–caliber gambling to the Phoenix area. Lots of slot machines, video poker, a card room, keno, and bingo. To reach the casino, take Exit 164 (Queen Creek Road) off I-10, turn right, and drive 17 miles to Maricopa.

12 Side Trips from Phoenix

THE APACHE TRAIL

There isn't a whole lot of desert or history left in Phoenix, but only an hour's drive to the east you'll find quite a bit of both. ☻ **The Apache Trail,** a winding, partially gravel road that snakes its way around the north side of the Superstition Mountains, offers some of the most scenic desert driving in central Arizona. Along the way are ghost towns and legends, saguaros and century plants, ancient ruins and artificial lakes.

This tour includes a lot of driving on a narrow, winding gravel road, and if you'd rather leave the driving to someone else, you can take a tour of the area with **Apache**

Trail Tours (☎ 480/982-7661), which offers four-wheel-drive tours of different lengths ($60 to $125 per person), as well as hiking trips ($10 per person per hour with a 4-hour minimum) into the Superstition Mountains.

To start this drive, head east on U.S. 60 to the town of Apache Junction and then head north on Arizona 88. Just 3¹/₂ miles north of Apache Junction, you'll come to **Goldfield Ghost Town,** a reconstructed 1890s gold-mining town. Although it's a bit of a tourist trap—gift shops, an ice-cream parlor, and the like—it's also home to the **Superstition Mountain/Lost Dutchman Museum** (☎ 480/983-4888), which has interesting exhibits about the history of the area. Of particular note is the exhibit on the Lost Dutchman gold mine, perhaps the most famous mine in the country despite the fact its location is unknown. Admission to the museum is $2 for adults, $1.50 for seniors, and 75¢ for children. **Goldfield Ghost Town and Mine Tours** (☎ 480/983-0333) provides guided tours of the gold mine beneath the town ($5 for adults, $3 for children ages 6 to 12). The company also operates a narrow-gauge railroad train, which circles the town (rides are $4 for adults, $2 for children ages 5 to 12). If it's lunchtime already, you can get a meal at the steakhouse/saloon.

Not far from Goldfield is **Lost Dutchman State Park** (☎ 480/982-4485), where you can hike into the rugged Superstition Mountains and see what the region's gold seekers have been up against. Park admission is $5 per vehicle, and there is a campground that charges $10 per site.

Continuing northeast, you'll next come to **Canyon Lake,** the first of three reservoirs you'll pass on this drive. The three lakes provide much of Phoenix's drinking water, without which the city would never have been able to grow as large as it is today. Here at Canyon Lake you can go for a swim or take a cruise on the *Dolly* steamboat (☎ 480/827-9144). A 90-minute cruise on this reproduction paddle wheeler costs $14 for adults and $8 for children 6 to 12. Dinner cruises are also available. Or, for a taste of the Old West, hold out for **Tortilla Flat** (☎ 480/984-1776), an old stagecoach stop that has a restaurant, saloon, and general store, all of which are papered with business cards and more than $50,000 worth of dollar bills left by travelers who have stopped here. If it's a hot day, don't miss the prickly pear ice cream (guaranteed spineless).

A few miles past Tortilla Flat, the pavement ends and the truly spectacular desert scenery begins. Among the rocky ridges, arroyos, and canyons of this stretch of road, you'll see saguaro cacti and century plants (a type of agave that dies after sending up its 15-foot-tall flower stalk). Next you'll come to **Apache Lake,** which is in a deep canyon flanked by colorful cliffs and rugged rock formations. This lake also has a marina, as well as a campground, motel, restaurant, and general store.

Shortly before reaching pavement again, you'll reach **Theodore Roosevelt Dam.** This dam, built in 1911, forms Roosevelt Lake and is the largest masonry dam in the world.

Continuing on Arizona 88, you'll next come to ✪ **Tonto National Monument** (☎ 520/467-2241), which preserves the southernmost cliff dwellings in Arizona. These pueblos were built between 1100 and 1400 by the Salado people, and are some of the few remaining traces of this tribe, which once cultivated lands now flooded by Roosevelt Lake. The lower ruins are ¹/₂ mile up a steep trail from the visitor center, and the upper ruins are a 3-mile round-trip hike from the visitor center. The lower ruins are open daily year-round except Christmas, and the upper ruins are open November through April by reservation (reserve at least a couple of weeks in advance). The park is open daily from 8am to 5pm (you must begin the lower ruin trail by 4pm), and admission is $4 per car.

Continuing on Arizona 88 will bring you to the copper-mining town of **Globe.** The mines here are open pits, and although you can't see the mines themselves, the tailings (remains of rock removed from the copper ore) can be seen piled high all around the

The Lost Dutchman of the Superstitions

The Superstition Mountains rise up to the east of Phoenix, dark and ominous, jagged and hot. Cacti bristle across the mountains' flanks, and water is almost nonexistent. Yet for more than a century, gold-crazed prospectors have been scouring these forbidding mountains for a gold mine that may not even exist. The power of a legend is strong, and few legends are as well documented as the legend of the Lost Dutchman gold mine.

The year was 1870 when two German miners, Jacob Waltz and Jacob Weiser, set off into the Arizona wilderness east of Phoenix in hopes of striking it rich. When these two "Dutchmen" (an appellation derived from the German word *Deutsch*) returned to civilization, they carried with them pouches filled with gold nuggets. Although unsavory prospectors tried to track them to their mother lode in hopes of claim jumping, none was successful. Through visits to saloons and brothels, the two Jacobs remained tight-lipped about their mine's whereabouts.

Jacob Weiser eventually disappeared from the scene amid speculation that his partner did him in so as to keep all the gold to himself. Waltz eventually gave up prospecting in the Superstitions in 1889 at the age of 80. On his deathbed in 1891, he gave detailed directions to a Phoenix woman he had befriended. She and her foster son and the foster son's father and brother spent the next 40 years searching fruitlessly for Waltz's Lost Dutchman mine. Waltz's dying directions just weren't good enough to lead the searchers through these rugged, uncharted mountains.

Clues to the mine's location abound, and hopeful prospectors and treasure hunters have followed every possible lead in their quest for the mine. However, gold fever has led more than a few to their deaths in this harsh wilderness. While skeptics say that there's no proof there ever was a Lost Dutchman mine, others see in the mine's continued elusiveness hope that they might one day be the prospector to find this fabled mother lode.

town. In Globe, be sure to visit ✪ **Besh-Ba-Gowah Archaeological Park** (☎ **520/425-0320**), which is on the eastern outskirts of town (open daily 9am to 5pm; admission $3 for adults and $2 for seniors; children 12 and under are free). This Salado Indian pueblo site has been partially reconstructed, and several rooms are set up to reflect the way they might have looked when they were first occupied about 700 years ago. These are among the most fascinating ruins in the state. To reach Besh-Ba-Gowah, head out of Globe on South Broad Street to Jesse Hayes Road.

From Globe, head west on U.S. 60. On the west side of Superior, you'll come to ✪ **Boyce Thompson Southwestern Arboretum,** 37615 U.S. 60 (☎ **520/689-2811**), which is dedicated to researching and propagating desert plants and instilling in the public an appreciation for desert plants (open daily, except Christmas, 8am to 5pm; admission $5 adults and $2 children 5 to 12; free for children 4 and under). This was the nation's first botanical garden established in the desert, and the cactus gardens are impressive. The setting in Queen Creek and Anett canyons is quite dramatic with cliffs for a backdrop and a stream running through the gardens. As you hike the miles of nature trails, watch for the two bizarre boojum trees

If after a long day on the road you're looking for a good place to eat, stop in at **Gold Canyon Golf Resort,** 6100 S. Kings Ranch Rd., Gold Canyon (☎ **480/982-9090**), which has a good formal dining room and a more casual bar and grill.

CAVE CREEK & THE OLD WEST

A drive north from Phoenix can give you glimpses into how the pioneers once lived—and how Hollywood imagines Western towns should look.

Head north out of Phoenix on I-17 for about 20 miles and take the Pioneer Road exit. Here you'll find the ✪ **Pioneer Arizona Living History Museum,** 3901 W. Pioneer Rd. (☎ **623/465-1052**). This museum includes nearly 30 original and reconstructed buildings, and on- site you'll find costumed interpreters practicing traditional frontier activities. There are also melodramas and gunfights staged daily. Among the buildings are a carpentry shop, a blacksmith shop, a miner's cabin, a stagecoach station, a one-room schoolhouse, an opera house, a church, farmhouses, and a Victorian mansion. The museum is open October through May, Wednesday to Sunday 9am to 5pm, and June through September, Friday to Sunday 5 to 9pm. Admission is $5.75 adults, $5.25 seniors and students, $4 children 6 to 12, and free for children under 4.

Heading back south on I-17, take Exit 223 and head east to **Cave Creek** and **Carefree.** Cave Creek, founded as a mining camp in the 1870s, clings to its Wild West image and looks something like the fake cow towns all over the Arizona desert. Carefree, on the other hand, is all New West retirees, mansions, and golf courses. To learn more about the history of this area, stop in at the **Cave Creek Museum** at the corner of Skyline Drive and Basin Road (☎ **480/488-2764**). The museum is open October through May, Wednesday to Sunday 1 to 4:30pm, and admission is by donation.

Cave Creek is home to several Western steakhouses, saloons, and shops selling Western and Native American crafts and antiques. When you've worked up a thirst or a hunger, wander over to **Crazy Ed's Satisfied Frog Saloon,** 6245 E. Cave Creek Rd. (☎ **480/488-3317**), where you can get some hearty Western fare and sample Cave Creek chile beer, each bottle of which has a whole chile pepper in it. For dining with a little more finesse, consider the **Tonto Bar & Grill,** 5734 E. Rancho Mañana Blvd. (☎ **480/488-0698**), which overlooks the Rancho Mañana golf course. Patio dining and a contemporary American menu make this place an inviting spot for a meal. Rancho Mañana Boulevard is at the west end of town just off Cave Creek Road; if you can, call for a reservation.

Carefree is a much more subdued place, a planned community established in the 1950s and popular with retirees. Ho Hum Road and Easy Street are just a couple of local street names that reflect the sedate nature of the town, which is home to the exclusive Boulders resort. Boasting one of the most spectacular settings of any resort in Arizona, The Boulders also has a couple of excellent restaurants.

On Easy Street, in what passes for downtown in Carefree, you'll find one of the world's largest sundials. The dial is 90 feet across, and the gnomon (the part that casts the shadow) is 35 feet tall. From the gnomon hangs a colored-glass star, and in the middle of the dial is a pool of water and a fountain. This elaborate timepiece shows the correct time on vernal and autumnal equinoxes, but on other days of the year, you have to consult a chart next to the sundial to determine the correct time.

In downtown Carefree, you'll also find a sort of reproduction Spanish village shopping area, and just south of town, adjacent to The Boulders resort, you'll find the upscale El Pedregal Festival Marketplace shopping center, where there are lots of interesting shops, art galleries, and a few restaurants.

If you'd like to do a bit of horseback riding while you're in the area, contact **Cave Creek Outfitters** (☎ **480/471-4635**), just off Dynamite Boulevard on 144th Street. They charge $55 to $65 for a 2-hour ride. There's also plenty of good mountain biking in the area, and if you'd like do a bit of fat-tire riding, you can rent a bike from **Cave Creek Bikes,** 6149 Cave Creek Rd. (☎ **480/488-5261**), which charges $35 to $45 a day for mountain bikes.

13 En Route to Tucson

Driving southeast from Phoenix on I-10 for about 60 miles will bring you to the Florence and Casa Grande area, where you can learn about Indian cultures both past and present and view the greatest concentration of historic buildings in Arizona.

To reach Florence, continue south on I-10 to Exit 185 (Ariz. 387) and head east. Before reaching Florence, near the town of Coolidge, you'll come to ♻ **Casa Grande Ruins National Monument** (☎ 520/723-3172). In Spanish, the name means "Big House," and that's exactly what you'll find. In this instance, the big house is the ruin of an earth-walled structure built 650 years ago by the Hohokam people. Although it's still not known what purpose this unusual structure served, the building provides a glimpse of a style of ancient architecture rarely seen. Instead of using adobe bricks or stones, the people who built this structure used layers of hard-packed soil that have survived the ravages of the weather. The Hohokam people who once occupied this site began farming the valleys of the Gila and Salt rivers about 1,500 years ago, and eventually built an extensive network of irrigation canals for watering their fields. By the middle of the 15th century, however, the Hohokam had abandoned both their canals and their villages and disappeared without a trace. The monument is open daily 8am to 5pm (closed Christmas), and admission is $2 for adults.

Continuing east, you'll soon come to the farming community of **Florence.** Although at first glance this town may seem like any other small town, closer inspection turns up more than 150 buildings on the National Register of Historic Places. The majority of these buildings are constructed of adobe and were originally built in the Sonoran style, a style influenced by Spanish architectural ideas. Most buildings were altered over the years and now display aspects of various architectural styles popular during territorial days in Arizona.

Before touring the town, stop in at the **Pinal County Historical Society Museum,** 715 S. Main St. (☎ 520/868-4382), to learn more about the history of the area. It's open Wednesday to Saturday 11am to 4pm and Sunday noon to 4pm (closed from mid-July through August). Admission is by donation.

At the corner of Main Street and Ruggles Street, you'll find the **McFarland State Historic Park** (☎ 520/868-5216), which is housed in a former Pinal County Courthouse built in 1878. It's open Thursday to Monday 8am to 5pm; admission is $2 adults, $1 children ages 12 to 18. The current county courthouse, built in 1891, rises above the center of town and displays an unusual combination of different architectural styles.

To find out more about the buildings of Florence, stop in at the **Florence Visitors Center,** 291 N. Bailey St. (☎ 800/437-9433 or 520/868-9433), housed in a historic 1891 bakery in the center of town.

If you're interested in shopping deals, there are a couple of **factory-outlet shopping malls** in the town of Casa Grande at exits 194 and 198 off I-10. They are only a short distance out of your way to the south if you are headed back to Phoenix.

If you are continuing south toward Tucson from Florence, we suggest taking the scenic **Pinal Pioneer Parkway** (Ariz. 79), which was the old highway between Phoenix and Tucson. Along the way you'll see signs identifying desert plants and a memorial to silent-film star Tom Mix, who died in a car crash here in October 1940.

Alternatively, if you're heading to Tucson by way of I-10, and it isn't too hot outside, consider a stop at ♻ **Picacho Peak State Park** (☎ 520/466-3183), which is 20 miles south of Casa Grande at Exit 219. Picacho Peak, a wizard's cap of rock rising 1,500 feet above the desert, is a visual landmark for miles around. Hiking trails lead around the lower slopes of the peak and up to the summit, and these trails are especially popular in spring, when the wildflowers bloom (the park is well known as one of the best places in Arizona to see wildflowers, in fact). In addition to its natural beauty, Picacho Peak was the site of the only Civil War battle to take place in Arizona. Park admission is $5 per car and campsites are $10, or $15 with electricity and water.

14 En Route to Northern Arizona

If your idea of a great afternoon is searching out deals at factory outlet stores, then you'll be in heaven at **Prime Outlets at New River,** 4250 W. Honda Bow Rd. (☎ **623/465-9500).** Among the stores here are Barneys, Ann Taylor, Bugle Boy, Gap, Geoffrey Beene, and Levi's. Take Exit 229 (Desert Hills Rd.) off I-17.

A little farther north, you'll find the town of Rock Springs, which is barely a wide spot in the road and is easily missed by drivers roaring up and down I-17. However, if you are a fan of pies, then *do not* miss Exit 242 off the Interstate. Here you'll find the **Rock Springs Cafe** (☎ **623/374-5794,** or 602/258-9065 in Phoenix), which has been in business since 1910. Although this aging nondescript building looks like the sort of place that would best be avoided, the packed parking lot says different. Why so popular? No, it's not the coffee or the "hogs in heat" barbecue or even the Bradshaw Mountain oysters. No, what keeps this place packed are Penny's pies, the most famous pies in Arizona (32,891 sold in 1998). No matter what your favorite type might be, you'll likely find it in the pie case. If one slice isn't enough, order a whole pie to go; you can enjoy it when your day's driving is over. As the menu says, this place is "worth the drive from anywhere."

If you have an interest in innovative architecture, don't miss the Cordes Junction exit (Exit 262) off I-17. Here you'll find ✪ **Arcosanti** (☎ **520/632-7135;** www.arcosanti.org), Italian architect Paolo Soleri's vision of the future—a "city" that merges architecture and ecology.

Soleri, who came to Arizona to study with Frank Lloyd Wright at Taliesin West, envisions a compact, energy-efficient city that disturbs the natural landscape as little as possible—and that's just what's rising out of the Arizona desert here at Arcosanti. The organic design of this city built of cast concrete will fascinate both students of architecture and those with only a passing interest in the discipline. Arcosanti has been built primarily with the help of students and volunteers who come and live here for various lengths of time.

To help finance the construction, Soleri designs and sells **wind-bells** cast in bronze or made of ceramic. These distinctive bells are available at the gift shop here.

If you'd like to stay overnight, there are basic accommodations ($30 to $75 double per night) available by reservation, but you must arrive before 5pm. You'll also find a bakery and cafe on the premises. Arcosanti is open daily 9am to 5pm, and **tours** are held hourly 10am to 4pm ($5 suggested donation).

Some 71,000 acres of land east of I-17 between Black Canyon City and Cordes Junction was, in early 2000, designated the **Agua Fria National Monument,** which is administered by the Bureau of Land Management, Phoenix Field Office, 2015 W. Deer Valley Rd., Phoenix, AZ 85027-2099 (☎ **623/580-5500).** The monument was created to protect the region's numerous prehistoric Native American ruin sites, which date from between A.D. 1250 and 1450 (at least 450 prehistoric sites are known to exist in this area). There is very limited access to the monument and no facilities for visitors. The only roads within the monument are rugged dirt roads, many of which require four-wheel-drive and high clearance.

Central Arizona 5

Let's say you're planning a trip to Arizona. You're going to fly in to Phoenix, rent a car, and head north to the Grand Canyon. Glancing at a map of the state, you might easily imagine that there is nothing to see or do between Phoenix and the Grand Canyon. This is the desert, right? Miles of desolate wasteland, that sort of thing. Wrong!

Between Phoenix and the Grand Canyon lies one of the most beautiful landscapes on earth, the red-rock country of Sedona. Don't get the idea that Sedona is some sort of wilderness waiting to be discovered. Decades ago Hollywood came to Sedona to shoot westerns; then came the artists and the retirees and the New Agers. Now it seems Hollywood is back, but this time the stars are building huge homes in the hills. There's even talk of Sedona becoming the next Aspen, albeit without a ski slope (although there is one not too far away on the other side of Flagstaff).

Central Arizona isn't just red rock and retirees, though. It also has the former territorial capital of Prescott, historic sites, ancient Indian ruins, old mining towns turned artists' communities, even a few good old-fashioned dude ranches out Wickenburg way. There are, of course, thousand of acres of cactus-studded desert, but there are also high mountains, cool pine forests, and a fertile river valley, appropriately named the Verde (Green) Valley. And, heading up from Sedona's red rocks, is Oak Creek Canyon, one of the most beautiful scenic drives in the state.

If you should fall in love with this country, don't be too surprised. People have been drawn to this region for hundreds of years. The Hohokam people farmed the fertile Verde Valley as long ago as A.D. 600, followed by the Sinagua and then the first white settlers. Although the early tribes had disappeared by the time the first white settlers arrived in the 1860s, Apache and Yavapai tribes inhabited the area. It was to protect settlers from these hostile tribes that the U.S. Army established Fort Verde here in 1871.

When Arizona became a U.S. territory in 1863, Prescott was chosen as its capital, due to its central location. Although the town would eventually lose that title to Tucson and then to Phoenix, it was the most important city in Arizona for part of the late 19th century. Wealthy merchants and legislators rapidly transformed this pioneer outpost into a beautiful town filled with stately Victorian homes surrounding an imposing county courthouse.

Settlers were lured to this region not only by fertile land but also by the mineral wealth that lay hidden in the ground. Miners founded a number of communities in central Arizona, among them Jerome. When the mines shut down, Jerome was almost completely abandoned, but now artists and craftspeople have moved in to reclaim and revitalize the old mining town.

Once called the dude ranch capital of the world, Wickenburg still clings to its Western roots and has restored much of its downtown to its 1880s appearance. It is here you find most of the region's few remaining dude ranches—now called "guest ranches."

1 Wickenburg

53 miles NW of Phoenix; 61 miles S of Prescott; 128 miles SE of Kingman

Once known as the Dude Ranch Capital of the World, the town of Wickenburg, located in the desert northwest of Phoenix, attracted celebrities and families from all over the country. Those were the days when the West had only just stopped being wild, and spending the winter in Arizona was an adventure, not just a chance to escape winter weather. Today, although the area has only a handful of dude (or guest) ranches still in business, Wickenburg clings to its Wild West image. The dude ranches that remain range from rustic to luxurious, but a chance to ride the range is still the area's main attraction.

Wickenburg lies at the northern edge of the Sonoran Desert on the banks of the Hassayampa River, one of the last free-flowing rivers in the Arizona desert. The town was founded in 1863 by Prussian gold prospector Henry Wickenburg, who discovered what would eventually become the most profitable gold and silver mine in Arizona: the Vulture Mine. However, the mine closed in 1942 and today is operated as a tourist attraction.

When the dude ranches flourished back in the 1920s and 1930s, Wickenburg realized that visitors wanted a taste of the Wild West, so the town gave the tenderfoots what they wanted—trail rides, hayrides, cookouts, the works. To play up its Western heritage, Wickenburg has preserved one of its downtown streets much as it may have looked in 1900. If you've come to Arizona searching for the West the way it used to be, Wickenburg is a good place to look. Just don't expect staged shoot-outs in the streets; this ain't Tombstone.

ESSENTIALS

GETTING THERE From Phoenix, take U.S. 60, which heads northwest and becomes U.S. 93/Ariz. 89. Ariz. 89 also comes down from Prescott in the north, while U.S. 60 comes in from I-10 in western Arizona. U.S. 93 comes down from I-40 in northwestern Arizona. **Airport Express of Wickenburg** (☎ **888/684-TOMS** or 520/684-0925) offers a shuttle from the Phoenix Sky Harbor Airport to Wickenburg for $75 for two people (with 24 hours' notice) or $85 without a reservation.

VISITOR INFORMATION For more information about Wickenburg, contact the **Wickenburg Chamber of Commerce,** 216 N. Frontier St., Wickenburg, AZ 85390 (☎ **800/942-5242** or 520/684-5479; www.wickenburgchamber.com).

SPECIAL EVENTS **Gold Rush Days,** held each year on the second full weekend in February, is the biggest festival of the year in Wickenburg. Events include gold panning, a rodeo, and shoot-outs in the streets. On the second full weekend in November, the **Bluegrass Festival** features contests for fiddle and banjo. Each year on the first weekend in December, Wickenburg holds its annual **Cowboy Poetry Gathering,** with lots of poetry and music.

Get Away For Less.

Avis features GM cars.

With great offers and services from Avis, you'll get more out of your vacation! And now you can **save $20 on a weekly rental**. All the information you need is on the coupon below. Plus most rentals come with free unlimited mileage to save you even more.

As an added touch you can count on our famous "We try harder." service for a fast, hassle-free rental. Because speed and personal service is what everyone at Avis is dedicated to delivering.

For more information and reservations, call your travel agent or Avis toll free at **1-800-831-8000**.

Save $20 On A Weekly Rental

Reserve an Avis Intermediate through Full Size 4-Door car for a minimum of five consecutive days. At time of rental, present this coupon at the Avis counter and you can save $20. **An advance reservation is required.** Subject to complete Terms and Conditions below. Rental must begin by 06/30/01.

For reservations and information, call your travel consultant or Avis toll free at **1-800-831-8000**.

Terms and Conditions: Coupon valid on an Intermediate (Group C) through a Full Size 4-Door (Group E) car. Dollars off applies to the cost of the total rental with a minimum of 5 days. A Saturday night overstay is required. Coupon must be surrendered at time of rental; one per rental. Coupon valid at Avis participating locations in the U.S. An advance reservation is required. Cars subject to availability. Taxes, local government surcharges, vehicle licensing and an airport recruitment fee at some locations, optional items such as LDW, additional driver fee and refueling fee are extra. Renter must meet Avis driver and credit requirements. Minimum age is 25 but may vary by location. Rental must begin by 6/30/01.

Coupon #: **MUNA002**

Rental Sales Agent Instructions
At checkout:
In AWD, enter AWD number.
In CPN, enter **MUNA002**.
Complete this information:
RA # _____
Rental location _____
Attach to COUPON tape.

AVIS

www.avis.com   11/99 DTPP

It's a Whole New World wit

Frommer's

Central Arizona

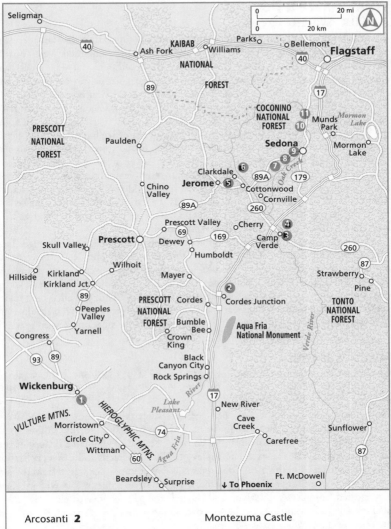

Arcosanti **2**

Boynton Canyon **9**

Crescent Moon/
   Red Rock Crossing **8**

Fort Verde State Historic Park **3**

Hassayampa River Preserve **1**

Jerome State Historic Park **5**

Montezuma Castle
   National Monument **4**

Oak Creek Canyon **11**

Red Rock State Park **7**

Slide Rock State Park **10**

Tuzigoot National Monument
   & Dead Horse Ranch State Park **6**

WHAT TO SEE & DO
A WALK AROUND TOWN

While Wickenburg's main attraction remains the several guest ranches outside town, a stroll around downtown Wickenburg provides a glimpse of the Old West. Most of the buildings were built between 1890 and the 1920s (although a few are older), and although not all of these old buildings look their age, there is just enough Western character to make a walk around on foot worthwhile (if the heat isn't too bad).

The old **Santa Fe train station** is now the Wickenburg Chamber of Commerce, which should be your first stop in town. You can pick up a map that tells a bit about the history of the town's older buildings. The brick **post office** building, almost across the street from the train station, once had a ride-up window providing service to people on horseback. **Frontier Street** is preserved as it looked in the early 1900s. The covered sidewalks and false fronts are characteristic of frontier architecture; the false fronts often disguised older adobe buildings that were considered "uncivilized" by settlers from back east. The oldest building in town is the **Etter General Store,** adjacent to the Gold Nugget Restaurant. The old adobe-walled store was built in 1864 and has long since been disguised with a false wooden front.

Two of the town's most unusual attractions aren't buildings at all. The **Jail Tree,** behind the Circle K store at the corner of Wickenburg Way and Tegner Street, is an old mesquite tree that served as the local hoosegow. Outlaws were simply chained to the tree. Their families would often come to visit and have a picnic in the shade of the tree. The second, equally curious, town attraction is the **Wishing Well,** which stands beside the bridge over the Hassayampa. Legend has it that anyone who drinks from the Hassayampa River will never tell the truth again. How it became a wishing well is unclear.

MUSEUMS & MINES

Desert Caballeros Western Museum. 21 N. Frontier St. ☎ **520/684-2272.** Admission $5 adults, $4 senior citizens, $1 children 6–16, free for children under 6. Mon–Sat 10am–5pm; Sun noon–4pm. Closed major holidays.

Wickenburg thrives on its Western heritage, and inside this museum you'll find Western art depicting life on the range in the days of "cowboys and Indians." Although it's not too large, the museum manages to convey a great deal about the history of this part of Arizona. There's an excellent display of colorful minerals and a small collection of Indian artifacts. On the main floor, dioramas depict important scenes from the history of the Wickenburg region. Downstairs, a 1900 street scene from a Western town is re-created, complete with saloon and general store. There are also regularly scheduled special exhibits and an art collection containing work by Remington, Russell, and members of the Cowboy Artists of America.

Robson's Arizona Mining World. Ariz. 71, 28 miles west of Wickenburg. ☎ **520/685-2609.** Admission $5 adults, $4.50 seniors, free for children 10 and under. Daily 10am–4pm. Closed May 1–Oct 15. Head west out of Wickenburg on U.S. 60 and, after 24 miles, turn north on Ariz. 71.

Boasting the world's largest collection of antique mining equipment, this private museum is a must for anyone who is fascinated by Arizona's rich mining history. Located on the site of an old mining camp, the museum consists of 26 buildings filled with antiques. More like a ghost town than a museum, Robson's buildings contain displays pertaining to life in a mining camp. In addition to touring the museum, you can pan for gold or hike to see Native American petroglyphs. A three-story hotel (no credit cards accepted) and a restaurant are also on the premises.

The Vulture Mine. Vulture Mine Rd. ☎ **602/859-2743.** Admission $5 adults, $4 children 6–12, free for children under 6. Oct–Mar Thurs–Mon 8am–4pm; Apr–Sept Fri–Sun 8am–4pm. Take U.S. 60 west out of town, turn left on Vulture Mine Rd. and drive 12 miles south.

Lying at the base of Vulture Peak (the most visible landmark in the Wickenburg area), the Vulture Mine was first staked by Henry Wickenburg in 1863. This mine fueled the small gold rush that helped populate this section of the Arizona desert. Today the Vulture Mine has the feel of a ghost town and can be explored by self-guided tour or guided tour with prior arrangements.

A BIRDER'S PARADISE

✪ **Hassayampa River Preserve.** 49614 U.S. 60 (3 miles south of Wickenburg on U.S. 60). ☎ **520/684-2772.** Admission $5 suggested donation (free for Nature Conservancy members). Mid-Sept to mid-May Wed–Sun 8am–5pm; mid-May to mid-Sept Wed–Sun 6am–noon. Closed major holidays.

At one time the Arizona desert was laced with rivers that flowed for most, if not all, of the year. In the past 100 years, however, these rivers, and the riparian (waterside) habitats they once supported, have disappeared at an alarming rate due to the damming of rivers and the lowering water tables caused by the large number of wells drilled throughout the state. Riparian areas support trees and plants that require more water than is usually available in the desert, and this lush growth provides food and shelter for hundreds of species of birds, mammals, and reptiles. Thus, the rapidly disappearing riparian areas of the state play an ever more important role in supporting wild plants and animals in the desert. Today, the riparian cottonwood-willow forests of the desert Southwest are considered the country's most endangered forest type.

The Nature Conservancy, a nonprofit organization dedicated to purchasing and preserving threatened and endangered habitats, owns and manages the Hassayampa River Preserve, which is now one of the state's most important bird-watching sites (more than 230 species of birds have been spotted within the preserve). Nature trails lead along the river beneath cottonwoods and willows and past the spring-fed Palm Lake. There is a visitor center and bookshop, and naturalist-guided walks are offered. Although the guided walks are free, reservations are required (call the preserve for the current schedule).

OUTDOOR PURSUITS

Even if you aren't staying at a guest ranch, you can go horseback riding in the Wickenburg area. **No Fences on Moonlight Mesa** (☎ 520/684-3308) is run by Dianna Tangen, who offers guided horseback rides on well-trained quarter horses. Two-hour rides cost $35 per person, and a 6-hour ride in Box Canyon costs $60.

Jeep tours of the area are available through **Wickenburg Jeep Tours,** 295 E. Wickenburg Way (☎ 800/596-5337 or 520/684-0438). Tour prices range from $50 to $70 for adults, and from $25 to $35 for children ages 12 and under.

If you want to play a round of golf, try **Los Caballeros Golf Club,** 1551 S. Vulture Mine Rd. (☎ 520/684-2704), which has been rated one of the best courses in the state. Greens fees are about $110 in peak season and $44 in the summer.

If you'd rather do some hiking, there are a couple of interesting options. Southwest of town at the end of Vulture Mine Road (off U.S. 60), you can climb **Vulture Peak,** which is a steep climb best done in the cooler months. However, the views from up top (or even just the saddle near the top) are well worth the effort. For an easier hike, stop by the Wickenburg Chamber of Commerce information center and get its map of **Box Canyon,** a scenic stretch of the Hassayampa River.

WHERE TO STAY
GUEST RANCHES

Flying E Ranch. 2801 W. Wickenburg Way, Wickenburg, AZ 85390. ☎ **520/684-2690.**
Fax 520/684-5304. www.flyingeranch.com. 17 units. A/C TV. $220–$285 double. Rates
include all meals. Minimum stay is 2–4 nights. No credit cards. Closed June–Oct. Drive 4 miles
west of town on U.S. 60.

Of the handful of guest ranches still operating in Wickenburg, this is the only real
working cattle ranch, and there are 20,000 high, wide, and handsome acres for you
and the cattle to roam. Family-owned since 1952, this ranch attracts plenty of repeat
business, with families finding it a particularly appealing and down-home kind of
place. The main lodge features a spacious lounge where guests like to gather by the
fireplace. The guest rooms vary in size, but all have Western-style furnishings. There
are either twin or king-size beds in the rooms.

Dining/Diversions: Three family-style meals are served in the wood-paneled dining room, but there's no bar, so you'll need to bring your own liquor. There are also
breakfast cookouts, lunch rides, and evening chuck-wagon dinners.

Amenities: Horseback riding ($25 to $35 per day additional), small outdoor pool,
whirlpool, sauna, exercise room, tennis court, shuffleboard, table tennis, horseshoes,
hayrides, guest rodeos.

✪ **Kay El Bar Guest Ranch.** Rincon Rd. (off U.S. 93; P.O. Box 2480), Wickenburg, AZ
85358. ☎ **800/684-7583** or 520/684-7593. Fax 520/684-4497. www.kayelbar.com. 10
units, 1 cottage. $275 double; $300 cottage for 2. Rates include all meals. Minimum stay may
apply. MC, V. Closed May 1 to mid-Oct.

This is the smallest and oldest of the Wickenburg guest ranches, and its old adobe
buildings, built between 1914 and 1925, are listed in the National Register of Historic
Places. New owners John and Nancy Loftis, who took over in 1997, have added two
new rooms. The rest of the ranch, which has been in business for more than 70 years,
remains unchanged. However, it is well maintained and quintessentially Wild West in
style and decor (telegraph poles hold up the ceiling of the main lodge, where there is a
large stone fireplace). The setting, on the bank of the (usually dry) Hassayampa River
bed, lends the ranch a surprisingly lush feel compared with the arid surrounding landscape. While the cottage and the new Casa Grande room are the most spacious here,
the smaller lodge rooms, in the adobe main lodge, have the original Monterey-style furnishings and other classic 1950s dude ranch decor. The ranch has only 60 acres, but it
abuts thousands of acres of public lands where guests can ride or hike.

Dining/Diversions: A tile floor and beehive fireplace in the dining room provide
an authentic Southwestern feel. The meals vary from Chinese to prime rib, and are
served in heaping portions. There's also a fully stocked bar.

Amenities: Horseback riding (included in rates), small outdoor pool.

✪ **Merv Griffin's Wickenburg Inn and Dude Ranch.** 34801 N. Hwy. 89, Wickenburg, AZ
85390. ☎ **800/942-5362.** Fax 520/684-2981. 63 units. www.merv.com. A/C TV TEL. Mid-
Feb to May (plus Thanksgiving and Christmas) $350–$410 double, $470–$840 casita; June–Sept
$236–$250 double, $280–$520 casita; Oct to mid-Feb (except Thanksgiving and Christmas)
$310–$365 double, $415–$792 casita (all rates plus 16% service charge). Rates include all meals
and horseback riding. 16% gratuity added to all bills. AE, CB, DC, DISC, MC, V.

Located 8 miles north of Wickenburg and 2 miles down a gravel road, the Wickenburg Inn is big country, just the sort of place people dream about when they think of
an Arizona ranch vacation. As you enter the ranch down its long driveway, the view
takes in nothing but miles of open desert. However, don't expect cowboy accommodations; this place is as luxurious as most resorts, just without the glitz. With its nature
center and educational programs for kids, it is also a good place to bring the family.

The casitas here are cottages built to resemble old Spanish colonial adobes, with red-tile roofs and porches made from rough-hewn logs. Inside are kitchenettes with tile counters, fireplaces, high-beamed ceilings, and wet bars. Deluxe suites have sundecks, and studios have similar styling to suites. Lodge rooms are fairly small, but they offer the most economical choice.

Dining/Diversions: Meals are a combination of Southwestern fare and steaks, and a couple of nights each week there are campfire cookouts in the desert.

Amenities: Horseback riding and lessons (all-day rides and cattle drives are an additional charge), lessons in roping and barrel racing, two pools (one with sand beach for kids), whirlpools, tennis courts, arts-and-crafts center, nature center, jogging trail, children's programs, baby-sitting, guided nature hikes.

Rancho de los Caballeros. 1551 S. Vulture Mine Rd. (off U.S. 60 west of town), Wickenburg, AZ 85390. ☎ **800/684-5030** or 520/684-5484. Fax 520/684-2267. www.SunC.com. 79 units. A/C TV TEL. Oct–Jan and May $289–$339 double, $399 suite; Feb–Apr $339–$399 double, $499 suite (all rates plus 15% gratuity). Rates include all meals (riding and golf packages also available). No credit cards. Closed mid-May to mid-Oct.

Located on 20,000 acres 2 miles west of Wickenburg, Rancho de los Caballeros is part of an exclusive country club–resort community and as such feels more like an exclusive resort than a guest ranch. However, the main lodge building itself, with its flagstone floor, large copper fireplace, and colorfully painted furniture, has a very Southwestern feel. Peace and quiet are the keynotes of a visit here, and most guests focus on golfing (the golf course is one of the best in the state) and horseback riding. Guest rooms are filled with handcrafted Southwestern-style furnishings and for the most part have a classically ranch character. Exposed-beam ceilings, Indian rugs, and, in some rooms, tile floors complete the Southwestern motif. Some rooms have their own fireplaces.

Dining/Diversions: While breakfasts and lunches here are quite casual, dinner is a rather formal affair, with proper attire required. After dinner, you can catch a little cowboy music or an old western movie in the ranch's "saloon."

Amenities: Horseback riding ($30 to $45 per ride), small outdoor pool, four tennis courts, 18-hole golf course ($90 greens fee with cart), pro shop, trap and skeet shooting ($30 per round), mountain bike rentals, star gazing, laundry service, in-room massages, children's programs, baby-sitting.

OTHER ACCOMMODATIONS

Best Western Rancho Grande. 293 E. Wickenburg Way, Wickenburg, AZ 85390. ☎ **800/854-7235** or 520/684-5445. Fax 520/684-7380. 80 units. A/C TV TEL. $63–$110 double. AE, CB, DC, DISC, MC, V. Pets accepted.

Located right in the heart of downtown Wickenburg, this Best Western is built in Spanish colonial style, with tile roofs, stucco walls, arched colonnades, and tile murals. There's a wide range of room types and prices. At the higher end you get a larger room, a larger bathroom (with a phone), large towels, and a coffeemaker. The hotel has an outdoor pool, a whirlpool, and a tennis court. Because this motel is right downtown, it's within walking distance of good restaurants and the town's historic sites.

WHERE TO DINE

Get a quick salad, sandwich, or juice right in the center of downtown Wickenburg at the friendly **Pony Espresso Café**, 233 E. Wickenburg Way (☎ **520/684-0208**).

✪ **Griff's at the Wickenburg Inn.** Ariz. 89 (Prescott Hwy.). ☎ **520/684-7811.** Reservations recommended. Lunch items $6–$9; main courses dinner $8–$24; barbecue cookouts Tues and Sat nights $25 adults, $15 children 11 and under. AE, CB, DC, DISC, MC, V. Daily 7–10am and 11:30am–2:30pm; Sun–Mon and Wed–Fri 6–10pm. 8 miles north of town on Ariz. 89. AMERICAN.

While most of the people eating here are usually guests of the ranch, the restaurant is open to the public by advance reservation and is one of the best places in the area for a meal if you aren't already staying at another guest ranch. The remote setting amid rolling desert hills and the old-fashioned Southwestern feel of the lodge make a meal here a very Arizona experience. Stone and raw wood give the dining room a rugged feeling, but creature comforts are not overlooked. Main courses are typically upscale ranch fare (steak, ribs, trout, burgers). The restaurant is closed on Tuesday and Saturday nights, when cookouts are offered. Call for cookout reservations and starting times.

House Berlin. 169 E. Wickenburg Way. ☎ **520/684-5044.** Main courses lunch $6–$11, dinner $9–$14. MC, V. Tues–Sun 11:30am–2pm and 5–9pm. GERMAN/CONTINENTAL.

For some strange reason, Germans seem to love the desert, so it shouldn't really come as a surprise that good German food is available in Wickenburg. The restaurant is small and casual and serves a mix of German and other continental dishes. Because of bad visibility when exiting from the restaurant's parking lot, it's a good idea to park on the street.

Rancho de los Caballeros. 1551 S. Vulture Mine Rd. ☎ **520/684-5484.** Reservations required. Jackets required for men. Lunch $11–$14, complete dinner $23. No credit cards. Mon–Sat 12:30–1:30pm and 6:30–8:30pm; Sun noon–2pm (buffet lunch) and 6:30–8:30pm. Closed mid-May to mid-Oct. CONTINENTAL/SOUTHWESTERN.

Wickenburg's most exclusive guest ranch also opens its restaurant to the public. The formerly conservative menu has been updated with contemporary Southwestern dishes, and although it changes daily, you always have a choice of several soups and salads, main courses, and half-a-dozen desserts. You might start your meal with *albondigas,* a Spanish-style meatball soup, or black bean soup with goat cheese, and then move on to chile-accented salmon with a cilantro and basil sauce or steak au poivre with a spinach soufflé. For dessert, you might choose crème brûlée or chocolate mousse pie. Men are required to wear a sports jacket or western vest, and women must also dress appropriately.

EN ROUTE TO PRESCOTT

Between Wickenburg and Prescott, Ariz. 89 climbs up out of the desert at the town of **Yarnell,** which lies at the top of a steep stretch of road. The landscape around Yarnell is a jumble of weather-worn granite boulders that give the town a unique appearance. Several little craft and antiques shops here are worth a stop, but the town's main claim to fame is the **Shrine of St. Joseph of the Mountains,** which is known for its carved stone stations of the cross.

2 Prescott

100 miles N of Phoenix; 60 miles SW of Sedona; 87 miles SW of Flagstaff

What attracts many people to Prescott, the former territorial capital of Arizona, is that it doesn't seem like Arizona at all. With its stately courthouse on a tree-shaded square, its well-preserved historic downtown business district, and its old Victorian homes, Prescott wears the air of the quintessential American small town, the sort of place where the Broadway musical *The Music Man* might have been staged. Prescott has just about everything a small town should have: a soda fountain (Déjà Vu), a burger shop (Kendall's), an 1890s saloon (The Palace), an old cattlemen's hotel (Hassayampa Inn), a brew pub (Prescott Brewing Company); a French crêperie (Provence), and a European-style cafe (Café St. Michaels). Add to this several small museums, a couple of historic hotels, and the nearby Prescott National Forest, and you have a town that appeals to visitors with a diverse range of interests.

The town's Anglo history dates from 1863, when the Walker party discovered gold in the mountains of central Arizona. Soon miners were flocking to the area to seek their own fortunes. A year later, in 1864, Arizona became a U.S. territory, and the new town of Prescott, located right in the center of Arizona, was made the territorial capital. Prescott later lost its statewide influence when the capital moved to Phoenix, but because of the importance of ranching and mining in central Arizona, Prescott continued to be a very important regional town. Today Prescott has become an upscale retirement community, as retirees rediscover Arizona's once-bustling territorial capital and the mild year-round climate here. In summer, Prescott is also a popular weekend getaway for Phoenicians, since it is usually 20° cooler here than it is in Phoenix.

ESSENTIALS

GETTING THERE   Prescott is at the junction of Ariz. 89, Ariz. 89A, and Ariz. 69. If you're coming from Phoenix, take the Cordes Junction exit (Exit 262) from I-17. If you're coming from Flagstaff, the most direct route is I-17 to Ariz. 169 to Ariz. 69. From Sedona, just take Ariz. 89A all the way.

There is regularly scheduled service between Prescott's Ernest A. Love Airport, on U.S. 89, and the Phoenix Sky Harbor Airport on **America West** airlines (☎ **800/235-9292** for schedule information).

Shuttle "U" provides shuttle service between Prescott and the Phoenix Sky Harbor Airport. The fare is $24 one way and $42 round-trip. Phone ☎ **800/304-6114** (out of the Prescott area) or 520/772-6114 for schedule information.

ORIENTATION   Ariz. 89 comes into Prescott on the northeast side of town, where it joins with Ariz. 69 coming in from the east. Five miles north of town, Ariz. 89A from Sedona also merges with Ariz. 89. The main street into town is **Gurley Street,** which forms the north side of the Courthouse Plaza. **Montezuma Street,** also known as Whiskey Row, forms the west side of the plaza. If you continue south on Montezuma Street, you'll be on Ariz. 89 heading toward Wickenburg.

VISITOR INFORMATION   For more information on Prescott, contact the **Prescott Chamber of Commerce,** 115 W. Goodwin St. (P.O. Box 1147), Prescott, AZ 86302 (☎ **800/266-7534** or 520/445-2000; www.prescott.org).

GETTING AROUND   If you need to rent a car, contact **Budget** (☎ **800/527-0700** or 520/778-3806) or **Enterprise Rent-A-Car** (☎ **800/RENT-A-CAR** or 520/778-6506). If you need a taxi, call **Ace City Cab** (☎ **520/445-1616**).

SPECIAL EVENTS   The ❸ **World's Oldest Rodeo** is held each year in early July as part of the city's Prescott Frontier Days celebration. Also included in this celebration are a Western art show, a golf tournament, a carnival, and a parade. Territorial Days, held in early to mid-June, is another big annual festival with special art exhibits, performances, tournaments, races, and lots of food and free entertainment. In mid-July, the Sharlot Hall Museum hosts the **Prescott Indian Art Market,** and on the third weekend in August the **Arizona Cowboy Poets' Gathering** takes place there as well. Prescott is also officially recognized as Arizona's Christmas City. During December, the city is decked out with lights, and there are numerous holiday events.

EXPLORING THE TOWN

A walk around the **Courthouse Plaza** should be your introduction to Prescott. The stately old courthouse in the middle of the tree-shaded plaza sets the tone for the whole town. The building, far too large for a small regional town such as this, dates from the days when Prescott was the capital of the Arizona Territory. Under the big shade trees of this plaza, you'll find several large bronze statues of cowboys and soldiers.

Surrounding the courthouse and extending north for a block is Prescott's **historic business district.** Stroll around admiring the brick buildings, and you'll realize that Prescott was once a very important place. Duck into an old saloon or the lobby of one of the town's two historic hotels, and you'll understand that the town was also part of the Wild West. After you've gotten a taste of Prescott, there are several museums, listed below, you might like to visit.

To learn more about the history of Prescott, contact **Prescott Historical Tours,** 815 Bertrand Ave. (☎ **520/445-4567**), which offers a historical tour of Prescott ($40 per couple) and a Victorian tea tour ($50 per couple). Call for a reservation.

Phippen Museum. 4701 U.S. 89N. ☎ **520/778-1385.** Admission $3 adults, $2 seniors and students, children 12 and under free. Mon and Wed–Sat 10am–4pm; Sun 1–4pm.

If you're a fan of classic Western art, you won't want to miss this small museum. Located on a hill a few miles north of town, the Phippen Museum exhibits works by both established Western artists and newcomers and is named after the first president of the prestigious Cowboy Artists of America organization. The museum also displays historical artifacts and photos that help place the artwork in the context of the history of the region. Each year on Memorial Day weekend the museum sponsors the **Phippen Western Art Show.** In the museum store, more than 100 Arizona artists are represented.

✪ **Sharlot Hall Museum.** 415 W. Gurley St. ☎ **520/445-3122.** Admission by suggested donation: $4 adult, $3 senior citizens, $5 family. Apr 1–Oct 31 Mon–Sat 10am–5pm, Sun 1–5pm; Nov 1–Mar 31 Mon–Sat 10am–4pm, Sun 1–5pm. Closed Thanksgiving, Christmas, and New Year's Day.

In 1882, at the age of 12, Sharlot Hall traveled to the Arizona territory with her parents. From an early age she was fascinated by frontier life. As an adult, she became a writer and historian and began collecting artifacts from Arizona's pioneer days. From 1909 to 1911 she was the territorial historian, an official government position. In 1928 she opened this museum in Prescott's **Old Governor's Mansion,** a log home built in 1864. Eventually, through the donations of others and the activities of the local historical society, the museum grew into the present complex of historic buildings and gardens.

In addition to the Old Governor's Mansion, which is furnished much as it might have been when it was built, there are several other interesting buildings that can be toured. The **Frémont House** was built in 1875 for the fifth territorial governor. Its traditional wood-frame construction shows how quickly Prescott grew from a remote logging and mining camp into a civilized little town. The 1877 **Bashford House** reflects the Victorian architecture that was popular throughout the country around the turn of the century. The **Sharlot Hall Building** was built of stone and pine logs in 1934 and now houses museum exhibits on prehistoric and historic Native American cultures and territorial Arizona. Other buildings of interest include a blacksmith's shop, a schoolhouse, a gazebo, a ranch house built by Sharlot Hall, and an old windmill.

The museum's rose garden honors famous women of Arizona. Every year in early summer, artisans, craftspeople, and costumed exhibitors participate in the **Folk Arts Fair.**

The Smoki Museum. 147 N. Arizona St. ☎ **520/445-1230.** Admission $4. May–Sept Mon–Sat 10am–4pm, Sun 1–4pm; Oct Fri–Sun 10am–4pm, Sun 1–4pm. Closed Nov–Apr.

This interesting little museum, which houses a collection of Native American artifacts in a historic stone building, is named for the fictitious Smoki tribe. The tribe was dreamed up in 1921 by a group of non-Indians who wanted to inject some new life into Prescott's July 4th celebrations. Despite its phony origins, the museum contains genuine artifacts and basketry from many different tribes, mainly Southwestern.

ENJOYING THE OUTDOORS

Prescott's most readily recognizable natural landmark is **Thumb Butte,** a rocky outcropping that towers over the forest just west of town. A trail leads nearly to the top of this butte, and from the saddle near the top of the butte is a panoramic vista of the entire region. To hike up Thumb Butte, head west out of town on Gurley Street, which becomes Thumb Butte Road. Follow the road until you see the National Forest signs, after which there's a parking lot, picnic area and a trailhead for the trail that leads up the butte. Parking costs $2. The trail itself is very steep but is paved much of the way. The summit of the butte is a popular rock-climbing spot. An alternative return trail makes a loop hike possible.

A few miles north of town on Ariz. 89 is an unusual and scenic area known as the **Granite Dells.** Here, jumbled hills of rounded granite suddenly jut up from the landscape, creating a maze of huge boulders and smooth rock. In the middle of this dramatic landscape lies Watson Lake, the waters of which push their way in among the boulders to create one of the prettiest lakes in the state. On the highway side of the lake, you'll find Watson Lake Park, which has picnic tables and great views. However, if you turn east onto Sun Dog Ranch Road, which is between Prescott and the Granite Dells, and follow this road for about 1 1/2 miles, you'll find a trailhead parking area for the Peavine Trail, a rails-to-trails path that extends for several miles through the middle of the Granite Dells. This trail is the best way to see the Granite Dells. Also accessible from this same trailhead is the Watson Woods Riparian Preserve, which has some short trails through the wetlands and riparian zone along Granite Creek.

Prescott is situated on the edge of a wide expanse of high plains with the pine forests of **Prescott National Forest** at its back. There are hiking trails, several lakes, and campgrounds within the national forest. Of particular note is the Granite Mountain Wilderness northwest of town. Here you'll find excellent hiking opportunities. For maps and information, stop by the Prescott National Forest Office, 344 S. Cortez St. (☎ 520/771-4700).

If you want to explore the area on horseback, there are several options. **Rafter 6 Outdoor Adventures,** P.O. Box 618, Chino Valley, AZ 86323 (☎ **520/636-5007**), does everything from 1 1/2-hour rides ($30) to overnight cowboy campouts ($160 per day) to chuck wagon rides ($65). **Prescott Ranch** (☎ **800/684-7433** or 520/636-9737), about 25 minutes north of Prescott off Ariz. 89 near the town of Paulden, offers guided trail rides in the Prescott National Forest. A 2-hour trail ride is $35. Reserve in advance. Also in the Paulden area, the **Double D Ranch** (☎ **520/636-0418**), which also operates a B&B, leads all-day rides into the Prescott National Forest. These rides visit ancient Indian ruins and even include a bit of six-gun and Winchester practice. Rides run $90 to $200 per person, depending on the number of people in the group, and include dinner.

Reasonably priced golfing is available at the **Antelope Hills Golf Courses,** 1 Perkins Dr. (☎ **800/972-6818** in Arizona or 520/776-7888).

SHOPPING

Downtown Prescott is filled with antiques stores, especially along North Cortez Street. In the Hotel St. Michael's shopping arcade, check out **Hotel Trading,** 110 S. Montezuma St. (☎ 520/778-7276), an Indian arts shop that carries some genuine antique Native American artifacts at reasonable prices. Also in this same block of Montezuma Street is the **Arts Prescott Cooperative Gallery,** 134 S. Montezuma St. (☎ **520/776-7717**), a cooperative of local artists. Prices here are very reasonable.

WHERE TO STAY
EXPENSIVE

Double D Ranch Bed & Breakfast & Horses. P.O. Box 334, Paulden, AZ 86334. ☎ **520/636-0418.** www.virtualcities.com. 2 units. $160 double for 1 night; $145 double for 2 nights or more; $60 each additional person; $160 per night double depending on availability. Rates include full breakfast. AE, DISC, MC, V.

Located out in the ranch country north of Prescott, this B&B is something of a miniature guest ranch—there are lots of horses, chickens, and other ranch animals, and guests tend to spend their days horseback riding. At the end of a day in the saddle, you can soak your sore muscles in the inn's unique "cowboy hot tub," which is made from a horse watering trough! Innkeepers Doug and Denise Dipietro (the Double Ds of the name) take only one group of guests at a time, so when you show up, you'll have the unusual rammed-earth ranch house all to yourself. With its flagstone floors and contemporary decor, the house is much more 1990s than 1890s. All-day rides into the adjacent national forest run $90 to $200 per person, including dinner, depending on the size of the group. For $40 per person, Denise, a certified chef, can prepare gourmet dinners. Family-style dinners are available for $15 per person.

✪ **Hassayampa Inn.** 122 E. Gurley St., Prescott, AZ 86301. ☎ **800/322-1927** or 520/778-9434. Fax 520/445-8590. www.hassayampainn.com. 68 units. A/C TV TEL. Apr–Oct $111–$141 double, $155–$195 suite; Nov–Mar $99–$129 double, $155–$195 suite. Rates include full breakfast. AE, DC, DISC, MC, V.

The Hassayampa Inn, which is listed on the National Register of Historic Places, was built as a luxury hotel in 1927 and evokes the time when Prescott was the bustling capital of the Arizona Territory. In the lobby, stenciled exposed ceiling beams, wrought-iron chandeliers, and arched doorways all reflect a Southwestern heritage. Each guest room is unique and features either original furnishings or antiques. One room is even said to be haunted, and any hotel employee will be happy to tell you the story of the ill-fated honeymooners whose ghosts are said to reside here.

Dining/Diversions: The Peacock Room exudes the same classic elegance as the rest of the hotel. A small lounge with art nouveau styling provides a quiet place to have a drink in the evening.

Amenities: Room service, laundry service, access to nearby health club.

Prescott Resort, Conference Center and Casino. 1500 Hwy. 69, Prescott, AZ 86301. ☎ **800/967-4637** or 520/776-1666. Fax 520/776-8544. www.prescottresort.com. 160 units. A/C TV TEL. $129–$159 double; $149–$179 suite. AE, MC, V.

This is Prescott's only full-service resort hotel; although its focus is on conferences, its small casino is aimed at siphoning off some of the business that once went to Laughlin or Las Vegas. Built high on a hill overlooking the city and the surrounding valley and mountains, the resort has the best view of any lodging in Prescott. However, the town's Western heritage is played up only in the overabundance of Western art that covers the walls leading out from the lobby. Public rooms aside, the guest rooms are spacious and comfortable, and each has its own balcony overlooking the valley.

Dining/Diversions: The dining room here offers a stunning panorama to accompany the fine meals. For a drink and conversation, there's a lobby lounge. The 24-hour casino is the resort's biggest draw for many guests.

Amenities: Outdoor pool, tennis courts, racquetball courts, exercise room, art gallery, salon services, room service, valet/laundry service.

MODERATE

Hotel Vendome. 230 S. Cortez St., Prescott, AZ 86303. ☎ **888/468-3583** or 520/776-0900. Fax 520/771-0395. www.vendomehotel.com. 21 units. AC TV TEL. $69–$169 double; $99–$189 suite. Rates include continental breakfast. AE, CB, DC, DISC, MC, V.

Built in 1917 as a lodging house, this restored two-story brick building is only 2 blocks from the action of Whiskey Row, but far enough away from the action that you can get a good night's sleep. The guest rooms are outfitted with new furnishings, but some still have original clawfoot tubs in the bathrooms. Others have modern oval tubs, and all have built-in water filters, air filters, and overhead fans. Of course, this hotel has its own resident ghost as well. Not quite as luxurious as the Hassayampa, yet not as basic as the St. Michael, the Vendome offers a good middle-price choice for anyone who wants to stay in a historic hotel.

The Marks House Victorian Bed & Breakfast. 203 E. Union St., Prescott, AZ 86303. ☎ **800/370-6275** or 520/778-4632. www.virtualcities.com/ons/az/r/azr2602.htm. 4 units. $85–$135 double. Rates include full breakfast. DISC, MC, V.

Located high on a hill only a block from the courthouse, this large Victorian inn has the best views of any B&B in town. While not as immaculate as some of the others, The Marks House has the most authentic atmosphere and some of the most interesting rooms. The Princess Victoria room features an unusual copper bathhouse-style tub, while in the Queen Anne room, you'll find a clawfoot tub in one corner of the room and a small turret sitting area in another. The evening social hour is a good time to get to know the innkeepers. So many B&Bs claim to be just like Grandma's house, but this one really is.

✪ Rocamadour Bed & Breakfast for (Rock) Lovers. 3386 N. Hwy. 89, Prescott, AZ 86301. ☎ **888/771-1933** or 520/771-1933. www.rocamadour-inn-arizona.com. 4 units. A/C TV TEL. $95–$135 double; $195 suite. Rates include full breakfast. AE, MC, V.

The Granite Dells, just north of Prescott, is the area's most amazing feature, and should you wish to stay amid these jumbled boulders, there is no better choice than Rocamadour. At this inn you'll enjoy luxurious surroundings in the midst of a fantastic landscape. Owners Mike and Twila Coffey honed their innkeeping skills as owners of a 40-room château in France before moving to Prescott, and pieces of antique furniture from the château can now be found throughout this inn. The most elegant pieces are in the Chambre Trucy, which has an amazing underlit whirlpool tub. For those who really want to be in the midst of the rocks, there is a cottage built into the boulders with a large whirlpool tub on its deck. The unique setting, engaging innkeepers, and thoughtful details everywhere you turn make this one of the state's must-stay inns. If you need more room and your own kitchen, there is the Suite Amérique, which is filled with Americana.

INEXPENSIVE

In addition to the following hotel, Prescott has several budget chain motels. Try the **Super 8 Motel,** 1105 E. Sheldon St. (☎ **520/776-1282**), charging $55 to $60 double, and **Motel 6,** 1111 E. Sheldon St. (☎ **520/776-0160**), charging $42 to $52 double.

Hotel St. Michael. 205 W. Gurley St., Prescott, AZ 86301. ☎ **800/678-3757** or 520/776-1999. Fax 520/776-7318. 75 units. A/C TV TEL. $42–$78 double; $75–$85 suite. Rates include continental breakfast. AE, DISC, MC, V.

Located right on Whiskey Row, this restored hotel complete with resident ghost and the oldest elevator in Prescott, offers a historic setting at budget prices (don't expect the best of mattresses or most stylish furnishings). All rooms are different; and some have bathtubs but no showers. Among the St. Michael's past guests are Teddy Roosevelt and Barry Goldwater. The casual Café St. Michael, where the complimentary breakfast is served, has brick walls and a pressed-tin ceiling and overlooks Courthouse Square.

WHERE TO DINE

The best place in town to savor a mocha and pastry while watching the world go by is at the **Café St. Michael,** 205 W. Gurley St. (☎ **520/776-1999**), on the ground floor of the historic hotel of the same name. With its high ceiling, brick walls, and battered wood floor, this place has the feel of an old saloon and offers a view of the city's 19th-century courthouse. Light meals are also available. For an authentic and tasty crêpe, try **Provence** (☎ **520/445-2325**), a little espresso bar at 108 W. Gurley St. For a milkshake, an ice cream soda, or an espresso, don't miss **Déjà Vu,** 134 N. Cortez St. (☎ **520/445-6732**), which is inside an old saloon that now houses an antiques store.

MODERATE

Murphy's. 201 N. Cortez St. (a block from Courthouse Plaza). ☎ **520/445-4044.** Reservations recommended for parties of 5 or more. Main courses lunch $7–$13, dinner $13–$27. AE, DISC, MC, V. Sun–Thurs 11am–9pm; Fri–Sat 11am–10pm. Stays open later in summer. AMERICAN.

Murphy's, housed in the oldest mercantile building in the Southwest, has long been Prescott's favorite special-occasion restaurant and is best known for its mesquite-broiled meats and excellent, traditional seafood dishes. The building, which is on the National Register of Historic Places, was built in 1890, and many of the shop's original shelves can be seen in the restaurant's lounge area. Sparkling leaded-glass doors usher diners into a high-ceilinged room with fans revolving slowly overhead. In keeping with the historical nature of the building, antiques are on display throughout the restaurant.

✪ **The Palace.** 120 S. Montezuma St. ☎ **520/541-1996.** Reservations suggested on weekends. Main courses $5–$10 at lunch, $11.50–$19 at dinner. AE, DISC, MC, V. Sun–Thurs 11am–3pm and 4:30–9:30pm; Fri–Sat 11am–3pm and 4:30–10:30pm. SOUTHWEST/STEAK/SEAFOOD.

The Palace is the oldest frontier bar in Arizona (in business for more than 120 years) and in 1996 was beautifully renovated and returned to the way it might have looked around the turn of the century. This grand hall tends to be noisy and bustling and is a good place for people watching. The menu includes choices such as a tasty appetizer of grilled tiger prawns wrapped in basil and prosciutto; citrus salmon; corn chowder; and generous portions of steak, pork chops, and seafood. The bar area in front is an alternative to waiting for a table, but it can be smoky. If you're in town for only one meal, have it here.

✪ **The Rose Restaurant.** 234 S. Cortez St. ☎ **520/777-8308.** Reservations recommended. Main courses $14–$27. AE, DISC, MC, V. Wed–Sun 5–9:30pm. CONTINENTAL.

Chef Linda Rose worked for nearly a decade at the Hassayampa Hotel's Peacock Room, and now she brings her creative flair to her own restaurant. The manicotti and double-cut lamb chops are house specialties well worth trying. The dining rooms here are small, and tables are close together, but that doesn't dissuade both locals and visitors from enjoying the excellent food and reasonably priced wines. Dishes are attractively presented (often with a rose of whipped yam on the plate), and there is usually a wide selection of desserts.

INEXPENSIVE

Gurley St. Grill. 230 W. Gurley St. ☎ **520/445-3388.** Reservations only for parties of 5 or more at dinnertime. Main courses $7–$15. AE, DISC, MC, V. Daily 11am–10pm; late-night menu daily 10am–midnight. ITALIAN/AMERICAN.

The Gurley St. Grill is located a block off Courthouse Plaza and run by the same people who operate Murphy's. Brick walls, ceiling fans, and beveled glass reflect the building's historic heritage. You'll see lots of families who have come for the pastas, pizzas, steaks, fish tacos, and rotisserie chicken. At lunch, the Sonoran corn chowder is a good bet; at dinner, the Cajun chicken with house-made fettuccine is not only delicious but plentiful. The restaurant's bar has many microbrews on tap and attracts a lively professional crowd.

Kendall's Famous Burgers & Ice Cream. 113 S. Cortez St. ☎ **520/778-3658.** Burgers $4–$6. AE, MC, V. Mon–Sat 11am–6pm; Sun 11am–6pm (later in summer). BURGERS.

Ask anyone in town where to get the best burger in Prescott, and you'll be sent to Kendall's on Courthouse Plaza. This bright and noisy luncheonette serves juicy burgers with a choice of more than a dozen condiments. A basket of fries is a mandatory accompaniment.

✪ Machu Picchu Peruvian Restaurant. 111 Grove St. ☎ **520/717-8242.** Reservations not accepted. Main courses $6.50–$13. AE, MC, V. Mon–Sat 11am–2pm and 4–9pm. PERUVIAN.

In America's quest for ever more exotic food, South America has for the most part been overlooked. However, here in Prescott, you can get a taste of Peruvian cooking, and chances are, you'll want to come back for more. This little cottage restaurant is great. Prices are beguilingly low, and the food is quite both flavorful and filling, somewhere between Spanish and Mexican. David Black, who spent time kayaking in Peru, and Analus Gomez de Black, who formerly had a restaurant and bakery in Peru, are the proprietors. Here in Prescott, Analus cooks, and David manages the house. For starters, the *ceviche*, with its piquant lime and chile flavorings, is pleasantly offset by the sweetness of an accompanying yam. For more intriguing flavors, try the fried rockfish, squid, shrimp, mussels, and potatoes covered with a spicy shredded onion salsa. For dessert, don't miss the *budin* (bread pie with raisins), which is flamed tableside with a blowtorch. The restaurant is small and quite popular, so expect a wait.

Prescott Brewing Company. 130 W. Gurley St. ☎ **520/771-2795.** Main courses $6–$13. AE, DISC, MC, V. Sun–Thurs 11am–10pm; Fri–Sat 11am–11pm (pub stays open 2 hours after kitchen closes). AMERICAN/PUB FOOD.

Popular primarily with a younger crowd, this brew pub keeps a good selection of its own beers and ales on tap, but is just as popular for its cheap and filling meals. Fajitas are a specialty, and of course there are such pub standards as fish and chips, bangers and mash, and not-so-standard spent-grain beer-dough pizzas and vegetarian dishes. The Caesar salad with chipotle dressing packs a wallop. And what better accompaniment to a good wheat beer than the house-made chocolate malted mousse?

PRESCOTT AFTER DARK

Back in the days when Prescott was the territorial capital and a booming mining town, it supported dozens of rowdy saloons, most of which were concentrated along Montezuma Street on the west side of Courthouse Plaza. This section of town was known as **Whiskey Row,** and legend has it there was a tunnel from the courthouse to one of the saloons so lawmakers wouldn't have to be seen ducking into the saloons during regular business hours. On July 14, 1900, a fire consumed most of Whiskey Row, including 25 saloons and bawdy houses. However, concerned cowboys and miners managed to drag the tremendously heavy bar of the Palace Saloon across the street before it was damaged by the fire. (The saloon continued to do business in its new open-air location.)

Today Whiskey Row is no longer the sort of place where respectable women shouldn't be seen, although it does still have a few noisy saloons with genuine Wild West flavor. Most of them feature live country music on weekends and are the dark, dank sorts of places that cowboys tend to gravitate to. If, however, you'd rather see what this street's saloons looked like back in the old days, drop by **The Palace,** 120 S. Montezuma St. (☎ **520/541-1996**), which still has a classic bar area up front (though it's now primarily a restaurant). Just push through the swinging doors and say howdy to the fellow with the six-guns or shotgun; he's the owner. A couple of times a month, The Palace presents dinner theatre performances; call to find out if anything is happening while you are in town. Just around the corner, you'll find the **Prescott Brewing Company,** 130 W. Gurley St. (☎ 520/771-2795), which is today's answer to the saloons of yore, brewing and serving its own tasty microbrews. Good pub fare is also served.

If you're feeling lucky, head up to **Bucky's Casino,** 1500 Hwy. 69 (☎ **800/ SLOTS-44**), located at the Prescott Resort. In addition to 300 slot machines, the casino has a poker room and keno. Across the street from the entrance to the Prescott Resort, you'll find the **Yavapai Casino,** which is under the same management and offers slot machines and bingo.

The **Prescott Fine Arts Association,** 208 N. Marina St. (☎ 520/445-3286), sponsors plays, music performances, children's theater, and art exhibits (tickets $9 to $12). The association's main building, a former church built in 1899, is on the National Register of Historic Places.

EN ROUTE TO OR FROM PHOENIX

If you crave a taste of the country life, stop by **Young's Farm** (☎ 520/632-7272), a country store at the intersection of Ariz. 69 and 169 between I-17 and Prescott. Located in the middle of the desert, this country farm stand sells a wide variety of produce as well as gourmet and unusual foods. You might find any of a number of various seasonal festivals going on here, such as a Pumpkin Festival during the month of October.

3 Jerome

35 miles NE of Prescott; 28 miles W of Sedona; 130 miles N of Phoenix

Clinging to the slopes of Cleopatra Hill high on Mingus Mountain, the former copper-mining town of Jerome beckons to today's travelers just as it once beckoned to miners. It was never easy mining the copper ore beneath Jerome. The high elevation made shipping ore an expensive proposition that eventually prompted mining interests to build a smelter at the base of the mountain. For many years the mountain's copper ore was mined using an 88-mile-long network of underground railroads. However, in 1918, a fire broke out in the mine tunnels, and mining companies were forced to abandon the tunnels in favor of open-pit mining. One unforeseen hazard of this type of mining was the effect dynamiting would have on a town built on a 30-degree slope. Buildings in downtown Jerome began sliding downhill, and eventually the town jail broke loose and slid 225 feet downhill (now that's a jailbreak).

Between 1883 and 1953, Jerome experienced an economic roller-coaster ride as the price of copper rose and fell. In the early 1950s, when it was no longer profitable to mine the copper ore of Cleopatra Hill, the last mining company shut down its operations, and almost everyone left town. By the early 1960s Jerome looked as though it were on its way to becoming just another ghost town, but then artists who had discovered the phenomenal views and dirt-cheap rents began moving in, and slowly the would-be ghost town developed a reputation as an artists' community. Soon tourists began visiting to see and buy the artwork that was being created in Jerome, and old storefronts turned into galleries.

Today Jerome is far from a ghost town, and on summer weekends the streets are packed with visitors shopping at galleries and crafts shops. The same remote and rugged setting that once made it difficult and expensive to mine copper here has now become one of the town's main attractions.

Jerome is divided into two sections by an elevation of 1,500 vertical feet, with the upper part of town 2,000 feet above the Verde Valley. On a clear day (of which there are quite a few), the view from up here is stupendous—it's possible to see for more than 50 miles, with the red rocks of Sedona, the Mogollon Rim, and the San Francisco Peaks all visible in the distance.

Because Jerome is built on a 30-degree slope, streets through town switch back from one level of houses to the next. Old brick and wood-frame buildings built into the side of the mountain have windows gazing out into the distance. Narrow streets, alleys, and stairways connect the different levels of town.

The entire town has been designated a National Historic Landmark, and in recent years people have been restoring Jerome's old buildings. Today residences, studios, shops, and galleries stand side by side looking (externally, anyway) much as they did when Jerome was an active mining town.

ESSENTIALS

GETTING THERE   Jerome is on Ariz. 89A roughly halfway between Sedona and Prescott. Coming from Phoenix, take Ariz. 279 from Camp Verde.

VISITOR INFORMATION   For information on Jerome, contact the **Jerome Chamber of Commerce,** P.O. Drawer K, Jerome, AZ 86331 (☎ **520/634-2900;** www.jeromechamber.com).

EXPLORING THE TOWN

Wandering the streets, soaking up the atmosphere, and shopping are the main pastimes in Jerome. However, before you launch yourself on a shopping tour, you can learn about the town's past at the **Jerome State Historic Park,** off U.S. 89A on Douglas Road in the lower section of town (☎ **520/634-5381**). Located in a mansion built in 1916 as a home for mine owner "Rawhide Jimmy" Douglas and as a hotel for visiting mining executives, the Jerome State Historic Park contains exhibits on mining and a few of the mansion's original furnishings. Built on a hill above Douglas's Little Daisy Mine, the mansion overlooks Jerome and, dizzyingly far below, the Verde Valley. Constructed of adobe bricks made on the site, the mansion contained a wine cellar, billiard room, marble shower, steam heat, and a central vacuum system. The mansion's library has been restored as a period room; other rooms have exhibits on copper mining and the history of Jerome. Various types of colorful ores are on display, along with the tools once used to extract the ore from the mountain. Admission is $2.50 for adults, $1 for children 7 to 13, and free for children 6 and under. It's open daily 8am to 5pm, except Christmas Day.

To get a wider perspective on both the mining history and Native American history of this area, try a four-wheel-drive tour with **Arizona Time Expeditions** (☎ **520/634-3497;** www.azhealingtours.com), which is operated by Clay Miller (who also works as a guide on the nearby Verde Canyon Railroad and is a fount of information on this region). Clay also offers hiking explorations and shamanistic counseling through his business **Soul Journey.** For that classic mining-town tourist-trap experience, follow the signs up the hill from downtown Jerome to the **Gold King Mine and Ghost Town,** where you can see lots of old, rusting, metal mining equipment.

However, most visitors come to Jerome for the shopping. The shops offer an eclectic blend of urban art, chic jewelry, one-of-a-kind handmade fashions, unusual imports and gifts, and the inevitable tacky souvenirs and ice cream (alas, no place stays undiscovered for long anymore; at least there's no McDonald's). To see what local artists are creating, stop in at the **Jerome Artists Cooperative** (☎ 520/639-4276), which is on the west side of the street where Hull Avenue and Main Street fork as you come up the hill into town. The **Raku Gallery,** 250 Hull Ave. (☎ 520/639-0239), has gallery space on two floors and walls of glass across the back of both floors. If you can tear your eyes from the view out the back (yes, those are the red rocks of Sedona in the distance), you'll find lots of interesting art by artists from around the country. The **Jerome Gallery,** 240 Hull Ave. (☎ 520/634-7033), also has good-quality ceramics, jewelry, and home furnishings. **Sky Fire,** 140 Main St. (☎ 520/634-8081), has a interesting collection of Southwestern and ethnic gifts and furnishings. On this same block, you'll also find ✪ **Nellie Bly,** 136 Main St. (☎ 520/634-0255), with a room full of colorful, handmade kaleidoscopes (ask to see the kaleidoscopes in the back room) and **Nellie Bly II,** 130 Main St. (☎ 520/634-7825), which specializes in jewelry made from semiprecious stones. **Guilt Complex** (also the House of Joy) on Hull Ave. (☎ 520/634-5339) stocks an eclectic assortment of greeting cards, hearts, handmade bears, and old tobacco art.

WHERE TO STAY

Ghost City Inn. 541 N. Main St. (P.O. Box 382), Jerome, AZ 86331. ☎ **888/63-GHOST** or 520/63-GHOST. www.ghostcityinn.com. 5 units (1 with private bathroom). TV. $85–$100 double. Rates include full breakfast. AE, DISC, MC, V.

With its long verandas on both floors, this restored old house is hard to miss as you drive into Jerome from Clarkdale. Most of the rooms, although rather plain and small, do have great views across the Verde River Valley, which makes a stay here memorable. There's a hot tub in the terraced backyard.

The Inn at Jerome. 309 Main St. (P.O. Box 901), Jerome, AZ 86331. ☎ **800/634-5094** or 520/634-5094. 8 units (2 with private bathroom). TV. $55–$85 double. AE, DISC, MC, V.

This B&B has similar styling to the Ghost City Inn, but its antiques-filled rooms lend quite a bit more character. One room has a rustic log bed so tall that you have to climb up into it. Other beds are equally attractive, including a wrought-iron bed, a spool bed, and a sleigh bed. All the rooms have terry robes, ceiling fans, and evaporative coolers (almost as good as air-conditioning), but only two rooms have valley views. Reception is at the restaurant downstairs. Note that breakfast is not included in the room rate.

✪ **The Surgeon's House.** 101 Hill St. (P.O. Box 998), Jerome, AZ 86331. ☎ **800/639-1452** or 520/639-1452. www.surgeonshouse.com. 3 units. A/C TV. $100–$150 suite. Rates include full breakfast. MC, V.

Built in 1917 as the home of Jerome's resident surgeon, this Mediterranean-style home has a jaw-dropping view of the Verde Valley and is surrounded by beautiful gardens. All three units are suites; but the old chauffeur's quarters ($150), located in a separate cottage across the inn's garden, is the one to request. This unconventionally designed room has a wall of glass opposite the bed so you can soak in the view from under the covers, an old tub in one corner, and a wall of glass blocks around the toilet. The two rooms in the main house are much more traditional and filled with antiques that conjure up Jerome's heyday. However, one of these rooms has a unique private bathroom that's so tiny everything gets wet when you shower; it's designed as a combination shower stall and toilet (strange but fun). The inn is on a narrow side lane toward the top of town.

WHERE TO DINE

The **House of Joy** on Hull Ave. (☎ 520/634-5339) has a bordello theme and may be open for dinner on Saturday and Sunday when you visit. Stop by or call for information.

Apizza Heaven. Near the corner of Main St. and Hull Ave. ☎ **520/649-1834.** Pizzas, pastas, sandwiches $6–$19. No credit cards. Wed–Mon 11am–8pm, sometimes later on Fri–Sat. PIZZA/SOUTHERN ITALIAN.

These folks specialize in East Coast–style pizza, which seems to taste good just about anywhere. We like to get it to go (this place isn't very big) and then grab a seat with a view at the nearby public park. You can also dig into such things as a hearty eggplant parmigiana dinner or a sausage and pepper sandwich.

Flatiron Café. In the Flatiron Building, at the fork in the road (corner of Main St. and Hull Ave.) ☎ **520/634-2733.** Breakfast, salads, and sandwiches $4–$8. No credit cards. Mon–Fri 7:30am–3pm; Sat–Sun 7:30am–5pm. BREAKFAST/LIGHT MEALS.

The tiny Flatiron Café is Jerome's outpost of urban flavors and serves breakfast and light meals such as black-bean hummus, grilled prosciutto panini, smoked-salmon quesadillas, fresh juices, and espresso drinks. It looks as though you could hardly squeeze in here, but there's more seating across the street. Definitely not your usual ghost town lunch counter.

4 The Verde Valley

Camp Verde: 30 miles S of Sedona; 95 miles N of Phoenix; 20 miles E of Jerome

With its headwaters in the Juniper Mountains of Prescott National Forest, the Verde River flows down through a rugged canyon before meandering slowly across the plains of the Verde Valley. This valley, named by early Spanish explorers who were impressed at the sight of such a verdant valley in an otherwise brown desert landscape, has long been a magnet for both wildlife and people. Today the valley is one of Arizona's richest agricultural and ranching regions and is quickly gaining popularity with retirees.

However, long before the first European explorers entered the Verde Valley, the Sinagua people were living by the river and irrigating their fields with its waters. Sinagua ruins can still be seen at Tuzigoot and Montezuma national monuments, and there are even primitive cave dwellings along the banks of the river. By the time the first pioneers began settling in this region, the Sinaguas had long since disappeared, but Apaches had claimed the river valley as part of their territory. Inevitably, there were clashes with the Apaches, and the U.S. Army established Fort Verde to protect the settlers. Today hundreds of years of Verde Valley history and prehistory can be viewed at sites such as Fort Verde State Park and Tuzigoot and Montezuma Castle national monuments. This valley is also the site of the most scenic railroad excursion in the state.

ESSENTIALS

GETTING THERE Camp Verde is just off I-17 at the junction with Ariz. 260. This latter highway leads northwest through the Verde Valley for 12 miles to Cottonwood.

VISITOR INFORMATION   For more information on the Verde Valley, contact the **Cottonwood/Verde Valley Chamber of Commerce,** 1010 S. Main St., Cottonwood, AZ 86326 (☎ **520/634-7593;** http://chamber.verdevalley.com).

EXPLORING THE VERDE VALLEY
A RAILWAY EXCURSION

✪   **Verde Canyon Railroad.** 300 N. Broadway, Clarkdale. ☎ **800/293-7245** or 520/639-0010. www.verdecanyonrr.com. Admission is $35.95 for adults, $32.95 for seniors, $20.95 for children 2–12; a first-class ticket is $54.95. Call for schedule and reservations.

When the town of Jerome was busily mining copper, a railway was built to link the booming town with the territorial capital at nearby Prescott. Because of the rugged mountains between Jerome and Prescott, the railroad was forced to take a longer but less difficult route north along the Verde River before turning back south toward Prescott. Today you can ride these same tracks aboard the Verde Canyon Railroad. The route through the Verde River Canyon traverses both the remains of a copper smelter and unspoiled desert that's inaccessible by car and is part of the Prescott National Forest. The views of the rocky canyon walls and green waters of the Verde River are quite dramatic, and if you look closely along the way, you'll see ancient Sinagua cliff dwellings. In the late winter and early spring, nesting bald eagles can also be spotted. Of the two excursion train rides in Arizona, this is by far the more scenic (although the Grand Canyon Railway certainly has a more impressive destination). Live music and a very informative narration make the ride entertaining as well.

INDIAN RUINS & AN ARMY FORT

Fort Verde State Historic Park. 125 Holloman St. ☎ **520/567-3275.** Admission $2 adults, $1 children 7 to 13, free for children under 7. Daily from 8am–5pm.

Just south of Montezuma Castle and Montezuma's Well, in the town of Camp Verde, you'll find Fort Verde State Historic Park. Established in 1871, Fort Verde was the third military post in the Verde Valley and was occupied until 1891, by which time tensions with the Indian population had subsided and made the fort unnecessary. The military had first come to the Verde Valley in 1865 at the request of settlers who wanted protection from the local Tonto Apache and Yavapai. The tribes, traditionally hunters and gatherers, had been forced to raid the settlers' fields for food after their normal economy was disrupted by the sudden influx of whites and Mexicans into the area. Between 1873 and 1875 most of the Indians in the area were rounded up and forced to live on various reservations. An uprising in 1882 led to the last clash between local tribes and Fort Verde's soldiers.

Today the state park, which covers 10 acres, preserves three officers' quarters, an administration building, and some ruins. The buildings that have been fully restored house exhibits on the history of the fort and what life was like here in the 19th century. With their white lattices and picket fences, gables, and shake-shingle roofs, the buildings of Fort Verde suggest that life at this remote post was not so bad, at least for officers.

There are costumed military reenactments here on the second Saturday in October.

✪ **Montezuma Castle National Monument.** Exit 289 off I-17. ☎ **520/567-3322.** Admission $2 adults, free for children 16 and under; there's no charge to see Montezuma Well. Late May–early Sept daily 8am–7pm; early Sept–late May daily 8am–5pm.

Despite the name, the ruins within this monument are neither castle nor Aztec dwelling—as the reference to Aztec ruler Moctezuma (traditionally Montezuma) implies. Rather, the Sinagua cliff dwelling, among the best preserved in Arizona, consists of two impressive stone pueblos. The more intriguing of the two is set in a shallow cave 100 feet up in a cliff overlooking Beaver Creek. Construction on this five-story, 20-room village began sometime in the early 12th century. Because Montezuma Castle has been protected from the elements by the overhanging roof of the cave in which it was built, the original adobe mud that was used to plaster over the stone walls of the dwelling is still intact. Another structure, containing 45 rooms on a total of six levels, stands at the base of the cliff. This latter dwelling, which has been subjected to rains and floods over the years, is not nearly as well preserved as the cliff dwelling.

For some as-yet-unknown reason, these buildings were abandoned by the Sinagua people, who disappeared without a trace in the early 14th century. The visitor center displays artifacts that have been unearthed at the ruins.

Located 11 miles north of Montezuma Castle (and part of the national monument), **Montezuma Well** is a water-filled sinkhole that has for centuries served as an oasis in the desert. Occupied first by the Hohokam and later by the Sinagua, this sunken pond was formed when a cavern in the porous limestone bedrock here collapsed. Underground springs quickly filled the sinkhole, which today contains a pond measuring 368 feet across and 65 feet deep. Over the centuries, the presence of year-round water attracted both the Hohokam and the Sinagua peoples, who built irrigation canals to use the water for growing crops. Some of these irrigation channels can still be seen. An excavated Hohokam pit house, built around 1100, and Sinagua houses and pueblos stand around the sinkhole.

Tuzigoot National Monument. Just outside Clarkdale off U.S. 89A. ☎ **520/634-5564.** Admission is $2 for adults, free for children 16 and under. Late May–early Sept daily 8am–7pm; early Sept–late May daily 8am–5pm.

Perched atop a hill overlooking the Verde River, this small, stone-walled pueblo was built by the Sinagua people, contemporaries of northern Arizona's Anasazi people, and was inhabited between 1125 and 1400. The *Sinagua* people, whose name is Spanish for "without water," were traditionally dry-land farmers relying entirely on rainfall to water their crops. When the Hohokam, who had been living in the Verde Valley since A.D. 600, moved on to more fertile land around 1100, the Sinagua moved into this valley. Their buildings progressed from individual homes called pit houses to communal pueblos.

An interpretive trail leads through the Tuzigoot ruins, explaining different aspects of Sinaguan life, and inside the visitor center is a small museum displaying many of the artifacts unearthed here. Desert plants, many of which were used by the Sinagua, are identified along the trail.

OTHER VERDE VALLEY ATTRACTIONS & ACTIVITIES
IN & AROUND CAMP VERDE

If you have an interest in 19th-century reenactments or antique cowboy and military gear, stop in at **Kicking Mule Outfitters,** 545 S. Main St., Camp Verde (☎ **520/ 567-2501**). This store specializes in reproduction Western leather holsters, gun belts, saddles, and the like. It also sells Western antiques and rents equipment to movie companies. Another place worth a look is **White Hills Indian Arts,** 567 S. Main St. (☎ **520/567-3490**), which is housed in an 1883 stagecoach stop and specializes in Native American arts and crafts.

Horseback Adventures (☎ **520/567-5502**), offers horseback rides ranging from 1 hour ($29) to all day ($120). The 1- and 2-hour rides along Beaver Creek are probably the most enjoyable if you haven't spent much time in the saddle.

For a completely different sort of entertainment in Camp Verde, drop by the **Cliff Castle Casino,** 353 Middle Verde Rd. (☎ **520/567-6956**), at exit 289 off of I-17.

If you want to do some wine tasting while you're in the area, drop by the **San Dominique Winery** (☎ 480/945-8583), 11 miles south of Camp Verde. To get to the winery, take exit 278 off I-17 (the Cherry Road exit), go east, and then before the road turns to gravel, turn right on the dirt road that leads to the winery. You might have to look hard to see the winery's small sign. There are always plenty of wines available for tasting at a quarter a taste. The winery also sells lots of garlic-flavored foods, as well as different types of pickles. Sandwiches and light meals are available.

In & Around Cottonwood & Clarkdale

Cottonwood, 6 miles from Jerome, isn't nearly as atmospheric as the old copper town, but there are a few blocks of historic buildings slowly filling up with interesting shops that seem to be spillovers from the old hippie days in Jerome. **Old Town Cottonwood's Main Street,** one side of which has a covered sidewalk, has several shops, galleries, and cafes and is a pleasant place to stroll. One of the most fascinating shops here is **Streck Family, Inc.,** at 1004 N. Main St. (☎ 520/639-3421) which previously was in Santa Fe. At their shop here in Cottonwood they specialize in rustic yet imaginative handmade furniture and fanciful punched-tin lampshades and chandeliers. Also here in town you'll find the **Clemenceau Heritage Museum,** 1 N. Willard St. (☎ 520/634-2868), housed in an old school building. The museum's most interesting display is a model railroad layout of the region's old system of mining railroads. The museum is open Wednesday 9am to noon, and Friday to Sunday 11am to 3pm. Admission is free.

On the outskirts of Cottonwood, not far from Tuzigoot National Monument, you'll find **Dead Horse Ranch State Park** (☎ 520/634-5283), which is set on the banks of the Verde River and offers picnicking, fishing, swimming, hiking, and camping. Trails beginning here lead into the adjacent national forest, so you can actually get in many miles of scenic hiking. Park admission is $4 per vehicle per day.

WHERE TO STAY

Cliff Castle Lodge & Casino. 333 Middle Verde Rd., Camp Verde, AZ 86322. ☎ **800/ 524-6343** or 520/567-6611. Fax 520/567-9455. 80 units. A/C TV TEL. $59–$79 double. AE, CB, DC, DISC, MC, V.

Although most people staying at this motel just off I-17 at Exit 289 are here to do a little gambling in the adjacent casino, the motel also makes a good base for exploring the Verde Valley. Rooms are standard motel issue, and there is a pool in summer and a whirlpool year-round.

WHERE TO DINE

Blazin' M Ranch Chuckwagon Suppers. Off 10th St., Cottonwood. ☎ **800/WEST-643** or 520/634-0334. Reservations recommended. $18.95 adults, $8.95 children age 10 and under. AE, DISC, MC, V. Call for days and times. AMERICAN.

Located adjacent to the Dead Horse State Park, the Blazin' M Ranch is more a slice of the Old West than just a place to have dinner. The chuck wagon suppers include not only a belly-fillin' heap o' food but also a Western variety show. Lots of fun for kids (pony rides, farm animals, a little cow town).

Gas Works Mexican Restaurant. 1033 N. Main St., Cottonwood. ☎ **520/634-7426.** Meals $3–$7. No credit cards. Sun–Fri noon–7pm. MEXICAN.

If you happen to be hungry and can't hold out for Jerome (or couldn't handle the crowds up at the top of the hill), check out this colorful and eclectic hole-in-the-wall in old-town Cottonwood. Basic homey cooking here includes burritos, enchiladas, and, for the vegetarians among us, vegetable tamales and salads.

Main Street Cafe. 315 S. Main St., Cottonwood. ☎ **520/639-4443.** Reservations recommended. Main courses $10–$22. DISC, MC, V. Tues–Sat 11am–3pm and 5–9pm; Sun 11am–2pm and 5–9pm. SOUTHWESTERN.

You'll find this casual and very reasonably priced restaurant between the modern strip malls and old-time Cottonwood. The menu is a mix of both the familiar (fajitas and lemon-pepper fettuccini) and more creative dishes. It is in the latter realm that the restaurant usually shines. The green corn tamale in chipotle cream sauce makes a savory starter, or try the Southwest corn chowder. Steak fans shouldn't miss the Southwest blackened sirloin with fresh salsa. Although many of the dishes here are pretty fiery, there are plenty of mild dishes as well, and the wine list is extensive.

Murphy's Grill. 747 S. Main St. ☎ **520/634-7272.** Main courses $6–$15. AE, DC, MC, V. Daily 11am–10pm; late-night menu served until midnight. AMERICAN.

The best thing about this place is that now folks in this neck of the desert can get food until midnight. With a cheerful and lively atmosphere reminiscent of other Murphy's properties in Prescott, the main focus here is on decently prepared salads, sandwiches, pastas, pizzas, and rotisserie chicken. Service is speedy, and there's a full bar.

✪ **Old Town Café.** 1025 "A" N. Main St.. ☎ **520/634-5980.** Sandwiches $5–$6. No credit cards. Tues–Fri 7am–4pm; Sat 8am–4pm. CAFE.

The almond croissants at this European-style cafe in downtown Cottonwood are the best we've ever had, period. If that isn't recommendation enough for you, there are also good salads and sandwiches, such as a grilled panini of smoked turkey, spinach, and tomatoes.

5 Sedona & Oak Creek Canyon

106 miles S of the Grand Canyon; 116 miles N of Phoenix; 56 miles NE of Prescott

Although in recent years housing developments and strip malls have sprawled across the hills at the mouth of Oak Creek Canyon, the town of Sedona can still claim the most beautiful setting in the Southwest. Red-rock buttes, eroded canyon walls, and mesas rise into blue skies. Off in the distance, the Mogollon Rim looms, its forests of juniper and ponderosa pine dark against the red rocks. Imagine Monument Valley with a wealthy southern California suburb, and you have a pretty good idea of Sedona today.

However, with national forest surrounding the city (and even extending fingers of forest into what would otherwise be the city limits), Sedona has some of the best outdoor access of any city in the Southwest. All over the city, alongside highways, and down side streets in suburban neighborhoods, there are trailheads. Head down any one of these trails, and you leave the city behind and enter the world of the red rocks. Just don't be too surprised if you come around a bend in the trail and find yourself in the middle of a wedding ceremony or a group of 30 people doing tai chi.

Located at the mouth of Oak Creek Canyon, Sedona was first settled by pioneers in 1877 and named for the first postmaster's wife (because her name fit on the cancellation stamp and previously submitted names did not). However, the word of Sedona's beauty did not begin to spread until Hollywood filmmakers began using the region's red rock as backdrop to their Western films. Next came artists, lured by the landscapes and desert light (it was here in Sedona that the Cowboy Artists of America organization was formed). However, although still much touted as an artists' community, Sedona's art scene these days is geared more toward tourists than toward collectors of fine art.

More recently, the spectacular views and mild climate were discovered by retirees. Today Sedona's hills are alive with the sound of construction as ostentatious retirement mansions and celebrity trophy homes sprout from the dust like desert toads after an August rainstorm. When quite a few years back a New Age channeler discovered the "Sedona vortexes," yet another group discovered that Sedona was where their cosmic energy fields converged. Most recently, mountain bikers have begun to ride the red rock, and the word is slowly spreading that the biking here is almost as good as up north in Moab, Utah.

The waters of Oak Creek were what first attracted settlers and native peoples to this area, and today this stream still lures visitors to Sedona—especially in the summer months, when the cool shade and even cooler creek waters are a glorious respite from the heat of the desert. Two of Arizona's finest swimming holes are located on Oak Creek, only a few miles from Sedona, and one of these, Slide Rock, has been made into a state park.

With its drop-dead scenery, dozens of motels and resorts, and plethora of good restaurants, Sedona makes an excellent base for exploring central Arizona. Several ancient Indian ruins (including an impressive cliff dwelling), the "ghost town" of Jerome, and the scenic Verde Canyon Railroad are all within easy driving distance, and even the Grand Canyon is but a long day trip away.

ESSENTIALS

GETTING THERE   Sedona is on Ariz. 179 at the mouth of scenic Oak Creek Canyon. From Phoenix, take I-17 to Ariz. 179 north. From Flagstaff, head south on I-17 until you see the turnoff for Ariz. 89A and Sedona. Ariz. 89A also connects Sedona with Prescott.

Sedona Phoenix Shuttle (☎ **800/448-7988** in Arizona, or 520/282-2066) operates several trips daily between the Phoenix Sky Harbor Airport and Sedona. The one-way fare is $35, and the round-trip fare is $60. Call for schedule information.

VISITOR INFORMATION   Contact the **Sedona–Oak Creek Chamber of Commerce,** P.O. Box 478, Sedona, AZ 86339 (☎ **800/288-7336** or 520/282-7722; www.sedonachamber.com), which also operates a visitor center on the corner of Ariz. 89A and Forest Road near uptown Sedona.

GETTING AROUND   Whether traveling in a car or on foot, you'll need to cultivate patience when trying to cross major roads in Sedona. Traffic here, especially on weekends, is some of the worst in the state. Also be prepared for slow traffic on roads that have good views; drivers are often distracted by the red rocks. You may hear or see references to the **"Y"** while you're in Sedona. The term refers to the intersection of Ariz. 179 and Ariz. 89A between the Tlaquepaque shopping plaza and uptown Sedona.

Rental cars are available in Sedona through **Enterprise Rent-a-Car** (☎ **800/ 325-8007** or 520/282-2052), **Practical Rent-a-Car** (☎ **800/464-8697** or 520/282-6702), and **Sedona Car Rentals** (☎ **800/879-JEEP or** 520/282-2227). For about $120 a day, you can also rent a Jeep from **Desert Jeep Rentals** (☎ **888/ GO-4-JEEP** or 520/284-1099) or **Sedona Jeep Rentals** (☎ **800/879-JEEP** or 520/282-2227).

For a taxi, call Bob's Sedona Taxi (☎ **520/282-1234**).

SPECIAL EVENTS   The **Sedona International Film Festival** (☎ **800/780-ARTS** or 520/203-4TIX; www.sedonaculturalpark.org), held in early March, has been getting good publicity across the state and has been booking quite a few interesting films.

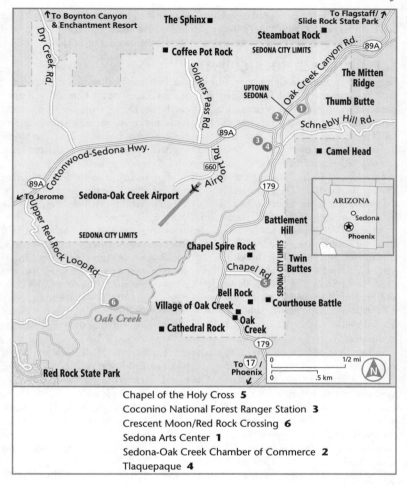

Chapel of the Holy Cross **5**
Coconino National Forest Ranger Station **3**
Crescent Moon/Red Rock Crossing **6**
Sedona Arts Center **1**
Sedona-Oak Creek Chamber of Commerce **2**
Tlaquepaque **4**

One of the year's biggest events is the world-class **Sedona Chamber Music Festival,** held each year in late May; contact the Sedona Chamber Music Society, P.O. Box 153, Sedona, AZ 86339-0153 (☎ **520/204-2415**), for details.

The **Jazz on the Rocks Benefit Festival** is held each year on the fourth weekend in September in an outdoor amphitheater with a superb view of the red rocks. Tickets range from $35 to $50. For more information, contact Sedona Jazz on the Rocks, P.O. Box 889, Sedona, AZ 86339 (☎ **520/282-1985;** www.sedonajazz.com).

In early October (usually a week after the jazz festival), an annual benefit for the Native American Scholarship Project called the **Verde Valley Music Festival** is staged by Jackson Browne. This concert always includes musical friends of Browne's, such as Bruce Cockburn, Crosby, Stills & Nash, and Marc Cohn. In the past the concert has been held at the Verde Valley School's Warren Amphitheater, but the venue may change when the Sedona Cultural Center is completed. For information, contact the Sedona Chamber of Commerce.

From Thanksgiving eve until early January, Sedona celebrates the **Festival of Lights** at Tlaquepaque (☎ **800/288-7336**) by lighting thousands of luminárias (paper bags partially filled with sand and containing a single candle) beginning at sunset.

EXPLORING RED ROCK COUNTRY

Rugged cliffs, needlelike pinnacles, and isolated buttes rise up from the green forest floor at the mouth of Oak Creek Canyon in Sedona. Layers of different-colored stone deposited during various prehistoric ages form bands through the cliffs above, the most prominent of these bands being the layer of red sandstone called the Schnebly Hill Formation. Because this rosy sandstone predominates around Sedona, the region has come to be known as the red rock country. Each evening at sunset the red rocks put on a light show that alone is reason enough for visiting Sedona.

Days can be spent exploring the red rock country in any of half a dozen different modes of transport. There are Jeep tours, hot-air-balloon flights, horseback rides, mountain-bike trails, hiking trails, and scenic drives suitable for standard cars. (See the following sections, "Organized Tours" and "Sports & Outdoor Pursuits.")

Although in the past it has been possible for passenger cars to drive **Schnebly Hill Road** for superb views of Sedona, as of press time the road is no longer regularly maintained. However, it is worth checking at the Sedona Visitor Center (see "Visitor Information," above) to see if it is once again passable in a regular passenger car. If so, head south out of Sedona on Ariz. 179, turn left after you cross the bridge over Oak Creek, and head up the unpaved road. The road climbs up into the hills above town, every turn yielding a new and breathtaking view, and eventually reaching the top of the Mogollon Rim. At the rim is the Schnebly Hill overlook, offering the very best view in the area.

Just south of Sedona, on Ariz. 179, you'll see the aptly named **Bell Rock** on the east side of the road. There's a parking area at the foot of Bell Rock and trails leading up to the top. From Bell Rock, you can see **Cathedral Rock** to the west. This rock is the most photographed formation in Sedona. Adjacent to Bell Rock is **Courthouse Rock,** and not far from Bell Rock and visible from Chapel Road, are **Eagle Head Rock** (from the front door of the Chapel of the Holy Cross—see "Attractions & Activities Around Town," below—look three-quarters of the way up the mountain to see the eagle's head), the **Twin Nuns** (two pinnacles standing side by side), and **Mother and Child Rock** to the left of the Twin Nuns.

If you head west out of Sedona on U.S. 89A and turn left onto Airport Road, you'll drive up onto ✪ **Airport Mesa,** which consists of three small hills commanding an unobstructed panorama of Sedona and the red rocks. About halfway up the mesa is a small parking area from which trails radiate out. The views from here are among the best in the region and the trails are very easy.

One of the most beautiful areas around Sedona is **Boynton Canyon.** To reach this spectacular canyon, drive west out of Sedona on U.S. 89A, turn right on Dry Creek Road, take a left at the T intersection, and at the next T intersection take a right. On the way to Boynton Canyon, look north from U.S. 89A, and you'll see **Coffee Pot Rock,** which is also known as Rooster Rock, rising 1,800 feet above Sedona. Three pinnacles, known as the **Three Golden Chiefs** by the Yavapai tribe, stand beside Coffee Pot Rock. As you drive up Dry Creek Road, on your right you'll see **Capitol Butte,** which resembles the U.S. Capitol building. Just outside the gates of Enchantment Resort is a parking area for the ✪ **Boynton Canyon Trail.** From the parking area the trail leads 3 miles up into the canyon. The ancient Sinagua people once lived in Boynton Canyon, and the ruins of their homes can still be seen.

Vortex Power

In recent years Sedona has been one of the world's centers for the New Age movement; large numbers of people come to experience the "power vortexes" of the surrounding red rock country. You'll see local bulletin boards and publications advertising such diverse New Age services as past-life regressions, crystal healing, angelic healing, tarot readings, reiki, axiatonal therapy, electromagnetic field balancing, soul recovery, channeling, aromatherapy, myofacial release, and aura photos and videos.

According to believers, a *vortex* is a site where the earth's unseen lines of power intersect to form a particularly powerful energy field. Page Bryant, an adherent of New Age beliefs, determined through channeling that there were four vortexes around Sedona. Scientists may scoff, but Sedona's vortexes have become so well known that the chamber of commerce visitor center has several handouts to explain them and a map to guide you to them. (Many of the most spectacular geological features of the Sedona landscape also happen to be vortexes.)

The four main vortexes include Bell Rock, Cathedral Rock, Airport Mesa, and Boynton Canyon. **Bell Rock** and **Airport Mesa** are both said to contain masculine or electric energy that boosts emotional, spiritual, and physical energy. **Cathedral Rock** is said to contain feminine or magnetic energy, good for facilitating relaxation. The **Boynton Canyon** vortex is considered an electromagnetic energy site, which means it has a balance of both masculine and feminine energy.

If you're not familiar with vortexes and want to learn more about the ones here in Sedona, consider a ✪ **vortex tour.** These are offered by several companies around town including **Earth Wisdom Tours** (☎ **520/282-4714**), **Spirit Steps** (☎ **800/728-4562** or 520/282-4562), and **Vortex Tours** (☎ **520/282-2733**). All three of these companies offer vortex tours that combine aspects of Native American and New Age beliefs. Tours last about 3 hours and cost about $55 to $60 per person.

You can also stock up on books, crystals, and other spiritual supplies at stores such as **Crystal Magic,** 2978 W. Hwy. 89A (☎ **520/282-1622**); **Center for the New Age,** 341 Hwy. 179 (☎ **520/282-2085**); and **The Eye of the Vortex Book Center,** 1405 W. Hwy. 89A (☎ **520/282-5614**).

In this same area, you can visit the well-preserved Sinagua cliff dwellings at **Palatki Ruins,** set in a beautiful canyon. To reach the ruins follow the directions to Boynton Canyon, but instead of turning right at the second T intersection, turn left onto unpaved Boynton Pass Road (FR 152), which is one of the most scenic roads in the area and is well worth driving even if you don't go to Palatki. Follow this road to another T intersection and go right onto FR (forest road) 125, then veer right onto FR 795, which dead-ends at the ruins. You can also get here by taking Ariz. 89A west from Sedona to FR 525, a gravel road leading north to FR 795. To visit Palatki, you'll need a Red Rock Pass (see "The High Cost of Red Rock Views" box feature for details); ruins are usually open daily 9:30am to 4:30pm. Don't try coming out here if the roads are at all muddy.

South of Ariz. 89A and a bit west of the turnoff for Boynton Canyon is Upper Red Rock Loop Road, which leads to **Crescent Moon Recreation Area** (formerly known as Red Rock Crossing), a National Forest Service recreation area that has become a

The High Cost of Red Rock Views

A quick perusal of any Sedona real estate magazine will convince you that property values around these parts are as high as the Mogollon Rim. However, red rock realty is also expensive for those who only want a glimpse of the rocks. With the land around Sedona split up into several types of National Forest Service day-use sites, state parks, and national monuments, visitors find themselves pulling out their wallets just about every time they turn around to look at another rock. So here's the low-down on what it's going to cost you to do the red rocks right.

Depending on how long you're spending in the area and how much you want to see, you'll want to get a **Red Rock Pass,** which will allow you to visit Palatki Ruins and the V-Bar-V petroglyph site and park at any national forest trailhead parking areas. These passes, which are good for everyone in your vehicle, cost $5 for a 1-day pass, $15 for a 7-day pass, and $20 for a 12-month pass. If you plan to be in the area for more than a week and also want to visit Grasshopper Point (a swimming hole), Banjo Bill (a picnic area), Call of the Canyon (the West Fork Oak Creek trailhead), and Crescent Moon recreation sites (Sedona's top photo-op site), you'll want to buy a **Red Rock Grand Pass** for $40. Individually, these sites each charge a $5 admission, so if you aren't planning on going to all of them or you don't expect to be around for more than a week, the Red Rock Grand Pass is not a good deal.

There are also two state parks in the area—Slide Rock and Red Rock—both of which charge $5 per car. However, you can also get, for $15, a pass good for admission to five state parks. Admission to Montezuma Castle or Tuzigoot national monuments, will cost you $2 per adult. However, if there are two or more of you traveling together and you are planning on visiting the Grand Canyon and three or four other national parks or monuments, you might want to consider getting a Golden Eagle Pass for $50. These passes are good for a year and will get you into any national park or national monument in the country. If you're 62 or older, you should definitely get a Golden Age Pass; they're only $10 and are good for the rest of your life. A Golden Age Pass will also get you a Red Rock Pass for half price.

must-see spot for almost everyone who visits Sedona these days. Its popularity stems from a beautiful photograph of Oak Creek, with **Cathedral Rock** in the background—an image that has been reproduced countless times in Sedona promotional literature and on postcards. Hiking trails beginning here lead up to Cathedral Rock. Admission is $5, unless you have previously purchased a Red Rock Grand Pass (see "The High Cost of Red Rock Views" box feature for details).

If you continue on Upper Red Rock Loop Road, it becomes gravel for a while before turning into Lower Red Rock Loop Road and reaching **Red Rock State Park** (☎ **520/282-6907**), which flanks Oak Creek. The views here take in many of the rocks listed above, and you have the additional bonus of being right on the creek (but no swimming or wading is allowed). Park admission is $5 per vehicle.

South of Sedona, near the junction of I-17 and Ariz. 179, you can visit an ancient petroglyph site at the **V Bar V Ranch.** To reach this site, head east several miles on the marked dirt road that leads to the Beaver Creek Campground. The entrance to the petroglyph site is just past the campground. From the parking area, it's about a 1/2-mile walk to the petroglyphs. The site is open Friday to Monday 9:30am to 4pm. To visit this site, you'll need to purchase a Red Rock Pass.

OAK CREEK CANYON

The **Mogollon Rim** is a 2,000-foot escarpment cutting diagonally across central Arizona and on into New Mexico. At the top of the Mogollon Rim are the ponderosa pine forests of the high mountains, while at the bottom the lowland deserts begin. Of the many canyons cutting down from the rim, Oak Creek Canyon is the best known.

Ariz. 89A runs down through the canyon from Flagstaff to Sedona, winding its way down from the rim and paralleling Oak Creek. Along the way there are overlooks, parks, picnic areas, campgrounds, cabin resorts, and small inns.

If you have a choice of how first to view Oak Creek Canyon, come at it from the north. Your first stop after traveling south from Flagstaff will be the **Oak Creek Canyon Vista,** which provides a view far down the valley to Sedona and beyond. The overlook is at the edge of the Mogollon Rim, and the road suddenly drops in tight switchbacks just south of here. You may notice that one rim of the canyon is lower than the other. This is because Oak Creek Canyon is on a geologic fault line; one side of the canyon is moving in a different direction from the other.

Although the top of the Mogollon Rim is a ponderosa pine forest and the bottom a desert, Oak Creek Canyon supports a forest of sycamores and other deciduous trees. There is no better time to drive scenic Ariz. 89A than between late September and mid-October when the canyon is ablaze with red and yellow leaves.

The most popular spot in all of Oak Creek Canyon is ✪ **Slide Rock State Park** (☎ **520/282-3034**). Located 7 miles north of Sedona on the site of an old homestead, this park preserves a natural waterslide. On hot summer days the park is jammed with people splashing in the water and sliding over the algae-covered sandstone bottom of Oak Creek. Sunbathing and fishing are other popular pastimes here. The park is open daily, and admission is $5 per vehicle. There's another popular swimming area at **Grasshopper Point,** several miles closer to Sedona. Admission to Grasshopper Point is $5 per vehicle, unless you have previously purchased a Red Rock Grand Pass.

Within Oak Creek Canyon several hikes of different lengths are possible. By far the most spectacular and popular is the 6-mile round-trip hike up the ✪ **West Fork of Oak Creek.** This is a classic canyon-country hike with steep canyon walls rising up from the creek. At some points the canyon is no more than 20 feet wide with walls rising up more than 200 feet. You can actually hike many more miles up the canyon, which is popular for overnight backpacking trips. The trailhead for the West Fork hike is at the Call of the Canyon Recreation Area, which charges a $5 day-use fee unless you have already purchased a Red Rock Grand Pass.

Stop by the Sedona–Oak Creek Chamber of Commerce to pick up a free map listing hikes in the area. The **Coconino National Forest** ranger station (☎ **520/282-4119**) on Brewer Road, just west of the intersection of Ariz. 89A and Ariz. 179, is also a good source of hiking information.

If you get thirsty while driving through the canyon, hold out for **Garlands General Store** in Indian Gardens, which is about 4 miles north of Sedona. Here you can get delicious organic apple juice made from apples grown in the canyon. For one last view down the canyon, stop at **Midgely Bridge** (just watch for the parked cars and small parking area at the north end of the bridge).

ATTRACTIONS & ACTIVITIES AROUND TOWN

Sedona's most notable architectural landmark is the ✪ **Chapel of the Holy Cross** (☎ **520/282-4069**), a small church built right into the red rock on the south side of town. If you're driving up from Phoenix, you can't miss the chapel. It sits high above the road just off Ariz. 179. With its contemporary styling, the chapel is one of the most architecturally important modern churches in the country. Marguerite Brunswig Staude, a devout Catholic painter, sculptor, and designer, had the inspiration for the chapel in 1932, but it wasn't until 1957 that her dream was finally realized. The chapel's design is dominated by a simple cross forming the wall that faces the street. The cross and the starkly beautiful chapel seem to grow directly from the rock, allowing the natural beauty of the red rock to speak for itself. The chapel is open daily 9am to 5pm.

The **Sedona Arts Center,** Ariz. 89A at Art Barn Road (☎ **520/282-3865** or 520/282-3809), near the north end of town, serves both as a gallery for artwork by local and regional artists and as a theater for plays and music performances. Art classes are also held here.

To learn a bit about the history of Sedona, stop by the **Sedona Heritage Museum,** 735 Jordan Rd. (☎ **520/282-7038**), in Jordan Historical Park. The museum, which is housed in a historic home, is furnished with antiques and also contains exhibits on the many movies that have been filmed in the area over the years. The farm was once an apple orchard and there is still apple-processing equipment in the barn. The museum is open Thursday to Monday 10am to 4pm, for a suggested donation of $3.

Out on the west side of town the new **Sedona Cultural Park** (☎ **800/780-2787** or 520/282-0747; www.sedonaculturalpark.com), which opened in May 2000, is home to an amphitheater and buildings for classes, workshops, and exhibitions. There are also nature trails and picnic areas.

If seeing the red rocks just isn't enough for you, there's always the **SuperVue Theater** (☎ **520/284-3214**), just off Ariz. 179 behind the factory outlet stores in the Village of Oak Creek. This big-screen theater is similar to an IMAX theater.

While Sedona isn't yet a resort destination on par with Phoenix or Tucson, it does have a few **spas** and treatment centers that might add just the right bit of relaxation and pampering to your Sedona vacation. **Therapy on the Rocks,** 676 N. Hwy. 89A (☎ **520/282-3002**), with its creek-side setting, is a long-time local favorite that offers myofacial release and great views of the red rocks. At Los Abrigados resort, you'll find the more traditional **Sedona Health Spa,** 160 Portal Lane (☎ **520/282-1777**), with a wide selection of body and beauty treatments, including body polishes, seaweed facials, and mineral wraps.

ORGANIZED TOURS

If you'd like to get an overview of Sedona, you can take a tour on the **Sedona Trolley** (☎ **520/282-5400**), which leaves several times each day on two separate tours. One tour visits Tlaquepaque, the Chapel of the Holy Cross, and several art galleries, while the other goes out through west Sedona to Boynton Canyon and Enchantment Resort. Tours are $7 for adults and $2 for children 12 and under. Call for the trolley stop nearest you.

The red rock country surrounding Sedona is the city's greatest natural attraction, and there's no better way to explore the red rock country than in a four-wheel-drive vehicle. If you're not inclined to rent your own Jeep, there's plenty of tour options. For more than 35 years, **Pink Jeep Tours,** 204 N. Hwy. 89A (☎ **800/873-3662** or 520/282-5000), has been heading deep into the Coconino National Forest. It offers nearly a dozen different tours ranging in length from 1¹/₂ hours ($35) to 3¹/₂ hours ($75). For a trip over the red rocks and for better value, you're best off springing for the 2-hour "Broken Arrow" tour ($60).

Sedona Red Rock Jeep Tours, 270 N. Hwy 89A (☎ **800/848-7728** or 520/282-6826), offers similar tours for $32 to $58. This latter company does helicopter-Jeep tours, horseback rides, and even a seasonal canoe tour to cave dwellings on the

Verde River. If you want some photographic tips while you tour the red rock country, try **Sedona Photo Tours,** 252 N. Hwy 89A (☎ **800/973-3662** or 520/282-4320), which charges comparable prices and operates the Kodak®-yellow Jeeps you see around town.

If you're interested in getting an aerial view of the area, you have several options. **Arizona Helicopter Adventures** (☎ **800/282-5141** or 520/282-0904) and **Sky-dance Helicopters** (☎ **800/882-1651** or 520/282-1651) both offer short flights to different parts of this colorful region. Prices start around $36 for a 10-minute flight. For a really memorable tour, try **Arizona Helicopter Adventures:** They will helicopter you to the top of a red-rock mesa for a romantic picnic and leave you there until you radio for pickup, all for only $1,295 per couple. **AeroVista** (☎ **520/ 282-7768**) and **West Wind Air Tours** (☎ **888/282-2037** or 520/282-2037) offer a variety of tours in small planes. These flights start at around $45 to $55 per person for a 25-minute flight. Flights as far afield as the Grand Canyon and Canyon de Chelly can be arranged.

However, our favorite tours are those of **Red Rock Biplane Tours** (☎ **888/ TOO-RIDE** or 520/204-5939), which operates two modern Waco open-cockpit biplanes. With the wind in your hair, you'll feel as though you've entered the world of *The English Patient.* A 20-minute tour is about $65 per person.

If something a bit slower is more your speed, **Red Rock Balloon Adventures** (☎ **800/ 258-3754** or 520/284-0040), **Northern Lights Balloon Expeditions** (☎ **800/ 230-6222** or 520/282-2274), and **Sky High Balloon Adventures** (☎ **800/ 551-SKYS** or 520/204-1395) offer peaceful hot-air-balloon rides over the canyons and sculpted buttes. Expect to pay around $145 for a 1- to 1¹/₂-hour ride.

SPORTS & OUTDOOR PURSUITS

Hiking is by far the most popular outdoor sport in the Sedona area, and with dozens of trails leading off into the red rocks, it's easy to understand why. Among the more popular and scenic hiking trails are those starting alongside Ariz. 179 just north of the Village of Oak Creek and leading up to Bell Rock. To explore the Cathedral Rock area, turn off Ariz. 179 at the sign for the Back o' Beyond housing development and watch for the trailhead at the end of the paved road. Another access to Cathedral Rock is from the National Forest Service's Red Rock Crossing recreation area off Upper Red Rock Loop Road on the west side of Sedona. Perhaps the most popular trails in the Sedona area are those that lead into Boynton Canyon (site of Enchantment Resort). Here you'll glimpse ancient Native American ruins built into the red rock cliffs. Also in this area are a pair of easy, though scenic, trails—the Fay Canyon Arch Trail and the Vultee Arch Trail. You'll find easy trails with great views about halfway to the top of Airport Mesa on Airport Road. For more information on hiking in Oak Creek Canyon (site of the famous West Fork Trail), see "Oak Creek Canyon," above. For more information on all these hikes, contact the **Coconino National Forest ranger station** (☎ **520/282-4119**) on Brewer Road, just west of the intersection of Ariz. 89A and Ariz. 179.

Sedona is rapidly becoming one of the **mountain-biking** meccas of the Southwest. The red rock here is every bit as challenging and scenic as the famed slick-rock country of Moab, Utah, and much less crowded. Using Sedona as a base, mountain bikers can ride year-round by heading up to Flagstaff in summer and down to the desert lowlands in winter. You can rent a mountain bike from **Sedona Sports,** Creekside Plaza below the "Y" (☎ **520/282-1317**), or **Mountain Bike Heaven,** 1695 W. Hwy. 89A (☎ **520/282-1312**). Rates are around $18 to $24 per half-day, or $25 to $39 per day. **Sedona Bike & Bean,** 6020 Hwy. 179 (☎ **520/284-0210**), across the street from the popular Bell Rock Pathway and its adjacent mountain-bike trails, rents bikes (and serves coffee). Bikes go for $24 for a half day and $39 for a full day. Any of these stores can sell you a map or guide to area rides.

Trail Horse Adventures at Kachina Stables, Lower Red Rock Loop Road (☎ 800/SADDLE-UP or 520/282-7252), offers guided horseback trail rides. Prices range from $30 for a 1-hour ride to $135 for an all-day ride (minimum two people; includes lunch). There are also breakfast, lunch, sunset, and multiday pack trips. Lower Red Rock Loop Road is west of Sedona on Ariz. 89A. **Sedona Red Rock Jeep Tours** (☎ 800/848-7728 or 520/282-6826) offers horseback riding ($42 for 1 hour, $55 for 2 hours). These rides include transportation by Jeep to the ranch where the rides are held.

Oak Creek is well known in Arizona as an excellent trout stream, and **fly fishing** is quite popular here. The creek is stocked with trout during the summer. If you're look-ing for a fly-fishing guide, call Jim McInnis of **Gon' Fishen** at ☎ **520/282-0788.** If you want to take the family fishing, try the **Rainbow Trout Farm** (☎ **520/ 282-3379**), 4 miles north of Sedona on Ariz. 89A.

Surprisingly, Sedona has not yet been ringed with **golf** courses. However, what few courses there are offer superb views to distract you from your game. The **Oak Creek Country Club,** 690 Bell Rock Blvd. (☎ **520/284-1660**), south of town off Ariz. 179, has stunning views from the course (greens fees $35 to $75). The ✪ **Sedona Golf Resort** (☎ **520/284-9355**), also located south of town on Ariz. 179, offers sim-ilar excellent views of the red rocks (greens fees $87 to $97).

The **tennis courts** at Poco Diablo Resort, on the south side of Sedona, are open to the public for $12 per hour. To make reservations, call the resort at ☎ **520/282-7333.**

SHOPPING

Ever since the famous Cowboy Artists of America organization was founded in Sedona back in 1965 (at what is now the Cowboy Club restaurant), this town has had a rep-utation as an artists' community. Today, with dozens of galleries around town, it is obvious that art is one of the driving forces behind the local economy. Most of Sedona's galleries specialize in traditional Western, contemporary Southwestern, and Native American art, and in some of the galleries around town, you'll see works by members of the Cowboy Artists of America. You'll find the greatest concentration of galleries and shops in the uptown area of Sedona (along Ariz. 89A just north of the "Y") and in the Tlaquepaque Arts and Crafts Village.

With more than 40 stores and restaurants, **Tlaquepaque Arts & Crafts Village** on Ariz. 179 (at the bridge over Oak Creek on the south side of Sedona), designed to resemble a Mexican village, is named after a famous arts-and-crafts neighborhood in the suburbs of Guadalajara, Mexico. The maze of narrow alleys, connecting court-yards, fountains, and even a chapel and a bell tower are worth a visit even if you aren't in a buying mood.

Unfortunately, many of Sedona's shops now specialize in cheap Southwestern gifts that have little to do with art, and weeding through the tacky gift shops to find the real galleries can be difficult. One place to start is at **Hozho,** where there are a couple of Sedona's better galleries, on Ariz. 179 just before you cross over the Oak Creek bridge in Sedona.

Compass Rose Gallery. Hillside Courtyard, 671 Ariz. 179. ☎ **520/282-7904.**

Oddly out of place, but certainly welcome on the overly souvenir-oriented Sedona shopping scene, this store sells old maps (up to $3,000), old prints, and Edward S. Curtis sepia-toned photos.

Cowboy Corral. 219 N. Hwy. 89A. ☎ **800/457-2279** or 520/282-2040.

If you've decided you want to adopt the Wyatt Earp or Annie Oakley look, this shop can outfit you. Definitely not your standard urban cowboy Western wear shop, Cowboy Corral goes for the vintage look. Classic firearms are available to accessorize your ensemble.

Garland's Indian Jewelry. At Indian Gardens, 4 miles north on Ariz. 89A. ☎ **520/282-6632.**

A great location in the shade of scenic Oak Creek Canyon and a phenomenal collection of concho belts, squash blossom necklaces, and bracelets make this a worthwhile stop.

✪ **Garland's Navajo Rugs.** 411 Hwy. 179. ☎ **520/282-4070.**

With a very large collection of both contemporary and antique Navajo rugs (claimed to be the biggest in the world), Garland's is the premier Navajo rug shop in Sedona. It also carries a line of Native American baskets and pottery, Hopi kachina dolls, and Navajo sandpaintings.

Hillside Courtyard. 671 Hwy. 179. ☎ **520/282-4500.**

This is a shopping center dedicated to art galleries, retail shops, and a couple of restaurants. Here you'll find the Clay Pigeon, with some nice ceramics and glass, and the Scherer Gallery (see below).

✪ **Hoel's Indian Shop.** 9440 N. Hwy. 89A. ☎ **520/282-3925.**

Located 10 miles north of Sedona in a private residence in Oak Creek Canyon (just past Hoel's Cabins), this Native American arts-and-crafts gallery is one of the finest in the region and sells pieces of the highest quality. Most customers are serious collectors. It's a good idea to call before coming out here to make sure the store will be open.

Prime Outlets. Hwy. 179, Village of Oak Creek. ☎ **888/545-7227** or 520/284-2150.

Yes, even Sedona (or, more correctly, the near community of the Village of Oak Creek) has an outlet mall. If you aren't in the market for art, but do need some cut-rate fashions, this is the place.

Scherer Gallery. Hillside Courtyard, 671 Hwy. 179. ☎ **520/203-9000** or 800/957-2673.

What makes this gallery unique is its collection of kaleidoscopes, which may be the largest in the country. More than a hundred kaleidoscope artists from around the world create the colorful concoctions here. You'll also find art glass, tasteful contemporary paintings, and Jack Acrey's large-format photographs of red rock landscapes.

Sedona Arts Center Gallery Shop. Ariz. 89A and Art Barn Rd. ☎ **520/282-3865.**

Located at the north end of uptown Sedona, this shop features works by area artists. You'll find everything from jewelry to fiber arts to photography to ceramics. This is the best place in town to see the work of Sedona artists. Since it's a nonprofit shop, you won't pay any tax here.

✪ **Son Silver West.** 1476 Hwy. 179 (on the south side of town). ☎ **520/282-3580.**

For those who love everything Southwestern, this shop is a treasure trove of all kinds of interesting stuff, from Native American and Hispanic arts and crafts to antique *santo* (saint) carvings and rifles to big imported pots, chili garlands (*ristras*), and garden art.

WHERE TO STAY

We have listed here some of our favorite of the many hotels, resorts, and B&Bs in the Sedona area. Sedona is one of the most popular tourist destinations in the Southwest and there are dozens of inexpensive and moderately priced motels in town. However, keep in mind that accommodations in the area are often relatively expensive for what you get. Blame it on the incomparable views.

EXPENSIVE

✪ **Briar Patch Inn.** 3190 N. Hwy. 89A, Sedona, AZ 86336. ☎ **888/809-3030** or 520/282-2342. Fax 520/282-2399. www.briarpatchinn.com. 18 units. $149–$295 double. Rates include full breakfast. AE, MC, V.

If you're searching for tranquility or a romantic retreat amid the cool shade of Oak Creek Canyon, this is the place. Located 3 miles north of Sedona on the banks of Oak Creek (there are even swimming holes here), this inn's cottages are set amid beautiful shady grounds where bird songs and the babbling creek set the mood. The cottages date from the 1930s but have all been attractively renovated and updated (some with flagstone floors). A Western style predominates, and some rooms have a fireplace and kitchenette. Breakfast is often served on a terrace above the creek, and there is a stone gazebo for creekside massages. All in all, the Briar Patch offers a delightful combination of solitude and sophistication—the quintessential romantic hideaway.

Canyon Villa. 125 Canyon Circle Dr., Sedona, AZ 86351. ☎ **800/453-1166** or 520/284-1226. Fax 520/284-2114. www.canyonvilla.com. 11 units. A/C TV TEL. $145–$225 double. Rates include full breakfast. AE, MC, V.

Located in the Village of Oak Creek, 6 miles south of Sedona, this big bed-and-breakfast offers luxurious accommodations and spectacular views of the red rocks. All rooms but one have views, as do the swimming pool area, living room, and dining room, so if you want to just hole up at the inn, you won't be missing the best of the area; it's right out your window. Guest rooms are varied—Victorian, Santa Fe, country, rustic, Americana, wicker—but no matter what the decor, the furnishings are impeccable, and there are such amenities as terry robes, whirlpool tubs, and double sinks. All the rooms have balconies or patios, and several have fireplaces. Breakfasts are lavish affairs meant to be lingered over, and in the afternoons there is an elaborate spread of snacks.

✪ **Enchantment Resort.** 525 Boynton Canyon Rd., Sedona, AZ 86336. ☎ **800/ 826-4180** or 520/282-2900. Fax 520/282-9249. www.enchantmentresort.com. 221 units. A/C MINIBAR TV TEL. $195–$325 double; $295–$425 casita parlor; $390–$650 1-bedroom suite; $655–$950 2-bedroom suite. AE, DC, DISC, MC, V.

Located at the mouth of Boynton Canyon, this resort more than lives up to its name. The setting is breathtaking, the pueblo-style architecture of the hotel blends in with the canyon landscape, and at press time a new spa was being planned. The individual casitas of this resort can be booked as two-bedroom suites, one-bedroom suites, or as single rooms, and it's worth booking a suite just so you can enjoy the casita living rooms, which feature high, beamed ceilings, beehive fireplaces, and Native American crafts. The large patios provide dramatic views of the canyon. The newest rooms, added in 1998, are worth requesting.

Dining/Diversions: Both the resort's main restaurant, the Yavapai Dining Room (see "Where to Dine," below), and a less formal bar and grill offer indoor dining and tables on the terrace. Lunch on the terrace is a meal not to be missed. The menu in both restaurants features innovative American cuisine.

Amenities: Although you won't find an 18-hole golf course here at Enchantment, you'll find just about everything else, including four pools, seven tennis courts, a croquet court, whirlpools, a fitness center, hiking trails, a six-hole pitch-and-putt course, and a putting green. The spa offers a wide variety of treatments and programs. The resort also offers a concierge, room service, tennis lessons, guided hikes, in-room massages, and children's programs.

✪ **The Graham Bed & Breakfast Inn & Adobe Village.** 150 Canyon Circle Dr., Sedona, AZ 86351. ☎ **800/228-1425** or 520/284-1425. Fax 520/284-0767. www.sedonasfinest. com. 10 units. A/C TV TEL. $169–$239 double; $249 suite; $329–$369 casita. Rates include full breakfast. AE, DISC, MC, V.

Located in the Village of Oak Creek, 6 miles south of Sedona, this inn lies almost at the foot of Bell Rock and features a variety of individually decorated rooms and suites. However, the casitas (and the newly added Sundance room) are the most impressive rooms in the Sedona area. From the outside, the four casitas look like an old adobe village arranged around courtyard gardens. Inside, however, each is very different. The Purple Lizard opts for a colorful Taos-style interior (lots of purple, teal, and magenta), has lots of Southwestern art, and an absolutely amazing rustic canopy bed. The Wilderness is a log cabin inside and has a fireplace that can be seen from both the living room and the double whirlpool tub. The Lonesome Dove is a sort of upscale cowboy cabin complete with wide plank floors, flagstone fireplace, potbelly stove, and swinging saloon doors leading into the bathroom, which has a round hot tub in a "barrel." The Sunset Casita features a sort of Mediterranean modern aesthetic that includes an elaborate wrought-iron four-poster bed with eight pillows and brocade bedspread, fireplaces in both the bathroom (beside the double whirlpool tub) and the living room, and a wall of glass. In addition to the whirlpool tubs, there are showers that have cascades of water rather than the usual spray you might expect. Can you say romantic?

✪ **The Inn on Oak Creek.** 556 Hwy. 179, Sedona, AZ 86336. ☎ **800/499-7896** or 520/282-7896. Fax 520/282-0696. www.sedona-inn.com. 11 units. A/C TV TEL. $160–$250 double. Rates include full breakfast. AE, DISC, MC, V.

Located right on Oak Creek and just around the corner from the Tlaquepaque shopping plaza, this luxurious modern inn offers the best of both worlds. A shady creekside setting lends it the air of a forest retreat, yet much of Sedona's shopping and many of its best restaurants are within walking distance. There is even a private little park on the bank of the creek. Guest rooms vary considerably in size, but all have interesting theme decors. Some of our personal favorites are the Garden Gate (with a picket fence headboard on the bed), Hollywood Out West (with old movie posters), the Rose Arbor (with creek views from both the tub and the bed), and the Angler's Retreat (with bentwood furniture, fly-fishing decor, and a fabulous view). Because the inn is built out over the creek, staying here is almost like staying on a cruise ship; you can look straight down into the water from your balcony. All the rooms come with VCRs and gas fireplaces, too.

Junipine Resort. 8351 N. Hwy. 89A, Sedona, AZ 86336. ☎ **800/742-PINE** or 520/282-3375. Fax 520/282-7402. www.junipine.com. 50 units. TV TEL. $170–$210 1-bedroom unit; $230–$265 2-bedroom unit (lower rates Nov–Feb). AE, DC, DISC, MC, V.

If you're coming up this way with the family and are looking for a place in the cool depths of Oak Creek Canyon (rather than amid the red rock views in Sedona proper), this condominium resort is a good bet. All the condos (here called creek houses) have loads of space (some with lofts), skylights, decks, stone fireplaces, decorative quilts on the walls, full kitchens, and contemporary styling. Some creek houses have hot tubs. Best of all, the creek is right outside the door of most units.

Dining/Diversions: The resort's dining room serves a surprisingly sophisticated Southwestern and regional American menu at reasonable prices, so there's no need to drive all the way into Sedona for a good meal.

Amenities: Room service.

L'Auberge de Sedona. 301 L'Auberge Lane (P.O. Box B), Sedona, AZ 86339. ☎ **800/ 272-6777** or 520/282-1661. Fax 520/282-2885. www.lauberge.com. 100 units. A/C TV TEL. Late Nov–Feb (excluding holidays) $160–$210 double, $220–$250 suite, $245–$355 cottage; Mar–late Nov and holidays $175–$240 double, $235–$280 suite, $315–$395 cottage. AE, CB, DC, DISC, MC, V.

Located in the heart of uptown Sedona, this resort claims an enviable location on a hillside above Oak Creek and amid the shade trees along the banks of the creek. However, the country French styling seems very inappropriate for such a quintessentially Southwestern setting. Likewise, room decor is for the most part quite fussy. However, if you had to forgo your vacation in France this year, you might enjoy a stay here. If you want spectacular views and sunsets, opt for a room in the resort's Orchards wing, which faces the red rocks but lacks the secluded setting of the main lodge or cottages. While the creek-side cottages set beneath shady sycamores look utterly rustic from the outside, the brown-painted log cabins actually hide rooms done in flowery country decor. With its two restaurants but only a pool and whirlpool for activities, this lodge is more romantic getaway than recreational resort.

Dining/Diversions: L'Auberge, serving six-course French dinners, is one of Sedona's most expensive restaurants. A more casual restaurant in the Orchards section serves simpler meals.

Amenities: Small outdoor pool, whirlpool, French boutique, concierge, room service, valet/laundry service, in-room massage, baby-sitting, access to nearby health club.

MODERATE

Best Western Inn of Sedona. 1200 W. Hwy. 89A, Sedona, AZ 86336. ☎ **800/292-6344** or 520/282-3072. Fax 520/282-7218. 110 units. A/C TV TEL. $85–$125 double. Rates include continental breakfast. AE, CB, DC, DISC, MC, V. Pets accepted.

Located about midway between uptown Sedona and west Sedona, this hotel has great views of the red rocks from its wide terraces and from the outdoor pool area. Unfortunately, although the guest rooms are comfortable enough, not all of them have views. However, the modern Southwestern styling of the hotel and the setting, surrounded by native landscaping and out of the tourist mainstream makes this an appealing choice. In addition to the outdoor pool, there's also a hot tub.

Doubletree Sedona Resort. 90 Ridge Trail Dr., Sedona, AZ 86351. ☎ **800/222-TREE** or 520/284-4040. Fax 520/284-6940. 225 units. A/C MINIBAR TV TEL $99–$199 double. AE, CB, DC, DISC, MC, V.

Opened in late 1998, this is Sedona's newest resort; affiliated with the Sedona Golf Resort, it has one of the most breathtaking golf courses in the state. While golf is the driving force behind most stays here, anyone looking for an active vacation will find something to keep him or her busy here. All the guest rooms are suites of varying sizes and come with microwaves, coffeemakers, and fireplaces. About the only drawback to this place is that it is quite a ways outside Sedona itself (actually south of the Village of Oak Creek), so it's a bit of a drive to Sedona's restaurants and shops and the beauties of Oak Creek Canyon.

Dining/Diversions: With its light California and Southwestern cuisine, the dining room places an emphasis on healthful cuisine and plays up its golf course and red rock views.

Amenities: 18-hole golf course; outdoor pool; fitness center; three racquetball and five tennis courts; full-service spa with whirlpool spas, saunas, steam rooms, and various spa treatments; room service; concierge.

✪ **Garland's Oak Creek Lodge.** P.O. Box 152, Sedona, AZ 86339. ☎ **520/282-3343.** www.garlandslodge.com. 16 units. $178–$198 double (all rates plus 15% gratuity). Rates include breakfast and dinner. 2-night minimum. MC, V. Closed mid-Nov to Mar 31 and Sun throughout the year.

Located 8 miles north of Sedona in the heart of Oak Creek Canyon, this lodge may be the hardest place in the area to get a reservation. People have been coming here for so many years and like it so much that they reserve a year in advance (last-minute cancellations do occur, so don't despair). What makes the lodge so special? Maybe it's that you have to drive *through* Oak Creek to get to your log cabin (don't worry—the water's shallow, and the creek bottom is paved). Maybe it's the beautiful gardens overlooking the creek. Or maybe it's the slow, relaxing atmosphere of an old-time summer getaway. Cabins have all been well maintained and are rustic but comfortable. The larger cabins have their own fireplaces.

Breakfast and dinner are included in the rates and are served in a rustic dining hall. Organic fruits and vegetables grown on the property are frequently used, and each evening features a different entree accompanied by soup, salad, homemade breads, and dessert. Cocktails and wine are available. Amenities include a tennis court and baby-sitting.

The Lodge at Sedona. 125 Kallof Place, Sedona, AZ 86336. ☎ **800/619-4467** or 520/204-1942. Fax 520/204-2128. www.lodgeatsedona.com. 14 units. A/C. $125–$175 double; $185–$245 suite. Rates include full breakfast. AE, DISC, MC, V.

Located in the West Sedona part of town, this large B&B is surrounded by desert landscaping that includes pine trees, rock gardens, waterfalls, sculptures, and a stone labyrinth. The rooms are all individually decorated; our personal favorites are the Lariat Room and the Master Suite (which is absolutely huge and has a stone fireplace). Upstairs rooms tend to be small and have showers only (instead of shower/tub combinations), so if you can afford to spend a little more, opt for a downstairs room, and ask for one with a whirlpool tub. With 14 rooms and suites, this lodging may seem large for a bed-and-breakfast, but size doesn't limit the hospitality of owners Barb and Mark Dinunzio, who make all their guests feel very much at home.

Poco Diablo. 1752 S. Hwy. 179 (P.O. Box 1709), Sedona, AZ 86339. ☎ **800/528-4275** or 520/282-7333. Fax 520/282-9712. www.pocodiablo.com. 137 units. A/C TV TEL. Mid-Feb to mid-Nov $115–$245 double, $265 suite; late Nov–early Feb $99–$235 double, $245 suite. AE, CB, DISC, MC, V.

Although not nearly as lavish as golf resorts down in Phoenix, this older golf and tennis resort, located on the southern outskirts of Sedona, benefited from a complete renovation a couple of years ago. Oak Creek runs through the 22-acre grounds, and the green fairways of the nine-hole golf course provide a striking contrast to the red rocks and blue skies. The views here are not as good as at some other comparable properties in the area, but the staff is courteous and helpful. With its Mission-style furnishings, contemporary Southwestern art, and Native American baskets and pottery, the lobby has the feel of a small inn, while the rest of the grounds all say resort. If you can afford to spend a bit more, be sure to ask for one of the rooms with a view of the golf course or the red rocks. These rooms have whirlpool tubs and fireplaces and are done in a modern rustic Southwest decor. The lower-end rooms are quite economical, but the upper-end rooms seem a bit overpriced.

The restaurant offers views of the golf course and red rocks and a Southwestern menu. The small, dark lounge is basically a sports bar. There are two small pools, three whirlpools, four tennis courts (two lighted), racquetball courts, nine-hole golf course, concierge, room service, valet/laundry service, and massages.

Rose Tree Inn. 376 Cedar St., Sedona, AZ 86336. ☎ **888/282-2065** or 520/282-2065. Fax 520/282-0083. www.rosetreeinn.com. 5 units. A/C TV TEL. $85–$135 double. AE, MC, V.

This little inn, only a block from Sedona's uptown shopping district, is tucked amid pretty gardens (yes, there are lots of roses) on a quiet street. The inn consists of an eclectic cluster of older buildings that have all been renovated. Four of the rooms have kitchenettes, which makes them good choices for families or for a longer stay. All the rooms are furnished a little bit differently—one Victorian, one Southwestern, another with a gas fireplace. There's also a whirlpool, and complimentary coffee and tea are available.

Saddle Rock Ranch. 255 Rock Ridge Dr., Sedona, AZ 86336. ☎ **520/282-7640.** Fax 520/282-6829. www.saddlerockranch.com. 3 units. A/C TV. $140–$175 double. Rates include full breakfast. No credit cards.

The stunning views alone would make this one of Sedona's better lodging choices, but on top of the views, you get classic Western ranch styling (the house was built in 1926) in a home that once belonged to Barry Goldwater. Walls of stone and adobe, a flagstone floor in the living room, huge exposed beams, and plenty of windows to take in the scenery are enough to enchant guests even before they reach their rooms. And the rooms don't disappoint, either. In one you'll find Victorian elegance, in another an English canopy bed and stone fireplace. Dressing areas and private gardens add to the charm. The third room is a separate little Western cottage with a lodgepole-pine bed, flagstone floors, and beamed ceiling. The pool and whirlpool are surrounded by a flagstone terrace and enjoy one of the best red rock views in town.

INEXPENSIVE

Canyon Portal Motel. 280 N. Hwy. 89A, Sedona, AZ 86336. ☎ **800/542-8484** or 520/282-7125. 20 units. A/C TV TEL. Summer and holidays $69–$89 double; $105–$150 suite or house (lower rates other times of year). DISC, MC, V.

Located behind the tourist shops and Jeep tour offices in uptown Sedona, this modest little motel can claim some of the best views in town. Most of the rooms, although quite basic, are large, and some have balconies. Just be sure you ask for a room with a view; they're only $10 more than the cheapest rooms. Behind the motel, you'll find a small pool and hot tub with the same great red-rock views.

Cedars Resort. 20 W. Hwy. 89A (P.O. Box 292), Sedona, AZ 86339. ☎ **520/282-7010.** Fax 520/282-5372. 38 units. A/C TV TEL. $69–$99 double. AE, CB, DC, DISC, MC, V.

Located right at the "Y" (where it is often difficult to get out of the parking lot) and within walking distance of uptown Sedona, this economical motel has a fabulous view across Oak Creek to the towering red rocks. It also has a small pool, a hot tub, and a long stairway (77 steps) leading down to Oak Creek. Guest rooms are large, and all have refrigerators. For the best views, ask for a king-size room.

Matterhorn Lodge. 230 Apple Ave., Sedona, AZ 86336. ☎ **520/282-7176.** Fax 520/282-0727. www.sedona.net/hotel/matterhorn. 23 units. A/C TV TEL. Mid-Feb to Nov $74–$99 double; Dec–early Feb $49–$79 double. AE, MC, V. Small pets accepted.

Located in the heart of the uptown shopping district, the Matterhorn is convenient to restaurants and shopping, and all rooms have excellent views of the red rock canyon walls. Guest rooms have modern furnishings and in-room amenities include coffeemakers, hair dryers, and refrigerators. You'll also find an outdoor pool and whirlpool. Although the hotel overlooks busy U.S. 89A, if you lie in bed and keep your eyes on the rocks, you'll never notice the traffic below. This motel may not have a lot of character, but it is a good value for Sedona.

Oak Creek Terrace Resort. 4548 N. Hwy. 89A, Sedona, AZ 86336. ☎ **800/224-2229** or 520/282-3562. Fax 520/282-6061. www.oakcreekterrace.com. 20 units. A/C TV TEL. $72–$165 double. AE, DISC, MC, V. Small dogs accepted, $25 nonrefundable fee.

Wedged between the highway and Oak Creek about 5 miles north of Sedona on Ariz. 89A, this is sort of a budget romantic getaway. For as little as $79 you can get a room with a fireplace, and for $89 you can get a room with an in-room whirlpool. There are hammocks beside the creek, so you can stretch out in the shade, and a picnic area with barbecue grills if you want to save money on your dining budget. Rooms range from cramped to spacious, and most have a modern woodsy feel to them (but with a bit of Southwest styling thrown in). To get closer to the creek and farther from the highway, ask for a room in back. There are even on-site Jeep rentals.

Sedona Motel. P.O. Box 1450 (almost at the intersection of Ariz. 179 and Ariz. 89A), Sedona, AZ 86339. ☎ **520/282-7187.** 16 units. A/C TV TEL. $49–$89 double. DISC, MC, V.

Although the Sedona Motel looks like any other older motel from the outside, once you check in, you'll find a few surprises. First and foremost is the view across the parking lot to the red rocks. You can pay twice as much in Sedona and not have views this good. Despite being right on the highway, the hotel's double-paned windows help keep the rooms quiet and cool. Furnishings and bathroom fixtures are usually a cut above motel standards, which adds up to comfort and a good value.

✪ **Sky Ranch Lodge.** Airport Rd. (P.O. Box 2579), Sedona, AZ 86339. ☎ **888/708-6400** or 520/282-6400. Fax 520/282-7682. www.skyranchlodge.com. 94 units. A/C TV TEL. $75–$200 double. AE, MC, V. Pets accepted; $10 charge.

This motel is located atop Airport Mesa and has the most stupendous view in town. From here you can see the entire red rock country, with Sedona filling the valley below. Of course, the rooms with the best views are also the most expensive ($129 to $179), but if you're willing to walk a few feet for your view, you can stay here for much less. Although the rooms are fairly standard motel-style, some have such features as gas fireplaces, barn-wood walls, and balconies. They all have coffeemakers.

CAMPGROUNDS

Within the reaches of Oak Creek Canyon along U.S. 89A, there are five National Forest Service campgrounds. Of these, **Bootlegger,** 9 miles north of town, is the largest, but **Manzanita,** 6 miles north of town, is the most pleasant (and the only one open in winter). Other Oak Creek Canyon campgrounds include **Pine Flat,** 13 miles north of town, and **Cave Springs,** 12 miles north of town. The **Beaver Creek Campground,** 3 miles east of I-17 on FR 618, which is an extension of Ariz. 179 (take exit 298 off I-17), is a pleasant camp spot near the V-Bar-V petroglyph site. For more information on area campgrounds, stop by the **Coconino National Forest ranger station** (☎ 520/282-4119) on Brewer Road, just west of the intersection of U.S. 89A and Ariz. 179. Reservations can be made for Pine Flat and Cave Springs campgrounds; contact the **National Recreation Reservation Service** (☎ 800/280-2267; www.reserveusa.com).

Super Sedona Sunset Spots

If you thought the rocks were beautiful at noon, wait 'til you see the way they glow in the setting sun. Some of the best spots for taking in Sedona's sunsets are the following:

- Airport Mesa (arrive early to get a parking space at the trailhead, which is near the top of the mesa).

- Bell Rock Pathway, which is at the foot of Bell Rock between Sedona and the Village of Oak Creek.

- Dry Creek and Boynton Pass roads, which are both near Enchantment Resort (avoid the latter if it's muddy).

- Enchantment Resort's restaurant, lounge, or adjacent terraces, all of which are very civilized and very popular.

- Crescent Moon Recreation Area on Red Rock Loop Road (west of Sedona off Ariz. 89A).

WHERE TO DINE

Restaurants in Sedona tend to be expensive, so your best bets for economical meals are sandwich shops or ethnic restaurants. For filling sandwiches, try **Sedona Memories,** 321 Jordan Rd. (☎ **520/282-0032**), 1 block off Ariz. 89A in the uptown shopping area. As you wait for your order you can also peruse the collection of old Western movie posters and photos. **Connelly's Sedona Market,** 162 Hwy. 179, at the "Y" (☎ **520/282-4226**), also makes up tasty inexpensive sandwiches to go. For breakfast, locals swear by the **Coffee Pot Restaurant,** 2050 W. Hwy. 89A (☎ **520/282-6626**). For baked goods such as croissants and bread made with organic flour, visit the **Desert Flour Bakery & Bistro,** in Oak Creek Village at 6446 Hwy. 179 (☎ **520/ 284-4633**), and in West Sedona at 3150 W. Hwy. 89A (☎ **520/204-9921**).

EXPENSIVE

✪ **Cowboy Club.** 241 N. Hwy. 89A. ☎ **520/282-4200.** Reservations recommended. Main courses $6–$13 at lunch, $12–$30 at dinner. AE, DISC, MC, V. Daily 11am–10pm. SOUTHWESTERN.

With its big green booths, huge steer horns over the bar, and cowboy gear adorning the walls, this place looks like a glorified cowboy steakhouse, but when you see the menu, you'll know it's more than your average meat-and-potatoes joint. This is big flavor country, and the menu isn't the sort any real cowboy would likely have anything to do with. To start out, you can have fried cactus strips with black-bean caramel gravy or deep-fried pieces of snake with prickly pear–tequila sauce. For an entree, grilled salmon with chipotle hollandaise or the buffalo meatloaf with smoked tomato sauce are almost too good to pass by. At lunch, burgers and sandwiches are mainstays, but you can also get baby back ribs with raspberry-plum barbecue sauce. Just don't miss the sweet potato fries. Service is relaxed and friendly. By the way, it was in this building that the Cowboy Artists of America organization was formed back in 1965.

Adjacent to the Cowboy Club is an upscale version of the same restaurant, the Silver Saddle. Decor is more luxurious, with huge suede-covered booths and Western paintings, and a similar but toned-down menu with higher prices.

◆ Dahl & DiLuca. 2321 W. Hwy. 89A (in West Sedona diagonally across from the Safeway Plaza). ☎ **520/282-5219.** Reservations recommended. Main courses $10–$24. AE, DISC, MC, V. Daily 5–10pm. ROMAN ITALIAN.

In an atmosphere that is both romantic and humorous, brightly colored cherubs dance across the ceiling amid opulent decor. Maybe they're joyous because they've just eaten some *pane romano*, which, as far as we're concerned, is the best garlic bread west of New York's Little Italy. Pasta predominates here, and portions are big. We like the linguine with calamari and mushrooms in a deep red basil sauce. The kitchen also serves up a panoply of deftly prepared seafood, chicken, and vegetarian dishes. Sauteed prawns in a garlic-parsley wine sauce are a real standout. Genial and efficient service, reasonably priced wines, and occasional live piano music make this place even more enjoyable. An amaretto crème brûlée or a deceptively light chocolate espresso mousse torte—that's the sort of difficult decision you'll have to make when it comes time for dessert.

René at Tlaquepaque. Tlaquepaque, Suite 118 (on Ariz. 179). ☎ **520/282-9225.** Reservations recommended. Main courses $8–$12 at lunch, $18–$29 at dinner. AE, MC, V. Mon–Thurs 11:30am–2:30pm and 5:30–8:30pm; Fri 11:30am–2:30pm and 5:30–9pm; Sat 11:30am–3pm and 5:30–9pm; Sun 11:30am–2:30pm and 5:30–8:30pm. Closes earlier weekdays in summer. CONTINENTAL/AMERICAN.

Slightly less expensive than the dining room at L'Auberge de Sedona resort, this elegant, traditional restaurant (lace curtains and paintings by Southwestern artists) offers the same sort of formal dining experience and traditional French fare. Located in Tlaquepaque, the city's upscale south-of-the-border–themed shopping center, René's is a great place for a special lunch or dinner. You might start off with traditional escargots or the spinach salad, followed by the house specialty rack of lamb or lamb chops with pistachio butter. More adventurous diners may want to try the excellent tenderloin of venison with whiskey–juniper berry sauce, or the roasted duck with sun-dried cherry sauce. Finish with a flambéed dessert and selections from the after-dinner drink cart, then settle back to enjoy a warm glow of well-being. At lunch you could try the coriander-crusted pork tenderloin or chicken cordon bleu, Southwest style.

◆ Yavapai Dining Room. In the Enchantment Resort, 525 Boynton Canyon Rd. ☎ **520/204-6000.** Reservations highly recommended. Main courses $10–$17 at lunch, $21–$37 at dinner. AE, DISC, MC, V. Daily 6:30am–2:30pm and 5:30–9:30pm; Sun brunch 10:30am–2:30pm ($28.50, reservations required). SOUTHWESTERN.

Because the view of the red rocks of Boynton Canyon are so much a part of the experience of dining here, we recommend coming out to this classy resort for lunch or, preferably, a sunset dinner. Much of the dinner menu changes regularly, but it usually includes a few popular signature dishes. Among such dishes are the surprisingly complex black-bean soup, which gets a special touch with applewood-smoked bacon and cumin-scented tortilla strips. As for the entrees, tasty standouts include rack of lamb with a pistachio crust. The dessert tray is, of course, enchantingly decadent.

MODERATE

Fournos Restaurant. 3000 W. Hwy. 89A. ☎ **520/282-3331.** Reservations highly recommended. Main courses $13–$16. No credit cards. Thurs–Sat seatings at 6 and 8pm. MEDITERRANEAN.

In contrast to the glitz and modern Southwest decor of so many other of Sedona's restaurants, Fournos is a refreshingly casual place run by the husband and wife team of Shirley and Demetrios Fournos. Pots and ladles hang from the kitchen ceiling in this tiny place where chef Demetrios cooks up a storm, preparing such dishes as Greek salads with homemade kalamata olives and shrimp flambéed in ouzo and baked with feta cheese. Many of the people who eat here are regulars, but even if this is your first time, Shirley will make you feel right at home. The menu is written on a chalkboard and includes specialties such as lamb Cephalonian with herbs and potatoes and poached fish Mykonos with a sauce of yogurt, onions, mayonnaise, and butter. Other specialties are rack of lamb and lamb Wellington, for a slightly higher price than the usual dinners. Greek pastries, such as a flourless semolina-honey sponge cake, come with ice cream and fruit for a delicious dessert.

✪ **The Heartline Cafe.** 1610 W. Hwy. 89A. ☎ **520/282-0785.** Reservations recommended. Main courses $6–$13 at lunch, $15–$28 at dinner. AE, CB, DC, DISC, MC, V. Fri–Mon 11am–3pm; daily 5–9:15pm. SOUTHWESTERN/INTERNATIONAL.

The heart line, from Zuni mythology, is a symbol of health and longevity; it is also a symbol for the food here—healthful and very creative. Service is great, and crusty rolls appears on the table immediately (accompanied by an unusual spread made from butternut squash). Attention to detail and creative flavor combinations are the order of the day. Large salads, such as watercress with grapes and pistachios or spinach with gorgonzola cheese and pecans, have sublime flavors and make tasty starters. Memorable entrees include halibut with ginger-lemongrass butter, and smoked mozzarella ravioli. Lunch fare leans toward imaginative sandwiches and salads. Those searching out variety in vegetarian choices will find it here; those on a budget might want to come at lunch when prices are a lot lower. A beautiful courtyard outside and a traditionally elegant interior are good places to savor a meal accompanied by a selection from the reasonably priced and well-chosen wine list, or desserts such as a fruit berry tart with warm hazelnut sauce.

Pietro's Italian Restaurant. 2445 W. 89A (in West Sedona diagonally across from the Safeway Plaza). ☎ **520/282-2525.** Reservations recommended. Main courses $16–$24; pastas $14–$18. AE, CB, DC, DISC, MC, V. Mar–Oct daily 5:30–9:30pm; Nov–Feb daily 5–9pm. TUSCAN.

Pietro's pushes the envelope of Italian creativity. You'll find appetizers such as calamari with smoked tomato-and-basil aïoli and grilled eggplant rolled with goat cheese in a red-pepper sauce. For a pasta you might try fettuccine with duck confit, shiitake mushrooms, and figs in a port-wine sauce. Main courses are not quite as daring, but such dishes as boneless game hen with fresh rosemary, lemon, and garlic are certainly tasty. A wide range of wines, including many rare Italian reds and American boutique wines, are available by the glass. Another good reason to come here is for house-made desserts, such as passion fruit–cinnamon sorbet, crêpes filled with fresh berries, and *zabaglione*, a heavenly traditional Italian custard. On Sunday through Wednesday from opening until 6:30pm, less expensive southern Italian dinners, such as lasagna, are served. Parking is in back of the restaurant—look sharp for the driveway, which is to the east of the building.

Robert's Creekside Café. Creekside Plaza, 251 Ariz. 179. ☎ **520/282-3671.** Reservations recommended. Main courses $6–$8 at lunch, $13–$19 at dinner. AE, DISC, MC, V. Sun–Thurs 11am–9pm; Fri–Sat 11am–10pm. SOUTHWEST.

This place bustles, and tables are small and close together, so we like to opt for a seat on the patio if it's available. At lunch, there are salads and sandwiches, such as a hearty eggplant sandwich with goat cheese and roasted red pepper. Dinner sees the likes of well-done seafoods and cracked-pepper steak. We especially like the nibble-perfect house smoked salmon pâté. There are more than the usual vegetarian choices here, especially in the realm of side dishes. Don't forget to top it all off with Robert's justifiably famous peach cobbler. And, if you show up on a weekend night, you just might catch some live music.

Sedona Swiss Restaurant & Cafe. 350 Jordan Rd. ☎ **520/282-7959.** Reservations recommended. Main courses lunch $5–$7, dinner $10–$25. AE, MC, V. Restaurant Mon–Sat 11am–2pm and 5:30–9:30pm; cafe Mon–Sat 7:30am–6pm. Shorter hours in winter. SWISS/EUROPEAN.

Chef Robert Ackermann, this restaurant's founder and formerly the executive chef at the Swiss embassy in Washington, D.C., is the raison d'être for this authentically Swiss restaurant in a quiet spot near old-town Sedona (although tourist buses tend to disembark near here). You'll find classic Swiss and French fare such as *Rahmschnitzel* (sauteed pork scaloppini in a mushroom-cream sauce), cheese fondue, and the house specialty, *Galgenspiess*—beef tenderloin dramatically flambéed at your table. You can dine inside the cozy restaurant or outside on the patio. Visit the cafe/pastry shop for dessert and coffee.

INEXPENSIVE

The Hideaway Restaurant. Country Square, Ariz. 179. ☎ **520/282-4204.** Reservations for 10 or more only. Main courses lunch $5.50–$8, dinner $8.50–$11. AE, DC, DISC, MC, V. Spring and summer daily 11am–10pm; fall and winter daily 11am–9pm. ITALIAN/DELI.

Hidden away at the back of a shopping plaza near the "Y," this casual family restaurant is as popular with locals as it is with visitors, despite the relatively high lunch prices. Pizzas, subs, sandwiches, salads, and pastas are the choices here, and although none of these dishes is particularly remarkable, the views from the deck certainly are. From the shady porch you can see the creek below and the red rocks rising up across the canyon. An early sunset dinner is your best bet here.

India Palace. 1910 W. Hwy. 89A ((next to Basha's). ☎ **520/204-2300.** Complete dinners $12–$14; entrees $7–$13. AE, DC, DISC, MC, V. Daily 11am–2:30pm and 5–10pm. NORTHERN INDIAN.

Good Indian food in a no-frills atmosphere is what you have here. We like the nicely marinated chicken tandoori and textural breads such as garlic naan and parantha stuffed with spicy vegetables. There are lots of veggie options here, even in the all-you-can-eat buffet lunch, which goes for $5.95 per person.

Javelina Cantina. 671 Hwy. 179 (in the Hillside Courtyard shopping plaza). ☎ **520/ 203-9514.** Reservations recommended at dinner. Main courses $8.50–$19. AE, DC, MC, V. Daily 11:30am–9:30pm. MEXICAN.

Although Javelina Cantina is part of a chain of Arizona restaurants, the formula works, and few diners go away disappointed. Sure the restaurant is touristy, but what it has going for it is good Mexican food, a lively atmosphere, decent views from the windows, and a convenient location in the Hillside shops (so you can do a bit of shopping before or after dining). Shrimp *albondigas* (meatball) soup comes in a rich and hearty broth, and the grilled fish tacos are tasty. There are also the usual combo dishes and fajitas, with plenty of different margaritas and tequilas to accompany your meal. Expect a wait.

SEDONA PERFORMING ARTS AND NIGHTLIFE

With the opening in May 2000 of the new **Sedona Cultural Park** (☎ **800/ 780-2787** or 520/282-0747; www.sedonaculturalpark.com), Sedona finally got a performing arts space that takes full advantage of the magnificent scenery. The main attraction of the cultural park is its amphitheater, which will host a wide variety of performances throughout each summer. During the summer, the **Shakespeare Sedona** festival stages plays both here at the cultural park and also at another venue in Sedona. Tickets are $16 to $22; for tickets or more information, contact Sedona Cultural Park or http://shakespearesedona.com.

You can also catch frequent music performances and theater productions at the **Sedona Arts Center,** U.S. 89A at Art Barn Road (☎ **520/282-3809**). Theater fans might also want to check the schedule of the **Actors Repertory Theater of Sedona** (☎ **520/204-2064**), Sedona's professional acting company.

If all the entertainment you need is a pleasant place for a sunset cocktail, you'll want to head out to the Enchantment Resort, where the lounge and adjacent patio boast some of the best sunsets in the state. (See "Where to Stay," above, for directions.) If it's microbrewed beer you're after, drop by the **Oak Creek Brewing Co.,** 2050 Yavapai Dr. (☎ **520/204-1300**), which is north of Ariz. 89A off Coffee Pot Drive.

The Grand Canyon & Northern Arizona

6

The Grand Canyon—the name is at once apt and inadequate. How can words sum up the grandeur of 2 billion years of the earth's history sliced open by the power of a single river? Once an impassable and forbidding barrier to explorers and settlers, the Grand Canyon is today a magnet that each year attracts millions of visitors from all over the world. The pastel layers of rock weaving through the rugged ramparts of the canyon, the interplay of shadows and light, the wind in the pines and the croaking of ravens on the rim are the sights and sounds that never fail to transfix the millions of visitors who annually gaze awestruck into the canyon's seemingly infinite depths.

Yet other parts of northern Arizona contain worthwhile, and less crowded, attractions. Only 60 miles south of the great yawning chasm stand the San Francisco Peaks, the tallest of which, Humphreys Peak, rises to 12,643 feet. These peaks, sacred to the Hopi and Navajo, are ancient volcanoes that today are popular with skiers, hikers, and mountain bikers. The eruption in this region of smaller volcanoes in the not-too-distant past helped turn the land northeast of Flagstaff into fertile farmland that supported Sinagua people, who have long since disappeared, leaving only the ruins of their ancient villages.

Amid northern Arizona's miles of windswept plains and ponderosa pine forests stands the city of Flagstaff, which at 7,000 feet in elevation is one of the highest cities in the United States. It's home to Northern Arizona University, whose students ensure that Flagstaff is a lively town. Born of the railroads and named for a flagpole, Flagstaff is best known as the jumping-off point for trips to the Grand Canyon. However, the city has preserved its Western heritage in its restored downtown historic district.

While it is the Grand Canyon that brings most people to northern Arizona, the region actually has much more to offer, and since most people spend only a day or so in Grand Canyon National Park, you may want to take a look at what else there is to do in this part of the state. If, on the other hand, you only want to visit the canyon, there are many different ways to accomplish this goal. You can do so in a group or alone, on foot or by raft, from a mule or a helicopter. Regardless of what you decide, you'll find that the Grand Canyon more than lives up to its name.

1 Flagstaff

150 miles N of Phoenix; 32 miles E of Williams; 80 miles S of Grand Canyon Village

At 7,000 feet above sea level, Flagstaff, a classic western mountain town, is one of the highest cities in the country and best known as the jumping-off point for trips to the South Rim of the Grand Canyon. However, with its wide variety of accommodations and restaurants, the great outdoors at the edge of town, three national monuments nearby, one of the state's finest museums, and a university that supports a lively cultural community, Flagstaff is an ideal base for exploring much of northern Arizona.

The San Francisco Peaks, just north of the city and the site of the Arizona Snowbowl ski area, are one of Arizona's main winter playgrounds. In summer, miles of trails on these same mountains attract hikers and mountain bikers, and it's even possible to ride the ski lift at Arizona Snowbowl for a panoramic vista that stretches 70 miles north to the Grand Canyon. Of the area's national monuments, two preserve ancient Indian ruins and one preserves an otherworldly landscape of volcanic cinder cones.

It was as a railroad town that Flagstaff made its fortunes, and after several years of renovation, the town's historic downtown offers a glimpse of the days when the city's fortunes rode the rails. The railroad still runs right through the middle of Flagstaff, much to the dismay of many visitors, who find that most of the city's inexpensive motels are too close to the busy tracks to allow them to get a good night's sleep.

ESSENTIALS

GETTING THERE   Flagstaff is on I-40, one of the main east-west interstates in the United States. I-17 starts here and heads south to Phoenix. U.S. 89A connects Flagstaff to Sedona by way of Oak Creek Canyon. U.S. 180 connects Flagstaff with the South Rim of the Grand Canyon, and U.S. 89 connects to Page.

Flagstaff's Pulliam Airport, 3 miles south of town off I-17, is served by **America West** (☎ 800/235-9292) from Phoenix.

Flagstaff is served by **Amtrak** (☎ 800/872-7245 or 520/774-8679 for schedule information) from Chicago and Los Angeles. The train station is at 1 E. Route 66.

VISITOR INFORMATION   For more information, contact the **Flagstaff Visitors Center,** 1 E. Route 66, Flagstaff, AZ 86001-5745 (☎ 800/842-7293 or 520/774-9541; www.flagstaffarizona.org).

GETTING AROUND   Car rentals are available from **Avis** (☎ 800/331-1212 or 520/774-8421), **Budget** (☎ 800/527-0700 or 520/779-5255), **Enterprise** (☎ 800/325-8007 or 520/526-1377), **Hertz** (☎ 800/654-3131 or 520/774-4452), and **National** (☎ 800/227-7368 or 520/774-3321).

If you need a taxi, call **Friendly Cab** (☎ 520/774-4444). **Pine Country Transit** (☎ 520/779-6624), provides public bus transit around the city; the fare is 75¢ for adults.

ORIENTATION   Downtown Flagstaff is just north of I-40. Milton Road, which at its southern end becomes I-17 to Phoenix, leads past Northern Arizona University on its way into downtown, where it becomes Route 66. Route 66 runs parallel to the railroad tracks. Downtown's main street is San Francisco Street; Humphreys Street leads north out of town toward the San Francisco Peaks and the South Rim of the Grand Canyon.

The Grand Canyon & Northern Arizona

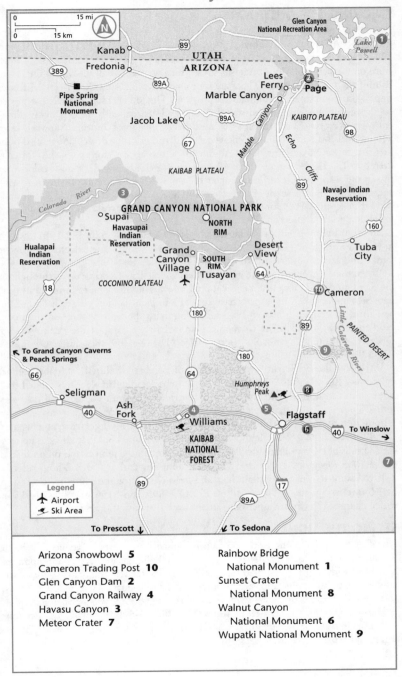

Legend
✈ Airport
⛷ Ski Area

Arizona Snowbowl **5**
Cameron Trading Post **10**
Glen Canyon Dam **2**
Grand Canyon Railway **4**
Havasu Canyon **3**
Meteor Crater **7**

Rainbow Bridge
  National Monument **1**
Sunset Crater
  National Monument **8**
Walnut Canyon
  National Monument **6**
Wupatki National Monument **9**

ENJOYING THE OUTDOORS

Flagstaff is northern Arizona's center for outdoor activities. Chief among them is snow skiing at **Arizona Snowbowl** (information ☎ **520/779-1951;** snow report 520/779-4577; snow report from Phoenix 602/957-0404; www.arizonasnowbowl. com) on the slopes of Mount Agassiz, from which you can see all the way to the North Rim of the Grand Canyon. There are four chair lifts, 32 runs, 2,300 vertical feet of slopes, ski rentals, and a children's ski program. This ski area has an excellent mix of beginner, intermediate, and advanced slopes, and consequently attracts many different types of skiers. As the ski area that's most accessible from Phoenix, Snowbowl sees a lot of weekend traffic from the snow-starved denizens of the desert. Snow conditions here are, however, very unreliable. All-day lift tickets are $37 for adults, $20 for children 8 to 12, $17 for seniors 65 to 69, and free for children under 8 and seniors over 69. In the summer you can ride a chair lift almost to the summit of Mount Agassiz and enjoy the expansive views across seemingly all of northern Arizona. The round-trip lift ticket price is $9 for adults, $6.50 for seniors, $5 for children 6 to 12, and free for children 5 and under.

Snowbowl also operates the **Flagstaff Nordic Center** (☎ **520/779-1951**), which is 16 miles north of Flagstaff and has 40 kilometers of groomed track. Equipment rentals and ski lessons are available. All-day trail passes are $10.

When there's no snow on the ground, there are plenty of **hiking trails** throughout the San Francisco Peaks, and many national forest trails are open to mountain bikes. Late September, when the aspens have turned a brilliant golden yellow, is one of the best times of year for a hike in Flagstaff's mountains. For information on the many excellent hiking trails in the Coconino National Forest, contact the **Peaks Ranger District,** Coconino National Forest, 5075 N. Hwy. 89, Flagstaff, AZ 86004 (☎ **520/526-0866**).

If you feel like saddlin' up and hittin' the trail, contact **Hitchin' Post Stables,** 4848 Lake Mary Rd. (☎ **520/774-1719**). This horseback-riding stable offers guided trail rides, sunset steak rides, and cowboy breakfast rides. The most popular trail ride goes into Walnut Canyon, site of ancient cliff dwellings. Ride prices range from $45 for a 2-hour ride to $95 for a full-day Walnut Canyon ride. **Flying Heart at Flagstaff** (☎ **520/526-2788**), 3¹/₂ miles north of Flagstaff Mall on U.S. 89, leads rides up into the foothills of the San Francisco Peaks and out through the juniper and piñon forests of the lower elevations. Rides are $25 for a 1-hour ride and $45 for a 2-hour ride.

If you want to rent a mountain bike and head out on the trails around town, stop by **Mountain Sports,** 1800 S. Milton Rd. (☎ **800/286-5156** or 520/779-5156), which charges $25 (front suspension) to $45 (full suspension) a day.

SEEING THE SIGHTS

Downtown Flagstaff along Route 66, San Francisco Street, Aspen Avenue, and Birch Avenue is the city's **historic district.** The old brick buildings of this neighborhood are now filled with shops selling Native American handcrafts, arts and crafts by local artisans, Route 66 souvenirs, and various other Arizona souvenirs such as rocks, minerals, and crystals. This historic area is worth a walkthrough even if you aren't shopping.

During the summer, **Nava-Hopi Tours** (☎ **520/774-5003**) operates a trolley tour that takes in most of the city's museums and other attractions. Tours cost $19.50 for adults and $9.50 for children ages 5 to 15.

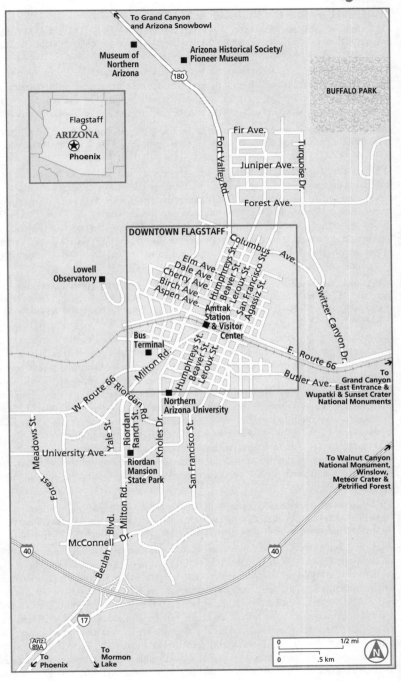

Flagstaff

To Grand Canyon
and Arizona Snowbowl

Museum of
Northern
Arizona

Arizona Historical Society/
Pioneer Museum

180

BUFFALO PARK

Flagstaff
ARIZONA
Phoenix

Fir Ave.

Juniper Ave.

Turquoise Dr.

Fort Valley Rd.

Forest Ave.

Lowell
Observatory

DOWNTOWN FLAGSTAFF

Columbus Ave.

Elm Ave.
Dale Ave.
Cherry Ave.
Birch Ave.
Aspen Ave.

Humphreys St.
Beaver St.
Leroux St.
San Francisco St.
Agassiz St.

Amtrak
Station
& Visitor
Center

Bus
Terminal

Milton Rd.

Humphreys St.
Beaver St.
Leroux St.

E. Route 66

Switzer Canyon Dr.

Butler Ave.

To
Grand Canyon
East Entrance &
Wupatki & Sunset Crater
National Monuments

W. Route 66

Riordan Rd.

Riordan
Ranch St.

Knoles Dr.

Northern
Arizona University

San Francisco St.

Meadows St.

Yale St.

University Ave.

Riordan
Mansion
State Park

To Walnut Canyon
National Monument,
Winslow,
Meteor Crater &
Petrified Forest

Forest

Milton Rd.

Beulah Blvd.

McConnell

40

40

17

Ariz
89A

To
Phoenix

To
Mormon
Lake

0   1/2 mi
0   .5 km

N

197

MUSEUMS, PARKS & CULTURAL ACTIVITIES

The Arboretum at Flagstaff. 4001 Woody Mountain Rd. ☎ **520/774-1442.** www.thearb.org. Admission $3 adults, $1 youths 6–17, free for children under 6. Daily 9am–5pm. Guided tours at 11am and 1pm. Closed mid-Dec to late Mar.

Covering 200 acres, this arboretum, the highest-elevation research garden in the United States, focuses on plants of the high desert, coniferous forests, and alpine tundra, all of which are environments found in the vicinity of Flagstaff. On the grounds, you'll find a butterfly garden, an herb garden, a shade garden, and a passive solar greenhouse.

Arizona Historical Society Pioneer Museum. 2340 N. Fort Valley Rd. ☎ **520/ 774-6272.** Admission by donation. Mon–Sat 9am–5pm. Closed Jan 1, Easter, Thanksgiving, and Dec 25.

The main museum building here is a large stone structure built in 1908 as a hospital for the indigent (Poor Farm). Today the old hospital houses a historical collection from northern Arizona's pioneer days. Among the exhibits are pieces of camera equipment used by Emery Kolb at his studio on the South Rim of the Grand Canyon. Many of Kolb's photos are on display. Several small exhibit rooms cover various aspects of life in northern Arizona during the pioneer days and later. You'll see a doctor's office filled with frightening instruments, barbed wire and brands, dolls, saddles, and trapping and timber displays.

✪ **Lowell Observatory.** 1400 W. Mars Hill Rd. ☎ **520/774-2096.** www.lowell.edu. Admission $3.50 adults, $3 seniors, $1.50 youth 5–17. Apr–Oct daily 9am–5pm (tours 10am, 1 and 3pm); Nov–Mar daily noon–5pm (tours 1 and 3pm). Call for hours and days of evening telescope viewings.

Located atop aptly named Mars Hill is one of the oldest astronomical observatories in the Southwest. Founded in 1894 by Percival Lowell, the observatory has played important roles in contemporary astronomy. Among the work carried out here was Lowell's study of the planet Mars and his calculations that led him to predict the existence of the planet Pluto. It wasn't until 13 years after Lowell's death that Pluto was finally discovered, almost exactly where he had predicted it would be. Today it is still an important research facility, but most astronomical observations are now carried out at Anderson Mesa, 10 miles farther away from the lights of Flagstaff.

The facility consists of several observatories, a large visitor center with numerous fun and educational exhibits, and outdoor displays. Keep in mind that the telescope domes are not heated, so if you come up to observe the stars, be sure to dress appropriately.

✪ **Museum of Northern Arizona.** 3101 N. Fort Valley Rd. (3 miles north of downtown Flagstaff on U.S. 180). ☎ **520/774-5213.** www.musnaz.org. Admission $5 adults, $4 seniors, $3 students, $2 children 7–17. Daily 9am–5pm. Closed Jan 1, Thanksgiving, and Dec 25.

This small but surprisingly thorough museum is the ideal first stop on an exploration of northern Arizona. Here you'll learn, through state-of-the-art exhibits, about the archaeology, ethnology, geology, biology, and fine arts of the region. The cornerstone of the museum is an exhibit that explores life on the Colorado Plateau from 15,000 B.C. to the present. Among the other displays are a life-size kiva ceremonial room and a small but interesting collection of kachinas. The large gift shop is full of contemporary Native American arts and crafts, and throughout the summer there are special exhibits focusing on Hopi, Navajo, and Zuni arts and crafts.

The museum building itself is made of native stone and incorporates a courtyard featuring vegetation from the six life zones of northern Arizona. Outside the museum is a short self-guided nature trail that leads through a narrow canyon strewn with boulders.

Riordan Mansion State Historic Park. 1300 E. Riordan Rd. (off Milton Rd./U.S. 89A, just north of the junction of I-40 and I-17). ☎ **520/779-4395.** Admission $4 adults, $2.50 ages 7–13, free for children 6 and under. May–Sept daily 8:30am–5pm; Oct–Apr daily 11:30am–5pm. Guided tours on the hour. Closed Dec 25.

Built in 1904 for local timber barons Michael and Timothy Riordan, this 13,000-square-foot mansion is actually two houses connected by a large central hall. Each of the two Riordan brothers and his family occupied one half of the house, and they had the rooflines constructed differently so that visitors could tell the two sides apart. The home is built in the Craftsman style, and although it looks like a log cabin, it's actually only faced with log slabs.

NEARBY ATTRACTIONS

If you find yourself traveling U.S. 89 between the entrances to Sunset Crater and Wupatki national monuments, keep an eye out for **Sacred Mountain Trading Post** (☎ 520/679-2255), which though small, has the look and feel of a trading post of 50 years ago. The shelves are full of Navajo pottery.

Sunset Crater Volcano National Monument. 18 miles north of Flagstaff off U.S. 89. ☎ **520/526-0502.** www.nps.gov/sucr. Admission $3 adults, free for children under 17 (admission also valid for Wupatki National Monument). Daily sunrise to sunset; visitor center daily 8am–5pm (6pm in summer). Closed Dec 25.

Dotting the landscape northeast of Flagstaff are more than 400 volcanic craters, of which Sunset Crater Volcano is the youngest. Taking its name from the sunset colors of the cinders near its summit, Sunset Crater Volcano stands 1,000 feet tall and began forming in A.D. 1064. Over a period of 100 years, the volcano erupted repeatedly, creating the red-and-yellow cinder cone we see today, and eventually covered an area of 800 square miles with ash, lava, and cinders. A mile-long interpretive trail here passes through a desolate landscape of lava flows, cinders, and ash as it skirts the base of this volcano. In the visitor center (at the west entrance to the national monument) you can learn more about the formation of Sunset Crater and about volcanoes in general. Near the visitor center is a small campground that's open spring to fall.

Walnut Canyon National Monument. 7 miles east of Flagstaff on Walnut Canyon Rd. (take Exit 204 off I-40). ☎ **520/526-3367.** www.nps.gov/waca. Admission $3 adults, free for children under 17. June–Aug, daily 8am–6pm; Mar–May and Sept–Nov, daily 8am–5pm; Dec–Feb, daily 9am–5pm; trail closes 1 hour earlier.

The undercut layers of limestone in this 400-foot-deep canyon east of Flagstaff proved ideal for building dwellings well protected from the elements and from enemies. Today, the remains of 300 small 13th-century Sinagua cliff dwellings can still be seen in the dry wooded canyon. The Sinagua were the same people who built and then abandoned the stone pueblos found in Wupatki National Monument to the north. It's theorized that when the land to the north lost its fertility, the Sinagua began migrating southward, settling for 150 years in Walnut Canyon.

A self-guided trail leads from the visitor center on the canyon rim down 185 feet to a section of the canyon wall where 25 cliff dwellings can be viewed up close (some can even be entered). Bring binoculars if you have them so you can scan the canyon walls for other cliff dwellings. There's a picnic area near the visitor center. Also, if you're interested in more hiking, you'll find a segment of the Arizona Trail 1.7 miles down a dirt road near the monument entrance.

✪ **Wupatki National Monument.** 36 miles north of Flagstaff off U.S. 89. ☎ **520/ 679-2365.** www.nps.gov/wupa. Admission $3 adults, free for children under 17. Daily sunrise–sunset; visitor center, daily 8am–5pm (6pm in summer). Closed Dec 25.

The landscape northeast of Flagstaff is desolate and windswept, a sparsely populated region carpeted with volcanic ash deposited in the 11th century. It comes as quite a surprise, then, to learn that this area contains hundreds of Native American habitation sites. The most impressive ruins are those left by the Sinagua (the name means "without water" in Spanish) people who inhabited this area from around A.D. 1100 until shortly after 1200. The Sinagua people built small villages of stone similar to the pueblos on the nearby Hopi reservation, and today the ruins of these ancient villages can be seen in this national monument.

The largest of the pueblos is Wupatki Ruin in the southeastern part of the monument. Here the Sinagua built a sprawling three-story pueblo containing nearly 100 rooms. They also constructed what is believed to be a ball court, which although quite different in design from the courts of the Aztec and Maya, leaves no doubt that a similar game was played. Another circular stone structure just below the main ruins may have been an amphitheater or dance plaza.

The most unusual feature of Wupatki, however, is a natural phenomenon: a blowhole, which may have been the reason this pueblo was constructed here. A network of small underground tunnels and chambers acts as a giant barometer, blowing air through the blowhole when the underground air is under greater pressure than the outside air. On hot days, cool air rushes out of the blowhole with amazing force.

Several other ruins within the national monument are easily accessible by car. They include Nalakihu, Citadel, and Lomaki, which are the closest to U.S. 89, and Wukoki, near Wupatki. Wukoki Ruin, built atop a huge sandstone boulder, is particularly picturesque. The monument's visitor center is adjacent to the Wupatki ruins. Here you'll find interesting exhibits on the Sinagua and Anasazi people who once inhabited the region.

ORGANIZED TOURS

Gray Line/Nava-Hopi Tours (☎ **877/467-3329** or 520/774-5003; www.navahopitours. com) operates several day-long tours of northern Arizona. These tours include excursions to the South Rim of the Grand Canyon ($42 adults, $21 children 5 to 15); Lake Powell and Page, with a float trip on the Colorado River ($109 adults, $59 children 5 to 15); Sedona and the Verde Valley ($40 adults, $20 children 5 to 15); the Navajo Indian Reservation ($74 adults, $37 children 5 to 15); and the Petrified Forest, Painted Desert, and Meteor Crater ($58 adults, $29 children 5 to 15).

JOINING AN ARCHAEOLOGICAL DIG

On the north side of Flagstaff on U.S. 89 is a small archaeological site called Elden Pueblo, which is open to the public free of charge. These Sinagua ruins are not much to look at, but if you're interested, you can help out with the excavation of the site. Each summer, the **Elden Pueblo Archaeological Project,** P.O. Box 3496, Flagstaff, AZ 86003 (☎ **520/527-3475**), hosts several public days as well as field schools for members of the Arizona Archaeological Society (AAS). Field schools cost $100 per week plus the $30 AAS membership dues.

WHERE TO STAY
EXPENSIVE

✪ **The Inn at 410.** 410 N. Leroux St., Flagstaff, AZ 86001. ☎ **800/774-2008** or 520/774-0088. Fax 520/774-6354. www.inn410.com. 9 units. A/C. $125–$175 double. Rates include full breakfast. MC, V.

Located only 2 blocks from downtown Flagstaff, this restored 1907 bungalow is one of the best B&Bs in Arizona and provides convenience, pleasant surroundings, comfortable rooms, and delicious breakfasts. A large front porch (complete with swing), a comfortably furnished living room and dining room, and a pleasant garden patio all add up to plenty of places to lounge about. Rooms feature distinctive themes, and eight have their own fireplaces. Some of the rooms are in a separate adjacent building, and one of them is wheelchair accessible. The Dakota Suite and the Southwest Room are our personal favorites since they conjure up the inn's Western/Southwestern heritage. Breakfasts are multicourse affairs, and if you're lucky, you might get innkeeper Sally Krueger's award-winning curried cornbread pudding with pumpkin sauce.

MODERATE

Arizona Mountain Inn. 4200 Lake Mary Rd., Flagstaff, AZ 86001. ☎ **520/774-8959.** Fax 520/774-8837. 20 units. $90–$110 double; $80–$110 cabin. AE, DISC, MC, V. Pets accepted, $5 per night. $50 refundable cleaning fee.

Located just a few minutes south of downtown Flagstaff, the Arizona Mountain Inn is a quiet mountain retreat set beneath shady pine trees. Although there are three bed-and-breakfast rooms in the main building, the rest of the accommodations are cabins that sleep 2 to 16 people. Many of the rustic cabins are A-frames or chalets, and each is a little bit different. The family-oriented inn sits on 13 acres, beyond which are miles of national forest. Facilities include volleyball and basketball courts, a playground, horseshoe pits, and a coin laundry.

✪ **Jeanette's Bed & Breakfast.** 3380 E. Lockett Rd., Flagstaff, AZ 86004-4043. ☎ **800/752-1912** or 520/527-1912. Fax 520/527-1713. www.bbonline.com/az/jbb. 4 units. May–Oct $99 double; Nov–April $85–$130 double. Rates include full breakfast. AE, DC, MC, V.

If you've ever wanted to step back in time and live in the early decades of the 20th century, then you might want to spend some time at this unusual B&B a few miles from downtown Flagstaff. Innkeepers Jeanette and Ray West built this new "old house" a few years ago, and their attention to details is astounding. There are vintage tubs and sinks, vintage heat grates, vintage light switches, and, of course, plenty of antique furniture. What you might not expect is that wardrobes, dressers, and trunks are filled with vintage clothing. The house is designed as a 1912 Victorian home that has been updated to a less cluttered 1920s look. One room has a fireplace, while another has a porch with a view of nearby Mt. Elden. Mornings start with coffee in the parlor and then an elaborate Victorian breakfast.

Little America. 2515 E. Butler Ave., Flagstaff, AZ 86004. ☎ **800/352-4386** or 520/779-7900. Fax 520/779-7983. 248 units. A/C TV TEL. $79–$119 double. AE, CB, DC, DISC, MC, V. Take Exit 198 off I-40.

At first it might seem as if Little America is little more than a giant truck stop, but on closer inspection you'll find that this one, a spread-out complex beneath the pines on the east side of Flagstaff, is an excellent economy hotel. The interior decor is dated but fun, with a sort of suburban French provincial styling. Rooms vary in size, but all have small private balconies. There's a casual dining room plus a more formal restaurant that serves steaks and continental dishes. The hotel offers room service, laundry/dry cleaning, a courtesy van, a pool, a fitness room, horseshoes, volleyball, croquet, and jogging trails.

Radisson Woodlands Hotel Flagstaff. 1175 W. Rte. 66, Flagstaff, AZ 86001. ☎ **800/333-3333** or 520/773-8888. Fax 520/773-0597. 183 units. A/C TV TEL. $89–$109 double; $109–$139 suite. AE, CB, DC, DISC, MC, V.

With its elegant marble-floored lobby, the Woodlands Hotel is easily the most upscale and luxurious hotel in Flagstaff. A white baby grand piano, crystal chandelier, traditional European furnishings, and contemporary sculpture all add to the unexpected luxury, as do intricately carved pieces of furniture and architectural details from different Asian countries. Guest rooms are comfortable but not overly luxurious.

One of the two restaurants here serves Japanese meals with table-side cooking and a sushi bar, while the other features traditional American fare with a few international and Southwestern dishes. The hotel offers room service, an outdoor pool, two whirlpools, a sauna, steam room, and fitness center.

✪ **The Sled Dog Inn.** 10155 Mountainaire Rd., Flagstaff, AZ 86001. ☎ **800/754-0664** or 520/525-6212. Fax 520/525-1855. www.sleddoginn.com. 10 units. A/C. $109–$149 double. Rates include full breakfast. AE, MC, V. No children under age 7.

For outdoor-sports enthusiasts, this is *the* place to stay in the Flagstaff area. Located on the edge of a meadow south of the city, the Sled Dog Inn is a contemporary building that abounds in wood, much of which was salvaged from buildings being torn down. The inn has more than a dozen Siberian huskies, and when there is enough snow in the winter, dog sled rides are offered. However, rock-climbing, cross-country skiing, and mountain-biking excursions are also on the program here. There's workout equipment in the upstairs lounge, and at the end of an active day, the hot tub out the back door is always welcome. Guest rooms are modern lodge rustic and are comfortable and uncluttered. Don't be surprised if you wake up and see elk grazing right outside your window.

INEXPENSIVE

In addition to the hotels listed below, you'll find numerous budget chain motels in Flagstaff. They include **Motel 6**, 2440 E. Lucky Lane (☎ **520/774-8756**), charging $44 to $52 for a double, and **Motel 6**, 2745 S. Woodlands Village (☎ **520/779-3757**), charging $46 to $56 for a double. Flagstaff has dozens of old Route 66 motels that aren't for the fussy, but usually charge under $30 for a double.

Hotel Monte Vista. 100 N. San Francisco St., Flagstaff, AZ 86001. ☎ **800/545-3068** or 520/779-6971. Fax 520/779-2904. 50 units (6 with shared bathrooms). TV TEL. $40 double with shared bathroom; $55–$75 double with private bathroom; $90–$120 suite (lower rates in winter). AE, DISC, MC, V.

If you don't mind roughing it a bit for a chance to sleep in a hotel once frequented by the likes of Clark Gable, John Wayne, Jane Russell, Spencer Tracy, Carole Lombard, and Gary Cooper, check out the Monte Vista. Originally opened in 1927, this hotel was renovated in the mid-1980s and today appeals mostly to a younger crowd, especially college students and young European travelers who appreciate the economical rates (and the hotel bar). In the small, dark lobby (a bit the worse for wear) are painted ceiling beams and Victorian furniture. The rooms vary in size, and many are furnished with oak furniture and ceiling fans. Although the hotel has plenty of old-fashioned flair, don't expect top-notch accommodations. Check out a room first to see if this is your kind of place.

Hotel Weatherford. 23 N. Leroux St., Flagstaff, AZ 86001. ☎ **520/779-1919**. Fax 520/773-8951. www.weatherfordhotel.com. 8 units, 5 with private bathroom; 2 dorms. $38–$44 double with shared bathroom, $49–$55 double with private bathroom. AE, CB, DC, DISC, MC, V.

For many years this historic hotel was known primarily as a youth hostel frequented by backpacking European travelers. However, as part of an ongoing 20-year restoration by owners Henry Taylor and Sam Green-Taylor, the hotel has risen above hostel level. Although only a few of the hotel's rooms have yet been renovated, for budget-conscious fans of historic hotels, these rooms are worth checking out. The distinctive stone-walled hotel, built in 1897, has a wraparound veranda on its second floor, where you'll find the beautifully restored Zane Grey Ballroom (now an elegant bar). Downstairs you'll find a diner and the ever-popular Charly's Pub & Grill, which has been booking live rock, blues, and jazz acts for 2 decades. This place isn't fancy but it has loads of character.

WHERE TO DINE
MODERATE

Chez Marc Bistro. 503 Humphreys St. ☎ **520/774-1343.** Reservations recommended. Main courses $22–$29. AE, MC, V. Sun–Thurs 5–9pm; lunch Thurs–Sun 11:30am–2:30pm in summer. FRENCH.

Housed in an elegant little cottage in downtown Flagstaff, this French restaurant could pass for a country inn if not for the busy road out front. However, once inside, you can easily forget where you are. For many years now, this has been northern Arizona bastion of all things Gallic. You want frogs legs in garlic butter or escargot in a phyllo tulip? You got 'em. However, other influences creep onto the menu, and you might find buffalo steak in a beaujolais sauce or guinea hens in sun-dried cranberry demiglace. Regardless of what you order, rest assured you won't find a more rarified atmosphere in Flagstaff. The wine list is excellent.

✪ **Cottage Place Restaurant.** 126 W. Cottage Ave. ☎ **520/774-8431.** Reservations recommended. 3-course meals $16.50–$27. AE, MC, V. Tues–Sun 5–9:30pm. CONTINENTAL/NEW AMERICAN.

Located on the south side of the railroad tracks in a neighborhood mostly frequented by college students, Cottage Place is just what its name implies—an unpretentious little cottage. But despite the casual appearance, dining is a formal affair. The menu, which tends toward the rich side, is primarily continental, but there are Southwestern and Middle Eastern influences as well. The house specialties are chateaubriand and rack of lamb (both served for two), and there are always several choices for vegetarians. The appetizer sampler, with stuffed mushrooms, charbroiled shrimp, and *tiropitas* (cheese-stuffed phyllo pastries) is a winner. There's a long wine list (priced on the high side).

Marc's Cafe Americain Brasserie & Wine Bar. 801 S. Milton Rd. ☎ **520/556-0093.** Reservations recommended. Main courses $7–$13 at lunch, $11–$20 at dinner. AE, DC, DISC, MC, V. Daily 11am–2:30pm and 4:30–9pm. AMERICAN/FRENCH.

This spin-off from Chez Marc (see above) is a more casual brasserie-style eatery in a strip mall along Milton Road and, despite its reasonable prices, is hardly a college hangout. Crêpes, pastas, and excellent rotisseried meats are the specialties, but you can also get bouillabaisse and a few other seafood dishes. Flavorful salad dressings, sauces, and spreads are a strong point, as are the brasserie fries, which shouldn't be missed. An open kitchen in the middle of the restaurant provides a bit of entertainment, and there are about a dozen wines available by the glass.

INEXPENSIVE

✪ **Beaver Street Brewery.** 11 S. Beaver St. ☎ **520/779-0079.** Main courses $7.50–$10. AE, DISC, MC, V. Sun 11:30am–10pm; Mon–Thurs 11:30am–11pm; Fri–Sat 11:30am–midnight. BURGERS/PIZZA.

This big microbrewery and cafe in a former supermarket on the south side of the railroad tracks in downtown Flagstaff serves up several good brews, but it also does great pizzas and salads. The Beaver Street pizza, made with roasted-garlic pesto, sun-dried tomatoes, fresh basil, and soft goat cheese, is particularly tasty. There are robust salads, such as a Mongolian beef salad with sesame-ginger dressing, and even fondue. This place stays packed with college students, but a good pint of ale helps any wait pass quickly, especially if you can grab a chair by the woodstove.

Café Espress. 16 N. San Francisco St. ☎ **520/774-0541.** Sandwiches/plates $4.50–$9. MC, V. Daily 7am–9pm. INTERNATIONAL/VEGETARIAN.

Grab a newspaper from the basket by the door, sit down at one of the tables by the front window, and ensconce yourself in college life all over again. If you happen to be a student (or one at heart), this place will become your favorite dining spot in Flagstaff. You can start the day with granola (or something much more substantial), grab a tempeh or turkey burger for lunch, and then have spanakopita or artichoke scampi for dinner. There are good sandwiches, a salad bar, and espresso as well.

Macy's European Coffee House & Bakery. 14 S. Beaver St. ☎ **520/774-2243.** Meals $3.50–$7. No credit cards. Sun 8am–7pm; Mon–Wed 6am–8pm; Thurs–Sat 6am–9pm. COFFEE/BAKERY.

Good espresso and baked goodies draw people in here the first time, but there are also decent vegetarian pasta dishes, soups, salads, and other old college-town standbys. This is Flagstaff's counterculture hang-out, and it attracts both students and professors. For the true Macy's experience, order one of the huge lattes and a scone or other pastry.

Pasto. 19 E. Aspen St. ☎ **520/779-1937.** Reservations recommended. Main courses $9–$16. AE, MC, V. Sun–Thurs 5–9pm; Fri–Sat 5–9:30pm (until 10pm in summer). ITALIAN.

Operated by the same folks who run Café Espress, Pasto is a health-conscious Italian restaurant in downtown Flagstaff and very popular with the hip and young at heart. Billing itself as "Fun Italian Dining," Pasto has a flamboyant decor and casual atmosphere. The menu includes a good assortment of pastas, of course, but there are also dishes such as chicken marsala and artichoke orzo.

FLAGSTAFF AFTER DARK

For events taking place during your visit, check *Flare* or *Flagstaff Live,* two free weekly arts-and-entertainment newspapers available at shops and restaurants downtown. The university has many musical and theatrical groups that perform throughout most of the year, and several clubs around town book a variety of live music acts.

The **Flagstaff Symphony Orchestra** (☎ 520/774-5107) provides the city with a full season of classical music. Most performances are held at Ardrey Auditorium on Knoles Drive on the campus of Northern Arizona University. Ticket prices range from $13 to $36.

The city's community theater group, **Theatrikos** (☎ 520/774-1662), performs at the Flagstaff Playhouse, 11 W. Cherry St. Tickets are $9 to $14.

For a livelier scene, check out the **Museum Club,** 3404 E. Route 66 (☎ 520/526-9434), a Flagstaff institution and one of America's classic roadhouses. Built in the early 1900s and often called the Zoo Club, this cavernous log saloon is filled with deer antlers, stuffed animals, and trophy heads. There's live music, predominantly country and western, most nights.

2 Williams

58 miles S of the Grand Canyon; 32 miles W of Flagstaff; 220 miles E of Las Vegas

Although it's almost 60 miles south of the Grand Canyon, Williams is still the closest real town. Consequently, it has dozens of motels catering to people who were unable to get a room at the park. However, Williams, founded in 1880 as a railroading and logging town, has a bit of Western history to boast about. Old brick commercial buildings dating to the late 19th century line the main street, and modest Victorian homes sit on the tree-shaded streets that spread south from the railroad tracks.

In recent years, mid–20th-century history has taken center stage. Williams was the last town on historic Route 66 to be bypassed by I-40, and consequently, the town plays up its Route 66 heritage.

Named for famed mountain man Bill Williams, the town sits at the edge of a ponderosa pine forest atop the Mogollon Rim, and surrounding the town is the Kaibab National Forest. Within the forest and not far out of town are good fishing lakes, hiking and mountain-biking trails, and a small downhill ski area.

Most important, Williams is where you'll find the Grand Canyon Railway depot. The excursion train that leaves from here provides not only a fun ride on the rails but is an alternative to dealing with traffic congestion in Grand Canyon National Park. Of course, there are the obligatory on-your-way-to-the-Grand-Canyon tourist traps nearby.

ESSENTIALS

GETTING THERE   Williams is on I-40 just west of the junction with Ariz. 64, which leads north to the South Rim of the Grand Canyon.

Amtrak (☎ **800/872-7245**) now has service to Williams on its *Southwest Chief* line. However, there is no station, and the train stops on the outskirts of town. Be sure you have previously arranged to have your hotel pick you up.

The **Grand Canyon Railway,** Grand Canyon Railway Depot, Grand Canyon Boulevard (☎ **800/843-8724** or 520/773-1976; www.thetrain.com), operates vintage steam and diesel locomotives and 1920s coaches between Williams and Grand Canyon Village. Round-trip fares range from $49.50 to $119.50 for adults and $24.95 to $94.95 for children 16 and under (fares do not include tax or national park entrance fee). Although this is primarily a day-excursion train, it's possible to ride up one day and return on a different day—just let the reservation clerk know. If you opt to stay overnight, you'll want to be sure you have a reservation at one of the hotels right in Grand Canyon Village; otherwise, you'll end up having to take a shuttle bus or taxi out of the park to your hotel, which can be inconvenient and add a bit to your daily costs. In conjunction with Farwest Airlines, Grand Canyon Railway offers air-rail packages from Phoenix, Las Vegas, and Los Angeles's Long Beach Airport.

VISITOR INFORMATION   For more information on the Williams area, including information on hiking, mountain biking, and fishing in the area, contact the **Williams–U.S. Forest Service Visitor Center,** 200 W. Railroad Ave., Williams, AZ 86046 (☎ **520/635-4061**). The visitor center, which includes some interesting historic displays, is open daily 8am to 5pm. The shop here carries books on the Grand Canyon and trail maps for the adjacent national forest.

WHAT TO SEE & DO: ROUTE 66 & BEYOND

These days, most people coming to Williams are here to board the Grand Canyon Railway (see "Getting There," above, for details).

Route 66 fans will want to drive Williams's main street, which, not surprisingly, is named Route 66. Along this stretch of the old highway, you can check out the town's vintage buildings, many of which now house shops selling Route 66 souvenirs. There are a few antiques stores selling collectibles from the heyday of Route 66.

Both east and west of town, there are other stretches of the "Mother Road" that you can drive. East of town, take Exit 167 off I-40 and follow the graveled Old Trails Highway (the predecessor to Route 66). A paved section of Route 66 begins at Exit 171 on the north side of the interstate and extends for 7 miles to the site of the Parks General Store. From Parks, you can continue to Brannigan Park on a graveled section of Route 66.

West of Williams, take Exit 157 and go south. If you turn east at the T intersection, you will be on a gravel section of the old highway; if you turn west, you'll be on a paved section. Another stretch can be accessed at Exit 106. If you continue another 12 miles west and take Exit 139, you will be on the longest uninterrupted stretch of Route 66 left in the country. It stretches from here through the town of Seligman, which has several interesting buildings, and all the way to Kingman.

WHERE TO STAY
MODERATE

Best Western Inn of Williams. 2600 W. Route 66, Williams, AZ 86046. ☎ **800/ 635-4445** or 520/635-4400. Fax 520/635-4488. 79 units. Late May–Dec $89–$129 double; Jan–late May $59–$99. Rates include full breakfast. AE, CB, DC, DISC, MC, V.

Although this modern motel is not within walking distance of historic downtown Williams, the contemporary styling and location in the pines at the west end of town make it a good bet for comfortable, quiet accommodations. You'll find a whirlpool spa and an outdoor pool that's kept heated throughout the year.

○ **Fray Marcos Hotel.** 235 N. Grand Canyon Blvd., Williams, AZ 86046. ☎ **800/ 843-8724** or 520/635-4010. Fax 520/773-1610. www.thecanyon.com. 196 units. A/C TV TEL. Mid-Mar to mid-Oct (and holidays) $119 double; late Oct–early Mar $79 double. Railroad packages available. AE, DISC, MC, V.

Named for Fray (Father) Marcos de Niza, who some say was the first European to set foot in what is today Arizona, this hotel is affiliated with the Grand Canyon Railway and is named for the Williams hotel once run by the famous Fred Harvey Company. The hotel combines modern comforts with the style of a classic Western railroad hotel, and the high-ceilinged lobby features a large flagstone fireplace and original paintings of the Grand Canyon. Guest rooms are very comfortable and feature Southwestern styling. Ask for a room in the new wing (which has a fitness room, a pool, and a hot tub). The hotel's elegant lounge, which features a 100-year-old English bar, serves simple meals, and there's an adjacent cafeteria-style restaurant. The original Fray Marcos now serves as the railway station (ticket office, gift shop, railroad museum, and display trains).

Quality Inn Mountain Ranch. 6701 E. Mountain Ranch Rd. (Exit 171 off I-40), Williams, AZ 86046. ☎ **800/228-5151** or 520/635-2693. www.thecanyon.com. 73 units. A/C TV TEL. Apr to mid-May and Oct $55–$85 double; mid-May to Sept $75–$105 double. Rates include full breakfast. AE, DC, DISC, MC, V. Supervised pets accepted. Closed Nov–Feb.

Located 6 miles east of town, this motel is surrounded by 26 acres of forest and meadow that give it a secluded feeling. This seclusion and the hotel's recreational amenities (horseback riding, a pool, a whirlpool, a sauna, two tennis courts, volleyball, basketball, and a putting green) make it the best choice in the Williams area. However, the rooms, although large and usually with views of forest and mountains, are strictly motel issue. There's a restaurant on the premises, so you don't have to drive into town to eat.

The Sheridan House Inn. 460 E. Sheridan Ave., Williams, AZ 86046. ☎ **888/635-9345** or 520/635-9441. www.thegrandcanyon.com/sheridan. 9 units. TV. $95–$225 double. Rates include full breakfast. AE, DISC, MC, V. Closed mid-Jan to mid-Feb.

Located on a pine-shaded hillside a few blocks from downtown Williams, this B&B isn't fancy but it's plenty comfortable. Innkeepers Steve and Evelyn Gardner make people feel right at home in a B&B with the amenities of a resort (hot tub on the flagstone patio, pool table and bar in the basement, fitness room, and plenty of video-tapes for watching on in-room VCRs). Guest rooms are comfortably furnished; our favorite room is the Cedar Room. Complimentary happy hour each evening includes enough hors d'oeuvres to make a meal (which somewhat offsets the relatively high rates for most of the rooms here), and the breakfast always includes an impressive array of fruits. This inn is child friendly, so it makes a good base of operations for families.

Terry Ranch Bed & Breakfast. 701 Quarterhorse St., Williams, AZ 86046. ☎ **800/ 210-5908** or 520/635-4171. Fax 520/635-2488. www.grand-canyon-lodging.net. 4 units. Apr–Sept $110–$140 double; Oct–Mar $100–$130 double. Rates include full breakfast. AE, DISC, MC, V.

This modern log inn on the edge of town looks as though it should be surrounded by a big cattle spread, but instead it's close to the train depot and the restaurants in down-town Williams. The guest rooms, furnished in Western-country style, have king beds and antiques and are named for brides who lived at the Terry Ranch in Utah back in the 1800s. Two rooms have clawfoot tubs, and two have whirlpool tubs. There are fire-places in two of the rooms.

INEXPENSIVE

In addition to the motels and B&Bs listed below, there are numerous budget chain motels in Williams, including two Motel 6s, two Super 8s, a Comfort Inn, an Econo Lodge, and a Travelodge.

The New Canyon Motel. 1900 Rodeo Rd., Williams, AZ 86046. ☎ **800/482-3955** or 520/635-9371. Fax 520/635-4138. 18 units. $40–$60 double; $89–$119 caboose double. AE, DISC, MC, V.

You'll find this recently restored old motel on the eastern outskirts of Williams tucked against the trees, and while the setting and new rooms in duplex stone cabins are nice enough, the real attractions here are the railroad cars parked in the front yard. You can stay in a caboose or a Pullman car, which makes this a fun place to stay if you're planning on taking the excursion train to the Grand Canyon. There's an indoor swimming pool.

Norris Motel. 1001 W. Rte. 66, P.O. Box 388, Williams, AZ 86046. ☎ **800/341-8000** or 520/635-2202. Fax 520/635-9202. 33 units. A/C TV TEL. Mid-May to mid-Sept $55–$107 double; Apr–early May and late Sept–Oct $44–$87 double; Nov–Mar $26–$59 double. AE, DISC, MC, V.

Run by a British family, the Norris Motel may not look like anything special from the street, but the friendliness of the welcome will immediately let you know this is not your ordinary motel. Most of the guest units have been remodeled and have a homey feel. Many rooms have refrigerators. There's even a hot tub for soaking away your aches and pains in the evening and a swimming pool for cooling off in during the hot summer months. Keep an eye out for the prairie dogs in the back field.

✪ **The Red Garter Bed & Bakery.** 137 W. Railroad Ave., Williams, AZ 86046. ☎ **800/ 328-1484** or 520/635-1484. www.redgarter.com. 4 units. $75–$110 double. Rates include continental breakfast. Lower rates off-season. AE, DISC, MC, V.

The Wild West lives again at this restored 1897 bordello, but these days the only tarts that come with the rooms are in the bakery downstairs. Located across the street from the Grand Canyon Railway terminal at the top of a steep flight of stairs, this B&B sports high ceilings, new carpets, attractive wood trim, and reproduction period fur-nishings. A couple of rooms even have graffiti written in the early 20th century by bor-dello visitors.

CAMPGROUNDS

There are several campgrounds near Williams in the Kaibab National Forest. They include Cataract Lake (2 miles northwest of Williams on Cataract Lake Road), Dogtown Lake (8 miles south of Williams off Fourth Street/County Road 73), Kaibab Lake (4 miles northeast of Williams off Ariz. 64), and Whitehorse Lake (15 miles south of Williams off Fourth Street/County Road 73). All campgrounds are first-come, first-served.

WHERE TO DINE

Cruiser's Café 66. 233 W. Rte. 66. ☎ **520/635-0631.** Main courses $6.50–$14. AE, DISC, MC, V. Daily 2–9:30pm (5–9:30pm in winter). AMERICAN.

If you're looking for a taste of old-fashioned Route 66 atmosphere, this is the place. Dig into some smoked baby back pork ribs or a platter of fajitas at Cruiser's, which is full of all manner of Route 66 memorabilia. Some tables are even flanked by a couple of old-fashioned gas pumps. The menu runs the gamut from steaks and spicy wings to pizza and calzones.

Rod's Steak House. 301 E. Rte. 66. ☎ **520/635-2671.** Reservations recommended. Main courses $8–$26. MC, V. Mar–Oct daily 11:30am–9:30pm; Nov–Feb Mon–Sat 11:30am–9:30pm. STEAKS/SEAFOOD.

If you're looking for a good dinner in Williams, just look for the red neon steer at the east end of town. This is the sign that beckons hungry canyon explorers to come on in and have a great steak. The menu, printed on a paper cutout of a steer, may be short, but the food is reliable. Prime rib au jus, the house specialty, comes in three different weights to fit your hunger. If you're not in a mood for a steak, there are trout, chicken, shrimp, and barbecued ribs.

3 The Grand Canyon South Rim

60 miles N of Williams; 80 miles NE of Flagstaff; 230 miles N of Phoenix; 340 miles N of Tucson

A mile deep, 277 miles long, and up to 18 miles wide, the Grand Canyon is truly one of the great wonders of the world. The cartographers who mapped this land were obviously deeply struck by the spiritual beauty of the canyon and named the landscape features accordingly. Their reverence is reflected in such names as Solomon Temple, Angels Gate, the Tabernacle, Apollo Temple, Venus Temple, Thor Temple, Zoroaster Temple, Horus Temple, Buddha Temple, Vishnu Temple, Krishna Temple, Shiva Temple, and Confucius Temple.

Something of this reverence infects nearly every first-time visitor to the Grand Canyon. Nothing in the slowly changing topography of the approach to the Grand Canyon prepares you for what awaits. You hardly notice the elevation gain or the gradual change from windswept scrubland to pine forest. Suddenly, it's there. No preliminaries, no warnings. Stark, quiet, a maze of colors and cathedrals sculpted by nature.

Banded layers of sandstone, limestone, shale, and schist give the canyon its colors, and the interplay of shadows and light from dawn to dusk creates an ever-changing palette of hues and textures. Written in these bands of stone are more than 2 billion years of history. Formed by the cutting action of the Colorado River as it flows through the Kaibab Plateau, the Grand Canyon is an open book exposing the secrets of the geologic history of this region. Geologists believe it has taken between 3 and 6 million years for the Colorado River to carve the Grand Canyon, but the canyon's history extends much further back in time.

Millions of years ago vast seas covered this region. Sediments carried by sea water were deposited and over millions of years were turned into limestone and sandstone. When the ancient seabed was thrust upward to form the Kaibab Plateau, the Colorado River began its work of cutting through the plateau. Today 21 sedimentary layers, the oldest of which is more than a billion years old, can be seen in the canyon. However, beneath all these layers, at the very bottom, is a stratum of rock so old that it has metamorphosed, under great pressure and heat, from soft shale to a much harder stone. Called Vishnu schist, this layer is the oldest rock in the Grand Canyon and dates from 2 billion years ago.

In the more recent past, the Grand Canyon has been home to several Native American cultures, including the Anasazi, who are best known for their cliff dwellings in the Four Corners region. About 150 years after the Anasazi and Coconino peoples abandoned the canyon in the 13th century, another tribe, the Cerbat, moved into the area. The Hualapai and Havasupai tribes, descendants of the Cerbat people, still live in and near the Grand Canyon on the south side of the Colorado River. On the North Rim lived the Southern Paiute, and in the west, the Navajo.

In 1540 Spanish explorer Garcia Lopez de Cárdenas became the first European to set eyes on the Grand Canyon. However, it would be another 329 years before the first expedition would travel through the entire canyon. John Wesley Powell, a one-armed Civil War veteran, was deemed crazy when he set off to navigate the Colorado River in wooden boats. His small band of men spent 98 days traveling 1,000 miles down the Green and Colorado Rivers. So difficult was the journey that when some of the expedition's boats were wrecked by powerful rapids, part of the group abandoned the journey and set out on foot, never to be seen again.

How wrong the early explorers were about this supposedly godforsaken landscape. Instead of being abandoned as a worthless wasteland, the Grand Canyon has become one of the most important natural wonders on the planet, a magnet for people from all over the world. By raft, by mule, on foot, and in helicopters and small planes—five million people each year come to the canyon to gaze into this great chasm.

However, there have been those in the recent past who regarded the canyon as mere wasted space, suitable only for filling with water. Upstream of the Grand Canyon stands Glen Canyon Dam, which forms Lake Powell, while downstream lies Lake Mead, created by Hoover Dam. The same thing could have happened to the Grand Canyon, but luckily, the forces for preservation prevailed. Today the Grand Canyon is the last major undammed stretch of the Colorado River.

The Colorado River, named by early Spanish explorers for the pinkish color of its muddy waters, once carried immense loads of silt. However, now, due to the Glen Canyon Dam, the water in the Grand Canyon is much clearer (and colder) than it once was and no longer flows murky and pink from heavy loads of eroding sandstone. The water that now rumbles through the Grand Canyon flows cold and clear from the bottom of the Glen Canyon Dam after it has had a chance to deposit its silt on the bottom of Lake Powell.

Glen Canyon Dam has had a much greater effect on the Grand Canyon than just changing the color and temperature of the Colorado. Due to changes in electricity demand, the outflow of water from Glen Canyon Dam can change dramatically over the course of a day. These frequent fluctuations have changed the natural cycle of flushing and depositing that once created beaches and backwaters within the canyon. In an attempt to reproduce the natural flooding process that once sustained the Grand Canyon's riparian environment, Glen Canyon Dam experimented in spring 1996 with larger drawdowns of water that more closely reproduced the natural cycle of spring flooding in the canyon. These drawdowns proved to be somewhat, but not entirely, successful in restoring the banks of the Colorado River to a more natural appearance. As a result of this study, daily fluctuations in the amount of water released from Glen Canyon Dam have been modified.

While the waters of the Colorado River are now clearer than before, the same cannot be said for the air in the canyon. Yes, you'll find smog here, smog that has been blamed on both Las Vegas and Los Angeles to the west and a coal-fired power plant to the east near Page. Scrubbers installed on the power plant's smokestacks should help the park's air quality, but there isn't much to be done about smog drifting up from Las Vegas.

However, the most visible and frustrating negative impact on the park in recent years has been the traffic congestion at the South Rim during the busy months from spring to fall. With five million visitors each year, traffic during the summer months has become almost as bad at the South Rim as it is during rush hour in any major city, and finding a parking space can be the biggest challenge of a visit to Grand Canyon National Park. However, this may all be changing in the next few years with the construction of a new light-rail system connecting the community of Tusayan with the South Rim. The light rail will in turn connect with buses operating along the South Rim. Current projections are that this new system will be in operation by 2004. As part of this new vision for the park, there are plans to build a multi-use greenway trail along the South Rim. With the implementation of these plans, it's hoped that the park's congestion problems will become a thing of the past.

Today the Canyon is at a turning point. With the implementation over the next few years of the Grand Canyon National Park General Management Plan, the park should become a far more enjoyable place to visit. Visitors in 2001 should be able to start their Grand Canyon visit at the new Canyon View Information Plaza. However, because the light rail and new bus system are not expected to be in place yet in 2001, you can still expect parking problems and traffic congestion, but don't let these inconveniences dissuade you from visiting. Despite the crowds, the Grand Canyon still more than lives up to its name and is one of the most amazing sights on earth.

GETTING THERE

BY CAR   In the past few years parking problems, traffic jams, and traffic congestion have become the norm at Grand Canyon Village during the popular summer months (and are becoming common in spring and fall as well). If at all possible, travel into the park by some means other than car. (Alternatives include taking the Grand Canyon Railway from Williams, flying into the Grand Canyon Airport and then taking the Tusayan–Grand Canyon Shuttle or a taxi, or taking the Nava-Hopi Tours bus service from Flagstaff.) There are plenty of scenic overlooks, hiking trails, restaurants, and lodges in the village area, and depending on the time of year, free shuttle buses operate along both the West Rim Drive and East Rim Drive.

If you do drive, be sure you have plenty of gasoline in your car before setting out for the canyon; there are few service stations in this remote part of the state. The South Rim of the Grand Canyon is 60 miles north of Williams and I-40 on Ariz. 64 and U.S. 180. Flagstaff, the nearest city of any size, is 78 miles away. From Flagstaff it's possible to take U.S. 180 directly to the South Rim or U.S. 89 to Ariz. 64 and the east entrance to the park.

Grand Canyon National Park is currently developing a combination light-rail and alternative-fuel bus system for transporting visitors to and around the South Rim and Grand Canyon Village. Plans are to have a light-rail system connect Tusayan, outside the park's south entrance, with the new Canyon View Information Plaza, which will become the South Rim's main transportation hub and orientation area for South Rim visitors. From this transit center, alternative-fuel buses will shuttle visitors to various points along the South Rim. By having day-use visitors leave their cars outside the park and take the light rail to the South Rim, much of the park's traffic congestion should be alleviated. This new transportation plan will be implemented over the next few years. At press time, the Canyon View Information Plaza was scheduled to open in late 2000.

BY PLANE   The Grand Canyon Airport is 6 miles south of Grand Canyon Village in Tusayan. It's served by **Air Vegas** (☎ **800/255-7474**), which charges $278 for round-trip flights. Airlines flying from Las Vegas to the Grand Canyon Airport include **Scenic Airlines** (☎ **800/446-4584**), which charges $222 round-trip. Alternatively, you can fly into Williams and take the Grand Canyon Railway excursion train to the canyon (see "Williams," above, for details) or fly into Flagstaff and then arrange another mode of transportation the rest of the way to the national park (see "Flagstaff," above, for details).

BY TRAIN   The **Grand Canyon Railway** operates excursion trains between Williams and the South Rim of the Grand Canyon. See "Williams," above, for details.

For long-distance connections, **Amtrak** (☎ **800/872-7245**) provides service to Flagstaff and Williams (although the Williams stop is undeveloped and is on the outskirts of town; if you plan to take the train all the way to Williams, be sure to arrange to get picked up by your hotel). From Flagstaff it's then possible to take a bus directly to Grand Canyon Village. From Williams, you can take the Grand Canyon Railway excursion train to Grand Canyon Village.

BY BUS   Bus service between Phoenix, Flagstaff, and Grand Canyon Village is provided by **Nava-Hopi Tours** (☎ **800/892-8687** or 520/774-5003; www.navahopitours. com). Round-trip fares are $76 between Phoenix and Grand Canyon Village and $28 between Flagstaff and Grand Canyon Village.

VISITOR INFORMATION

You can get information on the Grand Canyon before leaving home by contacting the **Grand Canyon National Park,** P.O. Box 129, Grand Canyon, AZ 86023 (☎ **520/638-7888;** www.thecanyon.com/nps).

Once there, you should stop by the **Grand Canyon National Park Visitor Center,** on Village Loop Drive 6 miles north of the south entrance. Here you'll find an information desk, brochures, exhibits about the canyon, and a bookshop selling maps as well as books about the canyon. The center is open daily. *The Guide,* a small newspaper crammed full of useful information about the park, is available at both South Rim entrances.

For information on service outside the park in Tusayan, contact the **Grand Canyon Chamber of Commerce,** P.O. Box 3007, Grand Canyon, AZ 86023 (☎ **520/638-2901;** www.grandcanyonchamber.com).

ORIENTATION

Grand Canyon Village is built on the South Rim of the canyon and divided roughly into two sections. At the east end of the village are the visitor center, Yavapai Lodge, Trailer Village, and Mather Campground. At the west end are El Tovar Hotel and Bright Angel, Kachina, Thunderbird, and Maswik lodges, as well as several restaurants, the train depot, and the trailhead for the Bright Angel Trail.

GETTING AROUND

As mentioned earlier, the Grand Canyon Village area can be extremely congested, especially during the summer months. If possible, you may want to use one of the transportation options below to avoid the park's traffic jams and parking problems. Just to give you an idea, in summer you can expect at least a 20- to 30-minute wait at the South Rim entrance gate just to get into the park. You can cut the waiting time here by acquiring a national park pass (Golden Eagle, Golden Age, or Golden Access) before arriving. With pass in hand, you can use the express lane for seasonal pass holders.

BY BUS   The **Cassi Grand Canyon–Tusayan Shuttle** (☎ 520/638-0821; www. cassitours.com) operates between the Grand Canyon Airport in Tusayan, at the park's south entrance, and Grand Canyon Village, with stops in Tusayan at the Canyon Squire Inn and Babbitt's Store and in Grand Canyon Village at Yavapai Lodge, Bright Angle Lodge, and Maswik Transportation Center. The fare is $4 each way, with service between 9:30am and 6:30pm (shorter hours outside of summer months).

Between mid-March and mid-October, free shuttle buses operate on three routes within the park. The Village Loop bus circles through Grand Canyon Village throughout the day with frequent stops at the visitor center, hotels, campgrounds, restaurants, the Yavapai Observation Center, and other facilities. The West Rim Loop bus takes visitors to eight canyon overlooks west of Bright Angel Lodge. The Yaki Point/South Kaibab Loop, which stops at Bright Angel Lodge, the Maswik Transportation Center (Backcountry Office), and Yavapai Lodge, provides the only access to Yaki Point, the trailhead for the South Kaibab Trail to the bottom of the canyon. Hikers needing transportation to or from Yaki Point when the bus is not running must use a taxi (☎ 520/638-2822).

Trans Canyon (☎ 520/638-2820) offers shuttle-bus service between the South Rim and the North Rim. The vans leave the South Rim at 1:30pm and arrive at the North Rim at 6:30pm. The return trip leaves the North Rim at 7am, arriving back at the South Rim at noon. The fare is $60 per person one way, $100 per person round-trip.

BY CAR   There are **service stations** outside the south entrance to the park in Tusayan, at Desert View near the east entrance (this station is seasonal), and east of the park at Cameron. Because of the long distances within the park and to towns outside the park, be sure you have plenty of gas before setting out on a drive. Gas at the canyon is very expensive.

BY TAXI   There is taxi service available to and from the airport, trailheads, and other destinations (☎ 520/638-2822). The fare from the airport to Grand Canyon Village is $10 for up to two adults.

Fast Facts: The Grand Canyon

Accessibility   The Grand Canyon National Park *Accessibility Guide* is available at the visitor center, Yavapai Observation Station, Tusayan Museum, and Desert View Information Center. The national park has wheelchairs available at no charge for temporary use inside the park. You can usually find one of these wheelchairs at the visitor center. You can get a temporary handicapped parking permit at the visitor center or Yavapai Observation Center. There are wheelchair-accessible tours offered by prior arrangement through any lodge transportation desk or by calling Grand Canyon National Park Lodges (☎ 520/638-2631). TDD phones are available for hotel guests who require them.

Admission   Admission to Grand Canyon National Park is $20 per car (or $10 per person if you happen to be coming in on a bus, by taxi, or on foot). Your admission ticket, which is good for 7 days, is nothing more than a small paper receipt similar to what you might get at a store. Don't lose it, or you'll have to pay again.

Banks & ATM Networks   There's an ATM at the Bank One in the shopping center near Yavapai Lodge. The bank is open Monday to Thursday 10am to 3pm and Friday 10am to 3pm and 4 to 6pm.

Bus Tours   If you'd rather leave the driving to someone else and enjoy more of the scenery, you can opt for a bus or van tour of one or more sections of the park. **Grand Canyon National Park Lodges** (☎ 520/638-2631) offers several different tours within the park. Tours can be booked by calling the above phone number or by stopping at one of the transportation desks, which are at the visitor center and at Bright Angel, Maswik, and Yavapai lodges (see "Where to Stay" in this section). Prices range from $11 for a 1¹/₂-hour sunset tour to $31.50 for a combination tour of the East Rim and West Rim.

Climate   The climate at the Grand Canyon is quite different from that of Phoenix, and between the rim and the canyon floor there's a considerable difference. Because the South Rim is at 7,000 feet, it gets very cold in the winter. You can expect snow anytime between November and May, and winter temperatures can be below 0°F at night, with daytime highs in the 20s or 30s. Summer temperatures at the rim range from highs in the 80s to lows in the 50s. The North Rim of the canyon, which is slightly higher than the South Rim and stays a bit cooler throughout the year, is open to visitors only from May to October because the access road is not kept cleared of snow.

On the canyon floor, temperatures are considerably higher. In summer the mercury can reach 120°F with lows in the 70s, while in the winter temperatures are quite pleasant with highs in the 50s and lows in the 30s. July, August, and September are the wettest months because of frequent afternoon thunderstorms. April, May, and June are the driest months, but it still might rain or even snow. Down on the canyon floor, there is much less rain year-round.

Drugstores   There's a pharmacy (☎ **520/638-2460**) in Grand Canyon Village on Clinic Drive, off Center Road. The drugstore is open Monday to Friday 8:30 to 5pm.

Emergencies   Dial ☎ **911.**

Festivals   The **Grand Canyon Music Festival** (☎ **800/997-8285** or 520/638-9215; www.grandcanyonmusicfest.org) is held each year in mid-September.

Hospitals/Clinics   The **Grand Canyon Clinic** (☎ **520/638-2551** or 520/638-2469) is on Clinic Drive, off Center Road (the road that runs past the National Park Service ranger office). The clinic is open Monday to Friday 8am to 5pm and Saturday 9am to noon. It provides 24-hour emergency service.

Laundry   A coin-operated laundry is located near Mather Campground in the Camper Services building.

Lost & Found   Report lost items or turn in found items at the visitor center or Yavapai Observation Station. Call ☎ **520/638-7798** Tuesday to Friday between 8am and 5pm. For items lost or found at a hotel, restaurant, or lounge, call ☎ **520/638-2631.**

Newspapers & Magazines   Current newspapers and magazines are available at souvenir stores and lodges in the village.

Parking   If you want to avoid parking headaches, try using the lot in front of the general store, which is up a side road across from the visitor center (near Yavapai Lodge). From this large parking area, a paved hiking trail leads to the historic section of the village in less than 1¹/₂ miles and most of the route is along the rim. Another alternative is to park at the Maswik Transportation Center parking lot, which is served by the Village Loop shuttle bus.

Photographic Needs   Film is available at all village curio shops.

Police   In an emergency, dial ☎ **911.** Ticketing speeders is one of the main occupations of the park's police force, so obey the posted speed limits.

Post Office   The post office is in the shopping center near Yavapai Lodge.

Radio   KSGC, **92.1 FM,** provides news, music, the latest weather forecasts, and travel-related information for the Grand Canyon area.

Road Conditions   Information on road conditions in the Grand Canyon area are available by calling ☎ **520/638-7888** or 520/779-2711.

Safety   The most important safety tip to remember is to be careful near the edge of the canyon. Footing can be unstable and may give way. Be sure to keep your distance from wild animals, no matter how friendly they may appear. Don't hike alone and keep in mind that the canyon rim is more than a mile above sea level (it's harder to breathe up here). Don't leave valuables in your car or tent.

GRAND CANYON VILLAGE & VICINITY: YOUR FIRST LOOK

Grand Canyon Village is the main destination of the vast majority of the more than five million people who visit the Grand Canyon every year. Consequently, it is the most crowded place in the park, but it has the most overlooks and visitor services. Its many historic buildings, while nowhere near as impressive as the canyon itself, are worth visiting.

For most visitors, that initial glimpse of the canyon comes at **Mather Point,** the first canyon overlook you reach if you enter the park through the south entrance. By the end of 2000, this viewpoint should be the first site you come to after leaving the new Canyon View Information Plaza. Continuing west toward the village proper, you next come to **Yavapai Point,** a favorite spot for sunrise and sunset photos and the site of the **Yavapai Observation Station.** This historic building houses a small museum and has excellent views through its large windows. Yavapai point is at the east end of a paved hiking trail that extends for almost 3 miles to the west side of Grand Canyon Village.

The next stop along Village Loop Drive is the **visitor center** (☎ **520/638-7888**), one of the busiest places in the park and usually the hardest place to find a parking space. The visitor center is open daily and, in addition to providing answers to all your questions about the Grand Canyon, houses exhibits on the canyon's natural history, human history, and exploration. An orientation slide presentation is shown here throughout the day. There's an excellent little bookstore where you can find books on all aspects of the canyon. In the center's courtyard are several boats that have navigated the canyon over the years.

In the historic district, in addition to numerous canyon viewpoints, you'll find the historic **El Tovar Hotel** and **Bright Angel Lodge,** both of which are worth brief visits.

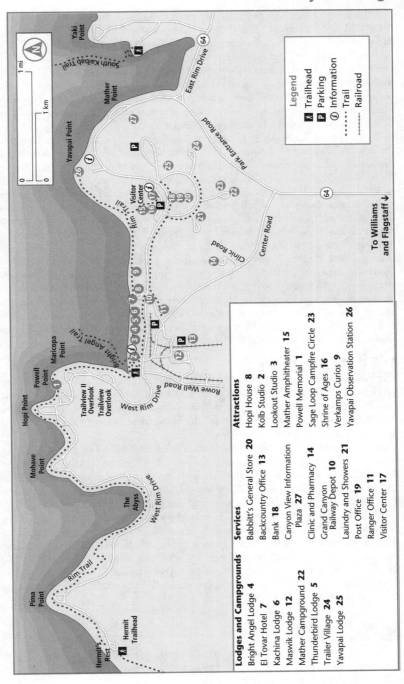

Grand Canyon Village

Legend
- 🪧 Trailhead
- 🅿 Parking
- ⓘ Information
- ••••• Trail
- ╫╫╫ Railroad

To Williams and Flagstaff ↓

Lodges and Campgrounds
Bright Angel Lodge **4**
El Tovar Hotel **6**
Kachina Lodge **7**
Maswik Lodge **12**
Mather Campground **22**
Thunderbird Lodge **5**
Trailer Village **24**
Yavapai Lodge **25**

Services
Babbitt's General Store **20**
Backcountry Office **13**
Bank **18**
Canyon View Information Plaza **27**
Clinic and Pharmacy **14**
Grand Canyon Railway Depot **10**
Laundry and Showers **21**
Post Office **19**
Ranger Office **11**
Visitor Center **17**

Attractions
Hopi House **8**
Kolb Studio **2**
Lookout Studio **3**
Mather Amphitheater **15**
Powell Memorial **1**
Sage Loop Campfire Circle **23**
Shrine of Ages **16**
Verkamps Curios **9**
Yavapai Observation Station **26**

Adjacent to El Tovar are two historic souvenir and curio shops. **Hopi House Gift Store and Art Gallery,** the first shop in the park, was built in 1905 to resemble a Hopi pueblo and to serve as a place for Hopi artisans to work and sell their crafts. Today it's full of Hopi and Navajo arts and crafts, including expensive kachinas, rugs, jewelry, and pottery. The second floor of the Hopi House is an art gallery. The nearby **Verkamps Curios** originally opened in a tent in 1898, but John Verkamp soon went out of business. However, the store reopened in 1905 and ever since has been the main place to look for souvenirs and crafts. Just inside the door is a 535-pound meteorite. Both shops are open daily; hours vary seasonally.

To the west of Bright Angel Lodge, two buildings cling precariously to the rim of the canyon. These are the **Lookout** and **Kolb studios,** both of which are listed on the National Register of Historic Places. **Kolb Studio** is named for Ellsworth and Emory Kolb, two brothers who set up a photographic studio on the rim of the Grand Canyon in 1904. The construction of this studio generated one of the Grand Canyon's first controversies—over whether buildings should be allowed on the canyon rim. Because the Kolbs had friends in high places, their sprawling studio and movie theater remained. Emory Kolb lived here until his death in 1976, by which time the building had been listed as a historic building. Today it serves as a bookstore, and the auditorium houses special exhibits. **Lookout Studio,** built in 1914 from a design by Mary Elizabeth Jane Colter, was the Fred Harvey Company's answer to the Kolb brothers' studio. Photographs and books about the canyon were sold at the studio, which incorporates architectural styles of the Hopi and the Anasazi. The use of native limestone and an uneven roofline allows the studio to blend in with the canyon walls and gives it the look of an old ruin. Today the studio houses a souvenir store and two lookout points. Both studios are open daily; hours vary seasonally.

THE WEST RIM DRIVE

The West Rim Drive is an 8-mile-long road leading west from Grand Canyon Village to Hermits Rest. From mid-March to mid-October, this road is closed to private automobiles, but a free shuttle operates frequently and stops at most of the overlooks. The rest of the year it's possible to drive this scenic road in your own car, stopping whenever and wherever you wish.

The first stops are **Trailview Overlook** and **Paiute Point.** From either of these points, you have a view of the Bright Angel Trail winding down into the canyon from Grand Canyon Village. The trail, which leads down to the bottom of the canyon, crosses the Tonto Plateau about 3,000 feet below the rim. This plateau is the site of Indian Garden, where there is a campground in a grove of cottonwood trees.

The next stop on the West Rim Drive is **Maricopa Point.** Here you can see the remains of the Orphan Mine, which began operation in 1893. The mine went out of business because transporting the copper to a city where it could be sold was too expensive. Uranium was discovered here in 1954, but in 1966 the mine was shut down, and the land became part of Grand Canyon National Park. If you look carefully at the bottom of the canyon, you can see black Vishnu schist, which is among the oldest exposed rock on earth.

<hr />

Impressions

We are imprisoned three quarters of a mile in the depths of the earth and the great unknown river shrinks into insignificance as it dashes its angry waves against the walls and cliffs that rise to the world above.
  —Maj. John Wesley Powell, on his successful trip through the Grand Canyon

Shooting the Canyon: Tips for Photographers

By the time most people leave the Grand Canyon they've shot several rolls of film. This is not at all surprising considering the beauty of this rugged landscape. But it's not always easy to capture the canyon's spirit. Here are some tips to help you bring back the best possible photos from your trip:

A polarizing filter is a great investment if you have the kind of camera that accepts lens filters. A polarizing filter reduces haze, lessens the contrast between shadowy areas and light areas, and deepens the color of the sky.

The best times to photograph the canyon are at sunrise and sunset, when filtered and sharply angled sunlight paints the canyon walls in beautiful shades of lavender and pink. At these times the shadows are at their most dramatic. To capture these ephemeral moments, it's best to use a tripod and a long exposure. The worst time to photograph the canyon is at noon when there are almost no shadows, and thus little texture or contrast. The National Park Service includes a table with sunrise and sunset times in *The Guide,* the park's official visitor newspaper.

Something else to keep in mind is that the Grand Canyon is immense. A wide-angle lens may leave the canyon looking on paper like a distant plane of dirt. Try zooming in on narrower sections of the canyon to emphasize a single dramatic landscape element. If you're shooting with a wide-angle lens, try to include something in the foreground (people or a tree branch) to give the photo perspective and scale.

When shooting portraits against a sunrise or sunset, use a flash to illuminate your subjects; otherwise, your camera meter may expose for the bright light in the background and leave your subjects in shadow.

The **Powell Memorial,** the next stop, is dedicated to John Wesley Powell, who, in 1869 with a party of nine men, became the first person to navigate the Colorado River through the Grand Canyon.

Next along the drive is **Hopi Point,** from which you can see a long section of the Colorado River. Because of the great distance, the river seems to be a tiny, quiet stream, but in reality the section you see is more than 100 yards wide and races through Granite Rapids.

Mohave Point is the next stop. From here you can see (and sometimes hear) Hermit Rapids, another section of white water. As with almost all rapids in the canyon, these are formed at the mouth of a side canyon where boulders loosened by storms and carried by flooded streams are deposited in the Colorado River.

The next stop is at the **Abyss,** the appropriately named 3,000-foot drop created by the Great Mojave Wall. This vertiginous view is one of the most awe-inspiring in the park. The walls of the Abyss are red sandstone that's more resistant to erosion than the softer shale in the layer below. Other layers of erosion-resistant sandstone have formed the freestanding pillars that are visible from here. The largest of these pillars is called the Monument.

From **Pima Point** it's possible to see the remains of Hermit Camp on the Tonto Plateau. Built by the Santa Fe Railroad, Hermit Camp was a popular tourist destination between 1911 and 1930 and provided cabins and tents. Today only foundations remain.

At the end of West Rim Drive is **Hermit's Rest,** named for Louis Boucher, a prospector who came to the canyon in the 1890s and was known as the Hermit. The log-and-stone Hermit's Rest building, designed by Mary Elizabeth Jane Colter and built in 1914, is on the National Register of Historic Places.

THE EAST RIM DRIVE

The East Rim Drive extends for 25 miles from Grand Canyon Village to Desert View. The first stop is **Yaki Point,** near the trailhead for the South Kaibab Trail, which leads to Phantom Ranch. The spectacular view from here encompasses a wide section of the central canyon. The large flat-topped butte to the northeast is Wotan's Throne, one of the canyon's easily recognizable features. From mid-March to mid-October, Yaki Point is closed to private vehicles and can be reached only by shuttle bus.

The next stop, **Grandview Point,** affords a view of Horseshoe Mesa, another interesting feature of the canyon landscape. The mesa was the site of the Last Chance Copper Mine in the early 1890s. Later that same decade the Grandview Hotel was built and served canyon visitors until its close in 1908.

Next along the drive is **Moran Point,** from which you can see a bright red layer of shale in the canyon walls. This point is named for 19th-century landscape painter Thomas Moran, who through his artwork shared the beauty of the West with people of the eastern cities.

The **Tusayan Museum** (open daily in summer, as staffing permits in other months; free admission) is the next stop along the East Rim Drive. This small museum is dedicated to the Hopi tribe and ancient Anasazi people who inhabited this region 800 years ago, and inside the museum are artfully displayed exhibits on various aspects of Anasazi life. Outside the museum is a short self-guided trail through the ruins of an Anasazi village. Free guided tours are available.

At **Lipan Point** you get one of the park's best views of the Colorado River; you can even see a couple of major rapids. From here you can see the Grand Canyon *supergroup:* several strata of rock tilted at an angle to the other layers of rock in the canyon. Their angle indicates there was a period of geological mountain building before the depositing of layers of sandstone, limestone, and shale. The red, white, and black rocks of the supergroup are composed of sedimentary rock and layers of lava. From **Navajo Point,** the Colorado River and Escalante Butte are both visible, and there's a good view of Desert Tower.

Desert View, with its trading post, general store, cafeteria, service station, information center, bookstore, and watchtower, is the end of this scenic drive. The road does continue east from here, but it soon leaves the park, although outside the park, there are still some good views to be had of the Little Colorado River. The scenery is breathtaking from anywhere at Desert View, but the very best perspective is from atop the Desert View Watchtower (open daily, admission 25¢). Although the watchtower looks as though it had been built centuries ago, it actually dates from 1932. Architect Mary Elizabeth Jane Colter, who is responsible for much of the park's historic architecture, designed the tower to resemble the prehistoric towers that dot the Southwestern landscape. Built as an observation tower and rest stop for tourists, the watchtower incorporates Native American designs and art. The curio shop on the ground floor is a replica of a kiva (sacred ceremonial chamber) and has lots of interesting souvenirs, Southwestern crafts, and books. The tower's second floor features artwork by Hopi artist Fred Kabotie. Covering the walls are pictographs incorporating traditional designs. On the walls and ceiling of the upper two floors are more traditional images by artist Fred Geary, this time reproductions of petroglyphs from throughout the Southwest. From the roof, the highest point on the South Rim (7,522 feet above sea level), it's possible to see the Colorado River, the Painted Desert to the northeast, the

San Francisco Peaks to the south, and Marble Canyon to the north. Coin-operated binoculars provide close-up views of some of the noteworthy landmarks of this end of the canyon. On the roof are several black-mirror "reflectoscopes" that provide interesting darkened views of some of the most spectacular sections of the canyon. The gift shop offers a pamphlet describing the watchtower in detail.

OTHER WAYS TO SEE THE CANYON
MULE RIDES

Mule rides into the canyon are some of the most popular activities in the Grand Canyon and have been since the turn of the century when the Bright Angel Trail was a toll road. However, after having a look at the steep drop-offs and narrow path of the Bright Angel Trail, you might decide this isn't exactly the place to trust your life to a mule. Never fear: Wranglers will be quick to reassure you they haven't lost a rider yet. Trips of various lengths and to different destinations are offered. The 1-day trip descends to Plateau Point, where there's a view of the Colorado River 1,300 feet below. This grueling trip requires riders to spend 6 hours in the saddle. Those who want to spend a night down in the canyon can choose an overnight trip to Phantom Ranch, where cabins and dormitories are available at the only lodge actually in the canyon. From mid-November to March there's a 3-day/2-night trip to Phantom Ranch. Mule trips range in price from $112.95 for a 1-day ride to Plateau Point to $325.95 for an overnight ride to Phantom Ranch to $444.90 for a 2-night ride to Phantom Ranch. Couples get discounts on overnight rides.

There are a few rider qualifications you should keep in mind before calling to make a reservation. You must weigh less than 200 pounds fully dressed, stand at least 4 feet 7 inches tall, and speak fluent English. Pregnant women are not allowed on mule trips.

Because these trail rides are very popular (especially in summer), they often book up 6 to 11 months in advance (reservations are taken up to 23 months in advance). You should try to make a reservation as soon as you know when you'll be visiting. For more information or to make a reservation, contact **Grand Canyon National Park Lodges/AMFAC Parks & Resorts** (☎ **303/297-2757**; fax 303/297-3175). If at the last minute (5 days or less from the day you want to ride) you decide you want to go on a mule trip into the Grand Canyon, contact Grand Canyon National Park Lodges at its Arizona phone number (☎ **520/638-3283**) for the remote possibility that there may be space available. If you arrive at the canyon without a reservation and decide that you'd like to go on a mule ride, stop by the Bright Angel Transportation Desk to get your name on the next day's waiting list.

ON HORSEBACK

Trail rides on the rim (but not into the canyon) are available from Moqui Lodge's **Apache Stables** (☎ **520/638-2891**; www.apachestables.com), at the south entrance to the park. There are rides of various lengths, with prices ranging from $30.50 for a 1-hour ride to $95.50 for a 4-hour ride. Evening wagon rides ($12.50) are also offered. The stables are usually open March to early December (depending on the weather).

RIDING THE RAILS

In the early part of the 20th century, most visitors to the Grand Canyon arrived by train, and today it's still possible to travel to the canyon along the steel rails. The ✪ **Grand Canyon Railway** (☎ **800/843-8724** or 520/773-1976; www.thetrain. com), which runs from Williams to Grand Canyon Village, uses turn-of-the-century steam engines (during the summer) and 1950s-vintage diesel engines (other months) to pull 1920s passenger cars as well as a dome coach car. Trains depart from the Williams Depot, housed in the renovated Fray Marcos Hotel. Built in 1908, the old hotel now houses a railroad museum, gift shop, and cafe. (Grand Canyon Railway also operates a new Fray Marcos Hotel, which really is a hotel.) At Grand Canyon Village, the trains use the 1910 log railway terminal in front of El Tovar Hotel.

Passengers have the choice of five classes of service: coach, club, first class, deluxe observation class (upstairs in the dome car), and luxury parlor car. Actors posing as cowboys provide entertainment, including music performances, aboard the train. The round-trip takes 8 hours (including 3$^{1}/_{4}$ hours at the Canyon), and fares range from $49.95 to $119.95 for adults and from $24.95 to $94.95 for children 16 and under (these rates do not include tax or the national park admission fee).

Not only is this a fun trip that provides great scenery and a trip back in time, but by taking the train, you can avoid the traffic congestion and parking problems in Grand Canyon Village. When booking your train trip, you can book a bus tour in the park, which will help you see more than you would on foot. The railway offers different room/train packages.

A BIRD'S-EYE VIEW

Despite controversies over noise and safety (there have been a few crashes over the years), airplane and helicopter flights over the Grand Canyon remain one of the most popular ways to see these natural wonders. Several companies operating out of the Grand Canyon Airport in Tusayan offer air tours lasting from 30 minutes to about 2 hours.

Companies offering air tours by small plane include **Air Grand Canyon** (☎ **800/ 247-4726** or 520/638-2686), **Sky Eye Air Tours** (☎ **888/275-9393** or 520/638-6454), **Airstar Airlines** (☎ **800/962-3869** or 520/638-2622), and **Grand Canyon Airlines** (☎ **800/528-2413** or 520/638-2407). Rates for 50-minute flights are between $70 and $90 for adults and $45 to $55 for children.

Helicopter tours are available from **Airstar Helicopters** (☎ **800/962-3869** or 520/638-2622), **Kenai Helicopters** (☎ **800/541-4537** or 520/638-2764), and **Papillon Grand Canyon Helicopters** (☎ **800/528-2418** or 520/638-2419). Rates range from around $94 for a 30-minute flight to around $161 for a 45- to 55-minute flight.

INTERPRETIVE PROGRAMS

Numerous interpretive programs are scheduled throughout the year at various South Rim locations. There are ranger-led walks that explore different aspects of the canyon, geology talks, lectures on the cultural and natural resources of the canyon, nature hikes, trips to fossil beds, and star-gazing gatherings. At Tusayan Ruin there are guided tours. Evening programs are held at Mather Amphitheater or the Shrine of the Ages. Consult your copy of *The Guide* for information on times and meeting points.

THE GRAND CANYON FIELD INSTITUTE

If you are the active type or you'd just like to turn your visit to the Grand Canyon into more of an educational experience, you may want to consider doing a trip with the **Grand Canyon Field Institute,** P.O. Box 399, Grand Canyon, AZ 86023 (☎ **520/ 638-2485;** e-mail: gcfi@grandcanyon.org). Cosponsored by Grand Canyon National Park and the Grand Canyon Association, the field institute schedules an amazing variety of guided, educational trips, such as challenging backpacking trips through the canyon (some for women only) and programs lasting anywhere from 2 to 10 days. Subjects covered include wilderness studies, geology, natural history, human history, photography, and art.

JEEP TOURS

If you'd like to see some parts of Grand Canyon National Park that most visitors never see, try a Jeep tour with **Grand Canyon Outback Jeep Tours** (☎ **800/320-JEEP** or 520/638-JEEP; www.thecanyon.com/gcjeeps), which offers three different tours that visit the park as well as the adjacent Kaibab National Forest. One of the tours stops at a lookout tower where you get an elevated view of the canyon, while another tour visits an Indian ruin and site of petroglyphs and cave paintings. Tour prices range from $30 to $54 for adults and $20 to $35 for children ages 12 and under.

✪ HIKING THE CANYON

There are no roads leading into the Grand Canyon, so if you want to visit the inner canyon you have to hike, ride a mule, or float. The least expensive of these options is to hike in. However, if you go very far down a trail into the canyon, you'll find out exactly why so many people content themselves with walking along the canyon's rim. Think of the Grand Canyon as an upside-down mountain. You start out by walking downhill, thus saving the harder uphill climb for the second half of your hike (when you're likely already tired out from the hike down). Don't underestimate the difficulty of hiking down into the canyon, and always carry plenty of water. However, these warnings aside, no visit to the canyon is complete without journeying below the rim. While the views don't get any better than they are from the top, they do change considerably. Gazing up at all those thousands of feet of vertical rock walls provides a very different perspective on the Grand Canyon. Should you venture far below the rim you stand a chance of seeing fossils, old mines, petroglyphs, wildflowers, and wildlife.

The Grand Canyon offers some of the most rugged and strenuous hiking anywhere in the United States, and for this reason anyone attempting even a short walk should be well prepared. Each year people are injured or killed because they set out to hike the canyon without preparing properly. Most of these injuries and fatalities are suffered by day hikers who set out without sturdy footgear and without food or adequate amounts of water. Take precautions—don't become another Grand Canyon statistic! Unless you have proper footgear and at least 1 quart of water, you won't even be allowed on the daily ranger-led nature walk along the South Kaibab Trail. Even a short 30-minute hike in the summer can dehydrate you, and a long hike into or out of the canyon in the heat can necessitate drinking more than a gallon of water. Remember while hiking that mules have the right of way. Don't attempt to hike from the rim to the Colorado River and back in 1 day. Many people who have tried this have died.

DAY HIKES

Loop-trail day hikes are not possible in the Grand Canyon, but the vastly different scenery in every direction makes a return trip on the same trail a totally new experience. The easiest day hikes are those along the rim. There's a 1¹/₂-mile paved trail leading from the Yavapai Museum to the Powell Memorial. From the Powell Memorial, the trail becomes dirt and continues another 8 miles to Hermits Rest, from which, between mid-March and mid-October, you can take a free shuttle back to Grand Canyon Village.

Trails leading down into the canyon include the Bright Angel Trail, the South Kaibab Trail, Grandview Trail, and the Hermit Trail. If you plan to hike for more than 30 minutes, carry 2 quarts of water per person. If you're game to do it, hiking into the canyon even just a short distance before doubling back will allow you to escape the ever-present crowds.

The ✪ **Bright Angel Trail** starts just west of Bright Angel Lodge in Grand Canyon Village. It's the main route down to Phantom Ranch and the most popular trail into the canyon. Day hikes on this trail include the trips to Indian Garden (9.2 miles round-trip) or Plateau Point (12.2 miles round-trip). Both of these trips are long and strenuous. There are rest houses at 1½ and 3 miles (during the summer they have water), which make good turn-around points for a 3-mile or 6-mile round-trip hike.

The **South Kaibab Trail** begins near Yaki Point east of Grand Canyon Village and is the alternative route to Phantom Ranch. This trail offers the best views of any of the day hikes in the canyon, so should you have time for only one day hike into the canyon, make it down this trail (not the more popular Bright Angel Trail). From the trailhead it's a 3-mile round-trip to Cedar Ridge or 6 miles round trip to Skeleton Point. The hike is very strenuous, and there's no water available along the trail.

The **Grandview Trail** is a steep, unmaintained trail that should be attempted only by people with experience hiking in the desert. It's a very strenuous 6-mile round-trip hike to Horseshoe Mesa, and there's no water available along the trail. Allow at least 7 hours for this rugged hike. Alternatively, you can do a 1.5-mile round-trip hike to Coconino Saddle.

The **Hermit Trail** begins near Hermits Rest and is steep and unmaintained. Don't attempt this trail if you don't have some experience hiking in the desert. It's a 5-mile round-trip to Santa Maria Springs and a 7-mile round-trip to Dripping Springs. Water from these springs must be treated with a water filter, iodine, or purification tablets or by boiling for at least 10 minutes.

BACKPACKING

Backpacking the Grand Canyon is an unforgettable experience. Although most people are content to simply hike down to Phantom Ranch and back, there are many miles of trails deep in the canyon. Keep in mind, however, that to backpack the canyon, you'll need to do a lot of planning. A **Backcountry Use Permit** is required of all hikers planning to overnight in the canyon unless you'll be staying at Phantom Ranch in one of the cabins or in the dormitory.

Because a limited number of hikers are allowed into the canyon on any given day, it's important to make reservations as soon as it is possible to do so. Reservations are taken in person, by mail, by fax (but not by phone), and over the Internet. Contact the **Backcountry Office,** Grand Canyon National Park, P.O. Box 129, Grand Canyon, AZ 86023 (☎ **520/638-7875** between 1 and 5pm for information; fax 520/638-2125; www.thecanyon.com/nps). Holiday periods are the most popular. The office begins accepting reservations on the first of every month for the following 5 months. If you want to hike over the Labor Day weekend, be sure you make your reservation on May 1! If you show up without a reservation, go to the Backcountry Office (open daily 8am to noon and 1 to 5pm), at the Maswik Transportation Center, and put your name on the waiting list. When applying for a permit, you have to specify your exact itinerary, and once in the canyon, you must stick to this itinerary. Backpacking fees include a nonrefundable $20 backcountry permit fee and a $4 per person per night backcountry camping fee.

There are **campgrounds** at Indian Garden, Bright Angel Campground (near Phantom Ranch), and Cottonwood, but hikers are limited to 2 nights per trip at each of these campgrounds (except November 15 to February 28 when 4 nights are allowed at each campground). Other nights can be spent camping at undesignated sites in certain regions of the park.

The *Backcountry Trip Planner* publication has information to help you plan your itinerary. It's available through the Backcountry Office. Maps are available through the **Grand Canyon Association,** P.O. Box 399, Grand Canyon, AZ 86023 (☎ **800/ 858-2808;** fax 520/638-2484; www.grandcanyon.org), and at bookstores within the national park. They are at the visitor center, Kolb Studio, Desert View Information Center, Yavapai Observation Station, Tusayan Museum, and, on the North Rim, in Grand Canyon Lodge.

The best times of year to backpack in the canyon are spring and autumn. During the summer, temperatures at the bottom of the canyon are frequently above 100°F, while in the winter ice and snow at higher elevations make footing on trails precarious (crampons are recommended equipment in winter). Also, plan to carry at least 2 quarts, and preferably 1 gallon, of water whenever backpacking in the canyon.

If you'd like to have a guide lead you on a backpacking trip through some of the more remote and little visited parts of the park, contact Bill Vercammen, owner of **Grand Canyon Trail Guides** (☎ **888/283-3194** or 520/638-3194; http://grandcanyontrailguides.com), who offers guided hikes in the backcountry for around $250 per person per day, which includes most of your supplies and gear (lower rates apply if you supply some of your own gear and food). Guided day hikes are available. A wide range of guided backpacking trips are offered by the Grand Canyon Field Institute (see above for details).

✺ RAFTING THE COLORADO RIVER

Rafting down the Colorado River as it roars and tumbles through the mile-deep gorge of the Grand Canyon is the adventure of a lifetime. Ever since John Wesley Powell ignored everyone who knew better and proved that it was possible to travel by boat down the tumultuous Colorado River, running the big river has become a passion and an obsession with adventurers. Today anyone from grade-schoolers to grandmothers can join the elite group who have made the run. However, be prepared for some of the most furious white water in the world.

There are 16 companies offering trips through various sections of the canyon. You can spend as few as 3 days on the river or as many as 19. You can go down the river in a huge motorized rubber raft, a paddled- or oar-powered raft, or a wooden dory. In a motorized raft, you can travel the entire canyon from Lees Ferry to Lake Mead in only 8 days. Should you opt for an oar- or paddle-powered raft or dory, expect to spend 5 or 6 days getting from Lees Ferry to Phantom Ranch or 7 to 9 days getting from Phantom Ranch to Diamond Creek, just above Lake Mead.

Most trips start from Lees Ferry near Page and Lake Powell. However, it's possible to start (or finish) a trip at Phantom Ranch, hiking in or out from either the North or South Rim. The main rafting season is April to October, but some companies operate year-round. Rafting trips tend to book up well in advance, and most companies begin taking reservations in April for the following year's trips. Expect to pay around $200 per day for your white-water adventure.

The following companies are currently authorized to operate trips through the Grand Canyon:

Aramark-Wilderness River Adventures, P.O. Box 717, Page, AZ 86040 (☎ 800/992-8022 or 520/645-3296; www.riveradventures.com)

Arizona Raft Adventures, 4050-FE Huntington Dr., Flagstaff, AZ 86004 (☎ 800/786-RAFT or 520/526-8200; www.azraft.com)

Arizona River Runners, P.O. Box 47788, Phoenix, AZ 85068-7788 (☎ 800/477-7238 or 602/867-4866; www.raftarizona.com)

Canyon Explorations/Canyon Expeditions, P.O. Box 310, Flagstaff, AZ 86002 (☎ 800/654-0723 or 520/774-4559; www.canyonx.com)

Canyoneers, P.O. Box 2997, Flagstaff, AZ 86003 (☎ 800/525-0924 or 520/526-0924; www.canyoneers.com)

Colorado River & Trail Expeditions, P.O. Box 57575, Salt Lake City, UT 84157-0575 (☎ 800/253-7328 or 801/261-1789; www.crateinc.com)

Diamond River Adventures, P.O. Box 1300, Page, AZ 86040 (☎ 800/343-3121 or 520/645-8866; www.diamondriver.com)

Grand Canyon Dories, P.O. Box 216, Altaville, CA 95221 (☎ 800/877-3679 or 209/736-0805; www.oars.com/gcdories)

Grand Canyon Expeditions Company, P.O. Box O, Kanab, UT 84741 (☎ 800/544-2691 or 435/644-2691; www.gcex.com)

Hatch River Expeditions, P.O. Box 1200, Vernal, UT 84078 (☎ 800/433-8966 or 435/789-3813; www.hatchriver.com)

High Desert Adventures, P.O. Box 40, St. George, UT 84771-0040 (☎ 800/673-1733 or 435/673-1733; www.funboat.com)

Moki Mac River Expeditions, P.O. Box 21242, Salt Lake City, UT 84121 (☎ 800/284-7280 or 801/268-6667; www.mokimac.com)

OARS, P.O. Box 67, Angels Camp, CA 95222 (☎ 800/346-6277 or 209/736-2924; www.oars.com)

Outdoors Unlimited, 6900 Townsend Winona Rd., Flagstaff, AZ 86004 (☎ 800/637-7238 or 520/526-4546; www.outdoorsunlimited.com)

Tour West, P.O. Box 333, Orem, UT 84059 (☎ 800/453-9107 or 801/225-0755; www.twriver.com)

Western River Expeditions, 7258 Racquet Club Dr., Salt Lake City, UT 84121 (☎ 800/453-7450 or 801/942-6669; www.westernriver.com).

For information on 1- and 2-day rafting trips at the west end of the Grand Canyon, see "South Rim Alternatives: Havasu Canyon & Grand Canyon West," below. For information on half- and full-day trips near Page, see "Lake Powell & Page" in chapter 7, "The Four Corners Region: Land of the Hopi & Navajo."

INTERESTING ACTIVITIES OUTSIDE THE CANYON

If you aren't completely beat at the end of the day, you might want to take in an evening of Navajo **storytelling and dancing** at the Grand Hotel (☎ **520/638-3333**) in Tusayan; call for schedule.

For a virtual Grand Canyon experience, take in a show at the **Grand Canyon IMAX Theater,** Ariz. 64/U.S. 180 (☎ **520/638-2203**), in Tusayan outside the south entrance to the park. A short IMAX film covering the history and geology of the canyon is shown throughout the day on the theater's seven-story screen. Admission is $8.50 for adults and $6.50 children ages 3 to 11. March to October, there are shows daily between 8:30am and 8:30pm; November to February, there are shows daily between 10:30am and 6:30pm.

WHERE TO STAY

Keep in mind that the Grand Canyon is one of the most popular national parks in the country, and hotel rooms both within and just outside the park are in high demand. Make reservations as far in advance as possible. Don't expect to find a room if you head up here in summer without a reservation. You'll likely wind up driving back to Williams or Flagstaff to find a vacancy. There, is, however, one long-shot option. See "Inside the Park," below, for details. Who knows? You might get lucky.

INSIDE THE PARK

All hotels inside the park are operated by **Amfac Parks & Resorts.** Reservations are taken up to 23 months in advance, beginning on the first of the month. If you want to stay in one of the historic rim cabins at Bright Angel Lodge, reserve at least a year in advance. However, rooms with shared bathrooms at Bright Angel Lodge are often the last rooms in the park to book up, and although these rooms are small and very basic, if you're trying to get a last-minute reservation, they're your best bet. The Yavapai Lodge, because it is set back from the rim, is a good bet for last-minute reservations.

For making reservations at any of the in-park hotels listed here (as well as Moqui Lodge, just outside the park), contact **Grand Canyon National Park Lodges/Amfac Parks & Resorts,** 14001 E. Iliff Ave., Aurora, CO 80014 (☎ **303/297-2757;** fax 303/297-3175; www.amfac.com or www.grandcanyonlodges.com). It is sometimes possible, due to cancellations and no-shows, to get a same-day reservation; it's a long shot, but it happens. Same-day reservations can be made by calling ☎ **520/ 638-2631.**

Amfac accepts American Express, Diners Club, Discover, JCB, MasterCard, and Visa credit cards.

Moderate

✪ **El Tovar Hotel.** 78 units. A/C TV TEL. $116–$174 double; $199–$284 suite.

El Tovar Hotel, which first opened its doors in 1905, is the park's premier lodge. Built of local rock and Oregon pine by Hopi craftsmen, it's a rustic yet luxurious mountain lodge that perches on the edge of the canyon (but with views from only a few rooms). The lobby, entered from a veranda set with rustic furniture, has a small fireplace, cathedral ceiling, and log walls on which moose, deer, and antelope heads are displayed. The guest rooms feature modern Mission-style furnishings that are somewhat in keeping with the period when the hotel was built. The standard rooms are rather small, as are the bathrooms. For more leg room, book a deluxe room. Suites, with their private terraces and stunning views, are extremely spacious and done mostly in new Southwestern style.

The El Tovar Dining Room (see "Where to Dine," below) is the best restaurant in the village and serves excellent continental and Southwestern cuisine. Just off the lobby is a cocktail lounge with a view. Room service is available, and there's a concierge and tour desk.

Maswik Lodge. 278 units, including 28 cabins (available summer only). TV TEL. $73–$136 double; $63 cabin.

Set back ¼ mile or so from the rim, the Maswik Lodge offers spacious rooms and rustic cabins. If you crave modern appointments, opt for one of the Maswik North rooms. If you don't mind roughing it a bit, the rustic old cabins have lots of character and are comfortable enough. These cabins have bathtubs but not showers. There's a large cafeteria, a tour desk, and a sports lounge.

Thunderbird & Kachina Lodges. 104 units. A/C TV TEL. $114–$132 double.

Despite the use of native sandstone in their construction, these 1960s-vintage motel-style lodgings are far from your idea of what a national park lodge should look like, and the dated "modern" styling clashes with the traditional design of the adjacent historic lodges. However, if you want "modern" amenities and a fairly large room, these should be your in-park choice in this price range. The rooms in both lodges have large windows, although you'll have to request a canyon-side room on the second floor if you want a view of something more than a parking lot (the canyon-view rooms are only $10 more than those without views and are well worth the extra cost). Thunderbird Lodge registration is handled by Bright Angel Lodge, and Kachina Lodge registration is handled by El Tovar Hotel.

Yavapai Lodge. 358 units. TV TEL. $88–$120 double.

Located in several buildings at the east end of Grand Canyon Village (a 1-mile hike from the main section of the village), the Yavapai is the largest lodge in the park, and consequently it's where you'll likely wind up if you wait too long to make a reservation. There are no canyon views here, which is why this lodge is less expensive than the Thunderbird and Kachina lodges. The rooms in the Yavapai East section of the hotel are set under shady pines and are more attractive than the rooms in the Yavapai West section (well worth the price difference). There's a cafeteria and a tour desk.

Inexpensive

✪ Bright Angel Lodge & Cabins. 89 units (20 with shared bathroom). $44 double with sink only, $50 double with sink and toilet, $60 double with bathroom; $70–$234 cabin.

Bright Angel Lodge, which began operation in 1896 as a collection of tents and cabins on the edge of the canyon, is the most affordable lodge in the park; with its flagstone-floor lobby and huge fireplace, it has a genuine, if crowded, mountain lodge atmosphere. This lodge offers the greatest variety of accommodations in the park and has undergone the most recent renovation. In addition to rooms with shared bathrooms, there are cabins, including rim cabins that are the lodge's best and most popular accommodations (book a year in advance for summer). Outside the winter months, other rooms should be booked at least 6 months in advance. Most of the rooms and cabins feature rustic furnishings but have been fairly recently renovated. The Buckey Suite, the oldest structure on the canyon rim, is arguably the best room in the park, with a canyon view, fireplace, and a king-size bed. However, the rim cabins with fireplaces aren't worth the extra cost since the fireplaces don't work very well. The lodge has a coffee shop, a steakhouse, and an ice cream parlor. A tour desk and museum account for the constant crowds in the lobby.

✪ Phantom Ranch. Reconfirmations ☎ **520/638-3283** or 520/638-2631. 11 cabins, 40 dorm beds. $65.96 double in the cabins; $22.87 dormitory bed. Mule-trip overnights (with all meals and mule ride included) $325.94 for 1 person, $583.79 for 2 people. 2-night trips are available mid-Nov to Mar.

Built in 1922, Phantom Ranch is the only lodge at the bottom of the Grand Canyon and has a classic ranch atmosphere. The accommodations are in rustic stone-walled cabins or 10-bedded gender-segregated dormitories. Evaporative coolers keep both the cabins and the dorms cool in the summer. Make reservations as early as possible (up to a year in advance) and don't forget to reconfirm. It's possible to get a room on the day of departure if there are any last-minute cancellations. To attempt this, you must put your name on the waiting list at the Bright Angel Lodge transportation desk the day before you want to stay at Phantom Ranch.

Family-style meals must be reserved in advance. The menu consists of beef-and-vegetable stew or vegetarian dinner for $17.60 or steak for $28.15. Breakfasts ($12.65) are hearty, and sack lunches ($7.95) are available. Between meals the dining hall becomes a canteen selling snacks, drinks, gifts, and necessities. After dinner, the dining hall becomes a beer hall. There's a public phone here, and mule-back baggage transfer between Grand Canyon Village and Phantom Ranch can be arranged ($46.15 each way).

TUSAYAN (OUTSIDE THE SOUTH ENTRANCE)

If you can't get a reservation for a room in the park, this is the next closest place to stay. Unfortunately, this area can be very noisy because of the many helicopters and airplanes taking off from the airport. Also, hotels outside the park are very popular with tour groups, which during the busy summer months keep many hotels full. All the hotels listed here are lined up along U.S. 180/Ariz. 64.

There is one other motel in town, the **Seven Mile Lodge** (☎ **520/638-2291**), which is usually the least expensive place in town ($68 double). However, this motel does not take reservations and is usually full by 2pm in the summer (it starts renting rooms at 9am).

Moderate

Best Western Grand Canyon Squire Inn. Ariz. 64, P.O. Box 130, Grand Canyon, AZ 86023-0130. ☎ **800/622-6966** or 520/638-2681. Fax 520/638-2782. www.thecanyon. com/squire. 250 units. A/C TV TEL. Apr to mid-Oct and Christmas holiday $105–$175 double; mid-Oct to Mar $60–$125 double. AE, CB, DC, DISC, MC, V.

If you prefer playing tennis to riding a mule, this may be the place for you. With two tennis courts, a pool, an exercise room, a whirlpool, a sauna, a bowling alley, a pool room, a video arcade, and a tour desk, this hotel has the feel of a resort and seems to want to distract guests from the canyon itself. The rooms are large and have comfortable easy chairs and large windows. The dining room serves continental cuisine, and there's a less expensive coffee shop and a lounge. There's even a sort of cowboy museum in the lobby.

✪ **Grand Hotel.** P. O. Box 3319, Grand Canyon, AZ 86023. ☎ **888/63-GRAND** or 520/638-3333. Fax 520/638-3131. www.canyon.com. 120 units. A/C TV TEL. $90–$139 double. AE, DISC, JCB, MC, V.

This is the newest hotel in Tusayan, and the hotel's lobby, with its mountain-lodge styling, is certainly quite grand. There's a flagstone fireplace, log-beam ceiling, and fake ponderosa pine tree trunks holding up the roof. Just off the lobby (past the large gift shop), there's a big dining room (with evening entertainment ranging from Native American dancers to country-music bands) and a small bar that even has a few saddles for barstools. Guest rooms are big, with a few Western decor touches, and some have small balconies. Try to get a room on the back side of the hotel; these face the forest rather than the parking lot. Amenities here include an indoor pool, a whirlpool, and a fitness room.

Holiday Inn Express—Grand Canyon. P.O. Box 3245, Grand Canyon, AZ 86023. ☎ **888/473-2269** or 520/638-3000. Fax 520/638-0123. www.gcanyon.com/HI. 198 units. A/C TV TEL. $69–$129 double; $80–$149 suite. Rates include continental breakfast. AE, DC, DISC, JCB, MC, V.

This is one of the newest lodgings in the area and has modern, well-designed, if a bit sterile and characterless, guest rooms. With no pool or restaurant, this place is really just somewhere to crash at the end of the day. The Holiday Inn Express manages an adjacent 32-suite property that has theme suites. Although these suites are fairly pricey, they're among the nicest rooms inside or outside the park.

Moqui Lodge. Amfac Parks & Resorts, 14001 E. Iliff Ave., Aurora, CO 80014. ☎ **303/297-2757.** Fax 303/297-3175. www.amfac.com. 136 units. TV TEL. $94–$118 double. AE, DC, DISC, JCB, MC, V. Closed Nov–Mar.

Managed by the same company that operates all the lodges within the park, this motel is just outside the south entrance to the park. With its tall A-frame construction, Moqui Lodge has the feel of a ski lodge at first, but unfortunately lacks the appropriate character. The best of accommodations here are standard motel-style rooms with large windows that for the most part look out onto the parking lot, while the worst are cramped, poorly furnished, and overpriced. There's a lounge and a dining room serving moderately priced Mexican and American food. There's also a tour desk.

Quality Inn & Suites Grand Canyon. P.O. Box 520, Grand Canyon, AZ 86023. ☎ **800/ 221-2222** or 520/638-2673. Fax 520/638-9537. www.thecanyon.com/gcqual. 232 units. A/C TV TEL. Apr to mid-Oct $118 double, $168 suite; late Oct–Mar $73 double, $123 suite. AE, CB, DC, DISC, MC, V.

This relatively luxurious hotel at the park's south entrance is built around two enclosed skylit courtyards, one of which houses a restaurant and the other a bar and large whirlpool (there's also an outdoor pool and whirlpool). The rooms are large and comfortable and have balconies or patios. Most have minibars. For extra space, there are suites with separate small living rooms, microwaves, refrigerators, and coffeemakers. The hotel is next to the IMAX Theater and is very popular with tour groups.

Rodeway Inn Red Feather Lodge. Ariz. 64 (P.O. Box 1460), Grand Canyon, AZ 86023. ☎ **800/228-2000** or 520/638-2414. Fax 520/638-9216. www.redfeatherlodge.com. 231 units. A/C TV TEL. $59–$119 double. AE, DC, DISC, MC, V. Pets accepted with $50 deposit, $45 refundable.

Try to get one of the newer rooms, which are a bit more comfortable than the older ones. But no matter which type you get, you'll be able to avail yourself of an outdoor pool (seasonal) and whirlpool, as well as a fitness room. Kids will appreciate the game room. There is a casual restaurant on the premises.

Other Area Accommodations

✪ **Cameron Trading Post Motel.** P.O. Box 339, Cameron, AZ 86020. ☎ **800/338-7385** or 520/679-2231. Fax 520/679-2350. www.camerontradingpost.com. 62 units. A/C TV TEL. Mar–Apr 30 $69–$79 double; May–Oct $74–$84 double; Nov–Feb $59–$69 double. Suites $145–$175 year-round. AE, CB, DC, DISC, MC, V. Well-behaved pets accepted.

Located 54 miles north of Flagstaff on U.S. 89 at the junction with the road to the east entrance of the national park, this motel offers some of the most attractive rooms in the vicinity of the Grand Canyon. The motel, adjacent to the historic Cameron Trading Post, is built around the old trading post's terraced gardens, which are a shady oasis. The rooms are furnished with Southwestern-style furniture and attractively decorated. Most have balconies, and some have views of the canyon of the Little Colorado River. There's a restaurant here as well as one of the best trading posts in the state.

Campgrounds
Inside the Park

On the South Rim, there are two campgrounds and an RV park. **Mather Campground,** in Grand Canyon Village, has 350 campsites. Reservations can be made up to 5 months in advance and are accepted for stays between March 1 and November 30 (other months reservations are not accepted). For reservations, contact the National Park Reservation Service (☎ **800/365-2267** or 301/722-1257; http://reservations. nps.gov). Between late spring and early fall, don't even think of coming up here without a campground reservation; you'll just be setting yourself up for disappointment. However, if you don't have a reservation, your next best bet is to arrive in the morning when campsites are being vacated. Campsite fees range from $10 to $15 depending on the season.

Desert View Campground, with 50 sites, is 26 miles east of Grand Canyon Village and open mid-May to mid-October only. No reservations are accepted for this campground. Campsites are $12 per night.

The **Trailer Village RV park,** with 192 RV sites, is in Grand Canyon Village and charges $20 per night for full hookup sites. Reservations can be made up to 23 months in advance; contact Amfac Parks & Resorts, 14001 E. Iliff Ave., Aurora, CO 80014 (☎ **303/297-2757;** fax 303/297-3175).

Outside the Park

Getting a campsite inside the park is no easy feat, and if you get shut out, your next best choices lie within a few miles of the south entrance to the park. In Tusayan, you'll find **Grand Canyon Camper Village,** P.O. Box 490, Grand Canyon, AZ 86023-0490 (☎ **520/638-2887**), open year-round. This is primarily an RV park, but it also has sites for tents. The only drawback is that you're right in town, which is probably not what you were dreaming of when you planned your trip to the Grand Canyon. Rates here range from $15 to $23.

Two miles south of Tusayan you'll find the U.S. Forest Service's **Ten-X Campground.** The campground is open May to September, and campsites are $10. This is usually your best bet for finding a campsite late in the day.

You can camp just about anywhere within the Kaibab National Forest, which borders Grand Canyon National Park, as long as you are more than ¼ mile away from Ariz. 64/U.S. 180. Several dirt roads lead into the forest from the highway, and although you won't find designated campsites or toilets along these roads, you will find spots where others have obviously camped before. This so-called dispersed camping is usually used by campers who have been unable to find sites in campgrounds. Anyone equipped for backpacking could just hike in a bit from any forest road rather than camping right beside the road. One of the most popular roads for this sort of camping is on the west side of the highway between Tusayan and the park's south entrance. For more information, contact the **Tusayan Ranger District,** Kaibab National Forest, P.O. Box 3088, Grand Canyon, AZ 86023 (☎ **520/638-2443**).

WHERE TO DINE

In addition to the restaurants listed below, which are all within the park, you'll find several restaurants just outside the south entrance in Tusayan. The best of these is the **Canyon Star** at the Grand Hotel and the **Coronado Dining Room** at the Best Western Grand Canyon Squire Inn. You'll find a steak house and a pizza place, as well as familiar chains such as McDonald's, Taco Bell, Pizza Hut, and Wendy's.

INSIDE THE PARK

Expensive

✪ **El Tovar Dining Room.** In the El Tovar Hotel. ☎ **520/638-2631,** ext. 6432. Reservations required at dinner. Main courses $15.50–$23. AE, DC, DISC, JCB, MC, V. Daily 6:30–11am, 11:30am–2pm, and 5–10pm. CONTINENTAL/SOUTHWESTERN.

If you're staying at El Tovar, you'll definitely want to have dinner here in the hotel's rustic-yet-elegant dining room. However, before booking dinner at the most expensive restaurant in the park, be aware that meals can be uneven, and few tables here have views of the canyon. With this knowledge in hand, you now must decide for yourself whether you want to splurge on a meal that will definitely be the best food available inside the park but that might not be as good as you would hope after seeing the prices. The menu leans heavily to the spicy flavors of the Southwest (crab-stuffed trout with jalapeño lobster sauce, blue corn tamales, orange-and-chile-marinated broiled shrimp). However, plenty of milder, more familiar dishes are thrown in as well. Service is generally quite good. Make reservations as soon as possible to get the dinner-time you want.

Moderate

Arizona Steakhouse. In the Bright Angel Lodge. ☎ **520/638-2631.** Reservations not accepted. Dinner $14–$22. AE, DC, DISC, JCB, MC, V. Daily 4:30–10pm. STEAKS.

Meals other than steaks here can be very uneven, so stick to the slabs of beef and hope for the best. Despite the lackluster food, this place is always packed (can you say captive audience?) primarily because the steaks are relatively cheap and there's a decent view out the window. There's almost always a wait for a table, so try to show up early if you can. Keep in mind that once the sun goes down, the view out the window is absolutely black (which means you could be dining anywhere). Arrive early and enjoy the sunset.

Bright Angel Coffee Shop. In the Bright Angel Lodge. ☎ **520/638-2631.** Reservations not accepted. Main courses $6–$18. AE, DC, DISC, JCB, MC, V. Daily 6:30–10:45am and 11:15am–10pm. AMERICAN.

As the least expensive of the three restaurants right on the rim of the canyon, this casual Southwestern-themed coffee house in the historic Bright Angel Lodge stays packed throughout the day. Meals are simple and none too memorable, but if you can get one of the tables near the windows, at least you get something of a view. Unfortunately, there just aren't that many tables with views. The menu includes everything from Southwestern favorites such as chili, tacos, and fajitas to spaghetti and meatballs (foods calculated to comfort tired and hungry hikers). Wines are available, and service is generally friendly and efficient.

Inexpensive

If you're looking for a quick, inexpensive meal, there are plenty of options. In Grand Canyon Village, choices include **cafeterias** at the Yavapai and Maswik lodges and a **delicatessen** at Babbitt's General Store (across from the visitor center). However, the **Bright Angel Fountain,** which is at the back of the Bright Angel Lodge and serves hot dogs, sandwiches, and ice cream, seems to be the most popular food outlet in the village. **Hermits Rest Fountain** on the West Rim Drive is a snack bar. At Desert View (on the East Rim Drive), there's the **Desert View Trading Post Cafeteria.** All of these places are open daily for all three meals, and all serve meals for $8 and under.

EAST OF THE CANYON

The **Cameron Trading Post** (☎ **800/338-7385** or 520/679-2231), at the crossroads of Cameron where Ariz. 64 branches off U.S. 89, is the best trading post in the state and should not be missed. The original stone trading post, a historic building, now houses a gallery of old and antique Indian artifacts, clothing, and jewelry. This gallery offers museum-quality pieces, and even if you don't have $10,000 or $15,000 to drop on a rug or basket, you can still look around. The main trading post is a more modern building and is the largest trading post in northern Arizona. Don't miss the beautiful old terraced gardens in back of the original trading post.

4 South Rim Alternatives: Havasu Canyon & Grand Canyon West

Havasu Canyon: 200 miles W of Grand Canyon Village; 70 miles N of Ariz. 66; 155 miles NW of Flagstaff; 115 miles NE of Kingman

Grand Canyon West: 240 miles W of Grand Canyon Village; 70 miles N of Kingman; 115 miles E of Las Vegas

With five million people each year visiting the South Rim of the Grand Canyon, and traffic congestion and parking problems becoming the most memorable aspects of most people's visits to the canyon, you might want to consider an alternative to the South Rim. For most people, this means driving around to the North Rim; however, it's open only from mid-May to late October and is already getting a lot more visitors than it did a few years ago.

There are a couple of other lesser-known alternatives. A visit to Havasu Canyon, on the Havasupai Indian Reservation, entails a 20-mile round-trip hike or horseback ride similar to that from Grand Canyon Village to Phantom Ranch, although with a far more spectacular setting at the bottom of the canyon. Visiting Grand Canyon West, on the Hualapai Indian Reservation, is much less strenuous, but you will have to spend 28 miles on gravel road to get there and back.

ESSENTIALS

GETTING THERE   Havasu Canyon   It isn't possible to drive all the way to Supai village or Havasu Canyon. The nearest road ends 8 miles from Supai at Hualapai Hilltop. This is the trailhead for the trail into the canyon and is at the end of Indian Route 18, which runs north from Ariz. 66. The turnoff is 6 miles east of Peach Springs and 21 miles west of Seligman. Many Arizona maps show an unpaved road between U.S. 180 and Hualapai Hilltop, but this road is not maintained on a regular basis and is passable only to four-wheel-drive vehicles *when* no fallen logs block the way.

The easiest and fastest (and by far the most expensive) way to reach Havasu Canyon is by helicopter from Grand Canyon Airport. Flights are operated by **Papillon Grand Canyon Helicopters** (☎ **800/528-2418**). The round-trip air-and-ground day excursion is $440, and the overnight excursion is $482.

Grand Canyon West   If you're headed to Grand Canyon West, you've got several options, two of which entail driving nearly 50 miles of gravel roads that aren't even passable if it has rained any time recently. The best route is to head northwest out of Kingman on U.S. 93, and in 27 miles turn right onto the Pearce Ferry Road (signed for Dolan Springs and Meadview). After 28 miles on this road, turn right again onto a gravel Diamond Bar Road, which is signed for Grand Canyon West. Another 14 miles down this road brings you to the Hualapai Indian Reservation (and a bit of paved road again). A little farther along, you'll come to the Grand Canyon West Terminal (there's actually an airstrip here) where visitor permits and bus tour tickets are sold.

You can drive to Grand Canyon West from Peach Springs via Antares Road, which adds another 32 miles of gravel to your trip (64 miles if you return this same way).

VISITOR INFORMATION   For information on Havasu Canyon, contact the **Havasupai Tourist Enterprises,** P.O. Box 160, Supai, AZ 86435 (☎ **520/448-2121**), which handles all campground reservations. For information on Grand Canyon West, contact **Hualapai Reservations,** P.O. Box 538, Peach Springs, AZ 86434 (☎ **888/255-9550** or 520/769-2230; fax 520/769-2372; www.hualapaitours.com).

○ HAVASU CANYON

Imagine hiking for hours through a dusty brown landscape of rocks and cacti. The sun overhead is blistering and bright. The air is hot and dry. Rock walls rise up higher and higher as you continue your descent through a mazelike canyon. Eventually the narrow canyon opens up into a wide plain shaded by cottonwood trees, a sure sign of water, and within a few minutes you hear the sound of a babbling stream. The water, when you finally reach it, is cool and crystal clear, a pleasant surprise. Following the stream, you pass through a dusty (usually cluttered and unkempt, some say dirty and depressing) Indian village of small homes. Not surprisingly in a village 8 miles beyond the last road, every yard seems to be a corral for horses. Passing through the village, you continue along the stream. As the trail descends again, you spot the first waterfall.

The previously crystal-clear water is now a brilliant turquoise blue at the foot of the waterfall. The sandstone walls look redder than before. No, you aren't having a heat-induced hallucination—the water really is turquoise, and it fills terraces of travertine that form deep pools of cool water at the base of three large waterfalls. Together these three waterfalls form what many claim is the most beautiful spot in the entire state.

This is Havasu Canyon, the canyon of the Havasupai tribe, whose name means "people of the blue-green waters." For centuries the Havasupai have called this idyllic desert oasis home.

The waterfalls are the main attraction here, and most people are content to go for a dip in the cool waters, sun themselves on the sand, and gaze for hours at the turquoise waters. When you tire of these pursuits, you can hike up the small side canyon to the east of Havasu Falls. Another trail leads along the west rim of Havasu Canyon and can be reached by carefully climbing up a steep rocky area near the village cemetery. There's a trail that leads all the way down to the Colorado River, but this is an overnight hike.

In Supai village, there is a small museum dedicated to the culture of the Havasupai people. Its exhibits and old photos will give you an idea of how little the lives of these people have changed over the years.

The Havasupai entry fee is $20 per person to visit Havasu Canyon, and everyone entering the canyon is required to register at the Tourist Office in the village of Supai. Because it's a long walk in to the campground, be sure you have a confirmed reservation before setting out from Hualapai Hilltop. It's good to make reservations as far in advance as possible, especially for holiday weekends. Havasupai Tourist Enterprises operates on a cash-only basis, so be sure to bring enough money for your entire stay.

If you plan to hike down into the canyon, start early to avoid the heat of the day. The hike is beautiful, but it's 10 miles to the campground. The steepest part of the trail is the first mile or so from Hualapai Hilltop. After this section it's relatively flat.

Through the **Havasupai Tourist Enterprises** (☎ **520/448-2121** or 520/448-2141), you can hire a horse to carry you or your gear down into the canyon from Hualapai Hilltop. Horses cost $75 each way. Many people who hike in decide that it's worth the money to ride out, or at least have their backpacks carried out. Be sure to confirm your horse reservation a day before driving to Hualapai Hilltop. Sometimes no horses are available, and it's a long drive back to the nearest town.

GRAND CANYON WEST

Located on the Hualapai Indian Reservation on the south side of the Colorado River, **Grand Canyon West** (☎ **520/699-0269**) overlooks the rarely visited west end of Grand Canyon National Park. Neither as high nor as spectacular as the South Rim, Grand Canyon West nonetheless offers the chance to observe the green waters of the Colorado River as it carves its way through the multicolored cliffs of the canyon. Here at Grand Canyon West, you have several options for seeing the area, including a stop at an overlook, a hike down into the canyon, a guided bus tour along the rim, and a helicopter ride below the rim. What you won't find here, however, are crowds. In part this is because of the distance from Grand Canyon Village and the South Rim, and in part because to reach Grand Canyon West you must drive a minimum of 14 miles on a gravel road (28 miles total for the round-trip). You won't find the sort of strip-mall development that mars Tusayan just outside the entrance to the South Rim. Instead, you'll drive through miles of wide-open desert before reaching the short stretch of paved road at Grand Canyon West. If you're looking to escape the hordes and see a little-visited corner of the Grand Canyon, this is a good alternative.

If you'd just like to take in the view from this end of the canyon, head to **Quarter-master Point,** after first purchasing your sightseeing permit ($10) at the Grand Canyon West terminal. At Quartermaster Point, you'll find a trail that leads down into the canyon.

To see more of this area, you'll have to take a **guided bus tour** that includes a barbecue lunch and time to do a bit of exploring at a canyon overlook. These bus tours stop at Eagle Point, where rock formations resemble various animals and people, and at Guano Point, where bat guano was once mined commercially. The tours, which operate daily throughout the year, cost $32.50 for adults and $22 for children 2 to 12. No reservations are accepted, so it's a good idea to arrive around 8am when Grand Canyon West opens (if you are coming from Kingman, leave yourself at least 1¹/₂ hours to get here).

Want to fly to the bottom of the Grand Canyon in a helicopter? Well, Grand Canyon West is the only place where it's legal to do so. **Scenic Airlines/Heli-USA** (☎ 520/699-3993) offers a quick tour to the bottom for $79 per person and a combination chopper tour plus bus tour and barbecue for $99 per person.

OTHER AREA ACTIVITIES

While most rafting trips in the Grand Canyon take 6 to 8 days, here at the west end of the canyon, it is possible to do half-day and full-day rafting trips that begin on the Hualapai Indian Reservation and are operated by **Hualapai River Runners,** P.O. Box 246, Peach Springs, AZ 86434 (☎ 800/622-4409 or 520/769-2210; www.riverrunners.com), a tribal rafting company. Expect a mix of white water and flat water (all of it very cold), and although perhaps not as exciting as longer trips in the main section of the canyon, you'll still plow through some pretty big waves. Be ready to get wet. These trips stop at a couple of side canyons where you can get out and do some exploring. At one of these stops, there is a warm creek that flows out of a cave at the back of which is a waterfall that pours through a skylight in the top of the cave. One-day trips cost $250 per person, and half-day trips cost $160; rafters can arrange discount rates on lodging at the Hualapai Lodge.

Also in this area, you can visit **Grand Canyon Caverns** (☎ 520/422-3223), which are just outside Peach Springs. The caverns, which are accessed via a 210-foot elevator ride, are open Memorial Day to October 15, daily 9am to 6pm, and October 16 to Memorial Day, daily 9:30am to 5pm. Admission is $9.50 for adults, $6.75 for children ages 4 to 12.

WHERE TO STAY & DINE
IN & NEAR PEACH SPRINGS

Grand Canyon Caverns Inn. P.O. Box 180, Peach Springs, AZ 86434. ☎ **520/422-3223.** 48 units. A/C TV TEL. Summer $50 double; winter $35 double. AE, DISC, MC, V. Pets accepted, $50 deposit.

If you're planning to hike or ride into Havasu Canyon, you'll need to be at Hualapai Hilltop as early in the morning as possible. Because it's a 3- to 4-hour drive to this spot from Flagstaff, you might want to consider staying here, one of only two lodgings for miles around. As the name implies, this motel is built on the site of the Grand Canyon Caverns, which are open to the public. There is a casual restaurant and cocktail lounge. Facilities include a pool, a gift shop, and a general store with camping supplies and food. For much of the year, this motel is used by Elderhostel and stays full.

Hualapai Lodge. 900 Rte. 66, P.O. Box 538, Peach Springs, AZ 86434. ☎ **888/255-9550** or 520/769-2230. Fax 520/769-2372. 60 units. A/C TV TEL. May–Sept $75–$85 double; Oct–Apr $60–$70 double. AE, DISC, MC, V.

Located in the Hualapai community of Peach Springs, this lodge is by far the most luxurious accommodation anywhere in this region. Guest rooms here are spacious and modern, with a few bits of regional decor for character. The dining room is just about the only place in town to get food and serves basic American dishes. Most people staying here are in the area to go to Grand Canyon West, to go rafting with Hualapai River Runners, or to hike in to Havasu Canyon.

IN HAVASU CANYON

Havasu Campground. Havasupai Tourist Enterprise, P.O. Box 160, Supai, AZ 86435. ☎ **520/448-2121.** 400 sites. $10 per person per night. MC, V.

The campground is 2 miles below Supai village, between Havasu Falls and Mooney Falls, and the campsites are mostly in the shade of cottonwood trees on either side of Havasu Creek. Picnic tables are provided, but no firewood is available. Cutting any trees or shrubs is prohibited, so be sure to bring a camp stove. Spring water is available, and although it's considered safe to drink, we advise treating it first.

Havasupai Lodge. P.O. Box 159, Supai, AZ 86435. ☎ **520/448-2201.** 24 units. A/C. $80 double. MC, V.

Located in Supai village, this lodge is, aside from the campground, the only accommodation in the canyon. The two-story building features standard motel-style rooms that are lacking only TVs and telephones, neither of which are much in demand at this isolated retreat. The only drawback of this comfortable-though-basic lodge is that it's 2 miles from Havasu Falls and 3 miles from Mooney Falls. The Havasupai Café, across from the general store, serves breakfast, lunch, and dinner. It's a very casual place, and the prices are high for what you get because all ingredients must be packed in by horse.

5 The Grand Canyon North Rim

42 miles S of Jacob Lake; 216 miles N of Grand Canyon Village (South Rim); 354 miles N of Phoenix; 125 miles W of Page/Lake Powell

Although the North Rim of the Grand Canyon is only 10 miles from the South Rim as the crow flies, it's more than 200 miles by road. It is this much greater distance from population centers such as Phoenix and Las Vegas that has helped keep this rim of the canyon much less crowded than the South Rim. Additionally, due to heavy snowfalls, the North Rim is open only from mid-May to late October or early November. There are far fewer activities on the North Rim than there are on the South Rim (no helicopter or plane rides, no IMAX theater, no McDonald's). For these reasons, most of the millions of people who annually visit the Grand Canyon never make it to this side of the canyon. And that is exactly why quite a few people think the North Rim is a far superior place to visit. If Grand Canyon Village was more human zoo than the wilderness experience you had expected, the North Rim will probably be much more to your liking, although crowds, traffic congestion, and parking problems are not unheard of here either.

The North Rim is on the Kaibab Plateau, which is more than 8,000 feet high on average and takes its name from the Paiute word for "mountain lying down." The higher elevation of the North Rim means that instead of the junipers and ponderosa pines of the South Rim, you'll find dense forests of ponderosa pines, Douglas firs, and aspens interspersed with large meadows. Consequently, the North Rim has a much more Alpine feel than the South Rim. The 8,000-foot elevation (1,000 feet higher than the South Rim) means that the North Rim gets considerably more snow in the winter than the South Rim does. The highway south from Jacob Lake is not plowed in winter; consequently, the Grand Canyon Lodge closes down.

ESSENTIALS

GETTING THERE   The North Rim is at the end of Ariz. 67 (the North Rim Parkway), reached from U.S. 89A.

Trans Canyon operates a shuttle between the North Rim and South Rim of the Grand Canyon during the months the North Rim is open. The trip takes 5 hours, and the fare is $60 one way and $100 round-trip. Call ☎ **520/638-2820** for more information.

VISITOR INFORMATION   For information before leaving home, contact **Grand Canyon National Park,** P.O. Box 129, Grand Canyon, AZ 86023 (☎ **520/638-7888;** www.thecanyon.com/nps).

There's an **information desk** in the lobby of the Grand Canyon Lodge, open daily 8am to 6pm. At the entrance gate you'll be given a copy of *The Guide,* a small newspaper with information on park activities. There's a separate edition of *The Guide* for the North Rim.

ADMISSION   The park admission fee is $20 per car and is good for 1 week. Remember not to lose the little paper receipt that serves as your admission pass.

Important note: Visitor facilities at the North Rim are open only from mid-May to mid-October. From mid-October to November (or until snow closes the road to the North Rim), the park is open for day use only. The campground may be open after mid-October, weather permitting.

EXPLORING THE AREA

While it's hard to beat the view from a rustic rocking chair on the terrace of the Grand Canyon Lodge, the best spots for viewing the canyon are Bright Angel Point, Point Imperial, and Cape Royal. **Bright Angel Point** is the closest to Grand Canyon Lodge, and from here you can see and hear Roaring Springs, which is 3,600 feet below the rim and is the North Rim's only water source. From Bright Angel Point you can see Grand Canyon Village on the South Rim. At 8,803 feet, **Point Imperial** is the highest point on the North Rim. A short section of the Colorado River can be seen far below, and off to the east the Painted Desert is visible.

However, as grand as these other vistas are, **Cape Royal** is the most spectacular setting on the North Rim; along the 23-mile road to this viewpoint you'll find several other scenic overlooks. Across the road from the **Walhalla Overlook** are the ruins of an Anasazi structure, and just before reaching Cape Royal you'll come to the **Angel's Window Overlook,** which gives you a breathtaking view of the natural bridge that forms Angel's Window. Once at Cape Royal, you can follow a trail across this natural bridge to a towering promontory overlooking the canyon.

Other than simply taking in the views, hiking along the rim is the most popular activity at the North Rim, and quite a few day hikes of varying lengths are possible here. The shortest is the half-mile paved trail to Bright Angel Point, and the longest is the North Kaibab Trail to Roaring Springs and back, which takes 6 to 8 hours.

If you want to see the canyon from a saddle, contact **Grand Canyon Trail Rides** (☎ **435/679-8665**), which offers mule rides varying in length from 1 hour to a full day. Prices range from $15 for an hour ride up to $95 for the all-day trip.

EN ROUTE TO OR FROM THE NORTH RIM

Between Page and the North Rim of the Grand Canyon, U.S. 89A crosses the Colorado River at **Lees Ferry** in Marble Canyon. Lees Ferry is the starting point for raft trips through the Grand Canyon and for many years was the only place to cross the Colorado River for hundreds of miles in either direction. This stretch of the river is legendary among anglers for its trophy trout fishing, and when the North Rim closes

Return of the Condors

California condors are among the most endangered bird species in North America, but the Grand Canyon is playing a part in helping these huge scavengers return from the brink of extinction. Since 1996, the Vermilion Cliffs have been home to a tiny population of California condors that have been released here in hopes of reestablishing a wild condor population. Condors have also been released at the eastern end of the canyon in the Hurricane Cliffs area, now part of the newly designated Grand Canyon–Parashant National Monument. So far, most of the birds released in the canyon have survived, and although the birds still rely somewhat on food left out for them, they are slowly becoming accustomed to their natural surroundings. Occasionally Grand Canyon visitors spot these huge birds. Should you be so lucky as to see a condor, do not approach the bird or offer it food.

and the rafting season comes to an end, about the only folks you'll find up here are anglers and hunters. Here at Lees Ferry, you'll find a campground (☎ **520/ 355-2234**).

Lees Ferry Anglers (☎ **800/962-9755** or 520/355-2261), 3 miles west of the bridge at Lees Ferry, is fishing headquarters for the region. Not only do they sell all manner of fly-fishing tackle and offer advice about good spots to try your luck, but they also operate a guide service and rent waders and boats. A guide will cost you $250 per day for one person or $300 for two people.

Continuing west, the highway passes under the **Vermilion Cliffs,** so named for their deep red coloring. At the base of these cliffs are huge boulders balanced on narrow columns of eroded soil. The balanced rocks give the area an otherworldly appearance. Along this unpopulated stretch of road are a couple of very basic lodges.

Seventeen miles west of Marble Canyon, you'll see a sign for **House Rock Ranch.** This wildlife area, managed by the Arizona Game and Fish Department, is best known for its herd of bison (American buffalo). From the turnoff it's a 22-mile drive on a gravel road to reach the ranch.

One last detour to consider before or after visiting the national park is an area known as the East Rim. This area lies just outside the park on Kaibab National Forest and can be reached by turning east on gravel Forest Service Road 610 across from the Kaibab Lodge a few miles north of the park entrance. For the best view, continue to the end of FR 610 and the Saddle Mountain Viewpoint. Another good view can be had from the Marble viewpoint at the end of FR 219, a dead-end spur road off FR 610. For more information, contact the **Kaibab Ranger District** (☎ **520/ 643-7395**).

NORTH OF THE PARK

If you'd like to learn more about the pioneer history of this remote and sparsely populated region of the state (known as the Arizona Strip), continue west from Jacob Lake 45 miles on Ariz. 389 to **Pipe Spring National Monument** (☎ **520/643-7105;** www.nps.gov/pisp), which preserves an early Mormon fort. During the summer, there are living history demonstrations here. The monument is open daily (except Thanksgiving, Christmas, and New Year's Day) 8am to 5:30pm, and admission is $2 per adult.

Southwest of Pipe Spring, in an area accessible only via long gravel roads, lies the newly designated Grand Canyon–Parashant National Monument. Dedicated by President Clinton in early 2000, this monument preserves a vast and rugged landscape north of the east end of Grand Canyon National Park. The monument has no facilities and no paved roads. For more information, contact the Arizona Strip Field Office of the **Bureau of Land Management,** 345 E. Riverside Dr., St. George, UT 84790-9000 (☎ **435/688-3200;** www.az.blm.gov).

WHERE TO STAY
INSIDE THE PARK

✪ **Grand Canyon Lodge.** Amfac Parks & Resorts, 14001 E. Iliff Ave., Aurora, CO 80014. ☎ **303/297-2757** or 520/638-2611 (for same-day reservations). Fax 303/297-3175. www.amfac.com. 200 units. $78–$108 double. AE, DC, DISC, JCB, MC, V. Closed Oct 15– May 15.

Perched right on the canyon rim, this classic mountain lodge is listed on the National Register of Historic Places and is as impressive a lodge as you will find in any national park. The stone-and-log main lodge building has a soaring ceiling and a viewing room set up with chairs facing a wall of glass, and on either side of this room are flagstone terraces set with rustic chairs that face out toward the canyon. The guest rooms vary from standard motel rooms to rustic mountain cabins to comfortable modern cabins. Our favorites are the little cabins, which, although cramped and paneled with dark wood, capture the feeling of a mountain retreat better than any of the other rooms. A few rooms have views of the canyon, but most are tucked back away from the rim.

A large dining hall with two walls of glass serves straightforward American food and is open daily for all three meals. A saloon and a snack bar are outside the lodge's front entrance, and there's a tour desk in the lodge's lobby.

OUTSIDE THE PARK

In addition to this hotel, and the other lodges mentioned below, you'll find numerous budget motels in Fredonia, Arizona (30 miles west of Jacob Lake), and Kanab, Utah (37 miles west of Jacob Lake).

Kaibab Lodge. P.O. Box 2997, Flagstaff, AZ 86003. ☎ **800/525-0924** or 520/638-2389 (May 15–late Oct only). Fax 520/638-9864. www.canyoneers.com. 29 units. Mid-May to late Oct $75–$125 double. DISC, MC, V. Closed late Oct to mid-May. Pets accepted.

Located 5 miles north of the entrance to the Grand Canyon's North Rim, the Kaibab Lodge was built around 1926 and is situated on the edge of a large meadow where deer can often be seen grazing. Nights here are cool even in summer, and a favorite pastime of guests is to sit by the fireplace in the lobby. The rooms are in small rustic cabins set back in the pines from the main lodge building. The lodge's dining room serves all meals, and the kitchen prepares box lunches. There are hiking-equipment and mountain-bike rentals, a whirlpool spa, a tour desk, and a gift shop.

EN ROUTE TO THE PARK

If you don't have a reservation at either of the North Rim area lodges listed here, you may want to stop at one of the lodges recommended below and continue on to the North Rim the next morning. Lodges near the canyon fill up early in the day if they aren't already fully booked with reservations made months in advance.

Cliff Dwellers Lodge. U.S. 89A (HC67-30), Marble Canyon, AZ 86036. ☎ **800/433-2543** for reservations, or 520/355-2228. Fax 520/355-2229. www.cliffdwellerslodge.com. 21 units. A/C. $57–$78 double. DISC, MC, V.

To give you some idea of how remote an area this is, the Cliff Dwellers Lodge is marked on official Arizona state maps. There just isn't much else out here, so a single lodge can be as important as a town. The newer, more expensive rooms here are standard motel rooms and have combination bathtub/showers, while the older rooms, in a stone-walled building, have more character but showers only. A small restaurant provides meals. The lodge is close to some spectacular balanced rocks, and it's about 11 miles east to Lees Ferry. The views here are great.

Lees Ferry Lodge. U.S. 89A (HC67-Box 1), Marble Canyon, AZ 86036. ☎ **520/355-2231.** www.leesferrylodge.com. 11 units. A/C. $50–$75 double. MC, V.

Located at the foot of the Vermilion Cliffs, $3^1/_2$ miles west of the Colorado River, the Lees Ferry Lodge, built in 1929 of native stone and rough-hewn timber beams, is a small place with rustic accommodations. However, the rafters and anglers who stay here don't seem to care much about the condition of the rooms, and besides, the patio seating area in front of all the rooms has fabulous views of the Vermilion Cliffs. Unfortunately, the highway is only a few yards away, so traffic noises can disturb the tranquility. There's a small dining room on the premises.

Marble Canyon Lodge. P.O. Box 6001, Marble Canyon, AZ 86036. ☎ **800/726-1789** or 520/355-2225. Fax 520/355-2227. 60 units. A/C TV. $60–$125 double. AE, DISC, MC, V. Pets accepted.

Located just 4 miles from Lees Ferry, the Marble Canyon Lodge was built in the 1920s and is popular with rafters preparing to head down the Grand Canyon. The room styles vary considerably in size and age, with some rustic rooms in old stone buildings and other newer motel-style rooms as well. You're right at the base of the Vermilion Cliffs here, and the views are great. There's a cozy restaurant and a trading post.

CAMPGROUNDS

Located just north of Grand Canyon Lodge, the **North Rim Campground,** with 82 sites and no hookups for RVs, is the only campground at the North Rim. The campground opens in mid-May and may stay open past the mid-October closing of other North Rim visitor facilities. Reservations can be made up to 3 months in advance by calling the **National Park Reservation Service** (☎ **800/365-2267**). The fee is $15 to $20 per site per night.

There are two nearby campgrounds outside the park in the Kaibab National Forest. They are **DeMotte Park Campground,** which is the closest to the park entrance and has only 22 sites, and **Jacob Lake Campground,** which is 30 miles north of the park entrance and has 53 sites. Both campgrounds charge $10 per night and do not take reservations. You can camp anywhere in the Kaibab National Forest as long as you're more than $1/_4$ mile from a paved road or water source. So if you can't find a site in a campground, simply pull off the highway in the national forest and park your RV or pitch your tent.

The **Kaibab Camper Village,** P.O. Box 3331, Flagstaff, AZ 86003 (☎ **520/643-7804** in summer or 520/526-0924 in winter), is a privately owned campground in the crossroads of Jacob Lake, 30 miles north of the park entrance. Rates are $12 per night for tent sites and $22 per night for RV sites with full hookups. Make reservations well in advance.

7

The Four Corners Region: Land of the Hopi & Navajo

There is only one place in the United States where you can stand in four states at the same time, and that spot is in northeast Arizona where Colorado, Utah, New Mexico, and Arizona all come together. Known as Four Corners, this spot is the site of a Navajo Tribal Park. However, Four Corners also refers to this entire region. Most of the land here is Navajo and Hopi reservation land, and it's also some of the most spectacular countryside in the state, with majestic mesas, rainbow-hued deserts, towering buttes, multicolored cliffs, deep canyons, a huge cliff-rimmed reservoir, and even a meteorite crater. Among the most spectacular of the region's landscape features are the 1,000-foot buttes of Monument Valley, which for years have symbolized the Wild West of John Wayne movies and car commercials.

The Four Corners region is also home to Arizona's most scenic reservoir—Lake Powell—which is sort of a flooded version of the Grand Canyon. With its miles of blue water mirroring red-rock canyon walls hundreds of feet high, Lake Powell is one of northern Arizona's curious contrasts—a vast artificial reservoir in the middle of barren desert canyons. Although 40 years ago there was a bitter fight over damming Glen Canyon to form Lake Powell, today the lake is among the most popular tourist attractions in the Southwest, attracting sightseers from all over the world.

While this region certainly offers plenty of spectacular scenery, it also provides one of the nation's most fascinating cultural experiences. This is Indian country, the homeland of both the Navajo and the Hopi, tribes that have lived on these lands for hundreds of years and have adapted different means of surviving in this arid region. The Navajo, with their traditional log homes scattered across the countryside, have become herders of sheep, goats, and cattle. The Hopi, on the other hand, have congregated in villages atop mesas and built houses of stone. They farm the floors of narrow valleys at the feet of their mesas in much the same way the indigenous peoples of the Southwest have done for centuries.

These two tribes are, however, only the most recent Native Americans to inhabit what many consider to be a desolate, barren wilderness. The ancient Anasazi (Ancestral Puebloans) left their mark throughout the canyons of the Four Corners region. Throughout the region are cliff dwellings dating back 700 years and more, the most spectacular in Arizona being the ruins in Canyon de Chelly and Navajo national monuments. No one is sure why the Anasazi moved up into the cliff walls, but there is speculation that unfavorable growing conditions brought on by drought may have forced them to use every possible inch of arable land. Likewise, no one today is certain why the Anasazi abandoned their cliff dwellings in the 13th century, and with no written record, the disappearance of the Anasazi may forever remain a mystery.

The Hopi, who claim the Anasazi as their ancestors, have for centuries now had their villages on the tops of mesas in northeastern Arizona. They claim that Oraibi, on Third Mesa, is the oldest continuously inhabited community in the United States. Whether or not this is true, several of the Hopi villages are quite old, and for this reason they have become tourist attractions. Most of the villages are built on three mesas, known simply as First, Second, and Third Mesa, which are numbered from east to west. These villages have always maintained a great deal of autonomy, which over the years has sometimes led to fighting. The appearance of missionaries and the policies of the Bureau of Indian Affairs have also created conflicts among and within villages. Today the Hopi Reservation is completely surrounded by the much larger Navajo Reservation.

Roughly the size of West Virginia, the Navajo Reservation covers an area of 25,000 square miles in northeastern Arizona, as well as parts of New Mexico, Colorado, and Utah. It's the largest Native American reservation in the United States and is home to nearly 200,000 Navajo. Although the reservation today has modern towns with supermarkets, shopping malls, and hotels, many Navajo still follow a pastoral lifestyle as herders of goats and sheep. As you travel the roads of the Navajo Reservation, you'll frequently encounter these flocks as well as herds of cattle and horses. These animals have free range of the reservation and often graze beside the highways.

Unlike the pueblo tribes such as the Hopi and Zuni, the Navajo are relative newcomers to the Southwest. Their Athabascan language is most closely related to the languages spoken by Native Americans in the Pacific Northwest, Canada, and Alaska. It's believed that the Navajo migrated southward from northern Canada beginning around A.D. 1000, arriving in the Southwest sometime after 1400. At this time the Navajo were still hunters and gatherers, but contact with the pueblo tribes, who had long before adopted an agricultural lifestyle, began to change the Navajo into farmers. When the Spanish arrived in the Southwest in the early 17th century, the Navajo acquired horses, sheep, and goats through raids and adopted a pastoral way of life, grazing their herds in the high plains and canyon bottoms.

The continued use of raids, made even more successful with the acquisition of horses, put the Navajo in conflict with the Spanish settlers who were beginning to encroach on Navajo land. In 1805, the Spanish sent a military expedition into the Navajo's chief stronghold, Canyon de Chelly, and killed 115 people, who, by some accounts, may have been all women, children, and old men. This massacre, however, did not stop the conflicts between the Navajo and Spanish settlers.

In 1846, when this region became part of the United States, American settlers encountered the same problems that the Spanish had. Military outposts were established to protect the new settlers, and numerous unsuccessful attempts were made to establish peace. In 1863, after continued Navajo attacks, a military expedition led by Col. Kit Carson burned crops and homes late in the summer, effectively obliterating the Navajo's winter supplies. Thus defeated, the Navajo were rounded up and herded 400 miles to an inhospitable region of New Mexico near Fort Sumner. This march became known as the Long Walk and had a profound influence on the Navajo. Living conditions at Fort Sumner were deplorable, and the land was unsuitable for farming. In 1868, the Navajo were allowed to return to their homeland.

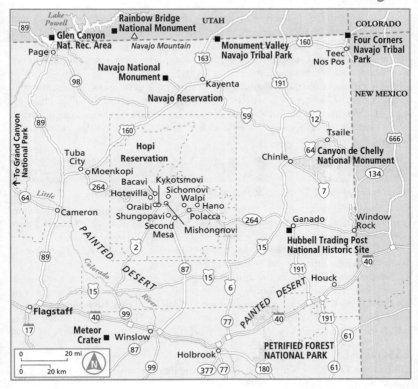

Upon returning home, and after continued clashes with white settlers, the Navajo eventually settled into a lifestyle of herding. In recent years, however, the Navajo have had to turn to different livelihoods. Although weaving and silver work have become lucrative businesses, the amount of money they garner for the tribe as a whole is not significant. Many Navajo now take jobs as migrant workers, and gas and oil leases on the reservation provide more income.

Although the reservation covers an immense area, much of it is of no value other than as scenery. Fortunately, the Navajo are recognizing the income potential of their spectacular land. Monument Valley is operated as a tribal park, as is the Four Corners park. Also, numerous Navajo-owned tour companies now operate on the reservation.

As you travel the Navajo reservation you may notice small hexagonal buildings with rounded roofs. These are *hogans,* the traditional homes of the Navajo, and are usually made of wood and earth. The doorway of the hogan always faces east to greet the new day. At the Canyon de Chelly and Navajo National Monument visitor centers you can look inside hogans that are part of the parks' exhibits. If you take a tour at Canyon de Chelly or Monument Valley, you may have an opportunity to visit a hogan that is still someone's home. Most Navajo now live in modest houses or mobile homes, but a family will usually also have a hogan for religious ceremonies.

All over the Navajo Reservation, you'll find roadside stalls selling jewelry and crafts. While you can sometimes find quality merchandise and bargain prices at these stalls, you'll usually find better quality at trading posts, museum and park gift shops, and established shops where you receive some guarantee of quality.

The Navajo and Hopi reservations cover a vast area and are laced with a network of good paved roads, as well as many unpaved roads that are not always passable to cars that don't have four-wheel drive. The main things to keep in mind when driving in this area are to keep your car gassed up, since distances are great, and to keep an eye out for livestock on the road, especially at night.

Before taking a photograph of a Navajo, always ask permission. If permission is granted, a tip of $1 or more is expected. Photography is not allowed at all in Hopi villages. Unlike the rest of Arizona, the Navajo Reservation observes daylight saving time. However, the Hopi Reservation does not. Also keep in mind that *alcohol is not allowed on either reservation.*

1 Winslow

55 miles E of Flagstaff; 70 miles S of Second Mesa; 33 miles W of Holbrook

It's hard to imagine a town that could build its entire tourist fortunes on a mention in a pop song, but that is exactly what Winslow has done for a couple of decades now ever since the Eagles sang about "standin' on a corner in Winslow, Arizona," in their hit song "Take It Easy." They've even building an official Standin' on a Corner Park (complete with a mural of girl in a flatbed Ford).

Popular songs aside, Winslow can claim a couple of more significant attractions. Right in town is one of the Southwest's historic railroad hotels, La Posada, which is in an ongoing renovation that has returned it to its original glory. Twenty miles west of town is a mile-wide Meteor Crater. And east of town is Homolovi Ruins State Park, which has ancient ruins as well as extensive petroglyphs.

ESSENTIALS

GETTING THERE   Winslow is on I-40 at the junction with Ariz. 87, which leads north to the Hopi mesas and south to Payson.

Amtrak (☎ **800/872-7245**) passenger trains stop in Winslow on East Second Street (at La Posada).

VISITOR INFORMATION   For more information on the area, contact the **Winslow Chamber of Commerce,** 300 W. North Rd., Winslow, AZ 86047 (☎ **520/289-2434, ext. 300;** www.winslowarizona.org).

THE ORIGINAL DEEP IMPACT

✪ **Meteor Crater.** 20 miles west of Winslow at exit 233 off I-40. ☎ **800/289-5898** or 520/289-2362. www.meteorcrater.com. Admission $10 adults, $9 seniors, $5 children 6–17, free for children under 6. May 15–Sept 15 daily 6am–6pm; Sept 16–May 14, daily 8am–5pm.

Northern Arizona has more than its fair share of natural attractions, and while most of the region's big holes in the ground were created by the slow process of erosion, there is one hole that has far more dramatic origins. At 570 feet deep and 3 miles in circumference, Meteor Crater, the best-preserved meteorite impact crater on earth, is billed as "this planet's most penetrating natural attraction." The meteorite, which estimates put at roughly 100 feet in diameter, was traveling at 45,000 miles per hour when it slammed into the earth 49,000 years ago. Within seconds, more than 300 million tons of rock had been displaced leaving a gaping crater and a devastated landscape. Today, you can stand on the rim of the crater and marvel at the power, equivalent to 15 million tons of TNT, that created this otherworldly setting. In fact, so closely does this crater resemble craters on the surface of the moon that in the 1960s, NASA came here to train Apollo astronauts.

On the rim you'll find a small museum full of exhibits on astrogeology and space exploration. There's a 1,400-pound meteorite as well as an Apollo space capsule on display. In the museum's theater, you can see a film on meteorites.

OTHER WINSLOW AREA ATTRACTIONS

In downtown Winslow, near that famous corner, you'll find the little **Old Trails Museum,** 212 N. Kinsley St. (☎ 520/289-5861), which has exhibits on Route 66 and the Harvey Girls (who once worked in the nearby La Posada hotel). From April to September, the museum is open Tuesday to Saturday 1 to 5pm (in summer it may open as early as 9am, depending on funding). Admission is free.

Even if you aren't planning on staying the night at the restored **La Posada Resort,** 303 E. Second St. (☎ 520/289-4366), you should be sure to stop by just to see this historic railway hotel. Self-guided tours are available for a $2 donation, and the hotel also arranges guided tours through Winslow's Harvey Girls association ($5 suggested donation).

On the windswept plains north of Winslow (1.3 miles north of I-40 at Exit 257), you'll find **Homolovi Ruins State Park** (☎ 520/289-4106), which preserves more than 300 ancient Anasazi archaeological sites, several of which have been partially excavated. Although these ruins are not nearly as impressive as those at Wupatki or Walnut Canyon, a visit here will give you a better understanding of the interrelationship of the many ancient pueblos of this region. Also in the park are numerous petroglyphs; ask directions at the visitor center. Admission is $4 per vehicle (up to four people, then $1 per person). The ruins are open from sunrise to sunset, but the visitor center is open only from 8am to 5pm daily. There is also a campground here.

Continuing north from the state park, you'll find the little known and little visited **Little Painted Desert,** a 660-acre county park. To reach the park and its viewpoint overlooking the painted hills of this stark yet colorful landscape, continue driving north on Ariz. 87 for another 12 miles. For information, contact Navajo County Parks (☎ 520/524-4251).

WHERE TO STAY

In addition to the historic hotel mentioned here, you'll find lots of budget chain motels in Winslow.

✪ **La Posada.** 303 E. 2nd St., on U.S. Rte. 66, Winslow, AZ 86047. ☎ **520/289-4366.** Fax 520/289-3873. www.laposada.org. 23 units. TV TEL. $79–$99 double. Rates include continental breakfast. AE, CB, DC, DISC, MC, V. Pets accepted, $5 fee.

Designed by Mary Elizabeth Jane Colter, who designed many of the buildings on the South Rim of the Grand Canyon, this railroad hotel opened in 1930. Colter designed La Posada to have the feel of an old Spanish hacienda and even created a fictitious history surrounding the building. Today the hotel is being restored and is itself reason enough to stay in Winslow. In the lobby are several pieces of original furniture as well as reproductions of pieces once found in the hotel. The public spaces are full of original art done by the managers of the hotel. The nicest guest rooms at this time are the large rooms named for famous guests of the hotel—Clark Gable, Howard Hughes, Gary Cooper, Charles Lindbergh, the Marx brothers. The management's artistic flare comes across in these rooms, one of which (the Frank & Joanne Randall Room) has wide plank floors, murals, a fireplace, a rustic bed and armoire, art-deco chairs, and a kilim rug. The bathroom is a classic of black-and-white tile and still has the original fixtures. By the time you read this, there should also be a restaurant and lounge on the premises.

WHERE TO DINE

Port Java. 703 Airport Rd. ☎ **520/289-0850.** Main dishes $4–$15. AE, MC, V. Tues–Fri 10am–8pm; Sat–Sun 8am–8pm. AMERICAN/INTERNATIONAL.

Unless you happened to be traveling in your own plane, you'd probably never find this out-of-the-way place at the Winslow airport. The specialty here is the $100 hamburgers ($5 for the burger and $95 for the airplane fuel to fly up and back from Phoenix). However, there are also good burritos and homemade pies. Evenings see nightly specials such as prime rib or surf and turf with shrimp and scallops.

2 The Hopi Reservation

250 miles NE of Phoenix; 67 miles N of Winslow; 100 miles SW of Canyon de Chelly; 140 miles SE of Page/Lake Powell

This remote region of Arizona, with its flat-topped mesas and rugged, barren landscape, is the center of the universe for the Hopi peoples. The Hopi Reservation is completely surrounded by the Navajo Reservation and has at its center the grouping of mesas upon which the Hopis have lived for nearly 1,000 years. Here the Hopi follow their ancient customs and many aspects of pueblo culture remain intact. However, much of the Hopi culture is hidden from the view of non-Hopi. Although the Hopi perform elaborate religious and social dances throughout the year, many of these dances are no longer open to outsiders.

Important note: When visiting the Hopi pueblos, remember that you are a guest and your privileges can be revoked at any time. Respect all posted signs at village entrances, and remember that *photographing, sketching, and recording are all prohibited in the villages and at ceremonies.* Also, kivas (ceremonial rooms) and ruins are off-limits.

ESSENTIALS

GETTING THERE   This section of Arizona is one of the state's most remote regions. Distances are great but the highways are generally in good condition. Ariz. 87 leads from Winslow to Second Mesa, and Ariz. 264 runs from Tuba City in the west to the New Mexico state line in the east.

The **Navajo Transit System** (☎ **520/729-4002**) operates a bus service Monday to Friday throughout the Navajo and Hopi reservations with service between the following towns: Farmington, Gallup, and Crown Point (all in New Mexico), and Window Rock, Kayenta, Chinle, and Tuba City. The route between Window Rock and Tuba City stops at several of the Hopi villages, including Second Mesa.

VISITOR INFORMATION   For more information before you leave home, contact the **Hopi Tribal Council,** P.O. Box 123, Kykotsmovi, AZ 86039 (☎ **520/734-3000;** www.hopi.nsn.us). You can also get information from the **Hopi Cultural Preservation Office** (☎ **520/734-2244;** www.nau.edu/~hcpo-p/).

Because each of the Hopi villages is relatively independent, you might want to contact the **Community Development Office** of a particular village for specific information on that village: **Bacavi** (☎ 520/734-9360), **First Mesa** (☎ 520/737-2670), **Hotevilla** (☎ 520/734-2420), **Kykotsmovi** (☎ 520/734-2474), **Mishongnovi** (☎ 520/737-2520), **Moenkopi** (☎ 520/283-8051), **Polacca** (☎ 520/737-2670), **Shipaulovi** (☎ 520/737-2570), **Shungopavi** (☎ 520/734-7135), and **Walpi** (☎ 520/737-5435). These offices are open Monday to Friday 8am to 5pm.

EXPLORING THE WORLD OF THE HOPI

Start your visit to the Hopi pueblos at the **Hopi Cultural Center,** on Ariz. 264 (☎ **520/734-6650**) in Second Mesa. This museum, motel, and restaurant is the tourism headquarters for the area. Here you can visit the museum and learn about Hopi culture and its history. Be sure to take notice of signs indicating when villages are open to visitors. The museum is open Monday to Friday 8am to 5pm and in the summer on Saturday and Sunday, 9am to 3pm. Admission is $3 for adults and $1 for children.

Although it's possible to get permission to visit most Hopi villages, the easiest to visit is ✪ **Walpi,** on First Mesa. Guided tours of this tiny village are offered daily (between 9am and 5pm in summer and between 9:30am and 4pm other months). Admission is $5 per adult, $4 ages 10 to 17, and $3 seniors and ages 5 to 10. To sign up for a tour, drive up to the top of First Mesa (in Polacca, take the road that says to First Mesa village) and continue through the village to **Punsi Hall Visitors' Center** (☎ **520/737-2262**) where you'll see signs for the tour. The 40-minute tours are led by Hopis who will tell you the history of the village and explain a bit about the local culture. On the third weekend in September is a harvest festival that features 2 days of dancing. As of this writing, the festival is open to the public.

THE VILLAGES

FIRST MESA   At the foot of First Mesa is **Polacca,** a settlement founded in the late 1800s by Walpi villagers who wanted to be closer to the trading post and school.

At the top of First Mesa is the village of **Walpi,** which was located lower on the slopes of the mesa until the Pueblo Revolt of 1680 brought on fear of reprisal from the Spanish. The villagers moved Walpi to the very top of the mesa so they could better defend themselves in the event of a Spanish attack. Walpi looks much like the Anasazi villages of the Arizona canyons. Small stone houses seem to grow directly from the rock of the mesa top and ladders jut from the roofs of kivas. The view from here stretches for hundreds of miles around.

Sichomovi was founded in 1750 as a colony of Walpi; **Hano** was founded by Tewa peoples either seeking refuge from the Spanish or offering aid to the people of Walpi.

SECOND MESA   Second Mesa is today the center of tourism in Hopiland, as the Hopi country is called, and this is where you'll find the Hopi Cultural Center.

Villages on Second Mesa include **Shungopavi,** which was moved to its present site after Old Shungopavi was abandoned in 1680 following the Pueblo Revolt against the Spanish.

Below Shungopavi is **Gray Spring.** The Snake Dance (actually a rain dance, and considered one of the most spectacular Native American ceremonies) is performed here in even-numbered years.

Mishongnovi, which means "place of the black man," is named for the leader of a clan that came here from the San Francisco Peaks around A.D. 1200. This village was also abandoned in 1680 and moved to its present location. The Snake Dance is held here in odd-numbered years.

Shipaulovi may also have been founded after the Pueblo Revolt of 1680.

THIRD MESA   **Oraibi,** which the Hopi claim is the oldest continuously occupied town in the United States, is located on Third Mesa. The village dates from 1150 and, according to legend, was founded by people from Old Shungopavi. A Spanish mission was established in Oraibi in 1629, and the ruins are still visible north of the village. Today Oraibi is a mix of old stone houses and modern ones, usually of cinderblock. With permission, you can wander around in Oraibi, where you'll likely be approached by village women offering to sell you various local crafts.

For centuries Oraibi was the largest of the Hopi villages, but in 1906 a schism occurred over Bureau of Indian Affairs policies and many of the villagers left to form

Hotevilla. This latter village is considered the most conservative of the Hopi villages and has had frequent confrontations with the federal government.

Kykotsmovi, also known as Lower Oraibi or New Oraibi, was founded in 1890 by villagers from Oraibi who wanted to be closer to the school and trading post.

Bacavi was founded in 1907 by villagers who had helped found Hotevilla but who later decided that they wanted to return to Oraibi. The people of Oraibi would not let them return, and rather than go back to Hotevilla, they founded a new village.

MOENKOPI   One last Hopi village, **Moenkopi,** is located 40 miles to the west. Founded in 1870 by people from Oraibi, Moenkopi sits in the center of a wide green valley where plentiful water makes farming more reliable. Moenkopi is only a few miles from Tuba City off U.S. 160.

CULTURAL TOURS

Perhaps the best way to see the Hopi mesas is on a guided small-group tour. With a guide, you will likely learn much more about this rather insular culture than you ever could on your own. Tour companies frequently use local guides and stop at the homes of working artisans. This all adds up to a more in-depth and educational visit to one of the oldest cultures on the continent. Gary Tso is one local guide who gives tours through his **Left-Handed Hunter Tour Co.** (☎ **520/734-2567;** e-mail: lhhunter58@hotmail.com). Gary will take you to Walpi, old Oraibi, a petroglyph site, and the studios of a kachina carver, a potter, and a silver- and goldsmith. All-day tours (including lunch, transportation, and entry fees) range from $175 for one person to $325 for four.

Other companies offering Hopi tours include **Crossing Worlds,** P.O. Box 623, Sedona, AZ 86339 (☎ **800/350-2693** or 520/649-3060; www.crossingworlds.com), **Discovery Passages,** 1161 Elk Trail (P.O. Box 630), Prescott, AZ 86303 (☎ **520/ 717-0519),**and **Native Highways Tour Company,** P.O. Box 1804, Sedona, AZ 86339 (☎ **888/282-8474** or 520/282-8474; www.nativehwystours.com). One-day tours to the Hopi Mesas run about $100 to $145 per person.

DANCES & CEREMONIES

The Hopi have developed the most complex religious ceremonies of any of the Southwest tribes. Masked kachina dances, for which they are most famous, are held from January to July. Social dances are held from August through February, and Snake Dances are held from August through December.

Kachinas, whether in the form of dolls or as masked dancers, are representative of the spirits of everything from plants and animals to ancestors and sacred places. More than 300 kachinas appear on a regular basis in Hopi ceremonies, and another 200 appear occasionally. The kachina spirits are said to live in the San Francisco Peaks to the south and at Spring of the Shadows in the east. According to legend, the kachinas lived with the Hopi long ago, but the Hopi people made the kachinas angry, causing them to leave. Before leaving, though, the kachinas taught the Hopi how to perform their ceremonies.

Today the kachina ceremonies, performed by men wearing elaborate costumes and masks, serve several purposes. Most important, they bring clouds and rain to water the all-important corn crop, but they also ensure health, happiness, long life, and harmony in the universe. As part of the kachina ceremonies, dancers often bring carved wooden kachina dolls to village children to introduce them to the various kachina spirits.

The kachina season lasts from the winter solstice until shortly after the summer solstice, with the actual dates for dances determined by the position of the sun and usually announced only shortly before the ceremonies are to be held. Preparations for the dances take place inside kivas (circular ceremonial rooms) that are entered from the roof by means of a ladder; the dances themselves are usually held in a village square or street.

With ludicrous and sometimes lewd mimicry, clowns known as *koyemsi, koshares,* and *tsukus* entertain spectators between the dances, bringing a lighthearted counterpoint to the very serious nature of the kachina dances. Be aware that non-Hopis at kachina dances often become the focus of attention for these clowns.

Despite the importance of the kachina dances, it is the **Snake Dance** that has captured the attention of many non-Hopis. The Snake Dance is held only every other year in any given village and involves handling both poisonous and nonpoisonous snakes. The ceremony takes place over 16 days with the first 4 days dedicated to collecting all the snakes from the four cardinal directions. Later, footraces are held from the bottom of the mesa to the top. On the last day of the ceremony, the actual Snake Dance is performed. Men of the Snake Society form pairs of dancers—one to carry the snake in his mouth and the other to distract the snake with an eagle feather. When all the snakes have been danced around the plaza, they are rushed down to their homes at the bottom of the mesa to carry the Hopi prayers for rain to the spirits of the underworld.

Due to the disrespectful attitude of some visitors in the past, many ceremonies and dances are now closed to non-Hopis. However, several Hopi villages do allow visitors to attend some of their dances. The best way to find out about attending dances is to contact the **Community Development Office** of the individual villages (see phone numbers under "Visitor Information," above).

SHOPPING

Most visitors come to the reservations to shop for Hopi crafts. There are literally dozens of small shops selling crafts and jewelry of different quality, and some homes have signs indicating that they sell crafts. Shops often sell the work of only a few individuals, so you should stop at several to get some idea of the variety of work available. Also, if you tour Walpi or wander around in Oraibi, you will likely be approached by villagers selling various crafts, including kachinas. The quality is not usually as high as in shops, but then, neither are the prices.

One of the best places to stop to get a quick education in Hopi art and crafts is **Tsakurshovi** (☎ 520/734-2478), a tiny shop 1¹/₂ miles east of the Hopi Cultural Center on Second Mesa. This shop has an amazing selection of crafts, old-style kachina dolls, native herbs, coil and wicker plaque baskets, and "Don't Worry, Be Hopi" T-shirts. The owners are very friendly and are happy to share their knowledge and expertise with visitors.

If you're in the market for Hopi silver jewelry, stop in at **Hopi Arts and Crafts-Silvercraft** (☎ 520/734-2463), 100 yards from the Hopi Cultural Center on Second Mesa. This arts-and-crafts cooperative shows work by artisans from all the villages of the Hopi mesas. The best time to shop here is in the summertime when the selection is most extensive. The **Honani Crafts Gallery** (☎ 520/737-2238), at the intersection of Highway 264 and the road up to Second Mesa, sells both silver and the less common gold jewelry.

If you're interested in kachina dolls, be sure to visit the **Monongya Gallery** (☎ 520/734-2344), a big turquoise and cream colored building on Ariz. 264 in Oraibi (west of the Hopi Cultural Center). This store usually has one of the largest selections of kachina dolls in the area and holds a Christmas Eve sale at 50% off.

A Native American Crafts Primer

The Four Corners region is taken up almost entirely by the Navajo and Hopi reservations, so Native American crafts are ubiquitous here. You'll see jewelry for sale by the side of desolate, windswept roads, Navajo rugs for sale in tiny trading posts, and Hopi kachinas being sold out of village homes. If you decide you want to take home a work by a local craftsperson, the information below will help you make an informed purchase. It is also possible now to shop for Native American crafts on the Internet at **www.hopimarket.com.**

Hopi Kachinas　　These elaborately decorated wooden dolls are representations of spirits of plants, animals, ancestors, and sacred places. Traditionally, they were given to children to initiate them into the pantheon of kachina spirits, who play important roles in ensuring rain and harmony in the universe. However, kachinas are also popular with collectors of Native American crafts, and Hopi kachina carvers have changed their style to cater to the new market. Older kachinas were carved from a single piece of cottonwood, sometimes with arms simply painted on. This older style of kachina is much simpler and stiffer than the currently popular style that emphasizes action poses and realistic proportions. A great deal of carving and painting goes into each kachina, and prices today are in the hundreds of dollars for even the simplest. Currently very popular with tourists and collectors are the *tsuku,* or clown, kachinas, which are usually painted with bold horizontal black and white stripes. The *tsukus* are often depicted in humorous situations or carrying slices of watermelon.

Navajo Silver Work　　While the Hopi create overlay silver work from sheets of silver and the Zuni use silver work simply as a base for their skilled lapidary or stone-cutting work, the Navajo silversmiths highlight the silver itself. Just as rug weaving did not begin until the latter part of the 19th century, silversmithing did not catch on with the Navajo until the 1880s, when Lorenzo Hubbell decided to hire Mexican silversmiths as teachers. When tourists began visiting the area after 1890, the demand for Navajo jewelry increased. The earliest pieces of Navajo jewelry were replicas of Spanish ornaments, but as the Navajo silversmiths became more proficient, they began to develop their own designs. Sandcasting, stamp work, repoussé, and file-and-chisel work give Navajo jewelry its unique look. The squash-blossom necklace, with its horseshoe-shaped pendant, is perhaps the most distinctive Navajo jewelry design. Wide bracelets and concha belts are also popular.

Hopi Overlay Silver Work　　Most Hopi silver work is done in the overlay style, which was introduced to Hopi artisans after World War II when the GI bill provided funds for Hopi soldiers to study silversmithing at a school founded by

Also in Oraibi you'll find **Old Oraibi Crafts** (no phone), which sells artwork and crafts based on kachina images. At Keams Canyon, almost 30 miles east of the cultural center, you'll find another great place to shop for kachina dolls. **McGee's Indian Art** (☎ 520/738-2295) is adjacent to a grocery store and has been a trading post for more than 100 years. There's always an outstanding selection of the best quality kachina dolls here.

WHERE TO STAY & DINE

The restaurant at the Hopi Cultural Center has a good salad bar and tasty traditional meals, such as Hopi stew with hominy, lamb, and green chile and *piki* bread (a paper-thin

Hopi artist Fred Kabotie. The overlay process basically uses two sheets of silver, one with a design cut from it. Heat fuses the two sheets, forming a raised image. Designs used in overlay jewelry are often borrowed from other Hopi crafts such as baskets and pottery, as well as from ancient Anasazi pottery designs. Belt buckles, earrings, bolo ties, and bracelets are all popular.

Hopi Baskets   Although the Tohono O'odham of central and southern Arizona are the state's best-known basketmakers, the Hopi also produce beautiful work. On Third Mesa, wicker plaques and baskets are made from rabbit brush and sumac and colored with bright aniline dyes, and on Second Mesa, coiled plaques and baskets are created from dyed yucca fibers. Throughout the reservation, yucca-fiber sifters are made by plaiting over a willow ring.

Hopi Pottery   With the exception of undecorated utilitarian pottery that's made in Hotevilla on Third Mesa, most Hopi pottery is produced on First Mesa. Contemporary Hopi pottery comes in a variety of styles, including a yellow-orange ware decorated with black-and-white designs. This style is said to have been introduced by the potter Nampeyo, a Tewa from the village of Hano who stimulated the revival of Hopi pottery in 1890. A white pottery with red-and-black designs is also popular. Hopi pottery designs tend toward geometric patterns.

Navajo Rugs   After they acquired sheep and goats from the Spanish, the Navajo learned weaving from the pueblo tribes, and by the early 1800s their weavings were widely recognized as being the finest in the Southwest. The Navajo women primarily wove blankets, but by the end of the 19th century the craft began to die out when it became more economical to purchase a ready-made blanket. When Lorenzo Hubbell set up his trading post, he immediately recognized a potential market in the East for the woven blankets if they could be made heavy enough to be used as rugs. Having great respect for Hubbell, the Navajo adapted his ideas and soon began doing a brisk business. Although today the cost of Navajo rugs, which take hundreds of hours to make, has become almost prohibitively expensive, there are still enough women practicing the craft to keep it alive and provide plenty of rugs for shops and trading posts all over Arizona.

The best rugs are those made with homespun yarn and natural vegetal dyes. However, commercially manufactured yarns and dyes are being used more and more to keep costs down. There are more than 15 regional styles of rugs and quite a bit of overlapping and borrowing. Bigger and bolder patterns are likely to cost quite a bit less than very complex and highly detailed patterns.

bread made from blue corn). Prices here are very reasonable, considering the remoteness of the location. If you've brought your food along, there are some picnic tables with an amazing view just east of Oraibi on top of the mesa.

Hopi Cultural Center Restaurant & Inn. P.O. Box 67, Second Mesa, AZ 86043. ☎ **520/ 734-2401.** Fax 520/734-6651. www.psv.com/hopi. 33 units. TV TEL. Mar 15–Oct 15 $95– $100 double; Oct 16–Mar 14 $65–$70 double. AE, DISC, MC, V.

Although it isn't much, this is the only lodging for miles around—so be sure you have a reservation before heading up here for an overnight visit. The rooms have all been recently remodeled and have new carpets, big TVs, and coffeemakers. The restaurant serves American and traditional Hopi meals, including *piki* bread. There's also a museum and a very basic campground.

3 The Petrified Forest & Painted Desert

25 miles E of Holbrook; 90 miles E of Flagstaff; 118 miles S of Canyon de Chelly; 180 miles N of Phoenix

Petrified wood has intrigued people for generations and although it can be found in almost every state, the "forests" of downed logs here in northeastern Arizona are by far the most extensive. When in the 1850s petrified wood was discovered scattered like kindling across this section of Arizona, enterprising people began exporting it wholesale to the East. By 1900 so much had been removed that in 1906 several areas were set aside as the Petrified Forest National Monument. Today, a 27-mile scenic drive winds through the petrified forest (and a small corner of the Painted Desert), providing a fascinating high desert experience.

It may be hard to believe when you drive across this arid landscape, but at one time this area was a vast humid swamp. That was 225 million years ago, when dinosaurs and huge amphibians ruled the earth and giant now-extinct trees grew on the high ground around the swamp. Fallen trees were washed downstream, gathered in piles in still backwaters, and were eventually covered over with silt, mud, and volcanic ash. As water seeped through this soil, it dissolved the silica in the volcanic ash and redeposited this silica inside the cells of the logs. Eventually the silica recrystalized into stone to form petrified wood. Minerals such as iron, manganese, and carbon contribute the distinctive colors.

This region was later inundated with water, and thick deposits of sediment buried the logs ever deeper. Eventually, the land was transformed yet again as a geologic upheaval thrust the lake bottom up above sea level. This upthrust of the land cracked the logs into the segments we see today. Wind and water gradually eroded the landscape to create the Painted Desert and northern Arizona's many other spectacular features, and the petrified logs were once again exposed on the surface of the land.

In gift shops throughout this region, you'll see petrified wood in all sizes and colors, natural and polished, being sold. This petrified wood comes from private land. No piece of petrified wood, no matter how small, may be removed from Petrified Forest National Park.

ESSENTIALS

GETTING THERE   The north entrance to Petrified Forest National Park is 25 miles east of Holbrook on I-40. The south entrance is 20 miles east of Holbrook on U.S. 180.

There is **Amtrak** passenger service to Winslow, 33 miles west of Holbrook. Call ☎ 800/872-7245 for schedules and rate information.

VISITOR INFORMATION   For further information on the Petrified Forest or the Painted Desert, contact **Petrified Forest National Park,** P.O. Box 2217, Petrified Forest, AZ 86028 (☎ 520/524-6228; www.nps.gov/pefo). The park is open daily 7:30am to 5pm (closed on Christmas; longer hours in summer). Admission is $10 per car.

For information on Holbrook and the surrounding region, contact the **Holbrook Chamber of Commerce,** 100 E. Arizona St., Holbrook, AZ 86025 (☎ 800/524-2459 or 520/524-6558).

EXPLORING A UNIQUE LANDSCAPE

Although Petrified Forest National Park has both a north and a south entrance, it is probably better to start at the southern entrance and work your way north along the park's 27-mile scenic road, which has more than 20 overlooks. This way, you'll see the most impressive displays of petrified logs early in your visit and save the Painted Desert overlooks for last.

Within the park are a visitor center and a museum, both of which sell maps and books about the region and also issue free backpacking permits. The **Rainbow Forest Museum,** at the south end of the park, features exhibits that chronicle the area's geologic and human history. There's also a display of letters written by people who took pieces of petrified wood and who later felt guilty and returned the stones. Adjacent to the Rainbow Forest Museum, there's a snack bar.

The best introduction to the park is the **Giant Logs self-guided trail,** which starts behind the Rainbow Forest Museum at the south end of the park. The trail winds across a hillside strewn with huge logs and certainly lives up to its name. Almost directly across the parking lot from the Rainbow Forest Museum is the entrance to the **Long Logs** and **Agate House** areas. On the 0.6-mile-long Long Logs trail, you can see more big trees, while at Agate House you will see the ruins of a pueblo built from colorful agatized petrified wood.

Heading north, you pass by the unusual formations known as **The Flattops.** These structures are caused by the erosion of softer soil deposits from beneath a harder and more erosion-resistant layer of sandstone. The Flattops is one of the park's wilderness areas. The **Crystal Forest** is the next stop to the north and is named for the beautiful amethyst and quartz crystals once found in the cracks of petrified logs. Concern over the removal of these crystals was what led to the protection of the petrified forest.

At the **Jasper Forest Overlook** you can see logs that include petrified roots, and a little bit farther north, at the **Agate Bridge** stop, you can see a petrified log that forms a natural agate bridge. Continuing north, you come to **Blue Mesa,** where pieces of petrified wood form capstones over easily eroded clay soils. As wind and water wear away at the clay beneath a piece of stone, the balance of the stone becomes more and more precarious until it eventually comes toppling down.

Erosion has played a major role in the formation of the Painted Desert, and to the north of Blue Mesa you'll see some of the most interesting erosional features of the area. It's quite evident why these hills of sandstone and clay are known as **The Teepees.** The layers of different color are due to different types of soils and stone and to minerals dissolved in the soil.

Human habitation of the area dates back more than 2,000 years, and at **Newspaper Rock** you can see a dense concentration of petroglyphs left by generations of Native Americans. At nearby **Puerco Pueblo,** the park's largest archaeological site, you can see the remains of homes built by the people who created the park's petroglyphs. This pueblo was abandoned some time around 1300.

North of Puerco Pueblo, the road crosses I-40. From here to the Painted Desert Visitor Center, there are eight overlooks onto the southernmost edge of the **Painted Desert.** Named for the vivid colors of the soil and stone that cover the land here, the Painted Desert is a dreamscape of pastel colors washed across a barren expanse of eroded hills. The colors are created by minerals dissolved in sandstone and clay soils that were deposited during different geologic periods. There's a picnic area at Chinde Point overlook, and at Kachina Point, you'll find the **Painted Desert Inn,** a restored historic building that's open daily 8am to 4pm. From here, there's access to the park's other wilderness area.

Just inside the northern entrance to the park, you'll find the **Painted Desert Visitor Center,** which showcases a 17-minute film that explains the process by which wood becomes fossilized. Adjacent to the visitor center are a cafeteria and a gas station.

OTHER REASONS TO LINGER IN HOLBROOK

Although the Petrified Forest National Monument is the main reason for visiting this area, you might also want to stop by downtown Holbrook's **Historic Courthouse Museum,** 100 E. Arizona St. (☎ 520/524-6558), which also houses the Holbrook Chamber of Commerce visitor center. This old and dusty museum in the town's historic courthouse has exhibits on local history, but is most interesting for having the town's old jail cells on display. June and July, the Holbrook Chamber sponsors Native American dancers weekday evenings on the lawn in front of the museum.

Although it is against the law to collect petrified wood inside Petrified Forest National Park, there are several **rock shops** in Holbrook where you can buy pieces of petrified wood in all shapes and sizes. These shops also sell plenty of other types of rocks as well. You'll find them lined up along the main street through town.

Three miles west of town, you'll find the **International Petrified Forest Visitor Center and Museum of the Americas,** 1001 Forest Dr. (☎ 520/524-9178), at exit 292 off I-40. Although this place may seem at first like just another Southwestern tourist trap, it actually contains the largest collection of pre-Columbian artifacts in the Southwest, with an emphasis on Maya and Aztec artifacts, but there are plenty of Anasazi and Hohokam pieces on display. There's also a "rock yard" full of petrified wood, dinosaur fossils, geodes, and other interesting rocks, and a 3-mile drive takes you past Triassic dig sites and lots more petrified wood. The museum is open 7am to 7pm in summer (shorter hours other months), and admission is $5. There's also a warehouse-size rock shop.

If you're a **Route 66** fan, you'll find plenty to keep you entertained here. Hopi Drive, the town's main street, is old Route 66, and it is here you will find the Wigwam Motel (see below). At **Julien's Roadrunner,** 109 W. Hopi Dr. (☎ 520/524-2388), you can investigate all manner of memorabilia, from Route 66 Highway signs to enameled replicas of old advertising signs for Mobil Gas and the Santa Fe Railroad. West of Holbrook at exit 269 off I-40, the **Jack Rabbit Trading Post** (☎ 520/288-3230) is another fun Route 66-era tourist trap worth a stop if you're a fan of the old highway. Here you'll find all kinds of fun, kitschy stuff straight out of the 1960s.

Also here in town (on the north side of I-40), you'll find **McGee's Gallery,** 2114 N. Navajo Blvd. (☎ 520/524-1977), a Native American crafts gallery with a wide selection of typical crafts at reasonable prices.

If you're interested in **petroglyphs,** you may want to schedule a visit to the ✪ **Rock Art Canyon Ranch** (☎ 800/524-2459 or 520/288-3260), which is southwest of Holbrook on part of the old Hashknife Ranch, which was the largest ranch in the country during the late 19th century. Within the bounds of this ranch, pecked into the rock walls of Chevelon Canyon, are hundreds of Anasazi petroglyphs. The setting, a narrow canyon that is almost invisible until you are right beside it, is enchanting, making this the single finest place in the state to view petroglyphs. Ranch visits are more than just a chance to see petroglyphs. You can also schedule a wagon ride, swimming, and rockhounding. Cowboy lunches and dinners, complete with music and storytelling, are also part of the Rock Art Canyon Ranch experience (available mid-May to mid-October). Tours are scheduled year-round, except for Sundays and Easter, Thanksgiving, and Christmas; guests can opt for their choice of the above-described activities, and prices vary depending on the activities and the size of the group.

WHERE TO STAY

Holbrook is the nearest town to Petrified Forest National Monument, and here you'll find lots of budget chain motels charging very reasonable rates.

✪ **Wigwam Motel.** 811 W. Hopi Dr. (P.O. Box 788), Holbrook, AZ 86025. ☎ **520/524-3048.** 15 units. A/C TV TEL. $32–$37 double. MC, V. Pets accepted.

If you're willing to sleep on a saggy mattress for the sake of reliving a bit of Route 66 history, don't miss this collection of concrete wigwams (teepees, actually). This unique motel was built in the 1940s when unusual architecture was springing up all along famous Route 66. Owned by the same family since it was built, the Wigwam was renovated a few years back. However, you'll still find the original rustic furniture in the small wigwam-shaped buildings.

WHERE TO DINE

Butterfield Stage Co. 609 W. Hopi Dr. ☎ **520/524-3447.** Main courses $9–$18. AE, MC, V. Daily 4–10pm. STEAK/SEAFOOD.

It's natural to assume that finding a decent meal in an out-of-the-way town might be nearly impossible, so the Butterfield Stage Co. is a pleasant surprise. The owners are from the former Yugoslavia, and we're not sure how they got to Holbrook, but we do know that meals here are pretty good, with a soup and salad bar that is usually fresh. Tables have historical panels with amusing information to read while waiting for your pepper steak or filet mignon. The restaurant is named for the famous overland stagecoach line that carried the mail from St. Louis to San Francisco in the mid-19th century.

4 The Window Rock & Ganado Areas

190 miles E of Flagstaff; 68 miles SE of Canyon de Chelly National Monument; 74 miles NE of Petrified Forest National Park; 91 miles E of Second Mesa

Window Rock, the capital of the Navajo nation, is less than a mile from the New Mexico state line and is named for a huge natural opening in a sandstone cliff just outside town. Today that landmark is preserved as the **Window Rock Tribal Park,** located 2 miles north of Ariz. 264. At one time there was a spring at the base of Window Rock, and water from the spring was used by medicine men performing the Tohee Ceremony, a water ceremony intended to bring the rains.

As the Navajo nation's capital, Window Rock is the site of government offices, a museum and cultural center, and a zoo. About a half hour's drive west of Window Rock is the community of Ganado, the location of two historic sites—St. Michael's Mission and the Hubbell Trading Post. Window Rock's Navajo Nation Inn makes a good base for exploring this corner of the reservation.

ESSENTIALS

GETTING THERE   To reach Window Rock from Flagstaff, take I-40 east to Lupton and go north on Indian Route 12.

There is **Amtrak** passenger service to Winslow, south of the reservation. Call ☎ 800/872-7245 for schedules and fares.

The **Navajo Transit System** (☎ 520/729-4002) operates bus service throughout the Navajo nation with service between the cities of Farmington, Gallup, and Crown Point (all in New Mexico), and Window Rock, Kayenta, Chinle, and Tuba City. Call for schedule information.

TIME   The Navajo nation observes daylight saving time, contrary to the rest of Arizona, so if you are coming from elsewhere in Arizona, the time here will be 1 hour later in months when daylight saving is in effect.

VISITOR INFORMATION   For more information before visiting, contact the **Navajo Nation Tourism Department,** P.O. Box 663, Window Rock, AZ 86515 (☎ 520/871-7371).

SPECIAL EVENTS   Unlike the village ceremonies of the pueblo-dwelling Hopi, Navajo religious ceremonies tend to be held in the privacy of family hogans. However, there are numerous fairs, powwows, and rodeos held throughout the year, and the public is welcome to attend. The biggest of these is the **Navajo Nation Fair** (☎ 520/ 871-6478), held in Window Rock in early September each year. At this fair are traditional dances, a rodeo, a powwow, a parade, a Miss Navajo Pageant (contestants are judged on, among other things, their sheep-butchering skills), and arts-and-crafts exhibits and sales.

AREA ATTRACTIONS

Hubbell Trading Post National Historic Site. Ariz. 264, Ganado. ☎ **520/755-3475.** Free admission. May–Oct daily 8am–6pm; Nov–Apr daily 8am–5pm.

Located just outside the town of Ganado, 26 miles west of Window Rock, the Hubbell Trading Post was established in 1876 by Lorenzo Hubbell and is the oldest continuously operating trading post on the Navajo Reservation. Hubbell did more to popularize the arts and crafts of the Navajo people than any other person and was in large part responsible for the revival of Navajo weaving in the late 19th century.

Although Hubbell Trading Post is still in use, today it is more of a living museum. You can tour the grounds on your own or take a guided tour, and in the visitor center, you can often watch Navajo weavers in the slow process of creating a rug.

The rug room here is filled with a variety of traditional and contemporary Navajo rugs. And although it's possible to buy a small 12-by-18-inch rug for around $100, most cost in the thousands of dollars. In another room, there are also baskets, kachinas, and several cases of jewelry by Navajo, Hopi, and Zuni artisans.

Glance around the general store, and you'll see basic foodstuffs (not much variety here) and bolts of cloth used by Navajo women for sewing their traditional skirts and blouses. Much more than just a place to trade crafts for imported goods, trading posts were for many years the main gathering spot for meeting people from other parts of the reservation and served as a sort of gossip fence and newsroom.

The Navajo Nation Museum. W. Ariz. 264, Window Rock (across from the Navajo Nation Inn). ☎ **520/871-6673.** Free admission. Oct–Apr Mon–Tues and Thurs–Fri 8am–5pm; Wed 8am–8pm (May–Sept also open Sat 8am–5pm.

Sponsored by the Navajo Nation Historic Preservation Society, this museum and cultural center is housed in a large modern building patterned after a traditional hogan. Inside, you'll find temporary exhibits of contemporary crafts and art, as well as exhibits on contemporary Navajo culture, a library, and gift shop. There are also plans to eventually add an exhibit of historical Navajo artifacts and old photos.

Navajo Nation Zoo & Botanical Park. Ariz. 264, Window Rock. ☎ **520/871-6573.** Free admission. Daily 8am–5pm. Closed Jan 1 and Dec 25.

Located in back of the Navajo Nation Inn, this zoo and botanical garden features animals and plants that are significant in Navajo history and culture. Bears, cougars, and wolves are among the animals you'll see here. The setting, which includes several sandstone "haystack" rocks, is very dramatic, and some of the animal enclosures are quite large and incorporate natural rock outcroppings. Also exhibited are examples of different styles of hogans. Well worth a stop.

St. Michael's Historical Museum. St. Michael's, just south of Ariz. 264. ☎ **520/ 871-4171.** Free admission. Memorial Day–Labor Day daily 9am–5pm. Closed the rest of the year.

Located in the town of St. Michael's, 4 miles west of Window Rock, this historical museum chronicles the lives and influence of Franciscan friars who started a mission in this area in the 1670s. The museum is in a small building adjacent to the impressive stone mission church.

A TOUR FROM THE NAVAJO PERSPECTIVE

The best way to understand the Navajo culture is through the eyes of a Navajo. Stanley M. Perry, a Navajo Indian born and raised on the reservation, is a storyteller and guide who will accompany you in your vehicle to tour the Window Rock, Canyon de Chelly, and Monument Valley areas. He can be reached at ☎ **520/871-2484** (best after 7pm). The rate is $100 per day for up to four people; for larger groups, rates depend on the number in the party.

SHOPPING

The Hubbell Trading Post, although it is a National Historic Site, is still an active trading post and has an outstanding selection of rugs, as well as lots of jewelry (see "Area Attractions," above).

In Window Rock, be sure to visit the **Navajo Arts and Crafts Enterprise** (☎ **520/ 871-4095**), which is next to the Navajo Nation Inn and has been operating since 1941. Here you'll find silver-and-turquoise jewelry, Navajo rugs, sandpaintings, baskets, pottery, and Native American clothing.

WHERE TO STAY

Navajo Nation Inn. 48 W. Hwy. 264 (P.O. Box 2340), Window Rock, AZ 86515. ☎ **800/ 662-6189** or 520/871-4108. Fax 520/871-5466. 56 units. A/C TV TEL. $67–$77 suite. AE, DC, MC, V. Pets accepted ($50 deposit).

Located on the edge of Window Rock, the administrative center of the Navajo Reservation, the Navajo Nation Inn is an older motel, but it's your only option in this area. The restaurant and coffee shop are open daily serving American and traditional Navajo dishes.

WHERE TO DINE

In Window Rock, your best bet for a meal is at the **Navajo Nation Inn.** In Ganado, you can get good, inexpensive cafeteria-style food at **Cafe Sage** (☎ **520/755-3411**) on the grounds of Ganado's health clinic, which is across Ariz. 264 and 1/2 mile east of the trading post.

5 Canyon de Chelly

222 miles NE of Flagstaff; 68 miles NW of Window Rock; 110 miles SE of Navajo National Monument; 110 miles SE of Monument Valley Navajo Tribal Park

It's hard to imagine narrow canyons less than 1,000 feet deep being more spectacular than the Grand Canyon, but in some ways ✪ **Canyon de Chelly National Monument** is just that. Gaze down from the rim of Canyon de Chelly at an ancient Anasazi cliff dwelling as the whinnying of horses and clanging of goat bells drift up from far below, and you will be struck by the continuity of human existence. For nearly 5,000 years people have called these canyons home, and today there are more than 100 prehistoric dwelling sites in the area.

Canyon de Chelly National Monument consists of two major canyons—Canyon de Chelly (which is pronounced canyon de *shay* and is derived from the Navajo word *tséyi*, meaning "rock canyon") and *Canyon del Muerto* (Spanish for "Canyon of the Dead")—and several smaller canyons. The canyons extend for more than 100 miles through the rugged slick-rock landscape of northeastern Arizona, draining the seasonal runoff from the snowmelt of the Chuska Mountains.

In summer, Canyon de Chelly's smooth sandstone walls of rich reds and yellows contrast sharply with the deep greens of corn, pasture, and cottonwood on the canyon floor. Vast stone amphitheaters form the caves in which the ancient Anasazi built their homes, and as you watch shadows and light paint an ever-changing canyon panorama, it's easy to see why the Navajo consider these canyons sacred ground. With mysteriously abandoned cliff dwellings and breathtaking natural beauty, Canyon de Chelly is certainly as worthy of a visit as the Grand Canyon.

From Memorial Day to Labor Day there are interpretive programs here at the national monument. Check at the **visitor center** for daily activities, such as campfire programs and natural-history programs, that might be scheduled.

ESSENTIALS

GETTING THERE   From Flagstaff, the easiest route to Canyon de Chelly is to take I-40 to U.S. 191 to Ganado. At Ganado, drive west on Ariz. 264 and then pick up U.S. 191 north to Chinle. If you're coming down from Monument Valley or Navajo National Monument, Indian Route 59, which connects U.S. 160 and U.S. 191, is an excellent road with plenty of beautiful scenery.

Chinle, 3 miles from the entrance to Canyon de Chelly National Monument, is served by the **Navajo Transit System** (☎ **520/729-4002**).

VISITOR INFORMATION   Before leaving home you can contact **Canyon de Chelly National Monument,** P.O. Box 588, Chinle, AZ 86503 (☎ **520/674-5500;** www.nps.gov/cach).

SPECIAL EVENTS   The **Central Navajo Fair** is held in Chinle each year in August.

ADMISSION   Park admission is free.

SEEING THE CANYON

Your first stop at Canyon de Chelly should be the **visitor center,** open daily May through September 8am to 6pm (on daylight saving time) and October through April 8am to 5pm. In front of the visitor center is an example of a traditional crib-style hogan, a hexagonal structure of logs and earth that Navajo use as both a home and a ceremonial center. Inside, a small museum acquaints visitors with the history of Canyon de Chelly, and there's often a silversmith demonstrating Navajo jewelry-making techniques. From here most people tour the canyon by car.

Very different views of the canyon are provided by the North Rim and South Rim drives. The North Rim Drive overlooks Canyon del Muerto, while the South Rim Drive overlooks Canyon de Chelly. Each of the rim drives is around 20 miles in each direction, and with stops it can easily take 3 hours to visit each rim.

THE NORTH RIM DRIVE

The first stop on the North Rim is the Ledge Ruin Overlook. On the opposite wall, about 100 feet up from the canyon floor, you can see the Ledge Ruin. This site was occupied by the Anasazi between A.D. 1050 and 1275. Nearby, at the Dekaa Kiva

Viewpoint, you can see a lone kiva (circular ceremonial building). This structure was reached by means of toeholds cut into the soft sandstone cliff wall.

The second stop is at the **Antelope House Overlook.** The Antelope House ruin takes its name from the paintings of antelopes on a nearby cliff wall. It's believed that the paintings were done in the 1830s. Beneath the ruins of Antelope House, archaeologists have found the remains of an earlier pit house dating from A.D. 693. Although most of the Anasazi cliff dwellings were abandoned sometime after a drought began in 1276, Antelope House had already been abandoned by 1260, possibly because of damage caused by flooding. Across the wash from Antelope House, an ancient tomb, known as the Tomb of the Weaver, was discovered in the 1920s by archaeologists. The tomb contained the well-preserved body of an old man wrapped in a blanket of golden eagle feathers and accompanied by cornmeal, shelled and husked corn, pine nuts, beans, salt, and thick skeins of cotton. Also visible from this overlook is Navajo Fortress, a red sandstone butte that the Navajo once used as a refuge from attackers. A steep trail leads to the top of Navajo Fortress, and through the use of log ladders that could be pulled up into the refuge, the Navajo were able to escape their attackers.

The third stop is at **Mummy Cave Overlook,** named for two mummies found in burial urns below the ruins. Archaeological evidence indicates that this giant amphitheater consisting of two caves was occupied for 1,000 years, from A.D. 300 to 1300. In the two caves and on the shelf between are 80 rooms, including three kivas. The central structure between the two caves is interesting because it includes a three-story building characteristic of the architecture in Mesa Verde in New Mexico. Archaeologists speculate that a group of Anasazi migrated here from New Mexico. Much of the original plasterwork of these buildings is still intact and indicates that the buildings were colorfully decorated.

The fourth and last stop on the North Rim is at the **Massacre Cave Overlook.** The cave got its name after an 1805 Spanish military expedition killed more than 115 Navajo at this site. The Navajo at the time had been raiding Spanish settlements that were encroaching on Navajo territory. Accounts of the battle at Massacre Cave differ. One account claims there were only women, children, and old men taking shelter in the cave, but the official Spanish records claim 90 warriors and 25 women and children were killed. Also visible from this overlook is Yucca Cave, which was occupied about 1,000 years ago.

THE SOUTH RIM DRIVE

The South Rim Drive climbs slowly but steadily along the South Rim of Canyon de Chelly, and at each stop you're a little bit higher above the canyon floor.

Near the mouth of the canyon, you'll find the Tunnel Overlook and, nearby, the **Tséyi Overlook.** *Tséyi* means "rock canyon" in Navajo, and that's just what you'll see when you gaze down from this viewpoint. A short narrow canyon feeds into Chinle Wash, which is formed by the streams cutting through the canyons of the national monument.

The next stop is at the **Junction Overlook,** so named because it overlooks the junction of Canyon del Muerto and Canyon de Chelly. Visible here is the Junction Ruin, with its 10 rooms and one kiva. The Anasazi occupied this ruin during the great pueblo period, which lasted from around 1100 until the Anasazi disappeared shortly before 1300. Also visible is First Ruin, which is perched precariously on a long narrow ledge. In this ruin are 22 rooms and two kivas.

The third stop, at **White House Overlook,** provides the only opportunity for descending into Canyon de Chelly without a guide or ranger. The ✪ **White House**

Ruins Trail descends 600 feet to the canyon floor, crosses Chinle Wash, and approaches the White House Ruins. These buildings were constructed both on the canyon floor and 50 feet up the cliff wall in a small cave. Although you cannot enter the ruins, you can get close enough to get a good look. You're not allowed to wander off this trail, and please respect the privacy of those Navajo living here. It's a 2¹/₂-mile round-trip hike and takes about 2 hours. Be sure to carry water. If you aren't inclined to hike the trail, you can view the ruins from the overlook. This is one of the largest ruins in the canyon and contains 80 rooms. It was inhabited between 1040 and 1275.

Notice the black streaks on the sandstone walls above the White House Ruins. These streaks, known as desert varnish, are formed by seeping water, which reacts with iron in the sandstone (iron is what gives the walls their reddish hue). To create the canyon's many petroglyphs, Anasazi artists would chip away at the desert varnish. Later the Navajo used paints to create pictographs of animals and historic events, such as the Spanish military expedition that killed 115 Navajo at Massacre Cave. Many of these petroglyphs and pictographs can be seen if you take one of the guided tours into the canyon.

The fifth stop is at **Sliding House Overlook.** These ruins are built on a narrow shelf and appear to be sliding down into the canyon. Inhabited from about 900 until 1200, Sliding House contained between 30 and 50 rooms. This overlook is already more than 700 feet above the canyon floor, with sheer walls giving the narrow canyon a very foreboding appearance.

The **Face Rock Overlook** provides yet another dizzying glimpse of the ever-deepening canyon. Here you gaze 1,000 feet down to the bottom of the canyon. The last stop on the South Rim is one of the most spectacular: **Spider Rock Overlook.** This viewpoint overlooks the junction of Canyon de Chelly and Monument Canyon, where the monolithic pinnacle called Spider Rock rises 800 feet from the canyon floor, its two freestanding towers forming a natural monument. Across the canyon from Spider Rock stands the similarly striking **Speaking Rock,** which is connected to the far canyon wall.

ALTERNATIVE WAYS OF SEEING THE CANYON

Access to the floor of Canyon de Chelly is restricted, and to enter the canyon *you must be accompanied by either a park ranger or an authorized guide* (unless you're on the White House Ruins trail). **Navajo guides** charge about $15 per hour with a 3-hour minimum and will lead you into the canyon on foot or in your own four-wheel-drive vehicle. **Canyon de Chelly Tours** (☎ 520/674-3772) charges $15 per hour to go out in your 4x4 vehicle (3-hour minimum); if they supply the vehicle, it's $100 total for three people. The visitor center also maintains a list of guides.

Another way to see Canyon de Chelly and Canyon del Muerto is from one of the **six-wheel-drive trucks** that operate out of **Thunderbird Lodge** (☎ 800/679-2473 or 520/674-5841). These trucks are equipped with seats in the bed and stop frequently for photographs and to visit ruins, Navajo farms, and rock art. Half-day tours cost $37 per person for a half-day ($28.50 for children 11 and under), and all-day tours cost $59.50 for all ages. Between April and October, half-day tours leave at 9am and 2pm; between November and March, they leave at 9am and, if demand warrants a second tour, at 1pm. All-day tours, offered in summer only, leave at 9am and return at 5pm. Locals call these ✪ **shake-and-bake tours,** and in summer they really live up to the name. In winter, the truck is enclosed to keep out the elements.

If you'd rather use a more traditional means of transportation for your tour of the inner canyon, you can go on a guided horseback ride. Stables offering horseback tours

Fred Harvey & His Girls

Unless you grew up in the Southwest and can remember back to pre–World War II days, you may never have heard of Fred Harvey and the Harvey Girls. However, if you spend much time in northern Arizona, you're likely to run into quite a few references to the Harvey Girls and their boss.

Fred Harvey was the Southwest's most famous mogul of railroad hospitality and an early promoter of tourism in the Grand Canyon State. Harvey, who was working for a railroad in the years shortly after the Civil War, had developed a distaste for the food served at railroad stations. He decided he could do a better job, and in 1876 opened his first Harvey House railway-station restaurant for the Santa Fe Railroad. At the time of his death in 1901, Harvey operated 47 restaurants, 30 diners, and 15 hotels across the West.

The women who worked as waitresses in the Harvey House restaurants came to be known as Harvey Girls. Known for their distinctive black dresses, white aprons, and black bow ties, Harvey Girls had to adhere to very strict behavior codes and were the prim and proper women of the late 19th- and early 20th-century American West. In fact, in the late 19th century, they were considered the only real "ladies" in the West, aside from schoolteachers. So celebrated were they in their day that in the 1940s, Judy Garland starred in a Technicolor MGM musical called *The Harvey Girls*. Garland played a Harvey Girl who battles the evil town dancehall queen (played by Angela Lansbury) for the soul of the local saloonkeeper.

---

into the canyon include **Justin's Horse Rental** (☎ 520/674-5678), which charges $10 per hour per person for a horse and $15 per hour per group for a guide (2-hour minimum). To visit a more remote part of the canyon (including the Spider Rock area), arrange a ride through **Tsotsonii Ranch** (☎ 520/755-6209), which is 1.6 miles past the end of the pavement on the South Rim Drive. Rides are $10 per hour per person for the horse and $10 per hour per group for the guide

SHOPPING

The large **Thunderbird Lodge Gift Shop** (☎ 520/674-5841) in Chinle is well worth a stop while you're in the area. It has a huge collection of rugs, as well as good selections of pottery and plenty of souvenirs. In the canyon wherever visitors gather (at ruins and petroglyph sites), you're likely to encounter craftspeople selling jewelry and other types of handiwork. These craftspeople, most of whom live here in the canyon, accept cash, personal checks, and traveler's checks and sometimes credit cards.

WHERE TO STAY & DINE

In addition to the motels listed below, another lodging option in the Canyon de Chelly area is **Coyote Pass Hospitality,** P.O. Box 91-B, Tsaile, AZ 86556 (☎ 520/724-3383; www.navajocentral.org/cppage.htm), which operates a very rustic sort of bed-and-breakfast operation. Guests stay in a traditional dirt-floored hogan and get a traditional breakfast in the morning. Lunch ($15) and dinner ($20) can be arranged in advance. Rates are $85 for one person and $15 for each additional person. At the time of making the reservation, guests can also arrange for customized, off-the-beaten path Navajo cultural and historic tours with the hosts.

Best Western Canyon de Chelly Inn. 100 Main St. (P.O. Box 295), Chinle, AZ 86503. ☎ **800/327-0354** or 520/674-5874. Fax 520/674-3715. 99 units. A/C TV TEL. May–Oct $96–$115 double; Nov–Apr $60–$74 double. AE, DC, DISC, MC, V.

This motel, located right in the center of Chinle, is both the farthest from the national monument and the least attractive of the three motels in town. Consequently, although the rooms are decent enough, you should make this your last choice here. The restaurant is large and reminiscent of a suburban chain restaurant, and the menu features moderately priced American and Navajo meals. There's also a seasonal indoor swimming pool.

Holiday Inn—Canyon de Chelly. Indian Rte. 7 (P.O. Box 1889), Chinle, AZ 86503. ☎ **800/HOLIDAY** or 520/674-5000. Fax 520/674-8264. 108 units. A/C TV TEL. July–Sept $109 double; Oct–June $79–$99 double. AE, CB, DC, DISC, JCB, MC, V.

Located between the town of Chinle and the national monument entrance, this is the newest hotel in Chinle. The hotel is on the site of the old Garcia Trading Post, which has been incorporated into the restaurant and gift shop building (although the building no longer has any historic character). The guest rooms all have patios or balconies and big windows and bathrooms, and most face the cottonwood-shaded pool courtyard. The hotel's restaurant serves moderately priced American and Navajo meals and is the best place in the area for dinner. Room service is available when the restaurant is open.

✪ **Thunderbird Lodge.** P.O. Box 548, Chinle, AZ 86503. ☎ **800/679-BIRD** or 520/674-5841. Fax 520/674-5844. www.tbirdlodge.com. 72 units. A/C TV TEL. $96–$101 double; $138 suite. Lower rates mid-Nov to Mar. AE, CB, DC, DISC, MC, V.

Built on the site of an early trading post right at the mouth of Canyon de Chelly, the Thunderbird Lodge is the most appealing of the hotels in Chinle and the closest to the national monument. The lodge's buildings back to a low hill and to one side is a large campground in a grove of cottonwoods. The red adobe construction of the lodge itself is reminiscent of ancient pueblos, and the presence on the property of an old stone-walled trading post gives this place more character than any of the other choices in Chinle. Guest rooms come in two sizes and have ceiling fans and air conditioners to keep the rooms cool in the hot summer months. The old trading post now serves as the lodge cafeteria, where American and Navajo meals are served. The lodge has a tour desk, gift shop, and rug room.

CAMPGROUNDS

Adjacent to the Thunderbird Lodge is the free **Cottonwood Campground,** which has 96 sites but does not take reservations. In the summer the campground has water and rest rooms, but in the winter you must bring your own water and only portable toilets are available. On South Rim Drive 10 miles east of the Canyon de Chelly Visitor Center, you'll also find the private **Spider Rock Campground,** P.O. Box 2509, Chinle, AZ 86503 (☎ **520/674-8261**), which charges $10 per night for campsites. The next nearest campgrounds are at **Tsaile Lake** and **Wheatfields Lake,** both of which are south of the town of Tsaile on Indian Route 12. Tsaile is at the east end of the North Rim Drive.

6 Monument Valley & Navajo National Monument

Monument Valley Navajo Tribal Park: 200 miles NE of Flagstaff; 60 miles NE of Navajo National Monument; 110 miles NW of Canyon de Chelly; 150 miles E of Page

Navajo National Monument: 140 miles NE of Flagstaff; 90 miles E of Page; 60 miles SW of Monument Valley; 110 miles NW of Canyon de Chelly

In its role as sculptor, nature has, in the north-central part of the Navajo Reservation, created a garden of monoliths and spires unequaled anywhere on earth. Whether you've ever been there or not, you almost certainly have seen ✪ **Monument Valley** before. This otherworldly landscape has been an object of fascination for years and has, since Hollywood director John Ford first came here in the 1930s, served as backdrop for countless movies, TV shows, and commercials.

Located 30 miles north of Kayenta and straddling the Arizona-Utah state line (you actually go into Utah to get to the park entrance), Monument Valley is a vast flat plain punctuated by natural sandstone cathedrals. These huge monoliths rise up from the sagebrush with sheer walls that capture the light of the rising and setting sun and transform it into fiery hues. Evocative names reflect the shapes the sandstone has taken under the erosive forces of nature: The Mittens, Three Sisters, Camel Butte, Elephant Butte, the Thumb, and Totem Pole are some of the most awe-inspiring natural monuments.

The Navajo have been living in the valley for generations, herding their sheep through the sagebrush scrublands, and some families continue to live here today. However, human habitation in Monument Valley dates much further back in time. Within the park are more than 100 ancient Anasazi archaeological sites, ruins, and petroglyphs dating from before A.D. 1300.

Navajo National Monument, although set in a less spectacular landscape, is no less interesting. It is here where you will find some of the largest cliff dwellings in Arizona. Located 30 miles west of Kayenta and 60 miles northeast of Tuba City, Navajo National Monument encompasses three of the best-preserved Anasazi cliff dwellings in the region: Betatakin, Keet Seel, and Inscription House. It's possible to visit both Betatakin and Keet Seel, but fragile Inscription House is closed to the public. The name Navajo National Monument is a bit misleading. Although the Navajo people do inhabit the area now, it was the ancient Anasazi who built the cliff dwellings. The Navajo arrived centuries after the Anasazi had abandoned the area.

The inhabitants of Tsegi Canyon were ancestral Hopi and Pueblo peoples known as the Kayenta Anasazi. For reasons unknown, the Anasazi began abandoning their well-constructed homes around the middle of the 13th century. Tree rings suggest that a drought in the latter part of the 13th century prevented the Anasazi from growing sufficient crops. However, in Tsegi Canyon there's another theory for the abandonment. The canyon floors were usually flooded each year by spring and summer snowmelt, which made farming quite productive, but in the mid-1200s weather patterns changed and streams running through the canyons began cutting deep into the soil, forming deep, narrow canyons called arroyos, which lowered the water table and made farming much more difficult.

ESSENTIALS

GETTING THERE   From Flagstaff, Navajo National Monument can be reached by taking U.S. 89 north to U.S. 160; Monument Valley Navajo Tribal Park is a bit farther on U.S. 160 and then north on U.S. 163.

The **Navajo Transit System** (☎ **520/729-4002**) operates bus service Monday to Friday throughout the Navajo nation with service between the cities of Farmington, Gallup, and Crown Point (all in New Mexico), and Window Rock, Kayenta, Chinle, and Tuba City. Call for schedule information.

VISITOR INFORMATION   For more information on Monument Valley, contact **Monument Valley Navajo Tribal Park,** P.O. Box 360289, Monument Valley, UT 84536 (☎ **435/727-3353**). The park is open May to September, daily 8am to 7pm; October to March, daily 8am to 5pm (8am to noon on Thanksgiving). Admission is

$2.50 for adults, $1 for seniors, and free for children 7 and under. *Please note:* The National Park Service's Golden Eagle Passport is *not* valid here because Monument Valley is a tribal park.

For more information on the national monument, contact **Navajo National Monument,** HC 71, Box 3, Tonalea, AZ 86044-9704 (☎ **520/672-2366;** www.nps.gov/nava). The park is open daily. There's no lodge at the national monument, but there is a campground. Park admission is free.

MONUMENT VALLEY NAVAJO TRIBAL PARK

This is big country, and, like the Grand Canyon, primarily a point-and-shoot experience for most visitors. Because this is reservation land and people still live in Monument Valley, backcountry or off-road travel is prohibited unless you have a licensed guide. So basically the only way to see the park is from the overlook at the visitor center; by driving the park's scenic (but very rough) 17-mile dirt loop road; or by taking a four-wheel-drive, horseback, or guided-hiking tour. At the park's valley overlook parking area, you'll find a small museum, gift shop, restaurant, snack bar, campground, and, in the parking lot, numerous Navajo tour companies that operate Jeep and hiking tours through the park.

If you want to do a four-wheel-drive tour, try **Roland's Navajoland Tours** (☎ **800/368-2785** or 520/697-3524), which offers three different tours of Monument Valley. Prices range from $30 for a 2^1/$_2$-hour tour to $45 for a half-day tour. **Sacred Monument Tours** (☎ **435/727-3218** or 520/691-6199) offers Jeep tours at comparable prices (hiking and horseback tours are also available).

If you want to see the park on foot, you can arrange a hiking tour through **Black's Hiking/Van Tours** (☎ **435/739-4226**) or **Totem Pole Tours** (☎ **800/345-8687** or 435/727-3313). A day-long guided hike will run you around $75 to $80 and can be physically demanding.

If nothing but the cowboy thing will do for you in this quintessential Wild West landscape, contact **Ed Black's Monument Valley Trail Rides** (☎ **435/739-4285**), which is located near the visitor center and charges $30 for a 1^1/$_2$-hour ride and $100 for an all-day ride.

Another option is to book with **Goulding's Tours,** P.O. Box 360001, Monument Valley, UT 84536 (☎ **435/727-3231**). This company has its office on the edge of the valley at Goulding's Lodge (see below), just a few miles from the park entrance. Half-day tours are $30.50 for 8 years and older; full-day tours are $60.50 for adults and $45.50 for children 8 and under.

ACTIVITIES OUTSIDE THE PARK

Before leaving the area, you might also want to visit **Goulding's Museum and Trading Post** at Goulding's Lodge. This old trading post was the home of the Gouldings for many years and is set up as they had it back in the 1920s and 1930s. There are also displays about the many movies that have been shot here. The trading post is usually open April to November daily 7:30am to 9pm; admission is $2. Also in the area is the **Oljato Trading Post & Museum** (☎ **435/727-3210**), which is 11 miles west of Monument Valley on the scenic stretch of road that leads past Gouldings. Although this trading post, which dates back to 1921, is in Utah, it was originally located in Arizona. The old building, which is open daily 7am to 7pm, still has a classic trading post feel and few tourists ever venture out this way. There's also a small museum here.

If you're interested in learning more about Navajo culture, you might want to stop at Kayenta's **Navajo Cultural Center,** U.S. 160 (☎ **520/697-3170**), located between the Burger King and the Hampton Inn. The center is basically just a display of hogans and other traditional Navajo structures, but the explanatory signs are very informative. During the summer, you might encounter Navajo artisans giving demonstrations here. Inside the adjacent Burger King, you'll also find an interesting exhibit on the Navajo code talkers of World War II. The code talkers were Navajo soldiers who used their own language to transmit military messages, primarily in the South Pacific. The Burger King display also includes lots of artifacts brought back from Japan after the war.

NAVAJO NATIONAL MONUMENT

Unlike Monument Valley, a visit to Navajo National Monument requires physical effort. The shortest distance you'll have to walk here is 1 mile, which is the round-trip distance from the visitor center to the Betatakin overlook. However, if you want to actually climb around inside these ruins, you're looking at strenuous day-long or overnight hikes.

Your first stop should be the **visitor center,** which has informative displays on the ancestral Pueblo and Navajo cultures, including numerous artifacts from Tsegi Canyon. You can watch a couple of short films or a slide show. The center is open daily 8am to 5pm (daylight saving time), and closed on New Year, Christmas, and Thanksgiving.

✪ **Betatakin,** which means "ledge house" in Navajo, is the only one of the three ruins that can be seen easily. Built in a huge amphitheater-like alcove in the canyon wall, Betatakin was occupied only from 1250 to 1300, and at its height of occupation may have housed 125 people.

A 1-mile round-trip paved trail from the visitor center leads to overlooks of Betatakin. The strenuous 5-mile round-trip hike to Betatakin itself is led by a ranger, takes about 5 hours, and involves descending more than 700 feet to the floor of Tsegi Canyon and later returning to the rim. These guided hikes are usually offered between Memorial Day and Labor Day and leave from the visitor center. All hikers should carry 2 quarts of water. This very popular hike is limited to 25 people per tour; many people line up at the visitor center an hour or more before the center opens.

✪ **Keet Seel,** which means "broken pieces of pottery" in Navajo, has a much longer history than Betatakin, with occupation beginning as early as A.D. 950 and continuing until 1300. At one point Keet Seel may have housed 150 people.

The 17-mile round-trip hike or horseback ride to Keet Seel is quite strenuous, and hikers may stay overnight at a primitive campground near the ruins. You must carry enough water for your trip (2 gallons), since none is available along the trail. Only 20 people a day are given permits to visit Keet Seel, and the trail is open only from Memorial Day to Labor Day.

WHERE TO STAY & DINE

In addition to the lodgings listed here, you'll find numerous budget motels 22 miles north of Monument Valley in Mexican Hat, Utah.

Best Western Wetherill Inn. 1000 Main St. (P.O. Box 175), Kayenta, AZ 86033. ☎ **800/ 528-1234** or 520/697-3231. Fax 520/697-3233. 54 units. A/C TV TEL. May 1–Oct 15 and Nov 16–Dec 31 $88–$98 double; Oct 16–Nov 15 and Mar 1–Apr 30 $63–$70 double; Jan 1–Feb 28 $50–$55 double. AE, DISC, JCB, MC, V.

Located in Kayenta 1 mile north of the junction of U.S. 160 and U.S. 163 and 20 miles south of Monument Valley, the Wetherill Inn offers neither the convenience of Goulding's Lodge nor the amenities of the nearby Holiday Inn. However, the rooms here are comfortable enough and do have coffeemakers. There's a year-round indoor pool and a cafe next door that serves Navajo and American food.

Country of Many Hogan Bed & Breakfast. c/o P.O. Box 2984, Tuba City, AZ 86045 ☎ **888/291-4397, PIN 4617** or 520/283-4125. www.navajoland.com/cmh. 2 units. $125 single or double. Rates include Navajo breakfast. DISC, MC, V.

Anyone accustomed to camping may want to consider spending the night in this traditional Navajo hogan. You'll sleep on sheepskins spread on the floor and awake in the morning to a traditional Navajo breakfast that includes tea made from local plants. The hogan is 10 miles southwest of Monument Valley Navajo Tribal Park on Navajo Rte. 6450. If you make arrangements in advance, you can also experience a traditional sweat lodge.

✪ **Goulding's Lodge.** P.O. Box 360001, Monument Valley, UT 84536-0001. ☎ **435/727-3231.** Fax 435/727-3344. www.gouldings.com. 62 units. A/C TV TEL. Mar 15–Oct 15 $138 double; Oct 16–Mar 14 $72 double. AE, CB, DC, DISC, MC, V.

This is the only lodge actually located in Monument Valley, and it offers superb views from the private balconies of the guest rooms furnished with Southwestern decor. Although the setting is memorable, the service can be somewhat lacking. A restaurant serves Navajo and American dishes, and the views from the restaurant are enough to make any meal an event. The hotel has a seasonal indoor pool, tour desk, museum, video library of films shot in Monument Valley, gift shop, coin laundry, and gas station.

Hampton Inn—Navajo Nation. U.S. 160 (P.O. Box 1217), Kayenta, AZ 86033. ☎ **800/HAMPTON** or 520/697-3170. Fax 520/697-3189. 73 units. A/C TV TEL. May–Sept $99–$106 double; Oct and mid-Mar to Apr $75–$84 double; Nov to mid-Mar $66–$74 double. Rates include continental breakfast. AE, DC, DISC, MC, V. Pets accepted.

Located in the center of Kayenta, this is the newest lodging in the area and as such should be your second choice after Gouldings. The hotel is adjacent to the small Navajo Cultural Center and a Burger King that has an interesting display on the Navajo code talkers of World War II. The hotel is built in a modern Santa Fe style and has large, comfortable rooms. There's also a restaurant open for lunch and dinner, a gift shop, and a small outdoor seasonal pool.

Holiday Inn—Kayenta. At the junction of U.S. 160 and U.S. 163 (P.O. Box 307), Kayenta, AZ 86033. ☎ **800/HOLIDAY** or 520/697-3221. Fax 520/697-3349. 160 units. A/C TV TEL. Apr–Oct $99–$129 double; Nov–Mar $79–$89 double. AE, DC, DISC, MC, V.

Located in the center of Kayenta, 23 miles south of Monument Valley and 29 miles east of Navajo National Monument, this Holiday Inn is very popular with tour groups and is almost always crowded. Although the grounds are dusty and a bit run-down, the rooms are spacious and clean. We like the poolside rooms best. Part of the motel's restaurant is designed to look like an Anasazi ruin, and the menu offers both American and Navajo meals. Room service is available, and the hotel has an outdoor pool, a tour desk, and a gift shop.

CAMPGROUNDS

If you're headed to Monument Valley Navajo Tribal Park, you can camp in the park at the **Mitten View Campground** (☎ **435/727-3287**), which has 100 campsites and charges $10 per night per site from April through September ($5 per night October through March, but there are no facilities and you must be self-contained), or just outside the park at **Goulding's Campground** (☎ **435/727-3231**), which charges $15 to $24 per night, is open mid-March through October, and even has an indoor swimming pool.

There's also a free campground at **Navajo National Monument** (☎ **520/672-2366**), west of Kayenta via U.S. 160 and Ariz. 564. There are only 30 campsites here, and the campground is open only from mid-May through October. In summer the spaces are usually full by dark.

DRIVING ON TO COLORADO OR NEW MEXICO: THE FOUR CORNERS MEET

Other attractions you might want to visit while you're in this part of the state include the **Four Corners Monument Navajo Tribal Park** (☎ 520/871-6647), north of Teec Nos Pos in the very northeast corner of the state. This is the only place in the United States where the corners of four states come together; consequently, you can stand in four states—Arizona, Colorado, Utah, and New Mexico—at the same time. The point is marked by a cement pad surrounded by flags, and in the park you'll also find a picnic ground and crafts vendors. The park is open daily 7am to 8pm between May and late August and 8am to 5pm between late August and April. Admission is $2 for adults, free for children 6 and under.

Also in the area, in the community of Teec Nos Pos, you'll find the **Teec Nos Pos Trading Post** (☎ 520/656-3224) and **Foutz Teec Nos Pos Arts and Crafts** (☎ 520/656-3228), both of which have good selections of rugs and other crafts.

DRIVING ON TO FLAGSTAFF OR THE GRAND CANYON

On the west side of the reservation, in Tuba City, you'll find the **Tuba Trading Post** (☎ 520/283-5441) on the corner of Main Street and Moenave Street. This octagonal trading post was built in 1906 of local stone and is designed to resemble a Navajo hogan (there's also a real hogan on the grounds). The trading post serves as both a small market and a store selling Native American crafts, with an emphasis on Pendleton blankets, books, music, and jewelry.

On the western outskirts of Tuba City, on U.S. 160, you'll find **Van's Trading Co.** (☎ 520/283-5343), in the corner of a large grocery store, which has a dead-pawn auction on the 15th of each month at 3pm. Pawned goods that are not reclaimed by the owner by a specified date.is called dead pawn. The auction provides opportunities to buy older pieces of Navajo silver-and-turquoise jewelry. In mid-October, Tuba City is the site of **Western Navajo Fair,** which provides another opportunity for buying Native American crafts.

West of Tuba City and just off U.S. 160, you can see **dinosaur footprints** preserved in the stone surface of the desert. There are usually a few people waiting at the site to guide visitors to the best footprints. These guides will expect a tip. Also in the area are red-rock sandstone formations that resemble petrified sand dunes.

The **Cameron Trading Post** (☎ 520/679-2231), 16 miles south of the junction of U.S. 160 and U.S. 89, is also well worth a visit. The main trading post is filled with souvenirs, but it has large selections of rugs and jewelry as well. In the adjacent stone-walled gallery, you'll find museum-quality Native American artifacts (with prices to match). The trading post also includes a motel (see "Where to Stay" under "The Grand Canyon South Rim" in chapter 6, "The Grand Canyon & Northern Arizona," for details).

WHERE TO STAY

Quality Inn Tuba City. Main St. and Moenave Ave. (P.O. Box 247), Tuba City, AZ 86045. ☎ **800/644-8383,** 800/228-5151, or 520/283-4545. 80 units. A/C TV TEL. Apr–Oct $95–$140 double; Nov–Mar $75–$105 double. AE, DISC, MC, V.

If you can't get a room at the Hopi Cultural Center, this is the next nearest acceptable motel, and at that, it's 62 miles from Second Mesa. Located on the Navajo Reservation adjacent to the historic Tuba City Trading Post, the motel offers comfortable, modern rooms. Its restaurant serves Mexican and American meals, as well as plenty of Navajo tacos. There's also an RV park.

7 Lake Powell & Page

272 miles N of Phoenix; 130 miles E of the Grand Canyon North Rim; 130 miles NE of Grand Canyon South Rim

Imagine the Grand Canyon filled with water instead of air, and you have a pretty good picture of Lake Powell. Had the early Spanish explorers of Arizona suddenly come upon this lake after traipsing for months across desolate desert, they would have either taken it for a mirage or fallen to their knees and rejoiced. Surrounded by hundreds of miles of parched desert land, this reservoir, created by the damming of the Colorado River at Glen Canyon, seems unreal when first glimpsed. Yet real it is, and, like a magnet, it draws everyone in the region toward its promise of relief from the heat.

Construction of the Glen Canyon Dam came about despite the angry outcry of many who felt that this canyon was even more beautiful than the Grand Canyon and should be preserved in its natural state. Preservationists lost the battle. Construction of the dam began in 1960 and was completed in 1963. It took another 17 years for Lake Powell to fill to capacity. Today the lake is a watery powerboat playground, and houseboats and skiers cruise where birds and waterfalls once filled the canyons with their songs. These days, however, most people seem to agree that Lake Powell is as amazing a sight as the Grand Canyon, and the lake draws almost as many visitors each year as its down-river neighbor.

While Lake Powell is something of a man-made wonder of the world, one of the natural wonders of the world—**Rainbow Bridge**—can be found on the shores of the lake. Called *nonnozhoshi*, or "the rainbow turned to stone," by the Navajo, this is the largest natural bridge on earth and stretches 275 feet across a side canyon of Lake Powell.

The town of Page, a work camp constructed to house the workers who built the dam, has now become much more than just a construction camp and, with its many motels and restaurants, is the main base for people who come to explore Lake Powell.

ESSENTIALS

GETTING THERE   Page is connected to Flagstaff by U.S. 89. Ariz. 98 leads southeast onto the Navajo Indian Reservation and connects with U.S. 160 to Kayenta and Four Corners.

Sunrise Airlines (☎ **800/347-3962**) flies to Page from Phoenix ($225 to $269 round-trip) and, between early May and mid-September, Las Vegas ($235 to $285 round-trip). The Page Airport is on the east side of town.

VISITOR INFORMATION   For further information on Page and Lake Powell, contact the **Page/Lake Powell Chamber of Commerce,** 644C N. Navajo Dr. (P.O. Box 727), Page, AZ 86040-0727 (☎ **888/261-7243** or 520/645-2741), or the **John Wesley Powell Museum and Visitor Information Center,** 6 N. Lake Powell Blvd. (P.O. Box 547), Page, AZ 86040-0547 (☎ **520/645-9496;** www.powellmuseum.org). You can also find out more about Lake Powell on the Web at www.powellguide.com.

GETTING AROUND   Rental cars are available at the Page Airport from **Avis** (☎ **800/331-1212** or 520/645-2024). Call **Lake Powell Taxi** (☎ **520/645-8540**) if you need a cab. One person will pay $15 from the airport to Wahweap Lodge.

GLEN CANYON NATIONAL RECREATION AREA

Until the flooding of Glen Canyon formed Lake Powell, this area was one of the most remote regions in the contiguous 48 states. However, with the construction of Glen

Canyon Dam at a spot where the Colorado River was less than ¹/₃ mile wide, this remote and rugged landscape became one of the country's most popular national recreation areas. Today the lake and much of the surrounding land is designated the Glen Canyon National Recreation Area and attracts nearly four million visitors each year. The otherworldly setting (imagine the Grand Canyon, only flooded) amid the slick-rock canyons of northern Arizona and southern Utah is a tapestry of colors, the blues and greens of the lake contrasting with the reds and oranges of the surrounding sandstone cliffs. This interplay of colors and vast desert landscapes easily makes Lake Powell the most beautiful of Arizona's many reservoirs.

Built to provide water for the desert communities of the Southwest and West, **Glen Canyon Dam** stands 710 feet above the bedrock and contains almost five million cubic yards of concrete. The dam also provides hydroelectric power, and deep within its massive wall of concrete are huge power turbines. Most visitors to the area are, however, more interested in water-skiing and powerboating than they are in drinking water and power production. Without the dam, however, there would be no lake, so any visit to this area ought to start with a tour of the dam and a stop at the **Carl Hayden Visitor Center** (☎ 520/608-6404), which is located beside the dam (on U.S. 89 just north of Page) and is open daily 7am to 7pm (between mid-May and mid-September) and 8am to 5pm other months. Here you can learn about the construction of the dam and then descend into the dam itself for a free guided tour that takes about an hour. The tour schedule varies with the time of year, so be sure to call ahead if you want to do the dam tour.

More than 500 feet deep in some places, and bounded by nearly 2,000 miles of shoreline, Lake Powell is a maze of convoluted canyons where rock walls often rise hundreds of feet straight out of the water. In places, long winding canyons are so narrow there isn't even room to turn a motorboat around. It is this otherworldly meeting of rock and water that has made this lake one of the most popular destinations in the Southwest.

For more information before leaving home, you can contact the **Glen Canyon National Recreation Area,** P.O. Box 1507, Page, AZ 86040-1507 (☎ 520/608-6404; www.nps.gov/glca). Admission to the national recreation area is $5 per car (pass good for 1 week), and there is also a $10-per-week boat fee if you bring your own boat. In addition to the Carl Hayden Visitor Center mentioned above, there is the **Bullfrog Visitor Center,** in Bullfrog, Utah (☎ 801/684-7400). This visitor center is open daily 8am to 5pm (open only Saturday and Sunday in March and closed November through February).

BOAT & AIR TOURS

There are few roads penetrating the Glen Canyon National Recreation Area, so the best way to appreciate this rugged region is by boat. If you don't have your own boat, you can at least see a small part of the lake on a boat tour. There are a variety of boat tours that depart from **Wahweap Marina** (☎ 800/528-6154 or 520/645-2433; www.visitlakepowell.com). The paddle wheeler *Canyon King* does a 1-hour tour ($11 adults, $8 children) that unfortunately doesn't really show you much more of the lake than you can see from shore. The *Canyon King* also does sunset ($25 adults, $22 children) and dinner cruises ($54). A better choice for anyone with limited time or finances would be the Navajo Tapestry Cruise ($37 adults, $28 children) or the Antelope Canyon Cruise ($24 adults, $20 children). However, to see the most of the lake, opt for the full-day tour to Rainbow Bridge (see below for details).

The Glen Canyon National Recreation Area covers an immense area, much of it inaccessible by car and only partially accessible by boat. If you'd like to see more of the area than is visible from car or boat, consider taking an air tour with **Lake Powell Airlines** (☎ **800/245-8668**), which offers several air tours of northern Arizona and southern Utah, including flights over Rainbow Bridge, the Escalante River, the Grand Canyon, Canyonlands, Bryce Canyon, Monument Valley, and the Navajo nation. Sample rates are $79 for a 30-minute flight over Rainbow Bridge and $160 for a 90-minute flight over Monument Valley.

RAINBOW BRIDGE NATIONAL MONUMENT

Roughly 40 miles up Lake Powell from Wahweap Marina and Glen Canyon Dam, in a narrow side canyon of the lake, rises **Rainbow Bridge,** the world's largest natural bridge and one of the most spectacular sights in the Southwest. Preserved in Rainbow Bridge National Monument, this natural arch of sandstone stands 290 feet high and spans 275 feet. Carved by wind and water over the ages, Rainbow Bridge is an awesome reminder of the powers of erosion that have sculpted this entire region into the spectacle it is today.

Rainbow Bridge is accessible only by boat or on foot (13-mile hike minimum), and traveling there by boat is by far the more popular route. **Lake Powell Resorts and Marinas** (☎ **800/528-6154** or 520/645-2433; www.visitlakepowell.com) offers daily half-day ($72 adults, $52 children) and full-day ($96 adults, $66 children) boat tours to Rainbow Bridge. Not only do these tours get you to Rainbow Bridge in comfort but they also cruise through some of the most spectacular scenery on earth. The full-day tours include box lunches and explore two other major canyons after visiting Rainbow Bridge.

Rainbow Bridge National Monument is administered by Glen Canyon National Recreation Area, and information is available from sources mentioned above for the recreation area. For information on hiking to Rainbow Bridge, contact the **Navajo Parks and Recreation Department,** P.O. Box 9000, Window Rock, AZ 86515 (☎ **520/871-6647**).

ANTELOPE CANYON

If you've spent any time in Arizona, chances are you've seen photos of a narrow sandstone canyon only a few feet wide. The walls of the canyon seem to glow with an inner light in these photos, and beams of sunlight slice down through the darkness of the deep slot canyon. Sound familiar? If you have seen such a photo, chances are you were looking at ✪ **Antelope Canyon** (also known as Corkscrew Canyon). Located 2¹/₂ miles outside Page off Ariz. 98 (at milepost 299), this famous photogenic canyon lies on the Navajo Indian Reservation at the end of a rough dirt and sand road. There are currently two options for visiting Antelope Canyon. The most convenient and reliable way is to take a 1¹/₂-hour tour with **Lake Powell Jeep Tours** (☎ **520/645-5501**), **Roger Ekis' Antelope Canyon Tours** (☎ **520/645-9102** or 520/645-8579), or **Grand Circle Adventures Scenic Tours** (☎ **520/645-5594**), all of which charge $20 per adult for a basic tour (photographic tours are $35). Alternatively, you can hire a Navajo guide through **Antelope Canyon Tours** (☎ **520/698-3384**), which usually has guides at the trailhead whenever the weather is safe for hiking into the canyon. This latter option will cost you $5 for a visitor's permit and $12.50 for the guide to drive you from the highway to the canyon and then pick you up again after your hike. If you want to stay longer to take pictures, it will cost an additional $5 per hour. Just remember that if there is even the slightest chance of rain anywhere in the region, you should not venture into this canyon, which is subject to flash floods. In the past, people who have ignored bad weather have been killed by flash floods in this canyon. For more information, contact the **Navajo Parks and Recreation Department,** P.O. Box 9000, Window Rock, AZ 86515 (☎ **520/871-6647**).

WATERSPORTS

While simply exploring the lake's maze of canyons on a narrated tour is satisfying enough for many visitors, houseboating, water-skiing, riding personal watercraft, and fishing are still the most popular activities, and five marinas (only Wahweap is in Arizona) help boaters explore the lake. You can bring your own boat or rent one here. At the **Wahweap Marina** (☎ **800/528-6154** or 520/645-2433; www.visitlakepowell. com) you can rent various types of boats, personal watercraft, and water skis and head out on your own to have some fun on the water. Rental rates in the summer high season range from about $72 to $359 per day depending on the type of boat you rent (low season rates from $46 to $215 per day). Weekly rates are also available. Small boats and personal watercraft can also be rented from **Lake Powell Water World,** 920 Hemlock St. (☎ **520/645-8845**), and from **Doo Powell,** 130 Sixth Ave. (☎ **800/ 350-1230** or 520/645-1230; www.doopowell.com). For information on renting houseboats, see "Houseboats" under "Where to Stay," below.

If roaring engines aren't your speed, you might want to consider exploring Lake Powell in a sea kayak. While afternoon winds can sometimes make paddling difficult, mornings are often quiet. With a narrow sea kayak, you can even explore canyons too small for powerboats. You can rent sea kayaks from **Twin Finn Diving Center,** 811 Vista Ave. (☎ **520/645-3114**). Sea kayaks rent for $45 per day, and sit-on-top kayaks rent for $35 to $48.50 per day.

While most of Glen Canyon National Recreation Area consists of the impounded waters of Lake Powell, within the recreation area there is also a short stretch of the Colorado River that still flows swift and free. If you'd like to see this stretch of river, try a float trip from Glen Canyon Dam to Lees Ferry. These raft trips are operated by **Wilderness River Adventures,** 50 S. Lake Powell Blvd. (☎ **800/528-6154** or 520/645-3279) between March and October and cost $54 for adults and $45 for children 12 and under for a half-day trip. All-day trips are also available ($75 adults, $65 children). Try to make reservations at least 2 weeks in advance.

If you have a boat (either your own or a rental), avail yourself of some excellent year-round **fishing.** Smallmouth, largemouth, and striped bass, as well as walleye, catfish, crappie, and carp are all plentiful. Because the lake lies within both Arizona and Utah, you'll need to know which state's waters you're fishing in whenever you cast your line out, and you'll need the appropriate license. (Also, be sure to pick up a copy of the Arizona and Utah state fishing regulations or ask about applicable regulations at any of the marinas on the lake.) You can arrange licenses to fish the entire lake at **Wahweap Lodge and Marina** (☎ **520/645-2433**), which also sells bait and tackle and can provide you with a bit of advice on fishing this massive reservoir. Other marinas on the lake also sell licenses, bait, and tackle. The best season is March through November, but walleye are most often caught during the cooler months. Throughout the year there are numerous fishing tournaments.

If you'd rather try your hand at catching enormous rainbow trout, try downstream of the Glen Canyon Dam, where cold waters provide ideal conditions for trophy trout. Unfortunately, there isn't much access to this stretch of river. You'll need a trout stamp to fish for the rainbows.

If you're just looking for a good place to go for a swim near Wahweap Lodge, take the Coves Loop just west of the marina. Of the three coves, the third one is the best, with a sandy beach. The Chains area, another good place to jump off the rocks and otherwise lounge by the lake, is just outside Page down a rough dirt road just before you reach Glen Canyon Dam. The view underwater at Lake Powell is as scenic as the view above it, and if you're interested in exploring the underwater regions of the canyon, contact **Twin Finn Diving Center,** 811 Vista Ave. (☎ **520/645-3114; www.twinfinn.com**), which charges $45 a day for scuba gear and also rents snorkling equipment.

MORE OUTDOOR FUN

While most activity within the national recreation area revolves around water, the short hike to the **Horseshoe Bend** viewpoint is not to be missed (be sure to bring your camera). Horseshoe Bend is a huge loop of the Colorado River, and the viewpoint is hundreds of feet above the water on the edge of a sheer cliff. Far below, you can often see people camped at a riverside campsite that is accessible only by boat. It's about $^{1}/_{2}$ mile to the viewpoint from the trailhead, which is 5 miles south of the Carl Hayden Visitor Center on U.S. 89 just south of milepost 545.

At Lees Ferry, 39 miles from Page at the southern tip of the national recreation area, you'll find three short trails (Cathedral Wash, River Trail, and Spencer Trail), as well as the southern trailhead for the famed **Paria Canyon,** a favorite of canyoneering backpackers. This latter trail is 37 miles long and follows the meandering route of a narrow slot canyon for much of its length. Most hikers start from the northern trailhead, which is in Utah on U.S. 89. At the Carl Hayden Visitor Center, you can also pick up brochures that describe several area day hikes.

The 27-hole **Lake Powell National Golf Course,** 400 Clubhouse Dr. (☎ **520/ 645-2023**), is one of the most spectacular golf courses in the state. The fairways wrap around the base of the red sandstone bluff atop which sits the town of Page. In places, walls of eroded sandstone come right down to the greens, and alongside one fairway, water is pumped up the rock to create a waterfall. The views stretch to forever. Greens fees range from $36 to $60 in the warmer months.

OTHER AREA ATTRACTIONS

In addition to the museum listed here, you can also learn about Navajo culture at the **Navajo Village,** a sort of living history center located on the south side of Page off Haul Road. Programs here, which run from May through October, start with a wagon ride from the Chamber of Commerce office in downtown Page; once at Navajo Village, you get to observe Navajo weavers, silversmiths, basket-makers, and potters. There are various presentations on different aspects of Navajo culture, and dinners are served as part of the evening tours. Tour prices range from $10 ($7 children ages 6 to 13) for a daytime tour to $49.95 ($34.95 children ages 6 to 13) for an evening tour that includes a wagon ride, dinner, and traditional dances. For information on the schedule or to make a reservation, contact the Page/Lake Powell of Commerce, 644C N. Navajo Dr. (☎ **520/645-2741** or 520/660-0304).

John Wesley Powell Memorial Museum & Visitor Information Center. 6 N. Lake Powell Blvd. ☎ **520/645-9496.** www.powellmuseum.org. By donation. May–Sept daily 8am–6pm; Nov to mid-Dec and mid-Feb to Apr Mon–Fri 9am–5pm. Closed mid-Dec to mid-Feb.

In 1869, John Wesley Powell, a one-armed Civil War veteran, and a small band of men spent more than 3 months fighting the rapids of the Green and Colorado rivers to become the first people to travel the length of the Grand Canyon. It is for this intrepid—some said crazy—adventurer that Lake Powell is named and to whom this small museum is dedicated. Besides documenting the Powell expedition with photographs, etchings, and artifacts, the museum displays Indian artifacts from Anasazi pottery to contemporary Navajo and Hopi crafts. The exhibit of fluorescent minerals is particularly interesting, and there are several informative videos shown in the museum's small auditorium. The museum also acts as an information center for Page, Lake Powell, and the region and has a small gift shop.

WHERE TO STAY
HOUSEBOATS

✪ **Lake Powell Resorts and Marinas.** P.O. Box 56909, Phoenix, AZ 85079. ☎ **800/528-6154.** Fax 602/331-5258. www.visitlakepowell.com. May to mid-Oct $1,616–$5,275 per week; mid-Oct to Apr $970–$3,165 per week (3-, 4-, 5-, and 6-night rates also available). AE, DISC, MC, V.

Although there are plenty of hotels and motels in and near Page, the most popular accommodations here are not waterfront hotel rooms but houseboats, which function as floating vacation homes. With a houseboat, which is as easy to operate as a car, you can explore Lake Powell's beautiful red-rock country, far from any roads. No special license or prior experience is necessary, and plenty of hands-on instruction is offered before you leave the marina. Because Lake Powell houseboating is extremely popular with people from all over the world, it's important to make reservations as far in advance as possible, especially if you plan to visit in the summer.

Houseboats range in size from 36 to 59 feet, sleep anywhere from 6 to 12 people, and come complete with hot showers, refrigerator/freezer, heating system (more expensive houseboats also have heat pumps or evaporative coolers), stove, oven, and gas grill. Kitchens come equipped with everything you need to prepare meals. The only things you really need to bring are bedding and towels.

HOTELS/MOTELS
Expensive

Wahweap Lodge. 100 Lakeshore Dr. (mailing address: P.O. Box 56909, Phoenix, AZ 85079). ☎ **800/528-6154** or 520/645-2433. Fax 602/331-5258. www.visitlakepowell.com. 350 units. A/C TV TEL. Apr–Oct $159–$169 double, $227 suite; Nov–Mar $111–$118 double, $158 suite. AE, DC, DISC, MC, V. Pets accepted.

The Wahweap Marina is a sprawling complex 5 miles north of Page on the shores of Lake Powell. As the biggest and busiest hotel in the area, Wahweap features many of the amenities and activities of a resort. The guest rooms are arranged in several long two-story wings, and all the rooms have either a balcony or a patio. However, only half the rooms have lake views, and of these, those in the west wing have the better views (the east wing overlooks the Navajo coal-fired power plant). This place stays packed with tour groups from around the world and getting a reservation can be difficult.

Dining/Diversions: The Rainbow Room (see "Where to Dine," below) offers fine dining with a sweeping panorama of the lake and desert. The menu is equally divided between American standards and Southwestern fare. A snack bar near the boat ramp provides light meals and snacks, and a lounge serves cocktails with a view.

Amenities: Two outdoor pools, whirlpool, boat ramp, boat rentals, boat tours, float trips, room service.

Moderate

Best Western Arizonainn. 716 Rimview Dr. (P.O. Box 250), Page, AZ 86040. ☎ **800/826-2718** or 520/645-2466. Fax 520/645-2053. 103 units. A/C TV TEL. Apr–Oct $80–$140 double; Nov–Mar $52–$77 double. AE, DC, DISC, MC, V. Pets accepted.

Perched right at the edge of the mesa on which Page is built, this modern motel has a fine view across miles of desert. Half the rooms have views, and of course, these are more expensive. The hotel offers free coffee in the lobby, an outdoor pool with a 100-mile view, a whirlpool, and an exercise room.

Best Western at Lake Powell. 208 N. Lake Powell Blvd. (P.O. Box 4899), Page, AZ 86040. ☎ **888/794-2888**, 800/528-1234, or 520/645-5988. Fax 520/645-2578. 132 units. A/C TV TEL. Mid-May to Sept $69–$99; Oct and Apr to mid-May $59–$79; Nov–Mar $49–$69. AE, DC, DISC, MC, V.

This hotel lies on the edge of town overlooking Lake Powell and is right next door to the Arizonainn. The rooms are comfortable and modern, and you'll find a pool with a great view, a hot tub, and an exercise room. There's no restaurant on the premises, but breakfast is available.

✔ ♻ **Courtyard by Marriott.** 600 Clubhouse Dr. (P.O. Box 4128), Page, AZ 86040. ☎ **800/851-3855**, 800/321-2211, or 520/645-5000. Fax 520/645-5004. 153 units. A/C TV TEL. July–early Sept $109–$139 double; early Sept–June $79–$109 double. AE, CB, DC, DISC, MC, V.

Located at the foot of the mesa on which Page is built and adjacent to the Lake Powell National Golf Course, this hotel is the closest you'll come to a golf resort in this corner of the state and is the top in-town choice. The rooms are larger than those at most motels, and there are king-size beds, separate seating areas, and dressing areas. You'll pay a premium for views of the golf course or lake. Moderately priced meals are served in a casual restaurant that has a terrace overlooking the distant lake, and there's also an adjacent lounge. The 18-hole golf course has great views of the surrounding landscape. An outdoor pool, whirlpool, exercise room, room service, and valet/laundry service round out the amenities here.

Lake Powell Motel. U.S. 89 near Wahweap Marina (mailing address: P.O. Box 56909, Phoenix, AZ 85079). ☎ **800/528-6154** or 520/645-2477. Fax 602/331-5258. www.visitlakepowell.com. 24 units. A/C TV TEL. $85 double. AE, DC, DISC, MC, V. Closed Nov–Mar. Pets accepted. Drive 3 miles west of the Wahweap Marina or 4 miles north of the Glen Canyon Dam on U.S. 89.

Located on a barren hill set back from the lake, the Lake Powell Motel offers an alternative away from the traffic and lights of downtown Page and the bustle of activity at the Wahweap Marina. The accommodations are standard motel rooms with two queen-size beds.

CAMPGROUNDS & RV PARKS

There are campgrounds and RV facilities at **Wahweap** (☎ **520/645-1059**) and **Lees Ferry** (☎ **520/608-6404**) in Arizona and at Bullfrog, Hite, and Halls Crossing in Utah. At Wahweap, there are separate campgrounds for tenters and for RVers. Some scrubby trees provide a bit of shade at the tenting campground, but the winds and sun make this a rather bleak spot in summer. However, because of the lake's popularity, these campgrounds stay packed for much of the year. Reservations are not taken.

WHERE TO DINE

For espresso and light meals, check out **Cactus & Tropicals Garden Cafe,** 809 N. Navajo Dr. (☎ **520/645-6666**), open Monday to Thursday 11am to 3pm and Friday and Saturday 11am to 9pm.

Butterfield Stage Co. 704 Rimview Dr. ☎ **520/645-2467**. Main courses $9–$19. AE, MC, V. Daily 4–9pm (until 10pm in summer). STEAKS/AMERICAN.

Located adjacent to the Best Western Arizonainn, this steak house is the only in-town restaurant with a view, and although the view is somewhat marred by the number of power lines that stretch out from the dam, it's still the best view in town. Sunrises and sunsets are gorgeous. Steaks and seafood are the menu mainstays.

The Dam Bar & Grille. 644 N. Navajo Dr. ☎ **520/645-2161.** Reservations recommended in summer. Main courses $9–$25. AE, DISC, MC, V. Wed–Sat 3–11pm (longer hours in summer). AMERICAN.

Page's first and only theme restaurant is a warehouse-size space designed to conjure up images of the Glen Canyon Dam. Big industrial doors are the first hint this is more than your usual small-town dining establishment. Inside, cement walls, hard hats, and a big transformer that sends out bolts of neon "electricity" put you in a dam good mood. Sandwiches, pastas, and steaks dominate the menu, with a smattering of seafood. There's a large lounge area that's a popular locals' hangout, and next door is an affiliated nightclub.

Rainbow Room. In the Wahweap Lodge, Lakeshore Dr. ☎ **520/645-1162.** Reservations recommended. Main courses $5–$8 at lunch, $10–$20 at dinner. AE, DC, DISC, MC, V. Daily 7am–2pm and 5–9pm (10pm in summer). AMERICAN/SOUTHWEST.

With sweeping vistas of Lake Powell out the walls of glass, the Rainbow Room at the Wahweap Lodge is Page's premier restaurant. As such, be prepared for a wait; this place regularly feeds busloads of tourists from around the world. The menu features American dishes, such as blackened chicken breast and Caesar salad, but there are also specials and dishes such as grilled rainbow trout with crab stuffing and lemon-caper sauce. If you're heading out on the water for the day, the kitchen will fix you a box lunch.

Zapata's. 614 N. Navajo Dr. ☎ **520/645-9006.** Main courses $7.50–$13.50. AE, DC, DISC, MC, V. Daily 11am–9pm. MEXICAN.

Zapata's, a little place in the shopping plaza diagonally across the intersection from the Powell Museum, serves some of the best Mexican food (and margaritas) in town. You can count on finding spicy chile verde burritos and somewhat milder, although flavorful, chicken enchiladas. At lunch there is a limited selection of specials for about $5. The crowd here is usually more local than tourist.

8 Eastern Arizona's High Country

When most people think of Arizona, they think of deserts and saguaro cacti. However, that's only part of the picture. Arizona actually has more mountainous country than Switzerland and more forest than Minnesota, and most of these mountains and forests are here in the highlands of eastern Arizona.

In this sparsely populated region, towns with such apt names as Alpine, Lakeside, and Pinetop have become summer retreats for the people who live in the state's low-lying, sun-baked deserts. Folks from Phoenix and its surrounding cities discovered long ago how close the cool mountain forests were to the desert. In only a few hours you can drive up from the cacti and creosote bushes to the meadows and pine forests of the White Mountains.

Dividing the arid lowlands from the cool pine forests of the highlands is the Mogollon Rim (pronounced *Mug-ee-un* by the locals), a 2,000-foot-high escarpment that stretches for 200 miles from central Arizona into New Mexico. Along this impressive wall, the climatic and vegetative change is dramatic. Imagine sunshine at the base and snow squalls at the top, and you have an idea of the Mogollon Rim's variety. This area was made famous by Western author Zane Grey, who lived in a cabin near Payson and set many of his novels in this scenic yet often-overlooked part of Arizona. Fans of Zane Grey's novels can follow in the author's footsteps and also visit a small museum dedicated to him.

Trout fishing, hiking, horseback riding, and hunting are the main warm-weather pastimes of eastern Arizona, and when winter weather reports from up north have Phoenicians dreaming about snow (it's true, they really do), many head up this way to the White Mountains for a bit of skiing. Sunrise Park Resort, operated by the White Mountain Apache Tribe, is the state's biggest and busiest downhill ski area, and there are also plenty of cross-country ski trails in the area.

A large chunk of eastern Arizona—1,664,874 acres to be exact—is Apache Reservation land. Recreational activities abound on the reservation, but just remember that the Apache tribe requires visitors to have reservation fishing permits and outdoor recreation permits. Fishing is particularly popular on the reservation, which isn't surprising considering there are 400 miles of trout streams and 25 lakes stocked with rainbow and brown trout.

1 Payson & the Mogollon Rim

94 miles NE of Phoenix; 90 miles SW of Winslow; 90 miles SE of Flagstaff; 100 miles W of Pinetop-Lakeside

Payson, 94 miles from Phoenix and 5,000 feet above sea level, is one of the closest places for Phoenicians to find relief from the summer heat. Payson may not be quite high enough to be considered the mountains, but it certainly isn't the desert (summer temperatures are 20° cooler than in the Valley of the Sun). The 2,000-foot-high, 200-mile-long Mogollon Rim is only 22 miles north of town, and the surrounding Tonto National Forest provides opportunities for hiking, swimming, fishing, and hunting. The nearly perfect climate of Payson has also made the town a popular retirement spot. Summer highs are usually in the 80s or 90s, while winter highs are usually in the 50°-to-60°F range.

ESSENTIALS
GETTING THERE   Payson is 94 miles from Phoenix on Ariz. 87, the Beeline Highway. Ariz. 87 also connects Payson to Winslow, which is 90 miles away. Ariz. 260 runs east from Payson, climbing the Mogollon Rim and continuing into the White Mountains.

VISITOR INFORMATION   For more information on Payson, contact the **Rim Country Regional Chamber of Commerce,** 100 W. Main St. (P.O. Box 1380), Payson, AZ 85547 (☎ **800/672-9766** or 520/474-4515; www.rimcountrychamber.com).

SPECIAL EVENTS   The ✪ **World's Oldest Continuous Rodeo** takes place each year on the third weekend in August, while another **PRCA Rodeo** is held in May.

ENJOYING THE OUTDOORS
The area's most popular attraction is **Tonto Natural Bridge State Park** (☎ **520/476-4202**), which is 15 miles north of Payson on Ariz. 87 and preserves the largest natural travertine bridge in the world. Discovered in 1877 by a gold prospector named David Gowan while he was being chased by Apaches, the bridge is 183 feet high and 150 feet across at its widest point. Although this all sounds very impressive, this natural bridge looks nothing like the sandstone arches in southern Utah. Tonto Natural Bridge creates something of a tunnel rather than a free-standing arch. This state park preserves not only the bridge, but a historic lodge built by Gowan's nephew and the nephew's sons. Today the lodge has been restored to the way it looked in 1927 but is not open for overnight accommodations. Admission to the park is $5 per car. The park is open daily 9am to 5pm in winter, 8am to 6pm in spring and fall, and 8am to 7pm Memorial Day to Labor Day.

If you'd like to go horseback riding between Memorial Day and late September, contact **O.K. Corral Stables** (☎ **520/476-4303**) in Pine, which is 14 miles north of Payson on Ariz. 87, or **Kohl's Ranch Stables,** located on Highway 260 17 miles north of Payson (☎ **520/478-0030**). Rates start at around $20 for a 1-hour ride.

The **Highline Trail** is a 51-mile-long hiking trail along the lower slope of the Mogollon Rim. You can find out more about this and other area trails at the **Payson Ranger Station** (☎ **520/474-7900**) on Ariz. 260 at the east end of town. At the ranger station, you can find out about area trails open to mountain bikes.

You can also hike this area in the company of llamas that will carry your gear for you. **Fossil Creek Llamas** (☎ **520/476-5178;** www.fossilcreekllamas.com) offers both day trips and overnight hikes starting at $55 per person. A tepee "bed-and-breakfast," wellness courses, and retreats are also offered.

MORE TO SEE & DO

About 5 miles north of town, off Ariz. 87 on Houston Mesa Road, you can visit the ruins of **Shoofly Village,** in the Tonto National Forest. This village was first occupied nearly 1,000 years ago by peoples related to the Hohokam and Salado cultures and contained 87 rooms. Today only rock foundations remain, but an interpretive trail helps bring the site to life.

To learn a bit more about the history of the area, stop in at the **Rim Country Museum,** 700 Green Valley Pkwy. (☎ **520/474-3483**), which has displays on the region as well as a special Zane Grey exhibit. The museum, located in Green Valley Park, is open Wednesday to Sunday noon to 4pm, and admission is $3 adults, $2.50 seniors, and $2 students 12 to 17 years old.

You'll find more Zane Grey memorabilia at the **Zane Grey Museum of Payson,** 503 W. Main St. (☎ **520/474-6243**). The museum is open Monday to Friday 10am to 3pm. The museum recently expanded from 800 to 3,000 square feet, and at press time the owners were considering instituting an admission fee for the first time. The museum includes a shop; Zane Grey book searches are a specialty.

If you feel lucky, you can spend some time and money at the **Mazatzal Casino** (☎ **800/777-PLAY**) ¹/₂ mile south on Ariz. 87. The casino is run by the Tonto Apaches.

SCENIC DRIVES

Scenic drives through this region are among the favorite pastimes of visitors. One of the most popular drives is along the top of the Mogollon Rim on 45-mile-long **Forest Road 300.** On the road, which clings to the edge of the Mogollon Rim, are numerous views of the forest far below and plenty of places to stop, including lakes, picnic areas, trailheads, and campgrounds. This is a good gravel road in summer and can be negotiated in a standard passenger car. However, in winter the road is not maintained. To access the rim road, head east on Ariz. 260 or north on Ariz. 87 for 30 miles and watch for signs.

About 15 miles north of Payson on Ariz. 87, you'll find the village of **Pine,** and another 3 miles beyond this, the village of **Strawberry.** Here, in a quiet setting in the forest, you'll find a few antiques and crafts shops and, in Pine, a small museum that chronicles the history of this area. In Strawberry, on the road that leads west from the center of the village, is the old Strawberry schoolhouse, a restored log building dating from 1885.

Another interesting drive starts west of the old Strawberry schoolhouse. If you continue west on this road, you will be on the Fossil Creek Road, a gravel road leading down a deep and spectacular canyon. It's a bit of a hair-raising drive, but if you like views, it's well worth the white knuckles and dust. At the bottom, **Fossil Creek** offers swimming and fishing.

WHERE TO STAY
IN TOWN

✪ **Majestic Mountain Inn.** 602 E. Ariz. 260, Payson, AZ 85541. ☎ **800/408-2442** or 520/474-0185. Fax 520/472-6097. www.majesticmountaininn.com. 50 units. A/C TV TEL. $67–$140 double. AE, CB, DC, DISC, MC, V.

Although it's located in town, this motel is built in an attractive, modern mountain-lodge design that makes it the most appealing place to stay right in Payson. There's a large stone chimney and fireplace in the lobby, and several of the deluxe rooms have

Eastern Arizona's High Country

fireplaces of their own. These deluxe rooms also have tile floors and double whirlpool tubs facing the fireplaces. The standard rooms aren't as spacious or luxurious, but are still quite comfortable. There's also a seasonal outdoor swimming pool.

OUTSIDE TOWN

✪ **Kohl's Ranch Lodge.** E. Ariz. 260, Payson, AZ 85541. ☎ **800/521-3131** or 520/478-4211. Fax 520/478-0353. www.ilxresorts.com. 49 units. A/C TV TEL. May 1–Sept 30 $95–$105 double, $230– $250 cabin; Oct 1–Apr 30 $75–$85 double, $200–$225 cabin. AE, DISC, MC, V.

Located 17 miles east of Payson on Ariz. 260, Kohl's Ranch is surrounded by pine forest on the banks of Tonto Creek and is the most comfortable mountain retreat in the area. Although the main lodge building looks like an aging mountain motel from the outside, this casual family-oriented resort makes an excellent base for exploring the Mogollon Rim region. All the guest rooms here feature a contemporary rustic look, and all the cabins and some of the smaller lodge rooms have fireplaces. The creek-side cabins are the best accommodations, but they seem somewhat overpriced. The dining room is done up like an old log cabin, and there's a lounge in the main lodge and a cowboy bar and pool hall across the parking lot. The hotel offers horseback riding, mountain-bike rentals, an outdoor pool, a fitness room, volleyball, putting green, bocce ball, a general store, and a playground.

CAMPGROUNDS

East of Payson on Ariz. 260 are several national forest campgrounds. These camp-grounds include (from west to east) Lower Tonto Creek and Upper Tonto Creek campgrounds (neither of which take reservations) and Christopher Creek Camp-ground (reservations through **National Recreation Reservation Service;** ☎ **800/ 280-2267;** www.reserveusa.com).

Information is available from the **Payson Ranger Station** (☎ 520/474-7900) on Ariz. 260 at the east end of town.

WHERE TO DINE

The Oaks Restaurant & Lounge. 302 W. Main St. ☎ **520/474-1929.** Reservations rec-ommended for dinner. Main courses $5–$7 at lunch, $13–$17 at dinner. AE, DISC, MC, V. Sun and Wed–Thurs 11am–2pm and 5–8pm; Fri–Sat 11am–2pm and 5–9pm. AMERICAN.

Taking its name from the grove of oak trees spreading over it, the Oaks Restaurant is a quiet, somewhat formal place for a meal in Payson, and the large patio dining area beside the grassy front lawn is a great spot for lunch or dinner on a warm night. The dinner menu is short and to the point: straightforward preparations of steaks and seafood, complemented by a selection of primarily California wines. The Caesar salad is good, as are the various cakes. The lunch menu features a variety of hot and cold sandwiches as well as several salads.

2 Pinetop-Lakeside

185 miles NE of Phoenix; 140 miles SE of Flagstaff; 50 miles S of Holbrook; 90 miles NE of Payson

With dozens of motels and cabin resorts strung out along Ariz. 260 as it passes through town, Pinetop-Lakeside, actually two towns that grew together over the years, is the busiest community in the White Mountains. At first glance it is easy to dismiss Pinetop-Lakeside as too commercial, what with all the strip malls, budget motels, and old cabin resorts, but this area has spent a lot of years entertaining families during the summer months, and it still has plenty of things to keep visitors busy. You just have to look a little harder than you might in other White Mountains communities.

With Apache-Sitgreaves National Forest on one side of town and the unspoiled lands of the White Mountain Apache Indian Reservation on the other, Pinetop-Lakeside is well situated for anyone who enjoys getting outside. Several lakes with good fishing; nearly 200 miles of hiking, mountain biking, and cross-country ski trails; horseback riding stables; and downhill skiing are all nearby, which makes this area a good base for a visit to the White Mountains. Although summer is the busy sea-son up here, Pinetop-Lakeside becomes a ski resort in the winter. Sunrise ski area is only 30 miles away, and on weekends the town is packed with skiers.

Pinetop-Lakeside is definitely the family destination of the White Mountains, so if you're looking for a romantic weekend or to just get away from it all, continue farther into the White Mountains to Greer or Alpine.

ESSENTIALS

GETTING THERE   Pinetop and Lakeside are both located on Ariz. 260. **Sunrise Airlines** (☎ **888/394-1851** or 520/532-8888) provides regularly scheduled air service between Scottsdale Airport and Show Low. Fares range from $154 to $194 round-trip.

GETTING AROUND   Rental cars are available in Show Low from **Enterprise Rent-a-Car** (☎ 520/537-5144).

VISITOR INFORMATION   For information on this area, contact the **Pinetop-Lakeside Chamber of Commerce,** 674 E. White Mountain Blvd. (P.O. Box 4220), Lakeside, AZ 85935 (☎ **800/573-4031** or 520/367-4290; www.pinetoplakesidechamber.com). For more information on the White Mountain Apache Reservation, contact the **White Mountain Apache Tribe Office of Tourism,** P.O. Box 710, Fort Apache, AZ 85926 (☎ **520/338-1230**).

ENJOYING THE OUTDOORS

Old forts and casinos aside, it is the outdoors (and the cool weather) that really draws people here. Fishing, hiking, mountain biking, and horseback riding are among the most popular activities in the Pinetop-Lakeside area.

If you want to saddle up, call **Porter Mountain Stable,** 4048 Porter Mountain Rd. (☎ **520/368-5306**), which charges $20 for a 1-hour ride.

In the forests surrounding Pinetop-Lakeside is the 180-mile **White Mountain Trail system.** Many of these trails are easily accessible (in fact, some are right in town) and are open to hikers and mountain bikers. The trails at **Woodland Lake Park** are among our favorites. The park is just off Ariz. 260 near the east end of Pinetop and has 6 miles of trails, including a paved trail around the lake. For a panoramic vista of the Mogollon Rim, you can hike the short **Mogollon Rim Nature Walk** off Ariz. 260 on the west side of Lakeside. For another short but pleasant stroll, check out the **Big Springs Environmental Study Area,** on Woodland Road in Lakeside. This quiet little preserve encompasses a small meadow through which flows a spring-fed stream. There is often good bird watching here. You can spot more birds at **Woodland Lake Park** in Pinetop and at **Jacques Marsh,** 2 miles north of Lakeside on Porter Mountain Road. For more information on area trails, contact the **Lakeside Ranger Station** (☎ **520/368-5111**) on Ariz. 260 in Lakeside or the **Pinetop-Lakeside Chamber of Commerce,** 674 E. White Mountain Blvd., Lakeside (☎ **520/367-4290**).

If you're up here to catch the big one, you've got plenty of options. Area lakes hold native Apache trout, as well as stocked rainbows, browns, and brookies. This is also the southernmost spot in the United States where you can fish for Arctic graylings. Right in the Pinetop-Lakeside area, try **Rainbow Lake,** which is a block south of Ariz. 260 in Lakeside and has boat rentals available; **Woodland Lake,** in Woodland Lake Park, which is toward the east end of Pinetop and just south of Ariz. 260; or **Show Low Lake,** which is east of Lakeside and north of Ariz. 260. On the nearby White Mountain Apache Indian Reservation, there is good fishing in **Hawley Lake** and at **Horseshoe Lake,** both of which are east of Pinetop-Lakeside and south of Ariz. 260. Be sure to get your reservation fishing license ($6 per day). They're available at the **Hon Dah Convenience Store** (☎ **520/369-4311**) at the junction of Ariz. 260 and Ariz. 73, and **Hawley Lake Store** (☎ **520/335-7511**), south of Ariz. 260 between Hon Dah and Sunrise.

Several golf courses in the area are open to the public, including **Pinetop Lakes Golf Club** (☎ **520/369-4531**), Buck Springs Road, Pinetop-Lakeside; **Silver Creek Golf Club** (☎ **520/537-2744**), White Mountain Lake Road, Show Low; and the **Show Low Country Club** (☎ **520/537-4564**), Ariz. 260 and Old Linden Road, Show Low.

About 50 miles south of Show Low, U.S. 60 crosses a bridge over the narrow, scenic canyon of the Salt River. This stretch of the Salt River is a favorite of white-water rafters, and several companies offer rafting trips of varying lengths on this stretch of the river. Some of these companies include **Far Flung Adventures** (☎ **800/231-7238** or 520/425-7272; www.farflung.com), **Sun Country Rafting** (☎ **800/272-3353** or 602/493-9011), and **Mild to Wild Rafting** (☎ **800/567-6745**). Prices range from around $80 to $100 for a day trip up to around $650 for a multiday trip.

MORE TO SEE & DO

Fort Apache Historic Park (☎ 520/338-4625), in the town of Fort Apache, which along with the White Mountain Apache Reservation was established in 1870 by the U.S. government. The park, approximately 22 miles south of Pinetop on Ariz. 73, now encompasses almost 300 acres, including more than 20 buildings, prehistoric ruins, a reconstructed Apache village, petroglyphs, and the Apache Museum/Cultural Center. The cultural center is open Monday to Friday 8am to 5pm (also on Saturday in the summer). Admission is $3 for adults and children 6 and older and $2 for seniors.

Also in this area, you'll find **Kinishba Ruins,** which are up a gravel road 1 mile west of Fort Apache on Ariz. 73. This 200-room pueblo ruin is more than 1,000 years old and was visited by Coronado when he passed through this region in search of the Seven Cities of Cíbola. Get directions to the ruins at the cultural center.

For more information on visiting the White Mountain Apache Reservation, contact the **White Mountain Apache Office of Tourism** (☎ 520/338-1230), which is also in Fort Apache Historic Park.

If you're looking for something to do after dark, you can head out to the **Hon-Dah Casino** (☎ 800/WAY-UP-HI or 520/369-0299), which is owned and operated by the White Mountain Apache Tribe. It's open daily around the clock and is at the junction of Ariz. 73 and Ariz. 260, about 4 miles east of Pinetop.

A PLEASANT VALLEY DETOUR

If you're looking for a bit of backroads adventure, you might want to head south from the Mogollon Rim to the remote community of Young, which sits in the middle of the aptly named Pleasant Valley. However, be prepared for a lot of miles on gravel roads. You see, although there are paved roads in Young itself, the town can be reached only via well-graded gravel roads (24 miles of gravel if you come from the north or 32 miles of gravel if you come from the south).

Why visit Young? Mostly people come here just to see the land that spawned the worst range war and family feud in the west. Known as the Pleasant Valley War or Graham-Tewksbury Feud, the range war, which likely erupted over conflicts over sheep grazing in the valley, was waged on this land in the 1880s and took dozens of lives. Zane Grey memorialized the feud in his novel *To the Last Man.*

You'll find Young on Ariz. 288, which runs from Ariz. 88 north of Globe (near Theodore Roosevelt Lake) to Ariz. 260 about midway between Payson and Heber.

WHERE TO STAY

Hon-Dah Resort. Ariz. 260 and Ariz. 73, Hon-Dah, AZ 85935. ☎ 800/WAY-UP-HI or 520/369-0299. Fax 520/369-7504. 130 units. A/C TV TEL. $79–$109 double; $150–$180 suite. AE, DISC, MC, V.

This hotel, adjacent to the Hon-Dah Casino a few miles east of Pinetop-Lakeside, is the largest and most luxurious hotel in the White Mountains, and, as with most casino hotels, this place is designed to impress. The portico is big enough to hold a basketball court, and inside the front door, there's an artificial rock wall on which are mounted stuffed animals, including a cougar, bobcat, bear, ducks, and even a bugling elk. Guest rooms are for the most part very large with big bathrooms and refrigerators. Amenities include two restaurants and two lounges, a year-round outdoor heated swimming pool, a whirlpool, and a sauna. The casino, however, is the hotel's main draw.

Lake of the Woods. Ariz. 260 (P.O. Box 777), Lakeside, AZ 85929. ☎ **520/368-5353.** www.privatelake.com. 27 units. TV. $49–$163 cabin for 2; $90–$294 house for 2. 3–5-night minimum summer and some holidays. DISC, MC, V.

Located on its own private lake right on Ariz. 260, Lake of the Woods is a rustic mountain resort that caters primarily to families. Cabins and houses range from tiny to huge, with rustic and modern side by side. The smallest sleep two or three, while the largest house sleeps 18, and several have kitchens and fireplaces. Some are on the edge of the lake while others are tucked away under the pines, so be sure to request a location away from the busy highway. Also, because cabins vary considerably in their quality, ask for a newer cabin. Kids in particular love this place. They can fish in the lake, row a boat, or play in the snow. The resort also offers a whirlpool, sauna, exercise equipment, table tennis, pool table, shuffleboard, horseshoes, a playground, and coin-operated laundry.

✪ **Rawhide & Roses.** 5130 S. Flores Dr. (P.O. Box 1153), Lakeside, AZ 85929. ☎ **888/418-5963** or 520/537-0216. www.rawhide-roses.com. 3 units. A/C TV. $95–$125 double. Rates include full breakfast. DISC, MC, V. From the hospital on Ariz. 260 west of Pinetop-Lakeside, go south on Cub Lake Rd., turn left on Flores Dr. and left again on S. Flores Dr.

Set among tall pines at the end of a rutted gravel road, this large log home is a surprising escape from the commercial clutter of Pinetop-Lakeside's main drag. Here, amid the pines, you'll find very tasteful Eddie Bauer–style decor and furnishings, and seemingly everywhere you turn are rock and wood architectural details. In the living room is a big stone fireplace, and in the dining room, an antler chandelier hangs above an alligator juniper table. In the high-ceilinged game room, you'll find a pool table, and out on the deck, there's a hammock for lazy afternoons. A split-log open staircase leads up to the second floor and to the three guest rooms, each of which has its own fireplace. Despite the name, Geronimo's Room, with its fireplace and adjacent rock-surrounded whirlpool tub, is the inn's most romantic room.

✪ **Sierra Springs Ranch.** HC 62, Box 32100, Pinetop, AZ 85935. ☎ **800/492-4059** or 520/369-3900. Fax 520/369-0741. www.sierrasspringsranch.com. 8 units. TV. $175 cabin for 2; $225 and up for larger cabins. 2-night minimum stay (longer minimum on holidays and in summer). AE, MC, V.

Located off a gravel road east of Pinetop, the Sierra Springs Ranch is the most upscale property around and as idyllic a mountain retreat as you'll find in Arizona. Set in a wide clearing in the forest, each of the eight cabins is a little bit different, but all are large and comfortable (the largest cabin sleeps 13). Our favorite is the honeymoon cottage, which is built of logs and has a stone fireplace. All the cabins have full kitchens, which make up for the lack of a restaurant on the premises.

On the ranch grounds you'll find a trout pond and meadows, a tennis court, and a walking/jogging path. Fishing gear, tennis racquets, and bicycles are all available for guests to use.

CAMPGROUNDS

There are four campgrounds in the immediate Pinetop-Lakeside area, including Show Low Lake, Fool Hollow, Lewis Canyon, and Lakeside. Of these, **Show Low Lake County Park** (☎ 520/537-4126) and **Fool Hollow Lake Recreation Area** (☎ 520/537-3680) are the nicest. There are also numerous campgrounds nearby on the White River Apache Indian Reservation. For information about these campgrounds, contact the **White Mountain Wildlife and Outdoor Recreation Division** (☎ 520/338-4385; www.wmatoutdoors.com) or the **Fort Apache Office of Tourism** (☎ 520/338-1230).

WHERE TO DINE

In addition to the places mentioned below and a few basic burger and steak places in town, there's **Eddie's Country Store,** on Ariz. 260 at the east end of Pinetop (☎ **520/ 367-2161**), where you can get an inexpensive breakfast and a variety of burgers and sandwiches made with applewood-smoked meats. Also, the food at the Hon-Dah Casino gets praises from locals, and the prices are very reasonable (if you can resist the temptation to spend some time at the slot machines).

Charlie Clark's Steak House. Ariz. 260 at Penrod Ave., Pinetop. ☎ **520/367-4900.** Main courses $10–$22. AE, DC, MC, V. Daily 5–9pm. STEAKS.

Charlie Clark's has been serving up thick, juicy steaks since 1938 and is the oldest steakhouse in the White Mountains. Mesquite-broiled steaks and chicken, as well as seafood and prime rib, fill the menu. To find Charlie Clark's, just look for the building with a fake horse on the roof.

The Christmas Tree Restaurant. 455 Woodland Rd., Lakeside. ☎ **520/367-3107.** Reservations recommended on Saturday. Main courses $10–$30. DISC, MC, V. Wed–Sun 5–9pm. AMERICAN/CONTINENTAL.

Located in a quiet setting off the main drag, this country restaurant serves good old-fashioned American food as well as a few standard continental offerings. Chicken and dumplings are the specialty of the house, but you can also get a good New York steak accompanied by your choice of seafood. Meals are large and filling and come with everything from delicious pickled beets to Boston clam chowder. As the name implies, a Christmas theme prevails here year-round, and there's also a country gift store.

3 Greer & Sunrise Park

51 miles SE of Show Low; 98 miles SE of Holbrook; 222 miles NE of Phoenix

The tiny community of Greer, set in the lush meadows on either side of the Little Colorado River and surrounded by forests, holds the distinction of being the most picturesque mountain community in Arizona. The elevation of 8,525 feet ensures plenty of snow in winter and pleasantly cool temperatures in summer, and together these two factors have turned Greer into a very popular vacation village. Greer has become something of an upscale mountain getaway town and is quite popular with wealthy, in-the-know Phoenix residents. Modern log homes are springing up all over the valley, but Greer is still free of the sort of strip-mall developments that have forever changed the character of Payson and Pinetop-Lakeside.

The Little Colorado River, which flows through the middle of Greer on its way to the Grand Canyon, is little more than a babbling brook up here. Still, it's well known for trout fishing, which is one of the main draws in these parts. Several lakes and ponds in the area also provide good fishing. In winter there are more than 12 miles of cross-country ski trails around Greer, and ice-skating, ice fishing, and sleigh rides are also popular. Additionally, Greer happens to be the closest town to the Sunrise ski area, which is what gives the village its ski resort atmosphere. There are several rustic mountain lodges and a number of rental-cabin operations here.

ESSENTIALS

GETTING THERE   From Phoenix, take U.S. 87 north to Payson and then go east on Ariz. 260, or take U.S. 60 east from Phoenix through Globe and Show Low to Ariz. 260 east. Greer is just a few miles south of Ariz. 260 on Ariz. 373.

VISITOR INFORMATION   For information on the Greer area, contact the **Round Valley Chamber of Commerce,** P.O. Box 31, Springerville, AZ 85938 (☎ 520/333-2123).

ENJOYING THE OUTDOORS

Winter is one of the busiest seasons in Greer, since it is so close to the **Sunrise Park Resort** ski area (☎ 520/735-7669; www.sunriseskipark.com). Located just off Ariz. 260 on Ariz. 273, this ski area, the largest and most popular in Arizona, is operated by the White Mountain Apache Tribe. The ski area usually opens in November, but winter thaws and long stretches without snow can make winters a bit unreliable (snowmaking machines enhance the sometimes sparse natural snowfall). Although there are some good advanced runs, beginner and intermediate skiers will be in heaven. We've rarely seen so many green runs starting from the uppermost lifts of a ski area, all of which translates into a very family-oriented ski area. At the top of 11,000-foot Apache Peak is a day lodge providing meals and a view that goes on forever. There's also a ski school that offers lessons for everyone from beginners to advanced skiers. Lift tickets are $34 for adults and $19 for children. Ski rentals are available here and at numerous shops in Pinetop-Lakeside.

Here at Sunrise, there are more than 13.5 kilometers of groomed cross-country ski trails that wind their way through forests of ponderosa pines and across high snow-covered meadows. These trails begin at the **Sunrise Sports Center,** located in the service station at the turnoff for the downhill area. There are also good opportunities for cross-country skiing in Greer, which has 35 miles of developed trails. At 8,500 feet, the alpine scenery here is quiet and serene. You can also go for a sleigh ride near Sunrise. They're offered by **Lee Valley Outfitters/High Country Stables** (☎ 520/735-7454), which charges $10 for a 20-minute ride or $16 for a 45-minute ride.

Come summer the cross-country ski trails in Greer become **mountain-bike trails,** and when combined with the nearby **Poll Knoll trail system,** provide mountain bikers with 35 miles of trails of varying degrees of difficulty. Sunrise Park Resort also opens up its slopes to mountain bikers. Bikes can be rented for $15 to $25 for 1 to 2 hours, and a lift ticket for the day will run you another $15.

This area offers some of the finest mountain **hiking** in Arizona, and most popular of all the area trails is the hike up 11,590-foot **Mount Baldy,** the second-highest peak in Arizona. This peak lies on the edge of the White Mountain Apache Indian Reservation and is sacred to the Apaches. Consequently, the summit is off limits to non-Apaches. There are two trailheads for the hike up Mount Baldy. The most popular and scenic route begins 6 miles south of Sunrise Ski Resort (off the gravel extension of Ariz. 273) and follows the West Fork of the Little Colorado River. This trail climbs roughly 2,000 feet and is moderately strenuous, although the high elevation often leaves lowland hikers gasping for breath. Hikers can also catch a lift to the top of the hill at Sunrise Ski Resort, which keeps its lifts running in the summer months for hikers and anyone else interested in the view from on high. A single-ride lift ticket is $6.

To explore the Greer area from the back of a horse, contact **Lee Valley Outfitters/High Country Stables** (☎ 520/735-7454), which is located between Greer and Ariz. 260 and offers rides of varying lengths ($20 for 1 hour, $32 for 2 hours). This company also does wagon rides and cookout rides.

The three Greer Lakes on the outskirts of town—Bunch, River, and Tunnel reservoirs—are popular fishing spots. All three lakes hold brown and rainbow trout. On River Reservoir, try fishing the shallows at the south end. On Tunnel Reservoir, you can often do well fishing from shore, especially if fly-fishing, but there is a boat launch.

However, it is Big Lake, south of Greer, that has the biggest fishing reputation around these parts. Fishing is also good on Sunrise Lake, but be sure to get a White Mountain Apache Indian Reservation fishing license (available at the Sunrise service station). If you'd like a guide to take you out for a day of fishing the Arizona high country, contact **Troutback Flyfishing Guide Service,** P.O. Box 864, Show Low, AZ 85902 (☎ **800/903-4092** or 520/532-3474; www.troutback.com), which charges $175 per day for one angler and $250 for two anglers.

Sunrise Lake, near the Sunrise ski area, is a popular spot in the summer when boat rentals (including small sailboats) are available. A fishing boat with an outboard motor rents for $45 per day.

A MUSEUM

The **Butterfly Lodge Museum** (☎ **520/735-7514**) is a restored historic cabin built in 1914. Once owned by James Willard Schultz (a writer) and his son Hart Merriam Schultz (a painter), the museum is a memorial to these two unusual and creative individuals who once called Greer home. The museum, located just off Ariz. 373 between Ariz. 260 and Greer, is open Friday to Sunday and holidays, 10am to 5pm.

WHERE TO STAY
IN GREER

Cattle Kate's Bed and Breakfast. 80 N. Main St. (P.O. Box 21), Greer, AZ 85927. ☎ **520/735-7744.** Fax 520/735-7386. www.wmonline.com/cattlekates. 9 units. $85 double; $125 suite. Rates include continental breakfast. AE, MC, V.

Consisting of several new log buildings with a classic mountain feel, Cattle Kate's seems to have patterned itself after the nearby Greer Lodge and is every bit as comfortable. The rooms, although spartanly furnished in classic Western style, have high ceilings and look out on small trout ponds (fly-fishing lessons available) and the meadows along the Little Colorado River. In the large breakfast room, an elk head is mounted over the fireplace, and an antler chandelier hangs from the ceiling. The only real drawback here is that you are right on the main road through Greer; however, this road is rarely very busy.

Greer Lodge. 44 Main St. (P.O. Box 244), Greer, AZ 85927. ☎ **888/475-6343** or 520/735-7216. Fax 520/735-7720. www.greerlodge.com. 11 units. $120 double; $95 cabin for 2; $210–$280 house. AE, DC, DISC, MC, V.

Located only 20 minutes from the Sunrise ski area and with its own trout ponds and section of the Little Colorado River, this old lodge is popular with both skiers and anglers. Rooms in the main lodge all have nice views of the mountains or river but tend to get quite a lot of noise from the lobby (which doubles as a TV room). If you're seeking quiet, request a cabin, although these have not been well maintained in recent years. The hotel also offers ice skating, cross-country ski trails, volleyball, horseshoes, a barbecue area, and fishing ponds. The lodge's multilevel restaurant has walls of glass that look out over a river, meadows, and a trout pond, and in the winter there's a cozy fireplace. Dinner entrees range from $13 to $21.

The Peaks at Greer. P.O. Box 132, Greer, AZ 85927. ☎ **800/556-9997** or 520/735-7777. Fax 520/735-7204. www.peaksresort.com. 19 units. $79–$119 double; $119–$159 suite; $99–$119 cabin for 2. Rates include continental breakfast. AE, DISC, MC, V. Pets accepted in cabins.

Located on a hill just past Greer Lodge, this is the most luxurious of Greer's handful of full-service hotels. In the high-ceilinged lobby are huge overstuffed chairs in front of the fireplace and exposed log beams overhead. Guest rooms are comfortable and modern, and many are quite large. Suites have their own fireplaces, as do the much more rustic cabins, which are a bit older than the rest of the hotel (but still fairly well maintained). La Ventana, the lodge's restaurant, is one of the best in town, and serves decent southwestern fare in the $10 to $20 range. There's also a small bar with a big deck and good views. Amenities include a hot tub and game room.

✪ **Red Setter Inn & Cottage.** P.O. Box 133, Greer, AZ 85927. ☎ **888/99-GREER** or 520/735-7441. Fax 520/735-7425. www.redsetterinn.com. 12 units. $130–$195 double; $550 cottage (8-person maximum). Rates include full breakfast. AE, MC, V.

If you're headed up to the mountains for a romantic weekend getaway, this three-story log lodge, the most luxurious in Greer, should be your first choice. Several of the guest rooms have fireplaces and whirlpool tubs that make them just right for a quiet weekend together. Other rooms have vaulted ceilings, some with skylights. The inn is built on the bank of the Little Colorado River, which is only steps away from the decks of some rooms. If you stay for 2 nights or more, you get a complimentary picnic lunch to take with you on an outing. Cases full of antique toys and a game room with old arcade games make this inn fun as well as romantic. There is also a housekeeping "cottage" with four bedrooms, three bathrooms, and three fireplaces.

✪ **Snowy Mountain Inn.** P.O. Box 337, Greer, AZ 85927. ☎ **520/735-7576.** Fax 520/735-7705. www.snowymountain.net. 14 units. $85–$100 double; $110–$285 cabin or house. Room rates include continental breakfast. 3- to 5-night minimums during busy times. MC, V. Short-haired pets accepted during summer ($15 per day).

Set back from the main road down a gravel driveway and shaded by tall pines, the Snowy Mountain Lodge has a very remote yet very comfortable feel about it. For couples, the lodge rooms are a good deal. Some of these rooms have gas fireplaces and/or whirlpool tubs. The large modern cabins are perfect for family vacations and come with gas fireplaces, porches, and sleeping lofts; some have private hot tubs. Surrounding the log cabins and main lodge building are 100 acres of private forest, so guests have plenty of room to roam, and the 1 1/2-acre trout pond is one of the largest in the area.

White Mountain Lodge Bed & Breakfast and Cabins. 140 Main St. (P.O. Box 143), Greer, AZ 85927. ☎ **888/493-7568** or 520/735-7568. Fax 520/735-7498. 11 units. $85–$95 double; $85–$195 cabin for 2. Lodge room rates include full breakfast. 2-night minimum on weekends, 3 to 4 nights on holidays. DC, DISC, MC, V. Pets accepted ($20 charge).

Situated on the road into Greer with a view across an open, marshy stretch of the valley, this recently remodeled lodge was built in 1892 and is the oldest building in Greer (but you'd never know it to look at it). Knotty pine throughout gives the lodge a classic cabin feel, but the many large windows prevent the rooms from feeling too dark. Guest rooms are done up in a Southwestern or country theme, and our favorite has a king-size bed and a view up the valley. However, the cabins, which are perfect for families or two couples, are even more comfortable. One has a stone fireplace and a porch swing.

IN MCNARY

Sunrise Park Lodge. Hwy. 273, near intersection of Hwy. 260 (P.O. Box 217), McNary, AZ 85930. ☎ **800/772-7669** or 520/735-7669. Fax 520/735-7315. www.sunriseskipark.com. 100 units. A/C TV TEL. Winter $59–$112 double, $195–$295 suite; summer $59–$72 double, $195 suite. AE, DC, DISC, MC, V.

Located 20 miles outside Greer in McNary, this is the closest lodge to the Sunrise ski area and thus a favorite of downhill skiers. About half the rooms overlook Sunrise

Lake, and they are worth requesting. The restaurant here is about your only dinner option in the vicinity; there's also a cozy lounge for après-ski drinks. The hotel offers a ski area shuttle bus, tiny indoor swimming pool, indoor and outdoor whirlpools, sauna, exercise room, volleyball, and rental bikes.

CAMPGROUNDS

In the immediate vicinity of Greer, there are three campgrounds on Apache-Sitgreaves National Forest. There are also several campgrounds nearby on the White Mountain Apache Indian Reservation (no reservations accepted). Reservations can be made for the Rolfe C. Hoyer Campground 1 mile north of Greer on Ariz. 373 and the Winn Campground 12 miles southwest of Greer on Ariz. 273 (the road past Sunrise Ski Resort) by contacting the **National Recreation Reservation Service** (☎ **800/ 280-2267;** www.reserveusa.com). Benny Creek, 2 miles north of Greer, does not take reservations. Because of its proximity to Greer and the Greer lakes, Rolfe C. Hoyer is the top choice in the area.

WHERE TO DINE

Your best bets for meals in Greer are the dining rooms at the Greer Lodge and The Peaks at Greer, both of which serve reasonably priced meals and have good views of the valley. Both restaurants serve a bit of Southwestern fare plus familiar American standards. Hours vary considerably with the seasons and the snowfall. See "Where to Stay," above, for details.

4 Springerville & Eagar

56 miles E of Show Low; 82 miles SE of Holbrook; 227 miles NE of Phoenix

Together the adjacent towns of Springerville and Eagar constitute the northeastern gateway to the White Mountains. Although the towns themselves are at the foot of the mountains, the vistas from around the two towns take in all the area's peaks. Springerville and Eagar like to play up their Wild West backgrounds, and in fact, John Wayne liked the area so much that he had a ranch along the Little Colorado River just west of Eagar. Today large ranches still run their cattle on the windswept plains north of the two towns.

It was volcanic activity between 300,000 and 700,000 years ago that gave the land north of Springerville and Eagar its distinctive character. This area is known as the Springerville Volcanic Field—the third largest volcanic field of its kind in the continental United States (the San Francisco Field near Flagstaff and the Medicine Lake Field in California are both larger). The Springerville Volcanic Field covers an area bigger than the state of Rhode Island and contains 405 extinct volcanic vents. However, it is the many cinder cones dotting the landscape that give this region such a distinctive appearance. For a brochure outlining a tour of the volcanic field, contact the Round Valley Chamber of Commerce (see "Visitor Information," below).

One other thing you might be curious about is that big dome—it's the Round Valley Ensphere, one of the only domed high school football stadiums in the country.

ESSENTIALS

GETTING THERE Springerville and Eagar are in the northeast corner of the White Mountains at the junction of U.S. 60, U.S. 180/191, and Ariz. 260. From the Phoenix area, there are two routes: Ariz. 87 north to Payson and then Ariz. 260 east, or U.S. 60 east to Globe and then north to Show Low and on to Springerville (alternatively, you can take Ariz. 260 from Show Low to Springerville). From Holbrook,

Cowboy Golf

If you've spent much time in Arizona souvenir shops, you've probably seen humorous drawings of cowboys playing golf on the range. Well, each year in June, the **X Diamond Ranch** (☎ **520/333-2286;** www.xdiamondranch.com) west of Springerville actually does hold a cowboy golf tournament. What sets cowboy golf apart from regular golf? Well, first of all, the caddies are horses. Then there's the golfers' attire—cowboy boots, blue jeans, and cowboy hats. And, of course, there are the coffee-can holes and the tall-grass fairways, which are really just cow pastures, filled with all the hazards one would expect in a cow pasture. (A chip shot on this golf course can be a very messy affair!)

take U.S. 180 southeast to St. Johns and U.S. 180/191 south to Springerville. From southern Arizona, U.S. 191 is slow but very scenic.

VISITOR INFORMATION   For information on the Springerville and Eagar areas, contact the **Round Valley Chamber of Commerce,** P.O. Box 31, Springerville, AZ 85938 (☎ **520/333-2123**).

ANASAZI RUINS

Casa Malpais Archaeological Park. 318 Main St., Springerville. ☎ **520/333-5375.** www.casamalpais.com. Guided tours $5 adults, $4 students and seniors, $3 children under 12. Daily 9am–4pm.

These Mogollon culture ruins, just outside Springerville, can also be visited, but you won't be able to do any digging. Casa Malpais is unique in that the pueblo, which dates from A.D. 1250 and was occupied until about 600 years ago, was built to take advantage of existing caves. Many of these caves form a system of catacombs under the pueblo. The Casa Malpais museum is located downtown; it is from here that tours start.

Lyman Lake State Park. 18 miles north of Springerville. ☎ **520/337-4441.** Admission $4 per car; tours $2 per person. Park, daily daytime hours; tours, May–September).

Within this state park are the early Anasazi ruins of Rattlesnake Point Pueblo, as well as petroglyphs that date back to 10,000 B.C. Some of the petroglyphs are accessible only by boat, and during the summer months you can see them on guided tours.

✪ **White Mountain Archaeological Center/Raven Site Ruin.** H.C. 30, Box 30, St. Johns, AZ 85936. ☎ **888/333-5859** or 520/333-5857. www.ravensite.com. Hands-on programs $59 adults, $39 children 9–17 (children under 9 not accepted); tours $4 adults, $3 seniors and children 12–17; petroglyph hikes $18 adults, $12 children. May 1–Oct 15, daily 10am–4pm. 12 miles north of Springerville off U.S. 180/191.

If you've ever dreamed of being an archaeologist, you've got a chance to do just that here in eastern Arizona. This field school and research center is located on a 5-acre pueblo site where Mogollon and Anasazi artifacts have been found. Hands-on archaeological programs allow visitors to assist in excavating this site while learning the basics of archaeology. Tours of the ruins, both guided and self-guided, and hikes to a nearby area rich in petroglyphs are also offered.

MUSEUMS

Also in the area are a couple of small museums worth a look if you have the time. The **Reneé Cushman Art Collection** is housed in the L.D.S. (Mormon) Church in

Springerville and consists of one woman's personal collection of European art and antiques. Among the works in the collection are an etching attributed to Rembrandt and three pen-and-ink drawings by Tiepolo. The antique furniture dates back to the Renaissance. The museum is open by appointment only; arrange a visit through the Round Valley Chamber of Commerce (☎ **520/333-2123**).

Local history and old automated musical instruments are the focus of the **Little House Museum** (☎ **520/333-2286**), 7 miles west of Eagar on South Fork Road, off Ariz. 260. Tales of colorful Wild West characters as told by your guide are as much a part of the museum as the displays themselves. The museum is open late May through Labor Day, with 90-minute tours offered Thursday to Sunday at 11am and 1pm. Tours cost $5 for adults and $2 for children 12 and under.

OUTDOOR ACTIVITIES

If you're interested in fishing, contact **Troutback Flyfishing Guide Service,** P.O. Box 864, Show Low, AZ 85902 (☎ **800/903-4092** or 520/532-3474; www.troutback. com), which charges $175 per day for one angler and $250 for two. Alternatively, you can head out to the **X Diamond Ranch** (☎ **520/333-2286**), which is off Ariz. 260 between Eagar and Greer (take County Road 4124). The ranch maintains a section of the Little Colorado River as a fishing habitat. A half-day of fishing here will cost $25, and a full day will cost $35.

Lyman Lake State Park (☎ **520/337-4441**), 18 miles north of Springerville, is also popular for lake fishing. And if it's high summer and you feel like swimming, this is the place to take a dip or even plan a day of water-skiing or sailing.

WHERE TO STAY

✪ **Paisley Corner Bed & Breakfast.** 287 N. Main St. (P.O. Box 458), Eagar, AZ 85938.
☎ **520/333-4665.** www.wmbba.com. 4 units. $65–$95 double. Rates include full breakfast. MC, V.

This lovingly restored 1910-vintage colonial-revival house in Eagar is one of the most authentic B&Bs we've visited and as such is one of our favorites in the state. (For authentic, read Victorian antiques and dark color schemes.) However, in contrast there is also a room done up to resemble an old soda fountain, complete with vintage jukeboxes and an old telephone booth in one corner. The inn's kitchen features a 1910 gas stove and looks as though it came straight out of a 1920s Sears and Roebuck catalog. Guest rooms on the second floor have antique beds, and two have bathrooms with clawfoot tubs and old pull-chain toilets.

X Diamond Ranch. P.O. Box 791, Springerville, AZ 85938. ☎ **520/333-2286.** Fax 520/333-5009. www.xdiamondranch.com. 5 units. $95–$175 double. DISC, MC, V. Off Ariz. 260 between Eagar and Greer (take County Road 4124).

Long known for its Little House Museum and trout fishing on the Little Colorado River, this ranch also rents a variety of cabins ranging from an updated old log cabin to a couple of new cabins. Ranch activities include fishing, horseback riding, and tours of the ranch's two archaeological sites (for $10 per hour, you can also help excavate these ruin sites). Perhaps most surprising of all, there's a small day spa on the ranch. There's no restaurant on the premises, but cabins have full kitchens.

CAMPGROUNDS

Lyman Lake State Park (☎ **520/337-4441**), 18 miles north of Springerville on U.S. 180/191, has a campground. However, it is very popular with water-skiers, so don't expect much peace and quiet.

WHERE TO DINE

There aren't a whole lot of dining options in this area; try **Booga Red's,** 521 Main St., Springerville (☎ **520/333-2640**), which serves burgers, steaks, and Mexican food in the $4 to $11 range.

5 The Coronado Trail

Alpine: 28 miles S of Springerville & Eagar; 95 miles N of Clifton & Morenci; 75 miles E of Pinetop-Lakeside

If you are not prone to car sickness, you may want to take a leisurely drive down the Coronado Trail (U.S. 191). This is one of the most remote and little-traveled paved roads in the state, winding southward from Springerville and Eagar to the Clifton and Morenci area. Because this road is so narrow and winding, it is slow going—the sort of road meant for people who aren't in a hurry to get anywhere anytime soon.

The Coronado Trail is named for the Spanish explorer Francisco Vásquez de Coronado, who came to Arizona in search of gold in the early 1540s. Although he never found it, his party did make it as far north as the Hopi pueblos and would have traveled through this region on their march northward from Mexico. Centuries later the discovery of huge copper reserves would make the fortunes of the towns of Clifton and Morenci, which lie at the southern end of the Coronado Trail.

However, it is **Alpine,** at the northern end of the Coronado Trail, that is the main base for today's explorers, who tend to be outdoor types in search of uncrowded trails and trout streams where the fish are still biting. In Alpine, which is not far from the New Mexico state line, you'll find a few basic lodges and restaurants and easy access to the region's many trails.

This area is known as the Alps of Arizona, and Alpine's picturesque setting in the middle of a wide grassy valley at 8,030 feet certainly lives up to this image. Alpine is surrounded by **Apache–Sitgreaves National Forest,** which has miles of hiking trails and several campgrounds. In spring, wildflowers abound and the trout fishing is excellent. In summer, there's hiking on forest trails. In autumn, the aspens in the Golden Bowl on the mountainside above Alpine turn a brilliant yellow, and in winter, there's cross-country skiing and ice fishing.

ESSENTIALS

GETTING THERE   Alpine is 28 miles south of Springerville and Eagar at the junction of U.S. 191, which continues south to Clifton and Morenci, and U.S. 180, which leads east into New Mexico.

VISITOR INFORMATION   For more information on this area, contact the **Alpine Area Chamber of Commerce,** P.O. Box 410, Alpine, AZ 85920 (☎ **520/ 339-4330**). For outdoor information, contact the Apache–Sitgreaves National Forest's **Alpine Ranger District,** P.O. Box 469, Alpine, AZ 85920 (☎ **520/339-4384**).

ENJOYING THE OUTDOORS

Fall, when the aspens turn the mountainside gold, is probably the most popular time of year in this area—there are only a few places in Arizona where fall color is worth a drive, and this is one of them.

Not far outside Alpine, there is cross-country skiing at the **Williams Valley Winter Recreation Area,** which doubles as a mountain-biking trail system in summer. On the first weekend in January, there are dog sled races in Alpine.

In Alpine you can also play a round of golf at the **Alpine Country Club** (☎ **520/ 339-4944**), 3 miles east of town off U.S. 180. At 8,500 feet in elevation, this is one of the highest golf courses in the country.

If you're looking for fish to catch, try **Luna Lake,** which is east of Alpine off U.S. 180. Here at the lake, you'll also find some easy to moderate mountain-bike trails that usually offer good wildlife-viewing opportunities.

The best hiking in the area is the trail up **Escudilla Mountain** just outside Alpine. It is here you'll see some of the best displays of aspens in the autumn.

Summer or winter, **Hannagan Meadows,** 23 miles south of Alpine, is the place to be. Here you'll find excellent hiking, mountain biking, and cross-country ski trails. Hannagan Meadows also provides access to the **Blue Range Primitive Area,** which is popular with hikers. The Eagle Trail, which starts 5 miles south of Hannagan Meadows off Eagle Creek Road, is another good place to spot wildlife. It is in the remote wilderness areas near here that a Mexican wolf recovery project has been underway for the past few years. The reintroduction has so far met with mixed success, as wolves have been killed by cars, people, disease, and even mountain lions. Some of the wolves have had to be recaptured because they had strayed out of the area set aside for them or because they had had encounters with humans.

WHERE TO STAY & DINE

Between Springerville/Eagar and Clifton/Morenci, there are nearly a dozen National Forest Service campgrounds. One particularly popular spot is **Luna Lake Campground** just east of Alpine on U.S. 180. The **Hannagan Meadows Campground** (no reservations) is also popular and makes a good base for exploring the Coronado Trail. Reservations are taken for Luna Lake Campground by contacting the **National Recreation Reservation Service** (☎ **800/280-2267;** www.reserveusa.com). For information on these campgrounds, contact the **Alpine Ranger District** (☎ **520/339-4384**).

If you're looking for someplace to eat, you'll find a couple of basic restaurants in Alpine.

Tal-Wi-Wi Lodge. U.S. 191 (P.O. Box 169), Alpine, AZ 85920. ☎ **520/339-4319.** Fax 520/339-1962. www.talwiwilodge.com. 20 units. $65–$95 double. 2-night minimum on holidays. MC, V. Dogs accepted ($5).

Located 3 miles north of Alpine on U.S. 191, the Tal-Wi-Wi Lodge is nothing fancy (just a rustic lodge popular with anglers and hunters), but it's the best place to stay in the Alpine area. The deluxe rooms come with their own hot tub or woodstove (one room comes with both), and these heat sources are well appreciated on cold winter nights (Alpine is often the coldest town in Arizona). The furnishings in the guest rooms are rustic and comfortable, and the wood-paneled walls and large front porches give the lodge a classic country flavor. The lodge's dining room serves country breakfasts and dinners.

Tucson 9

Encircled by mountain ranges and bookended by the two units of Saguaro National Park, Tucson is Arizona's second largest city, and for the vacationer it has everything that Phoenix has to offer plus a bit more. There are world-class golf resorts, excellent restaurants, art museums and galleries, an active cultural life, and, of course, plenty of great weather. However, Tucson has a long history that melds Native American, Hispanic, and Anglo roots, and perhaps even more important, Tucson, with a national park, a national forest, and other natural areas just beyond the city limits, is a city that celebrates its Sonoran Desert setting.

At Saguaro National Park, you can marvel at the massive saguaro cacti that have come to symbolize the desert Southwest, while at the Arizona–Sonora Desert Museum (actually a zoo), you can acquaint yourself with the myriad flora and fauna of this region. Take a hike or a horseback ride up one of the trails that leads into the wilderness from the edge of the city, and you might even meet up with a few desert denizens on their own turf. Look beyond the saguaros and prickly pears, and you'll find a desert oasis, complete with waterfalls and swimming holes, and, a short drive from the city, a pine forest that's home to the southernmost ski area in the United States.

Founded by the Spanish in 1775, Tucson is built on the site of a much older Native American village. The city's name comes from the Pima Indian word *chukeson,* which means "spring at the base of black mountain," a reference to the peak now known simply as "A Mountain." From 1867 to 1877, Tucson was the territorial capital of Arizona, but eventually the capital was moved to Phoenix. Consequently, Tucson did not develop as quickly as Phoenix and still holds fast to its Hispanic and Western heritage.

Tucson has a history of valuing quality of life over development. Back in the days of urban renewal, Tucson's citizens turned back the bulldozers and managed to preserve at least some of the city's old Mexican character. Likewise, today, in the face of the sort of sprawl that has given Phoenix the feel of a landlocked Los Angeles, advocates for controlled growth are fighting hard to preserve both Tucson's desert environment and the city's unique character.

The struggle to retain an identity distinct from other Southwestern cities is ongoing, and despite long, drawn-out attempts to breathe life into the city's downtown core area, known as the Tucson Downtown

Arts District, the past few years have seen the loss of downtown's vibrancy as shops, galleries, and restaurants have moved out to the suburbs. However, downtown Tucson still has its art museum, convention center, and historic neighborhoods, and there is still a belief that this part of the city will one day find its stride.

Despite this minor shortcoming, Tucson remains Arizona's most beautiful and most livable city. With the Santa Catalina Mountains for a backdrop, the city boasts one of the most dramatic settings in the Southwest, and whether you're taking in the mountain vistas from the tee box of the 12th hole, the saddle of a palomino, or a table for two, we're sure you'll agree that Tucson makes a superb winter vacation destination.

1 Orientation

Not nearly as large and spread out as Phoenix and the Valley of the Sun, Tucson is small enough to be convenient, yet large enough to be sophisticated. Compared to Phoenix, the mountains ringing the city of Tucson are bigger and closer to town, and the desert is equally close.

ARRIVING

BY PLANE   Located 6 miles south of downtown, **Tucson International Airport** (☎ 520/573-8000) is served by many airlines, including **Aero México** (☎ 800/237-6639), **America West** (☎ 800/235-9292), **American** (☎ 800/433-7300), **Continental** (☎ 800/525-0280), **Delta** (☎ 800/221-1212), **Northwest/KLM** (☎ 800/225-2525), **Shuttle by United** (☎ 800/748-8853), **Skywest** (☎ 800/453-9417), **Southwest** (☎ 800/435-9792), and **United** (☎ 800/241-6522).

At the airport you'll find car-rental desks, regularly scheduled shuttle vans to downtown, and taxis. In both baggage-claim areas there is a **visitor information center** where you can pick up brochures about Tucson and reserve a hotel room if you haven't done so already.

Many resorts and hotels in Tucson provide airport shuttle service and will pick you up and return you to the airport either for free or for a competitive fare, so check with your hotel. **Arizona Stagecoach** (☎ **520/889-1000**) operates a daily 24-hour van service to downtown Tucson and the foothills resorts. You'll find the vans outside the center of the baggage-claim area. Fares for two people range from about $14 to downtown to up to $32 to the foothills resorts. To return to the airport, it's best to call at least a day before your scheduled departure.

You'll find taxis waiting in the same area, or you can call **Yellow Cab** (☎ **520/624-6611**) or **Allstate Cab** (☎ **520/798-1111**). A taxi to downtown costs around $16 and to the resorts about $24 to $38.

Sun Tran (☎ **520/792-9222**), the local public transit, operates a bus service to and from the airport, although you'll have to make a transfer to reach downtown. The bus at the airport is no. 25 (ask for a transfer when you board); at the Roy Laos Transit Center you should transfer to no. 16 for downtown. The fare is 85¢. Route 25 from the airport operates daily Monday to Friday between about 6:30am and 7:30pm, on Saturday between about 7:30am and 7:30pm, and on Sunday between about 8:30am and 7:30pm. Departures are every hour.

BY CAR   **I-10,** the main east-west interstate across the southern United States, passes through Tucson as it swings north to Phoenix. **I-19** connects Tucson with the Mexican border at Nogales. **Arizona 86** heads southwest into the Papago Indian Reservation, and **Arizona 79** leads north toward Florence and eventually connects with **U.S. 60** into Phoenix.

If you're headed downtown, take the Congress Street exit off I-10. If you're headed for one of the foothills resorts north of downtown, you'll probably want to take the Ina Road exit.

BY TRAIN   Tucson is served by **Amtrak** passenger rail service (☎ **800/872-7245** in the United States and Canada). The Sunset Limited, which runs between Orlando, Florida and Los Angeles, stops in Tucson. The **train station** is at 400 E. Toole Ave. (☎ **520/623-4442**) in the heart of downtown Tucson and is within walking distance of the Tucson Convention Center, El Presidio Historic District, and a few hotels. You'll find taxis waiting to meet the train.

BY BUS   **Greyhound Lines** (☎ **800/231-2222** or 520/792-3475) connects Tucson to the rest of the United States through its extensive system. The bus station is at 2 S. Fourth Ave., across the street from the Hotel Congress in the Downtown Arts District.

VISITOR INFORMATION

The **Metropolitan Tucson Convention and Visitors Bureau (MTCVB),** 130 S. Scott Ave., Tucson, AZ 85701 (☎ **800/638-8350,** 888/2-TUCSON, or 520/624-1817; www.visittucson.org), is an excellent source of information on Tucson and environs. You can contact the bureau before leaving home or stop in at the visitor center, which is stocked with brochures and has helpful people at the desk to answer your questions. The visitor center is open Monday to Friday 8am to 5pm and Saturday and Sunday 9am to 4pm. At press time there were plans to move the visitor center to La Placita Village, 110 S. Church St. (on the corner of Broadway), so you might want to call ahead for the current address.

CITY LAYOUT

MAIN ARTERIES & STREETS   Tucson is laid out on a grid that's fairly regular in the downtown areas but becomes less orderly the farther you go from the city center. In the foothills, where Tucson's most recent growth has occurred, the grid system breaks down completely because of the hilly terrain. Major thoroughfares are spaced at 1-mile intervals, with smaller streets filling in the squares created by the major roads.

The **main east-west roads** are (from south to north) 22nd Street, Broadway Boulevard, Speedway Boulevard, Grant Road (with Tanque Verde Road as an extension), and Ina Road/Skyline Drive. The **main north-south roads** are (from west to east) Miracle Mile/Oracle Road, Stone/Sixth Avenue, Campbell Avenue, Country Club Road, and Alvernon Road. **I-10** cuts diagonally across the Tucson metropolitan area from northwest to southeast.

In **downtown Tucson,** Congress Street and Broadway Boulevard are the main east-west streets and Stone Avenue, Fourth Avenue, and Sixth Avenue are the main north-south streets.

FINDING AN ADDRESS   Because Tucson is laid out on a grid, finding an address is relatively easy. The zero (or starting) point for all Tucson addresses is the corner of Stone Avenue, which runs north and south, and Congress Street, which runs east and west. From this point, streets are designated either north, south, east, or west. Addresses usually, but not always, increase by 100 with each block, so that an address of 4321 E. Broadway Blvd. should be 43 blocks east of Stone Avenue. In the downtown area, many of the streets and avenues are numbered, with numbered streets running east and west and numbered avenues running north and south.

STREET MAPS   The best way to find your way around Tucson is to pick up a map at the visitor information center at the airport or at the MTCVB (see "Visitor

Tucson at a Glance

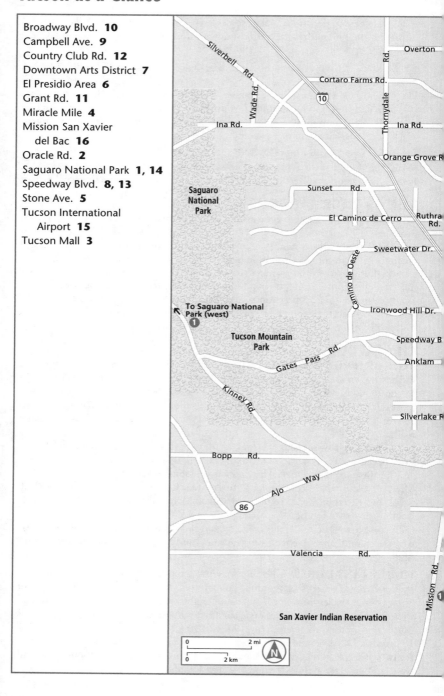

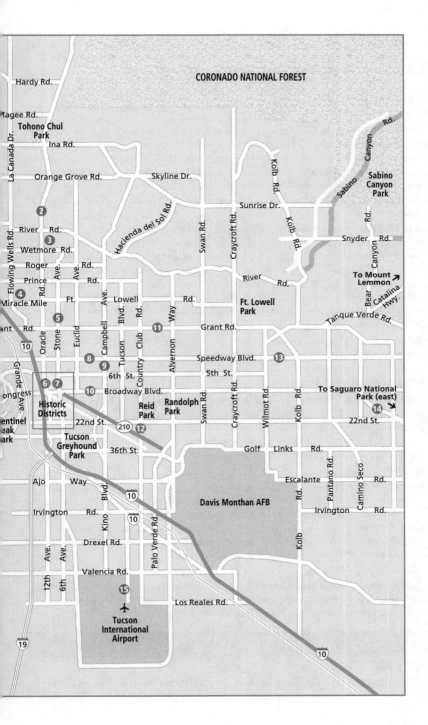

Information," above) for $2. The MTCVB offers a free map in the *Tucson Official Visitors Guide*. The maps handed out by car-rental agencies are not very detailed, but will do for some purposes. Local gas stations also sell detailed maps.

Neighborhoods in Brief

El Presidio Historic District   Named for the Spanish military garrison that once stood on this site, the neighborhood is bounded by Alameda Street on the south, Main Avenue on the west, Franklin Street on the north, and Church Avenue on the east. El Presidio was the city's most affluent neighborhood in the 1880s, and many large homes from that period have been restored and now house restaurants, arts-and-crafts galleries, and a bed-and-breakfast inn. The Tucson Museum of Art anchors the neighborhood.

Barrio Histórico District   Another 19th-century neighborhood, the Barrio Histórico is bounded on the north by Cushing Street, on the west by the railroad tracks, on the south by 18th Street, and on the east by Stone Avenue. The Barrio Histórico is characterized by Sonoran-style adobe rowhouses that directly abut the street with no yards, a style typical in Mexican towns. Although a few restaurants and art galleries dot the neighborhood, most restored buildings serve as offices. This is still a borderline neighborhood where restoration is a slow, ongoing process, so try to avoid it late at night.

Armory Park Historic District   Bounded by 12th Street on the north, Stone Avenue on the west, 19th Street on the south, and Second Avenue and Third Avenue on the east, the Armory Park neighborhood was Tucson's first historic district. Today this area is undergoing a renaissance.

Downtown Arts District   This neighborhood encompasses a bit of the Armory District, a bit of El Presidio District, and the stretch of Congress Street and Broadway Boulevard west of Toole Avenue. Although the area is home to several galleries, nightclubs, and hip cafes, as of 2000, it had lost most of its best businesses and was struggling to survive as an arts district. Today it is mostly frequented by the young and the homeless.

Fourth Avenue   Running from University Boulevard in the north to Ninth Street in the south, Fourth Avenue is the favored shopping district of cash-strapped college students. Shops specialize primarily in ethnic and used/vintage clothing and handcrafted items from around the world. Twice a year, in spring and late fall, the street is closed to traffic for a colorful street fair. Plenty of restaurants, bars, and nightclubs make this street the city's favorite college nightlife district as well.

The Foothills   Encompassing a huge area of northern Tucson, the foothills contain the city's most affluent neighborhoods. Elegant shopping plazas, modern malls, world-class resorts, golf courses, and expensive residential neighborhoods are surrounded by hilly desert at the foot of the Santa Catalina Mountains.

2 Getting Around

BY CAR

Unless you plan to stay by the pool or on the golf course, you'll probably want to rent a car. See "Getting Around," in chapter 2, "Planning a Trip to Arizona: The Basics," for details on renting a car in Arizona. Luckily, rates are fairly economical, especially if you can skip the collision-damage waiver. At press time, Budget was charging $136 per week or $28 per day for a compact car with unlimited mileage in Tucson.

The **car-rental agencies** below have offices at Tucson International Airport: **Alamo** (☎ 800/327-9633), **Avis** (☎ 800/331-1212), **Budget** (☎ 800/527-0700), **Dollar** (☎ 800/800-4000), **Enterprise** (☎ 800/736-8222, **Hertz** (☎ 800/654-3131), **National** (☎ 800/227-7368), **Payless** (☎ 800/237-2804), and **Thrifty** (☎ 800/367-2277). Several companies have offices in other parts of the city as well, so be sure to ask if they have a more convenient location for pickup or drop-off of your car.

Downtown Tucson is still a relatively easy place to find a parking space, and parking fees are low. There are two huge parking lots at the south side of the Tucson Convention Center, a couple of small lots on either side of the Tucson Museum of Art (one at Main Avenue and Paseo Redondo, south of El Presidio Historic District, and one at the corner of Council Street and Court Avenue), and parking garages beneath the main library and El Presidio Park. You'll find plenty of metered parking on the smaller downtown streets. Almost all Tucson hotels and resorts provide free parking.

Lanes on several major avenues in Tucson change direction at rush hour to facilitate traffic flow, so pay attention to signs hung over the street. These tell you the time and direction of traffic in the lanes.

BY PUBLIC TRANSPORTATION

BY BUS   Covering much of the Tucson metropolitan area, **Sun Tran** (☎ 520/792-9222) public buses cost only 85¢ for adults, 60¢ for students, and 35¢ for senior citizens, and are free for children 5 and under. Monthly bus passes are available.

Bus stops are marked by signs with information on which buses stop there, the major streets they serve, and their final destinations. The **Downtown-Ronstadt Transit Center,** at the corner of Congress Street and Sixth Avenue, is served by about 30 regular and express bus routes to all parts of Tucson.

The bus system does not extend to such tourist attractions as the Arizona–Sonora Desert Museum, Old Tucson, Saguaro National Park, or the foothills resorts and, consequently, is of limited use to visitors. However, Sun Tran does provide a shuttle for sports games and special events. Call ☎ **520/792-9222** for information.

BY TROLLEY   Although they don't go very far, the restored electric streetcars of **Old Pueblo Trolley** (☎ 520/792-1802) are a fun way to get from the Fourth Avenue shopping district to the University of Arizona. The trolleys operate on Friday 6pm to 10pm, on Saturday noon to midnight, and on Sunday noon to 6pm. The fare is $1 for adults and 50¢ for children 6 to 12; children under 5 ride free. All-day passes are $2.50 for adults and $1.25 for children.

BY TAXI

If you need a taxi, you'll have to phone for one. **Yellow Cab** (☎ **520/624-6611**) and **Allstate Cab** (☎ **520/798-1111**) provide service throughout the city. Fares start at about $1.25, and after that it's about $1.50 per mile. Although distances in Tucson are not as great as those in Phoenix, it's still a good 10 or more miles from the foothills resorts to downtown Tucson, so expect to pay at least $10 for any taxi ride. Most resorts offer or can arrange taxi service to the major tourist attractions around Tucson.

Shoppers should keep in mind that several Tucson shopping malls offer free shuttle service from hotels and resorts. Be sure to ask at your hotel before paying for a ride to a mall.

ON FOOT

Downtown Tucson is compact and easily explored on foot. Many old streets in the downtown historic neighborhoods are narrow and much easier to appreciate if you leave your car in a parking lot. On the other hand, several major attractions, including the Arizona–Sonora Desert Museum, Old Tucson Studios, Saguaro National Park, and Sabino Canyon, require quite a bit of walking, often on uneven footing, so be sure to bring a good pair of walking shoes.

Fast Facts: Tucson

Baby-Sitters   Most hotels can arrange a baby-sitter for you, and many resorts feature special programs for children on weekends and throughout the summer. If your hotel can't help, call **A-1 Messner Sitter Service** (☎ **520/881-1578**), which will send a sitter to your hotel.

Car Rentals   See "Getting Around," earlier in this chapter.

Climate   See "When to Go," in chapter 2.

Dentist   Call the **Arizona Dental Association** (☎ **800/866-2732**) or **Dental Referral Service** (☎ **800/577-7317**) for a dentist referral.

Doctor   For a doctor referral, call ☎ **800/230-CARE.**

Emergencies   For fire, police, or medical emergency, phone ☎ **911.**

Eyeglasses   **Alvernon Optical** has several stores around town where you can have your glasses repaired or replaced. Locations include 440 N. Alvernon Way (☎ **520/327-6211**), 7043 N. Oracle Rd. (☎ **520/297-2501**), and 7123 E. Tanque Verde Rd. (☎ **520/296-4157**).

Hospitals   The **Tucson General Hospital** is at 3838 N. Campbell Ave. (☎ **520/318-6300**), the **Tucson Medical Center** is at 5301 E. Grant Rd. (☎ **520/327-5461**), and the **University Medical Center** is at 1501 N. Campbell Ave. (☎ **520/694-0111**).

Information   See "Visitor Information" in "Orientation," earlier in this chapter.

Internet Access   The hot spot in downtown Tucson is **The Library of Congress** at the Hotel Congress, 311 E. Congress St. (☎ **520/622-2708**). The rates for Internet access is $6 per hour (pro-rated to the $^1/_2$).

Lost Property   If you lose something and you don't know where, try the **Tucson Police Department Found-Recovered Property Office** (☎ **520/791-4458**). If you lose something at the airport, call ☎ **520/573-8156;** if you lose something on a Sun Tran bus, call ☎ **520/792-9222.**

Newspapers/Magazines   The *Arizona Daily Star* is Tucson's morning daily, and the *Tucson Citizen* is the afternoon daily. The *Tucson Weekly* is the city's weekly news-and-arts journal; it's published on Thursday. **Crescent Tobacco Shop and Newsstand,** 7037 E. Tanque Verde Rd. (☎ **520/296-3102**), and downtown at 200 E. Congress St. (☎ **520/622-1559**), carries newspapers and magazines from all over the country.

Pharmacies   Walgreens has stores all over Tucson. Call ☎ **800/WALGREENS** for the Walgreens pharmacy that's nearest you or that's open 24 hours a day.

Photographic Needs   NuArt Photo, at 7090 N. Oracle Rd. (☎ **520/ 797-2493**), and El Con Mall, 3601 E. Broadway Blvd. (☎ **520/327-7062**), can supply camera needs or repairs.

Police   In case of an emergency, phone ☎ **911.**

Post Office   There's a post office in downtown Tucson at 141 S. 6th Ave. (☎ **800/275-8777**), open Monday to Friday 8:30am to 5pm and Saturday 9am to noon.

Radio   **KXCI** (91.3 FM) has an alternative mix of programming and is a favorite with local Tucsonans, while **KUAT** (90.5 FM) has all-classical programming and is a good station for news. **KUAZ** (89.1 FM) is National Public Radio.

Safety   Tucson is surprisingly safe for a city of its size. However, the Downtown Arts District isn't all that lively after dark, and you should be particularly alert in this area if you're down here for a performance of some sort. An exception is on the nights of Downtown Saturday Night festivities. Just to the south of downtown Tucson lies a poorer section of the city that's best avoided after dark unless you are certain of where you're going. Otherwise, take the same precautions you would in any other city.

When driving, be aware that many streets in the Tucson area are subject to flooding when it rains. Heed warnings about possible flooded areas and don't try to cross a low area that has become flooded. Find an alternative route instead.

Taxes   In addition to the 5% state sales tax, Tucson levies a 2% city sales tax. State car-rental tax is 5% (plus there are other taxes and surcharges on car rentals). The hotel room tax is 9.5% (plus $1 per day occupancy tax) in Tucson. Outside the city limits, you'll likely pay 7.5% to 8.5%

Taxis   See "Getting Around," earlier in this chapter.

Transit Information   For information on **Sun Tran** public buses, phone ☎ **520/792-9222.**

Weather   Phone ☎ **520/881-3333** for the local weather forecast.

3 Where to Stay

Although Phoenix still holds the title of Resort Capital of Arizona, Tucson is not far behind, and this city's resorts boast much more spectacular settings than many comparable resorts in Phoenix and Scottsdale. As far as non-resort accommodations go, Tucson has a wider variety of accommodations than Phoenix—partly because several historic neighborhoods around Tucson have become home to bed-and-breakfast inns. The presence of several guest ranches within a 20-minute drive of Tucson adds to the city's diversity of accommodations. Business and budget travelers are well served with all-suite and conference hotels, as well as plenty of budget chain motels.

If you're looking to stay in a bed-and-breakfast inn while in Tucson, you can contact several agencies. The **Arizona Association of Bed and Breakfast Inns,** P.O. Box 22086, Phoenix, AZ 86002-2086 (☎ **800/284-2589;** www.arizona-bed-breakfast. com), has several members in Tucson. **Advance Reservations Inn Arizona/Mi Casa-Su Casa Bed & Breakfast Reservation Service,** P.O. Box 950, Tempe, AZ 85280-0950 (☎ **800/456-0682** or 480/990-0682; www.azres.com), will book you into one of its many homestays in the Tucson area (or elsewhere in the state), as will **Arizona Trails Bed & Breakfast Reservation Service,** P.O. Box 18998, Fountain Hills, AZ 85269-8998 (☎ **888/799-4284** or 480/837-4284; fax 480/816-4224; www.arizonatrails.com), which books tour and hotel reservations.

Tucson Accommodations

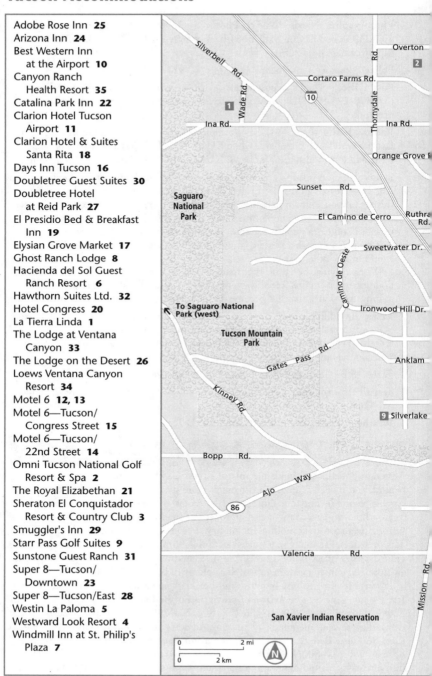

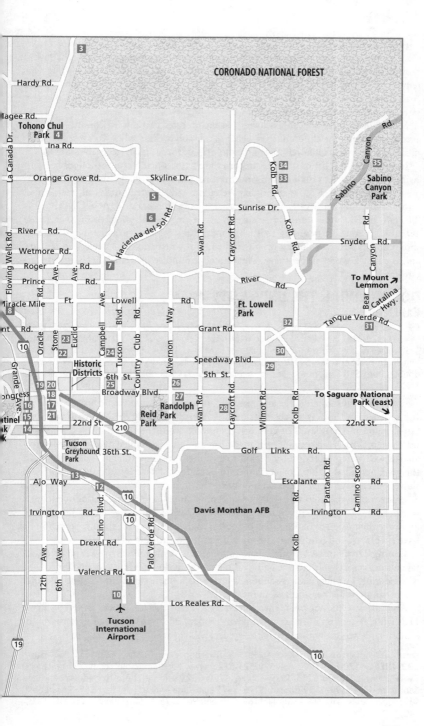

At the more expensive hotels and resorts, summer room rates, usually in effect from some time in May to some time in September or October, are often less than half what they are in winter. Surprisingly, temperatures usually aren't unbearable in May or September, which makes these good times to visit if you're looking to save money on an Arizona vacation. When making late spring reservations, always be sure to ask when rates are scheduled to go up or down.

Most hotels offer special packages, weekend rates, various discounts, and free accommodations for children, so it helps to ask about these when you reserve. Keep in mind that nearly all hotels have nonsmoking and wheelchair-accessible rooms.

In the following listings, price categories are based on the rate for a double room (with tax included) in high season (most resorts and hotels charge the same for a single or double room). Keep in mind that the rates listed are what hotels call "rack rates." Various discounts are often available that reduce these rates (ACCOMMODA-TIONS, AARP, and so on), so be sure to ask if any specials or discounted rates are available. If you aren't coming to Tucson specifically for the winter gem and mineral shows, then you'll save quite a bit on your room if you avoid the last week in January and the first 2 weeks in February, when hotels around town generally charge exorbitant rates.

DOWNTOWN & THE UNIVERSITY AREA
EXPENSIVE

✪ **Arizona Inn.** 2200 E. Elm St., Tucson, AZ 85719. ☎ **800/933-1093** or 520/325-1541. Fax 520/320-2182. www.arizonainn.com. 86 units, 3 houses. A/C TV TEL. Mid-Jan to mid-Apr $195–$245 double, from $267 suite; mid-Apr to May 31 $170–$230 double, from $207 suite; June 1 to mid-Sept $98–$110 double, from $120 suite; mid-Sept to mid-Dec $130–$186 double, from $184 suite; mid-Dec to mid-Jan $150–$196 double, from $204 suite. AE, DC, MC, V.

With its pink stucco buildings and immaculately tended gardens, the historic Arizona Inn, opened in 1930, is an absolute oasis. If you're searching for old Arizona charm but demand modern levels of comfort, then look no further. Most guest rooms here have original furniture (much of it made for the inn by disabled World War I veterans) as well as reproductions of period furnishings. Strolling the grounds, relaxing in the antiques-filled library, or cozying into your room, it's easy to conjure up those slower paced days when guests would spend the entire winter here.

Guest rooms are often very spacious, and most suites have private patios or enclosed sun porches, as well as sitting rooms. Although bathrooms are generally fairly small and have their original fixtures, this only adds to the charm of the rooms. Some rooms have fireplaces, and hair dryers, irons, and ironing boards are standard.

Dining/Diversions: The inn's main dining room, which serves primarily continental cuisine, is a casually elegant hall with plenty of outdoor seating as well. The lounge is filled with greenery and Audubon prints, and a pianist performs in the evening. There is a poolside bar and restaurant.

Amenities: Outdoor pool (surrounded by fragrant flowering trees and vines), two Har-Tru clay tennis courts, croquet lawn, modern and well-equipped exercise room, saunas, table tennis, concierge, room service, massages.

Doubletree Hotel at Reid Park. 445 S. Alvernon Way, Tucson, AZ 85711. ☎ **800/222-TREE** or 520/881-4200. Fax 520/323-5225. www.doubletreehotels.com. 295 units. A/C TV TEL. Nov–early Apr $215–$279 double, $250–$375 suite; mid-Apr to mid-May and late Sept to mid-Dec $99–$159 double, $175–$375 suite; late May to mid-Sept $59–$79 double, $175–$250 suite; late Dec–early Jan $69–$99 double, $175–$250 suite. AE, CB, DC, DISC, MC, V. Pets accepted ($50 deposit).

Located across the street from Randolph Park municipal golf course, the Doubletree is midway between the airport and downtown Tucson and can be thought of as an in-town budget golf resort. Although the hotel does a lot of convention business and sometimes feels crowded, the gardens, with their citrus trees and roses, are almost always tranquil. The rooms are divided between a nine-story building that offers views of the valley (even-numbered rooms face the pool, odd-numbered rooms face the mountains) and a two-story building with patio rooms overlooking the garden and pool area. All rooms are comfortably appointed with contemporary furnishings and have coffeemakers.

Dining/Diversions: The Cactus Rose Restaurant serves Southwestern cuisine (and one of the best Sunday brunches in Tucson), and the Javelina Cantina, a livelier place, serves Mexican food and mega-margaritas. There's a quieter lobby lounge.

Amenities: Outdoor pool, whirlpool, exercise room, tennis courts, golf course, and jogging trail (all at Reid Park); boutiques, room service, valet/laundry service.

The Lodge on the Desert. 306 N. Alvernon Way, Tucson, AZ 85711. ☎ **800/456-5634** or 520/325-3366. Fax 520/327-5834. www.lodgeonthedesert.com. 35 units. A/C TV TEL. Mid-Jan to May $169–$249 double; June–Sept $69–$139 double; Oct to mid-Jan $119–$189 double. Rates include full breakfast. AE, CB, DC, DISC, MC, V. Pets accepted, $5 per day and $50 deposit.

Dating from 1936, The Lodge on the Desert was, until several years ago, a dated hotel that appealed primarily to families who had been coming here for generations. However, under new management, the hotel is being transformed into a romantic getaway. The lodge consists primarily of hacienda-style adobe buildings in a garden compound shaded by palm, orange, and eucalyptus trees, and the neatly manicured lawns and flower gardens offer a lush and relaxing retreat. In the rooms—some with tile floors, others carpeted—you'll find a mix of contemporary and Southwestern furnishings, as well as coffeemakers and hair dryers. Many rooms have beamed ceilings or fireplaces.

Dining/Diversions: Cielos, the lodge's upscale dining room, serves imaginative cuisine and has a very pleasant patio.

Amenities: Although the pool (the original) is very small, it has a good view of the Catalinas.

MODERATE

Adobe Rose Inn. 940 N. Olsen Ave., Tucson, AZ 85719. ☎ **800/328-4122** or 520/318-4644. Fax 520/325-0055. 5 units. A/C TV. Mid-Dec to May $95–$125 double; June–Aug $65–$85 double; Sept to mid-Dec $75–$95 double. Rates include full breakfast. AE, DC, MC, V.

Located in a quiet residential neighborhood only a few blocks from the University of Arizona campus, this B&B, with its strikingly angular adobe buildings, has the feel of a little village. Our favorite room is right off the entrance hall and has a brick floor, beehive fireplace, and colorful stained-glass windows. For extra privacy, you can opt for the room in the cottage out back. Almost the first thing you see as you step through the front door is the blue of the swimming pool outside a large picture window. There's also a hot tub. Furnishings throughout the inn are of peeled lodgepole pine logs for a sort of contemporary Southwestern rustic look.

Catalina Park Inn. 309 E. 1st St., Tucson, AZ 85705. ☎ **800/792-4885** or 520/792-4541. www.catalinaparkinn.com. 6 units. A/C TV TEL. $104–$124 double (lower rates in summer and fall). Rates include full breakfast. AE, DISC, MC, V.

Located close to downtown and overlooking a shady park, this bed-and-breakfast inn has the look of a Mediterranean villa. Built in 1927, the home has been lovingly restored by owners Mark Hall and Paul Richard, and many interesting and playful touches enliven the classic interior (a crystal chandelier in a bathroom, beautifully lit display cases in the living room, a formal dining room, and a rustic breakfast room). The huge basement room is one of our favorites. Not only does it conjure up the inside of an adobe, but there is also a whirlpool tub in a former cedar closet and a separate toilet room with a display of colorful Fiestaware. Two of the rooms are in a separate cottage across the back garden, and they offer more contemporary styling than do the rooms in the main house. Two upstairs rooms have balconies.

○ **El Presidio Bed & Breakfast Inn.** 297 N. Main Ave., Tucson, AZ 85701. ☎ **800/ 349-6151** or 520/623-6151. Fax 520/623-3860. 3 units. TV TEL. $105–$125 double. Rates include full breakfast. 2-night minimum. No credit cards.

Built in 1886 and lovingly restored by innkeeper Patti Toci and her husband, Jerry, El Presidio is a mix of Victorian and adobe architectural styles. This old house, only steps from the Tucson Museum of Art, Old Town Artisans, and El Charro Cafe, is the quintessential Tucson territorial home and is now filled with interesting antiques. There is one high-ceilinged guest suite in the main house, while the other two, both with kitchenettes, are arranged around a shady courtyard at the center of which is a Mexican-style fountain. All three suites are decorated with antiques and original art (much of it by Jerry) and have kitchenettes. In addition to the filling breakfast in the sunroom, there are complimentary drinks, fruit, and treats in the afternoon and evening.

Elysian Grove Market. 400 W. Simpson St., Tucson, AZ 85701. ☎ **520/628-1522.** www. bbonline.com/az/elysiangrove. 2 units. $75 double. Rates include continental or Mexican breakfast. No credit cards. Well-supervised pets accepted.

Located in the Barrio Histórico just a block away from El Tiradito shrine, this former general store (the building still has the old store name painted on the front wall) is now an unusual little inn filled with rustic Mexican antiques and Hispanic folk art. The two suites consist of high-ceilinged living rooms that incorporate all manner of salvaged architectural details, colorful textiles, folk art, and original grocery store fixtures (including an old walk-in meat locker that has now been turned into a kitchen). Each suite has a bedroom on the ground level and a second bedroom (rather dark but cool) down a flight of steps. Although this funky barrio B&B isn't for everyone, the old Mexican atmosphere and abundance of art will appeal to travelers searching for a place with the feel of old Tucson.

○ **The Royal Elizabethan.** 204 S. Scott Ave., Tucson, AZ 85701. ☎ **877/670-9022** or 520/670-9022. Fax 520/629-9710. www.royalelizabeth.com. 6 units. A/C TV TEL. Sept–May $120–$170 double; June–Aug $85–$115 double. Rates include full breakfast. AE, DISC, MC, V.

Located only a block away from the Temple of Music and Art in downtown Tucson, this inn is housed in an 1878 vintage Victorian adobe home. The odd combination of architectural styles makes for a uniquely Southwestern-style inn. In classic 19th-century Tucson style, the old home looks thoroughly unpretentious from the outside. However, inside you'll find beautiful woodwork and gorgeous Victorian-era antique furnishings. Guest rooms open off a large, high-ceilinged central hall, and in the guest rooms, you'll find TVs and VCRs hidden in old armoires. Four of the rooms have separate sitting rooms and are extremely spacious. Rooms have safes and refrigerators. Out back, there's a pool and a whirlpool.

INEXPENSIVE

In addition to the inexpensive hotels listed below, you'll find dozens of budget chain motels along I-10 as it passes through downtown Tucson. Among the better choices are **Days Inn Tucson,** 222 S. Freeway, Exit 258 (☎ **520/791-7511**), charging $55 to $135 double; **Motel 6—Tucson/Congress Street,** 960 S. Freeway, Exit 258 (☎ **520/628-1339**), and **Motel 6—Tucson/22nd Street,** 1222 S. Freeway, Exit 259 (☎ **520/624-2516**), both charging $40 to $50 double; and **Super 8—Tucson/Downtown,** 1248 N. Stone St., Exit 257 (☎ **520/622-6446**), charging $39 to $59 double.

Clarion Hotel & Suites Santa Rita. 88 E. Broadway Blvd., Tucson, AZ 85701. ☎ **800/CLARION** or 520/622-4000. Fax 520/620-0376. 153 units. A/C TV TEL. $84–$154 double; $114–$194 suite. Rates include continental breakfast. AE, CB, DC, DISC, MC, V. Pets accepted.

This hotel, only a block from the convention center and close to El Presidio Historic District, isn't exactly luxurious, and you'd never know that it's nearly 100 years old. However, it was completely remodeled and updated a few years ago, and makes a decent, economical downtown address. Although the Clarion stays busy with conventioneers, it can be a good choice for vacationers. Benefits of staying here include the complimentary breakfast, an evening cocktail hour, and free local phone calls. Best of all, however, is that this hotel is home to Cafe Poca Cosa, Tucson's most innovative Mexican restaurant. Some of the guest rooms have balconies, and most have coffeemakers, refrigerators, microwaves, and irons and ironing boards. Facilities include a fitness center, saunas, and a pleasant little pool.

✪ **Ghost Ranch Lodge.** 801 W. Miracle Mile, Tucson, AZ 85705. ☎ **800/456-7565** or 520/791-7565. Fax 520/791-3898. www.ghostranchlodge.com. 83 units. A/C TV TEL. Jan–Apr $86–$124 double; May–June and Nov–Dec $54–$98 double; July–Oct $42–$76 double. Rates include continental breakfast. AE, DISC, MC, V. Pets accepted.

Although Miracle Mile was once Tucson's main drag, today it's looking a bit shabby. One exception is the Ghost Ranch Lodge, which opened in 1941 and was for many years one of Tucson's desert resorts catering to northern visitors who stayed for the winter. If you're looking for affordable Old Tucson, this is it. Situated on 8 acres, the lodge has a justly famous cactus garden, orange grove, and extensive lawns that together create an oasis atmosphere. The guest rooms were refurbished recently but retain a bit of Western flavor, with beamed ceilings, painted brick walls, and patios

---

⊕ Family-Friendly Hotels

Loews Ventana Canyon Resort *(see p. 308)*   With a playground, kids' club, croquet court, table tennis, basketball hoop, and its own waterfall, this resort has plenty to keep the kids busy. There's a hiking trail that starts from the edge of the property, and Sabino Canyon Recreation Area is nearby.

Smuggler's Inn *(see p. 306)*   Built around a large central courtyard with a very tropical feel, this hotel is a good choice for families on a budget. In addition to a pool and whirlpool, there are lawns for the kids to play on and a meandering pond that's home to fish and ducks.

Westin La Paloma *(see p. 309)*   Kids get their own lounge and games room. In the summer and during holiday periods there are special programs for the kids so parents can have a little free time. There's a great waterslide in the pool area.

Guest Ranches   The Tucson area has several guest ranches, most of which are family-oriented. Kids can play cowboy to their hearts' content, riding the range and singing songs by campfire.

covered by red-tile roofs. The lodge's dining room serves Southwestern-style meals and offers dining on a poolside patio or inside with a view of the Santa Catalina Mountains. Facilities include a small pool and a whirlpool.

Hotel Congress. 311 E. Congress St., Tucson, AZ 85701. ☎ **800/722-8848** or 520/622-8848. Fax 520/792-6366. www.hotcong.com. 40 units. TEL. $20–$70 double; $15.45 per person in shared hostel rooms. AE, DISC, MC, V. Pets accepted ($50 deposit).

Located in the heart of downtown Tucson, the Hotel Congress, built in 1919 to serve railroad passengers, once played host to John Dillinger. Today the hotel, conveniently near the Greyhound and Amtrak stations, operates as a budget hotel and youth hostel catering primarily to European backpack travelers. Although the hotel is far from luxurious, the lobby has been restored to its original Southwestern elegance (straight out of a film noir set). With antique telephones and old radios that really work, guest rooms remain true to their historical character, so don't expect anything fancy (like TVs). Some bathrooms have bathtubs only, and others have showers only. There's a classic little diner/cafe off the lobby (think Edward Hopper meets Gen X), as well as a tiny though very genuine Western bar. At night the Club Congress is a popular (and loud) dance club (guests can pick up free earplugs at the front desk). There's even a cybercafe called the Library of Congress.

EAST TUCSON
MODERATE

Doubletree Guest Suites. 6555 E. Speedway Blvd., Tucson, AZ 85710. ☎ **800/222-TREE** or 520/721-7100. Fax 520/721-1991. www.doubletreehotels.com. 304 suites. A/C TV TEL. $75–$154 double. Rates include full breakfast. AE, CB, DC, DISC, MC, V. Pets accepted ($25 nonrefundable fee).

With surprisingly reasonable rates throughout the year, this all-suite hotel is a good choice for both those who need plenty of space and those who want to be in the east-side business corridor. The five-story brick building is arranged around two long garden courtyards, one of which has a large pool and whirlpool. The pool and gardens, along with the full breakfast and evening cocktail hour, are the best reasons for vacationers to stay here. The two-room suites feature contemporary furnishings, and all have refrigerators, coffeemakers, hair dryers, and irons and ironing boards (most have microwaves). Food in the hotel's restaurant is uneven, but the cookies you get at check-in are great! Amenities include an exercise room (and access to a nearby health club), room service, and valet/laundry service.

Hawthorn Suites Ltd. 7007 E. Tanque Verde Rd., Tucson, AZ 85715. ☎ **800/527-1133** or 520/298-2300. Fax 520/298-6756. www.hawthornsuitesaz.com. 90 units. A/C TV TEL. Jan–Mar $99–$125 double; Apr–May and Oct–Dec $79–$89 double; June–Sept $49–$59 double. Rates include full breakfast. AE, CB, DC, DISC, MC, V. Pets accepted ($25 nonrefundable fee).

Although it looks rather stark from the outside, the Hawthorn Suites Ltd., built around four tranquil and lushly planted garden courtyards, is surprisingly pleasant inside. Most rooms are quite large and have coffeemakers and irons and ironing boards (some have kitchenettes). There's no restaurant on the premises, but numerous excellent restaurants are nearby (Tanque Verde is Tucson's restaurant row), which makes this a good choice for a foodie on a budget. Facilities include a pool and whirlpool (and access to a nearby fitness center). There's a complimentary cocktail reception each evening.

Smuggler's Inn. 6350 E. Speedway Blvd. (at Wilmot), Tucson, AZ 85710. ☎ **800/ 525-8852** or 520/296-3292. Fax 520/722-3713. www.smugglersinn.com. 150 units. A/C TV TEL. Jan–Mar $99–$119 double, $125–$135 suite; Apr $89–$109 double, $125 suite;

May–Sept $69–$79 double, $89 suite; Oct–Dec $79–$89 double, $99 suite. Rates include continental breakfast. AE, DC, DISC, MC, V.

Built around an attractive garden and pond, the Smuggler's Inn is a very comfortable and economically priced hotel, and the neatly trimmed lawns and tall palm trees give the garden a tropical look. There's nothing about this place to remind you that you're in the middle of the desert, but the grounds are much nicer than you'll find at most other comparably priced hotels in the area. Amid these tropical surroundings you'll find the pool, whirlpool, and putting green. Guest rooms are spacious, and all have modern furnishings and a balcony or patio. There are such amenities as coffeemakers and video games on the TVs. A fairly recent renovation has kept the rooms in good shape. There's a restaurant and cocktail lounge on the premises. Room service and health club privileges are available.

✪ **Sunstone Guest Ranch.** 2545 N. Woodland Rd., Tucson, AZ 85749. ☎ **520/ 749-1928.** Fax 520/749-2456. www.azstarnet.com/~sunston. 11 units. A/C TEL. Sept 1–May 31 $145 double; June 1–Aug 31 $95 double. Rates include breakfast. MC, V.

Although not exactly a guest ranch, this inn offers a beautiful ranchlike setting in a pocket of grassland surrounded by desert and suburbs. Although you'll feel as if you're on a remote spread, the gourmet dining of Tucson's restaurant row is only a 10-minute drive away. Basically, it's the best of both worlds—a little bit of country and a little bit of city. Accommodations are in a pair of 1920s baked-adobe buildings fronted by long verandas. Rooms are large and decorated in modern Southwest style with the occasional Mission-style antique. Bathrooms, though small, are functional. Surrounding these buildings are lush green lawns and huge old mesquite trees that keep the grounds delightfully shady. A heated pool, whirlpool, tennis court, basketball courts, volleyball, and horseshoe pits provide plenty of recreational opportunities.

THE FOOTHILLS
VERY EXPENSIVE

The Lodge at Ventana Canyon. 6200 N. Clubhouse Lane, Tucson, AZ 85750. ☎ **888/ GRAN-BAY** or 520/577-1400. Fax 520/577-4065. 50 units. A/C TV TEL. Oct–late Jan and Apr–early May $299–$399 1-bedroom suite, $499–$599 2-bedroom suite; late Jan–early Apr $399–$499 1-bedroom suite, $599–$699 2-bedroom suite; early May–late May $219–$299 1-bedroom suite, $399–$499 2-bedroom suite; late May–Sept $129–$199 1-bedroom suite, $199–$259 2-bedroom suite (all rates plus $16 nightly service charge). AE, DC, DISC, MC, V.

Golf is the name of the game at this small boutique resort, set within a gated country-club community at the base of the Santa Catalina Mountains. Although small, the lodge manages to offer plenty of big-resort amenities and places an emphasis on its personal service. Although there are a dozen tennis courts here, this resort appeals almost exclusively to avid golfers, thanks to the two highly acclaimed and spectacular Tom Fazio golf courses. (The Mountain Course's third hole plays across a deep ravine and is one of the most photographed holes in the West.) The accommodations are in spacious suites, most with walls of windows so you can enjoy the views of the Catalinas. Furnishings are modern Mission style, and all suites include small kitchens and large bathrooms with two sinks, separate changing rooms, and oversized tubs (sometimes old-fashioned footed tubs). Some suites have balconies, cathedral ceilings, and spiral stairs that lead to sleeping lofts.

Dining/Diversions: The dining room, a few steps from the lobby, offers fine dining with a view of the Catalinas. Drinks are served in two lounges, and there's a poolside snack bar.

Amenities: In addition to the golf courses and tennis courts, amenities include a pool, whirlpools, exercise and aerobics rooms, steam rooms, saunas, pro shop, concierge, room service, golf and tennis lessons, massages and other spa treatments, baby-sitting, and valet/laundry service.

✪ **Loews Ventana Canyon Resort.** 7000 N. Resort Dr., Tucson, AZ 85750. ☎ **800/ 23-LOEWS** or 520/299-2020. Fax 520/299-6832. www.loewshotels.com. 398 units. A/C TV TEL. Early Dec–late May $245–$385 double, $750–$2,400 suite; late May–early Sept $95–$150 double, $245–$1,200 suite; early Sept–early Dec $220–$345 double, $700–$1,800 suite. AE, CB, DC, DISC, JCB, MC, V.

For breathtaking scenery, fascinating architecture, and superb resort amenities (including two excellent Tom Fazio golf courses and a full-service spa), no other Tucson resort can compare with Loews Ventana Canyon. The Santa Catalina Mountains rise up in rugged contrast to the genteel comforts of this haven of luxury, and despite its many amenities, the resort is firmly planted in the desert and uses desert plants in much of its landscaping. Flagstone floors in the lobby and tables with boulders for bases give the resort's public rooms a rugged but luxurious appeal, and just off the lobby, a short path leads to a waterfall.

The guest rooms are designed to impress, with beds angled out from corners and drapes hung from the headboards. Private balconies overlook either the city lights or the mountains, and some rooms have fireplaces. Bathrooms are designed for convenience and comfort, and include tiny TVs, travertine floors, and bathtubs built for two.

Dining/Diversions: The Ventana Room (see "Where to Dine," below), is one of the finest restaurants in Tucson, while the Flying V is popular as much for its food as for the views from its large deck. There's a casual cafe with a waterfall view and a poolside snack bar. The lobby lounge serves afternoon tea and then becomes an evening piano bar.

Amenities: Two 18-hole golf courses, two pools with mountain views, whirlpools, eight tennis courts, croquet lawn, jogging track, nature trails, health spa (including a lap pool, aerobics room, exercise machines and free weights, steam rooms, saunas, and full assortment of spa services), bike rentals, car-rental desk, tour desk, concierge, 24-hour room service, valet/laundry service, playground, and kids' club.

Omni Tucson National Golf Resort & Spa. 2727 W. Club Dr. (off Magee Rd.), Tucson, AZ 85742-8919. ☎ **800/528-4856** or 520/297-2271. Fax 520/297-7544. www. omnihotels.com. 167 units. A/C MINIBAR TV TEL. Jan–Mar $260–$280 double, $280–$350 suite; Apr–late May $190–$210 double, $210–$280 suite; late May–early Sept $100–$110 double, $110–$160 suite; early Sept–Dec $170–$190 double, $190–$260 suite (plus $7 nightly service charge). AE, CB, DC, DISC, MC, V.

As the name implies, golf is the driving force behind most stays at this boutique resort, which is the site of the annual Tucson Open PGA golf tournament. If you haven't got your own set of clubs, you might feel a bit out of place here. Then again, you could just avail yourself of the full-service health spa, which is one of the best in Arizona. There are two pools and a tennis complex.

Most of the spacious guest rooms cling to the edges of the golf course and have their own patios or balconies. Hand-carved doors and Mexican tile counters in the bathrooms give the rooms a Spanish colonial feel, but furnishings have a classically modern Mediterranean style. For convenience there are double vanities and large dressing areas in all the rooms. Aside from the least expensive rooms, the accommodations here are the best and most luxurious in Tucson.

Dining/Diversions: The resort dining room serves good regional American fare, while a second restaurant serves reasonably priced Southwestern fare. A lobby lounge provides distant views of the Santa Catalina Mountains, and an upscale sports bar looks out over the golf course.

Amenities: Championship 27-hole golf course, four tennis courts, two pools, basketball and volleyball courts, pro shop, full-service health spa (with exercise machines, free weights, an aerobics room, steam rooms, saunas, whirlpools, and numerous spa treatments), concierge, 24-hour room service, valet/laundry service.

Sheraton El Conquistador Resort & Country Club. 10000 N. Oracle Rd., Tucson, AZ 85737. ☎ **800/325-7832** or 520/544-5000. Fax 520/544-1222. www.sheratonelconquistador. com. 428 units. A/C MINIBAR TV TEL. Jan–late May $249–$398 double, $329–$1,250 suite; late May–early Sept $89–$230 double, $169–$1,250 suite; late Sept–Dec $179–$360 double, $259–$1,250 suite (all rates plus $7 service fee). AE, CB, DC, DISC, MC, V. Pets accepted.

With the Santa Catalina Mountains rising up directly behind the property, this resort in Tucson's northern foothills boasts one of the most spectacular settings in the state. Just keep in mind that if you stay here, you'll be at least 30 minutes from downtown. The majority of the guest rooms are built around a central courtyard with a large pool and manicured lawns. However, this area is often taken over by conventions, and those seeking peace and quiet may want to opt for a room in the separate casitas area, which has its own pool. While golf on the resorts' three courses is the favorite pastime here, nongolfers have plenty of options, too. Golfers should note that one of the courses was renovated in 1999 and the other is currently being renovated, with completion scheduled for October 2000.

Guest rooms feature Southwestern-influenced contemporary furniture and have spacious marble bathrooms. All rooms have a balcony or patio, and in most suites, you'll find a fireplace. For the full Tucson experience, ask for a mountain-view room.

Dining/Diversions: In the lively Mexican restaurant, strolling mariachis entertain, while in the steak house, cowboy vittles and cancan dancers are the order of the day. A casual cafe offers patio dining and moderate prices, and the country club's restaurant capitalizes on its outstanding view.

Amenities: Three golf courses (45 holes total), 28 tennis courts, seven racquetball courts, four pools, six whirlpools, sauna, two health clubs, jogging trails, volleyball and basketball courts, rental bikes, car-rental desk, tour desk, concierge, room service, valet/laundry service, baby-sitting, massages, shopping shuttle, horseback riding, and children's programs in summer.

✪ Westin La Paloma. 3800 E. Sunrise Dr., Tucson, AZ 85718. ☎ **800/WESTIN-1** or 520/742-6000. Fax 520/577-5878. www.westin.com. 487 units. A/C MINIBAR TV TEL. Jan–late May $289–$329 double, from $379 suite; late May–early Sept $129–$149 double, from $199 suite; early Sept–Dec $229–$269 double, from $319 suite. AE, CB, DC, DISC, EURO, JCB, MC, V.

If grand scale is what you're looking for in a resort, this is the place. Everything about the Westin is big—big portico, big lobby, big lounge, big pool area, big views. The resort's sunset-pink Mission-revival buildings are set in the middle of Tucson's prestigious foothills and offer sweeping panoramas. While adults appreciate the resort's tennis courts, exercise facilities, and abundant poolside lounge chairs, kids love the 170-foot waterslide.

Guest rooms are situated in 27 low-rise buildings surrounded by desert landscaping. Couples should opt for the king rooms, which have the bed angled out from the corner of the room to best take in the views (ask for a mountain or golf course view if you don't mind spending a bit more). Bathrooms are extremely spacious, with separate tubs and showers, two sinks, and telephones.

Dining/Diversions: French-inspired Southwestern cuisine is the specialty at Janos, one of Tucson's finest restaurants (see "Where to Dine," below), and the affiliated J Bar. There's casual dining with a view just off the lobby. Snack bars are convenient to tennis and golf, and there's even a swim-up bar and grill.

Amenities: 27-hole golf course, three swimming pools (one for adults only), water-slide, three whirlpools, 12 tennis courts, racquetball court, golf and tennis pro shops, volleyball and croquet courts, bike rentals, children's lounge and game room, shopping arcade, spa services, health club (with exercise machines, aerobics room, and steam room), concierge, 24-hour room service, valet service.

EXPENSIVE

✪ **Hacienda del Sol Guest Ranch Resort.** 5601 N. Hacienda del Sol Rd., Tucson, AZ 85718. ☎ **800/728-6514** or 520/299-1501. Fax 520/299-5554. www.haciendadelsol.com. 30 units, 3 casitas. A/C TV TEL. Jan 1–Apr 30 $155 double, $190 hacienda, $290 suite, $325–$425 casita; May to mid-Dec $115 double, $140 hacienda, $200 suite, $250–$350 casita. Rates include continental breakfast. AE, MC, V.

With its colorful Southwest styling, historical character, mature desert gardens, and ridge-top setting, Hacienda del Sol is one of the most distinctive hotels in Tucson. The small resort, once a guest ranch (and later a private girls' school), exudes the sort of Old Tucson atmosphere available at only a couple of other lodgings in the city. The lodge's basic rooms are evocative of Spanish posadas and old Mexican inns and have rustic and colorful Mexican character, with a decidedly artistic flare. These rooms are in the lodge's oldest buildings, set around flower-filled courtyards. If you prefer more modern, comfortable, and spacious accommodations, ask for a suite; if you want loads of space and the chance to stay where Katherine Hepburn and Spencer Tracy may have once stayed, ask for a casita.

Dining/Diversions: With views over the foothills and large terraces for alfresco dining, The Grill is one of Tucson's most popular restaurants (see "Where to Dine," below). There's an adjacent lounge.

Amenities: The small pool has a great view of the Catalinas. Amenities include a tennis court, a whirlpool, horseback riding, nature walks, and massages.

✪ **Westward Look Resort.** 245 E. Ina Rd., Tucson, AZ 85704. ☎ **800/722-2500** or 520/297-1151. Fax 520/297-9023. www.westwardlook.com. 244 units. A/C MINIBAR TV TEL. Mid-Jan to Apr $199–$299 double; May $149–$189 double; June to mid-Sept $99–$129 double; mid-Sept to early Jan $109–$149 double. AE, CB, DC, DISC, MC, V. Pets accepted.

Built in 1912 as a dude ranch, the Westward Look is the oldest resort in Tucson and one of the most reasonably priced resorts in the city. The resort, set in the Catalina foothills, is surrounded by desert, and although it doesn't have its own golf course, it does have an excellent health spa and plenty of tennis courts. There are jogging and nature trails and a fitness center. If you aren't a golfer but do enjoy resort amenities, this is one of your best Tucson choices. Upstairs from the lobby, you'll find an interesting little natural history exhibit, which is part of this resort's emphasis on nature and the outdoors.

The guest rooms, all of which were recently renovated, are quite large and have private patios or balconies. Spanish colonial–style furnishings with an antique look give rooms here a classic Southwestern flavor. Many have exposed-beam ceilings and great views of the city.

Dining/Diversions: The Gold Room restaurant serves reliably excellent continental and Southwestern cuisine and has a great view of Tucson. A casual bar and grill, with live music on weekends, benefits from the same views.

Amenities: Three pools, eight tennis courts, three whirlpools, basketball and volleyball courts, a jogging trail, pro shop, large fitness center and full-service health spa (offering a wide variety of spa treatments and exercise, tai chi, and yoga classes), rental bikes, tour desk, concierge, room service, valet/laundry service, tennis lessons, horseback riding, guided hikes, baby-sitting.

MODERATE

Windmill Inn at St. Philip's Plaza. 4250 N. Campbell Ave., Tucson, AZ 85718. ☎ **800/547-4747** or 520/577-0007. Fax 520/577-0045. www.windmillinns.com. 122 units. A/C TV TEL. Mid-Jan to mid-Apr $135–$145 double; late Apr–early June and mid-Sept to mid-Jan $99–$120 double; early June to mid-Sept $65–$85 double. AE, DC, DISC, MC, V.

Located in St. Philip's Plaza, which has several great restaurants and an array of upscale shops, this hotel has a good location and spacious accommodations. All the rooms are suites and contain couches, work desks, two TVs, three telephones (one in the bathroom), double vanities, wet bars, small refrigerators, and microwaves. Basically there's everything to make the business traveler or vacationer comfortable for a long stay, and local phone calls are free. Amenities here include an outdoor pool, a whirlpool, a lending library, and complimentary use of bicycles (the Rillito River bike path starts in back of the hotel).

WEST OF DOWNTOWN
EXPENSIVE

✪ **La Tierra Linda Guest Ranch Resort.** 7501 N. Wade Rd., Tucson, AZ 85743. ☎ **888/872-6241** or 520/744-7700. Fax 520/579-9742. www.latierralinda.com. 14 units. A/C TV TEL. Early Dec to mid-May $155–$165 double, $215–$335 suite; mid-May to early Sept $90–$100 double, $125–$200 suite; early Sept to early Dec $115–$125 double, $160–$250 suite. Rates include full breakfast. AE, DC, DISC, MC, V.

Set on 30 acres in northwestern Tucson and adjacent to Saguaro National Park, this guest ranch was completely renovated a few years back and is now a surprisingly resortlike property. Originally opened as a dude ranch back in the 1930s, La Tierra Linda went through many incarnations before its most recent face-lift. Lots of mature desert landscaping gives La Tierra Linda a distinctive desert feel. Guest rooms vary a lot in size and layout, and the suites, which give you plenty of extra room, are generally worth the added expense. Throughout the property, there's lots of interesting stonework incorporated into the buildings. A viewing deck provides an excellent view of Sombrero Peak in the Tucson Mountains.

Dining/Diversions: The Ranch House Grill, in the main ranch house, serves Southwestern fare, of course. There's a small bar with the feel of a mine shaft.

Amenities: Small outdoor pool, whirlpool in a stone-walled gazebo, tennis court, volleyball court, horseshoe pits, and horseback riding.

Starr Pass Golf Suites. 3645 W. Starr Pass Blvd., Tucson, AZ 85745. ☎ **800/503-2898** or 520/670-0500. Fax 520/670-0427. www.starrpasstucson.com. 105 units. A/C TV TEL. Mid-Jan to mid-May $179 double, $309 suite, $429 casita; mid-May to Sept $89 double, $139 suite, $199 casita; Oct to mid-Jan (except Dec 24–Jan 1) $119 double, $179 suite, $249 casita; Dec 24–Jan 1 $169 double, $299 suite, $419 casita. AE, CB, DC, DISC, MC, V.

Located off West 22nd Street, 3 miles west of I-10, Starr Pass is the closest golf resort to downtown and the most economically priced golf resort in the city. However, it is a condominium resort, and you won't find the sort of service you get at Tucson's other resorts. On the other hand, you won't pay nearly as much. Accommodations are in privately owned Santa Fe–style casitas that can be broken down into a master suite and a standard hotel-style room or that can be rented as two-bedroom units. The master suites are the larger, more comfortable rooms and have fireplaces, full kitchens, and a general Southwestern style throughout. Bathrooms are large and have separate showers and tubs. The smaller rooms are a bit cramped and much less lavish in their appointments.

Dining: The dining room looks out over the golf course and surrounding hills and serves a mix of continental and Southwestern dishes at reasonable prices.

Amenities: The desert-style 18-hole golf course is best known for its 15th hole, which plays through a pass that was once a stagecoach route. Large pro shop, outdoor pool, exercise room, two tennis courts, whirlpool spa, hiking/biking trails, and valet/laundry service.

MODERATE

Casa Tierra. 11155 W. Calle Pima, Tucson, AZ 85743. ☎ **520/578-3058.** Fax 520/ 578-8445. 4 units. Sept–May $105–$165 double; $175–$300 suite (lower rates in summer). Rates include full breakfast. 2-night minimum. AE, MC, V.

If you've come to Tucson to be in the desert and you really want to be a *part* of the desert, then this secluded B&B is well worth considering. Built to look as if it has been here since Spanish colonial days, Casa Tierra, a modern adobe home, is surrounded by 5 acres of cactus and *palo verde* on the west side of Saguaro National Park. There are great views across a landscape full of saguaros to the mountains to the north, and sunsets are often enough to take your breath away. Surrounding a landscaped central courtyard is a covered seating area off of which the guest rooms open. The outdoor whirlpool spa makes a perfect stargazing spot, and there's a very well-equipped exercise room.

NEAR THE AIRPORT
MODERATE

Best Western Inn at the Airport. 7060 S. Tucson Blvd., Tucson, AZ 85706. ☎ **800/ 772-3847** or 520/746-0271. Fax 520/889-7391. 149 units. A/C TV TEL. Jan–Mar $89–$119 double; Apr–May and mid-Sept to Dec $59–$99 double; June to mid-Sept $59–$79 double. Rates include continental breakfast. AE, CB, DC, DISC, MC, V.

If you're the type who likes to get as much sleep as possible before getting up to catch a plane, this motel right outside the airport entrance will do it for you—there's no place closer. The rooms are comfortable, and the restaurant and lounge ensure that guests don't go hungry or thirsty. There's a small courtyard pool and a whirlpool as well as a fitness room and a tennis court.

Clarion Hotel Tucson Airport. 6801 S. Tucson Blvd., Tucson, AZ 85706. ☎ **800/ 526-0550** or 520/746-3932. Fax 520/889-9934. 191 units. A/C TV TEL. Jan–Apr $79–$129 double; May–Aug $59–$79 double; Sept–Oct $69–$79 double; Nov–Dec $59–$79 double. Rates include full breakfast. AE, CB, DC, DISC, MC, V.

Located just outside the airport exit, this low-rise hotel provides convenience and some great amenities, including a nightly complimentary cocktail reception and late-night snacks. The rooms are generally quite large, and the "king" rooms are particularly comfortable. The poolside rooms, in addition to being convenient for swimming and lounging, have small refrigerators. The restaurant, with its eclectic menu, offers moderately priced meals in casual surroundings. There's an adjacent lounge. Amenities include a pool, a whirlpool, an exercise room, room service, valet service, and a complimentary airport shuttle.

INEXPENSIVE

There are numerous budget motels near the Tucson Airport. They include **Motel 6,** 755 E. Benson Hwy., Exit 262 off I-10 (☎ **520/622-4614**), and **Motel 6,** 1031 E. Benson Hwy., Exit 262 (☎ **520/628-1264**), both charging $42 to $48 double; and **Super 8—Tucson/East,** 1990 S. Craycroft Rd., Exit 265 off I-10 (☎ **520/ 790-6021**), charging $43 to $80 double.

OUTLYING AREAS
NORTH OF TUCSON

✪ "Across The Creek" at Aravaipa Farms. 89395 Aravaipa Rd., Winkelman, AZ 85292.
☎ 520/357-6901. 3 units. $225 double. Rates include all meals. No credit cards.

Located 60 miles north of Tucson on one of the only year-round streams in southern Arizona, this B&B is a romantic getaway near one of the state's most spectacular desert wilderness areas. Because the inn is 3 miles up a gravel road and then across a stream (high-clearance vehicle recommended), it's a long way to a restaurant. Consequently, innkeeper Carol Steele, who formerly operated restaurants in the Scottsdale area, provides all meals. Guests entertain themselves hiking in the nearby Aravaipa Canyon Wilderness, bird watching, and cooling off in Aravaipa Creek. The three casitas here are eclectically designed and decorated in a mix of international folk art, rustic Mexican furniture, and original works of art. There are tile floors, stone-walled showers, and shady verandas. For either a romantic getaway or a vigorous weekend exploring the desert, this inn makes an ideal base.

C.O.D. Ranch. P.O. Box 241, Oracle, AZ 85623. ☎ 800/868-5617 or 520/615-3211. Fax 520/896-2271. www.codranch.com. 12 units (2 with shared bathroom). $95–$225 double. MC, V.

Located 45 minutes north of Tucson, this lodge is primarily used by groups and family reunions, but with its two restored 1880s adobe houses and remote setting overlooking the San Pedro Valley, the C.O.D. Ranch, lovingly restored by Steve Malkin, is an ideal spot for a tranquil getaway between the desert and the mountains. The decor is a mix of rustic Mexican furnishings and contemporary art by regional artists, and four of the casitas have full kitchens and two have fireplaces. Within a few miles of the ranch, you'll find a section of the Arizona Trail, and horseback rides along the trail can be arranged. At an additional cost and with prior arrangement, meals can be provided for guests staying more than 1 night.

SOUTH OF TUCSON

Santa Rita Lodge. HC 70, Box 5444, Sahuarita, AZ 85629. ☎ 520/625-8746. Fax 520/648-1186. www.maderacanyon.net. 12 units. $73–$93 double in the lodge; $83–$93 double in cabins. AE, MC, V. Pets accepted Sept–Nov only.

Located in the shade of Madera Canyon, this lodge is used almost exclusively by bird watchers, and getting a room here in late spring, when the birds are out in force, can be difficult. Book early. The rooms and cabins are large and fairly comfortable; natural history programs and guided bird walks are offered between March and August.

SPAS

Canyon Ranch Health Resort. 8600 E. Rockcliff Rd., Tucson, AZ 85750. ☎ 800/726-9900 for information, 800/742-9000 for reservations, or 520/749-9000. Fax 520/749-7755. www.canyonranch.com. 180 units. A/C TV TEL. Late Sept–early June 4-night package from $3,720 double; early June–late Sept 4-night package from $2,680 double (all rates plus 18% service charge). Rates include all meals and a variety of spa services and programs. AE, DC, DISC, MC, V. No children under 14 accepted (with exception of infants in the care of personal nannies).

Canyon Ranch, one of America's premier health spas, offers the sort of complete spa experience that's available at only a handful of places around the country. On staff are doctors, nurses, psychotherapists and counselors, fitness instructors, massage therapists, and tennis, golf, and racquetball pros. Services offered include health and fitness assessments; health, nutrition, exercise, and stress-management consultations, seminars, presentations, and evaluations; fitness classes and activities; massage therapy; herbal and aroma wraps; facials, manicures, pedicures, haircuts, and styling; private sports lessons; makeup consultations; cooking demonstrations; and art classes. There are a variety of spacious and very comfortable accommodations.

Dining/Diversions: Three gourmet low-calorie meals are served daily with options for total daily caloric intake. Don't worry, you won't go hungry.

Amenities: 62,000-square-foot spa complex that includes seven gyms, aerobics and strength-training rooms, squash and racquetball courts, yoga/meditation room, saunas, steam rooms, inhalation rooms, whirlpools, cold plunges, private sunbathing areas, and skin care and beauty salons. There's an aquatic center, several other pools, eight tennis courts, and a basketball court. A concierge is available, and airport transfers are included in the rates.

Miraval. 5000 E. Via Estancia Miraval, Catalina, AZ 85739. ☎ **800/232-3969** or 520/825-4000. Fax 520/825-5163. www.miravalresort.com. 106 units. A/C MINIBAR TV TEL. Oct–early June $790–$1,040 double, $1,440–$1,740 suite; early June–Sept $590–$890 double, $1,140–$1,440 suite (all rates plus 17.5% service charge). Rates include all meals and a variety of spa services and programs. AE, DISC, MC, V.

Focusing on what it calls "life balancing," Miraval emphasizes stress management, self-discovery, and relaxation rather than facials and mud baths. To this end, activities at the all-inclusive resort include meditation, tai chi, Pilates, and yoga, but for more active types, there is hiking, mountain biking, and rock climbing (on an outdoor climbing wall). Of course, such desert classics as horseback riding, tennis, volleyball, and swimming are available. However, staying busy isn't really the objective here; learning a new way of life is the ultimate goal at Miraval.

Throughout the resort, Southwestern styling predominates, and there are unequaled views of the Santa Catalina Mountains to be had from all over the grounds. Guest rooms, many of which have mountain views, are done in a Southwestern style and have very large bathrooms that, for the most part, have showers but no tubs.

Dining/Diversions: With two restaurants and two snack lounges, no one need fear going hungry here. However, rest assured that everything served is healthful as well as delicious.

Amenities: Two exercise pools and a three-tiered leisure pool surrounded by waterfalls and desert landscaping are among the most popular facilities here, but you'll also find a superbly equipped exercise room, rock-climbing wall, tennis courts, volleyball court, riding stables, whirlpool spas, saunas, and steam rooms. Miraval offers lifestyle management workshops, fitness/nutrition consultations, cooking demonstrations, exercise classes, an "equine experience" program, massage, and skin care and facials. Airport transfers are included in the rates.

GUEST RANCHES

Lazy K Bar Ranch. 8401 N. Scenic Dr., Tucson, AZ 85743. ☎ **800/321-7018** or 520/744-3050. Fax 520/744-7628. www.lazykbar.com. 23 units. A/C. Oct to mid-Dec $218–$248 double; mid-Dec to Apr $248–$308 double; May–Sept $190–$230 double (all rates plus 16% service charge). Rates include all meals. 3-night minimum. AE, DISC, MC, V.

Homesteaded in 1933 and converted to a dude ranch in 1936, the Lazy K Bar Ranch covers 160 acres adjacent to Saguaro National Park. There are plenty of nearby hiking and riding trails, and if you have a hankering for city life, downtown Tucson is only 20 minutes away. Ranch activities include horseback riding twice daily, hayrides, lunch rides, and cookouts. There are also nature talks and star viewing. The guest rooms vary in size and comfort level (some have whirlpool tubs), and the newest rooms are absolutely gorgeous, so try to get one of them.

Dining/Diversions: Meals are served family style in a dining room that features Mexican tile floors and an open-pit fireplace. The food is hearty American ranch style with cookouts some nights. There's a nightly happy hour at the ranch's BYOB bar.

Amenities: Horseback riding and lessons, cattle drives, pool, whirlpool, two tennis courts, volleyball and basketball courts, horseshoe pits, stables, mountain bikes, rappelling, guided hikes, complimentary airport transfer.

✪ **Tanque Verde Ranch.** 14301 E. Speedway Blvd., Tucson, AZ 85748. ☎ **800/234-DUDE** or 520/296-6275. Fax 520/721-9426. www.tanqueverderanch.com. 75 units. A/C TEL. Mid-Dec to Apr $315–$415 double; May–Sept $260–$345 double; Oct to mid-Dec $270–$355 double. Rates include all meals. AE, DISC, MC, V.

Far and away the most luxurious guest ranch in Tucson (some people say this is a resort with horses), Tanque Verde Ranch, founded in the 1880s, still has some of its original buildings. The ranch borders both Saguaro National Park and the Coronado National Forest, which ensures plenty of room for guided horseback rides. In addition to riding, the bird watching here is excellent (more than 220 species have been seen on the ranch) and birders are well served. There are nature trails, wildlife-viewing ramadas (shaded patios), and a nature center with displays of live snakes and other desert critters. The guest rooms are spacious and comfortable, but don't expect a TV here—ranch policy encourages guests to participate in various activities. Many rooms have fireplaces and patios, and the bathrooms are large. The new casitas are absolutely huge and among the most luxurious accommodations in the state.

Dining/Diversions: The large dining room, which overlooks the Rincon Mountains, sets impressive buffets. There are breakfast horseback rides, poolside luncheons, and cookout rides. An old foreman's cabin houses a cantina.

Amenities: Indoor and outdoor pools, riding stables, five tennis courts, exercise room, saunas, whirlpool, horseshoes, basketball and volleyball courts, tennis pro shop, rodeo arena, nature trails, complimentary riding and tennis lessons, evening lectures and performances, nature hikes, children's programs, baby-sitting, and complimentary airport shuttle with 4-night stay.

White Stallion Ranch. 9251 W. Twin Peaks Rd., Tucson, AZ 85743. ☎ **888/977-2624** or 520/297-0252. Fax 520/744-2786. www.wsranch.com. 39 units. A/C. Oct 1–Dec 18 $224–$260 double, $276–$316 suite; Dec 19–May 31 $244–$300 double, $316–$356 suite (all rates plus 15% service charge). Rates include all meals. 4- to 6-night minimum stay in winter. No credit cards. Closed June–Sept.

Set on 3,000 acres of desert just over the hill from Tucson, the White Stallion Ranch is perfect for those who crave wide-open spaces. Operated since 1965 by the True family, this spread has a more authentic ranch feel than any other guest ranch in the area. Three or four horseback rides are offered daily (except Sunday), and a petting zoo keeps kids entertained. The guest rooms vary considerably in size and comfort, from the tiny, spartan single rooms to deluxe two-bedroom suites.

Dining/Diversions: All meals, mostly traditional, familiar American fare, are served family style in the main dining room, which is housed in a 90-year-old building. There's an honor bar with cowhide stools and a longhorn steer head on the wall.

Amenities: Horseback riding and lessons, team cattle penning, outdoor pool, hot tub, two tennis courts, basketball and volleyball courts, nature trails, guided nature walks and hikes, games room, hayrides, airport pickup, tours available at additional charge.

4 Where to Dine

Variety, they say, is the spice of life, and Tucson certainly dishes up plenty of variety when it comes to eating out. Tucson is a city that lives for spice, and in the realm of spicy foods, Mexican reigns supreme. There's historic Mexican at El Charro Café and El Minuto, nouveau Mexican at Café Poca Cosa and J Bar, Mexico City Mexican at

Tucson Dining

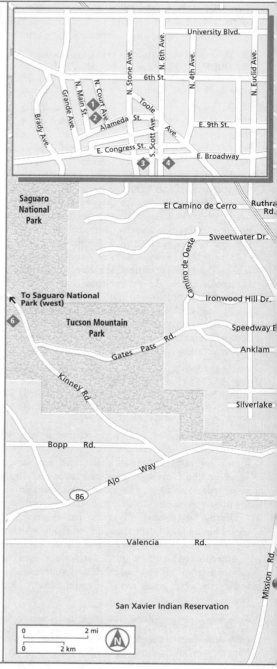

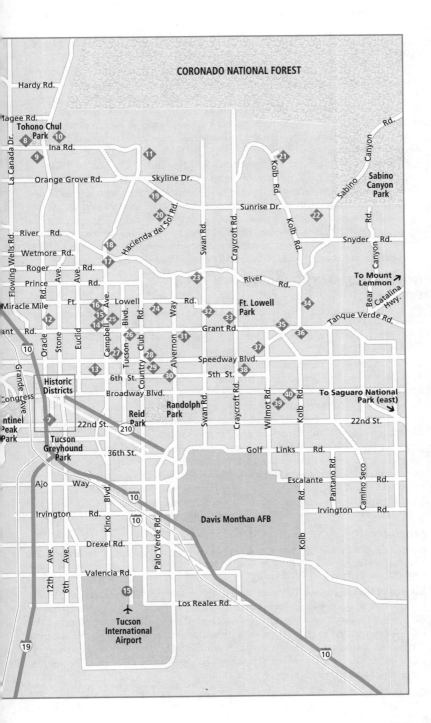

CORONADO NATIONAL FOREST

Hardy Rd.

Magee Rd.
Tohono Chul
Park

Ina Rd.

La Canada Dr.

Orange Grove Rd.

Skyline Dr.

Kolb Rd.

Sabino Canyon Rd.

Sabino
Canyon
Park

Sunrise Dr.

Kolb Rd.

Snyder Rd.

River Rd.

Flowing Wells Rd.

Wetmore Rd.

Roger Rd.

Prince Rd.

Miracle Mile

Ft. Lowell
Park

River Rd.

To Mount
Lemmon

Bear Canyon Rd.

Catalina Hwy.

ant Rd.

Oracle Rd.

Stone Ave.

Euclid Ave.

Ft. Lowell Rd.

Campbell Ave.

Way Rd.

Grant Rd.

Tanque Verde Rd.

Country Club Rd.

Alvernon Way

Speedway Blvd.

5th St.

Historic
Districts

6th St.

Broadway Blvd.

Randolph
Park

Swan Rd.

Craycroft Rd.

Wilmot Rd.

Kolb Rd.

To Saguaro National
Park (east)

Congress

Grande Ave.

ntinel
Peak
Park

Tucson
Greyhound
Park

22nd St.

Reid
Park

22nd St.

210

36th St.

Golf Links Rd.

Ajo Way

Irvington Rd.

Kino Blvd.

Palo Verde Rd.

Davis Monthan AFB

Escalante Rd.

Pantano Rd.

Camino Seco Rd.

Irvington Rd.

Kolb

Drexel Rd.

12th Ave.

6th Ave.

Valencia Rd.

Tucson
International
Airport

Los Reales Rd.

19

10

317

La Parilla Suiza, and family-style Mexican at Casa Molina. So if you like Mexican food, you'll find plenty of places here in Tucson to get all fired up.

On the other hand, if Mexican leaves you cold, don't despair—there are dozens of other restaurants serving everything from the finest French cuisine to innovative American, Italian, and Southwestern food. Southwestern cuisine is almost as abundant in Tucson as Mexican food, and you should be sure to dine at a Southwestern restaurant early in your visit. This cuisine, a more cultured cousin to Mexican, can be brilliantly creative, and after trying it you may want *all* your meals to be Southwestern. Keep in mind, however, that this food tends to be both pricey and spicy.

Foodies fond of the latest culinary trends will find plenty of places in Tucson to satisfy their cravings. Try almost any of the restaurants along East Tanque Verde Road, which is Tucson's restaurant row, or at any of the foothills resort restaurants. Elsewhere around the city, trendsetting restaurants include Pastiche, Firecracker, and Wildflower. On the other hand, if you're on a tight dining budget, you might want to avoid the trendy places and instead look for early-bird dinners, which are particularly popular with retirees. Although these economical early-evening dinners are more often offered during the summer months, some places have them year-round.

DOWNTOWN & THE UNIVERSITY AREA
EXPENSIVE

✪ **Arizona Inn.** 2200 E. Elm St. ☎ **520/325-1541.** Reservations recommended. Main courses $6–$15 at lunch, $18–$28 at dinner. AE, DC, MC, V. Mon–Sat 7–10am, 11:30am–2pm, and 6–10pm; Sun 7–10am, 11am–2pm (brunch), and 6–10pm. CONTEMPORARY AMERICAN.

The dining room at the Arizona Inn, one of the state's first resorts, has established itself as a consistently excellent restaurant with reasonable prices. The rose-pink stucco pueblo-style buildings are surrounded by neatly manicured gardens that have aged gracefully, and it's romantic to dine in the courtyard or overlooking the colorful gardens on the bar patio. The menu is not extensive, but every dish, such as roast confit of duck with an orange-coffee glaze and Grand Marnier sauce, is perfectly prepared. Flavors are predominantly Southwestern, with hints of Mediterranean and Asian. Because the Arizona Inn is a class act and doesn't have to work too hard to impress, presentation is artistic but not overly so, and fresh ingredients are emphasized more than sauces. The bouillabaisse is beautiful yet simple and homemade ice creams, such as ginger-cappuccino, are fabulous. On weekends, you might catch some live music. Lunches include quiche, pastas, salads, and sandwiches.

MODERATE

Barrio. 135 S. 6th Ave. ☎ **520/629-0191.** Reservations recommended for dinner. Main courses $7–$18. AE, DC, MC, V. Tues–Thurs 11am–10pm; Fri 11am–midnight; Sat 5pm–midnight; Sun 5–9pm. SOUTHWESTERN.

Located at the edge of the Barrio Histórico, this neighborhood restaurant is popular with downtown professionals and the art crowd. On the whole, the food is pleasantly spicy and served with zippy Southwestern accents. If you're not too hungry, one of the little plates, such as the tasty Anaheim chile stuffed with black beans, garlic, and goat cheese on a red-pepper cream sauce will do. For fans of burgers, the jalapeño burger is thick, juicy, and just spicy enough. Looking for an interesting mélange of flavors? Try the pork tenderloin with a mango-ginger chutney.

✪ **Café Poca Cosa.** Clarion Hotel & Suites Santa Rita, 88 E. Broadway Blvd. ☎ **520/622-6400.** Reservations highly recommended. Main courses $7.50–$9 at lunch, $11.50–$17 at dinner. MC, V. Mon–Thurs 11am–9pm; Fri–Sat 11am–10pm. MEXICAN.

North-of-the-Border Margaritaville

Jimmy Buffet may have had a problem keeping his flip-flops on after a few margaritas, but he certainly knew a good thing when he tasted it. Nothing takes the heat out of a hot desert day like an icy, limey margarita. While the rest of the country is busy sipping single malts and designer martinis, Tucson has quietly become a north of the border Margaritaville.

Today, with dozens of premium tequilas making their way north from Mexico, tequila is no longer something to be slammed back as quickly as possible with enough salt and lime to hide its flavor. A margarita makes far better use of salt and lime, which, when combined with a dash of Triple Sec or Cointreau, produce the perfect drink for the desert. When the tequila in a margarita is a premium *reposado* (rested or aged), 100% blue agave tequila and the lime juice is fresh-squeezed instead of from a bottle or a margarita mix, you have the makings of the perfect margarita. Of course, the question of on the rocks or frozen is a matter of personal taste; we prefer our margaritas on the rocks. It allows the flavors to better express themselves. And, yes, with salt. However, we do make an exception for prickly pear margaritas. These hot-pink concoctions, made with the fruit of the prickly pear cactus, are best when they're served blended.

The following are some restaurants and bars that we think make the best margaritas in Tucson and where you, too, can ponder the question, "Is this the perfect margarita?"

Barrio, 135 S. 6th Ave. (☎ **520/629-0191**). Downtown bars and margaritas just seem to go together. At the Barrio, you can sip your sour-and-salty with Tucson's art crowd.

Presidio Grill, 3352 E. Speedway Blvd. (☎ **520/327-4667**). Long one of Tucson's favorite restaurants for creative cuisine, the Presidio Grill serves good margaritas (although martinis still hold sway here).

Café Poca Cosa, 88 E. Broadway Blvd. (☎ **520/622-6400**). Great food, great atmosphere, and you never wonder if the bartender forgot the tequila in your margarita.

Casa Molina, 6225 E. Speedway Blvd. (☎ **520/886-5468**). Long the most popular margaritas in Tucson, and strong. They go well with the fiery salsa and chips here. No pretension.

Flying V Bar & Grill, in Loews Ventana Canyon Resort, 7000 N. Resort Dr. (☎ **520/299-2020**). While the prickly pear margaritas here aren't necessarily better than others around town, the view from the deck is superb. Not only does all of Tucson spread out below you, but you can watch the golfers double bogey the 18th hole of the Canyon Course.

¡Toma!, 311 N. Court Ave. (☎ **520/622-1922**). Another downtown favorite next door to El Charro Café, Tucson's famous *carne seca* restaurant. These margaritas are just plain good.

Created by owner-chef Suzana Davila, the food here is not just *any* Mexican food; it's imaginative and different, and the flamboyant atmosphere of red and purple walls and Mexican/Southwestern artwork is equally unusual. The cuisine here—which has been compared to the dishes dreamed up in *Like Water for Chocolate*—consists of creations such as grilled beef with a jalapeño chile and tomatillo sauce, and chicken with a dark *mole* (pronounced *mole*-ay) sauce made with Kahlua, chocolate, almonds, and chiles. The menu changes daily, but there is always something wonderful to try. The service staff is courteous and friendly and will recite the menu for you in both Spanish and English. This lively restaurant is an excellent value, especially at lunch (which is served until 4pm).

Another (smaller and simpler) Café Poca Cosa, 20 S. Scott St., is open for breakfast and lunch Monday to Friday 7:30am to 2:30pm.

The Dish Bistro & Wine Bar. 3200 E. Speedway Blvd. (at the Rumrunner). ☎ **520/ 326-1714.** Reservations highly recommended. Main courses $14.50–$25; smaller dishes $7–$9. AE, DC, MC, V. Tues–Sat 5–10pm. NEW AMERICAN.

Located in the rear of the Rumrunner Wine and Cheese Co. (and part of the same operation), this tiny, minimalist restaurant is brimming with urban chic. On a busy night, the space could be construed as either cozy or crowded, so if you like it more on the quiet side, come early or late. The chef has a well-deserved reputation for daring, and turns out such dishes as a butternut squash flan on puff pastry with Swiss chard; colorful and well-composed salads; sauteed crawfish tails with olives and goat cheese; and grilled chicken with pumpkin seed pesto. Naturally, the wine list is great, and the servers, who are well informed about the menus, will be happy to help you choose a bottle. Dishes come from small to large to suit your appetite.

✪ **El Charro Café.** 311 N. Court Ave. ☎ **520/622-1922.** Reservations recommended for dinner. Main courses $4–$14. AE, CB, DC, DISC, MC, V. Sun–Thurs 11am–9pm; Fri–Sat 11am–10pm. SONORAN MEXICAN.

El Charro, in an old stone building in El Presidio Historic District, claims to be Tucson's oldest family operated Mexican restaurant. A front porch has been glassed in for a greenhouse-like dining area overlooking the street, and there's dining downstairs. Look at the roof of El Charro as you approach, and you might see a large metal cage containing beef drying in the sun. This is the main ingredient in *carne seca*, El Charro's well-known specialty (like beef jerky), which is oft copied but never duplicated at other Mexican restaurants around town. You'll rarely find *carne seca* on a Mexican menu outside Tucson, so indulge in it while you're here. *A warning:* The cafe can be packed at lunch, so arrive early or late. The family runs the adjacent ¡Toma!, a colorful bar/cantina next door.

Other El Charro Cafe branches can be found at 6310 E. Broadway (☎ **520/ 745-1922**) and in the Tucson International Airport (☎ **520/573-8222**).

✪ **Kingfisher.** 2564 E. Grant Rd. ☎ **520/323-7739.** Reservations recommended on weekends. Main courses $7–$10 at lunch, $13.50–$20 at dinner. AE, CB, DC, DISC, MC, V. Mon–Fri 11am–midnight; Sat–Sun 5pm–midnight. SEAFOOD.

If you're serious about seafood, head for the Kingfisher. The freshest seafood, artfully blended with bright flavors and imaginative ingredients, is deftly prepared as appetizers, sandwiches, and main dishes. You may have difficulty deciding whether to begin with Umpqua Bay oysters (there's a full-service raw bar), seared ahi tuna salad, or the delicately smoked red trout—so why not tackle them all? Fans of outstanding salads will flip over the warm cabbage salad with mesquite bacon and spiced pecans, and meat eaters as well as vegetarians will find items on the menu. The atmosphere is upscale and lively, and the bar and late-night menu are a hit with night owls.

La Cocina/Two Micks Cantina. 201 N. Court St. ☎ **520/622-0351.** Reservations recommended. Main courses $6–$12 at lunch, $11–$22 at dinner. AE, CB, DC, DISC, MC, V. Mon 11am–2pm; Tues–Fri 11am–2pm and 4:30–9pm; Sat 11am–3pm and 4:30–9pm; Sun 4:30–8pm. SOUTHWESTERN.

Housed in the same historic 1850s adobe building as the Old Town Artisans shopping plaza, La Cocina is one of the few good restaurants left in downtown Tucson. Its convenience to both shopping and the Tucson Museum of Art makes it imminently recommendable. The restaurant's tree-shaded patio dining area, in the courtyard of the old adobe, is surrounded by colorful gardens and is an excellent place for a light lunch (salads, sandwiches, and Mexican specialties). The more formal indoor dining room, decorated with regional artwork, is most popular in the evening, when you might start your meal with an avocado and chile stuffed quesadilla, then move on to chicken with a blue cornmeal crust or ahi tuna topped with pecan-lime butter. On the far side of the courtyard from the dining room is the restaurant's rustic cantina.

Le Bistro. 2574 N. Campbell Ave. ☎ **520/327-3086.** Reservations recommended for dinner. Main courses $6–$10 at lunch, $9–$19 at dinner. AE, DISC, MC, V. Mon–Fri 11am–2:30pm and 5–10pm; Sat–Sun 5–10pm. FRENCH/EUROPEAN.

Etched mirrors, lace, and live palm trees full of twinkling lights set the scene for some casual bistro cuisine. European specialties include the likes of duck pâté, roast quail, blackened sea scallops, and bouillabaisse. Salads are quite good, there are dozens of choices for wine, and prices are reasonable. On the extravagant side is the showcase of desserts, with names such as Tuxedo (a double-chocolate mousse), Opera (a creation with hazelnut and mocha crème), and bombé (a chocolate-covered mountain of cream puffs), which frequently stops passersby dead in their tracks. The bar here is a good place to come for a glass of wine and one of these rich, decadent desserts.

Pastiche Modern Eatery. 3025 N. Campbell Ave. ☎ **520/325-3333.** Reservations recommended. Main courses $7–$19. AE, DC, DISC, MC, V. Mon–Sat 11:30–midnight; Sun 4:30pm–midnight. NEW AMERICAN.

Situated in a shopping plaza with lots of Tucson character, this high-energy bistro is currently one of *the* places to dine in Tucson. The colorful artwork and vibrant contemporary food scream *trendy*. However, the main reason for the restaurant's popularity is probably its variety of menu offerings. There are small plates, split plates, sandwiches, and full-size entrees—something to satisfy every appetite. Grilled ahi tuna with an aïoli sauce and crunchy wontons is terrific, as are the bold flavors of fusilli pasta with andouille sausage and gorgonzola cheese. The crowded bar is a popular watering hole that turns out some tasty margaritas.

✪ **Presidio Grill.** 3352 E. Speedway Blvd. ☎ **520/327-4667.** Reservations recommended. Main courses $7–$11 at lunch, $13–$22 at dinner. AE, DC, DISC, MC, V. Mon–Thurs 11am–3pm and 5–9pm; Fri–Sat 11am–3pm and 5–11pm; Sun 5–9pm. AMERICAN REGIONAL.

This ever-trendy restaurant, modern and upbeat in both cuisine and interior design, is in the Rancho Center shopping plaza, along busy Speedway Boulevard. Whether you want seafood, pasta, or something from the grill, the dishes here show a variety of international influences. One friend of ours claims that the warm brie and roasted garlic appetizer makes a perfect lunch, but for a heartier dish, try the Presidio chicken pasta with prosciutto, poblano chiles, asiago cheese, and roma tomatoes on linguine (which was featured on the cover of *Bon Appétit* magazine). The restaurant is usually packed at lunchtime during the week, so make a reservation if possible. There's an excellent selection of wines and liquors at very reasonable prices.

INEXPENSIVE

El Minuto Cafe. 354 S. Main Ave. ☎ **520/882-4145**. Main courses $6–$12. AE, MC, V. Daily 11am–10pm. MEXICAN.

El Minuto, downtown at the edge of the Barrio next to the El Tiradito shrine, is a meeting ground for both Anglos and Latinos who come here for the lively atmosphere and Mexican home cooking. In business since 1939, this place is a neighborhood landmark and a prototype that other Mexican restaurants often try to emulate. Cheese crisps (Mexican pizza) are a specialty, and enchiladas, especially *carne seca,* are tasty. This is a fun place for people-watching—you'll find all types from kids to guys in suits.

Miami Tropical Cafeteria. 1045 E. 6th St. ☎ **520/623-8020.** Main courses $4–$6.25. No credit cards. Mon–Sat 11am–8pm. CUBAN.

With just a few tables in a storefront near the University of Arizona, this casual place feels like a Cuban restaurant straight out of Miami. At lunch, the proprietor will dish you up a daily special from the steam table (perhaps chicken seasoned with olives, garlic, and bay leaves accompanied by black beans and rice). The Cuban sandwich is a meat- and cheese-filled baguette, pressed and warmed on the grill. Also worth trying are the fried plantains and yummy fruit shakes made with mango, banana, or *guanabana.*

✪ **Native Café.** 3073 N. Campbell Ave. ☎ **520/881-8881.** Salads and sandwiches $5.50–$9. MC, V. Mon–Sat 8am–9pm; Sun 8am–4:30pm. NATURAL FOODS.

With a mellow, arty atmosphere and a comfortable patio, the Native Café is a good place for a leisurely light meal or snack. Opulent salads brimming with the freshest of veggies and delicious sandwiches garnished with huge, crunchy sunflower sprouts are the norm here (the sandwiches are basically salads between slices of handcrafted bread). There are plenty of choices for everyone from vegans to meat eaters—and it's all healthful and impeccably fresh. Dinner specials include pad Thai or tempeh tacos. You can choose among juices, smoothies, or coffees to accompany a sweet treat of scones or cardamom-cinnamon coffee cake.

EAST TUCSON
EXPENSIVE

Cielos. At Lodge on the Desert, 306 N. Alvernon Way. ☎ **520/325-3366.** Reservations recommended. Main courses $13–$25; Sunday brunch $19.95. AE, DISC, MC, V. Mon–Sat 7–10am, noon–2pm, and 5–10pm; Sun 7–10am, 11am–2pm, and 5–10pm. CONTINENTAL.

Arriving at Cielos is like taking a step back to a more tranquil time. Against a backdrop of rosy terra-cotta walls, the colorful gardens, table candlelight, and fragrant woods burning in the open fireplaces create a romantic ambience. Ask for a table on the terrace, where you'll have garden and fireplace views. Cielos tends to be popular with an older clientele and families out on special occasions, so perhaps for that reason the menu has become more conservative of late. Look for familiar favorites such as well-prepared pork tenderloin or filet mignon with whipped potatoes and a port wine sauce. Salads are simple yet tasty. Wines both by the glass and by the bottle are fairly reasonably priced, as are the entrees.

Dakota Café. 6541 E. Tanque Verde Rd. (in Traildust Town). ☎ **520/298-7188.** Reservations recommended. Main courses $6–$9 at lunch, $6–$19 at dinner. AE, CB, DC, DISC, MC, V. Mon–Thurs 11am–9pm; Fri–Sat 11am–10pm. Also open Sun 11am–4pm Oct–May. INTERNATIONAL.

Located in a mock cow town favored by families with small children, this restaurant, with its contemporary cowboy decor, lures a fairly sophisticated and adult crowd. Start your meal out on the patio with fruity apricot iced tea (very refreshing on a hot day) and tempura coconut shrimp with chutney marmalade. The grilled ahi tuna sandwich with herbed aïoli and pickled ginger is tasty and well textured and comes with a generous side of crispy coleslaw. For dinner, we like the grilled pork tenderloin sauced with chipotle, honey, and molasses. The food here is hearty yet inventive enough to try on a regular basis, and vegetarians will find many meatless choices. Reasonable prices and a comfortable atmosphere add up to a good value.

Fuego. 6958 E. Tanque Verde Rd. (in Santa Fe Square). ☎ **520/886-1745.** Reservations recommended. Main courses $14–$25. AE, MC, V. Sun–Thurs 5:30–10pm; Fri–Sat 5–10:30pm. CONTEMPORARY AMERICAN/SOUTHWEST.

The name Fuego means fire, and there really *are* flambéed dishes on the menu here, especially among the extensive list of appetizers. Overall, though, the food here is more Southwestern than fiery. The atmosphere is slightly formal but unpretentious, with tables set close together. Waiters bustle about serving such uniquely flavored dishes as the signature Field of Greens salad, with blue cheese, chile-roasted walnuts, and dried cranberries, or prickly pear pork tenderloin that is so tender you can cut it with a fork. Great sauces, such as a rich, smoky chipotle cream sauce on chicken capellini, emerge from this kitchen. Artful food presentation can be amusing, if a little difficult to approach with a fork. Lively yet intimate, Fuego appeals to couples, families, and retirees alike, and as for attire, casual to dressy fits in just fine.

Le Rendez-Vous. 3844 E. Ft. Lowell Rd. (at Alvernon Way). ☎ **520/323-7373.** Reservations recommended. Main courses $7–$12 at lunch, $14–$26 at dinner. AE, DC, DISC, MC, V. Tues–Fri 11:30am–2pm; Tues–Sun 6–9:30pm. FRENCH.

While this rather casual French restaurant serves all the usual dishes you would expect (escargots, pâté, vichyssoise, veal sweetbreads), it has become legendary among Tucson's foodies for its phenomenal duck à l'orange, and you would be remiss if someone at your table didn't order this dish. However, rest assured there are other dishes worth ordering. To leave more room for a selection from the pastry tray, you can even order from the limited spa menu. At lunch, try the classic *moules marinieres* (mussels cooked in white wine) and the ultimate spinach salad. You might expect such rich savory fare to be served amid rarefied elegance, but Le Rendez-Vous is housed in an unpretentious little stucco cottage and the atmosphere is strictly bistro.

Vivace Restaurant. 4811 E. Grant Rd. ☎ **520/795-7221.** Reservations recommended. Main courses $12–$22. AE, DC, DISC, MC, V. Mon–Thurs 11:30am–9pm, Fri–Sat 11:30am–10pm. CONTEMPORARY NORTHERN ITALIAN.

With a casual but upscale setting in a shopping plaza, this Italian restaurant serves reasonably priced, creative dishes. The restaurant can be noisy at times, owing to its popularity—you'll find a mixed crowd here, both young and old. First, crusty bread comes with a basil-infused olive oil. Then one of the possible appetizers is a large luscious antipasto platter for two containing garlic-flavored spinach, roasted red peppers, marinated chilled shrimp, and goat cheese. The dish is visually appealing and tastes as good as it looks. The bustling waitstaff doesn't waste time in getting your order from the open kitchen to you. Pasta dishes, such as penne with sausage and roasted-pepper sauce, come served on a very large dish. Salads are generous, the wine list is good and reasonable, and the server will recite a long litany of desserts: crème brûlée, tiramisu, chocolate espresso mousse, and molten chocolate cake (the last a popular dessert here in Tucson).

INEXPENSIVE

Casa Molina. 6225 E. Speedway Blvd. (near the northwest corner with Wilmot Rd.). ☎ **520/886-5468.** Reservations recommended. Dinners $12–$18; à la carte $3–$12. AE, DC, DISC, MC, V. Daily 11am–10pm. MEXICAN.

For years this has been Tucson's favorite family-run Mexican restaurant. You can't miss it—just watch for the larger-than-life-size bull and bullfighter in front. Casa Molina sports a festive atmosphere and is usually abuzz with families, groups, and couples.

The margaritas are among the best in town, and the *carne seca* (sun-dried beef) shouldn't be missed. Lighter eaters will enjoy a layered topopo salad made with tortillas, refried beans, chicken, lettuce, celery, avocado, tomato, and jalapeños. The food is good, and the service is efficient; the only complaint is that prices are a little on the high side for Mexican cookery. The patio is pleasant in almost any weather.

There are other locations at 3001 N. Campbell Ave. (☎ **520/795-7593**) and 4240 E. Grant Rd. (☎ **520/326-6663**).

La Parilla Suiza. 5602 E. Speedway Blvd. ☎ **520/747-4838.** Main courses $6–$15. AE, DC, DISC, MC, V. Sun–Thurs 11am–10pm; Fri–Sat 11am–11pm. MEXICAN.

Most Mexican food served in the United States is limited to Sonoran style, originating just south of the border. Actually, however, the cuisine of Mexico is nearly as varied as that of China, and the meals served at La Parilla Suiza are based on the style popular in Mexico City, where most of the chain's restaurants are located. Many menu items are sandwiched between two tortillas, much like a quesadilla, but the charcoal broiling of meats and cheeses lends the sandwiches special status. Fried green scallions with lime is a favorite appetizer.

There's another La Parilla Suiza at 2770 N. Oracle Rd. (☎ **520/624-4300**).

Little Anthony's Diner. 7010 E. Broadway Blvd. (in back of the Gaslight Plaza). ☎ **520/296-0456.** Pizza and burgers $4–$7. MC, V. Mon 11am–9pm; Tues–Thurs 11am–10pm; Fri 11am–11pm; Sat 8am–11pm; Sun 8am–10pm. AMERICAN.

This is a place for kids, although big kids like us enjoy the 1950s music and decor. The staff is good with children, and there's a video-games room and a rocket ship outside to ride. How about a jailhouse rock burger or hound dog hotdog with a tower of onion rings? Daily specials and bottomless soft drinks make feeding the family fairly inexpensive. Beer and wine are served, and Friday and Saturday nights there's a DJ along with the dinner. The gaslight melodrama theater next door makes a perfect night out for the family.

THE FOOTHILLS
EXPENSIVE

Anthony's in the Catalinas. 6440 N. Campbell Ave. ☎ **520/299-1771.** Reservations highly recommended. Main courses $10–$15 at lunch, $20–$33 at dinner. AE, DC, MC, V. Mon–Fri 11am–2pm and 5:30–10pm; Sat–Sun 5:30–10pm. NEW AMERICAN/CONTINENTAL.

Anthony's, housed in a modern Italianate-style building overlooking the city, exudes Southwestern elegance from the moment you drive up and let the valet park your car. The waiters are smartly attired in tuxedos, and guests (the cigar and single-malt Foothills set) are nearly as well dressed. In such a rarefied atmosphere you'd expect only the finest meal and service, and that's exactly what you get. Shrimp stuffed with horseradish and wrapped in bacon with a caper sauce is a fitting beginning, followed by the likes of lamb Wellington baked in puff pastry with pâté and prosciutto. Wine is not just an accompaniment but a reason for dining out at Anthony's; at more than 70 pages, the wine list may be the most extensive in the city. Don't miss out on the next best part of a meal here (after the wine): the day's soufflé (order early).

If you're looking for something a little out of the ordinary, dinner is served in Anthony's underground wine cellar. For a $1,000 minimum, up to 14 people can dine in the dirt-floored cellar. Call for more information.

Daniel's Restaurant & Trattoria. In St. Philip's Plaza, 4340 N. Campbell Ave. ☎ **520/742-3200.** Reservations recommended. Pastas $17.50–$25; main courses $23–$32. AE, CB, DC, DISC, MC, V. Daily 5–10pm. NORTHERN ITALIAN/MEDITERRANEAN.

Although the elegant atmosphere here translates into as good a place for a romantic evening out as Anthony's, above, Daniel's appeals to an equally affluent but younger and more casual crowd who come for the contemporary northern Italian cuisine. For an appetizer, we recommend the intriguing *frutti di mare in pasticceria,* a puff pastry stuffed with seafood, leeks, and goat cheese. The signature dish is rack of lamb, but it's difficult to pass up a luscious linguine with shrimp, scallops, mussels, and calamari in a deeply flavored broth. OK, say it's possible to consume both pasta and an entree, but you must save room for the warm chocolate truffle cake with vanilla-bean gelato. An outstanding wine list emphasizes Italian wines and includes about 30 wines by the glass, many of them fairly inexpensive. Lots of single malts, too, and insanely decadent after-dinner coffee drinks.

The Gold Room. In the Westward Look Resort, 245 E. Ina Rd. ☎ **520/297-1151.** Reservations recommended. Main courses $10–$13.50 at lunch, $20–$42 at dinner; Sunday brunch $23.50. AE, DC, DISC, MC, V. Daily 7am–2pm and 5:30–9:30pm. REGIONAL AMERICAN/CONTINENTAL.

Located in the Westward Look Resort, the Gold Room is a tastefully casual restaurant featuring Southwestern ranch decor and a terrace for alfresco dining. Despite the casual decor, the place settings are elegant and the service is very professional. Satisfying all tastes, the menu is equally divided between classic dishes (filet mignon and roast rack of lamb) and regional specialties, all of which are beautifully presented. We favor the regional cuisine—tender mesquite-grilled buffalo with purple Peruvian potatoes or pan-seared duck breast with blue corn polenta—which emphasizes flavor over fire. The length of the wine list is staggering, and there's a welcome range of prices. Desserts are delectably rich and amusingly presented—the chocolate bombé is an event in itself. Lunch prices are less expensive than those at dinner, but the restaurant is most remarkable at night when the cityscape of Tucson twinkles below.

✪ The Grill. At the Hacienda del Sol Guest Ranch Resort, 5601 N. Hacienda del Sol Rd. ☎ **520/529-3500.** Reservations recommended. Main courses $20–$38; Sunday brunch $24.95. AE, CB, DC, DISC, MC, V. Daily 5–10pm; Sun brunch 10am–2pm. REGIONAL AMERICAN.

Located in a 1920s hacienda-style building at a former foothills dude ranch, The Grill has been one of Tucson's hottest restaurants for a couple of years now. Not only do you get well-prepared meats and vegetables grilled over pecan wood, but you also get great views of the city and a classically styled Southwestern setting. For openers, consider the roasted tomato soup, which comes with garlic and goat cheese crostini and is among the most satisfying starters on the menu. The dry-aged Angus New York strip steak is the most popular entree, but anyone seeking greater creativity would do well to opt for the perfectly done ahi tuna with wasabi orzo. To top things off, try one of the extravagant desserts, such as the flourless chocolate torte with layers of hazelnut buttercream and chocolate ganache. The patio overlooks the Catalinas and the fairways of the Westin La Paloma's golf course. Sunday brunch here is a treat.

✪ Janos. At the Westin La Paloma, 3770 E. Sunrise Dr. ☎ **520/615-6100.** Reservations highly recommended. Main courses $24–$36; 5-course tasting menu $65 ($100 with wines). AE, CB, DC, MC, V. Mon–Sat 5:30–9pm. SOUTHWESTERN/REGIONAL.

Janos Wilder is Tucson's most celebrated chef and has been satisfying Tucsonans' tastes for creative cuisine for many years now. Janos started out downtown in a historic adobe but now exercises his culinary imagination in a luxuriously appointed dining room just outside the front door of the Westin La Paloma. The menu changes both daily and seasonally, with Chef Janos regularly creating such complex dishes as chile relleno stuffed with brie, mushrooms, and dried tomatoes and served with a tower of jicama salad, and a pistachio-crusted rack of lamb with couscous and fig baklava. At least one vegetarian entree with sophisticated embellishments appears on the menu nightly. During the summer there's sometimes a low-priced sampler menu that is one of Tucson's best values. This is about as formal a restaurant as you'll find in this otherwise very casual city. There's an award-winning wine list

If you really want to experience the food here but can't afford the high prices, try Janos' adjacent J Bar, which dishes up equally memorable flavor combinations at much more moderate prices (see below under "Moderate").

McMahon's Prime Steakhouse. 2959 N. Swan Rd. ☎ **520/327-7463.** Reservations recommended. Main courses $20–$34. AE, DC, DISC, MC, V. Mon–Fri 11am–10pm; Sat–Sun 5–10pm. STEAKS/SEAFOOD.

If a perfectly done steak is your idea of a memorable meal out, then you'll enjoy McMahon's. With a decidedly nineties opulence that's a far cry from steak houses of yore, McMahon's boasts an atmosphere that's calculated to impress. A large glass-walled wine room dominates the main dining room, which is ringed with large plush booths. You can drop a bundle on dinner here, but no more than you'd spend at such high-end restaurants as Janos, the Tack Room, or the Ventana Room. The main difference is that here your choices are simpler: steak, seafood, or steak and seafood. You'd be wasting a night out, though, if you didn't order a steak; the aged prime-beef steaks here are the best we've ever had. Although the steaks come with a wedge of iceberg lettuce, everything else is à la carte. For those whose tastes run to after-dinner entertainments, there is a separate piano lounge and cigar bar.

✪ **The Tack Room.** 7300 E. Vactor Ranch Trail. ☎ **520/722-2800.** Reservations recommended. Main courses $26.50–$37. AE, CB, DC, DISC, MC, V. Feb to mid-May daily 6–10pm; mid-May to Jan Tues–Sun 6–10pm. SOUTHWESTERN/CONTEMPORARY AMERICAN.

Housed in an older Southwestern-style hacienda with a casually elegant atmosphere, The Tack Room is Tucson's most prestigious restaurant. This is a place to feel pampered. From the time that little marinated salads appear on the table to the moment the last bit of chocolate is savored, service (by a bevy of tuxedoed waiters) is attentive and discreet. Although the filet mignon (perhaps served with a charred tomato and oregano sauce) is the most popular dish on the menu, plump Guaymas shrimp shows up regularly in various incarnations and is always delicious. Crispy yet succulent duck, topped with pistachios and sitting on a pile of not-too-sweet fig-and-orange chutney, is another perennial favorite here. Coffee, which comes with a condiment tray that includes whipped cream and crumbled Belgian chocolate, could double as dessert, but don't let it. Of course, you'll pay for all this, but you'll leave truly satisfied with your dining experience.

Ventana Room. In Loews Ventana Canyon Resort, 7000 N. Resort Dr. ☎ **520/299-2020.** Reservations highly recommended. Jacket recommended for men. Main courses $28–$45; chef's 4-course tasting menu $70 without wine, $100 with wine; 4-course spa menu $55. AE, CB, DC, DISC, MC, V. Daily 6–10pm. CONTEMPORARY AMERICAN.

Ventana means "window" in Spanish, and the views through the windows of this restaurant are every bit as memorable as the food that comes from the kitchen. Whether you're seated overlooking the resort's waterfall or the lights of Tucson far below, you'll likely have trouble concentrating on your food, but do try; you wouldn't want to miss any of the subtle nuances of such dishes as the velvety fillet of Dover sole with truffles. The house smoked salmon, translucent and moist, and the baby spinach Caesar salad on a Parmesan wafer are other dishes not to be missed. With such creations as an indecently rich crème brûlée with raspberry sauce, the dessert cart should not be allowed to bypass you. In the restaurant's rarified atmosphere, you'll be pampered by a bevy of waitstaff providing professional and unobtrusive service.

MODERATE

✪ **Café Terra Cotta.** Until early 2001, in St. Philip's Plaza, 4310 N. Campbell Ave. (at River Rd.). After early 2001, at 3500 Sunrise Dr. ☎ **520/577-8100.** Reservations recommended. Main courses $7–$22. AE, DC, DISC, MC, V. Sun–Thurs 11am–9:30pm; Fri–Sat 11am–10pm. SOUTHWESTERN.

Café Terra Cotta is Arizona's original Southwestern restaurant, and for years has been one of Tucson's most highly acclaimed restaurants. The combination of a casual atmosphere and creative cooking appeals to trendy Tucsonans, who stop by for dinner or to pick up gourmet food to go. A large brick oven is used to make imaginative pizzas, while salads, sandwiches, small plates, and main dishes flesh out the long menu. With so many choices, it's often difficult to decide, but for starters the must-have signature dish is garlic custard, served with a warm salsa vinaigrette. Other standouts include the grilled eggplant and portobello sandwich with red bell peppers, basil, and goat cheese on focaccia and the pork tenderloin *adobado* (spicy red sauce) with apricot-chile conserve. For dessert, the chocolate mousse pie requires a Herculean effort to resist.

Note that sometime in early 2001, Café Terra Cotta plans to move to 3500 Sunrise Drive. Be sure to check its address before heading here for a meal.

Firecracker. 2990 N. Swan Rd. (at Ft. Lowell). ☎ **520/318-1118.** Reservations recommended. Main courses $9–$16. AE, DISC, MC, V. Mon–Thurs 11:30am–10pm; Fri 11:30am–11pm; Sat 4pm–11pm; Sun 4–10pm. Sunset dinners 4–6pm daily. PAN ASIAN.

With a menu that knows no boundaries and a wild decor that includes flames issuing from torches atop the building and faux tree trunks in the bar, Firecracker is currently one of Tucson's hot spots. Large portions and very reasonable prices contribute to this restaurant's popularity. The spicy-chicken lettuce-cup appetizers (sort of roll-your-own burritos) are a fun finger-food starter. Seafood is definitely the strong suit here, and the huge wok-charred chunks of salmon covered with cilantro pesto is just about the best thing on the menu. Needless to say, the coconut crème brûlée is rich and creamy and deliciously unhealthful. Expect a wait even if you have a reservation.

Flying V Bar & Grill. In Loews Ventana Canyon Resort, 7000 N. Resort Dr. ☎ **520/299-2020.** Reservations recommended at dinner. Main courses $10–$16 at lunch, $16–$23 at dinner. AE, DC, DISC, MC, V. Tues–Sat 11am–2:30pm and 5–10pm; Sun 11am–2pm and 5–10pm; tapas daily 2:30–10pm. SOUTHWESTERN.

If it's bold Southwestern fare you're after, you won't do better than the Flying V. Take a seat out on the large deck and watch the koi in the pond below or the golfers struggling not to double bogey on the 18th hole of the Canyon Course. Mixing creative Southwestern and gourmet Mexican, this is one of only a couple of menus in Tucson that competes with the flair of downtown's Café Poca Cosa. There aren't too many places where you'll find ostrich fajitas, venison nachos, and duck tacos. The guacamole prepared table side is a lot of fun, as are the hot-pink prickly pear margaritas. Keep an eye out for stray golf balls, and don't miss the red-chile onion rings.

✪ **J Bar.** At the Westin La Paloma, 3770 E. Sunrise Dr. ☎ **520/615-6100.** Reservations highly recommended. Main courses $12.50–$16. AE, CB, DC, MC, V. Mon–Sat 5:30–10pm. SOUTHWESTERN.

The mouthwatering culinary creations of celebrity chef Janos Wilder at half price? Sounds impossible but that's pretty much what you'll find here at J Bar, Chef Janos's casual bar and grill adjacent to his famed foothills restaurant. Ask for a seat out on the heated patio, and with the lights of Tucson twinkling in the distance, dig into the best nachos you'll ever taste—here made with chorizo sausage and chili con queso. No matter what you order, you'll likely find that the ingredients and flavor combinations are most memorable. Who can forget spicy jerked pork with cranberry-habañero chili pepper chutney or blue corn–crusted *cabrilla* fish with *huitlacoche* mushrooms? There are plenty of drink options, and the margaritas are tasty (and strong). You won't want to miss sampling one of the *postres* (desserts). The *cajeta* (Mexican caramel) sundae with Kahlua ice cream is a delicious spin on an old favorite.

Keaton's Arizona Grill. 7401 N. La Cholla Blvd. (in the Foothills Mall). ☎ **520/297-1999.** Reservations recommended on weekends. Main courses $6–$10 at lunch, $8–$18 at dinner. AE, DISC, MC, V. Daily 11am–10pm. CONTEMPORARY AMERICAN.

Keaton's, in a shopping mall in the northern suburbs, is a good place for innovative and moderately priced food. The setting is casual yet classy, with cozy lighting and booths, a comfortable spot for conversation with friends. Be forewarned, however, that both the crunchy sourdough and the zucchini bread at Keaton's are so good that it's virtually impossible to save room for your meal (just say no to more bread). To balance out your overly zealous attack on the bread basket, try the chicken salad with sun-dried cherries or the applewood house-smoked salmon. If you were able to control yourself, consider the barbecued baby back ribs or pasta with mesquite-grilled chicken and pesto-cream sauce. You might not want to miss the great selection of margaritas and cocktails served here.

Ovens. At St. Philip's Plaza, corner of Campbell Ave. at River Rd. ☎ **520/577-9001.** Reservations recommended. Main courses $8–$19. AE, MC, V. Sun–Thurs 11am–9:30pm; Fri–Sat 11am–10pm. INTERNATIONAL.

Here at Ovens, the wood-fired oven turns out pizzas topped with practically every imaginable ingredient, from green chiles to grilled eggplant sauced with *chipotle* (a smoky jalapeño flavor). Or if you'd rather, there are salads, handmade pasta dishes, and grilled meats and fish. Like Café Terra Cotta across the way, there is an outdoor patio on the mall and a lounge inside, where you can sample one of the many wines by the glass. Whimsical art on the walls lends a playful atmosphere.

✪ **Wildflower.** 7037 N. Oracle Rd. (in the Casa Adobes Shopping Plaza between Oracle and Ina roads). ☎ **520/219-4230.** Reservations recommended. Main courses $7–$9 at lunch, $10.50–$22 at dinner. AE, DC, DISC, MC, V. Mon–Thurs 11:30am–2:30pm and 5–9pm; Fri–Sat 11:30am–2:30pm and 5–10pm; Sun 5–9pm. CONTEMPORARY AMERICAN.

Stylish comfort foods in gargantuan proportions are the order of the day at this chic and casually elegant north Tucson bistro. A huge wall of glass creates minimalist drama, and large flower photographs on the walls enhance the bright and airy decor.

ⓕ Family-Friendly Restaurants

Hidden Valley Inn *(see p. 329)*   It's a false-fronted cow town in bright colors with an authentic dance hall and stable, which are the dining rooms. Kids will love the miniature action dioramas of funny Western scenes.

Little Anthony's Diner *(see p. 324)*   This is a place for kids, although big kids like us enjoy the 1950s music and decor. The staff is good with children, and there's a video-games room and a rocket ship outside to ride. The gaslight melodrama theater next door makes a perfect night out for the family.

Pinnacle Peak Steakhouse *(see p. 330)*   Dinner here is a Wild West event, with an entire Western town outside and a carousel. Kids love it.

The marinated Chinese chicken salad tossed with Napa cabbage and wontons and the heaping plate of fried calamari with mizuna greens are both well worth trying. Dinner offers similar appetizers and entrees as at lunch. They run the gamut from rack of lamb with a Dijon crust to a simple roasted chicken. Pasta and salmon both show up in various guises. With so many tempting, reasonably priced dishes to sample, Wildflower is a foodie's delight.

INEXPENSIVE

Tohono Chul Tea Room. 7366 N. Paseo del Norte (1 block west of the corner of Ina Rd. and Oracle Rd. in Tohono Chul Park). ☎ **520/797-1222.** Reservations accepted for 6 or more. Main courses $6–$8. AE, MC, V. Daily 8am–5pm. REGIONAL AMERICAN.

Located in a brick territorial-style building in 37-acre Tohono Chul Park, this is one of the most tranquil restaurants in the city. The garden setting provides a wonderful chance to experience the desert. Before or after lunching on grilled raspberry-chipotle chicken or some tortilla soup, you can wander through the park's desert landscaping admiring the many species of cacti. The tearoom's patios, surrounded by natural vegetation and plenty of flowers in pots, are frequented by many species of birds. The adjacent gift shop is packed with Mexican folk art, nature theme toys, household items, T-shirts, and books. For a description of the park, see "Parks, Gardens & Zoos" under "Seeing the Sights," below.

WEST TUCSON

Ocotillo Café. At the Arizona–Sonora Desert Museum, 2021 N. Kinney Rd. ☎ **520/883-5705.** Reservations required Sat nights. Main courses $11.50–$16. AE, MC, V. Jan 15–Apr daily 11am–3pm; May Sat–Sun 11am–3pm; June–Sept Sat 5–11pm; Dec 26–Jan 14, call for hours. REGIONAL AMERICAN.

With a terrace set in a beautiful desert garden and backed by colorful walls, the Ocotillo Café could be a destination in itself. Add to that the experience of visiting the Arizona–Sonora Desert Museum (see below under "The Top Attractions") and you have a superb day's outing. You can watch a hummingbird drink from a penstemon flower while you dine on a delicious salad made with salmon, jicama, chayote squash, toasted pumpkin seeds, and nopalito (pads of the prickly pear cactus). Chile-crusted pork loin is another winner. During the summer, the cafe is open Saturday nights only, which is a good time to view the museum's desert inhabitants in their more active nocturnal state.

COWBOY STEAK HOUSES

El Corral Restaurant. 2201 E. River Rd. ☎ **520/299-6092.** Reservations not accepted. Complete dinner $8–$13. AE, DC, DISC, MC, V. Mon–Thurs 5–10pm; Fri–Sun 4:30–10pm. STEAKS.

Owned by the same folks who brought you Tucson's Pinnacle Peak Steakhouse, El Corral is another inexpensive steak house. What you'll find here is good steak, cheap, which makes the place very popular with retirees and families. The restaurant doesn't accept reservations, so expect long lines or come before or after regular dinner hours. Inside, the hacienda building has a genuine old-timey feeling, with flagstone floors and wood paneling that make it dark and cozy, while outside in the bright sunlight a cactus garden flourishes. In keeping with the name, there's a traditional corral fence of mesquite branches around the restaurant parking lot. Prime rib is the house specialty, but there are steaks, chicken, pork ribs, and burgers for the kids.

✪ **Hidden Valley Inn.** 4825 N. Sabino Canyon Rd. ☎ **520/299-4941.** Reservations not accepted. Main courses $6–$20. AE, MC, V. Daily 11am–3pm and 4:30–10pm. STEAKS.

Kids will love this brightly colored, false-fronted cow town, whose most entertaining feature are the walls of glass cases containing miniature action dioramas of humorous Western scenes. A very authentic dance hall and stable serve as dining rooms, and the Red Garter Saloon is a place for adults to imbibe. This steak house is the kind where people come to celebrate a family birthday and inevitably leave with large doggie bags. Cowpuncher-size steaks and barbecued ribs are the main attraction, although there are some seafood and chicken choices.

Pinnacle Peak Steakhouse. 6541 E. Tanque Verde Rd. ☎ **520/296-0911.** Reservations not accepted. Main courses $5.50–$14. AE, DC, MC, V. Mon–Thurs 5–10pm; Fri–Sun 4:30–10pm. STEAKS.

Located in Trail Dust Town, a Wild West–themed shopping and dining center, the Pinnacle Peak Steakhouse specializes in family dining in a fun cowboy atmosphere. Be prepared for crowds—this place is very popular with tour buses. Stroll the wooden sidewalks past the opera house and saloon to the grand old dining rooms of the Pinnacle Peak Steakhouse. You'll be surprised at the authenticity of the restaurant, which really does resemble a dining room in Old Tombstone or Dodge City.

LATE-NIGHT NOSHING

If the movie didn't let out until 10pm and the popcorn wasn't enough to fill you up, where do you go to satisfy your hunger? Try **Barrio,** 135 S. 6th Ave. (☎ **520/629-0191**); **Kingfisher,** 2564 E. Grant Rd. (☎ **520/323-7739**); **Pastiche,** 3025 N. Campbell Ave. (☎ **520/325-3333**); **Presidio Grill,** 3352 E. Speedway Blvd. (☎ **520/327-4667**); or **Firecracker,** 2990 N. Swan Rd. (☎ **520/318-1118**), all of which stay open on weekends until 11pm or midnight.

QUICK BITES, CAFES & COFFEEHOUSES

A student hangout near the University of Arizona, **Café Paraíso,** 820 E. University Blvd. (☎ **520/624-1707**), has a shady, cool patio and delectable salads and sandwiches. **Cuppuccinos,** 3400 E. Speedway Blvd. (☎ **520/323-7205**), bills itself as a Seattle-style coffeehouse, and **The Epic Café,** 745 N. Fourth Ave. (☎ **520/624-6844**), is a good hangout place with wild artwork, delicious scones, and other light fare. Look for the mural out front. For eight-layer cakes and light food in an edgy atmosphere, we buzz on over to **The Cup** at Club Congress, 311 E. Congress St. (☎ **520/798-1618**). With comfy couches and a place to plug in your laptop, the **Coffee X Change,** 2415 N. Campbell Ave. (☎ **520/327-6784**), makes a good stop between downtown and the foothills. The **Bristol Espresso Bus,** a 1937 British double-decker bus and probably the oldest double-decker bus in the United States, is parked at 5775 E. Broadway (no phone), waiting to serve you espresso. The bus will probably be closed during the summer.

You can't beat the cheap breakfast specials on our favorite bagels at **The Bagelry,** 5319 E. Speedway Blvd. (☎ **520/322-0223**) and 2575 N. Campbell Ave. (☎ **520/881-6674**). When we need a quick lunch, we dart over to **Baggins Gourmet Sandwiches** for a delicious sandwich. Baggins has several locations, three of which are at Kolb Road and Speedway Boulevard (☎ **520/290-9383**), Campbell Avenue and Ft. Lowell Road (☎ **520/327-1611**), and downtown at Church Avenue and Pennington Street (☎ **520/792-1344**). Call for the one nearest you. **Beyond Bread,** 3055 North Campbell Ave. (☎ **520/322-9965**), will make you up the likes of a roast beef and brie sandwich on their ultrafresh bread. The best pizza in town can be had at **Magpies Gourmet Pizza,** downtown at Fourth Avenue and Fifth Street (☎ **520/628-1661**), Speedway Boulevard and Swan Road (☎ **520/795-5977**), Broadway

Boulevard and Pantano Road (☎ **520/751-9949**), and Ina and Oracle roads (☎ **520/297-2712**). **Wild Oats Market** is a good place to get picnic supplies. They have organic fruit, delicious baked goods, cheese, meats, and wine, the kind of things you'd expect from a specialty market. They're at 3360 E. Speedway Blvd. (☎ **520/ 795-9844**), at Oracle and Ina roads (☎ **520/297-5394**), and in the foothills at Sunrise Drive and Swan Road (☎ **520/299-8858**).

5 Seeing the Sights

THE TOP ATTRACTIONS

While there are plenty of interesting things to see and do all over the Tucson area, anyone interested in the desert Southwest or the cinematic Wild West should go west—to Tucson's western outskirts, that is. Here you'll find not only the west unit of Saguaro National Park (with the biggest and best stands of saguaro cactus) but also the Arizona–Sonora Desert Museum (one of Arizona's most popular attractions) and Old Tucson Studios (film site over the years for hundreds of westerns). Together these three attractions make a great day's outing.

THE TUCSON AREA'S (MOSTLY) NATURAL WONDERS

✪ **Arizona–Sonora Desert Museum.** 2021 N. Kinney Rd. ☎ **520/883-2702** or 520/ 883-1380. www.desertmuseum.org. Admission $9.95 adults, $1.75 children 6–12, free for children 5 and under. Oct–Feb daily 8:30am–5pm; Mar–Sept daily 7:30am–6pm. From downtown Tucson, go west on Speedway Blvd., which becomes Gates Pass Rd., and follow the signs.

Don't be fooled by the name. This is a zoo, and it's one of the best in the country. The Sonoran Desert, which encompasses much of central and southern Arizona as well as parts of northern Mexico, contains within its boundaries not only arid lands but also forested mountains, springs, rivers, and streams. To reflect this diversity, exhibits here encompass the full spectrum of Sonoran Desert life—from plants to insects to fish to reptiles to mammals—and all are on display in very natural settings. Coyotes and javelinas (peccaries) seem very much at home in their "invisi-fence" compounds, which are surrounded by almost invisible wire mesh fences that make it seem as though there is nothing between you and the animals. These display areas are along the new Desert Loop Trail, which currently has numerous new exhibits under construction. In only slightly less natural surroundings, you'll find black bears and mountain lions, beavers and otters, frogs and fish, tarantulas and scorpions, prairie dogs and desert bighorn sheep. However, our personal favorite exhibit is the walk-in hummingbird aviary. The tiny birds buzz past your ears and stop only inches in front of your face. A separate aviary contains many other bird species, and there is a garden devoted specifically to displays on pollinators (insects, birds, and mammals that pollinate desert flowers).

You'll find this zoological park 14 miles west of downtown near Tucson Mountain Park, Saguaro National Park West, and Old Tucson Studios. The museum has two restaurants, Ironwood Terraces (cafeteria style) and the Ocotillo Cafe (a sit-down restaurant), which both serve good food. The grounds here are extensive, so wear good walking shoes; a sun hat of some sort is advisable. Don't be surprised if you end up staying here hours longer than you had intended; there's an awful lot to see and do.

Colossal Cave Mountain Park. 22 miles east of Tucson in Vail. ☎ **520/647-7275.** Admission $7.50 adults, $4 children 6–12, in addition to $3 per car for park entry. Mar 16–Sept 15 Mon–Sat 8am–6pm, Sun and holidays 8am–7pm; Sept 16–Mar 15 Mon–Sat 9am–5pm, Sun

Tucson Attractions

Silverbell Rd.

Overton

Cortaro Farms Rd.

Wade Rd.

10

Thornydale Rd.

Ina Rd.

Ina Rd.

Orange Grove R

Sunset Rd.

Saguaro
National
Park

El Camino de Cerro

Ruthra
Rd.

Sweetwater Dr.

Camino de Oeste

Ironwood Hill Dr.

**To Saguaro National
Park (west)**

1

**Tucson Mountain
Park**

3

Speedway E

2

Gates Pass Rd.

Anklam

Downtown & the Historic Districts

W. 6th St.

N. Main Ave.

Church Ave.

N. Stone Ave.

N. 6th Ave.

N. 4th Ave.

Toole Ave.

E. 6th St.

N. 1st Ave.

Silverlake

E. 7th St.

E. 8th St.

Franklin St.

**El Presidio
Area**

19

Alameda St.

Pennington St.

Grande Ave.

**Downtown
Arts District**
Congress St.
Broadway Blvd.

E. 9th St.

**Tucson
Convention
Center**

20

10

Cushing St.

S. Stone Ave.

E. 12th St.

22

E. 13th St.

E. 14th St.

Armory Park Historic Area

Simpson St.

21

**Barrio
Historico**
Kennedy St.

E. 15th St.

E. 16th St.

W. 17th St.

E. 17th St.

S. 3rd Ave.

Osborne Ave.

W. 18th St.

E. 18th St.

S. 4th Ave.

S. 6th Ave.

W. 19th St.

S. 4th Ave.

E. 19th St.

W. 20th St.

E. 20th St.

Mission Rd.

W. 21st St.

E. 21st St.

W. 22nd St.

E. 22nd St.

E. 23rd St.

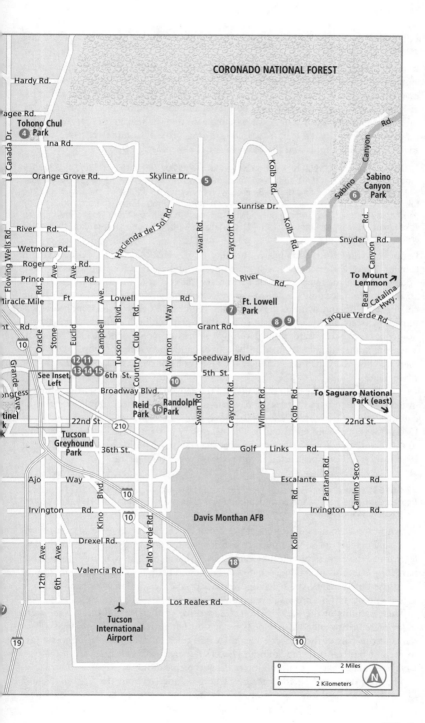

CORONADO NATIONAL FOREST

Hardy Rd.

agee Rd.

Tohono Chul
④ Park

Ina Rd.

La Canada Dr.

Orange Grove Rd.

Skyline Dr. ⑤

Sabino
Canyon
Park

Sunrise Dr.

Kolb Rd.

Sabino Canyon Rd.

⑥

River Rd.

Wetmore Rd.

Roger Rd.

Prince Rd.

Miracle Mile

nt Rd.

⑩

Grande

ongress

tinel
k

Hacienda del Sol Rd.

Swan Rd.

Craycroft Rd.

Kolb Rd.

Snyder Rd.

To Mount
Lemmon

Catalina Hwy.

Bear Canyon Rd.

Ft. Lowell
Way

Lowell Blvd.

Ft. Rd.

Rd.

⑦ Ft. Lowell
Park

Grant Rd.

⑧ ⑨

Tanque Verde Rd.

Oracle

Stone

Euclid

Campbell Ave.

Tucson Blvd.

Country Club Rd.

Alvernon Way

Speedway Blvd.

5th St.

⑫⑪
⑬⑭⑮ 6th St.

See Inset,
Left

Broadway Blvd.

⑩

Reid
Park

Randolph
⑯ Park

22nd St.

Tucson
Greyhound
Park

36th St.

Ajo Way

Irvington Rd.

Swan Rd.

Craycroft Rd.

Wilmot Rd.

Kolb Rd.

To Saguaro National
Park (east)

22nd St.

Golf Links Rd.

Escalante Rd.

Irvington Rd.

Pantano Rd.

Camino Seco Rd.

Davis Monthan AFB

Kolb Rd.

Drexel Rd.

Valencia Rd.

Kino Blvd.

Palo Verde Rd.

12th Ave.

6th Ave.

⑱

Los Reales Rd.

✈ Tucson
International
Airport

⑲

⑦

| 0 | | 2 Miles |
| 0 | | 2 Kilometers |

N

333

and holidays 9am–6pm. Take Old Spanish Trail southeast from east Tucson or take I-10 and get off at the Vail exit.

It seems nearly every cave in the Southwest has its legends of bandits and buried loot, and Colossal Cave is no exception. A tour through this dry cavern, which isn't exactly colossal but is certainly impressive, combines a bit of Western lore with a bit of geography for an experience that both kids and adults enjoy. Not surprisingly for this desert location, this is a dry cave, which means that the stalactites, stalagmites, and other formations are no longer actively growing. The 45-minute tour of the cave covers about half a mile, and the temperature is a comfortable 70° to 72°F.

✪ **Sabino Canyon.** 5900 N. Sabino Canyon Rd. ☎ **520/749-2861** or 520/749-2327 for moonlight reservations. Free admission. Sabino Canyon tram ride, $6 adults, $2.50 children 3–12, free for children 2 and under; Bear Canyon tram ride, $3 adults, $1 children 3–12, free for children 2 and under. Park, daily dawn–dusk. Sabino Canyon tram rides, daily 9am–4:30pm; Bear Canyon tram rides, daily 9am–4pm (both trams more limited in summer). Take Grant Rd. east to Tanque Verde Rd., continuing east; at Sabino Canyon Rd., turn north and watch for the sign.

Located in the Santa Catalina Mountains of Coronado National Forest, Sabino Canyon is a desert oasis that has attracted people and animals for thousands of years. Today it's by far the most spectacular and accessible corner of the desert in the Tucson area, containing not only impressive desert scenery, but hiking trails and a stream. The chance to splash and swim in the canyon's waterfalls and pools (water conditions permitting) attracts many canyon visitors, but it is equally enjoyable simply to gaze at the beauty of crystal-clear water flowing through a rocky canyon guarded by saguaro cacti. There are numerous picnic tables in the canyon, and many miles of hiking trails wind their way into the Catalinas from here, making it one of the best places in the city for a day hike.

A road once allowed cars to drive up into the canyon, but today cars are prohibited; instead, a narrated tram shuttles visitors up and down the lower canyon throughout the day. Moonlight tram rides take place three times each month between April and December (but not July or August). The Bear Canyon tram is used by hikers heading to the picturesque Seven Falls, which are at the end of a 2.6-mile hiking trail. Bring at least 1 quart of water per person if you plan to do any hiking here.

✪ **Saguaro National Park.** East district visitor center, 3693 S. Old Spanish Trail. ☎ **520/733-5153.** West district visitor center, 2700 N. Kinney Rd. ☎ 520/733-5158. $4 per car, $2 per hiker (charged on the east section only). Park open daily 7am–sunset; visitor centers daily 8:30am–5pm; open to hikers 24 hours a day.

Saguaro cactus are the quintessential symbol of the American desert and occur naturally only here in the Sonoran Desert. Sensitive to fire and frost and exceedingly slow to mature, these massive, tree-like cacti grow in great profusion around Tucson but have long been threatened by both development and plant collectors. In 1933, to protect these desert giants, the federal government set aside two large tracts of land as a saguaro preserve. This preserve eventually became Saguaro National Park.

The two units of the park, one on the east side of the city and one on the west, today preserve not only dense stands of saguaros, but also the many other wild inhabitants of this part of the Sonoran Desert. A visit to either unit provides opportunities to become familiar with the Sonoran Desert's flora and fauna. Both units of the park have loop roads, nature trails, hiking trails, and picnic grounds.

The west unit of the park, because of its proximity to both the Arizona–Sonora Desert Museum and Old Tucson Studios, is the more popular area to visit. This happens to be where you'll see the most impressive stands of saguaros. Coyotes, foxes, squirrels, and javelinas all eat the sweet fruit of the saguaro, and near the west unit's Red Hills Information Center you'll find a water hole that attracts these and other wild animals, which you're most likely to see at dawn, dusk, or night. To reach the west unit of the park, take Speedway Boulevard west from downtown Tucson (it becomes Gates Pass Boulevard).

The east section of the park contains an older area of saguaro "forest" at the foot of the Rincon Mountains. This section is popular with hikers because most of it has no roads. However, there is a visitor center, a loop scenic drive, and a picnic area. This section of the park has a trail open to mountain bikes (and the loop drive is a great bike ride). To reach the east unit of the park, take Speedway Boulevard east, then head south on Freeman Road to Old Spanish Trail.

HISTORIC ATTRACTIONS BOTH REAL & REEL

✪ **Mission San Xavier del Bac.** 1950 W. San Xavier Rd. ☎ **520/294-2624.** Free admission. Daily 8am–5pm. Take I-19 south to Exit 92 and turn right.

Called the White Dove of the Desert, Mission San Xavier de Bac, a blindingly white adobe building rising from a sere, brown landscape, is considered the finest example of mission architecture in the Southwest. The beautiful church, which was built between 1783 and 1797, incorporates Moorish, Byzantine, and Mexican Renaissance architectural styles. The church, however, was never actually completed, which becomes apparent when the two bell towers are compared. One is topped with a dome, while the other has none. The mission underwent an extensive restoration in recent years, and much of the elaborate interior decoration has taken on a new luster. Restored murals cover the interior walls, and behind the altar are colorful and elaborate decorations. To the left of the main altar, in a glass sarcophagus, is a statue of Saint Francis Xavier, the mission's patron saint, who is believed to answer the prayers of the faithful. A visit to San Xavier's little museum provides a bit of historical perspective and a chance to explore a bit more of the mission.

To the east of the church, atop a small hill, you'll find not only an interesting view of the church but also a replica of the famous grotto in Lourdes, France. This is an active Roman Catholic church serving the San Xavier Indian Reservation. Masses are held daily at 8:30am, Saturday at 5:30pm, and Sunday at 8am, 11am, and 12:30pm.

Old Tucson Studios. 201 S. Kinney Rd. ☎ **520/883-0100.** www.emol.org/emol/tucson/oldtucson/otindex.html. Admission $14.95 adults, $12.95 children 4–11 (Pima County residents $12.95 adult and $8.95 children). Daily 10am–6pm. Closed Thanksgiving and Dec 25. Take Speedway Blvd. west, continuing in the same direction when it becomes Gates Pass Blvd., and turn left on S. Kinney Rd.

Despite the name, this is not the historic location of the old city of Tucson—it's a Western town originally built as the set for the 1939 movie *Arizona*. In the years since then, Old Tucson has been used during the filming of John Wayne's *Rio Lobo, Rio Bravo,* and *El Dorado;* Clint Eastwood's *The Outlaw Josey Wales;* Kirk Douglas's *Gunfight at the O.K. Corral;* Paul Newman's *The Life and Times of Judge Roy Bean;* and, more recently, *Tombstone* and *Geronimo.*

Today, however, Old Tucson is far more than just a movie set. In addition to serving as a site for frequent film, TV, and advertising productions (call ahead to find out if any filming is scheduled), it has become a Wild West theme park with diverse family-oriented activities and entertainment. Throughout each day there are staged shoot-outs in the streets, stunt shows, cancan performances, medicine shows, and other performances. There are train rides, stagecoach rides, kiddie rides, restaurants, and gift shops. Educational shows explain the history of the West, and several multimedia and video presentations complement the various live performances.

MORE TO SEE & DO
ART MUSEUMS

Center for Creative Photography. University of Arizona campus, east of the corner of Park Ave. and Speedway Blvd. ☎ **520/621-7968.** www.creativephotography.org. $2 suggested donation. Mon–Fri 9am–5pm; Sat–Sun noon–5pm. Bus: 1, 4, 5, 6, 9X, 102, 103, 200, or 250.

Have you ever wished you could see an original Ansel Adams print up close, or perhaps an Edward Weston or a Richard Avedon? You can at the Center for Creative Photography. Originally conceived by Ansel Adams, the center now holds more than 500,000 negatives, 200,000 study prints, and 60,000 master prints by the world's greatest photographers, making it one of the best and largest collections in the world. Although the center mounts excellent photography exhibits year-round, it's also a research facility that preserves the complete photographic archives of various photographers, including Adams. Prints may be examined in a special room. It's highly recommended that you make an appointment and decide beforehand whose works you'd like to see. You're usually limited to two photographers per visit.

De Grazia Gallery in the Sun. 6300 N. Swan Rd. ☎ **800/545-2185** or 520/299-9191. Free admission. Daily 10am–4pm.

Southwestern artist Ettore "Ted" De Grazia is a Tucson favorite son, and his gallery, set in an adobe home in the foothills, is a Tucson landmark. De Grazia is said to be the most reproduced artist in the world because many of his impressionistic images of big-eyed children were used as greeting cards during the 1950s and 1960s. Connected to the gallery is a small adobe chapel that De Grazia built in honor of the missionary explorer Father Eusebio Kino. No original works are for sale, but there are many reproductions and other objects with De Grazia images.

Tucson Museum of Art & Historic Block. 140 N. Main Ave. ☎ **520/624-2333.** www.tucsonarts.com. Admission $2 adults, $1 students and seniors, free for children 12 and under; free for everyone Sunday. Mon–Sat 10am–4pm; Sun noon–4pm. Closed Mon Memorial Day–Labor Day and all national holidays. All downtown-bound buses.

The Tucson Museum of Art is situated in a large modern building surrounded by historic adobes and a spacious plaza frequently used to display sculptures. The museum boasts an excellent collection of pre-Columbian art, representing 3,000 years of life in Mexico and Central and South America. There's a large collection of Western art, depicting cowboys, horses, and the wide-open spaces of the American West. In addition, the museum hosts temporary exhibitions, such as the annual *American Women Artists and the West.* The museum has preserved five historic homes on this same block, and they are open to the public. See "History Museums & Landmark Buildings," below, for details.

○ **The University of Arizona Museum of Art.** University of Arizona campus, Park Ave. and Speedway Blvd. ☎ **520/621-7567.** Free admission. Mon–Fri 9am–5pm; Sun noon–4pm. Closed major holidays. Bus: 1, 4, 5, 6, 9X, 102, 103, 200, or 250.

With European and American works from the Renaissance to the 20th century, this collection is even more extensive and diverse than that of the Tucson Museum of Art. Tintoretto, Rembrandt, Piranesi, Picasso, O'Keeffe, Warhol, and Rothko are all represented here. Another attraction, the *Retable of Ciudad Rodrigo,* consists of 26 paintings from 15th-century Spain and was originally placed above a cathedral altar. The museum has an extensive collection of 20th-century sculpture that includes more than 60 clay and plaster models and sketches by Jacques Lipchitz.

HISTORY MUSEUMS & LANDMARK BUILDINGS

In addition to the museums and buildings listed below, downtown Tucson has a couple of historic neighborhoods that are described in "A Walking Tour—Downtown Historic Districts," below. Among the more interesting buildings are those maintained by the Tucson Museum of Art and located on the block surrounding the museum. These restored homes date from between 1850 and 1907 and are all built on the former site of the Tucson presidio. A map and descriptive brochures about the houses are available at the museum's front desk, and free (with admission to the museum) guided tours of the historic block are available.

Arizona Historical Society Tucson Museum. 949 E. 2nd St. ☎ **520/628-5774.** Admission by donation. Mon–Sat 10am–4pm; Sun noon–4pm. Closed major holidays. Bus: 1, 4, 5, 6, 9X, 102, 103, 200, or 250.

As the state's oldest historical museum, this repository of all things Arizonan is a treasure trove for the history buff. If you've never explored a real mine, you can do the next best thing by looking at the museum's full-scale reproduction of an underground mine tunnel. You'll see an assayer's office, miner's tent, stamp mill, and blacksmith's shop in the mining exhibit. A transportation exhibit, displaying stagecoaches and horseless carriages that revolutionized life in the Southwest, and temporary exhibits covering a wide range of topics give a pretty good idea of what it was like back then. The museum has a research library and a good gift shop.

Arizona State Museum. University of Arizona campus, University Blvd. and Park Ave. ☎ **520/621-6302.** Free admission, donations accepted. Mon–Sat 10am–5pm; Sun noon–5pm. Closed major holidays. Bus: 1, 4, 5, 6, 9X, 102, 103, 200, or 250.

Founded in 1893, the Arizona State Museum houses an extensive collection of artifacts from prehistoric and contemporary Native American cultures of the Southwest. A Paleo-Indian exhibit displays 12,000-year-old spear points that were found embedded in the bones of mammoths, now long extinct, and a large exhibit covers the Hohokam, an ancient farming culture that lived in the desert and built extensive networks of irrigation canals before disappearing mysteriously around 1450. Across the street in the North Building, an exhibit explores the lifestyles and cultural traditions of Indians living in Arizona today. In the year 2000, there is a plan for exhibits in the main museum to undergo remodeling, at which time only the North Building will be open.

Sosa-Carillo-Frémont House Museum. 141 S. Granada Ave. (in the Tucson Convention Center complex). ☎ **520/622-0956.** Free admission. Wed–Sat 10am–4pm. Closed all major holidays. All downtown-bound buses.

Located on the shady grounds of the modern Tucson Convention Center, the Sosa-Carillo-Frémont House is a classic example of Sonoran-style adobe architecture. Originally built in 1858 as a small adobe house, the structure was enlarged after 1866. In 1878 it was rented to territorial governor John Charles Frémont, who had led a distinguished military career as an explorer of the West. The building has been restored in the style of this period, with the living room and bedrooms opening off a large central hall known as a *zaguán*. All rooms are decorated with period antiques. The flat roof is made of pine beams called *vigas,* covered with saguaro cactus ribs, and topped by a layer of hard-packed mud. From November to March, this museum offers Saturday tours ($5) of historic Tucson.

SCIENCE & TECHNOLOGY MUSEUMS

○ Biosphere 2. Ariz. 77, mile marker 96.5. ☎ **800/828-2462** or 520/825-1289. www. bio2.edu. Admission $12.95 adults, $8.95 children 13–17, $6 children 6–12, free for children 5 and under. Discounts for students and seniors. Daily 8:30am–6pm. Closed Dec 25. Take Oracle Rd. north out of Tucson and continue north on Ariz. 77 until you see the Biosphere sign.

For 2 years, beginning in September 1991, four men and four women were locked inside this airtight, 3-acre greenhouse in the desert 35 miles north of Tucson near the town of Oracle. During their tenure in Biosphere 2 (earth is considered Biosphere 1), they conducted experiments on how the earth, basically a giant greenhouse, manages to support all the planet's life forms. Although there are no longer people living in Biosphere 2, similar experiments continue. This giant science project is a major tourist attraction.

Tours of the facility are offered daily, including a tour of part of the interior of Biosphere 2. You can learn about the project at an orientation center and then take a guided tour that includes the Ocean Viewing Gallery, the test module, demonstration labs, and multimedia presentations. An interactive display area provides entertainment for children. The latest addition here is a 24-inch telescope that allows nighttime visitors to do a bit of stargazing. Whether you consider it science or a tourist attraction, there's plenty to see and do. Also on the grounds are a hotel, restaurant, cafe, and gift shop.

Flandrau Science Center & Planetarium. University of Arizona campus, Cherry Ave. and University Blvd. ☎ **520/621-STAR.** www.flandrau.org. Admission to exhibits $3 adults, $2 children 13 and under. Telescope viewing free. Planetarium $5 adults, $4.50 seniors and students, $4 children 13 and under. Daytime daily 9am–5pm; evenings Wed–Sat 7–9pm. Telescope viewing Wed–Sat 7–10pm (weather permitting). Closed major holidays. Bus: 9.

Located on the campus of the University of Arizona, the Flandrau Planetarium offers stargazers a chance to learn more about the universe. The planetarium theater presents programs on the stars as well as very popular laser shows set to music. Exhibit halls contain a mineral collection (the largest in the state) and hands-on science exhibits for people of all ages. On clear nights, you can gaze through the planetarium's 16-inch telescope. (Arizona has become a magnet for stargazers, and several famous telescopes are near Tucson. See "Starry Starry Nights," in chapter 10, "Southern Arizona," for information on the Kitt Peak National Observatory.)

Pima Air & Space Museum. 6000 E. Valencia Rd. ☎ **520/574-0462.** www.pimaair.org. Admission $7.50 adults, $6.50 seniors and military, $4 children 7–12, free for children 6 and under. Daily 9am–5pm. Closed Thanksgiving, Dec 25. Take the Valencia Rd. exit from I-10 and then drive east 2 miles to the museum entrance.

Located just south of Davis Monthan Air Force Base, the Pima Air & Space Museum houses one of the largest collections of historic aircraft in the world. On display are more than 250 aircraft, including an SR-71 Blackbird, several Russian MiGs, World War II combat gliders, a "Superguppy," a B-17G "Flying Fortress," and numerous experimental aircraft, including a backpack helicopter known as the "Hopicopter." The collection includes replicas of the Wright brothers' 1903 Wright Flyer and the X-15, the world's fastest aircraft. Tours are available.

The museum offers guided tours of Davis Monthan's AMARC (Arizona Maintenance and Regeneration Center) facility, which goes by the name of The Boneyard. Here, thousands of mothballed planes are lined up in neat rows under the Arizona sun. Tours last just under an hour and cost $6 for adults, $5 for seniors, and $3 for children. Tour reservations (☎ **520/618-4806**) should be made 2 or 3 days in advance.

Titan Missile Museum. Duval Mine Rd., Green Valley (Exit 69 from I-19). ☎ **520/ 625-7736.** Admission $7.50 adults, $6.50 seniors, $4 children 7–12, free for children 6 and under. May 1–Oct 31, Wed–Sun 9am–5pm; Nov 1–Apr 30, daily 9am–5pm. Closed Thanksgiving, Dec 25. Take I-19 south to Green Valley. Take exit 69 west ¹/₁₀ mile to main entrance.

Operated by the Pima Air & Space Museum and located south of Tucson in the retirement community of Green Valley, this museum is a deactivated intercontinental ballistic missile (ICBM) silo and is the only such museum in the world. Tours lead you down into the silo itself so you can get a firsthand look at what it would be like to have your finger on the button. Advance reservations are recommended.

PARKS, GARDENS & ZOOS

See "Seeing the Sights," at the beginning of this section, for full details on the Arizona–Sonora Desert Museum, the region's premier zoo.

Reid Park Zoo. Lake Shore Lane and 22nd St. (between Country Club Rd. and Alvernon Way). ☎ **520/791-4022.** Admission $4 adults, $3 seniors, 75¢ children 5–14, free for children 4 and under. Daily 9am–4pm. Closed Dec 25. Bus: 7 or 14.

Although small and overshadowed by its neighbor, the Arizona–Sonora Desert Museum, the Reid Park Zoo is an important breeding center for several endangered species. Among the animals in the zoo's breeding programs are giant anteaters, white rhinoceroses, tigers, ruffed lemurs, and zebras. A new South American exhibit features a capybara (the largest rodent in the world), piranhas, and black jaguars. Get here early when the animals are more active and before the crowds hit. There's a good playground in the adjacent park.

✪ Frommer's Favorite Tucson Experiences

Visiting the Arizona–Sonora Desert Museum. One of the world's finest zoos, the museum focuses exclusively on the animals and plants of the Sonoran Desert of southern Arizona and northern Mexico.

Taking a Full-Moon Desert Hike. There's no better time to explore the desert than at night (when the desert comes alive) under a full moon. Drive to the east or west section of Saguaro National Park for your hike, where the parking lots at the east ends of Speedway and Broadway are open 24 hours a day. It's also possible to park on Old Spanish Trail outside the main entrance to the east unit of the park. There are places on the west side where you can park outside the gates and walk into the park.

✪ **Making the Drive to Mount Lemmon.** From the desert, the road twists and turns up into the Santa Catalina Mountains, with cactus and *palo verde* gradually replaced by pine and juniper. You'll have breathtaking views of Tucson along the way.

Spending Time in Sabino Canyon. Biking, hiking, swimming, birding— Sabino Canyon has it all. The canyon, carved by a creek that flows for most of the year, is an oasis in the desert. Although popular with both locals and tourists, it still offers delightful opportunities for escaping the city.

Bird Watching in Madera Canyon. Located south of the city in the Santa Rita Mountains, this canyon attracts many species of birds, some of which can be seen in only a handful of other spots in the United States. Even if you're not into birding, there are hiking trails and lots of shade here.

The Shrine That Stopped a Freeway

The southern Arizona landscape is dotted with roadside shrines, symbols of the region's Hispanic and Roman Catholic heritage. Most are simple crosses decorated with plastic flowers and dedicated to people who have been killed in auto accidents. However, one shrine in particular stands out from all the rest. It is Tucson's El Tiradito (The Castaway), which is dedicated to a sinner, and not too long ago stopped a freeway.

El Tiradito, on South Granada Avenue at West Cushing Street, is the only shrine in the United States dedicated to a sinner buried in unconsecrated soil. Several stories tell of how this shrine came to be, but the most popularly accepted tells of a young shepherd who fell in love with his mother-in-law some time in the 1880s. When the father-in-law found his wife in the arms of this young man, he shot the son-in-law. The young shepherd stumbled from his in-laws' house and fell dead beside the dusty street. Because he had been caught in the act of adultery and died without confessing his sins, his body could not be interred in the church cemetery, so he was buried where he fell.

The people of the neighborhood soon began burning candles on the spot to try to save the soul of the young man, and eventually people began burning candles in hopes that their own wishes would come true. They believed that if the candle burned through the night their prayers would be answered. The shrine eventually grew into a substantial little structure and in 1927 was dedicated by its owner to the city of Tucson. In 1940, the shrine became an official Tucson monument.

However, such status was not enough to protect the shrine from urban renewal, and when the federal government announced that it would level the shrine when it built a new freeway through the center of Tucson, the city's citizens were outraged. Their activities and protest led the shrine to be named to the National Register of Historic Places. Thus protected, the shrine could not be destroyed, and the freeway was moved a few hundred yards to the west.

To this day, devout Catholics from the surrounding neighborhood still burn candles at the shrine that stopped a freeway.

Tohono Chul Park. 7366 N. Paseo del Norte. ☎ **520/575-8468.** Admission by suggested donation, $2. Grounds, daily 7am–sunset. Exhibit house, Mon–Sat 9:30am–5pm; Sun 11am–5pm. Tearoom, daily 8am–5pm. Off Ina Rd. west of the intersection with Oracle Rd.

Although this public park is fairly small, it provides an excellent introduction to the plant and animal life of the desert. You'll see a forest of cholla cactus and a garden of small and complex pincushion cactus. The park includes an ethnobotanical garden; a garden for children that encourages them to touch, listen, and smell; a demonstration garden; natural areas; an exhibit house for art displays; a tea room that is great for breakfast, lunch, or afternoon tea; and a very good gift shop. From mid-February to April, the wildflower displays here are gorgeous (if enough rain has fallen in the previous months), and guided tours are offered.

Tucson Botanical Gardens. 2150 N. Alvernon Way. ☎ **520/326-9686.** www. tucsonbotanical.org. Admission $4 adults, $3 seniors, $1 children 6–11, free for children under 6. Daily 8:30am–4:30pm; Memorial Day–Labor Day 7:30am–4:30pm. Closed Jan 1, July 4, Thanksgiving, and Dec 24–25. Bus: 11.

Located amid residential neighborhoods in midtown Tucson, these gardens are an oasis of greenery and, though small, are well worth a visit if you are interested in desert plant life, landscaping, or gardening. On the 5¹/₂-acre grounds are several small gardens that not only have visual appeal but are also historical and educational. If you live in the desert, you might want to visit just to learn about harvesting rainfall for your desert garden and designing a water-conserving landscape. The sensory garden stimulates all five senses, while in another garden traditional Southwestern crops are grown for research purposes. In the greenhouse, you'll see "useful" plants from tropical forests. There's a gift shop here as well.

ESPECIALLY FOR KIDS

In addition to the museum listed below, two of the greatest places to take kids in the Tucson area are the Arizona–Sonora Desert Museum and Old Tucson Studios. Kids will get a kick out of the tram ride at Sabino Canyon, the Reid Park Zoo, Flandrau Science Center and Planetarium, and the Pima Air & Space Museum. All are described in detail above.

They'll also enjoy **Trail Dust Town,** 6541 E. Tanque Verde Rd., a Wild West–themed shopping and dining center. It has a full-sized carousel, a scaled-down train to ride, shoot-out shows, and a minigolf course next door. Basically, it's a sort of scaled-down Old Tucson. If the kids are into miniature golf, they'll probably love **Magic Carpet Golf,** 6125 E. Speedway Blvd. (☎ **520/885-3691**), as much as we do. Putt balls under and around a sphinx, a skull, a giant Easter Island head, and a huge snake.

Tucson Children's Museum. 200 S. 6th Ave. ☎ **520/792-9985.** Admission $5.50 adults, $4.50 seniors, $3.50 children 2–16, free for children under 2; free for everyone on the 3rd Sun of each month. Tues and Thurs 9am–5pm; Wed and Fri 9:30am–5pm; Sat 10am–5pm; Sun noon–5pm. Closed Jan 1, Easter Sunday, Thanksgiving, and Dec 25. All downtown-bound buses.

This museum is in the old Carnegie Library in downtown Tucson and is filled with fun and educational hands-on activities. Exhibits change every year or so, but have included a doctor's office, a fire station, and a bubble factory. Expect to find such perennial kid favorites as a fire truck, a police motorcycle, and dinosaur sculptures. Weekends generally feature special performances and programs.

DOWNTOWN SATURDAY NIGHT

Throughout the year, on the first and third Saturday of each month, the Downtown Arts District—which includes East Pennington Street, East Congress Street, and East Broadway Boulevard between Fourth Avenue and Stone Avenue—comes alive from about 7 to 10pm. On these nights there are art gallery openings, music performances on the street and in cafes, and late-evening shopping. For more information, call the **Tucson Arts District Partnership** (☎ **520/624-9977**).

A Walking Tour—Downtown Historic Districts

Start: Old Town Artisans.
Finish: Hotel Congress.
Time: 5 hours.
Best Times: Weekends, when restaurants aren't packed at lunch.
Worst Times: Summer, when it's just too hot to do any walking.

Tucson has a long and varied cultural history, which is most easily seen on a walking tour of the downtown historic neighborhoods. Start your explorations in the El

Presidio Historic District, which is named for the Presidio of San Augustín del Tucson (1775), the Spanish garrison built here to protect the San Xavier del Bac Mission from the Apaches. For many years it was the heart of Tucson, and although no original buildings are still standing, there are numerous buildings from the mid-19th century.

After finding a parking space at the large public parking lot at the corner of Court Avenue and Council Street, walk south on Court Avenue to the corner of Washington Street. Here you'll find Tucson's premier crafts market:

1. **Old Town Artisans,** 186 N. Meyer Ave. In this adobe building dating from 1862 are numerous rooms full of handmade Southwestern crafts (see "Shopping," below, for details). The central courtyard has shady gardens. You could spend hours browsing through the amazing assortment of crafts here, but keep in mind you've still got a long walk ahead of you. Across Meyer Avenue from this building's southwest corner is:

2. **La Casa Cordova,** 175 N. Meyer Ave., which dates from about 1848 and is one of the oldest buildings in Tucson. Although the art museum owns five historic homes on this block, this is the only one that has been restored to look as it might have in the late 1800s. Each year from November to March, there is a very elaborate *nacimiento,* a Mexican folk-art nativity scene, with images from the Bible and Latin American history all rolled up into one miniature landscape full of angels, greenery, and Christmas lights. Through a colorful gate just to the south of La Casa Cordova is the entrance to the:

3. **Tucson Museum of Art.** This modern building houses collections of pre-Columbian and Western art, as well as exhibits of contemporary works. A visit to the museum will not only allow you to see plenty of art, but you should be able to see inside a couple of historic buildings that now house some of the museum's galleries. After touring the museum, walk back up North Meyer Avenue and at the end of the block you will find the:

4. **Romero House,** which was built in 1868 and may incorporate part of the original presidio wall. This house was altered numerous times over the years and at one time served as a gas station. The Romero House now contains the Tucson Museum of Art School.

From the Romero House, turn left onto Washington Street and then left again onto Main Avenue. The first building you'll come to on this side of the art museum's historic block is the:

5. **Corbett House,** 180 N. Main Ave., a restored Mission revival–style building built in 1906. The house, which is set back behind a green lawn, is strikingly different from the older, Sonoran-style adobe homes on this block. Today the Corbett House has been furnished with Mission-style furniture and is open for tours.

Next door to this home stands the:

6. **Stevens House,** 150 N. Main Ave., a Sonoran-style rowhouse completed in 1866. This building currently houses the museum's cafe. Next door is the:

7. **Fish House,** 120 N. Main Ave., which was built in 1867 on the site of old Mexican barracks. Named for Edward Nye Fish, a local merchant, this building now houses the museum's Western art collection. Some of the walls of this house are 2 feet thick and ceilings in some places are made from old packing crates.

From here, head back up Main Avenue and at the far end of the next block, you will come to the:

8. **Julius Kruttschnidt House,** 297 N. Main Ave., which dates from 1886 and now houses El Presidio Bed and Breakfast Inn. Victorian trappings, including a long veranda, disguise the adobe origins of this unique and beautifully restored home.

Walking Tour—Downtown Historic Districts

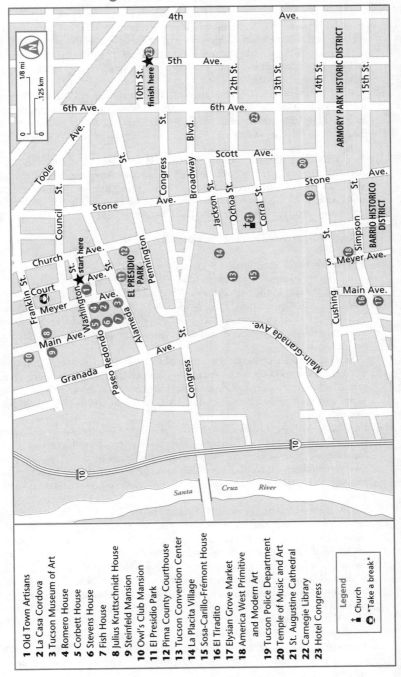

1 Old Town Artisans
2 La Casa Cordova
3 Tucson Museum of Art
4 Romero House
5 Corbett House
6 Stevens House
7 Fish House
8 Julius Kruttschnidt House
9 Steinfeld Mansion
10 Owl's Club Mansion
11 El Presidio Park
12 Pima County Courthouse
13 Tucson Convention Center
14 La Placita Village
15 Sosa-Carillo-Frémont House
16 El Tiradito
17 Elysian Grove Market
18 America West Primitive
    and Modern Art
19 Tucson Police Department
20 Temple of Music and Art
21 St. Augustine Cathedral
22 Carnegie Library
23 Hotel Congress

Legend
✝ ■ Church
○ "Take a break"

Across Main Avenue from the B&B stands the:

9. Steinfeld House, 300 N. Main Ave., which was built in 1900 in California Mission–revival style and was designed by Henry Trost, Tucson's most noted architect. This building served as the original Owl's Club, a gentlemen's club for some of Tucson's most eligible turn-of-the-century bachelors. Another block north on Main Avenue stands the:

10. Owl's Club Mansion, 378 N. Main Ave., which was built in 1902 and designed by Henry Trost in the Mission-revival style, albeit with a great deal of ornamentation. This impressive mansion replaced the Steinfeld House as home to the bachelors of the Owl's Club.

TAKE A BREAK   If you started your tour late in the morning, you're probably hungry by now. Backtrack down Main Avenue, cross the street, and walk east on Franklin Street to Court Avenue. Turn right onto Court, and you will come to **El Charro Cafe,** Tucson's oldest Mexican restaurant. Be sure to order *carne seca,* the house specialty. (See "Where to Dine," above, for details.)

From here, continue south on Court Avenue and cross Alameda Street to reach:

11. El Presidio Park, once the parade ground for the presidio and now a shady gathering spot for everyone from the homeless to downtown office workers.

Just to the east of the park is the very impressive:

12. Pima County Courthouse, 115 N. Church St. Built in 1928, the courthouse incorporates Moorish, Spanish, and Southwestern architectural features, including a colorful tiled dome. A portion of the original presidio wall is in a glass case on the second floor.

From the courthouse, continue south 2 blocks, and you will come to the:

13. Tucson Convention Center, a sprawling complex that includes a sports arena, grand ballroom, concert hall, theater, pavilions, meeting halls, gardens, restaurants, and craft and souvenir vendors. It is here you will find the colorfully painted:

14. La Placita Village, 110 S. Church Ave., a complex of offices and restaurants designed to resemble a Mexican village. This complex incorporates the Samaniego House, a Sonoran-style rowhouse that dates from the 1880s. By the time you do this tour, La Placita Village should be home to Tucson's Visitor Center. Near the fountains in the center of the convention center complex is the historic:

15. Sosa-Carillo-Frémont House, 151 S. Granada Ave., an adobe structure built in the 1850s and later the home of territorial governor John C. Frémont. The restored building is open to the public and is furnished in the style of the period.

Continue south through the grounds of the convention center complex, and you will come to Cushing Street, across which lies the Barrio Histórico District. With its 150 adobe rowhouses, this is the largest collection of 19th-century Sonoran-style adobe architecture in the United States. However, the entire neighborhood was almost razed in the name of urban renewal and highway construction. About half of downtown Tucson, including the neighborhoods that once stood on the site of today's convention center, was razed before the voices for preservation and restoration were finally heard. In fact, if it had not been for the activism of the residents of the Barrio Histórico, Interstate 10 would now run right through much of this area.

Start your exploration of the northern (and more restored) blocks of this neighborhood by crossing Cushing Street and then turning down Main Avenue, where you will find, on the west side of the street in the first block:

16. El Tiradito. This is the only shrine in the United States dedicated to a sinner buried in unconsecrated soil. People still light candles here in hope of having their wishes come true (see "The Shrine That Stopped a Freeway" box, above). Continuing south to the corner of W. Simpson Street, you will see the:

17. Elysian Grove Market, 400 W. Simpson St. This dilapidated-looking old adobe building is actually one of the most interesting and artistically decorated bed-and-breakfast inns in the city (see "Where to Stay," above).

Wander a while through the Barrio Histórico District, admiring the Sonoran-style homes that are built right out to the street. Many of these homes sport colorfully painted facades, signs of the ongoing renovation of this neighborhood.

Before leaving the Barrio, you may want to stop in at:

18. America West Primitive and Modern Art, 363 S. Meyer Ave. Not only will you get a glimpse inside one of these buildings, but the collection of art for sale in this gallery is fascinating. From the corner of Cushing Street and South Meyer Avenue, walk 2 blocks east to South Stone Avenue, where you'll find the:

19. Tucson Police Department, 270 S. Stone Ave. While most people like to give police stations a wide berth, this one is worth a visit. In the lobby you'll find a display of John Dillinger memorabilia (Dillinger's capture took place not long after an eventful stay at the nearby Hotel Congress). Continue another block east on Cushing Street and you will come to the:

20. Temple of Music and Art, 330 S. Scott Ave, which was built in 1927 as a movie and stage theater and is the home of the Arizona Theatre Company (see "Tucson After Dark," below, for details). From here, walk north on South Scott Avenue, turn left on McCormick Street/13th Street and then right onto South Stone Avenue, which will bring you to:

21. St. Augustine Cathedral, built in 1896 and modeled after the Cathedral of Queretaro, Mexico. Above the door of the cathedral, you'll see a statue of Saint Augustine as well as symbols of the Arizona desert—the horned toad, the saguaro, and the yucca. From here, walk east on Corral Street, turn left on South Scott Avenue, and then right on 12th Street and right again on South Sixth Avenue to reach the front of the old:

22. Carnegie Library, which dates from 1901 and was designed by Henry Trost. The building now houses the Tucson Children's Museum (see "Especially for Kids," above, for details). From here, head north on South Sixth Avenue for 2 blocks and turn right on Congress Street. In 1 block, you will see on the far side of the street the:

23. Hotel Congress, 311 E. Congress St., which was built as a railroad hotel in 1919 and once played host to John Dillinger, infamous public enemy number one. Today the restored budget hotel is popular with European travelers and students and has a classically Western-styled lobby. There's a cybercafe and a regular cafe here. The lobby is well worth a stroll-through.

6 Organized Tours

To get an overview of Tucson, you can take a 1½-hour guided city tour with **Tucson Tours** (☎ **520/297-2911**) for $18. The tours head up to the top of A Mountain for a look at the city from above, then visit the three downtown historic districts and the University of Arizona. The same company offers a shuttle service to the

Arizona–Sonora Desert Museum and Old Tucson Studios and tours to Mission San Xavier del Bac, Bisbee, Tombstone, Nogales, and Sedona.

To learn more about the history of Tucson, attach yourself to one of Ken Scoville's **Old Pueblo Walking Tours** (☎ **520/323-9290**) of downtown (he usually does tours for groups). Mr. Scoville is a wealth of information about the city and offers tours that focus on the original presidio site, El Presidio Historic District, and Tucson after the arrival of the railroad. Two-hour tours cost $10 and are offered November to May or on request; call for a reservation first.

Laurel Cooper at **Desert Paths Tours** (☎ **520/327-7235**) has a Ph.D. in anthropology and many years' experience in leading history, art, and culture-oriented field trips. She offers customized tours of the Saguaro National Monument and Southeastern Arizona, among other places.

Learning Expeditions, a program run by the **Arizona State Museum,** occasionally offers scholar-led archaeological tours, including a trip to view rock art in Tucson. For more information, call the marketing department at Arizona State Museum (☎ **520/626-8381;** www.statemuseum.arizona.edu), P.O. Box 210026, Tucson, AZ 85721.

If you'd like to learn more about the native peoples who lived in the Tucson area hundreds of years ago, take a tour with the **Center for Desert Archaeology** (☎ **520/885-6283** or 520/881-2244; www.cdarc.org; e-mail: connie@desert.com), a nonprofit educational and research organization that can take you to view petroglyphs in the foothills of the Tucson Mountains or Hohokam sites in Catalina State Park. Tours cost $40 for a half day and $70 for a full day and are usually led by Connie Allen-Bacon, who is a wealth of information on the ancient residents of this region. The Hohokam sites tour includes the chance to throw a spear using an *atlatl* and a chance to grind mesquite bean pods in an ancient mortar and pestle.

Tours of the Sabino Canyon Ruin are offered by the **Old Pueblo Archaeology Center** (☎ **520/798-1201**), which offers opportunities to assist in the excavation of the site. Two-hour tours (offered seasonally) provide an introduction to the site and cost $10. Day-long programs that include an orientation, a tour of the ruin site, excavation, and time in the lab cost $35 per person. Call for dates and reservations.

For a look at a completely different sort of excavation, head south from Tucson 15 miles to the **ASARCO Mineral Discovery Center,** exit 80 off I-19 to Pima Mine Road (☎ **520/625-7513**), where you can tour a huge open-pit copper mine and learn about copper mining past and present. The Mineral Discovery Center is open Tuesday to Saturday 9am to 5pm and admission is free. One-hour mine tours, which leave the Discovery Center every 20 to 30 minutes, are $6 for adults, $5 for seniors, and $4 for children 5 to 12.

Trail Dust Adventures (☎ **520/747-0323**), which charges $49 for a half-day tour, will take you into the desert on a private Jeep trail. Along the way you can stop to visit a 1,000-year-old archaeological site. With **Sunshine Jeep Tours** (☎ **520/742-1943**), which charges $48 for adults, you'll head out through the saguaros northwest of Tucson and visit an archaeological site.

7 Outdoor Pursuits

BALLOONING **Balloon America** (☎ **520/299-7744;** www.balloonridesusa. com) offers breakfast flights over the foothills of the Santa Catalina Mountains, with free pickups at selected resorts and a champagne toast at the end of the flight. Flights cost $150 to $250 per person and the ballooning season runs October to June.

Southern Arizona Balloon Excursions (☎ 520/624-3599) offers similar flights for $125 per person ($110 between Thanksgiving and Christmas).

BIKING   Tucson is one of the best bicycling cities in the country, and the dirt roads and trails of the surrounding national forest and desert are perfect for mountain biking. Bikes can be rented for $25 to $45 a day at **Full Cycle,** 3302 E. Speedway Blvd. (☎ 520/327-3232), or **Basement Bike,** 428 N. Fremont Ave. (☎ 520/ 628-1015), which is near the university. Either of these bike stores can set you up with a bicycling map of the area.

If you'd rather confine your pedaling to paved surfaces, there are some great options around town. The number-one choice in town for cyclists in halfway decent shape is the road up **Sabino Canyon** (see "Seeing the Sights," above). Keep in mind, however, that bicycles are allowed on this road only 5 days a week and then only before 9am and after 5pm, 5 days a week (the road's closed to bikes all day on Wednesday and Saturday). For a much easier ride, try the **Rillito River Park path,** a 4-mile trail that parallels River Road and the usually dry bed of the Rillito River between Campbell Avenue and La Cholla Boulevard. If you've got knobby tires, you can continue west on this trail after the pavement ends. Another option close to downtown is the 4-mile **Santa Cruz River Park path,** which extends from West Grant Road to 29th Street. Once again, this trail parallels a usually dry riverbed.

BIRD WATCHING   Southern Arizona has some of the best bird watching in the country, and although the best spots are south of Tucson, there are a few places around the city that birders will enjoy seeking out. **Agua Caliente County Park,** 4002 N. Soldier Trail, at the corner of Roger Road in the northeast corner of the city, is just about the best place in the city to see birds. The year-round warm springs here are a magnet for dozens of species, including waterfowl, great blue herons, black phoebes, soras, and vermilion flycatchers. To find the park, follow Tanque Verde Road east 6 miles from the intersection with Sabino Canyon Road and turn left onto Soldier Trail. Watch for signs.

Other good places include **Sabino Canyon Recreation Area** and the path to the waterfall at **Loews Ventana Canyon Resort.**

However, the best area bird watching is in ❂ **Madera Canyon National Forest Recreation Area** (☎ 520/281-2296), which is about 40 miles south of the city in the Coronado National Forest. Because of the year-round water to be found here, Madera Canyon attracts a surprising variety of bird life. Avid birders flock to this canyon from around the country in hopes of spotting more than a dozen species of hummingbirds, an equal number of flycatchers, warblers, tanagers, buntings, grosbeaks, and many rare birds not found in any other state.

However, before birding became a hot activity, this canyon was popular with families looking for a way to escape the heat down in Tucson, and the shady picnic areas and trails still get a lot of use by those who don't carry binoculars. If you're heading out here for the day, arrive early—parking is very limited. To reach Madera Canyon, take Exit 39 off I-19; from the exit, it's another 12 miles southeast. The canyon is open daily dawn to dusk for day use, but there is also a campground ($10 per night). On weekends a $2 donation is requested for use of the recreation area. For information on the canyon's Santa Rita Lodge, see "Where to Stay," in this chapter.

GOLF   Although there aren't quite as many golf courses in Tucson as in Phoenix, this is still a golfer's town. For last-minute tee-time reservations, contact **Standby Golf** (☎ 520/882-2665).

In addition to the public and municipal links, there are numerous resort courses that allow non-guests to play. Perhaps the most famous of these are the two 18-hole courses at ✪ **Ventana Canyon Golf and Racquet Club,** 6200 N. Clubhouse Lane (☎ **520/577-1400**). These Tom Fazio–designed courses offer challenging desert target–style play that is nearly legendary. The third hole on the Mountain Course here is one of the most photographed holes in the west ($189 winter; $95 summer). However, as famous as Ventana Canyon courses are, it is the 27-hole ✪ **Omni Tucson National Golf Resort and Spa,** 2727 W. Club Dr. (☎ **520/575-7540**), a traditional course, that is perhaps more familiar to golfers as the site of the annual Tucson Open ($149 winter; $59 summer). The **El Conquistador Country Club,** 10555 N. La Cañada Dr. (☎ **520/544-1800**), with two 18-hole courses and a nine-hole course, offers stunning (and very distracting) views of the Santa Catalina Mountains ($99 winter; $45 summer). At the **La Paloma Resort and Country Club,** 3660 E. Sunrise Dr. (☎ **520/299-1500**), golfers will find 27 holes designed by Jack Nicklaus ($165 winter; $90 summer). At ✪ **Starr Pass Golf Club,** 3645 W. Starr Pass Blvd. (☎ **520/ 670-0400**), players are seduced by the deceptively difficult 15th hole that plays right through the narrow Starr Pass, which was once a stagecoach route ($135 winter; $48 summer).

There are many other public courses around town. The **Raven Golf Club at Sabino Springs,** 9777 E. Sabino Greens Dr. (☎ **520/749-3636**), incorporates stands of cactus and rocky outcroppings into the course layout ($140 winter; $55 summer). At the **Golf Club at Vistoso,** 955 W. Vistoso Highlands Dr. (☎ **520/797-9900**), you'll find a championship desert course ($135 winter; $55 summer). **Heritage Highlands Golf & Country Club,** 4949 W. Heritage Club Blvd. (☎ **520/579-7000**), is a new championship desert course at the foot of the Tortolita Mountains ($115 winter; $45 summer). **The Links at Continental Ranch,** 8480 N. Continental Links Dr. (☎ **520/744-7443**), is a rolling links-style course reminiscent of Scottish courses ($79 winter; $39 summer).

Tucson Parks and Recreation operates five municipal golf courses, of which the **Randolph North** and **Dell Urich,** 600 S. Alvernon Way (☎ **520/325-2811**), are the premier courses. The former is the site of the LPGA Open. Other municipal courses include **Trini Alvarez/El Rio,** 1400 W. Speedway Blvd. (☎ **520/623-6783**); **Silverbell,** 3600 N. Silverbell Rd. (☎ **520/743-7284**); and **Fred Enke,** 8251 E. Irvington Rd. (☎ **520/296-8607**). Nonresident greens fees for 18 holes are $37 between November and May (about $20 in summer). Golf carts are available for $18.

HIKING   Tucson is nearly surrounded by mountains, most of which are protected as city and state parks, national forest, or national park, and within these public areas are hundreds of miles of hiking trails.

Saguaro National Park flanks Tucson on both the east and west with units accessible off Old Spanish Trail east of Tucson and past the end of Speedway Boulevard west of the city. In these areas you can observe Sonoran Desert vegetation and wildlife and hike among the huge saguaro cacti for which the park is named. For saguaro-spotting the west unit is the better choice.

Tucson Mountain Park, at the end of Speedway Boulevard, is adjacent to Saguaro National Park and preserves a similar landscape. The parking area at Gates Pass, on Speedway, is a favorite sunset spot.

Sabino Canyon, off Sabino Canyon Road, is Tucson's most popular recreation area. A cold mountain stream here cascades over waterfalls and forms pools that make great swimming holes. The ✪ **Seven Falls Trail,** which follows Bear Canyon deep into the mountains, is a 5.2-mile round-trip hike and the most popular hike in the recreation area. You can take a tram to the trailhead or add extra miles by hiking from the main parking lot.

With Tucson's city limits pushing right out to the boundary of the Coronado National Forest, there are some excellent hiking options in Tucson's northern foothills. The **Ventana Canyon Trail** begins at a parking area adjacent to the Loews Ventana Canyon Resort (off Sunrise Drive west of Sabino Canyon Road) and leads into the Ventana Canyon Wilderness. Over near the Westward Look Resort is the **Pima Canyon Trail,** which leads into the Ventana Canyon Wilderness and is reached off Ina Road just east of Oracle Road. Both of these trails provide classic desert canyon hikes of whatever length you feel like hiking (a dam at 3 miles on the latter trail makes a good turnaround point).

Catalina State Park, 11570 N. Oracle Rd. (☎ **520/628-5798**), is set on the rugged northwest face of the Santa Catalina Mountains, between 2,500 and 3,000 feet high. Hiking trails here lead into the Pusch Ridge Wilderness; however, the favorite park day hike is to Romero Pools, a refreshing destination on a hot day. Admission to the park is $5. There are horseback riding stables adjacent to the park, and within the park is an ancient Hohokam ruin. Guided hikes are offered in the cooler months.

One of the reasons Tucson is such a livable city is the presence of the cool (and, in winter, snow-covered) pine forests of 8,250-foot Mount Lemmon. Within the **Mount Lemmon Recreation Area,** at the end of the Catalina Highway, there are many miles of hiking trails, and the hearty hiker can even set out from down in the lowland desert and hike up into the alpine forests. For a more leisurely hike, drive to the top to start your hike. Keep in mind, however, that in winter, when the weather is pleasant in Tucson, people may be skiing up here. There is a $5-per-vehicle charge to use any of the sites within this recreation area. Even if you only plan to pull off at a roadside parking spot and ogle the view of the desert far below, you'll need to stop at the roadside ticket kiosk at the base of the mountain and pay your fee.

HORSEBACK RIDING   If you want to play cowboy or just go for a leisurely ride through the desert, there are plenty of stables around Tucson where you can saddle up. In addition to renting horses and providing guided trail rides, all the stables below offer sunset rides with cookouts. Although reservations are not always required, they're a good idea. You can opt to stay at a guest ranch and do almost as much riding as your muscles can stand.

Pusch Ridge Stables, 13700 N. Oracle Rd. (☎ **520/825-1664**), is adjacent to Catalina State Park and Coronado National Forest. Rates are $20 for 1 hour, $35 for 2 hours. This stable has a satellite stable at the Sheraton El Conquistador.

In the same area, you'll find **Walking Wind Stables,** 10811 N. Oracle Rd. (☎ **520/742-4422**) at Catalina State Park. Rates here are $18 for 1 hour, $35 for 2 hours, and $55 for 3 hours. Reservations are suggested.

Big Sky Rides, 6501 W. Ina Rd. (☎ **520/744-3789**), is 2 miles west of I-10 and offers a variety of rides in the Tucson Mountains and Saguaro National Park West. Rates range from $20 for 1 hour to $80 for a full day with lunch. Reservations are requested.

If your idea of fun is doing the city slicker thing, call the **Cocoraque Ranch,** 6255 N. Diamond Hills Lane (☎ **520/682-8594**). This working cattle ranch dates from the 1890s and now offers cattle drives. Rates depend on the number of people, and there is a 12-person minimum, but it is sometimes possible to join another group. Trail rides that go out to check on the cattle ($30 for 2 hours) are available. The ranch is near the Arizona–Sonora Desert Museum and Old Tucson Studios.

SKIING   Located 1 hour (35 miles) from Tucson, **Mount Lemmon Ski Valley** (☎ **520/576-1321**) is the southernmost ski area in the United States and offers 15 runs for experienced downhill skiers as well as beginners. The season here isn't very reliable, and locals recommend not using your own skis or snowboard (too many exposed rocks). The ski area often opens only after a new dump of snow (at which time the Mount Lemmon Highway is usually closed), so be sure to call the road condition information line (☎ 520/547-7510) before driving up. The ski season runs December to April. Full-day lift tickets are $28 to $32 for adults and $12 for children. Half-day rates are $23 to $27 for adults, $11 for children.

TENNIS   The **Randolph Tennis Center,** 50 S. Alvernon Way (☎ 520/791-4896), convenient to downtown, offers 25 lighted courts. During the day, court time is $2 per person; at night it's $6 per court. Many of the city's hotels and resorts provide courts for guest use.

WILDFLOWER VIEWING   Bloom time varies from year to year, but April and May are good times to view native wildflowers in the Tucson area. While the crowns of white blossoms worn by saguaro cacti are among the most visible blooms in the area, other cacti are far more colorful. Saguaro National Park and Sabino Canyon are among the best local spots to see saguaros, other cacti, and various other wildflowers in bloom. If you feel like heading farther afield, the wildflower displays at Picacho Peak State Park, between Tucson and Casa Grande, are considered the most impressive in the state.

8 Spectator Sports

BASEBALL   The **Colorado Rockies** (☎ 520/327-9467) pitch spring-training camp in March at Hi Corbett Field, 3400 E. Camino Campestre, in Reid Park (at South Country Club Road and East 22nd Street). Tickets are $2 to $10. Both the **Chicago White Sox** and the **Arizona Diamondbacks** have their spring training camps and exhibition games at Tucson Electric Park, 2500 E. Ajo Way (☎ 520/434-1111 for ticket information), which is on the south side of the city near the airport. Tickets for the two latter teams are available through **ETM Ticketing/Dillard's** (☎ 800/638-4253).

Tucson Electric Park is where you can watch the **Tucson Sidewinders** (☎ 520/434-1021), the Arizona Diamondbacks ACCOMMODATIONS team in the Pacific Coast League. The season runs April to August, and tickets are $4.50 to $8.

FOOTBALL   The **University of Arizona Wildcats** (☎ 520/621-2287), a PAC-10 team, play at UA's Arizona Stadium.

GOLF TOURNAMENTS   In mid-March, women golfers compete for big prizes at the **Welch's/Circle K LPGA Championship** (☎ 520/791-5742), which is held at the Randolph North Golf Course. Daily tickets are $10. The **Touchstone Energy Tucson Open** (☎ 800/882-7660), Tucson's main PGA tournament, is held in mid-February at the Omni Tucson National Golf Resort and Spa. Daily tickets are around $15.

GREYHOUND RACING   Greyhounds race year-round at **Tucson Greyhound Park,** 36th Street at Fourth Avenue (☎ 520/884-7576). Admission is $1.25. To reach the track, take Exit 261 off I-10.

HORSE RACING   Rillito Park (☎ 520/293-5011 during racing season, or 520/740-2690 other months), on First Avenue between River and Limberlost roads, was the birthplace of both the photo finish and organized quarter-horse and Arabian racing and has now been restored for both quarter-horse and thoroughbred racing. The ponies run on weekends in February and March, and admission is $2.50.

TENNIS TOURNAMENTS   The **Tucson Classic Celebrity Golf & Tennis Tournament** (☎ **520/623-6165**) takes place at the Sheraton El Conquistador in mid-May, when 20 to 30 celebrity tennis players take on the locals. There's a golf tournament and a celebrity golf shootout. Tickets are $5.

9 Day Spas

If you'd rather opt for a massage than a round on the links, consider spending a few hours at a day spa. While full-service health spas can cost $400 to $500 or more per person per day, for less than $100, you can avail yourself of a spa treatment or two (massages, facials, seaweed wraps, loofah scrubs, and the like) and maybe even get to spend the day lounging by the pool at some exclusive resort. Spas are great places to while away an afternoon if you couldn't get a tee time at that golf course you wanted to play or if it happens to be raining. While spas in general still cater primarily to women, those mentioned below also have special programs for men.

For variety of services and gorgeous location, you just can't beat the Spa & Tennis Center at **Loews Ventana Canyon Resort,** 7000 N. Resort Dr. (☎ **520/299-2020**), which is wedged between the rugged Catalinas and manicured fairways of some of the most fabled golf courses in the state. Soothed by the scent of aromatherapy, you can treat yourself to herbal wraps, mud body treatments, seaweed body masks, different styles of massage, specialized facials, complete beauty salon services, and much more. Treatments run $70 to $95. With any body treatment, you get use of the spa's fitness facilities and pool and can attend any fitness classes being held the day of your treatment.

For an equally luxurious day at the spa, you can opt to visit the **Omni Tucson National Golf Resort & Spa,** 2727 W. Club Dr. (☎ **520/575-7559**) off Magee Road in the northwestern foothills. Services and prices here are comparable to those at Loews, and once again, with any body treatment or massage, you have full use of the spa's facilities. Try the hot stone massage!

With five locations around the Tucson area, **Gadabout Day Spa** offers the opportunity to slip a relaxing visit to a spa into a busy schedule. Mud baths, facials, and massages as well as hair and nail services are available. You'll find Gadabout at the following locations: St. Philip's Plaza, 1990 E. River Rd. (☎ **520/577-2000**); 6393 E. Grant Rd. (☎ **520/885-0000**); Rancho Center, 3382 E. Speedway Blvd. (☎ **520/325-0000**); Sunrise–Kolb, 6960 E. Sunrise Dr. (☎ **520/615-9700**); and Plaza Escondida, 7888 N. Oracle Rd. (☎ **520/742-0000**). Body treatments and massages range from about $50 to $150. There are half-day and full-day spa getaways.

10 Shopping

Tucsonans have a very strong sense of their place in the Southwest, and this is reflected in the city's shopping scene. Southwestern clothing, food, crafts, furniture, and art abound (and often at reasonable prices), as do shopping centers built in a Southwestern architectural style.

Although Tucson is overshadowed by Scottsdale and Phoenix, the city provides a very respectable diversity of merchants. Its population center has moved steadily northward for some years, so it is in the northern foothills you'll find most of the city's large enclosed shopping malls as well as expensive shops selling the best-quality merchandise.

On Fourth Avenue, between Congress Street and Speedway Boulevard, more than 100 shops, galleries, and restaurants make up the **North Fourth Avenue historic**

shopping district. The buildings here were built in the early 1900s, and there has been an attempt to keep the neighborhood humming and maintain Tucson's downtown vitality. However, these days the area could best be described as the used-clothing capital of the world. Through the underpass at the south end of Fourth Avenue is Congress Street, the heart of the **Downtown Arts District,** where there are a few art galleries. However, despite the city's best efforts for several years now, neither of these neighborhoods seems to have caught on very fast with Tucson shoppers, and both neighborhoods seem to be primarily hangouts for college students.

El Presidio Historic District around the Tucson Museum of Art is the city's center for crafts shops. This area is home to Old Town Artisans and the Tucson Museum of Art museum shop. The **"Lost Barrio"** on the corner of Southwest Park Avenue and 12th Street (a block off Broadway) is a good place to look for Mexican imports and Southwestern-style home furnishings at good prices. Stores include Rústica, Colonial Frontiers, and Magellan Trading.

ANTIQUES

In addition to the shops listed below, you'll find concentrations of antiques shops along Speedway Boulevard between Swan and Craycroft roads and along Grant Road between Campbell Avenue and Alvernon Way.

Antique Center. 5001 E. Speedway Blvd. ☎ **520/323-0319.**

This mall has about 70 dealers and claims to be the largest antiques mall in southern Arizona. For sale are all manner of collectibles and antiques, including old radios and telephones and lots of copper and glassware collectibles.

ART

Tucson's art gallery scene is not as concentrated as it is in many other cities. While there are a handful of galleries downtown, most Tucson galleries have in the past few years abandoned downtown in favor of the foothills and other more affluent suburbs. The current art hot spot is the corner of Campbell Avenue and Skyline Drive, where you'll find El Cortijo Arts Annex, which has several art galleries and an upscale restaurant.

One of the best ways to take in the downtown Tucson art scene is on the free Thursday night docent-led ArtWalk tours that take place between 5:30 and 7:00pm. These walks are held the first and third Thursdays of the month between September and May and are sponsored by the **Tucson Arts District Partnership** (☎ **520/ 624-9977**). Call for information on tour starting point.

Dinnerware Contemporary Art Gallery. 135 E. Congress St. ☎ **520/792-4503.**

Contemporary is the key word at this gallery in the downtown arts district. Artists represented here tend to have a very wide range of styles and media, so you never know what you'll find. However, you can be sure it will be at the cutting edge of Tucson art.

El Presidio Gallery. 3001 E. Skyline Dr. ☎ **520/299-1414.**

One of Tucson's premier art galleries, El Presidio Gallery deals primarily in traditional and contemporary paintings of the Southwest, and has recently moved to a large, modern gallery space in the new El Cortijo Arts Annex. Contemporary works tend toward the large and bright and are favorites for decorating foothills homes. Also at Santa Fe Square, 7000 E. Tanque Verde Rd. ☎ **520/733-0388.**

✪ **Etherton Gallery.** 135 S. 6th Ave. ☎ **520/624-7370.**

For more than 16 years this gallery has been presenting some of the finest new art to be found in Tucson, including contemporary and historic photographs. Etherton Gallery, a favorite of museums and serious collectors, isn't afraid to present work with strong themes. The gallery has exhibition space upstairs from the B&B Café at the Temple of Music and Art, 330 S. Scott Ave.

✪ **Mark Sublette Medicine Man Gallery.** In Santa Fe Square, 7000 E. Tanque Verde Rd. ☎ **520/722-7798.**

This gallery has the finest and most tasteful traditional western art you'll find just about anywhere in Arizona. Artists represented here include Ed Mell and Howard Post, and most of the gallery's artists have received national attention. There's an excellent selection of Native American crafts here as well. The shop is near a branch of the El Presidio Gallery (see above). See "Native American Arts & Crafts" below for more details.

Philabaum Contemporary Art Glass. 711 S. 6th Ave. ☎ **520/884-7404.**

Visitors can stop by Tom Philabaum's glass studio to watch vases, perfume bottles, and bowls being blown, then browse the gallery full of lovely art glass pieces by Philabaum and more than 100 other artists from around the country.

✪ **Primitive Arts Gallery.** 3026 E. Broadway (in Broadway Village) ☎ **520/326-4852.**

This is the best gallery in Tucson for pre-Columbian art, with an eclectic mix of ancient artifacts focusing on ceramics. You'll find a smattering of other artifacts, from Greek urns to contemporary Argentinian maté gourds.

BOOKS

Chain bookstores in the Tucson area include **Barnes & Noble,** 5130 E. Broadway Blvd. (☎ **520/512-1166**) and 7325 N. La Cholla Blvd., in the Foothills Mall (☎ **520/742-6402**), and **Borders,** 4235 N. Oracle Rd. (☎ **520/292-1331**) and 5870 E. Broadway at the Park Place Mall (☎ **520/584-0111**).

Settlers West Book & Print Gallery. 3061 N. Campbell Ave. ☎ **520/323-8838.**

An impressive selection of books about the West, for both adults and children, is the main attraction here, but there are lots of interesting prints of Western themes.

CRAFTS

Details & Green Shoelaces. 2990 N. Swan Rd. (in Plaza Palomino). ☎ **520/323-0222.**

If you enjoy highly imaginative and colorful crafts with a sense of humor, you'll get a kick out of this place. Imaginative and unexpected objets d'art turn up in the form of clocks, ceramics, glass, and other mediums.

Obsidian Gallery. 4340 N. Campbell Ave. (at River Rd. in St. Philip's Plaza). ☎ **520/577-3598.**

Contemporary crafts by artists of national renown fill this gallery. You'll find luminous art glass, unique and daring jewelry, imaginative ceramics, and much more.

✪ **Old Town Artisans.** 186 N. Meyer Ave. ☎ **800/782-8072** or 520/623-6024.

Housed in a restored 1850s adobe building covering an entire city block of El Presidio Historic District are 15 rooms brimming with traditional and contemporary Southwestern designs by more than 400 artisans.

Pink Adobe Gallery. 6538 E. Tanque Verde Rd. (in La Plaza Shoppes). ☎ **520/298-5995.**

This contemporary crafts gallery sells unique and whimsical works produced by artists from all over the United States. On a recent visit there were hand-tinted photos, glass, ceramics, one-of-a-kind pieces of furniture, and cases full of unique jewelry. They feature fine-crafted Judaica. Many of the items here make great gifts.

Tucson Museum of Art Shop. 140 N. Main Ave. ☎ **520/624-2333.**

The museum's gift shop offers a colorful and changing selection of Southwestern arts and crafts, mostly by local and regional artists.

FASHIONS

See also "Western Wear," below.

FOR BOTH MEN & WOMEN

The Buffalo Exchange. 2001 E. Speedway Blvd. ☎ **520/795-0508.**

A big hit with the college students, this resale shop originated in Tucson and has grown into a chain with stores across the West. Browse through racks of resale and new clothing at fairly reasonable prices, and you're sure to find something to fit your needs. This is a good place to pick up a pair of cowboy boots if you're heading out on the trail. There's another Buffalo Exchange at 7045 E. Tanque Verde Rd. (☎ **520/885-8392**).

FOR MEN

Individual Man. In St. Philip's Plaza, 4320 N. Campbell Ave. ☎ **520/577-2121.**

Unique ties, silk and other natural-fiber shirts, and cotton slacks are casual and of a sophisticated palette, with styles by European, American, and Canadian designers.

FOR WOMEN

Jasmine. 3025 N. Campbell. ☎ **520/323-1771.**

Natural fibers, including washable silks and some hand-loomed fabrics, are the specialty here. There are plenty of styles to browse from on the crowded racks, from classic to exotic, and Southwestern accessories and jewelry to go with the clothes. There's a second store at 423 N. Fourth Ave. (☎ **520/629-0706**).

Maya Palace. In Plaza Palomino, El Mercado de Boutiques, 6332 E. Broadway Blvd. ☎ **520/748-0817.**

This shop features lushly ethnic but very wearable women's clothing in natural fabrics. The friendly staff helps customers of all ages put together a complete look, from casual to dressy. A second shop is at 2960 N. Swan Rd. (☎ **520/325-6411**).

✪ **Rochelle K Fine Women's Apparel.** 5350 E. Broadway Blvd. in The Plaza at Williams Centre (southwest corner of Broadway and Craycroft). ☎ **520/745-4600.**

With everything from the latest in the little black dress to casual and drapey silks and linens, Rochelle K attracts a well-heeled clientele. There are beautiful accessories and jewelry.

GIFTS/SOUVENIRS

B&B Cactus Farm. 11550 E. Speedway Blvd. ☎ **520/721-4687.**

This plant nursery is devoted exclusively to cacti and succulents. The store can pack your purchase for traveling or can ship it anywhere in the United States. The farm is worth a visit just to see the amazing variety of cacti on display. It's a good place to stop on the way to or from Saguaro National Monument east.

✪ **Native Seeds/SEARCH.** 526 N. Fourth Ave. ☎ **520/622-5561.** www.nativeseeds.org.

Gardeners, cooks, and just about anyone in search of an unusual gift will likely be fascinated by this tiny shop. The shelves are full of heirloom beans, corn, chiles, and other seeds from a wide variety of native desert plants. There are gourds and inexpensive Tarahumara Indian baskets, bottled sauces and salsas made from native plants, and books about native agriculture. Proceeds from the store go toward preserving the biodiversity offered by native Southwest seeds.

✪ **Picánte.** 2932 E. Broadway. ☎ **520/320-5699.**

There's a plethora of Hispanic-theme icons and accessories here, including *milagros,* Day of the Dead skeletons, Mexican crosses, jewelry, greeting cards, and folk art from around the world.

Tohono Chul Gift Shop and Tea Room. 7366 N. Paseo del Norte (1 block west of the corner of Ina Rd. and Oracle Rd. in Tohono Chul Park). ☎ **520/797-1222.**

This gift shop is packed with Mexican folk art, nature theme toys, household items, T-shirts, and books and makes a good stop after a visit to the surrounding Tohono Chul Park, which is landscaped with desert plants. Add a meal at the park's tea room, and you've got a good afternoon's outing. For a description of the park, see "Parks, Gardens & Zoos" under "Seeing the Sights."

JEWELRY

In addition to the stores mentioned below, see the Obsidian Gallery under "Crafts" in this section.

Beth Friedman Jewelry. 186 N. Meyer Ave. ☎ **520/622-5013.** Also Joesler Village, 1864 E. River Rd. ☎ **520/577-6858.**

Located in the Old Town Artisans complex, this shop sells a well-chosen collection of jewelry by Native American craftspeople and international designers. The shop carries some extravagant cowgirl getups in velvet and lace.

✪ **Turquoise Door.** In St. Philip's Plaza, 4330 N. Campbell Ave. (at River Rd.). ☎ **520/299-7787.**

The Southwestern contemporary jewelry here is among the most stunning in the city and is made with opals, diamonds, lapis lazuli, amethyst, and the ubiquitous turquoise.

MALLS/SHOPPING CENTERS

Foothills Mall. 7401 N. La Cholla Blvd. ☎ **520/742-7191.**

This large foothills mall went out of business a few years back but has now been revived as an outlet mall and discount shopping center. You'll find a Nike Factory Store, Off 5th Saks Fifth Avenue Outlet, and Donna Karan Company Store, as well as Keaton's Arizona Grill.

Plaza Palomino. 2970 N. Swan Rd. ☎ **520/795-1177.**

Built in the style of a Spanish hacienda with a courtyard and fountains, this shopping center is home to some of Tucson's fun little specialty shops, galleries, and restaurants. A courtesy hotel shuttle (☎ **520/750-0365**) is available.

✪ **St. Philip's Plaza.** 4280 N. Campbell Ave. (at River Rd.). ☎ **520/529-2775.**

This upscale Southwestern-style shopping center includes two or three excellent restaurants, a luxury beauty salon, and numerous shops and galleries, including Bahti Indian Arts and Turquoise Door jewelry. A great one-stop Tucson outing locale.

The Tucson Mall. 4500 N. Oracle Rd. ☎ **520/293-7330.**

The foothills of northern Tucson have become shopping-center central, and this is the largest of the malls. You'll find more than 200 merchants in this busy two-story skylit complex.

MEXICAN & LATIN AMERICAN IMPORTS

In addition to the shops mentioned below, the **"Lost Barrio"** on the corner of Southwest Park Avenue and 12th Street (a block off Broadway) is a good place to look for Mexican imports and Southwestern-style home furnishings at good prices.

Antigua de Mexico. 7037 N. Oracle Rd. (in the Casa Adobes Plaza). ☎ **520/742-7114.**

This is a place for arts and crafts from Mexico—big household items, such as oversized ceramics and painted plates, wooden and wrought-iron furniture, and punched-metal frames and framed mirrors. Smaller items include crucifixes and candlesticks. There are plans afoot for this business to close at this location and reopen in a new warehouse/showroom at 3235 W. Orange Grove Rd. The new showroom should offer similar items and craft demonstrations. Call the above number for more information.

La Buhardilla ("The Attic"). 2360 E. Broadway Blvd. ☎ **520/622-5200**.

OK, so you just cashed out of your place in California, you bought a big house, and you need some sizable furniture to fill up all that space. Buhardilla has it—the hand-carved Spanish Baroque furniture is big—as well as 10-foot-high carved wood doors and larger-than-life-size carvings of angels and archangels. There are Latin American arts and crafts pieces to accessorize all that furniture.

Zocalo. 3016 E. Broadway Blvd. ☎ **520/320-1236.**

Visiting Zocalo is a good reason to wander around Broadway Village, the pleasant shopping plaza where this store is located. They've got big stuff here, such as colonial-style furniture, and household decorator items such as Mexican ceramics, glassware, and Mexican-style paintings.

NATIVE AMERICAN ARTS & CRAFTS

Bahti Indian Arts. In St. Philip's Plaza, 4300 N. Campbell Ave. ☎ **520/577-0290.**

Family owned for more than 40 years, this store sells fine pieces—jewelry, baskets, sculpture, paintings, books, weavings, kachina dolls, Zuni fetishes, and much more.

Gallery West. 6420 N. Campbell Ave. (corner of Skyline Dr. and N. Campbell Rd.). ☎ **520/529-7002.**

Located right below Anthony's restaurant, this very small shop specializes in very expensive Native American artifacts (mostly pre-1940s), such as pots, Apache and Pima baskets, 19th-century Plains Indian beadwork, Navajo weavings, and kachinas. They've recently added both historic and contemporary jewelry.

Indian Territory. 5639 N. Swan Rd. (on the northwest corner with Sunrise Dr.). ☎ **520/577-7961.**

Despite the location in the foothills in a shopping plaza, it's a bit like an old museum in here, with hardwood floors and antique display cases full of Plains and Southwest Indian arts and crafts and regalia. Although much of the store is devoted to new works, you'll find rare old pieces, such as beaded gauntlets and moccasins. Don't come on Monday when the store is closed.

The Kaibab Shops. 2841 N. Campbell Ave. ☎ **520/795-6905**.

This store has been in business for almost 50 years and offers one of the best selections of Native American arts and crafts in Tucson. You can find high-quality jewelry, Mexican pottery and folk arts, home furnishings, glassware, kachinas, and rugs.

✪ **Mark Sublette Medicine Man Gallery.** In Santa Fe Square, 7000 E. Tanque Verde Rd. ☎ **520/722-7798.**

Collectors of old Navajo rugs seem to agree that this rug shop has the best and biggest selection in the city and perhaps even the entire state. There are Mexican and other Hispanic textiles, Acoma pottery, basketry, and other Indian crafts, as well as artwork by cowboy artists.

✪ **Morning Star Traders.** 2020 E. Speedway Blvd. (next door to the Plaza Hotel). ☎ **520/881-2112.**

With hardwood floors and a museum-like atmosphere, this store features museum-quality goods: antique Navajo rugs, kachinas, furniture, and a huge selection of old Native American jewelry. This just may be the best store of its type in the entire state.

An adjoining shop, **Morning Star Antiques,** at 2000 E. Speedway Blvd. (☎ **520/881-3060**), carries an astounding selection of antique Spanish Mission and Mexican furniture as well as WPA and South American pieces.

Primitive Arts Gallery. 3026 E. Broadway (in the Broadway Village). ☎ **520/326-4852.**

This is the best gallery in Tucson for pre-Columbian art, with an eclectic mix of ancient artifacts and some contemporary pieces as well, such as colorful Huichol Indian bead work. You'll find everything from Mayan pots to Greek urns to Argentinian maté gourds here.

Silverbell Trading. In Casas Adobes Plaza, 7007 N. Oracle Rd. ☎ **520/797-6852.**

Not your usual run-of-the-mill crafts store, this shop specializes in regional Native American artwork, such as baskets and pottery, and carries unique items that the shop's owner has obviously sought out. Small items such as stone Navajo corn maidens, Zuni fetishes, and figures carved from sandstone shouldn't be overlooked.

TOYS

Yikes! Toy Store. 2930 E. Broadway. ☎ **520/320-5669.**

If you love wild and wacky toys that are as much fun for adults as they are for kids, you won't want to miss Yikes!, which has a huge selection of rubber bugs, lizards, snakes, and frogs, as well as yo-yos, marbles, wind-up toys, and other absurd playthings.

WESTERN WEAR

Arizona Hatters. 3600 N. 1st Ave. ☎ **520/292-1320.**

Arizona Hatters carries important names in cowboy hats, from Stetson to Bailey to Tilles. Employees custom fit and shape the hat to the wearer's head and face. You'll find bolo ties, western belts, and other accessories here.

Western Warehouse. 3030 E. Speedway Blvd. ☎ **520/327-8005.**

If you want to put together your Western-wear ensemble under one roof, this is the place. It's the largest Western-wear store in Tucson and can deck you and your kids out in the latest cowboy fashions, including hats and boots. There are branches at 3719 N. Oracle Rd. (☎ **520/293-1808**) and 6701 E. Broadway Blvd. (☎ **520/885-4385**).

11 Tucson After Dark

Tucson after dark is a much easier landscape to negotiate than the vast cultural sprawl of the Phoenix area. Instead of having numerous performing arts centers all over the suburbs as in the Valley of the Sun, Tucson has a more concentrated nightlife scene. The **Downtown Arts District** is the center of all the action, with the Temple of Music and Art, the Tucson Convention Center Music Hall, and several nightclubs. The **University of Arizona campus,** only a mile away, is another hot spot for entertainment.

The best place to look for entertainment listings is in the *Tucson Weekly.* Here you'll find thorough listings of concerts, theater and dance performances, and club offerings. The newspaper is free and can be picked up in convenience stores and record stores, among other places. The "Starlight" section of the Thursday edition of *The Arizona Daily Star* is another good source.

THE CLUB & MUSIC SCENE
MARIACHI MUSIC

Tucson is the mariachi capital of the United States, and no one should visit without spending at least one evening listening to some of these strolling minstrels.

✪ **La Fuente.** 1749 N. Oracle Rd. ☎ **520/623-8659.** No cover.

La Fuente is the largest Mexican restaurant in Tucson and serves up good food, but what really draws the crowds is the live mariachi music. The music starts at 6pm, and if you just want to listen and not have dinner, you can hang out in the lounge. The mariachis perform Wednesday to Sunday.

COUNTRY

Cactus Moon Café. 5470 E. Broadway Blvd. (on the east side of town at the corner of Craycroft Rd.). ☎ **520/748-0049.** Cover $2–$4.

A younger to middle-aged crowd frequents this large and glitzy nightclub primarily for country music. However, you'll find top 40 dance music and hip-hop here.

The Maverick, King of Clubs. 4702 E. 22nd. St. (at Swan Rd.). ☎ **520/748-0456.** No cover.

This country-and-western place is tiny, which as far as a lot of people are concerned makes The Maverick a great place to go dancing. Basically it attracts an older crowd, but there's usually a mix of people. The house band plays Tuesday to Saturday.

ROCK, BLUES & REGGAE

Berky's Bar. 5769 E. Speedway Blvd. ☎ **520/296-1981.** Cover $3 Fri–Sat.

There's live music wailing 7 nights a week in this dark and smoky tavern. Monday nights are open jam nights, so you never know who or what you might hear.

Boondocks Lounge. 3306 N. 1st Ave. ☎ **520/690-0991.** Cover $3–$10.

Long a popular dive bar, this place north of downtown is now one of the city's best spots to hear live blues and reggae. There's even a swing night complete with dance lessons. Just look for the giant Chianti bottle out front.

Chicago Bar. 5954 E. Speedway Blvd. ☎ **520/748-8169.** Cover $3 Thurs–Sat.

Transplanted Chicagoans love to watch their home teams on the TVs at this neighborhood bar, but there's live music nightly. Sure, blues gets played a lot, but so do reggae and rock and about everything in between.

✪ **Club Congress.** 311 E. Congress St. ☎ **520/622-8848.** Cover $3–$15.

Just off the lobby of the restored Hotel Congress (now a budget hotel and youth hostel), Club Congress is Tucson's main alternative-music venue. There are usually a couple of nights of live music each week.

The Rialto Theatre. 318 E. Congress St. ☎ **520/740-0126.** Tickets $5–$25.

This recently renovated 1919 vaudeville theater, although not a nightclub, is now Tucson's main venue for performances by bands that are too big to play Club Congress (Los Lobos, Big Bad Voodoo Daddy, NRBQ).

JAZZ

To find out what's happening on the jazz scene in Tucson, call the **Tucson Jazz Society** (☎ **520/743-3399**). Its jazz hotline will give you up-to-date information on jazz clubs and jazz performances, which it sponsors throughout the year.

A COMEDY CLUB

Laffs Comedy Caffè. The Village, 2900 E. Broadway Blvd. ☎ **520/881-8928** or 520/323-8669. Cover Wed–Thurs and Sun $6, Fri–Sat $9.

This stand-up comedy club has local comedians and professional comedians from around the country performing Wednesday to Sunday nights. They have a full bar and a full menu.

DANCE CLUBS/DISCOS

El Parador. 2744 E. Broadway. ☎ **520/881-2808.** Cover $3–$5.

Tropical decor and an overabundance of potted plants here set the mood for lively Latin jazz performances and salsa lessons (Saturday nights) complete with a salsa band. Customers' ages range from the 20s to the 60s, giving new meaning to the term "all ages" club. Admission is free if you're having dinner here.

Metro. 296 N. Stone Ave. ☎ **520/622-3206.** Cover $3–$15.

It's big, it's loud, it's crowded, and under one name or another, this space has long been a favorite of the college crowd. Currently there are two distinctly different dance clubs under one roof here, and between the two, you'll find plenty of Top 40, R&B, house, alternative, and hip-hop.

THE BAR, LOUNGE & PUB SCENE

The Arizona Inn. 2200 E. Elm St. ☎ **520/325-1541.**

If you're looking for a quiet, comfortable scene, the jazz or acoustic music in the Audubon Lounge at the Arizona Inn is sure to soothe your soul. The gardens here are beautiful.

Cascade Lounge. In Loews Ventana Canyon Resort, 7000 N. Resort Dr. ☎ **520/299-2020.**

This is Tucson's ultimate piano bar. With a view of the Catalinas and a happy hour (daily 5 to 7pm), the plush lounge is perfect for romance or relaxation at the start or end of a night on the town. A couple of nights each week, a harpist performs instead of a pianist, and on the weekends, you'll find a trio here.

Gentle Ben's Brewing Co. 865 E. University Blvd. ☎ **520/624-4177.**

Located just off the UA campus, Gentle Ben's, a big modern place with plenty of outdoor seating, is Tucson's favorite microbrewery. The crowd is primarily college students, and there are daily food and drink specials.

Nimbus Brewing. 3850 E. 44th St. (2 blocks east of Palo Verde Rd.). ☎ **520/745-9175.**

Located in a warehouse district on the south side of Tucson, this brew pub is basically the front room of Nimbus's brewing and bottling facility. The furniture is straight out of Goodwill, but the beer is good, and there's live rock and jazz several nights a week. Hard to find, and definitely a local scene.

Presidio Grill. 3352 E. Speedway Blvd. ☎ **520/327-4667.**

With its hip contemporary decor, Presidio Grill attracts a young upscale crowd. Although best known as one of the city's premier restaurants, the bar is a great place for a cocktail.

Thunder Canyon Brewery. 7401 N. La Cholla Blvd. ☎ **520/797-2652.**

Located in the Foothills Mall and affiliated with the Prescott Brewing Co., this brew pub is your best bet in Tucson for hand-crafted ales and is the most convenient brew pub for anyone staying at a foothills resort.

✪ **¡Toma!** 311 N. Court Ave. ☎ **520/622-1922.**

Located in El Presidio Historic District and owned by the family who operates El Charro Café next door, this cafe has a humorous, festive atmosphere complete with a Mexican hat fountain/sculpture in the courtyard. Drop by for cheap margaritas during the daily happy hour from 3 to 7pm (only in the bar).

COCKTAILS WITH A VIEW

Just about all the best views in town are at foothills resorts, but luckily they don't mind sharing with non-guests. In addition to those listed below, the lounge at Anthony's in the Catalinas has a great view. See "Where to Dine," earlier in this chapter, for details.

Desert Garden Lounge. In the Westin La Paloma, 3800 E. Sunrise Dr. ☎ **520/742-6000.**

If you'd like a close-up view of the Santa Catalina Mountains, drop by the Desert Garden Lounge (at sunset perhaps). The large lounge, with its multicolored hardwood floors, affects a sort of Casablanca ambience, and there's live piano music several nights a week.

✪ **Flying V Bar & Grill.** In Loews Ventana Canyon Resort, 7000 N. Resort Dr. ☎ **520/299-2020.**

If you can't afford the lap of luxury, you can at least pull up a chair. Set it next to a waterfall just outside the front door of this popular resort watering hole for a view over the golf course and Tucson far below. The view is one of the best in the city.

Lookout Bar & Grille. In the Westward Look Resort, 245 E. Ina Rd. ☎ **520/297-1151.**

The Westward Look is one of Tucson's oldest resorts and took to the hills long before it became the fashionable place to be. The nighttime view of twinkling city lights and stars is unmatched. On weekend nights there's live music.

SPORTS BARS

Famous Sam's. 3620 N. 1st Ave. ☎ **520/292-0314.**

With 10 branches around the city, Famous Sam's keeps a lot of Tucson's sports fans happy with their cheap prices and large portions. Other convenient locations include 1830 E. Broadway Blvd. (☎ **520/884-0119**), 7930 E. Speedway Blvd. (☎ **520/290-9666**), and 4801 E. 29th St. (☎ **520/748-1975**).

GAY & LESBIAN BARS

To find out about other gay bars around town, keep an eye out for *The Observer,* Tucson's newspaper for the gay, lesbian, and bisexual community. You'll find it at **Antigone Books,** 411 N. Fourth Ave. (☎ 520/792-3715), as well as at the bars listed here.

Ain't Nobody's Bizness. 2900 E. Broadway Blvd. ☎ **520/318-4838.**

Located in a small shopping plaza in midtown, this somewhat upscale bar is *the* lesbian gathering spot in Tucson and has been for several years. There's a dance floor, two pool tables, and a quiet smoke-free room where you can duck out of the noise.

IBT's. 616 N. Fourth Ave. ☎ **520/882-3053.**

Located on funky Fourth Avenue, IBT's has long been the most popular gay dance bar in town. The music ranges from eighties retro to techno, and there are regular drag shows. There's always an interesting crowd.

THE PERFORMING ARTS

To a certain extent, Tucson is a clone of Phoenix when it comes to the performing arts. Three of Tucson's major performance companies—the Arizona Opera Company, Ballet Arizona, and the Arizona Theatre Company—spend half their time in Phoenix. This means that whatever gets staged in Phoenix also gets staged in Tucson. This city does, however, have its own symphony, and Tucson manages to sustain a diversified theater scene as well.

The best way to purchase tickets in Tucson is directly from the company's box office, but tickets to many concerts and theater performances are also available at **Dillard's** department store box offices or by calling **ETM Ticketing/Dillard's** (☎ 800/638-4253). Tickets to Tucson Convention Center events and other venues around town may be available by calling the TCC box office at ☎ 520/791-4266. **Ticketmaster** (☎ 520/321-1000; www.ticketmaster.com) sells tickets to some Tucson performances.

CLASSICAL MUSIC, OPERA & DANCE

Both the **Tucson Symphony Orchestra** (☎ 520/882-8585), which is the oldest continuously performing symphony in the Southwest, and the **Arizona Opera Company** (☎ 520/293-4336), the state's premier opera company, perform at the Tucson Convention Center (TCC) Music Hall, 260 S. Church Ave. Symphony tickets run $10 to $30, and opera tickets run about $19 to $69.

Tucson's dance scene is dominated by **Ballet Arizona** (☎ 888/322-5538), which splits its season between Tucson and Phoenix. Productions usually include well-known ballets as well as new works by regional choreographers, and performances are at different venues around town, including the Tucson Convention Center. Most tickets are $16 to $40.

If your interests run more to modern dance, find out if **Orts Theatre of Dance** (☎ 520/624-3799) or **Tenth Street Danceworks** (☎ 520/795-6980) will be performing in town during your visit.

THEATER

Tucson doesn't have a lot of theater companies, but what few it does have stage a surprisingly diverse sampling of both classic and contemporary plays.

Arizona Theatre Company (ATC) (☎ 520/622-2823), which performs at the Temple of Music and Art, 330 S. Scott Ave., splits its time between here and Phoenix and is the state's top professional theater company. Each season sees a mix of comedy, drama, and Broadway-style musical shows; tickets cost about $20 to $32.

For experimental theater, there's the **Invisible Theatre,** 1400 N. 1st Ave. (☎ **520/ 882-9721**), a tiny theater in a converted laundry building that has been home to Tucson's most experimental theater for 25 years (it does off-Broadway shows and musicals). Tickets go for about $12 to $19.

The West just wouldn't be the West without good old-fashioned melodramas, and the **Gaslight Theatre,** 7010 E. Broadway Blvd.(☎ **520/886-9428**), is where evil villains, stalwart heroes, and defenseless heroines pound the boards. You can boo and hiss, cheer and sigh as the predictable stories unfold on stage. It's all great fun for kids and adults. Tickets are $13.95 for adults, $11.95 for students and senior citizens, and $6.40 for children 12 and under. Performances are held Tuesday to Sunday, with two shows nightly on Friday and Saturday and a Sunday matinee.

PERFORMING ARTS CENTERS & CONCERT HALLS

Tucson's largest performance venue is the **Tucson Convention Center Music Hall,** 260 S. Church Ave. (☎ **520/791-4266**). It's the home of the Tucson Symphony Orchestra and where the Arizona Opera Company and Ballet Arizona usually perform when they're in town. This hall hosts many touring companies. The box office is open Monday to Friday 10am to 6pm.

However, the **Temple of Music and Art,** 330 S. Scott Ave. (☎ **520/622-2823**), a restored historic theater dating from 1927, is the centerpiece of the Tucson theater scene. The 605-seat Alice Holsclaw Theatre is the Temple's main stage, but there's also the 90-seat Cabaret Theatre. You'll find an art gallery and a gift shop here. Free tours of the Temple of Art and Music are given on Saturday mornings. The box office is open Monday to Friday 10am to 6pm (it's open Saturday and Sunday and later in the evening Tuesday to Friday during performance weeks).

Centennial Hall, University Boulevard and Park Avenue (☎ **520/621-3341**), on the UA campus, is Tucson's other main performance hall and stages performances by touring national musical acts, international performance companies, and Broadway shows. A large stage and excellent sound system permit large-scale productions. The box office is open Monday to Friday 10am to 5pm and Saturday noon to 5pm.

Also downtown, you'll find the **Tucson Center for the Performing Arts,** 408 S. 6th Ave., which stages a wide variety of performances, providing an alternative stage for small productions and concerts.

The **Center for the Arts,** Pima Community College (West Campus), 2202 W. Anklam Rd. (☎ **520/206-6988**), is another good place to check for classical music performances. It offers a wide variety of shows, including performances by Ballet Arizona and the Tucson Symphony Chamber Orchestra. The box office is open Monday to Friday 10am to 4pm.

OUTDOOR VENUES & SERIES

Weather permitting, Tucsonans head to Reid Park's **DeMeester Outdoor Performance Center,** at Country Club Road and East 22nd Street (☎ **520/791-4079**), for performances under the stars. This amphitheater is the site of performances by the Parks and Recreation Community Theatre and other production companies, as well as frequent music performances.

The **Tucson Jazz Society** (☎ **520/743-3399**), which manages to book a few well-known jazz musicians each year, sponsors different outdoor music series at various locations around the city with the summer series at St. Philip's Plaza shopping center being the most popular. Over the course of the year the society presents around 40 concerts. Tickets are about $11 to $25.

There are various outdoor concert series downtown throughout the year. The most popular of them are the concerts held in conjunction with the Downtown Saturday/Downtown Saturday Night events. Check in the *Tucson Weekly* for details.

FILM

The Loft Cinema. 3233 E. Speedway Blvd. ☎ **520/795-7777.**

If *Star Wars* wasn't your idea of the best movie ever made, this is the place for you. The screen here is one of the largest around, just right for watching a new independent or foreign release.

The Screening Room. 127 E. Congress St. ☎ **520/622-2262.**

Operated by the Arizona Center for Media Arts, this theater in the downtown arts district specializes in classic art-house films and contemporary independent and foreign films. This is the place to catch *That Obscure Object of Desire, The Night of the Iguana,* or *Woman in the Dunes* one more time.

CASINOS

Casino of the Sun. 7406 S. Camino de Oeste. ☎ **800/344-9435** or 520/883-1700.

Located 15 miles southwest of Tucson and operated by the Pascua Yaqui tribe, this is southern Arizona's largest casino and offers slot machines, keno, bingo, and a card room.

Desert Diamond Casino. 7350 S. Nogales Hwy. ☎ **520/294-7777.**

Operated by the Tohono O'odham tribe and only 3 miles from Mission San Xavier del Bac, this casino offers the same variety of slot and video poker machines found at other casinos in the state. A card room, bingo, and keno round out the options here.

10 Southern Arizona

Although southern Arizona has its share of prickly pears and saguaros, much of this region has more in common with the Texas plains than it does with the Sonoran Desert. In the southeastern corner of the state, the mile-high grasslands, punctuated by forested mountain ranges, have long supported vast ranches where cattle range across wide-open plains. It was also here that much of America's now-legendary Western history took place. Wyatt Earp and the Clantons shot it out at Tombstone's O.K. Corral, Doc Holliday played his cards, and Cochise and Geronimo staged the last Indian rebellions. Cavalries charged, and prospectors searched for the mother lode. Today, ghost towns litter the landscape of southeastern Arizona, but the past is kept alive by people searching for a glimpse of the Wild West.

Long before even the prospectors and outlaws arrived in this corner of the state, this region had gained historical importance as the first part of the Southwest explored by the Spanish. This first Spanish expedition, led by Francisco Vásquez de Coronado in 1540, marched up the San Pedro River valley past present-day Sierra Vista, where today a national memorial commemorates his unfruitful search for the Seven Cities of Cíbola. These cities were rumored to be filled with gold and precious jewels, but all Coronado found were simple Indian pueblos.

Nearly 150 years later Father Eusebio Francisco Kino founded a string of Jesuit missions across the region the Spanish called the Pimeria Alta, an area that would later become northern Mexico and southern Arizona. Converting the Indians and building mission churches, Father Kino left a long-lasting mark on this region. Two of the missions founded by Father Kino—San Xavier del Bac (see chapter 9, "Tucson") and San José de Tumacacori (see the section on Amado, Tubac, and Tumacacori, below)—still stand to this day.

More than 450 years after Coronado marched through this region, the valley of the San Pedro River is undergoing something of a population explosion, especially in the town of Sierra Vista, where retirement communities now sprawl across the landscape. Nearby, in the once nearly abandoned copper-mining town of Bisbee, famous for its Bisbee Blue turquoise, a different sort of boom is underway. Urban refugees and artists have been taking up residence and opening art galleries and B&Bs, making this one of the most interesting small towns in the state.

The combination of low deserts, high plains, and even higher mountains has given this region a fascinating diversity of landscapes. Giant saguaros cover the slopes of the Sonoran Desert throughout much of southern Arizona, and in the western reaches of this region, organ pipe cacti, similar to saguaros, reach the northern limit of their range. In the cool mountains, cacti give way to pines and passing clouds bring snow and rain. Narrow canyons and broad valleys, fed by the rain and snowmelt, provide habitat for an astounding variety of birds and other wildlife unique to the region. This is the northernmost range for many species of birds usually found only south of the border. Consequently, southeastern Arizona has become one of the most important bird-watching spots in the United States. Even nonbirders can appreciate the possibility of seeing more than a dozen different species of hummingbirds.

The region's mild climate has also given rise to the state's small wine industry. Throughout southeastern Arizona, there are now quite a few vineyards and wineries, and touring the wine country is a favorite weekend excursion for residents of Tucson and Phoenix.

1 Organ Pipe National Monument

135 miles S of Phoenix; 185 miles SE of Yuma; 140 miles W of Tucson

Located roughly midway between Yuma and Tucson, ✪ **Organ Pipe Cactus National Monument,** a preserve for the rare organ pipe cactus, is one of Arizona's least visited and most remote national monuments. Organ pipe cactuses resemble saguaro cactuses in many ways, but instead of forming a single main trunk, organ pipes have many trunks, some 20 feet tall, that resemble—you guessed it—organ pipes.

This is a rugged region with few towns or services. To the west lie the inaccessible **Cabeza Prieta Wildlife Refuge** and the **Barry M. Goldwater Air Force Range** (a bombing range), and to the east lies the large Papago Indian Reservation. The only services and motels in the area are in the small town of Ajo. This former company town was built around a now-abandoned copper mine, and the downtown plaza, with its tall palm trees and arched and covered walkways, has the look and feel of a Mexican town square. Be sure to gas up your car before leaving Ajo.

ESSENTIALS

GETTING THERE   From Tucson, take Ariz. 86 west to Why and turn south on Ariz. 85. From Yuma, take I-8 east to Gila Bend and then drive south on Ariz. 85.

VISITOR INFORMATION   For information before leaving home, contact **Organ Pipe Cactus National Monument,** Route 1, Box 100, Ajo, AZ 85321-9626 (☎ 520/387-6849; www.nps.gov/orpi). There is a visitor center open daily 8am to 5pm, although the park itself is open 24 hours a day.

ADMISSION   Park admission is $4 per car.

SEEING THE MONUMENT

Two well-graded one-way gravel roads loop through the park. The Puerto Blanco Drive is a 53-mile loop, and the Ajo Mountain Drive is only 21 miles long. On the Puerto Blanco Drive, you'll pass **Quitobaquito Spring,** which was relied on by Native Americans and pioneers as the only year-round source of water for miles around. This large spring offers great bird-watching opportunities, but cars are subject to break-ins (a highway is only 100 yards from the parking lot). Quitobaquito Spring can also be reached at the end of a 15-mile two-way section of the Puerto Blanco Drive. Guides available at the park's visitor center explain natural features of the landscape along both the loop roads. There are a number of hiking trails along both these roads.

WHERE TO STAY

There is one campground within the park (although non-vehicle camping is allowed in the backcountry with a permit). Campsites are $8 per night. The nearest lodgings are in Ajo, where there are several old and very basic motels as well as a B&B. There are also plenty of budget chain motels in the town of Gila Bend, 70 miles north of the monument. They include a **Best Western** and a **Super 8.**

Guest House Inn Bed & Breakfast. 700 Guest House Rd., Ajo, AZ 85321. ☎ **520/ 387-6133.** Fax 520/387-3995. 4 units. A/C. $79 double. Rates include full breakfast. DC, MC, V.

Built in 1925 as a guesthouse for mining executives, this B&B has attractive gardens in the front yard, a mesquite thicket off to one side, and a modern Southwestern feel to its interior decor. Guest rooms are cool and dark, which is often appreciated in the desert heat here in Ajo. However, there are also sunrooms on both the north and the south side of the house.

2 Amado, Tubac, Tumacacori & Buenos Aires National Wildlife Area

45 miles S of Tucson; 21 miles N of Nogales; 84 miles W of Sierra Vista

Located in the fertile valley of the Santa Cruz River 45 miles south of Tucson, Tubac and Tumacacori together sum up the early experiences of the Spanish, who were the first Europeans to settle in this region. Established in 1691 by Fr. Eusebio Francisco Kino, Tumacacori was one of the first Spanish missions in what would eventually become Arizona. At that time, Tubac was a Pima village, but by the 1730s, the Spanish had begun settling here in the region they called Pimeria Alta. After a Pima uprising in 1751, Spanish forces were sent into the area to protect the settlers, and in 1752 Tubac became a presidio (fort). Between 1752 and the present, seven different flags have flown over Tubac, including those of Spain, Mexico, the United States, the New Mexico Territory, the Confederacy, the U.S. Territory of Arizona, and the state of Arizona.

Although the European history of this area is more than 300 years old, the area's human habitation actually dates far back into prehistory. Archaeologists have found evidence that there have been people living along the nearby Santa Cruz River for nearly 10,000 years. The Hohokam lived in the area from about A.D. 300 until their mysterious disappearance around 1500, and when the Spanish arrived some 200 years later, they found the Pima people inhabiting this region.

Tubac's other claim to fame is as the site from which Juan Bautista de Anza III, the second commander of the presidio, set out in 1775 to find an overland route to California. De Anza led 240 settlers and more than 1,000 head of cattle on this grueling expedition, and when the group finally reached the coast of California, they founded the settlement of San Francisco. One year later, the garrison was moved from Tubac

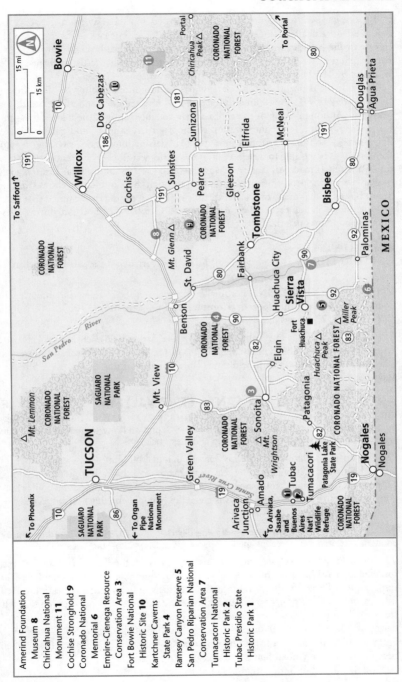

Amerind Foundation
Museum **8**
Chiricahua National
Monument **11**
Cochise Stronghold **9**
Coronado National
Memorial **6**
Empire-Cienega Resource
Conservation Area **3**
Fort Bowie National
Historic Site **10**
Kartchner Caverns
State Park **4**
Ramsey Canyon Preserve **5**
San Pedro Riparian National
Conservation Area **7**
Tumacacori National
Historic Park **2**
Tubac Presidio State
Historic Park **1**

to Tucson, and, with no protection, Tubac's settlers moved away from the area. Soldiers were once again stationed here beginning in 1776, but lack of funds caused the closure of the presidio when in 1821 Mexican independence brought Tubac under a new flag. It was not until this region became U.S. territory that settlers returned to the area, and by 1860, Tubac was the largest town in Arizona.

Today, Tubac is one of Arizona's largest arts communities. The town's old buildings house more than 80 shops selling fine arts, crafts, unusual gifts, and lots of Southwest souvenirs. Although many of the shops are thoroughly touristy, there are a few gems worth seeking out. This concentration of shops, artists' studios, and galleries makes Tubac one of southern Arizona's most popular destinations, and a small retirement community is beginning to develop in the area. After visiting Tubac Presidio State Historic Park and Tumacacori National Monument to learn about the area's history, you'll probably want to spend some time browsing through these interesting shops. Keep in mind, however, that many of the local artists leave town during the summer, so it's best to visit on weekends then. The busy season is October to May, and during these months shops are open daily.

ESSENTIALS

GETTING THERE   Amado, Tubac, and Tumacacori are all due south of Tucson on I-19.

VISITOR INFORMATION   For further information about Tubac and Tumacacori, contact the **Tubac Chamber of Commerce,** P.O. Box 1866, Tubac, AZ 85646 (☎ **520/398-2704;** www.tubacaz.com).

SPECIAL EVENTS   The **Tubac Festival of the Arts** is held each year in February. Artists from all over the country participate. In October, on the weekend nearest to the 23rd, **De Anza Days** commemorate Captain Juan Bautista de Anza's 1775 trek to found San Francisco.

ART & HISTORY IN THE SANTA CRUZ VALLEY

Tubac Center of the Arts. 9 Plaza Rd. ☎ **520/398-2371.** $2 donation suggested. Early Sept to mid-May Tues–Sat 10am–4:30pm, Sun 1–4:30pm; mid-Nov to mid-Apr same hours plus Mon 10am–4:30pm. Closed June–Aug and major holidays.

Tubac is an arts community, and this Spanish colonial building serves as its center for cultural activities. Throughout the season there are workshops, traveling exhibitions, juried shows, an annual crafts show, theater and music performances, and a gift shop. The quality of the art at these shows is generally better than what's found in the surrounding shops.

Tubac Presidio State Historic Park. Presidio Dr. ☎ **520/398-2252.** Admission $2 adults, $1 children 7–13, free for children 6 and under. Daily 8am–5pm. Closed Dec 25.

The Tubac Presidio has a long and fitful history. Although the Tumacacori mission was founded in 1691, it was not until 1752 that the Tubac Presidio was established in response to a Pima uprising. In 1775, the presidio's military garrison was moved to Tucson and, with no protection from raiding Apache, most of Tubac's settlers also left the area. A military presence was reestablished in 1787, but after Mexican independence in 1821, insufficient funds led to the closing of the presidio. Villagers once again abandoned Tubac because of Apache attacks. After the Gadsden Purchase, Tubac became part of the United States and was again resettled.

Although little but buried foundation walls remains of the old presidio, Tubac Presidio State Historic Park has exhibits that explain the history of the presidio. There are displays on the Spanish soldiers, Native Americans, religion, and contemporary Hispanic culture in southern Arizona. Also on the grounds is the old Tubac School, which was built in 1885 and is the oldest schoolhouse in Arizona.

There are living history presentations from October to March on Sundays between 1 and 4pm. Among the characters you'll meet are Spanish soldiers, settlers, and friars.

Tumacacori National Historical Park. Frontage Rd. ☎ **520/398-2341.** Admission $2 per person or $4 per carload, free for children 16 and under. Daily 8am–5pm. Closed Thanksgiving and Dec 25. Take I-19 to Exit 29; you'll find Tumacacori 3 miles south of Tubac.

These mission ruins are a silent reminder of the role that Spanish missionaries played in settling the Southwest. The Tumacacori mission was founded by Jesuit missionary and explorer Fr. Eusebio Francisco Kino in 1691 to convert the Pima people. Much of the old adobe mission church still stands, and the Spanish architectural influences can readily be seen. A small museum contains exhibits on mission life and the history of the region.

On weekends, Native American and Mexican craftspeople give demonstrations of indigenous arts. The **Tumacacori Fiesta,** a celebration of Indian, Hispanic, and Anglo cultures, is held the first weekend of December.

SHOPPING

While tourist brochures like to tout Tubac as an artists' community, the town is more of a Southwest souvenir mecca, something of a land of a million Kokopellis (before the petroglyph-inspired flute player took over the souvenir scene, it was howling coyotes). There are a few genuine art galleries here, but you have to look hard amid the many tourist shops to find the real gems.

With so many shops and tastes, it's hard to recommend specific stops in the Tubac area. But if you want to take the flavor of the area home, stop in at **The Chile Pepper** (☎ **520/398-2921**) on Tubac Road in downtown Tubac for gourmet foods with a Southwestern accent. Down near Tumacacori National Historical Park, you'll find all things hot (chiles, hot sauces, salsas) arranged on the shelves of one of the more genuine Tubac institutions, the ✪ **Santa Cruz Chile and Spice Co.** (☎ **520/398-2591**), a combination store and packing plant. There's an amazing assortment of familiar and obscure spices for sale. In the back, you can see various herbs being prepared and packaged. The shop is closed on Sunday.

The **Sonora Trading Company** (☎ **520/398-9016**), in Plaza Antigua on Tubac Street in downtown Tubac, is another interesting shop that specializes in carved Zuni fetishes. Some of the better fine art in Tubac is found at the **Karin Newby Gallery,** Mercado de Baca, 19 Tubac Rd. (☎ **520/398-9662**).

ENJOYING THE OUTDOORS

Linking Tubac with Tumacacori is the 8-mile-long **Anza Trail,** which follows the Santa Cruz River for much of its route and passes through forests and grasslands. This trail is part of the Juan Bautista de Anza National Historic Trail, which stretches from Nogales to San Francisco. Along the trail is an excavation of part of the Spanish colonial settlement of Tubac. However, bird watching is the most popular activity along the trail. The most convenient trailhead is beside Tubac Presidio State Historic Park. An interesting way to see this trail is on horseback rides offered by **Rex Ranch** (☎ **520/398-2696**), which charges $20 per hour per person (offered mid-October to mid-May).

If golf is more your speed, you can play a round at the **Tubac Golf Resort** (☎ **520/398-2021**), just north of Tubac off East Frontage Road. Greens fees range from $22 to $66.

Factoid

To find out what, if any, rare birds have been spotted at the time of your visit, call the Tucson Audubon Society's Rare Bird Hotline (☎ **520/698-1005**).

BUENOS AIRES NATIONAL WILDLIFE REFUGE

If you're a bird watcher, you'll definitely want to make the trip over to ✪ **Buenos Aires National Wildlife Refuge,** P.O. Box 109, Sasabe, AZ 85633 (☎ **520/ 823-4251**), which is about 28 miles from Tubac. To get to the refuge, first head north from Tubac on I-19 to Arivaca Junction and then drive west on a winding but paved two-lane road. The refuge begins just outside the small community of Arivaca.

Your first stop should be at **Arivaca Cienega,** ¹/₄ mile east of Arivaca. *Cienega* is a Spanish word for "marsh." This particular marsh is fed by seven springs that provide year-round water and consequently attract an amazing variety of bird life. This is one of the few places in the United States where you can see a gray hawk. Vermilion flycatchers are also common here. A boardwalk leads across the marsh.

Other good birding spots within the refuge include **Arivaca Creek,** 2 miles west of Arivaca, and **Aguirre Lake,** ¹/₂ mile north of the refuge headquarters and visitor center, which is off Ariz. 286 north of Sasabe. The visitor center is a good place to spot one of the refuge's rarest birds, the masked bobwhite quail. These quail disappeared from Arizona in the late 19th century but have been reintroduced in the refuge. Other birds you might spot outside the visitor center include Bendire's thrasher, Chihuahuan ravens, canyon towhees, and green-tailed towhees. Other wildlife in the refuge includes pronghorn antelopes, javelinas, coatimundis, white-tailed deer, mule deer, and coyotes.

The visitor center is open daily from dawn to dusk. There is also a refuge information center in Arivaca, but this center is open only when volunteers are available to staff it.

Guided birding and other tours at the refuge are offered weekends throughout the year. Call for details; reservations are required. There is primitive camping within the refuge at more than 100 designated spots along rough gravel roads. At the refuge information center is a catalog that shows pictures of the campsites and provides accessibility information. Look for the brown campsite signs along the road and bring water. There is good mountain biking on these roads. If you're looking for a strenuous hike, try the **Mustang Trail,** which has its trailhead 2 miles west of Arivaca. The trail climbs up from Arivaca Creek into the surrounding dry hills and makes for a 5-mile round-trip hike.

If you enjoy scenic drives and don't mind gravel roads, you won't want to pass up the opportunity to drive the Ruby Road through Coronado National Forest to **Peña Blanca Lake** and **Nogales.** This road winds its way through the mountains just north of the Mexican border, passing Arivaca Lake and the privately owned ghost town of Ruby before reaching picturesque Peña Blanca Lake, where there are a couple of campgrounds and the paved road picks up again.

WHERE TO STAY
AMADO

✪ **Amado Territory Inn Bed & Breakfast.** 3001 E. Frontage Rd. (P.O. Box 81), Amado, AZ 85645. ☎ **888/398-8684** or 520/398-8684. Fax 520/398-8186. www.amado-territory-inn.com. 10 units. A/C. Nov–June $105–$135 double, $250 suite; July–Oct $90–$105 double, $175 suite. Rates include full breakfast. MC, V. No children under 12.

This modern inn just off I-19 in the crossroads of Amado is built in the territorial style and succeeds in capturing the feel of old Arizona ranch houses. A spacious high-ceilinged lobby has a big leather couch in front of the fireplace—welcome warmth on cool winter nights. Guest rooms are furnished in a mix of reproduction East Coast antiques and Mexican rustic furnishings, much the way homes would have been furnished in Arizona 100 years ago. While a bit spartan, the rooms have plenty of character; those on the second floor have balconies with views across the farm fields of the Santa Cruz Valley. The suite is a large apartment with a full kitchen. Breakfast is served in a sunny breakfast room, and there's a flagstone patio out back under the mesquite trees. Next door is a similarly designed restaurant affiliated with the inn.

The Rex Ranch. 131 Amado Montosa Rd. (P.O. Box 636), Amado, AZ 85645. ☎ **888/ REX RANCH** or 520/398-2914. Fax 520/398-8229. www.rexranch.com. 28 units. A/C. Oct–May $125–$225 double; June–Sept $105–$205 double. Rates include continental breakfast. AE, CB, DC, DISC, MC, V.

Just getting to this remote and economical health spa is something of an adventure, since you have to drive *through* the Santa Cruz River to reach it. With its classic Southwestern styling and location adjacent to the de Anza Trail, this place is truly a getaway, and although not all the guest rooms are as attractively decorated as the public areas, the new rooms and the more recently renovated rooms are quite comfortable. Primarily a conference center and health spa, the family-run ranch offers a wide variety of spa treatments and massages. The attractive little dining room is one of this area's best restaurants. Horseback riding and mountain bike rentals are available.

TUBAC

Tubac Golf Resort. 1 Otero Rd. (P.O. Box 1297), Tubac, AZ 85646. ☎ **800/848-7893** or 520/398-2211. Fax 520/398-9261. www.arizonaguide.com/tubac. 46 units. A/C TV TEL. $75–$145 double; $100–$190 suite. AE, DISC, MC, V.

The Tubac Golf Resort is built on the Otero Ranch, which in 1789 became the first Spanish land grant in the Southwest. The old ranch stables, which now house the resort's restaurant, are the ranch's oldest buildings and date from the turn of the century. Red-tile roofs and brick archways remind you that this was once a Spanish hacienda. The guest rooms are all in much newer buildings set amid expansive lawns that seem a bit out of place here in the desert. The casitas have two patios, tile bathroom counters, beamed ceilings, and beehive fireplaces. Newer rooms are worth requesting. The dining room has booths that resemble horse stalls, and the menu focuses on mesquite-broiled steaks and seafood, but there's enough variety that you won't get bored if you stay here for a few days. In the lounge, a wall of glass looks out to the golf course and mountains. Facilities include an 18-hole golf course (used in the film *Tin Cup*), a swimming pool, hot tub, a tennis court, and a pro shop.

Valle Verde Ranch Bed & Breakfast. 1/4 mile south of Tubac on E. Frontage Rd., P.O. Box 157, Tumacacori, AZ 85640. ☎/fax **520/398-2246.** 5 units. TV. $80–$95 double; $100–$135 casita. Rates include full breakfast, unless you stay in a casita. No credit cards. Closed Memorial Day to October. No children.

Until recently, this inn on the outskirts of Tubac had a delightfully secluded feel. However, with the construction of a new housing development immediately next to the inn's property, the B&B no longer feels so secluded. However, this Mission-revival ranch house, built in 1937 and painted pink with blue trim, is still an eyeful. Interior walls are painted beautiful Southwestern colors. Antiques from around the world give the inn a pleasantly cluttered feel, and one room has been turned into a delightful little bar where guests can hang out. European furnishings predominate in the guest

Starry, Starry Nights

Southern Arizona likes to brag about how many sunny days it has each year, but those clear sunny days give way to clear starry nights. The absence of lights in the surrounding desert makes the night sky here as brilliant as anywhere on earth. This fact has not gone unnoticed by the world's astronomers—the Tucson vicinity has a greater concentration of astronomical observatories than any other region on earth, and Southern Arizona has come to be known as the Astronomy Capital of the World.

Many of these observatories are open to the public. In addition to the ones listed below, the Flandrau Science Center in Tucson offers public viewings, as does Biosphere 2, north of Tucson (see "Seeing the Sights" in chapter 9, "Tucson," for details). In Flagstaff, there are public viewing programs at the Lowell Observatory (see the "Flagstaff" section in chapter 6, "The Grand Canyon & Northern Arizona," for details).

Observatories

Fred Lawrence Whipple Observatory. Near Amado. ☎ **520/670-5707.** Tours $7 adults, $2.50 children ages 6–12, no children under age 6 allowed. Reservations are required and can be made up to 2 months in advance. Visitor center Mon–Fri 8:30am–4:30pm; tours mid-Mar to Nov, Mon, Wed, and Fri 9am–3pm. Take I-19 south from Tucson to exit 56, then follow E. Frontage Rd. south 3 miles to Elephant Head Rd. Turn left on this road and then right on Mt. Hopkins Rd. Continue 7 miles to visitor center.

Located atop 8,550-foot Mt. Hopkins, this is the largest observatory operated by the Smithsonian Astrophysical Observatory. Tours last 6 hours, and no food is available here, so be sure to bring a picnic lunch.

✪ **Kitt Peak National Observatory.** Off Ariz. 86. ☎ **520/318-8200,** or 520/318-8726 for stargazing reservations. Admission by donation ($2 suggested). Nighttime stargazing program (reservations required; see below) $35 adults; $25 students, seniors, and children under 18. Daily 9am–4pm (tours at 10 and 11:30am and 1:30pm). Closed Jan 1, Thanksgiving, and Dec 24–25. Take Ariz. 86 southwest from Tucson for about 40 miles to the turnoff for Kitt Peak.

Kitt Peak National Observatory is the largest and most famous astronomical observatory in this region. Located in the Quinlan Mountains, 56 miles southwest of Tucson, the observatory sits atop 6,882-foot Kitt Peak. There are five major telescopes operating at Kitt Peak, including the McMath telescope, the world's largest solar telescope. This telescope's system of mirrors channels an image of the sun deep into the mountain before reflecting it back up to the observatory, where scientists study the resulting 30-inch-diameter image. The 158-inch Mayall telescope features a 30,000-pound quartz mirror and is used

rooms. In one of the casitas you'll find a whirlpool bath, but if you don't stay in that particular one, you can still relax in the inn's outdoor whirlpool spa.

SASABE

✪ **Rancho de la Osa.** P.O. Box 1, Sasabe, AZ 85633. ☎ **800/872-6240** or 520/823-4257. Fax 520/823-4238. www.guestranches.com/ranchodelaosa. 18 units. $310 double; $375 suite (all rates plus 15% service charge). 3- to 4-night minimum. Rates include all meals and horseback riding. DISC, MC, V.

Steeped in history and sharing a fence line with the Mexican border, this ranch dates from roughly 200 years ago and was one of the last Spanish haciendas built in what for studying distant regions of the universe. This is the area's only major observatory to offer public nighttime viewing. Day visitors must be content with a visitor center and museum that provide information on the facility. A box meal is supplied with evening stargazing programs; day visitors need to pack a lunch.

In the winter high season, reservations are recommended a month in advance, but sometimes it's possible to slip in on someone else's cancellation.

Mt. Graham International Observatory & Discovery Park's Gov Aker Observatory. Near Safford. ☎ **520/428-6260.** www.discoverypark.com. Tours $30. Reservations required; call at least 2 weeks in advance. Mount Graham International Observatory tours offered mid-May to mid-Nov (weather permitting) on specific Saturdays 10am–4pm. Gov Aker Observatory open to the public Tues–Wed 1–4pm and Thurs–Sat 1–9pm.

This controversial observatory, one of the nation's newest, stands atop Mt. Graham and is partly operated by the Vatican and partly by the University of Arizona. The facilities include the Vatican Advanced Technology Telescope, the Heinrich Hertz Sub-millimeter Telescope, and the Large Binocular Telescope, which was still under construction at press time. When completed, this last telescope will be the most powerful on earth. Tours of the facility last 6 hours and include lunch, but do not include actual viewing through the telescopes at the observatory (although the telescopes at Gov Aker Observatory at Discovery Park are open to the public).

Where to Stay

Skywatcher's Inn. ℅ 5655 N. Via Umbrosa, Tucson, AZ 85750-1357. ☎/fax **520/615-3886.** www.communiverse.com/skywatcher. 4 units. $75–$160 double. Rates include full breakfast. MC, V. Pets accepted with limitations.

Situated on the grounds of the privately owned Vega-Bray Observatory, an amateur observatory with six telescopes and a planetarium, this has to be the most unusual lodging in the state of Arizona. The inn provides guests with not only a bed for the night, but also a chance to observe both the night sky and the sun through the observatory's telescopes. Although experienced amateur astronomers can rent the facilities for $35 per night, inexperienced guests should opt for one of the astronomer-assisted programs, which range from $85 to $150 per night per group. The observatory includes a small science and astronomy museum and a whirlpool spa. A kitchen is available to guests. The inn is 4 miles outside Benson; call for directions.

later became the United States. Today the ranch is owned by Richard and Veronica Schultz, who gave up their law practices in Scottsdale to live out their dream of restoring and operating a historic ranch. As avid art collectors, the Schultzes have brought to the ranch an artistic aesthetic unknown at other guest ranches in the state. The adobe buildings are painted in vibrant shades of pink and turquoise with blue trim, and guest rooms, which also have distinctive paint jobs, are in sun-baked adobe buildings and furnished with rustic Mexican antiques. Most have fireplaces and patios. Meals are gourmet Southwestern fare, and there's a rustic little saloon in what may be the oldest building in the state. Although horseback riding is the traditional favorite activity, the ranch attracts birders due to its proximity to Buenos Aires National Wildlife Refuge. A swimming pool and whirlpool are refreshing after a long day of riding the range.

WHERE TO DINE

In addition to the restaurants mentioned below, the **Tubac Golf Resort** has a good restaurant. See "Where to Stay," above, for details.

AMADO

Amado Café. 3001 E. Frontage Rd., Amado (Exit 48 off I-19). ☎ **520/398-9211.** Main courses $6–$9 at lunch, $10–$20 at dinner. AE, DISC, MC, V. Tues–Sun 11am–2pm and 5–8pm. Closed Mon–Tues in summer and also for 2–3 weeks in July. GREEK/AMERICAN.

There aren't a lot of dining options out here, so this restaurant, in a handsome territorial-style building just off I-19, is an asset to the community. The best part of the experience is sitting out back on the rustic flagstone patio, listening to the gurgling fountain, and contemplating the view of the mountains in the distance. The menu includes sandwiches, salads, and more filling fare, such as leg of lamb and prime rib. The family who owns the restaurant is Greek, so such dishes as Greek salad, a gyro sandwich, and stuffed grape leaves are good bets. The dessert tray usually has some tempting treats, including baklava.

✪ **Cantina Romantica.** At the Rex Ranch, 6 miles north of Tubac in Amado. ☎ **520/398-2914.** Reservations recommended for dinner. Main courses $6.50–$9 at lunch, $18–$24 at dinner. AE, DC, DISC, MC, V. Sun–Mon noon–2pm and 4–6:30pm; Tues–Sat noon–2pm and 5:30–9pm. Call before coming during extreme heat in the summer; restaurant may be closed. SOUTHWESTERN/CONTEMPORARY AMERICAN.

Located in a historic adobe hacienda, Cantina Romantica is a culinary oasis in this neck of the woods. The chef arrived here by way of other famous restaurant kitchens in Tucson and brings a metropolitan flair to the menu, which includes the likes of pecan-crusted pork and grilled citrus chicken with Guaymas shrimp in a tequila–prickly pear sauce. A gargantuan grilled chicken salad and a vegetarian portabello mushroom, avocado, and Brie sandwich are both delicious sensory overloads. The setting is rustic and colorful, and the inn is reached by driving *through* the Santa Cruz River.

TUBAC

Melio's Trattoria. 12 Plaza Rd. ☎ **520/398-8494.** Reservations recommended for dinner. Main courses lunch $7–$8, dinner $7.50–$17. AE, MC, V. Wed–Sun 11am–3pm and 5–8 or 9pm. ITALIAN.

With candles flickering in wax-covered Chianti bottles, Italian music playing, and a friendly ambience, this little Tubac trattoria has the feel of a neighborhood restaurant in Little Italy. At lunch you'll find pastas and sandwiches made with Italian meats, and at dinner more pastas (spaghetti *alla carbonara,* penne with smoked salmon) and familiar Italian favorites such as veal with lemon sauce.

Shelby's Bistro. 19 Tubac Rd. ☎ **520/398-8075.** Reservations recommended for dinner. Main courses $6–$18. AE, DISC, MC, V. Tues–Wed 9am–4pm; Thurs–Mon 9am–4pm and 5–9pm. AMERICAN.

With only about a dozen tables and tucked into the back of the Mercado de Baca shopping plaza, this casual place is usually crammed with tourists at lunch when the pizza and sandwiches really pack 'em in. At dinner, in addition to the aforementioned options, more upscale cuisine, such as sesame-encrusted pork tenderloin and salmon médaillons, is offered. Friday and Saturday nights are prime rib night.

3 Nogales

175 miles S of Phoenix; 63 miles S of Tucson; 65 miles W of Sierra Vista

Situated on the Mexican border, the twin towns of Nogales, Arizona, and Nogales, Sonora, Mexico (known jointly as Ambos Nogales) form a bustling border town. All day long U.S. citizens cross into Mexico to shop for bargains on Mexican handicrafts, pharmaceuticals, and tequila, while Mexican citizens cross into the United States to buy products not available in their own country. Nogales is also the busiest produce port in the world. During the harvest season, more than 700 truckloads of produce cross into the United States from Mexico each day.

ESSENTIALS

GETTING THERE   Nogales is the last town on I-19 before the Mexican border. Arizona 82 leads northeast from town toward Sonoita and Sierra Vista.

VISITOR INFORMATION   For further information on Nogales, contact the **Nogales–Santa Cruz County Chamber of Commerce,** Kino Park, Nogales, AZ 85621 (☎ **520/287-3685;** www.nogaleschamber.com).

EXPLORING NORTH & SOUTH OF THE BORDER

Most people who visit Nogales, Arizona, are here to cross the border to Nogales, Mexico. The favorable exchange rate makes shopping in Mexico very popular with Americans, although most of the items for sale in Mexico are actually cheaper in Tucson. Many people now cross the border specifically to purchase prescription drugs, and pharmacies line the streets near the border crossing.

If you'd like to learn more about the history of this area, stop by the **Pimeria Alta Historical Society,** at the corner of Grand Avenue and Crawford Street (☎ **520/287-4621**), near the border crossing in downtown Nogales. The historical society maintains a small museum, library, and archives on this region of northern Mexico and southern Arizona, which was once known as Pimeria Alta. It's open Friday and Saturday 10am to 4pm. Admission is by donation.

Just a couple of miles outside Nogales on the road to Patagonia, you'll see signs for the **Arizona Vineyard Winery** (☎ **520/287-7972**), open daily 10am to 5pm. You may not think of Arizona as wine country, but the Spanish began growing grapes and making wine as soon as they arrived in the area several centuries ago. You can taste free samples of white burgundy, Grand Canyon White, Desert Dust, and Rattlesnake Red, among others.

As you can probably guess, Nogales, Mexico, is a typical border town filled with tiny shops selling Mexican crafts and souvenirs and dozens of restaurants serving simple Mexican food. Some of the better deals are on wool rugs, which cost a small fraction of what a Navajo rug costs, but are not nearly as well made. Pottery is another popular buy. Our personal favorites are the ceramic sinks and the handblown drinking glasses and pitchers.

All the shops and restaurants in Nogales, Mexico, are within walking distance of the border, so unless you're planning to continue farther into Mexico, it's not a good idea to take your car. There are numerous pay parking lots and garages on the U.S. side of the border where your vehicle will be secure for the day. If you should take your car into Mexico, be sure to get Mexican auto insurance before crossing the border—your U.S. auto insurance is not valid. There are plenty of insurance companies set up along the road leading to the border.

Most shops and restaurants in Nogales, Mexico, accept U.S. dollars. You may bring back $400 worth of merchandise duty free, including 1 liter of liquor (if you are 21 or older). U.S. citizens need only a driver's license to walk across the border. (For those under driving age, birth certificates are recommended, but not required.)

WHERE TO STAY

Although your best bet is to make this a day trip from Tucson, Tubac, or Patagonia, there are a few budget chain motels in Nogales, including a **Best Western,** a **Motel 6,** a **Super 8,** and a **Days Inn.** There is, however, one attractive golf resort nearby.

✪ **Rio Rico Resort & Country Club.** 1069 Camino Caralampi, Rio Rico, AZ 85648. ☎ **800/288-4746** or 520/281-1901. Fax 520/281-7132. www.rioricoresort.com. 180 units. A/C TV TEL. Jan–Mar $165–$185 double; Apr–May and Sept–Dec $135–$175 double; June–Aug $100–$150 double; $205–$1,000 suite. AE, CB, DC, DISC, MC, V.

Located a few miles north of Nogales, Rio Rico is a secluded hilltop golf resort that attracts quite a few retirees contemplating relocating to this area. If you're looking for someplace where you can feel you've gotten away from it all, this is a good bet. While the setting is far from the madding crowd, the accommodations and amenities are the equal of many of the resorts in Tucson, and the views are almost as good. All the guest rooms have excellent views over the golf course and desert (third-floor rooms have the best views). An abundance of Mexican tile work gives these rooms a little sense of place, too.

Dining/Diversions: The resort's dining room, which has those same great views, serves a mix of Southwestern and Mediterranean dishes, and the lavish Sunday brunch is extremely popular. There is also a large adjacent lounge.

Amenities: 18-hole golf course, Olympic-size pool, whirlpool, sauna, exercise room, four tennis courts, pro shop, horseback riding ($20 for 1 hour), mountain bike rentals.

WHERE TO DINE

✪ **La Roca Restaurant.** Calle Elias 91, Nogales, Mexico. ☎ **888/527-0220** toll-free in the U.S., or (52) 631/2-08-91. Main courses $8–$18. MC, V. Daily 11am–midnight. MEXICAN.

La Roca is as unexpected a restaurant as you're ever likely to find in a border town. Built into a cliff and cool as a cave, the restaurant conjures up images of colonial Mexico. White-jacketed waiters provide a level of professional service found only in the most expensive restaurants north of the border. Folk art and large paintings in the spacious rooms seem to make the interior glow, and at night the place is lit with candles ensconced on the stone walls. The Guaymas shrimp and chicken mole are our longtime favorites. The shrimp are reliably succulent, and the mole sauce is a brilliantly flavorful balance between chile and chocolate. Don't miss the margaritas—small but zesty with lime and full of tequila.

To find La Roca, walk through the border checkpoint, continue 100 yards or so, cross over the railroad tracks on your left, and look for a narrow side street along the base of the cliff you see as you cross into Mexico. The restaurant is about 100 feet down this street.

4 Patagonia & Sonoita

Patagonia: 171 miles SE of Phoenix; 60 miles SE of Tucson; 50 miles SW of Tombstone; 19 miles NW of Nogales

A mild climate, numerous good restaurants, bed-and-breakfast inns, and a handful of wineries have turned the small communities of Patagonia and Sonoita into a favorite weekend getaway area for Tucsonans. However, Sonoita Creek, one of the only perennial streams in southern Arizona, is also a major draw for the area, attracting bird watchers from all over the country. Because this creek flows year-round, it attracts an amazing variety of bird life.

ESSENTIALS
GETTING THERE   Sonoita is at the junction of Ariz. 83 and Ariz. 82. Patagonia is 12 miles southwest of Sonoita on Ariz. 82.

VISITOR INFORMATION   For further information on Patagonia and Sonoita, contact the Patagonia Community Association, **Patagonia Visitors Center,** P.O. Box 241, Patagonia, AZ 85624 (☎ **888/794-0060** or 520/394-0060; www.patagoniaaz. com). The visitor center is in the center of town at 305 McKeown Ave., in the building with Mariposa Bookstore and next to the lobby of the Stage Stop Inn. At press time, there was a good chance the visitor center would be moving next door to 307 McKeown Ave.

BIRD WATCHING, WINE TASTING & OTHER AREA ACTIVITIES
Patagonia, 18 miles north of Nogales on Ariz. 82, is a historic old mining and ranching town 4,000 feet up in the Patagonia Mountains. Surrounded by higher mountains, the little town has for years been popular with film and television crews. Among the films that have been shot here are *Oklahoma, Red River, A Star Is Born,* and *David and Bathsheba.* Television programs filmed here have included "Little House on the Prairie," "The Red Badge of Courage," and "The Young Riders." Today, however, bird watching and tranquility draw people to this remote town.

The **Patagonia–Sonoita Creek Preserve** (☎ **520/394-2400**) is a nature preserve owned by the Nature Conservancy and protects $1^1/_2$ miles of Sonoita Creek riparian (riverside) habitat, which is important to migratory birds. More than 250 species of birds have been spotted on the preserve, which makes it a very popular spot with birders from all over the world. Among the rare birds that can be seen here are 22 species of flycatchers, kingbirds, and phoebes, and the Montezuma quail. A forest of cottonwood trees, some of which are 100 feet tall, lines the creek and is one of the best remaining examples of such a forest in southern Arizona. At one time these forests grew along all the rivers here. The sanctuary is just outside Patagonia on a dirt road that parallels Ariz. 82. Hours are Wednesday to Sunday 7:30am to 4pm. A $5 donation is suggested if you're not a Nature Conservancy member. On Wednesdays at 8am and Saturdays at 9am, there are naturalist-guided walks through the preserve; reservations aren't required. If the reserve should be closed when you visit, you are welcome to bird along the road bordering the preserve from dawn to dusk.

Avid birders will also want to visit the **Empire-Cienega Resource Conservation Area** (☎ **520/722-4289**), which has grasslands, wetlands, and oak forests. This is a good place to look for the rarely seen gray hawk. Access is off the east side of Ariz. 83—about 7 miles north of Sonoita.

Patagonia Lake State Park (☎ **520/287-6965**), about 7 miles south of Patagonia off Ariz. 82, is a popular boating and fishing lake formed by damming Sonoita Creek. The lake is $2^1/_2$ miles long and stocked in the winter with trout. Bass, crappie, bluegill, and catfish can also be found in the lake. Park facilities include a picnic ground, a campground, and a swimming beach.

Sonoita proper is little more than a crossroads with a few shops and restaurants. Surrounding the community are miles of rolling grasslands that are primarily cattle ranches. However, recent years have seen the planting of several wine vineyards in the area, and the Sonoita area is slowly becoming Arizona's wine country. The **R. W. Webb Winery** (and Dark Mountain Brewery) (☎ 520/762-5777), the most accessible of the area's wineries, does a fairly nice sherry. Its attractive little tasting room is 27 miles north of Sonoita at Exit 279 off I-10. In the ghost town of Elgin, you'll find the **Village of Elgin Winery** (☎ 520/455-9309), and 3 miles south of Elgin, **Sonoita Vineyards** (☎ 520/455-5893) on Canelo Road. **Callaghan Vineyards** (☎ 520/455-5322) is open for tastings with more limited hours than other tasting rooms. They're usually open Sundays 11am to 4pm from November to May. This vineyard is 5 miles south of Elgin; call for directions.

Despite the proliferation of vineyards in the area, this is still ranch country. If you'd like to ride the open range, there are a couple of area horseback riding stables that will get you back in the saddle again. In Patagonia, contact **Arizona Trail Tours** (☎ 800/477-0615; www.aztrailtours.com), which offers everything from 2¹/₂-hour rides ($40) to 4-day pack trips ($750). These rides head up into the Patagonia Mountains and the San Rafael Valley. In Sonoita, contact **Sonoita Stables** (☎ 520/455-9266), which offers 1-hour to half-day rides into the Empire-Cienega Resource Conservation Area on Peruvian Paso horses. Rates range from $30 for 1 hour to $120 for a half day. Expect to see antelope on your ride.

WHERE TO STAY
In Patagonia

○ Circle Z Ranch. Patagonia, AZ 85624. ☎ **888/854-2525** or 520/394-2525. Fax 520/394-2058. www.circlez.com. 24 units. Weekly rates: $1,500–$1,980 double (slightly higher rates for shorter stays). Rates include all meals and horseback riding. 3-night minimum. Lower rates for ages 17 and under. No credit cards. Closed May 15–Oct 30.

Located on Ariz. 82 between Nogales and Patagonia, this guest ranch has been in business since 1925 and is the oldest working cattle ranch in Arizona. Over the years it has served as a backdrop for numerous movies and TV shows, including "Gunsmoke" and John Wayne's *Red River*. The 6,000-acre ranch on the banks of Sonoita Creek is bordered by the Nature Conservancy's Patagonia–Sonoita Creek Sanctuary, Patagonia State Park, and the Coronado National Forest. Miles of trails ensure everyone gets in plenty of riding in a variety of terrains, from desert hills to grasslands to the riparian forest along the creek. The adobe cabins provide that authentic ranch feel that is appreciated by guests hoping to find a genuine bit of the Old West. There's a wide variety of accommodation styles, including large cottages for families. The ranch has a pool and tennis court, and there's a special kids' cantina complete with video games, jukebox, and a pool table.

Duquesne House B&B. 357 Duquesne Ave., P.O. Box 772, Patagonia, AZ 85624. ☎ **520/394-2732** or 520/394-0054. 4 units. $75 double. Rate includes full breakfast. No credit cards.

This old adobe building with a long shady porch across the front was built at the turn of the century as a miner's boarding house and has been renovated and converted into a B&B. Each guest room has its own entrance off the front porch and both a sitting room and a bedroom. Our personal favorite room has an ornate woodstove and clawfoot bathtub. At the back of the house is a screened porch that overlooks the garden and a fishpond. The owner of the B&B also owns a local art gallery, and artists will feel right at home here.

Stage Stop Inn. 303 W. McKeown St., P.O. Box 777, Patagonia, AZ 85624. ☎ **800/923-2211** inside Arizona, or 520/394-2211. Fax 520/394-2212. 43 units. A/C TV TEL. $69 double. AE, DISC, MC, V.

Although nothing fancy, this small hotel in the center of town is large enough that it usually has a few rooms available. Furnishings are motel basic, but there's a small pool in the courtyard if you happen to be here in the heat of summer. A bit of Western styling adds a touch of character to the lobby, where you'll usually find information on local attractions and activities.

IN SONOITA

Sonoita Inn. P.O. Box 99, Sonoita, AZ 85637. ☎ **520/455-5935.** Fax 520/455-5069. www.sonoitainn.com. 18 units. A/C TV TEL. $99–$125 double. Rates include continental breakfast. AE, DC, DISC, MC, V. Pets accepted ($25).

Housed in a barnlike building at the intersection of Ariz. 82 and Ariz. 83, the Sonoita Inn plays up the area's ranching history. The building was originally built by the owner of the famed Triple Crown–winning thoroughbred Secretariat, but in 1999 was converted into an inn. The large lobby, with its wooden floors, huge fireplace, and ranch brands for decoration, is cool and dark and is where breakfasts and afternoon snacks are served. Guest rooms feature rustic beds, Indian rugs, and big windows, with 1950s-inspired bedspreads for a retro cowboy touch. Although the inn is right on Sonoita's main road, the fascinating interior decor more than makes up for the less-than-quiet location. There is a popular steak house adjacent to the inn.

The Vineyard Bed & Breakfast. 92 S. Los Encinos Rd., P.O. Box 1227, Sonoita, AZ 85637. ☎ **520/455-4749.** 4 units. $95 double; $105 casita. Rates include full breakfast. No credit cards.

Set atop a hill just south of Sonoita, the heart of southeast Arizona's wine country, this B&B is in a pink adobe ranch house built in 1916. There are expansive views from the property and about half an acre of vineyards beside the inn. The sweeping views of plains and mountains are the biggest selling point of this inn, so if you're looking for high, wide, and handsome, this is it. The house itself has an unpretentious farm/ranch feel. The casita is well worth the little extra it costs and has its own patio and saltillo tile floors. Inn pets include a talking parrot, peacocks, a burro, and very friendly black labs. You'll also find a whirlpool and a koi pond with waterfalls in the backyard.

WHERE TO DINE
IN PATAGONIA

✪ **Cose Buone.** 436 Naugle Ave. ☎ **520/394-2366.** Reservations highly recommended. $20 for 3-course meal. MC, V. Fri–Tues 5:30 until closing. Best to call for hours. Reduced hours June–July and Sept–Oct, closed Aug. ITALIAN.

It's not often you have a fine dining experience in a building that also houses a Laundromat, but here it is. Intimate seating (there are only 20 chairs), and a relaxed atmosphere (the owner is willing to stop and chat) combine for an experience that seems worlds away from the urban glitz to the north. The menu changes weekly, but the first

---

Please *Do* Feed the Tourists

If you think dining at good restaurants is an integral part of any vacation, you shouldn't head down this way on a Monday or Tuesday. Most of the best restaurants in southeastern Arizona are closed on those days of the week. To be absolutely certain of getting good food during your visit, plan to come between Thursday and Sunday (and make a reservation, if possible), but you should be on your way somewhere else by Sunday afternoon because most of the good restaurants aren't open Sunday night either.

course might be a full-flavored antipasto of assorted untraditional vegetables, including a dollop of creamy mashed potatoes, or a rustic mushroom soup. For *secondi,* expect risotto or pasta, and for a third course, smoked mozzarella and prosciutto stuffed pork tenderloin with a marsala sauce. A finale of light and airy tiramisu is liberally dusted with cocoa powder. Add an extensive and reasonably priced list of wines, with an emphasis on Italian vintages, and you'll think you've died and gone to Tuscany.

Marie's European Cuisine. 340 Naugle Ave. ☎ **520/394-2812.** Reservations recommended. Main courses $11–$14. DISC, MC, V. Wed–Sat 5–9pm; Sun 1–7pm. EUROPEAN.

Located in the center of Patagonia, this little restaurant sits behind a low wall in a colorful cottage with a few tiled tables and folk art in a "secret garden" setting. The menu offers simple yet very flavorful rustic European food and ranges the continent from the Adriatic to the Baltic. Marie is the chef here and whips up the likes of leek tart, broccoli soufflé, chicken with olives and dried fruit in white-wine sauce, roast lamb so tender it cuts with a fork, and even roast suckling pig. Don't miss the chicken pâté or the house-blended Château Marie wine. Portions are large, but if you want vegetables, order a salad. This is a small two-person operation, so be prepared to relax.

Velvet Elvis Pizza Company. 292 Naugle Ave. ☎ **520/394-2102.** Pizzas $13–$23. MC, V. Jan–June Thurs 5–8pm, Fri–Sun noon–8pm; July–Dec Fri–Sun noon–8pm. Closed Thurs other months. ITALIAN.

Marie's and Cose Buone are just the sort of restaurants you might expect to find in wine country, but Velvet Elvis strikes a very different chord. Faux-finished walls ooze artiness, and paeans to pop culture include shrines to both the Virgin Mary and Elvis. There's even a genuine velvet Elvis painting on display. This casual hangout features pizzas heaped with veggies, cheeses, and meats. Add a salad for even more vegetables (your mom would be proud) and accompany it with a fresh juice, microbrew, or espresso.

IN SONOITA

Café Sonoita. 3280 Ariz. 82. ☎ **520/455-5278.** Reservations recommended for dinner for 5 or more. Main courses $6–$15. MC, V. Wed 5–8pm; Thurs–Sat 11am–2:30pm and 5–8pm; Sun 10am–2:30pm. INTERNATIONAL.

A tiny place with just a handful of tables, this cafe is a great favorite with locals. In spite of the casual atmosphere, the kitchen here actually turns out some very tasty and creative dishes, and the prices are great. For dinner, try roast duckling with dark cherry port sauce, sauteed jumbo shrimp with artichoke hearts and bacon, or a bowl of green chile corn chowder. Lunchtime sandwiches are huge and delicious. You'll find Café Sonoita in an old building at the east end of Sonoita.

Karen's Wine Country Café. 3266 Ariz. 82. ☎ **520/455-5282.** Reservations recommended. Main courses $7–$10 at lunch, $18–$20 at dinner; chef's 4-course wine dinner $39.95. MC, V. Daily 11am–4pm; Thurs–Sat 5–8pm. SOUTHWESTERN.

With crisp blue-and-white tablecloths and expansive windows, this bright room looks out on panoramic rangeland that, framed by the windows, seems almost surreal. The view is of the Empire Cienega Ranch, a grassland ringed by mountain ranges—you might see antelope grazing here. And inside, instead of dusty, beer-drinking cowboys, there are well-dressed urbanites sipping wine and grazing on pistachio-wheat bread. You can order dishes such as pork tenderloin with raspberry-chipotle glaze or New York steak with blue cheese. Salads of organic greens are good and liberally dosed in vinaigrette dressing (which is a specialty here, along with local jams and jellies; all available for purchase).

5 Sierra Vista & the San Pedro Valley

189 miles SE of Phoenix; 70 miles SE of Tucson; 33 miles SW of Tombstone; 33 miles W of Bisbee

Located at an elevation of 4,620 feet above sea level, Sierra Vista is blessed with the perfect climate—never too hot, never too cold. This fact more than anything else has contributed in recent years to Sierra Vista becoming one of the fastest-growing cities in Arizona. Although Sierra Vista itself is a modern, sprawling community outside the gates of the U.S. Army's Fort Huachuca, it is wedged between the Huachuca Mountains and the San Pedro River valley. Consequently, Sierra Vista, with its many inexpensive motels, can be used as a base for exploring the region's natural attractions.

Within a few miles' drive of town are the San Pedro Riparian National Conservation Area, Coronado National Memorial, and the Nature Conservancy's Ramsey Canyon Preserve. No other area of the United States attracts more attention from birders, who come in hopes of spotting some of the 300 bird species that have been sighted here in southeastern Arizona. Also not far north of town is Kartchner Caverns State Park, the region's biggest attraction, located near Benson.

ESSENTIALS
GETTING THERE   Sierra Vista is at the junction of Ariz. 90 and Ariz. 92 about 35 miles south of I-10.

America West (☎ **800/235-9292**) has regular flights from Phoenix to the Fort Huachuca Airport (also called the Sierra Vista Airport), 2100 Airport Dr.

VISITOR INFORMATION   For further information on Sierra Vista, contact the **Sierra Vista Convention and Visitors Bureau,** 21 E. Wilcox Dr., Sierra Vista, AZ 85635 (☎ **800/288-3861** or 520/458-6940; www.visitsierravista.com). Follow the signs for Visitor Information/Chamber of Commerce. Turn onto Carmichael Avenue from Fry Boulevard; the office is 2 blocks off Fry Boulevard on the left.

SPECIAL EVENTS   Cowboy poets, singers, and musicians come together to tell their stories at the **Cochise Cowboy Poetry & Music Gathering** in February (☎ **520/459-3868** or 800/288-3861; www.cowboypoets.com).

ATTRACTIONS AROUND BENSON
While Kartchner Caverns are the big attraction in the Benson area, there are a few other attractions in the area you might want to check out as well. North of town a few miles is the **Singing Wind Bookshop** (☎ **520/586-2425**), a remarkable bookstore on a ranch down a dirt road. The bookstore is the brainchild of Winifred Bundy, who, with her late husband, began the business more than 25 years ago with only a couple of shelves of books. Now the inventory is well into the thousands, with an emphasis on the Southwest. To reach the bookstore, take Exit 304 from I-10 in Benson. Drive north 2¼ miles and take a right (east) at the sign that says SINGING WIND ROAD. Drive to the end, opening and closing the green gate.

Also north of town is **Gammon's Gulch Movie Set and Tour Town** (☎ **520/ 212-2831;** www.gammonsgulch.com), a reconstruction of an old western town. Many authentic buildings were used in the town's construction, and there is a private collection of John Wayne memorabilia. Kids will love this place. Gammons Gulch is open Wednesday to Sunday 9am to 5pm, with guided tours four times a day. Admission is $5. To reach Gammons Gulch, take exit 306 off I-10 and go north to Cascabel Road. Continue to milepost 7, and then turn left on East Rockspring Road.

۞ Kartchner Caverns State Park. Off Ariz. 90, 10 miles south of Benson. ☎ **520/586-4100** (information), 520/586-CAVE (tour reservations), or 602/542-4174 (Arizona State Parks). www.pr.state.az.us. Admission $10 per car to enter the park and visit aboveground exhibits; cave tours $14 adults, $6 children 7–13, free for children under 7. Call ahead for reservations. Park hours daily 7:30am–6pm; cave tours approximately every 15 minutes 8:30am–4:30pm.

These caverns, which opened to the public in 1999, were discovered in 1974 and kept secret for 14 years. The reason for the secrecy was to protect what are among the largest and most beautiful caverns in the country. These are wet caverns, which means that all the cave formations, including stalactites, stalagmites, soda straws, cave popcorn, and "cave bacon" are still growing. To ensure that the cave formations continue to grow as they have for thousands of years, extensive measures, including the construction of air-lock doors, were taken before the caverns were opened to the public. The great effort expended to protect these caverns is in large part the cause of the high admission prices.

Seven acres of the caverns are currently open to the public, and within this area are two huge rooms, each larger than a football field with ceilings more than 100 feet high. In the first room, the Rotunda Room, are thousands of delicate soda straws. In fact, Kartchner Caverns contain the longest soda straw formation in the U.S. (21 feet, 2 inches). However, the highlight of the cave tour is the Throne Room, at the center of which is a 58-foot-tall column known as Kubla Khan. Within the park are several miles of hiking trails through the hills that hide the caverns, and there is a campground charging $15 per night per site.

Because the caverns are a popular attraction and tours are limited, you should try to make a reservation as much as 3 months before you plan to visit, especially if you want to visit on a weekend. However, it is sometimes possible to get tickets on the same day you want to tour the caverns, so if you happen to be passing by, you could see if any spaces are available.

ATTRACTIONS AROUND SIERRA VISTA

Arizona Folklore Preserve. 44 Ramsey Canyon Rd. (Ariz. 92 south of Sierra Vista). ☎ **520/378-6165.** www.arizonafolklore.com. Admission by donation. Showtimes Sat–Sun 2pm. Reservations required.

Set beneath the shady cottonwoods and sycamores of Ramsey Canyon, the Arizona Folklore Preserve is an ongoing project, the brainchild of Dolan Ellis, Arizona's official state balladeer, and his wife, Rose. Ellis, who started out with the folk group The New Christy Minstrels, was first appointed state balladeer back in 1966 and has been writing songs about Arizona for more than 30 years. As the name implies, the objective of the center is to preserve the folklore of Arizona, and to that end, Ellis takes to the stage most weekends to sing his songs of life in Arizona. He often welcomes guests to the stage (currently in an old house on the property). In the past there have been cowboy poets, folk artists, a fiddle maker, saddle makers, and musicians. If all goes according to plan, there will eventually be a small but impressive theater tucked amid the trees here.

Fort Huachuca Museum. Inside the Fort Huachuca U.S. Army base, Grierson Rd., Sierra Vista. ☎ **520/533-5736.** Free admission ($2 donation suggested). Mon–Fri 9am–4pm; Sat–Sun 1–4pm.

Fort Huachuca, an army base at the mouth of Huachuca Canyon northeast of Sierra Vista, was established in 1877 and, although it has been closed a couple of times, is active today. The buildings of the old post have been declared a National Historic

Landmark, and one is now a museum dedicated to the many forts that dotted the Southwest in the latter part of the 19th century. Interesting aspects of the exhibits include the quotes by soldiers that give an idea of what it was like to serve in the Southwest in the latter half of the 19th century. Near the museum stands a row of Victorian officers' quarters. Also nearby is the **U.S. Army Military Intelligence Museum** (☎ 520/533-1127), which is located at the corner of Hungerford and Cristi streets. On display are early code machines, surveillance drones, and other pieces of equipment formerly used by the Army for intelligence gathering. The museum is open Monday, Wednesday, and Friday from 10am to 2pm, and admission is free.

BIRDING HOT SPOTS & OTHER NATURAL AREAS

Birding has become big business in this area over the past few years, with birders' B&Bs, bird refuges, and even birding festivals. The **Southwest Wings Birding Festival** (☎ 800/288-3861 or 520/459-EVNT) is held in Sierra Vista each year in August.

If you'd like to join a guided bird walk along the San Pedro River or up Carr Canyon in the Huachuca Mountains, an owl-watching night hike, or a hummingbird banding session, contact the **Southeastern Arizona Bird Observatory,** P.O. Box 5521, Bisbee, AZ 85603-5521 (☎ 520/432-1388; www.sabo.org). Most of these activities take place between March and May and cost between $8 and $55 (hummingbird banding sessions are by donation). Workshops and tours are also offered.

Serious birders who want to be sure of adding lots of rare birds to their life lists might want to visit this area on a guided tour. These tours are available through **High Lonesome Ecotours** (☎ 800/743-2668; www.hilonesome.com), which charges about $850 to $1,050 per person for a 4-day birding trip.

In addition to the birding hot spots listed below, there are a few other spots in the area that serious birders should not miss. **Garden Canyon,** on Fort Huachuca, has 8 miles of trails, and 350 species of birds have been sighted. There are also Indian pictographs along one of the trails through the canyon. This is a good place to look for elegant trogons and Mexican spotted owls. Get directions to Garden Canyon at the fort's front gate, and be prepared to show your license, vehicle registration, and proof of vehicle insurance. The canyon is open to the public daily during daylight hours but is sometimes closed due to military maneuvers, so you must check with the **Range Control Office** (☎ 520/533-7100 or 520/533-7093) before heading out here.

South of Ramsey Canyon off Ariz. 92, you'll find **Carr Canyon,** which has a road that climbs up through the canyon to some of the higher elevations in the Huachuca Mountains. This is a good place to look for buff-breasted flycatchers, red crossbills, and red-faced warblers. The road is one lane, narrow and windy (usually passable by passenger car), and not for the acrophobic. It climbs 5 miles up into the mountains and goes to Reef Townsite, an old mining camp.

The **Sierra Vista Wastewater Wetlands,** 3.1 miles east of Ariz. 92 on Ariz. 90, is a good place to see yellow-headed blackbirds, ducks, peregrines, and harriers from fall through spring. The area is open Monday to Friday 7am to 3pm, Saturday and Sunday 7am to 1pm.

Coronado National Memorial. Montezuma Canyon Rd. ☎ **520/366-5515.** Free admission. Daily 8am–5pm.

About 20 miles south of Sierra Vista is a 5,000-acre memorial dedicated to Francisco Vásquez de Coronado, the first European to explore this region. Coronado, leading more than 700 people, left Compostela, Mexico, on February 23, 1540, in search of the fabled Seven Cities of Cíbola. These cities were said to be rich in gold and jewels, and Coronado had dreams of becoming wealthy from his expedition. Coronado led his band of weary men and women up the valley of the San Pedro River sometime between 1540 and 1542. The forested Montezuma Pass, in the center of the memorial, is situated at 6,575 feet and provides far-reaching views of Sonora, Mexico, to the south, the San Pedro River to the east, and several mountain ranges and valleys to the west. A visitor center tells the story of Coronado's fruitless quest for riches and features a wildlife observation area where you might see some of the memorial's 140 or more species of birds.

✪ **Ramsey Canyon Preserve.** 27 Ramsey Canyon Rd. (off Ariz. 92 south of Sierra Vista). ☎ **520/378-2785.** www.tnc.org/arizona. $5 suggested donation (free for Nature Conservancy members). Mar–Oct daily 8am–5pm; Nov–Feb daily 9am–5pm. Closed Thanksgiving, Christmas, and New Year's Day.

Located 5 miles south of Sierra Vista off Ariz. 92, this wildlife preserve is owned by the Nature Conservancy and is internationally known as home to 14 species of hummingbirds—more than anywhere else in the United States. In late spring, a buzzing fills the air in Ramsey Canyon, but it's not mosquitoes; it's the buzzing of curious hummingbirds. Wear bright red clothing when you visit this preserve, and you're certain to attract the curious little avian dive bombers, which will mistake you for the world's largest flower.

Situated in a wooded gorge in the Huachuca Mountains, the preserve covers only 380 acres. However, because Ramsey Creek, which flows through the canyon, is a year-round stream, it attracts a wide variety of wildlife, including bears, bobcats, and nearly 200 species of birds. A short nature trail leads through the canyon, with an explanatory guidebook that points out the reasons for and difficulties in preserving Ramsey Canyon; a second trail leads higher up the canyon. There are guided walks as well. April and May are the busiest times of year here, and August and May are the best times to see hummingbirds.

The preserve also operates the adjacent bed-and-breakfast inn (see "Where to Stay," below, for details).

✪ **San Pedro Riparian National Conservation Area.** Ariz. 90. ☎ **520/458-3559.** Free admission. Parking areas open sunrise to sunset.

Located 8 miles east of Sierra Vista, the San Pedro Riparian National Conservation Area is a rare example of a natural riverside habitat. Over the past 100 years the Southwestern landscape has been considerably altered by the human hand. Most deleterious of these changes has been the loss of 90% of the region's free-flowing year-round rivers and streams that once provided water and protection to myriad plants, animals, and even humans. Fossil findings from this area indicate that people were living along this river 11,000 years ago. At that time this area was not a desert, but a swamp, and the San Pedro River is all that remains of this ancient wetland. (Today there isn't much water on the surface, because most of the river water has flowed underground since an earthquake a century ago.) The conservation area is particularly popular with birders, who have a chance of spotting more than 300 species of birds here. Also living in this region are 80 species of mammals, 14 species of fish, and 40 species of amphibians and reptiles.

There are three main parking areas for the conservation area at the bridges over the San Pedro River on Ariz. 92, Ariz. 90, and Ariz. 82. This last parking area is in the ghost town of Fairbank. At the Ariz. 90 parking area, the San Pedro House, a 1930s ranch, operates as a visitor center and bookstore. It's open daily 9am to 4:30pm.

OTHER OUTDOOR ACTIVITIES

The near-perfect climate of Sierra Vista has made it a popular retirement community in recent years, and has also made Sierra Vista a great place to play golf. You can play a round at the **Pueblo del Sol Country Club,** St. Andrew's Drive (☎ **520/ 378-6444),** which is off Ariz. 92 on the east side of town and has a great view of the Huachuca Mountains. Greens fees run from $18 to $38, and a cart is extra.

Horseback riding at Fort Huachuca's Buffalo Corral is a good deal, with rates of $18 per person for a 2-hour trail ride and special family rates. Call ☎ **520/533-5220** for hours of operation and additional details.

Hikers will find numerous trails in the Huachuca Mountains, which rise up to the west of Sierra Vista. There are trails at Garden Canyon near Fort Huachuca, at Ramsey Canyon Preserve, at Carr Canyon in Coronado National Forest, and at Coronado National Memorial. See "Birding Hot Spots & Other Natural Areas," above, for details on all these natural areas. For information on hiking in the Coronado National Forest, contact the **Sierra Vista Ranger District** (☎ **520/378-0311)** at 5990 S. Hwy. 92, 8 miles south of Sierra Vista in Hereford.

WHERE TO STAY
IN BENSON

If you're looking for someplace to stay close to Kartchner Caverns, try the **Holiday Inn Express,** 630 South Village Loop, Benson, AZ 85602 (☎ **888/263-CAVE** or 520/586-8800), which charges $89 for a double.

IN SIERRA VISTA

In addition to the moderately priced Sierra Vista hotel listed below, you'll find numerous budget chain motels in Sierra Vista, including a **Motel** and a **Super 8 Motel.** In addition to the moderately priced Sierra Vista hotel listed below, you'll find numerous budget chain motels in Sierra Vista, including a Motel 6 and a Super 8 Motel.

Windemere Hotel & Conference Center. 2047 S. Hwy. 92, Sierra Vista, AZ 85635. ☎ **800/825-4656** or 520/459-5900. Fax 520/458-1347. 149 units. A/C TV TEL. $73 double; $150–$195 suite. Rates include full breakfast. AE, CB, DC, DISC, MC, V. Pets accepted ($50 deposit).

This three-story conference hotel on the south side of town is one of Sierra Vista's best lodgings and one of the closest to Ramsey Canyon. However, although it makes a good choice for avid bird-watchers, it is much more popular with conventions. Guest rooms feature contemporary furnishings, coffeemakers, refrigerators, large closets, and plenty of counter space in the bathrooms. There's a casual restaurant, a lounge, an outdoor pool, and a whirlpool. The hotel also offers room service, complimentary evening cocktail hour, and access to a nearby health club.

IN HEREFORD

Casa de San Pedro. 8933 S. Yell Lane, Hereford, AZ 85615. ☎ **800/588-6468** or 520/366-1300. Fax 520/366-0701. www.naturesinn.com. 10 units. A/C. $119 double (2-night minimum); June–July $100 double. Rates include full breakfast. DISC, MC, V.

Built with bird-watching tour groups in mind, this modern inn is set on the west side of the San Pedro River on 10 acres of land that border the river. While the setting doesn't have as much historical character as that of the San Pedro River Inn (see below), the rooms are large, modern, hotel-style accommodations. Built in the territorial style around a courtyard garden, the inn has a large common room where birders gather to swap tales of the day's sightings. This is by far the most upscale inn in the region.

✪ **Ramsey Canyon Inn Bed & Breakfast.** 29 Ramsey Canyon Rd., Hereford, AZ 85615. ☎ **520/378-3010.** Fax 520/803-0819. www.tnc.org/ramseycanyon/ramseycanyoninn. E-mail: lodging@theriver.com. 6 units; 2 apts. $110–$132 double (including full breakfast); $132–$142 apt. (breakfast not included). MC, V.

Located just outside the gates of the Nature Conservancy's Ramsey Canyon Preserve and operated by the conservancy, this inn is the most convenient lodging choice for avid birders. The inn's property straddles Ramsey Creek. Guest rooms are in the main house, while apartments are in small cabins reached by a footbridge over the creek. Hummingbird feeders set up on the inn's front porch attract 14 species of hummers. A large country breakfast is served in the morning, and in the afternoon you're likely to find a fresh pie made with fruit from the inn's orchard. Breakfast is not included in the apartment rates because they have their own kitchens. Very popular, book early.

San Pedro River Inn. 8326 S. Hereford Rd., Hereford, AZ 85615. ☎ and fax **520/366-5532.** www.sanpedroriverinn.com. 4 units. $105 double. Rates include continental breakfast. $5 fee for dogs and horses. No credit cards.

With the character of a small guest ranch, this family-friendly inn is a casual place that will please avid birders who prefer old Arizona character over spotless modern accommodations. Located on the east side of the San Pedro Riparian National Conservation Area, the four cottages here are set beneath huge old cottonwood trees. Surrounding the grounds are acres of grasslands and expansive vistas. All the cottages, which are rather eclectically furnished, have kitchens so you can do your own cooking.

CAMPGROUNDS

You'll find two Coronado National Forest campgrounds—Reef Townsite and Ramsey Vista—up the winding Carr Canyon Road south of Sierra Vista off Ariz. 92. At Fort Huachuca there are a few campsites and a couple of rustic cabins available in Garden Canyon. To reserve a site or a cabin, contact the **Sportsmen Center** (☎ **520/533-7085**) on base.

WHERE TO DINE

Because Sierra Vista is home to a military base and many of the servicemen have Asian wives, the town supports quite a number of good Asian restaurants, with an emphasis on Chinese, Japanese, and Korean cuisine. Otherwise, it's only 30 minutes or so to Bisbee or Sonoita, where in each place there are a couple of dining choices.

The Outside Inn. 4907 S. Ariz. 92. ☎ **520/378-4645.** Reservations recommended. Main courses $6–$7 at lunch, $11–$21 at dinner. AE, MC, V. Mon–Fri 11am–1:30pm and 5–9pm; Sat 5–9pm. STEAKS/SEAFOOD/ITALIAN.

It's difficult to find a decent meal in Sierra Vista, so the Outside Inn comes as a pleasant surprise. Long the special-occasion restaurant in town, it's south of town just north of the turnoff for Ramsey Canyon. You'll find the Outside Inn in a cottage-like building, surrounded by nondescript suburban shopping plazas. In the main dining room or out on the patio, you can dine on such fare as salmon with spinach fettuccine, blackened swordfish, or mahi-mahi with a macadamia nut crust. The lunch menu offers a variety of homemade soups, salads, and sandwiches, and desserts are American favorites, such as mud pie and cheesecake as well as lighter choices such as fruit tortes and mousses.

6 Tombstone

181 miles SE of Phoenix; 70 miles SE of Tucson; 24 miles N of Bisbee

Tombstone, "the town too tough to die," is one of Arizona's most popular tourist attractions, but we'll leave it up to you to decide whether it deserves its reputation (either as a tough town or as a tourist attraction). All it took was a brief blaze of gunfire more than a century ago to seal the fate of this former silver-mining boomtown. It was on this town's very streets, at a livery stable known as the O.K. Corral, that Wyatt Earp, his brothers Virgil and Morgan, and their friend Doc Holliday took on the outlaws Ike Clanton and Frank and Tom McLaury on October 26, 1881.

Tombstone was named by Ed Schieffelin, a silver prospector who ventured into this region at a time when the resident Apaches were fighting to preserve their homeland. Schieffelin was warned that all he would find here was his own tombstone, so when he discovered a mountain of silver, he named it Tombstone. Within a few years Tombstone was larger than San Francisco, and between 1880 and 1887, an estimated $37 million worth of silver was mined here. Such wealth created a sturdy little town, and as the Cochise County seat of the time, Tombstone boasted a number of imposing buildings, including the county courthouse, which is now an Arizona state park. In 1887, an underground river flooded the silver mines, and despite attempts to pump the water out, the mines were never reopened. With the demise of the mines, the boom times came to an end and the population rapidly dwindled.

Today Tombstone's historic district consists of both original buildings that went up after the town's second fire and newer structures built in keeping with the architectural styles of the time. Most of them house souvenir shops and restaurants, which should give you some indication that this place is a classic tourist trap, but kids (and adults raised on Louis L'Amour and John Wayne) love it, especially when the famous shootout is reenacted.

ESSENTIALS

GETTING THERE   From Tucson, take I-10 east to Benson, from which Ariz. 80 heads south to Tombstone. From Sierra Vista, take Ariz. 90 north to Ariz. 82 heading east.

VISITOR INFORMATION   Contact the **Tombstone Chamber of Commerce,** Allen Street, P.O. Box 280, Tombstone, AZ 85638 (☎ **888/457-3929** or 520/457-3929; www.tombstone.org). The Chamber also operates a **visitor information center** on the corner of Allen Street and Fourth Street.

SPECIAL EVENTS   Tombstone's biggest annual celebrations are **Territorial Days,** held the third weekend of March; **Wyatt Earp Days,** held in late May; and **Helldorado Days,** held on the third weekend in October. The latter celebrates the famous gunfight at the O.K. Corral and includes countless shoot-outs in the streets, mock hangings, a parade, and contests.

GUNSLINGERS & SALOONS: IN SEARCH OF THE WILD WEST

As portrayed in novels, movies, and TV shows over the years, the shoot-out has come to epitomize the Wild West, and nowhere is this great American phenomenon more glorified than here in Tombstone, where the star attraction is the famous ✪ **O.K. Corral.** Located on Allen Street near the corner of Third Street, the O.K. Corral, site of a brief gun battle, has taken on mythic proportions over the years despite the brevity of the shoot-out that took place here. Today fans of Western lore flock to this site as if on a pilgrimage. Inside the corral, you'll find life-size figures set up in the spots where all the famous gunslingers are thought to have been standing when the fight took place. Next door you'll find **Tombstone's Historama,** a sort of multimedia affair that rehashes the well-known history of Tombstone's "bad old days." Admission is $2.50 at both places.

However, you need not settle for static figures and dioramas. All over Arizona there are regular reenactments of gunfights, with the sheriff in his white hat always triumphing over the bad guys in black hats, and nowhere else in the state are there so many modern-day gunslingers entertaining so many people with their blazing six-guns as in Tombstone. Shoot-outs occur fairly regularly around town between noon and 4pm. Expect to pay about $3 for any of these shows.

When the smoke cleared in 1881, three men lay dead. They were later carted off to the **Boot Hill Graveyard** on the edge of town. The cemetery is open to the public and is entered through a gift shop on Ariz. 80 just north of town. The graves of Clanton and the McLaury brothers, as well as those of others who died in gunfights or by hanging, are well marked. Entertaining epitaphs grace the gravestones here; among the most famous is that of Lester Moore—"Here lies Lester Moore, 4 slugs from a 44, No Les, no more."

When the residents of Tombstone weren't shooting each other in the streets, they were likely to be found in the saloons and bawdy houses that lined Allen Street. The most famous of them is the **Bird Cage Theatre,** so named for the cagelike cribs (actually what most people would think of as box seats) that are actually suspended from the ceiling. These velvet-draped cages were used by prostitutes to ply their trade. Also here in the Bird Cage, you can see the poker table where the longest running poker game in the west was played. For old Tombstone atmosphere, this place is hard to beat.

If you're looking for someplace to down a cold beer, Tombstone has a couple of very lively saloons that are popular with visitors. The **Crystal Palace** (☎ 520/457-3611), at the corner of Allen and Fifth streets, was built in 1879 and has been completely restored. This is one of the favorite hangouts for the town's costumed actors and other would-be cowboys and cowgirls. **Big Nose Kate's,** on Allen Street between Fourth and Fifth streets (☎ 520/457-3107) is an equally entertaining spot full of Wild West character and characters.

Tombstone has long been a tourist town, and its streets are lined with souvenir shops selling wind chimes, Beanie Babies, and other less-than-wild western souvenirs. However, there are also several small museums scattered around town. At the **Rose Tree Inn Museum,** at Fourth and Toughnut streets, you can see what may be the world's largest rose bush (a "Lady Banksia" rose, actually more of a tree). The shrub is indeed impressive as it sprawls across an arbor and covers 8,000 square feet. Inside the museum, you'll see antique furnishings from Tombstone's heyday in the 1880s.

The most imposing building in town is the **Tombstone Courthouse State Park,** at the corner of Third and Toughnut streets. Built in 1882, the courthouse is now a state historical park and museum, containing artifacts, photographs, and newspaper clippings chronicling Tombstone's lively past. In the courtyard, the gallows that once ended the lives of outlaws and bandits still stands.

Factoid

If you're interested in learning more about Arizona's most notorious town, consider reading *Tombstone's Early Years* (Bison Books, 1995), by John Myers.

At the **Tombstone Epitaph Museum,** on Fifth Street between Allen and Fremont streets, you can inspect the office of the town's old newspaper. To see what life was like for the common folk in the old days, pay a visit to the **Pioneer Home Museum,** on Fremont Street (Ariz. 80) between Eighth and Ninth streets.

Of the dozens of shops in town, one that stands out is **G. F. Spangenberg,** 17 S. Fourth St. (☎ 520/457-9229), a gun shop dealing in antique and modern six-shooters, as well as other guns, holsters, and the sundry necessities of the cowboy life. This is the town's most authentic shop and has been in business since 1880. One other shop well worth a visit is the **Tombstone Smithy,** 302 E. Fremont St. (☎ **520/457-2326**), where a wide variety of Western-theme metalwork is crafted. Here you'll find such imagery as petroglyphs and gun-totin' cowboys.

At several places along Allen Street, you can hop aboard a reproduction **stage-coach or covered wagon,** and for a few dollars get a narrated tour of town. With their rubber tires, these wagons and stagecoaches are much more comfortable than the originals.

WHERE TO STAY

Best Western Lookout Lodge. Ariz. 80 W. (P.O. Box 787), Tombstone, AZ 85638. ☎ **877/652-6772** or 520/457-2223. Fax 520/457-3870. www.tombstone1880.com/bwlookoutlodge. 40 units. A/C TV TEL. $65–$80 double. Rates include continental breakfast. AE, CB, DC, DISC, MC, V. Pets accepted ($5 a night plus deposit).

The biggest and most comfortable motel in Tombstone is 1 mile north of town overlooking the Dragoon Mountains. Stone walls, porcelain doorknobs, Mexican tiles in the bathrooms, and old-fashioned "gas" lamps give the spacious rooms an Old West feel. In summer the pool is very welcome after a long hot day. Ask for a room with a view of the Dragoon Mountains.

Priscilla's Bed & Breakfast. 101 N. 3rd St., P.O. Box 700, Tombstone, AZ 85638. ☎ **520/457-3844.** www.tombstone1880.com/priscilla. 4 units (1 with private bathroom). $59 double with shared bathroom; $69 double with private bathroom. Rates include full breakfast. AE, CB, DC, DISC, JCB, MC, V.

Located 2 blocks from the O.K. Corral, this small Victorian farmhouse has been completely restored and is set behind a white picket fence. Built in 1904, the home reflects a less notorious period of Tombstone's past, a time when lawyers could build houses such as this. Lace curtains hang in the windows, and throughout the house, oak trim and oak furniture set a Victorian mood.

Tombstone Boarding House. 108 N. Fourth St., P.O. Box 906, Tombstone, AZ 85638-0906. ☎ **888/225-1319** or 520/457-3716. Fax 520/457-3038. 8 units. $60–$80 double. Rates include full breakfast. AE, DISC, MC, V.

Housed in two whitewashed 1880s adobe buildings with green trim, this inn is 2 blocks from busy Allen Street in a quiet residential neighborhood. The main house was originally the home of Tombstone's first bank manager, while the guest rooms are in an old boarding house. Rooms are comfortable and very clean, with good beds and country decor. Hardwood floors and antiques lend a period feel to these rooms. Two

---

Impressions

From the hygienic point of view, whiskey and cold lead are mentioned as the leading diseases at Tombstone.

—A Tombstone visitor in the 1880s

guest rooms have clawfoot tubs, and one is in an old miner's cabin. At press time, the inn had plans to open a restaurant as well.

WHERE TO DINE

Don Teodoro's Mexican Restaurant. 15 N. 4th St. ☎ **520/457-3647.** Reservations not taken; phone 30 minutes ahead. Main courses $5–$13. AE, MC, V. Sun–Thurs 11am–9pm; Fri–Sat 11am–10pm. SONORAN MEXICAN.

We heard the sweet strains of a guitar wafting through Tombstone, and followed the sound to Don Teodoro's, a little restaurant with a real south-of-the-border atmosphere (and with live music many nights of the week). We dined on the enclosed patio, and the experience as a whole was slightly better than the food, which consisted of adequately prepared dishes such as burritos, chile rellenos, and *carne asada*. What's really good is the Sonoran-style enchilada, a thick corn tortilla covered with enchilada sauce and jack cheese; the tortilla soup is okay, but too salty. This is actually one of the better options for dining in Tombstone.

OK Café. 220 E. Allen St. (corner of 3rd and Allen sts.). ☎ **520/457-3980.** Main courses $4–$7. MC, V. Daily 7am–2pm. AMERICAN.

Sure it's touristy, since it's on the main drag in Tombstone, but we really enjoy the buffalo burgers and homemade soups. Along with the buffalo burgers, you'll find ostrich, emu, and veggie burgers and, of course, beef burgers, as well as chicken and BLTs. It's also a good place for breakfast—the service is bustling, and the people who work here are friendly.

7 Bisbee

205 miles SE of Phoenix; 94 miles SE of Tucson; 24 miles NW of Douglas

Arizona has a wealth of ghost towns that boomed on mining profits and then quickly went bust when the mines played out, but none is as impressive as Bisbee, which is built into the steep slopes of Tombstone Canyon on the south side of the Mule Mountains. Between 1880 and 1975, Bisbee's mines produced more than $6 billion worth of metals. However, when the Phelps Dodge Company shut down its copper mines here, Bisbee nearly went the way of other abandoned mining towns, but because Bisbee is the Cochise County seat, it was saved from disappearing into the desert dust.

Bisbee's glory days date back to the late 19th and early 20th century, and because the town stopped growing in the early part of the 20th century, it is now one of the best-preserved historic towns anywhere in the Southwest. Old brick buildings line the narrow winding streets, and miners' shacks sprawl across the hillsides above downtown. Television and movie producers years ago discovered these well-preserved streets, and over the years Bisbee has doubled as New York City, Spain, Greece, Italy, and, of course, the Old West.

The rumor of silver in "them thar hills" is what first attracted prospectors to the area in 1877, and within a few years the diggings attracted the interest of some San Francisco investors, among them Judge DeWitt Bisbee, for whom the town is named. However, it was copper and other less-than-precious metals that would make Bisbee's fortune. With the help of outside financing, large-scale mining operations were begun in 1881 by the Phelps Dodge Company. By 1910, the population had climbed to 25,000, and Bisbee was the largest city between New Orleans and San Francisco. The town boasted that it was the liveliest spot between El Paso and San Francisco—and the presence of nearly 50 saloons and bordellos along Brewery Gulch backed up the boast.

Tucked into a narrow valley surrounded by red hills, Bisbee today has a very cosmopolitan air. Many artists now call the town home, and urban refugees have been dropping out of the rat race to restore the town's old buildings, opening small inns, restaurants, and art galleries. Between the rough edges left over from its mining days and this new cosmopolitan atmosphere, Bisbee is rapidly becoming one of Arizona's most interesting towns.

ESSENTIALS

GETTING THERE   Bisbee is on Ariz. 80, which begins at I-10 in the town of Benson, 45 miles east of Tucson.

VISITOR INFORMATION   For further information on Bisbee, contact the **Bisbee Chamber of Commerce,** 31 Subway St. (P.O. Box BA), Bisbee, AZ 85603 (☎ **520/ 432-5421;** www.bisbeearizona.com).

SPECIAL EVENTS   Each year Bisbee puts on **coaster races** on the Fourth of July, **Brewery Gulch Days** in September, a **Gem and Mineral Show** and **the 1000 Stair Climb** in October, a Historic Homes tour on Thanksgiving weekend, and **an Arts Festival** in the spring and fall. Ask the Bisbee Chamber of Commerce for specific information.

EXPLORING THE TOWN

At the Bisbee Chamber of Commerce visitor center, located in the middle of town, you can pick up walking-tour brochures that will lead you past the most important buildings and sites in town. There's parking available around the downtown area.

Your first stop should be the **Bisbee Mining and Historical Museum,** 5 Copper Queen Plaza (☎ 520/432-7071), which is housed in the 1897 Copper Queen Consolidated Mining Company office building. This small museum features an exhibit on the history of Bisbee and other exhibits that change annually. The museum is open daily 10am to 4pm, and admission is $4 for adults, $3.50 for seniors, and free for anyone 16 and under.

For another look at early life in Bisbee, visit the **Muheim Heritage House,** 207 Youngblood Hill (☎ 520/432-7071), which was built between 1902 and 1915 and has an unusual semicircular porch. Inside the house is decorated with period furniture. You'll find the historic home up Brewery Gulch. The Muheim House is usually open Thursday to Tuesday 10am to 4pm, and a $2 donation is suggested.

On the second floor of the **Copper Queen Library,** across the street from the visitor center, are some great old **photographs** that give a pretty good idea of what the town looked like in the past century.

If you climb up to the top of **OK Street,** there's a path that takes you up to a hill above town for an excellent panorama of the jumble of old buildings. Atop this hill are numerous small colorfully painted shrines built into the rocks and filled with candles, plastic flowers, and pictures of the Virgin Mary. It's a steep climb on a rocky, very uneven path, but the views and the fascinating little shrines make it well worth the effort. After you've seen the old town, you might want to drive out to the Warren district, where the wealthier citizens of Old Bisbee built their homes.

You can also see what it was like to work inside one of Bisbee's copper mines by taking one of the ✪ **Queen Mine Tours** (☎ 520/432-2071). You can choose either the underground Queen Mine tour or the surface mine and historic tour. Tours are offered daily 9am to 3:30pm. Underground Queen Mine tours cost $10 for adults, $3.50 for children 7 to 15, $2 for children 3 to 6; surface mine and historic tours cost $7 per person; children under 3 are admitted free. You'll find the ticket office and mine just south of the Old Bisbee business district at the Ariz. 80 interchange.

If you're interested in a personally guided tour of the area, contact **Mary's Walking Tours** (☎ 520/432-9039). She's a wealth of information about the area and good with families to boot.

There are lots of interesting ✪ **shops and galleries** in Bisbee—all you have to do is walk around to explore—but there are a couple of places we especially like. **Optimo Custom Hat Works,** 47 Main St. (☎ 520/432-4544), sells Panama hats woven by hand in Ecuador and custom-fitted with finesse. The hats sold here range from about $20 for a low-grade model to several thousand dollars for a grade 20 "fino fino" (but many are much more reasonably priced). One of the best galleries in town is **Jane Hamilton Fine Art,** 29 Main St. (☎ 520/432-3660), showing a wide variety of art styles. If you're interested in having a look at some of the quality jewelry created from the minerals mined in the Bisbee area, stop by **Czar Minerals** (☎ 520/432-2698), up at the top of Tombstone Canyon Road and Clausen Avenue, or **Bisbee Blue** (☎ 520/432-5511), at the Lavender Pit View Point on Ariz. 80. At the former, the specialty is gold- and silversmithing; the latter is an exclusive dealer of the famous Bisbee Blue turquoise, which is a byproduct of copper mining and comes from the Lavender Pit mine. The proprietor here will be happy to tell you about the stones.

WHERE TO STAY

✪ **Bisbee Grand Hotel.** 61 Main St., P.O. Box 825, Bisbee, AZ 85603. ☎ **800/421-1909** or 520/432-5900. www.bisbeegrand.com. 13 units. $55–$78 double; $95–$175 suite. Rates include breakfast. AE, DISC, MC, V.

The Bisbee Grand Hotel is the sort of place you'd expect Wyatt Earp and his wife to patronize. At street level is a historical saloon with a high pressed-tin ceiling and an 1880s back bar from Tombstone. Upstairs are beautifully decorated turn-of-the-century guest rooms. The Oriental Suite has an incredibly ornate Chinese wedding bed, a clawfoot tub, and a skylight; the Victorian Suite has a red-velvet canopy bed. Other, smaller rooms are equally attractive and sport their own themes, and while they all have private bathrooms, some of them are not in the room but across the hall. For 1890s atmosphere, this hotel can't be beat.

Copper Queen Hotel. 11 Howell Ave., P.O. Drawer CQ, Bisbee, AZ 85603. ☎ **520/432-2216.** Fax 520/432-4298. 45 units. A/C TV TEL. $75–$135 double. AE, DC, DISC, MC, V.

Located in the center of Bisbee, the Copper Queen Hotel was built just after the turn of the century by the Copper Queen Mining Company and in those years played host to such notables as Theodore Roosevelt and General "Black Jack" Pershing. Today, the atmosphere here is casual and authentic. The old safe behind the check-in desk has been there for years, as has the oak rolltop desk. Spacious halls, with their own lounges, lead to guest rooms furnished with antiques. Rooms vary considerably in size (the smallest being quite cramped), and while most have been renovated and are attractively furnished, the renovation is an ongoing project. Ask for a renovated room. The hotel's dining room serves decent food, and out front there's a terrace for alfresco dining. And what would a mining-town hotel be without its saloon? For cooling off, there's even a swimming pool.

✪ **High Desert Inn.** 8 Naco Rd., P.O. Box 145, Bisbee, AZ 85603-9998. ☎ **800/281-0510** or 520/432-1442. Fax 520/432-1410. www.highdesertinn.com. 6 units. A/C TV TEL. $70–$95 double. DISC, MC, V.

Although small, this is Bisbee's most luxurious hotel, housed in the former Cochise County Jail (ca. 1901). The guest rooms vary in size, but all feature high ceilings, a cool and sophisticated color scheme, and contemporary furnishings, including wrought-iron headboards on the beds. Small bathrooms have modern fixtures. The inn's dining room is one of the best restaurants in town.

Shady Dell RV Park. 1 Douglas Rd., P.O. Box 1432, Bisbee, AZ 85603. ☎ **520/432-3567.** 8 units. $30–$75 per trailer (1–2 people). No credit cards. No pets or children under 10.

Yes, this really is an RV park, but you'll find neither shade nor dell at this roadside location just south of the Lavender Pit mine. What you will find are eight vintage trailers that have been lovingly restored by owners Ed Smith and Rita Personett. Although the trailers don't have their own private bathrooms (there's a bathhouse in the middle of the RV park), they do have all kinds of vintage decor and furnishings (even tapes of period music and radio shows). After numerous write-ups in national publications, the Shady Dell has become so famous that reservations need to be made far in advance. At press time, there were plans to add a vintage Chris Craft boat and a 1947 Flexible Clipper bus that once belonged to the Sacramento Solons baseball team. Also here at the Shady Dell is **Dot's Diner** (☎ **520/432-2046**), a 1957 vintage diner.

WHERE TO DINE

On nights when Café Roka and the High Desert Inn are closed (see below for both), the dining room at the **Copper Queen Hotel** is going to be your best bet for a decent meal. (See above for both.) For good coffee and a mining-theme decor, check out the **Bisbee Coffee Co.** (☎ **520/432-7879**) at the Convention Center. For burgers and homemade sweet potato pie in a 1957 vintage diner, drop by **Dot's Diner,** 1 Douglas Rd. (☎) **520/432-2046**), which is open Tuesday through Saturday. Call for directions.

✪ Café Roka. 35 Main St. ☎ **520/432-5153.** Reservations highly recommended. Main courses $13.50–$18.50. AE, MC, V. Mid-Oct to mid-May Wed–Sat 5–9pm; mid-May to mid-Oct nights of operation may be more limited, so call for hours. Sun brunch served mid-May to mid-Oct 11am–3pm. CONTEMPORARY CALIFORNIAN.

Ask almost anyone in southern Arizona where to eat in Bisbee, and this is where they'll send you. Café Roka is a casual and hip find in out-of-the-way Bisbee, and offers good value as well as imaginatively prepared food. Every main course comes with a soup, salad, and sorbet, with quite an elegant presentation, and portions are small enough so that you don't feel too full when you're finished. You'll find a lively mix of locals and out-of-towners here having dinner or sitting at the bar in the middle of the room. Menu offerings include the likes of grilled salmon with a gorgonzola crust and angel-hair pasta with shrimp and chipotle aïoli. There's usually a vegetarian dish or two. Flourless chocolate cake with raspberry sauce is an exquisite ending. Local artists display their works, and on some evenings jazz musicians perform.

✪ High Desert Inn Restaurant. 8 Naco Rd. ☎ **520/432-1442** or 800/281-0510. Reservations recommended a week in advance. Main courses $14.50–$18.50. DISC, MC, V. Thurs–Sat (and major holiday Sun) 5:30–9pm. INTERNATIONAL.

Along with Café Roka, this is the most upscale restaurant in Bisbee. It's housed in what was formerly the Cochise County Jail—the back patio used to be the jail cells. In a genteel, romantically lit setting, you'll dine on food that draws its inspiration from around the globe. Such entrees as roasted chicken with rosemary and cracked pepper, sesame-coated mahi-mahi, and curried vegetables *en croûte* are representative of the sort of dishes that show up on the menu here.

8 Exploring the Rest of Cochise County

Willcox: 192 miles SE of Phoenix; 81 miles E of Tucson; 74 miles N of Douglas

Although the towns of Bisbee, Tombstone, and Sierra Vista all lie within Cochise County, much of the county is taken up by the vast Sulphur Springs Valley, which is bounded by multiple mountain ranges. It is across this wide-open landscape that Apache chiefs Cochise and Geronimo once rode, and gazing out across this landscape today, it is easy to understand why the Apaches fought so hard to keep white settlers out of this area. Although relatively unknown outside the region, the Chiricahua and Dragoon mountains offer some of the most spectacular scenery in the Southwest. In these mountain ranges that flank the Sulphur Springs Valley on the east and west, massive boulders litter the mountainsides, creating bizarre and fascinating landscapes. The Chiricahua Mountains also have the distinction of being a favorite destination of avid bird watchers, for it is here that the colorfully plumed elegant trogon reaches the northern limit of its range.

In the southern part of this region lies the town of Douglas, which is an important gateway to Mexico. However, unless you're heading to Mexico, there aren't many reasons to visit Douglas. But if you do find yourself passing through town, be sure to stop in at the historic Gadsden Hotel (see "Where to Stay," below, for more information), and if you don't mind driving on gravel roads, the Slaughter Ranch is well worth a visit.

ESSENTIALS

GETTING THERE   Willcox is on I-10, with Ariz. 186 heading southeast toward Chiricahua National Monument.

VISITOR INFORMATION   For more information on this area, contact the **Willcox Chamber of Commerce and Agriculture,** 1500 N. Circle I Rd., Willcox, AZ 85643 (☎ **800/200-2272** or 520/384-2272; www.willcoxchamber.com).

SPECIAL EVENTS   **Wings over Willcox,** a festival celebrating the return to the area of more than 12,000 sandhill cranes and other migratory birds, takes place in January. For information, contact the Willcox Chamber of Commerce and Agriculture (☎ **520/384-2272**).

IN WILLCOX

Railroad Avenue in downtown Willcox is slowly developing into something of a little historical district. It is here you will find the town's two museums, plus the recently restored **Southern Pacific Willcox Train Depot,** 101 S. Railroad Avenue, a redwood railway depot built in 1880. Inside the old depot, you'll find a small display of Willcox historic photos.

Chiricahua Regional Museum & Research Center. 127 E. Maley St. (in downtown Wilcox). ☎ **520/384-3971** or 800/200-2272. Free admission. Mon–Sun 1–4pm.

If you want to learn more about the history and geology of southeastern Arizona, stop by this small museum, now in its temporary location in an old hardware store. Exhibits done in a folksy and personal style inform the visitor about pioneers, the U.S. Army, and the Chiricahua Apaches, including one dedicated to Cochise.

Rex Allen Museum. 155 N. Railroad Ave. ☎ **520/384-4583.** Admission $2 per person, $3 per couple, or $5 per family. Daily 10am–4pm.

If you grew up in the days of singing cowboys, then you're probably familiar with Willcox's favorite hometown star. It was Rex Allen who made famous the song "Streets of Laredo," and here at the small museum dedicated to Allen, you'll find plenty of Rex Allen memorabilia as well as a Cowboy Hall of Fame exhibit. Each year in October, Willcox celebrates Rex Allen Days.

SOUTHWEST OF WILLCOX

While Chiricahua National Monument claims the most spectacular scenery in this corner of the state, there are a couple of areas southwest of Willcox in the Dragoon Mountains that are almost as impressive. The first of these, **Texas Canyon,** lies right along I-10 between Benson and Willcox and can be enjoyed from the comfort of a speeding car. Here, huge boulders are scattered across a rolling desert landscape. South of the community of Dragoon, which is now known for its many pistachio farms (most of which are open to the public), lies a much less accessible area of the Dragoon Mountains. It is not without good reason that this corner of these mountains has come to be called **Cochise Stronghold.** This rugged jumble of still more giant boulders, almost as spectacular as the nearby Chiricahua National Monument, is reached by a rough gravel road, at the end of which you'll find a campground, picnic area, and hiking trails. A hike among these incredible rock formations is an opportunity to muse on the history of this area.

The Apache peoples first moved into this region of southern Arizona sometime in the early 16th century. They pursued a hunting and gathering lifestyle that was supplemented by raiding neighboring tribes for food and other booty. When the Spanish arrived in the area, the Apache acquired horses and became even more efficient raiders. They attacked Spanish, Mexican, and eventually American settlers, and despite repeated attempts to convince them to give up their hostile way of life, the Apache refused to change. Not long after the Gadsden Purchase of 1848 made Arizona U.S. soil, more people than ever before began settling in the region. The new settlers immediately became the object of Apache raids, and eventually the U.S. Army was called in to put an end to the attacks.

By the mid-1880s only Cochise and Geronimo and their Chiricahua Apache were continuing to attack settlers and fight the U.S. Army. Cochise used this rugged section of the Dragoon Mountains as his hideout and managed to elude capture for years, the granite boulders and pine forests making it impossible for the army to track him and his followers. Cochise eventually died and was buried at an unknown spot somewhere in the area now called Cochise Stronghold.

More Native American history is on display at the following museum.

✪ **Amerind Foundation Museum.** Dragoon. ☎ **520/586-3666.** Admission $3 adults, $2 seniors and children 12–18, free for children 11 and under. Sept–May daily 10am–4pm; June–Aug Wed–Sun 10am–4pm. Closed major holidays. 64 miles east of Tucson between Benson and Willcox, take the Triangle T-Dragoon exit (Exit 318) from I-10 and continue 1 mile east.

It may be out of the way and difficult to find, but this museum is well worth seeking out. Established in 1937, the Amerind Foundation is dedicated to the study, preservation, and interpretation of prehistoric and historic Indian cultures. To that end, the foundation has compiled the nation's finest private collection of archaeological artifacts and contemporary items. There are exhibits about the dances and religious ceremonies of the major Southwestern tribes, including the Navajo, Hopi, and Apache, and exhibits that contain archaeological artifacts amassed from the numerous Amerind Foundation excavations over the years. Many of the pieces came from right here in Texas Canyon. Fascinating ethnology exhibits include amazingly intricate beadwork from the Plains tribes, a case full of old Zuni fetishes, Pima willow baskets, old kachina dolls, 100 years of Southwestern tribal pottery, and Navajo weavings. The art gallery displays works by 19th- and 20th-century American artists, such as Frederic Remington, whose works focused on the West. The museum store is small but has a surprisingly good selection of books and Native American crafts and jewelry.

EAST OF WILLCOX

If you'd like to explore the Chiricahua Mountains on horseback, contact **Sunglow Guest Ranch** (☎ 520/824-3334), which offers rides of anywhere from 1 hour ($18) to all day ($85). Lessons are also available. Reservations are required.

In the town of Bowie, the **Fort Bowie Vineyard,** 156 N. Jefferson St. (☎ 520/847-2593), has a wine-tasting room and sells locally grown pecans and walnuts.

✪ Chiricahua National Monument. Ariz. 186, 30 miles southwest of Willcox. ☎ **520/824-3560.** Admission $6. Visitor center open daily 8am–5pm.

Sea Captain, China Boy, Duck on a Rock, Punch and Judy—these may not seem like appropriate names for landscape features, but this is no ordinary landscape. These gravity-defying rock formations—called "the land of the standing-up rocks" by the Apache and the "wonderland of rocks" by the pioneers—are the equal of any of Arizona's many amazing rocky landmarks. Rank upon rank of monolithic giants seem to have been turned to stone as they marched across the forested Chiricahua Mountains. Big Balanced Rock and Pinnacle Balanced Rock threaten to come crashing down at any moment. Formed about 25 million years ago by a massive volcanic eruption, these rhyolite (a very acidic, volcanic rock) badlands were once the stronghold of renegade Apache. If you look closely at Cochise Head peak, you can even see the famous chief's profile. If you're in good physical condition, don't miss the chance to hike the **✪ Heart of Rocks Trail,** which can be accessed from several trailheads. However, no matter where you start, you'll have to hike 7 to 10 miles to see this spectacular scenery.

Within the monument are a visitor center, campground, picnic area, many miles of hiking trails, and a scenic drive with views of many of the most unusual rock formations.

Fort Bowie National Historic Site. Off Ariz. 186. ☎ **520/847-2500.** Free admission. Visitor center, daily 8am–5pm; grounds, daily dawn–dusk. Closed Christmas. From Willcox, drive southeast on Ariz. 186, and after about 20 miles, watch for the signs; it's another 8 miles up a dirt road to the trailhead. Alternatively, drive east from Willcox to Bowie and drive 11 miles south on Apache Pass Rd. From the trailhead, it is a 1^1/$_2$-mile hike to the fort.

The Butterfield Stage, which carried mail, passengers, and freight across the Southwest in the mid-1800s, followed a route that passed through the heart of Apache territory in the Chiricahua Mountains. Fort Bowie was established in 1862 near the mile-high Apache Pass to ensure the passage of this slow-moving stage as it traversed this difficult region, and to protect the water source for cavalry going east to fight the Confederate army in New Mexico. Later, it was from Fort Bowie that federal troops battled Geronimo until the Apache chief finally surrendered in 1886. Today there's little left of Fort Bowie but some crumbling adobe walls, but the hike along the old stage route to the ruins conjures up the ghosts of Geronimo and the Indian Wars.

IN & NEAR DOUGLAS

In addition to the historic site listed below, the town of Douglas abounds in old buildings, and although not many of them are restored, they hint at the diverse character of this community. Just across the border from Douglas is Agua Prieta, Sonora, where Pancho Villa lost his first battle. Whitewashed adobe buildings, old churches, and sunny plazas provide a contrast to Douglas. Curio shops and Mexican restaurants abound. At the **Douglas Chamber of Commerce,** 1125 Pan American Ave. (☎ **888/ 315-9999** or 520/364-2477; www.discoverdouglas.com), you can pick up a map to the town's historic buildings, as well as a rough map of Agua Prieta. There are also walking tours to Agua Prieta that originate from this office.

✪ **Slaughter Ranch Museum. ☎ 520/558-2474.** Admission $3 adults, children under 14 free. Wed–Sun 10am–3pm. From Douglas, go east on 15th St., which runs into Geronimo Trail; keep going east for 14 miles.

About 14 miles east of Douglas, down a dusty gravel road, lies a little known Southwestern landmark—the Slaughter Ranch. If you're old enough, you might remember a Walt Disney TV show about Texas John Slaughter. Well, this was his ranch (and you can watch videos of the old shows in the ranch's little theater). In 1884, former Texas Ranger John Slaughter bought the San Bernardino Valley and turned it into a cattle ranch, one of the finest in the West. Slaughter later went on to become the sheriff of Cochise County and helped rid the region of the unsavory characters who had flocked to the many mining towns of this remote part of the state. Today the ranch is a National Historic Landmark and has been restored to its turn-of-the-century look. Long shady porches, whitewashed walls, and dark green trim give the ranch a well-manicured look, while inside, antique furnishings present a picture of life as it was then. Surrounding the ranch buildings are wide lawns and a large pond that together attract a wide variety of birds, making this one of the best winter birding spots in the state. For the-way-it-was tranquility, this old ranch can't be beat.

BIRDING HOT SPOTS

At the Willcox Chamber of Commerce, 1500 N. Circle I Rd. (☎ **520/384-0293**), you can pick up several **birding maps** and **checklists** for the region.

To the east of Chiricahua National Monument, on the far side of the Chiricahuas, lies ✪ **Cave Creek Canyon,** one of the most important bird-watching spots in America. It's here that the colorful elegant trogon reaches the northern limit of its range. Other rare birds that have been spotted here include sulfur-bellied flycatchers and Lucy's, Virginia's, and black-throated gray warblers. Stop in at the visitor center for information on the best birding spots in the area. If you'd like a guide to help you identify the area's many bird species, contact David Jasper, P.O. Box 16430, Portal, AZ 85632 (☎ **520/558-2307**). Cave Creek Canyon lies just outside the community of Portal and in summer can be reached by driving over the Chiricahuas from the national monument on graded gravel roads. However, in the winter you'll have to drive around the mountains, which entails going south to Douglas and then 60 miles north to Portal or north to I-10 and then south 35 miles to Portal.

The ✪ **Cochise Lakes** (actually the Willcox sewage ponds) are another great bird-watching spot in this region. Here bird watchers can see a wide variety of waterfowl and shorebirds, including avocets and ibises. To find the ponds, head south out of Willcox on Ariz. 186, turn right onto Rex Allen Jr. Drive at the sign for the Twin Lakes golf course, and go past the golf course.

Between October and March, as many as 12,000 sandhill cranes gather in the Sulphur Springs Valley south of Willcox, and in January the town holds the Wings over Willcox festival, a celebration of these majestic birds. There are a couple of good places in the area to see sandhill cranes during the winter. Southwest of Willcox on U.S. 191 near the Apache Station electric generating plant and the community of Cochise, you'll find the Apache Station Wildlife Viewing Area. About 60 miles south of Willcox off U.S. 191 near the town of Elrida, you'll find the Whitewater Draw Wildlife

Area. To reach the viewing area, go south from Elfrida on Central Highway, turn right on Davis Road, and in another 2.5 miles, turn left on Coffman Road and continue another 2 miles. The last 2 miles is on a dirt road that is not recommended after it has rained. The Sulphur Springs Valley is also well known for its large wintering population of raptors, including ferruginous hawks and prairie falcons.

Near Douglas, the **Slaughter Ranch,** which has a large pond, and the adjacent **San Bernardino National Wildlife Refuge** are good birding spots in both summer and winter. See the Slaughter Ranch Museum description in "In & Near Douglas," above, for directions.

North of Willcox, at the end of a 30-mile-long gravel road, lies the **Muleshoe Ranch Cooperative Management Area** (☎ **520/586-7072** or 520/622-3861), a Nature Conservancy preserve that contains seven perennial streams. These streams support endangered aquatic life as well as riparian zones that attract a large number of bird species. To reach the ranch, take Exit 340 off I-10 and go south; take a right on Bisbee Avenue and then take another right onto Airport Road. After 15 miles watch for a fork in the road and take the right fork. If the road is dry, it is usually passable in passenger cars. The headquarters, which includes the visitor center, is open mid-February to mid-May daily 8am to 5pm. Mid-May to mid-February the headquarters is closed Tuesday and Wednesday. The backcountry is accessible all year-round 24 hours a day. Overnight accommodations in casitas ($85 to $125 double) are available by reservation, but are closed June through August.

WHERE TO STAY
IN & NEAR WILLCOX

Budget chain motels are the only options right in Willcox (you'll find all of the ones listed below off I-10 at Exit 340). They include the **Best Western Plaza Inn,** 1100 W. Rex Allen Dr. (☎ **520/384-3556**), charging $69 to $89 double; **Days Inn,** 724 N. Bisbee Ave. (☎ **520/384-4222**), charging $40 to $50 double; **Motel 6,** 921 N. Bisbee Ave. (☎ **520/384-2201**), with rates of $42 double; and **Super 8,** 1500 Fort Grant Rd. (☎ **520/384-0888**), charging $48 double.

✪ **Cochise Hotel.** P.O. Box 27, Cochise, AZ 85606. ☎ **520/384-3156.** 5 units. $50–$65 double. Rates include full breakfast. No credit cards. Take Exit 331 off I-10 onto Ariz. 191 and drive south 5 miles to Cochise.

Built in 1882, this historic hotel is about the most authentic in the state. The atmosphere is totally uncontrived, and although all the rooms have private bathrooms, the rooms are as simply furnished as travelers on the Southern Pacific Railroad might have found them 100 years ago. In the hotel's parlor, you'll find a working Victrola (guests often end up dancing to old 78 records) and a velvet sofa said to have belonged to Jenny Lind. On 2-day notice the hotel can prepare dinners of either baked chicken ($8) or grilled steaks ($10). Although this hotel is certainly not for everyone, it is a genuine step back in time. If you're a light sleeper, bring earplugs; the trains still run right past the front door.

IN DOUGLAS

Gadsden Hotel. 1046 G Ave., Douglas, AZ 85607. ☎ **520/364-4481.** Fax 520/364-4005. www.theriver.com/gadsdenhotel. 156 units. A/C TV TEL. $40–$60 double; $70–$85 suite. AE, CB, DC, DISC, MC, V.

Built in 1907, the Gadsden bills itself as "the last of the grand hotels," and its listing on the National Register of Historic Places backs up that claim. The marble lobby, although dark, is a classic. Vaulted stained-glass skylights run the length of the ceiling, and above the landing of the wide Italian marble stairway is a genuine Tiffany stained-glass window. Although the carpets in the halls are well worn and rooms aren't always spotless, many rooms have been renovated and refurnished. The bathrooms are, however, a bit worse for the wear. The lounge is a popular local hangout, with more than 200 cattle brands painted on the walls. The dining room serves Mexican and American food, and there's also a coffee shop.

IN PORTAL

Portal Peak Lodge, Portal Store & Cafe. P.O. Box 364, Portal, AZ 85632. ☎ **520/558-2223.** Fax 520/558-2473. www.portalproduction.com/portalpeaklodge. 16 units. A/C TV. $65 double. AE, DISC, MC, V.

This motel-like lodge is behind the general store/cafe in the hamlet of Portal. The guest rooms are fairly new and face each other across a wooden deck. All have two double beds and coffeemakers. Meals are available in the adjacent cafe. If you are seeking utterly predictable accommodations, you'll find them here.

✪ **Southwestern Research Station, The American Museum of Natural History.** P.O. Box 16553, Portal, AZ 85632. ☎ **520/558-2396.** Fax 520/558-2396. 15 units. $122 double (discounts for children). Rates include 3 meals. No credit cards.

Located far up into Cave Creek Canyon, this is a field research station that takes guests when the accommodations are not filled by scientists doing research here in the canyon. As such, it is the best place in the area for serious bird watchers, who will find the company of researchers to be a fascinating addition to a stay here. Accommodations are in simply furnished cabins scattered around the open grounds of the research center. Spring and fall are the easiest times to get reservations and the best times for bird watching.

AREA GUEST RANCHES

Grapevine Canyon Ranch. P.O. Box 302, Pearce, AZ 85625. ☎ **800/245-9202** or 520/826-3185. Fax 520/826-3636. www.gcranch.com. 12 units. $240–$360 double. Rates include all meals. 3-night minimum. Various weeklong packages available. AE, DISC, MC, V. No children under 12 accepted.

Located in the foothills of the Dragoon Mountains adjacent to Cochise Stronghold about 35 miles southwest of Willcox, this guest ranch can be either a quiet hideaway where you can enjoy the natural setting or a place to experience traditional ranch life—horseback riding, rounding up cattle, mending fences. The landscape of mesquite and yucca conjures up images of the high chaparral, and a wide variety of rides are offered, with an emphasis on those for experienced riders. The small cabins (with only showers in their bathrooms) and larger casitas (with combination baths) are set under groves of manzanita and oak trees, and there are decks from which you can view wildlife and the night sky. Unfortunately, furnishings and carpets are old, and rooms lack Western character. There's a swimming pool, and if you don't care to go horseback riding, sightseeing excursions can be arranged.

✪ **Sunglow Guest Ranch.** HC 1, Box 385, Turkey Creek Rd., Pearce, AZ 85625. ☎ **520/824-3334.** Fax 520/824-3176. www.sunglowranch.com. 10 units, including 1 house. $69–$89 double; $149 for 4 in house. AE, DISC, MC, V.

Located in the western foothills of the Chiricahua Mountains roughly 40 miles southeast of Willcox, this remote and tranquil ranch is surrounded by Coronado National Forest. A small lake lies just downhill from the ranch buildings, and rising up behind this lake are the peaks of the Chiricahuas. Back in the 1880s, Sunglow was a logging boom town, but all that remains today is an adobe cottage said to have been the home of outlaw Johnny Ringo's girlfriend. Today the old adobe building is the ranch's dining hall. A reproduction of an old mission church serves as a recreation hall and lounge. Guest rooms are all quite large and have kitchenettes, and most also have woodstoves. However, you won't find TVs or telephones in the rooms. This guest ranch is much less structured than so many others in the state and consequently rates are much lower. Horseback riding is an additional $18 per hour for guests ($25 per hour for riding lessons). There's also great bird watching here on the ranch and in the nearby hills. Meals are available if arranged in advance ($26 per person per day). Daily maid service is not provided.

CAMPGROUNDS

Campgrounds in the area include one at **Chiricahua National Monument** (☎ 520/ 824-3560) on Ariz. 186 and a small campground at **Cochise Stronghold** in the Coronado National Forest on the road to Portal. For information on these national forest campgrounds, contact the **Douglas Ranger District** (☎ 520/364-3468). Reservations are not accepted for any of these campgrounds.

WHERE TO DINE
IN WILLCOX

Right across the parking lot from the Willcox Chamber of Commerce Visitor Center/ Museum of the Southwest (off I-10 at Exit 340), you'll find **Stout's Cider Mill** (☎ 520/384-3696), which makes delicious concoctions with apples. There's cider, cider floats, "cidersicles," apple cake, and the biggest (and contender for the best) apple pie in the world. It's open daily 8am to 6pm.

Rodney's. 118 N. Railroad Ave. ☎ **520/384-5180.** Main courses $5–$8.50. Tues–Sun 11am–9pm or later, depending on business. BARBECUE.

Willcox doesn't have much in the way of good restaurants, but if you're a fan of barbecue, you'll want to be sure to schedule a stop at Rodney's. This little hole-in-the-wall on Railroad Avenue near the Rex Allen Museum is so nondescript that you can easily miss it. Inside, you'll find Rodney Brown, beaming with personality, and dishing up lip-smackin' pork barbecue sandwiches and plates of ribs, shrimp, and catfish.

IN DOUGLAS

The Grand Café. 1119 G Ave. ☎ **520/364-2344.** Reservations not necessary. Main courses $6–$15. MC, V. Sun–Thurs 10am–10pm; Fri–Sat 10am–11pm. SONORAN MEXICAN.

The most interesting part of this cafe is the flamboyant interior and the Marilyn Monroe pictures all over the walls. There are plenty of familiar Mexican choices—enchiladas, tacos, fajitas, and posole, a chile stew with hominy and chicken or pork—with steak and the occasional Italian dish thrown in for good measure. We like the chicken mole, if it's available, with an appetizer of grilled green onions. The guacamole had cottage cheese in it, which seemed rather strange, but the green corn tamales are quite good. Don't expect snappy service here.

Western Arizona 11

Separating Arizona from California and Nevada are 340 miles of Colorado River waters, most of which are impounded in huge reservoirs that provide the water and electricity to such sprawling Southwestern boomtowns as Phoenix and Las Vegas. Because of this watery border, this region has come to be known as Arizona's West Coast.

Lake Havasu, Lake Mohave, and Lake Mead are the largest and most popular of these reservoirs, and due to convolutions in the landscape, these lakes offer thousands of miles of shoreline. In some ways Arizona's West Coast is actually superior to California's Pacific Ocean coastline. Although there aren't many waves on this stretch of the Colorado River, both the weather and the water are warmer than in California. Consequently, watersports of all types are extremely popular, and the fishing is some of the best in the country.

While the Colorado River has always been the lifeblood of this region, it was not water that first attracted settlers to this rugged region. A hundred years ago, prospectors ventured into this sun-baked landscape hoping to find gold in the desert's mountains. Some actually hit pay dirt. Mining towns sprang up overnight, only to be abandoned a few years later when the gold ran out. Today, Oatman is the most famous of these mining boomtowns, but it has too many people and wild burros to be called a ghost town (there's even an active mine or two here).

People are still venturing into this region in hopes of striking it rich, but now they head for the casinos in Laughlin, Nevada, just across the Colorado River from Bullhead City, Arizona. Here a miniature version of Las Vegas has grown up on the Nevada shore of the Colorado River.

As with any warm coastline, Arizona's West Coast is lined with lakefront resorts, hotels, RV parks, and campgrounds. Arizona's West Coast is for the most part a vacation destination for desert residents, so you won't find any hotels or resorts even remotely as upscale or expensive as those in Phoenix, Tucson, or Sedona. You will, however, find plenty of houseboats for rent. These floating vacation homes are immensely popular for family and group vacations. With a houseboat, you can get away from the crowds. When you find a remote cove, the best fishing, or the most spectacular views, you can just drop anchor and kick back. You can even houseboat to the London Bridge, which is no longer falling down, but instead bridges a backwater of Lake Havasu and is now one of Arizona's biggest tourist attractions.

1 Kingman

90 miles SE of Las Vegas; 180 miles SW of Grand Canyon Village; 150 miles W of Flagstaff; 30 miles E of Laughlin

Although Lt. Edward Fitzgerald Beale, leading a special corps of camel-mounted soldiers, passed through this area in 1857, Kingman was not founded until 1882, by which time the railroad had already arrived in this region. Gold and silver were discovered in the nearby mountains in the 1870s, and mining continued well into the 1920s until the mines became unprofitable and were abandoned (although a few mines are still operating today).

During the 1930s, Kingman was a stop on the road to the promised land of California, as tens of thousands of unemployed people followed Route 66 from the Midwest to Los Angeles. Route 66 has long since been replaced by I-40, but the longest remaining stretch of the old highway runs between Kingman and Ash Fork. Over the years Route 66 has taken on legendary qualities, and today people come from all over the world searching for pieces of this highway's historic past.

Remember Andy Devine? No? Well, Kingman is here to tell you all about its squeaky-voiced native-son actor. Devine starred in hundreds of short films and features in the silent-screen era, but he's perhaps best known as cowboy sidekick Jingles on the 1950s TV Western "Wild Bill Hickok." In the 1950s, and 1960s, he hosted "Andy's Gang," a popular children's TV show. In the 1960s, he played Captain Hap on the popular program "Flipper." Devine died in 1977, but here in Kingman his memory lives on—in a room in the local museum, on an avenue named after him, and every October when the town celebrates Andy Devine Days.

ESSENTIALS

GETTING THERE   Kingman is on I-40 at the junction with U.S. 93 from Las Vegas. One of the last sections of old Route 66 (Ariz. 66) connects Kingman with Seligman, Arizona.

America West (☎ **800/235-9292**) flies between Phoenix and Kingman Airport. Car rental is available here through Enterprise (☎ **800/325-8007**), Hertz (☎ **800/654-3131**), and Thrifty (☎ **800/367-2277**).

There is **Amtrak** (☎ **800/872-7245**) passenger service to Kingman from Chicago and Los Angeles. The railway station is at 120 W. Andy Devine Ave. in downtown Kingman.

VISITOR INFORMATION   For more information about Kingman, contact the **Kingman Area Chamber of Commerce,** 333 W. Andy Devine Ave., P.O. Box 1150, Kingman, AZ 86402 (☎ **520/753-6106;** www.arizonaguide.com/visitkingman). The chamber of commerce also operates the Tourist Information Center in the restored 1907 powerhouse at 120 W. Andy Devine Ave. This center is open daily 9am to 6pm.

EXPLORING THE KINGMAN AREA

There isn't much to do right in Kingman, but while you're in town, you can learn more about local history at the **Mohave Museum of History and Arts,** 400 W. Beale St. (☎ **520/753-3195**). There's also plenty of Andy Devine memorabilia on display. The museum is open Monday to Friday 9am to 5pm and Saturday and Sunday 1 to 5pm. Admission is $3. After touring the museum, take a drive or a stroll around downtown Kingman to view the town's many historic buildings. (You can pick up a map at the museum.)

If you're interested in historic homes, you can tour the **Bonelli House,** 430 E. Spring St., a two-story stone home built in 1915 and now furnished much as it may have been when it was constructed. The house is open to the public Thursday to Monday 1 to 4pm, but before heading over to the Bonelli House, check at the Mohave Museum of History and Arts to see if there will be a guide to show you around the historic home. Admission is by donation.

A new **Route 66 Museum** is also under construction in the renovated powerhouse at 120 W. Andy Devine Ave. However, at press time, the Historic Route 66 Association of Arizona (☎ 520/753-5001) had not yet been able to raise enough money to finish the museum, but there were hopes it would open some time in 2001.

When you're tired of the heat and want to cool off, head southeast of Kingman to **Hualapai Mountain Park,** on Hualapai Mountain Road (☎ 877/757-0915 or 520/757-0915), which is at an elevation of 7,000 feet and offers picnicking, hiking, camping, and rustic rental cabins built in the 1930s by the Civilian Conservation Corps.

GHOST TOWNS OF THE KINGMAN AREA

Located 30 miles southwest of Kingman on what was once Route 66 is the busy little ghost town of **Oatman,** a classic Wild West ghost-town tourist trap full of shops selling tacky souvenirs. Founded in 1906 when gold was discovered here, Oatman quickly grew into a lively town of 12,000 people and was an important stop on Route 66—even Clark Gable and Carole Lombard once stayed here (on their honeymoon, no less). However, when the U.S. government closed down many of Arizona's gold-mining operations in 1942 because gold was not essential to the war effort, Oatman's population plummeted. Today there are fewer than 250 inhabitants, and the once-abandoned old buildings have been preserved as a ghost town. The historic look of Oatman has attracted filmmakers for years; among the movies filmed here was *How the West Was Won.*

One of the biggest attractions of Oatman is its population of almost-wild burros. These animals, which roam the streets of town begging for handouts, are descendants of burros used by gold miners. Be careful—they bite!

There are daily staged shoot-outs in the streets and dancing to country music on weekend evenings. Special events include bed races in January, a Fourth of July high-noon sidewalk egg fry, a Labor Day burro biscuit toss, and a December Christmas bush festival (bushes along the highway are decorated with tinsel and Christmas ornaments). Saloons, restaurants, and a very basic hotel (where you can view the room Clark and Carole rented on their wedding night) provide food and lodging if you decide you'd like to soak up the Oatman atmosphere for a while. For more information, contact the **Oatman Chamber of Commerce,** P.O. Box 423, Oatman, AZ 86433 (☎ 520/768-6222).

Chloride, yet another almost-ghost town, is about 20 miles northwest of Kingman. The town was founded in 1862 when silver was discovered in the nearby Cerbat Mountains and is named for a type of silver ore that was mined here. By the 1920s, there were 75 mines and 2,000 people in Chloride. When the mines shut down in 1944, the town lost most of its population. Today there are about 300 residents.

Much of the center of the town has been preserved as a historic district and includes the oldest continuously operating post office in Arizona, the old jail, the Silverbelle Playhouse, and the Jim Fritz Museum. Many of the downtown buildings now serve as gift shops.

On the first and third Saturday of each month, Chloride comes alive with **staged gunfights** in the streets (at high noon, of course) and an afternoon **vaudeville show** at the Town Hall (but there's no show during July and August). On the last Saturday in June, the town celebrates **Old Miners' Day** with a parade, shoot-outs, melodramas, music, and dancing.

Chloride's biggest attractions are the **Chloride murals,** painted by artist Roy Purcell in 1966. The murals, sort of colorful hippie images, are painted on the rocks on a hillside about a mile outside town. To find them, drive through town on Tennessee Avenue and continue onward after the road turns to dirt. You can also see old petroglyphs created by the Hualapai tribe on the hillside opposite the murals.

For more information about Chloride, contact the **Chloride Chamber of Commerce,** P.O. Box 268, Chloride, AZ 86431 (☎ **520/565-2204;** www.oldwesttowns.com).

WHERE TO STAY

In addition to the accommodations listed below, most of the budget motel chains have facilities in Kingman.

✪ **Hotel Brunswick.** 315 E. Andy Devine Ave., Kingman, AZ 86401. ☎ **520/718-1800.** Fax 520/718-1801. www.hotel-brunswick.com. 22 units (13 with private bathroom). A/C TV TEL. $25 single with shared bathroom; $50 double with private bathroom; $75–$95 suite. Rates include deluxe continental breakfast. AE, DC, DISC, MC, V.

Built in 1909 and located in downtown Kingman, the Brunswick Hotel reopened in 1997 after a complete renovation and is Kingman's only historic lodging (and the only historic hotel in at least a 100-mile radius). Back when the hotel's imposing tufa-stone building was constructed, the railroad was the lifeblood of this town, and inside you'll find rooms furnished with antiques and vintage character from those days. The guest rooms vary considerably in size, and most of those with shared bathrooms have only single beds. The rooms are quite comfortable, and suites are extremely spacious. Although the railroad tracks are right across the street, triple-paned windows keep the rooms pretty quiet. The restaurant on the premises serves excellent continental fare, and there is a small bar at the back of the high-ceilinged lobby. New owners have brought more than 3 decades of hotel experience to the management of this hotel.

Quality Inn—Kingman. 1400 E. Andy Devine Ave., Kingman, AZ 86401. ☎ **800/228-5151** or 520/753-4747. 97 units. A/C TV TEL. $50–$68 double. Rates include continental breakfast. AE, CB, DC, DISC, MC, V.

Andy Devine Avenue used to be the famous Route 66, and this motel, 2 miles south of I-40, cashes in on the fame of this historic highway. There are antique gas pumps and other Route 66 memorabilia around the motel's public spaces and a breakfast room done up like a 1950s soda shop. The rooms here are a bit cramped, but are clean and have coffeemakers and two sinks in the bathrooms. The motel also offers an outdoor pool, a whirlpool, a sauna, and a fitness room.

WHERE TO DINE

If you're desperate for an espresso, try **Oldtown Coffeehouse,** 616 E. Beale St. (☎ **520/753-2244**), in an old cottage in downtown Kingman. Need a microbrew? Try the Iguana Amber Ale at **Your Mother's,** 301 N. Fourth St. (☎ **520/753-3615**), a brew pub and restaurant in the historic 1904 Elks Lodge building.

DamBar & Steak House. 1960 E. Andy Devine Ave. ☎ **520/753-3523.** Reservations recommended on weekends and in summer. Lunch items $6–$13; main courses $10–$17 at dinner. AE, MC, V. Sun–Thurs 11am–10pm; Fri–Sat 11am–11pm. STEAK.

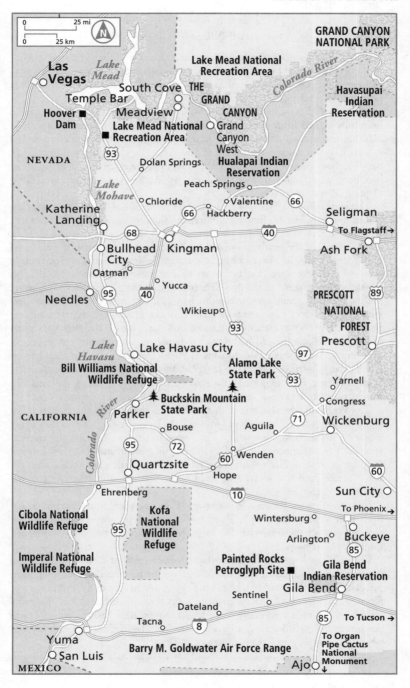

Western Arizona

GRAND CANYON NATIONAL PARK

Lake Mead National Recreation Area

Colorado River

Las Vegas

Lake Mead

South Cove

THE GRAND

CANYON

Havasupai Indian Reservation

Temple Bar

Meadview

Hoover Dam

Lake Mead National Recreation Area

Grand Canyon West

NEVADA

93

Dolan Springs

Hualapai Indian Reservation

Lake Mohave

Peach Springs

Chloride

Valentine

66

Katherine Landing

66

Hackberry

Seligman

68

Kingman

40

To Flagstaff →

Bullhead City

Ash Fork

Oatman

95

Yucca

PRESCOTT

89

Needles

40

Wikieup

NATIONAL

93

FOREST

97

Prescott

Lake Havasu

Lake Havasu City

Alamo Lake State Park

93

Yarnell

Bill Williams National Wildlife Refuge

Congress

River

Buckskin Mountain State Park

71

Wickenburg

CALIFORNIA

Parker

Bouse

Aguila

95

72

Wenden

60

Quartzsite

60

Hope

Sun City

Colorado

Ehrenberg

10

Cibola National Wildlife Refuge

Kofa National Wildlife Refuge

Wintersburg

To Phoenix →

95

Arlington

Buckeye

85

Imperial National Wildlife Refuge

Painted Rocks Petroglyph Site

Gila Bend Indian Reservation

Gila Bend

Sentinel

Dateland

85

To Tucson →

Tacna

8

To Organ Pipe Cactus National Monument

Yuma

Barry M. Goldwater Air Force Range

San Luis

Ajo

MEXICO

Get Your Kicks on Route 66

It was the Mother Road, the Main Street of America, and for thousands of Mid-westerners devastated by the dust bowl days of the 1930s, Route 66 was the road to a better life. On the last leg of its journey from Chicago to California, Route 66 meandered across the vast empty landscape of northern Arizona.

Officially dedicated in 1926, Route 66 was the first highway in America to be uniformly signed from one state to the next. Less than half of the highway's 2,200-mile route was paved, and in those days the stretch between Winslow and Ash Fork was so muddy in winter that drivers had their cars shipped by railroad between those two points. By the 1930s, however, the entire length of Route 66 had been paved, and the westward migration that characterized the Great Depression was under way.

The years following World War II saw Americans take to Route 66 in unprece-dented numbers, but this time for a different reason. Steady jobs, a new prosperity, and reliable cars made travel a pleasure, and Americans set out to discover the West—many on the newly affordable family vacation. Motor courts, cafes, and tourist traps sprang up along its length, and these businesses turned to increasingly more eye-catching signs and billboards to lure passing motorists. Neon lights abounded, looming out of the dark Western nights on lonely stretches of highway.

By the 1950s, Route 66 just couldn't handle the amount of traffic it was see-ing. With President Eisenhower's initiation of the National Interstate Highway System, Route 66 was eventually replaced by a four-lane divided highway. Many of the towns along the old highway were bypassed, and motorists stopped fre-quenting such roadside establishments as Pope's General Store and the Oatman Hotel. Many closed, and others were replaced by their more modern equivalents. Some, however, have managed to survive, and they appear along the road like strange time capsules from another era, vestiges of Route 66's legendary past.

The **Wigwam Motel** is one of the most distinctive Route 66 landmarks. For many miles out from the town of Holbrook, billboards along I-40 beckon weary motorists to "sleep in a wigwam." The wigwams in question (actually teepees) were built out of concrete around 1940 and still contain many of their original furnishings. Also in Holbrook are several rock shops with giant signs—and life-size concrete dinosaurs—that date from Route 66 days. Nighttime here comes alive with vintage neon.

Continuing west, between Winslow and Flagstaff, you'll find a landmark that made it into *Forrest Gump*. The Twin Arrows truck stop, now little more than an old cafe just off the interstate, has as its symbol two giant arrows constructed from telephone poles.

Flagstaff, the largest town along the Arizona stretch of Route 66, became a major layover spot. Motor courts flourished on the road leading into town from the east. Today this road has been officially renamed Route 66 by the city of Flagstaff, and many of the old motor courts remain. Although you probably wouldn't want to stay in many of these old motels, their neon signs were once beacons in the night for tired drivers. Downtown Flagstaff has quite a few shops where you can pick up Route 66 memorabilia.

Operated by the same people who run Murphy's in Prescott, this steak house has long been Kingman's favorite place for dinner out. It's hard to miss the DamBar—just

About 65 miles west of Flagstaff begins the longest remaining stretch of old Route 66. Extending for 160 miles from Ash Fork to Topock, this lonely black-top passes through some of the most remote country in Arizona (and also goes right through the town of Kingman). In the community of Seligman, at the east end of this stretch of the highway, you'll find the **Snow Cap Drive-In,** where owner Juan Delgadillo serves up fast food and quick wit amid outrageous decor. You can't miss it. Next door at **Angel's Barber Shop,** owned by Juan's brother Angel, you'll be entertained by one of the Route 66's most famous residents and an avid fan of the old highway. Angel still cuts hair, and his one-chair barber-shop's walls are covered with photos and business cards of happy customers, many of whom traveled thousands of miles to get their hair cut here. Angel's place also serves as something of a Route 66 information center and souvenir shop, and Angel is president emeritus of the Route 66 Association of Arizona.

After leaving Seligman, the highway passes through such waysides as Peach Springs, Truxton, Valentine, and Hackberry. Before reaching Peach Springs, you'll come to **Grand Canyon Caverns,** once a near-mandatory stop for families traveling Route 66. At Valle Vista, near Kingman, the highway goes into a curve that continues for 7 miles. Some people claim it's the longest continuous curve on a U.S. highway.

After driving through the wilderness west of Seligman, Kingman feels like a veritable metropolis, and its bold neon signs once brought a sigh of relief to the tired and the hungry. Today there are dozens of modern motels in Kingman, but our favorite is the **Quality Inn** on Andy Devine Avenue. The motel has lots of Route 66 memorabilia on display, and the breakfast room is done up like a 1950s malt shop. **Mr. D'z Route 66 Diner,** a modern rendition of a 1950s diner (housed in an old gas station/cafe), serves burgers and blue plate specials and usu-ally has a few classic cars parked out front. Across the street you'll find the newly restored powerhouse, which dates from 1907 and is now home to the Kingman Area Chamber of Commerce Tourist Information Center, a 1950s-style malt shop, and the **Historic Route 66 Association of Arizona** (☎ **520/753-5001**), which has been raising money for years to open a Route 66 Museum here in Kingman's old powerhouse. Each year in late April or early May, Kingman is the site of the **Route 66 Fun Run Weekend,** which consists of a drive along 150 miles of old Route 66 between Topock and Seligman.

The last stretch of Route 66 in Arizona heads southwest out of Kingman through the rugged Sacramento Mountains. This stretch of the old highway passes through **Oatman,** once almost a ghost town after the local mining industry collapsed and the new interstate pulled money out of town. Today mock gunfights and nosy wild burros (watch out; they bite) entice motorists to stop, and shops playing up Route 66's heritage line the wooden sidewalks.

Dropping down out of the mountains, the road once crossed the Colorado River on a narrow metal bridge. The bridge is still there, but now it carries a pipeline instead of traffic, and cars must return to the bland I-40 to continue their journey into the promised land of California.

watch for the steer on the roof of a rustic wooden building as you drive along Andy Devine Avenue. Inside, the atmosphere is very casual, with sawdust on the floor and wooden booths. Mesquite-broiled steaks are the name of the game here, but there are plenty of other hearty dishes as well (Louisiana catfish, margarita grilled chicken, baby back ribs).

Hubb's Café. At the Hotel Brunswick, 315 E. Andy Devine Ave. ☎ **520/718-1800.** Lunch items $4–$11; main courses $10–$16 at dinner. AE, DC, DISC, MC, V. Wed–Mon 11am–9pm. CONTINENTAL.

Hubb's, a downtown restaurant located in an authentically restored historic 1909 hotel, offers menu items not normally seen in Kingman. Scallops *waterzooï*, a traditional Belgium dish, is rich, creamy, and flavorful, while Indonesian-style chicken curry is done with finesse. If these sound too exotic for your tastes, you'll find steak, chicken, and pastas on the menu. Desserts are calculated to be small enough so that you end your dinner feeling satisfied, not stuffed. Lunchtime is also a good opportunity to soak up the historic atmosphere you'll find at this hotel.

Mr. D'z Route 66 Diner. 105 E. Andy Devine Ave. ☎ **520/718-0066.** Sandwiches $3–$7; blue plate specials $7–$9. AE, DC, DISC, MC, V. Daily 10am–5pm. AMERICAN.

This 1990s version of a vintage roadside diner is housed in an old gas station now painted an eye-catching turquoise and pink. The retro color scheme continues inside where you can snuggle into a pink-and-turquoise booth or grab a stool at the counter. This place is a big hit with car buffs and people doing Route 66, and there are usually a some hot rods and vintage cars in the parking lot. Punch in a few 1950s tunes on the jukebox, order up a Corvette burger and a root beer float, and you've got an instant trip down memory lane Route 66 style.

Portofino Ristorante Italiano. 318 Oak St. ☎ **520/753-7504.** Lunch items $5–$8; main courses $8–$20 at dinner. MC, V. Mon 5–9pm; Tues–Fri 11am–2pm and 5–9pm; Sat 5–9pm. ITALIAN.

Housed in an old territorial-style cottage in the historic section of downtown Kingman, this friendly neighborhood restaurant is a favorite spot for a meal. They do a nice job here with Italian standards, including a fresh mozzarella plate with tomato and basil. From there you can move on to a selection from the long pasta menu, such as fettuccine with shrimp and mushrooms in a spicy cream sauce, or a choice from the short selection of filling main courses. Of course, there's an excellent, very light and airy tiramisu with which to finish things off.

2 Lake Mead National Recreation Area

30 miles SE of Las Vegas; 70 miles NW of Kingman; 256 miles NW of Phoenix

Constructed between 1931 and 1935, Hoover Dam was the first major dam on the Colorado River, and by supplying huge amounts of electricity and water to Arizona and California, it set the stage for the phenomenal growth the region experienced in the second half of the 20th century. But Lake Mead, the massive reservoir impounded by Hoover Dam's gargantuan cement wall, provides far more than just water and power. As the focal point of Lake Mead National Recreation Area, it is one of Arizona's (and Nevada's) favorite aquatic playgrounds. Every year more than eight million people visit this national recreation area to boat, ski, fish, swim, and camp on both Lake Mead and Lake Mohave. This latter lake, impounded by Davis Dam, is much smaller than Lake Mead but also lies within the boundaries of the National Recreation Area, which encompasses parts of both Arizona and Nevada.

ESSENTIALS

GETTING THERE   U.S. 93, which runs between Las Vegas and Kingman, crosses over Hoover Dam, and traffic backups at the dam can be horrendous. Don't be surprised if you get stuck for an hour just trying to get across the dam. Several small secondary roads lead to various marinas on the lake. There are also many miles of unpaved roads within the recreation area. If you have a high-clearance vehicle or four-wheel-drive, these roads can take you to some of the least visited shores of the two lakes.

VISITOR INFORMATION   For more information, contact the **Lake Mead National Recreation Area,** 601 Nevada Hwy., Boulder City, NV 89005-2426 (☎ **702/293-8906**), or stop by the **Alan Bible Visitor Center** (☎ **702/293-8990**), between Hoover Dam and Boulder City, Nevada.

DAM, LAKE & RIVER TOURS

Standing 726 feet tall, from bedrock to the roadway atop it, and tapering from a thickness of 660 feet at its base to only 45 feet at the top, **Hoover Dam** is the tallest concrete dam in the western hemisphere. Behind this massive dam lie the waters of **Lake Mead,** which at 110 miles long and with a shoreline of more than 550 miles is the largest artificial lake in the United States. U.S. 93 runs right across the top of the dam, and there's a visitor center that chronicles the dam's construction. The visitor center is open daily 8:30am to 5:30pm (closed Thanksgiving and Christmas). Two different guided tours of the dam are offered. The basic tours last 35 minutes and cost $8 for adults, $7 for seniors, and $2 for children ages 6 to 16. The Hardhat Tour, a more behind-the-scenes tour, lasts about an hour and costs $25.

If you'd like to tour the lake and the dam, book passage on one of **Lake Mead Cruise's** (☎ **702/293-6180**) paddle-wheeler excursions on the *Desert Princess.* These cruises leave from Lake Mead Cruises Landing off Lakeshore Drive on the Nevada side of Hoover Dam. Day tours, which go to the dam, last 1¹/₂ hours and are $16 for adults and $6 for children ages 2 to 11. There are also weekend breakfast cruises ($21 adults and $10 children), dinner cruises ($29 adults and $15 children), and weekend dinner-and-dancing cruises ($43).

One of the most interesting ways to see a remote section of Lake Mohave is to take a kayak trip with **Back Bay Canoes & Kayaks,** 1450 Newberry Dr. (at Ariz. 95), Bullhead City (☎ **888/KAYAKEN** or 520/758-6242), which offers full-day and half-day river trips in the Laughlin-Bullhead City area. **Black Canyon Raft Tours** (☎ **800/696-7238** or 702/293-3776) offers 3-hour motorized raft trips through Black Canyon, below Hoover Dam. Trips cost $65 for adults, $40 for children ages 12 and under (includes lunch, but transportation to and from major hotels costs extra). This is an easy float trip rather than a white-water run.

OUTDOOR RECREATION

As you would expect, swimming, fishing, water-skiing, sailing, windsurfing, and powerboating are the most popular activities in Lake Mead National Recreation Area. On Arizona shores, there are swimming beaches at Lake Mohave's Katherine Landing (outside Bullhead City) and Lake Mead's Temple Bar (north of Kingman off U.S. 93). Picnic areas can be found at these two areas and also at Willow Beach on Lake Mohave and more than half a dozen spots on the Nevada side of Lake Mead.

Fishing for monster striped bass (up to 50 lbs.) is one of the most popular activities on Lake Mead, and while Lake Mohave's striped bass may not reach these awesome proportions, fish in the 25-pound range are not uncommon. However, largemouth bass and even rainbow trout are plentiful in the National Recreation Area's waters due to the diversity of habitats. Try for big rainbows in the cold waters that flow out from Hoover Dam through Black Canyon and into Lake Mohave. To fish from shore, you need a fishing license from either Arizona or Nevada (depending on which shore you're fishing from). To fish from a boat, you need a license from one state and a special use stamp from the other. Most Lake Mead marinas sell both licenses and stamps.

The fishing season for striped bass starts around the beginning of April when the water starts to warm up. If you don't have your own boat, try fishing from the shore of Lake Mohave near Davis Dam, where the water is deep. Anchovy pieces work well as bait, but be sure to put some shot on your line to get it down to the depths where the fish are feeding. You can get bait, tackle, licenses, and fishing tips at the **Lake Mohave Resort marina** (☎ 520/754-3245), at Katherine Landing.

In Arizona, **marinas** can be found at Katherine Landing on Lake Mohave (just outside Bullhead City), near the north end of Lake Mohave at Willow Beach (best access for trout angling), and at Temple Bar on Lake Mead. There is also a boat ramp at South Cove, north of the community of Meadview at the east end of Lake Mead. This latter boat ramp is the closest to the Grand Canyon end of Lake Mead. On the Nevada side of Lake Mohave, you'll find a marina at Cottonwood Cove, and on the Nevada side of Lake Mead, you'll find marinas at Boulder Beach, Las Vegas Bay, Callville Bay, and Echo Bay. These marinas offer resorts, restaurants, general stores, campgrounds, and boat rentals. At both **Temple Bar** (☎ 520/767-3211 or 800/752-9669) and **Lake Mohave Resort** (☎ 520/754-3245 or 800/752-9669), you can rent ski boats, fishing boats, and patio boats for between $100 and $250 per day. Personal watercraft are available and rent for about $50 an hour or $270 a day.

Despite the area's decided water orientation, there's quite a bit of mountainous desert here that's home to bighorn sheep, roadrunners, and other wildlife. This land was once home to several indigenous tribes who left reminders of their presence in **petroglyphs.** The best place to see these carvings is at Grapevine Canyon, due west of Laughlin, Nevada, in the southwest corner of the National Recreation Area. To reach Grapevine Canyon, take Nev. 163 west from Laughlin to milepost 13 and turn right on the marked dirt road. From the highway, it's about 1 1/2 miles to the turnoff for the parking area. From here it's less than 1/4 mile to the petroglyph-covered jumble of rocks at the mouth of Grapevine Canyon. Covering the boulders are thousands of cryptic symbols, as well as ancient illustrations of bighorn sheep. To see these petroglyphs, you have to do a lot of scrambling, so wear sturdy shoes (preferably hiking boots).

For information on other **hikes,** contact any of the ranger stations within the National Recreation Area (Katherine Landing, Cottonwood Cove, Temple Bar, Las Vegas Bay, Callville Bay, Echo Bay, or Overton Beach).

WHERE TO STAY

All three of the accommodations listed below are operated by Seven Crown Resorts, which also operates two other resorts on the Nevada side of the lake. For more information, contact **Seven Crown Resorts** (☎ 800/752-9669).

HOUSEBOATS

Seven Crown Resorts. Mailing address: P.O. Box 16247, Irvine, CA 92623-6247. ☎ **800/752-9669.** www.sevencrown.com. A/C. $1,150–$2,750 per week. DISC, MC, V.

Why pay extra for a lake-view room when you can rent a houseboat that always has a 360-degree water view? There's no better way to explore Lake Mead than on one of these floating vacation homes. You can cruise for miles, tie up at a deserted cove, and have a wilderness adventure with all the comforts of home. Houseboats come complete with full kitchens, air-conditioning, and room to sleep up to 14 people. The scenery here isn't quite as spectacular as on Lake Powell, Arizona's other major houseboating lake.

MOTELS

Lake Mohave Resort. Katherine Landing, Bullhead City, AZ 86430. ☎ **800/752-9669** or 520/754-3245. 51 units. A/C TV TEL. Mar–Oct $72–$100 double; Nov–Feb $40–$75 double. DISC, MC, V. Pets accepted ($25 deposit plus $5 per day).

Just up Lake Mohave from Davis Dam and only a few minutes outside Bullhead City, the Lake Mohave Resort is an older motel, but the huge rooms are ideal for families on vacation. Most of the rooms have some sort of view of the lake, which is across the road from the motel. Tail O' the Whale, the resort's nautical-theme restaurant and lounge, overlooks the marina where giant carp loll just below the surface waiting for people to feed them. The resort offers boat rentals, a convenience store, and a tackle-and-bait store.

Temple Bar Resort. Temple Bar, AZ 86443. ☎ **800/752-9669** or 520/767-3211. 22 units. A/C TV. $50–$95 double. DISC, MC, V. Pets accepted ($25 deposit plus $5 per night).

Although basically just a motel, the Temple Bar Resort has a wonderfully remote setting that will have you thinking you're on vacation in Baja California. With a beach right in front, great fishing nearby, and 40 miles of prime skiing waters extending out from the resort, this place makes an excellent getaway. Directly across from Temple Bar is the huge Temple monolith from which this area gets its name. A restaurant and lounge overlook the lake and provide economical meals. The resort offers ski rentals, powerboat rentals, and a convenience store. There are also four very basic fishing cabins here that share shower rooms and toilets.

CAMPGROUNDS

In Arizona, there are campgrounds at Katherine Landing on Lake Mohave and at Temple Bar on Lake Mead. Both of these campgrounds have been heavily planted with trees so they provide some semblance of shade during the hot, but popular, summer months. In Nevada, you'll find campgrounds at Cottonwood Cove on Lake Mohave and at Boulder Beach, Las Vegas Bay, Callville Bay, Echo Bay, and Overton Beach on Lake Mead.

3 Bullhead City & Laughlin, Nevada

30 miles W of Kingman; 216 miles NW of Phoenix; 60 miles N of Lake Havasu City

You may find it difficult at first to understand why anyone would ever want to live in Bullhead City. According to the U.S. Weather Service, this is the hottest town in the country, with temperatures regularly topping 120°F during the summer. However, to understand Bullhead City, you need only gaze across the Colorado River at the gambling mecca of Laughlin, Nevada, where the slot machines are always in action and the gaming tables are nearly as hot as the air outside. Laughlin is the southernmost town in Nevada and before the advent of Indian casinos, was the closest place to Phoenix to do any gambling. The dozen or so large casino hotels across the Colorado in Nevada still make Bullhead City one of the busiest little towns in Arizona.

Laughlin is a perfect miniature Las Vegas. High-rise hotels loom above the desert like so many glass mesas, miles of neon lights turn night into day, and acres of asphalt are always covered with cars and RVs as hordes of hopeful gamblers go searching for Lady Luck. Cheap rooms and meals lure people into spending on the slot machines what they save on food and a bed. It's a formula that works well. Why else would anyone endure the heat of this remote desert?

ESSENTIALS

GETTING THERE   From Phoenix, take U.S. 60, which becomes U.S. 93, northwest to I-40. From Kingman, take Ariz. 68 west to Bullhead City.

The Bullhead City–Laughlin Airport is in Bullhead City and is served from Phoenix by **America West** (☎ **800/235-9292**).

There are also shuttle bus services operating between Laughlin and the Las Vegas airport. For information or a reservation, call **Super Shuttle** (☎ **800/801-8687** or 520/704-9000), which charges $34 one-way.

VISITOR INFORMATION   For more information on Bullhead City and Laughlin, Nevada, contact the **Bullhead Area Chamber of Commerce,** 1251 Hwy. 95, Bullhead City, AZ 86429 (☎ **800/987-7457** or 520/754-4121). For information in Laughlin, stop by the **Laughlin Visitor Bureau,** 1555 S. Casino Dr., P.O. Box 502, Laughlin, NV 89029 (☎ **800/452-8445** or 702/298-3321; www.visitlaughlin.com).

GETTING AROUND   Car rentals are available in Bullhead City/Laughlin from **Avis** (☎ **800/831-2847** or 520/754-4686), **Enterprise** (☎ **800/325-8007** or 520/ 754-2700), **Hertz** (☎ **800/654-3131** or 520/754-4111), and **Thrifty** (☎ **800/ 367-2277** or 520/704-0193). **Citizens Area Transit (CAT)** provides public bus service within Laughlin. The fare is $1.50. There is also a shuttle service that operates between the casinos and a ferry that shuttles gamblers back and forth across the river from Bullhead City to Laughlin.

CASINOS & OTHER INDOOR PURSUITS

Laughlin is a very popular weekend destination for Phoenicians and other Arizonans, who have limited gambling in their own state. The casinos of Laughlin are known for having liberal slots—that is, the slot machines pay off frequently. There's also keno, blackjack, poker, craps, off-track betting, and sports betting. If you want to learn how to play a game that requires a bit more thinking than slot machines, you can take a lesson in poker, blackjack, or craps at most of the casinos. All the hotels in Laughlin offer live entertainment of some sort, including an occasional headliner (Roy Clark, Doobie Brothers, Mills Brothers), but gambling is still the main event after dark as far as most people are concerned.

If you'd like to learn more about the history of this area, visit the **Colorado River Museum,** 355 Hwy. 95, Bullhead City (☎ **520/754-3399**), which is ^{1}/$_2$ mile north of the Laughlin Bridge. The museum is open September to June daily 10am to 4pm; closed July and August. Admission is free, but donations are welcome.

BOAT TOURS

If you'd like to get away from the noise of the casinos and see a bit of the Colorado River, there are daily "paddle wheeler" cruises available at the **Flamingo Hilton** and **Edgewater** (☎ **800/228-9825** or 702/298-5111). These cruises cost $11 for adults and $6 for children (dinner cruises for $26 are also available). At the **Riverside Resort** (☎ **702/298-2535**), you can take a tour on a 65-foot double decker boat to Davis Dam, which takes about the same length of time as the "paddle wheeler" tours and costs $10 for adults and $6 for children.

If you'd rather look at natural surroundings instead of casino towers, consider booking a jet-boat tour with **London Bridge Jet Boat Tours** (☎ **888/505-3545** or 702/298-5498). The trip leaves from Laughlin's Pioneer Casino and goes down river to Lake Havasu City to see London Bridge. On the way, the boat passes through scenic Topock Gorge. These powerful boats cruise at up to 40 m.p.h. and make the 58-mile trip in 2 hours. Round-trip fares are $49 for adults and $30 for children ages 12 and under.

OUTDOOR RECREATION

If you'd like to do some guided kayaking, contact **Back Bay Canoes & Kayaks,** 1450 Newberry Dr., Bullhead City (☎ **888/KAYAKEN** or 520/758-6242), which offers full-day and half-day river kayak trips in the Laughlin-Bullhead City area.

For information on fishing in nearby Lake Mohave, see the "Lake Mead National Recreation Area" section above. If you'd rather just feed the fish, check out the carp that hang out at the dock behind the Edgewater Hotel & Casino. There are machines dispensing carp chow so you can feed these aquatic vacuums.

In Laughlin golfers can play a round at the scenic and challenging **Emerald River Golf Course** (☎ **702/298-0061**), 2 miles south of Harrah's. Greens fees range from $25 to $85, depending on when you play. The **Mojave Resort Golf Club,** 9905 Aha Macav Pkwy. (☎ **702/535-4653**), adjacent to the Avi Resort & Casino, is the area's newest golf course and charges greens fees of $55 to $65. In Bullhead City, try the **Desert Lakes Golf Course** (☎ **520/768-1000**), 15 miles south of town off Ariz. 95 on Joy Lane in Fort Mohave. Greens fees range from $45 to $65 and are usually lower during the hot summer months. There are also three 9-hole courses near Bullhead City. These include **Riverview Resort & Golf Club,** 2000 E. Ramar Rd. (☎ **520/ 763-1818**); **Chaparral Country Club,** 1260 E. Mohave Dr. (☎ **520/758-6330**); and **Willow Springs Golf Course,** 8011 Hwy. 95, Mohave Valley (☎ **520/ 768-4414**).

Bird watching is excellent in **Havasu National Wildlife Refuge,** which is a wintering area for many species of waterfowl. However, much of this refuge lies within the scenic Topock Gorge and is accessible only by boat. The most accessible birding areas are along the marshes in the vicinity of the communities of Golden Shores and Topock, which are both north of the I-40 bridge over the Colorado. Topock Gorge, one of the most scenic stretches of the lower Colorado River, is a 15-mile stretch of the Colorado River bordered by multicolored cliffs that rise up from the river.

WHERE TO STAY
IN BULLHEAD CITY

Bullhead City has numerous budget chain motels, including a **Days Inn,** a **Super 8,** and a **Comfort Inn.**

IN LAUGHLIN, NEVADA

Laughlin, Nevada, currently has 10 huge hotel-and-casino complexes, 8 of which are right on the west bank of the Colorado River (the 9th is across the street from the river, and the 10th is on the river but several miles south of town). All offer cheap rooms (usually $15 to $30 on weeknights) to lure potential gamblers. In addition to huge casinos with hundreds (even thousands) of slot machines and every sort of gaming table, these hotels have several restaurants (with ridiculously low prices in at least one restaurant, which usually has long lines), bars and lounges (usually with live country or pop music nightly), swimming pools, video arcades for kids, ferry service to parking lots on the Arizona side of the river, valet parking, room service, car-rental desks, airport shuttles, gift shops, and gaming classes. The only real difference between most of these places is the theme each has adopted for its decor.

Should you wish to stay at one of these hotels, here's the information you'll need:

Avi Hotel & Casino, 10000 Aha Macav Pkwy., P.O. Box 77011, Laughlin, NV 89029-7011 (☎ 800/284-2946 or 702/535-5555; www.aviresort.com)

Colorado Belle Hotel & Casino, 2100 S. Casino Dr., Laughlin, NV 89028 (☎ 800/47-RIVER or 702/298-4000; www.coloradobelle.com)

Edgewater Hotel & Casino, 2020 S. Casino Dr., P.O. Box 30707, Laughlin, NV 89029 (☎ 800/67-RIVER or 702/298-2453; www.edgewater-casino.com)

Flamingo Hilton, 1900 S. Casino Dr., Laughlin, NV 89029 (☎ 800/ FLAMINGO or 702/298-5111; www.flamingolaughlin.com)

Golden Nugget, 2300 S. Casino Dr., Laughlin, NV 89028 (☎ 800/237-1739 or 702/298-7111; www.gnl.com)

Harrah's Laughlin, 2900 S. Casino Dr., Laughlin, NV 89028 (☎ 800/ 447-8700 or 702/298-4600; www.harrahs.com)

Pioneer Hotel & Gambling Hall, 2200 S. Casino Dr., P.O. Box 29664, Laughlin, NV 89029 (☎ 800/634-3469 or 702/298-2442); www.santafegaming.com/pio)

Ramada Express, 2121 S. Casino Dr., Laughlin, NV 89029 (☎ 800/ 243-6846 or 702/298-4200; www.ramadaexpress.com)

River Palms Resort & Casino, 2700 S. Casino Dr., P.O. Box 77700, Laughlin, NV 89028-7700 (☎ 800/835-7903 or 702/298-2242; www.rvrpalm.com)

Riverside Resort Hotel & Casino, 1650 S. Casino Dr., P.O. Box 500, Laughlin, NV 89029 (☎ 800/227-3849 or 702/298-2535; www.riversideresort.com)

WHERE TO DINE

The dozens of inexpensive casino hotel restaurants are usually the top choice of visitors to Laughlin and Bullhead City. Cheap steaks, prime ribs, and all-you-can-eat buffets are the specialties of these places.

4 Lake Havasu & the London Bridge

200 miles NW of Phoenix; 60 miles S of Bullhead City; 61 miles S of Kingman; 150 miles S of Las Vegas

Once upon a time London Bridge really was falling down, but that was before Robert McCulloch, founder of Lake Havasu City, hit upon the brilliant idea of buying the bridge in the late sixties and having it shipped to his undertouristed little town in the middle of the Arizona desert. Today the London Bridge sits like a mirage on the banks of Lake Havasu. An unlikely place for a bit of British heritage, true, but Lake Havasu City and the London Bridge have become the second most popular tourist destination in Arizona (only the Grand Canyon attracts more visitors).

Lake Havasu was formed in 1938 by the building of the Parker Dam, but it wasn't until 1963 that the town of Lake Havasu City was founded by McCulloch. Not too many people were keen on spending time out in this remote corner of the desert, where summer temperatures are often over 110°F. Despite its name, Lake Havasu City at the time was little more than an expanse of desert with a few mobile homes on it. It was then that McCulloch began looking for ways to attract more people to his little city on the lake. His solution proved to be a stroke of genius.

In recent years, Lake Havasu City has become very popular with college students across Arizona, especially during spring break. The city is sort of a Fort Lauderdale in the desert, and businesses cater primarily to young partiers. Be prepared for a lot of noise if you are here on a weekend or during a holiday.

ESSENTIALS

GETTING THERE   From Phoenix, take I-10 west to Ariz. 95 north. From Las Vegas, take U.S. 93 south to Kingman and then I-40 west to Ariz. 95 south.

America West (☎ **800/235-9292**) has regular flights to Lake Havasu City from Phoenix.

The **Havasu/Vegas Express** (☎ **800/459-4884** or 520/453-4884) operates a shuttle van between Lake Havasu City and Las Vegas. Fares are $49 one-way and $87 round-trip.

VISITOR INFORMATION   For more information on this area, contact the **Lake Havasu Area Chamber of Commerce/Lake Havasu Tourism Bureau,** 314 London Bridge Rd., Lake Havasu City, AZ 86403 (☎ **800/242-8278** or 520/855-4115; www.arizonaguide.com/lakehavasu). There is also a tourist information center at 420 English Village (☎ **520/855-5655**).

GETTING AROUND   Taxi service is available from **City Transit Service** (☎ **520/453-7600**). Car rentals are available from **Avis** (☎ **800/831-2847** or 520/764-3001), **Enterprise Rent-a-Car** (☎ **800/325-8007** or 520/453-0033), and **Hertz** (☎ **800/654-3131** or 520/764-3994). There is also the **River City Trolley,** a trolley-style bus that loops past many of the city's shopping centers, motels, and tourist attractions.

LONDON BRIDGE

In the mid-1960s, the British government decided to sell the London Bridge, which was indeed falling down—or, more correctly, sinking—into the Thames River because of too much heavy car and truck traffic. McCulloch and his partner paid $2,460,000 for the famous bridge; had it shipped 10,000 miles to Long Beach, California; and then trucked it to Lake Havasu City. Reconstruction of the bridge was begun in 1968, and the grand reopening was held in 1971. Oddly enough, the 900-foot-long bridge was not built over water; it just connected desert to more desert on a peninsula jutting into Lake Havasu. It wasn't until after the bridge was rebuilt that a mile-long channel was dredged through the base of the peninsula, thus creating an island offshore from Lake Havasu City.

The London Bridge has a long history, although the bridge that now stands in Arizona is not very old by British standards. The first bridge over the Thames River in London was probably a pontoon bridge built by the Romans in A.D. 43. However, the first written record of a London Bridge comes from the mention of a suspected witch being drowned at the bridge in 984. In 1176, the first stone bridge over the Thames was built. They just don't build 'em like that bridge anymore—it lasted for more than 600 years but was eventually replaced in 1824 by the bridge that now stands in Lake Havasu City.

At the base of the bridge sits **English Village,** which is done up in proper English style and has shops, restaurants, and a waterfront promenade. It's here you'll find several cruise boats and small-boat rental docks.

LAND, RIVER & LAKE TOURS

There are several companies offering different types of boat tours on Lake Havasu. **Bluewater Charters** (☎ **888/855-7171** or 520/855-7171) offers jet-boat tours that leave from the London Bridge and spend 2 hours cruising up the Colorado River to the Topock Gorge, a scenic area 25 miles from Lake Havasu City. The tours are $35 for adults, $32 for seniors, $17.50 for children 10 to 16, and free for children 9 and under.

You can also cruise on the *Dixie Belle* (☎ 520/453-6776), a small replica paddle-wheel riverboat. Cruises are $12 for adults and $5 for children 6 to 12.

One of the most interesting and beautiful boat tour destinations is Copper Canyon, a flooded canyon 9 miles from Lake Havasu City. The *Kon Tiki* (☎ 520/453-6776), a pontoon boat berthed at English Village, makes the trip regularly and charges $12 for adults and $5 for children 6 to 12.

For an even more scenic tour, but one that entails a bit of effort, contact **Western Arizona Canoe and Kayak Outfitter** (☎ 520/855-6414 or 520/680-9719), which offers kayak trips through the beautiful and rugged Topock Gorge, where you can see ancient petroglyphs and possibly bighorn sheep. Trips are $39 for self-guided and $44 for a guided trip per person. **Jerkwater Canoe Company** (☎ 520/768-7753) offers a similar Topock Gorge trip and also arranges other canoe trips of varying lengths. With Jerkwater, the Topock Gorge self-guided trip is $35 per person. Another popular trip is through Black Canyon, but advance planning is required to get the necessary permit. It's much easier to get a permit for Black Canyon midweek than it is on a weekend. Both companies provide boats, paddles, life jackets, maps, and shuttles to put-in and take-out points, but most often no guide (the maps make it easy for you to find your own way). Some trips include additional overnight campground or bunkhouse bed-and-breakfast fees.

If you'd like to explore the desert surrounding Lake Havasu City, you can arrange a four-wheel-drive tour through **Outback Off-Road Adventures** (☎ 520/680-6151), which charges $65 for a half-day tour and $130 for a full-day tour.

WATERSPORTS

While the London Bridge is what made Lake Havasu City, these days watersports on 45-mile-long Lake Havasu are the area's real draw. Whether you want to go for a swim, take a leisurely pedal-boat ride under the London Bridge, go parasailing, or spend the day water-skiing, there are plenty of places to arrange to get wet.

The best beach in the area is the **London Bridge Beach,** in a county park behind the Island Inn Resort off West McCulloch Boulevard. This park has a sandy beach, lots of palm trees, and views of both the London Bridge and the distant desert mountains. There are also picnic tables and a snack bar, which make this park a great place to spend the whole day. There are more beaches at the **Windsor Beach Unit of Lake Havasu State Park,** 2 miles north of the London Bridge, and **Cattail Cove State Park,** 15 miles south of Lake Havasu City. Lake Havasu State Park also has 20 miles of shoreline to the south of Lake Havasu City, but there are no roads to this shoreline. If you have your own boat, you'll find lots of secluded little beaches.

The cheapest way to get out on the water in Lake Havasu also happens to involve the greatest expenditure of energy. At the **Fun Center** (☎ 520/453-4386) in English Village you can rent pedal boats and aqua cycles for $15 an hour. If kayaking or canoeing is more your style, contact **Western Arizona Canoe and Kayak Outfitter** (☎ 520/855-6414), which rents canoes and kayaks on the lake beginning at $25 a day.

If you didn't bring your own boat, you can rent one at **Blue Water Rentals,** in English Village beside the bridge (☎ 520/453-9613 or 520/855-7171). The company offers rentals of ski boats (starting at $280 per day) and pontoon boats (starting at $190 per day). Boats are also available at **Fun Time Boat Rentals,** 1633 Industrial

Blvd. (☎ **800/680-1003** or 520/680-1003). Ski boats come with water skis or knee boards.

If your main reason for getting out on the water is to catch some fish, you'll likely come away from a visit to Lake Havasu with plenty of fish stories to tell. Striped bass, also known as stripers, are the favorite quarry of anglers here. These fish have been known to reach almost 60 pounds in these waters, so be sure to bring the heavy tackle. Largemouth bass in the 2- to 4-pound range are also fairly common, and giant channel catfish of up to 35 pounds have been caught in Topock Marsh. The best fishing starts in midspring when the water begins to warm up, but there is also good winter fishing.

GOLF

And what would an Arizona desert community be without its golf courses? Lake Havasu City has four, all of which are open to the public. Panoramic views are to be had from each of the courses here, and there's enough variety to accommodate golfers of any skill level.

London Bridge Golf Club, 2400 Club House Dr. (☎ **520/855-2719**), with two 18-hole courses, is the area's premier championship course. High-season greens fees (with cart) top out at $79 (with cart) on the West Course and $53 on the East Course. The **Havasu Island Golf Course,** 1040 McCulloch Blvd. (☎ **520/855-5585**), is a 4,012-yard, par-61 executive course with lots of water hazards. The 9-hole **Bridgewater Links,** 1477 Queen's Bay Rd. (☎ **520/855-4777**), at the London Bridge Resort, is the most accessible and easiest of the area courses.

Golfers also won't want to miss the ✪ **Emerald Canyon Golf Course,** 72 Emerald Canyon Dr., Parker (☎ **520/667-3366**), which is about 30 miles south of Lake Havasu City. This municipal course is the most spectacular course in the region and plays through rugged canyons and past red-rock cliffs, from which there are views of the Colorado River. One hole even has you hitting your ball off a cliff to a green 200 feet below you! Greens fees range from about $27 to about $45.

WHERE TO STAY
HOUSEBOATS

Havasu Springs Resort. 2581 Hwy. 95, Parker, AZ 85344. ☎ **520/667-3361.** Fax 520/667-1098. Mar 1–Sept 30 $1,853–$2,432 per week; Oct 1–Feb 28 $1,166–$1,690 per week. No credit cards.

One of the most popular ways to enjoy Lake Havasu is on a rented houseboat. You can spend your days motoring from one good fishing or swimming hole to the next, and there are beaches and secluded coves where you can drop anchor and stay for days. If you feel like doing a bit of sightseeing or shopping, you can cruise right up to the London Bridge. Houseboats come in several sizes, with the large boats providing much more luxury. Boats sleep 10 to 12 people and are very popular with families.

HOTELS & MOTELS

In addition to the accommodations listed here, Lake Havasu City has numerous budget chain motels, including **Motel 6, Super 8,** and **Days Inn.**

Bridgeview Motel. 101 London Bridge Rd., Lake Havasu City, AZ 86403. ☎ **520/855-5559.** Fax 520/855-5564. 37 units. A/C TV TEL. $38–$72 double (higher on holidays). MC, V.

If you're just looking for a clean and inexpensive place to stay, this motel fits the bill and offers a view of the bridge. It's also quiet here (usually), and there's a small pool.

Island Inn. 1300 W. McCulloch Blvd., Lake Havasu City, AZ 86403. ☎ **800/243-9955** or 520/680-0606. Fax 520/680-4218. 117 units. A/C TV TEL. Mar 1–Oct 31 $65–$95 double, $130–$180 suite; Nov 1–Feb 28 $49–$59 double, $98 suite. AE, DC, DISC, MC, V. Pets accepted with extra charge.

The Island Inn is across the London Bridge from downtown and has one of the nicest hotel settings in Lake Havasu City. Although it's not right on the water, this hotel is close to one of the area's best public beaches. The rooms are large and spartan, and they seem to have seen a lot of wear and tear, but they are slowly ugrading the carpets. Most rooms have balconies (ask for one of these), and those on the upper floors have the better views (and higher prices). Facilities include an outdoor pool and a whirlpool.

♦ **London Bridge Resort.** 1477 Queens Bay, Lake Havasu City, AZ 86403. ☎ **800/ 624-7939** or 520/855-0888. Fax 520/855-9209. www.londonbridgeresort.com. 122 units. A/C TV TEL. $104–$164 studio; $124–$199 1- or 2-bedroom condo. Higher rates on holidays. AE, DISC, MC, V.

It doesn't take much to figure out that this resort was built after the London Bridge made its historic move to the Arizona desert. Merrie Olde England was once the theme here, with Tudor half-timbers jumbled up with turrets, towers, ramparts, and crenellations. However, England is giving way to the tropics and the desert as the resort strives to please its young, partying clientele (who tend to make a lot of noise and leave the hotel looking much the worse for wear). Although the bridge is just out the hotel's back door, and a replica of Britain's gold State Coach is inside the lobby, guests seem more interested in the three pools, the tropical-theme outdoor nightclub, and the Mexican cantina. Even the dining room now serves Southwestern food. The rooms are large and have gotten a Southwestern face-lift as the hotel has converted to time-share ownership. In addition to the three pools, recreational options include an executive golf course, tennis courts, whirlpools, and a beach.

CAMPGROUNDS

In the Lake Havasu City area, there are two state park campgrounds. **Lake Havasu State Park's Windsor Beach Unit** (☎ 520/855-2784) is 2 miles north of the London Bridge on London Bridge Road, and **Cattail Cove State Park** (☎ 520/ 855-1223) is 15 miles south of Lake Havasu City off Ariz. 95. The former campground has no hookups and charges $12 per night per vehicle, and the latter charges $15 for a full hookup per vehicle. Reservations for camping are not accepted. In addition to sites in these campgrounds, there are about 160 boat-in campsites within Lake Havasu and Cattail Cove state parks.

WHERE TO DINE

Chico's Tacos. In the Basha's Center, 1641 McCulloch Blvd. ☎ **520/680-7010.** Main courses $2.50–$6. MC, V. Sun–Thurs 10:30am–9:30pm; Fri–Sat 10:30am–10pm. MEXICAN.

This Mexican fast-food place is great for a quick, cheap bite to eat. The carne asada and chicken carbón are excellent, and there's a fresh salsa bar for you to do your own doctoring of your meal. Be forewarned that the burritos are big and messy!

City of London Arms Pub & Restaurant. 422 English Village. ☎ **520/855-8782.** Reservations recommended. Main courses $8–$20. AE, DC, DISC, MC, V. Mon–Thurs 11am–8:30pm; Fri–Sat 11am–9:30pm; Sun noon–8:30pm (buffet 8am–noon. PUB FARE/STEAKS.

A British pub atmosphere reigns here, with a Tudor-style interior and British comfort food on the menu—fish-and-chips, steak-and-mushroom pie, and banger rolls. It's a cool retreat from the blazing sun and kind of an odd place in which to find oneself (since this is the desert). This pub was actually built by the City of London, and here you'll be competing with other tourists on the London Bridge scene for a table either inside or on the patio overlooking the river. If you desire something non-British, take heart—the menu includes seafood, steaks, pizza, and pasta. The restaurant serves Guinness stout, but this place is also a brew pub (with a separate but similar menu) serving a half-dozen different beers and ales brewed on the premises.

Shugrue's. 1425 McCulloch Blvd. (at the Island Mall). ☎ **520/453-1400.** Reservations recommended. Main courses $7–$25. AE, DC, MC, V. Daily 11am–3pm and 4:30–9pm (sometimes later on weekend nights). STEAK/SEAFOOD.

Located just across the London Bridge from the English Village shopping complex, Shugrue's seems to be popular as much for its view of the London Bridge as it is for its food. The large restaurant has been built so that most diners get a view of the bridge. In addition to the seafood, prime rib, burgers, and sandwiches, there's a short list of pastas. This place is a favorite of vacationing retirees and families—there's also a children's menu including such items as chicken tenders or a minipizza. Shugrue's operates the Barley Brothers Brewery and Grill in the same shopping center as well.

DRIVING DOWN TO YUMA
THE PARKER AREA

About 16 miles south of Lake Havasu City stands the **Parker Dam,** which holds back the waters of Lake Havasu and is said to be the deepest dam in the world because 73% of its 320-foot height is below the riverbed. Beginning just above the dam and stretching south to the town of Parker is one of the most beautiful stretches of the lower Colorado River. Just before you reach the dam, you'll come to the **Bill Williams National Wildlife Refuge,** which preserves the lower reaches of the Bill Williams River. This refuge offers some of the best bird watching in western Arizona. Keep your eyes out for vermilion flycatchers, Yuma clapper rails, soras, Swainson's hawks, and white-faced ibises.

Continuing south, you'll come to a dam overlook and the Take-Off Point boat launch, where you can also do some fishing from shore. Below the dam, the river becomes narrow, and red-rock canyon walls close in. Although this narrow gorge is lined with mobile home parks, the most beautiful sections have been preserved in two units of **Buckskin Mountain State Park** (☎ **520/667-3231**). Both units—Buckskin Point and River Island—have campgrounds ($15 for campsites and $20 for cabanas at Buckskin and $12 at River Island) as well as day-use areas ($6) that include river beaches and hiking trails leading into the Buckskin Mountains. Reservations for camping are not accepted. In this area is the spectacular Emerald Canyon Golf Course (see "Golf," above, for details).

For more information on the Parker area, contact the **Parker Area Chamber of Commerce,** 1217 California Ave., Parker, AZ 85344 (☎ **520/669-2174;** www.coloradoriverinfo.com/parker).

THE QUARTZSITE AREA

For much of the year, the community of **Quartzsite** is little more than a few truck stops at an interstate off-ramp. However, the population explodes each year with the annual influx of winter visitors (also known as snowbirds), and from early January to mid-February the community is the site of numerous gem-and-mineral shows that attract more than a million rock hounds. Among these shows is the **Quartzsite Pow Wow,** which is held in late January and is one of the largest gem-and-mineral shows in the country. If you're passing through during these months, you might want to check out one of these shows. During the winter months, Quartzsite sprouts thousands of vendor stalls, as flea markets and the like are erected along the town's main streets. A variety of interesting food makes it a great place to stop for lunch or dinner. For more information, contact the **Quartzsite Chamber of Commerce,** 1490 Main Event Lane, P.O. Box 85, Quartzsite, AZ 85346 (☎ **520/927-5600;** www.quartzsitechamber.com).

For information on parking your RV in the desert outside Quartzsite, contact the **Bureau of Land Management,** Yuma Field Office, 2555 East Gila Ridge Rd., Yuma, AZ 85365 (☎ **520/317-3200**). Alternatively, you can get information and camping permits at the Long-Term Visitor Area entrance stations just south of Quartzsite on U.S. 95. The season here runs September 15 to April 15, with permits going for $100 for the season and $20 for 7 consecutive days.

If ancient rock art interests you, be sure to watch for Plomosa Road as you travel between Parker and Quartzsite. Off this road, you'll find a 30-foot-long intaglio (or geoglyph) known as the **Bouse Fisherman.** This primitive image of a person spearing fish was formed by scratching away the rocky crust of the desert soil. Its origin and age are unknown, but it is believed to have been created centuries ago by native peoples and may depict the god Kumastamo, who created the Colorado River by thrusting a spear into the ground. To find this intaglio, drive 8 miles up Plomosa Road, which is approximately 6 miles north of Quartzsite, and watch for a wide parking area on the north side of the road. From here, follow the trail $1/4$ mile over a small hill.

Right in Quartzsite you'll find **Hi Jolly's Last Camp,** the pyramid-shaped stone monument and tomb of Hadji Ali (Hi Jolly), the Syrian camel driver who tended the camels of the U.S. Army's experimental camel corps from 1856 to 1864. You'll find the monument at the west end of town off Main Street, and although it's not particularly impressive, it commemorates a fascinating desert experiment of the 19th century.

There are only three places in Arizona where palm trees grow wild, and if you'd like to visit one of these spots, watch for the Palm Canyon turnoff 18 miles south of Quartzsite. Palm Canyon lies within the boundaries of the **Kofa National Wildlife Refuge,** which was formed primarily to protect the desert bighorn sheep that live here in the rugged Kofa Mountains. The palms are 8 miles off U.S. 95 in a narrow canyon a short walk from the end of the well-graded gravel road, and although there are only a couple of dozen trees, the hike to see them provides an opportunity to experience these mountains up close. Keep your eyes peeled for desert bighorn sheep. Incidentally, the Kofa Mountains took their name from the King of Arizona Mine. For maps and more information, contact the **Kofa National Wildlife Refuge,** 356 W. First St., Yuma, AZ 85364 (☎ **520/783-7861**).

5 Yuma

180 miles SW of Phoenix; 180 miles E of San Diego; 240 miles W of Tucson

Although you may never have heard of Yuma, Arizona, it was once one of the most important towns in the region, known as the Rome of the Southwest because all roads led to Yuma Crossing—the shallow spot along the Colorado River where Yuma was founded. Quechan Indians, Spanish missionaries and explorers, Kit Carson and his mountain men, '49ers heading for the gold fields of California, pioneers, and soldiers all passed through this narrow spot on the lower Colorado River. Despite its location in the middle of the desert, Yuma became a busy port town duirng the 1850s as shallow-draft steamboats traveled up the Colorado River from the Gulf of California. From here, during the Apache wars of the 1870s and 1880s, military supplies were transported overland to the many forts and camps throughout the Southwest. When the railroad pushed westward into California in the 1870s, it passed through Yuma. Even today I-8, which connects San Diego with Tucson and Phoenix, crosses the Colorado at Yuma.

Even hotter than Phoenix, Yuma often records summer temperatures in excess of 120°F, and the U.S. Weather Service says Yuma is the sunniest city in the United States. Yuma's warm winters have made it the winter destination of tens of thousands of snowbirds, who drive their RVs from as far away as Canada.

Despite having more than a dozen golf courses and two important historic sites, Yuma has had to struggle to attract visitors. For whatever reason, many people just don't take this city seriously as a winter vacation destination. However, in the hopes of luring more people off the interstate, Yuma has in the past few years been working hard to restore its downtown historic buildings, expand its historic sites, and preserve its natural setting on the Colorado River. More developments along these lines are in store for 2001, so you might want to contact the Yuma Convention and Visitors Bureau (see below) to find out what's new in town when you're in the area.

ESSENTIALS

GETTING THERE   Yuma is on I-8, which runs from San Diego, California, to Casa Grande, Arizona.

The Yuma Airport is at 2191 32nd St. and is served by **America West** (☎ **800/235-9292**) from Phoenix.

There's **Amtrak** (☎ **800/872-7245**) passenger service to Yuma from Los Angeles and New Orleans. The station is on Gila Street.

VISITOR INFORMATION   For more information about Yuma, contact the **Yuma Convention and Visitors Bureau,** 377 S. Main St., Yuma, AZ 85364 (☎ **800/293-0071** or 520/783-0071; www.visityuma.com).

GETTING AROUND   For a taxi, call **Yuma City Cab** (☎ **520/782-0111**). Rental cars are available in Yuma from **Avis** (☎ **800/831-2847** or 520/726-5737), **Budget** (☎ **800/527-0700** or 520/344-1822), **Enterprise** (☎ **800/325-8007** or 520/344-5444), and **Hertz** (☎ **800/654-3131** or 520/726-5160).

SPECIAL EVENTS   The Yuma area is a major producer of lettuce and celebrates this in the **Lettuce Festival** held in late January. **Yuma Crossing Days,** held in late February, features historical reenactments, historic site tours, and railroad rides.

HISTORIC SITES

Arizona Historical Society Century House Museum. 240 S. Madison Ave. ☎ **520/782-1841.** Free admission; $2 suggested donation. Tues–Sat 10am–4pm.

If you'd like to find out more about pioneer life in Yuma, stop by this territorial-period home, which is full of historical photographs and artifacts and surrounded by lush gardens and aviaries full of exotic birds. Adjacent to the museum is the Garden Cafe, an excellent lunch spot.

✪ **Yuma Crossing State Historic Park.** 201 N. 4th Ave. (at the Colorado River). ☎ **520/329-0471.** Admission $3 adults, $2 children 7–13, free for children 6 and under. Daily 9am–5pm (Apr–Oct closed Tues–Wed). Closed Dec 25.

In 1865, Yuma Crossing, the narrow spot in the Colorado River where the town of Yuma sprang up, became the site of the military's Quartermaster Depot. Yuma was a busy river port during this time, and after supplies shipped from California were unloaded, they went to military posts throughout the region. When the railroad arrived in Yuma in 1877, the Quartermaster Depot began losing its importance in the regional supply network, and by 1883, the depot had been closed. Today the depot's large wooden buildings have been restored, and although they are now set back from the current channel of the Colorado River, it's easy to imagine being stationed at this hot and dusty outpost in the days before air-conditioning. Exhibits tell the story of those who lived and worked at Yuma Crossing.

Yuma Territorial Prison State Historic Park. 1 Prison Hill Rd. ☎ **520/783-4771.** Admission $3 adults, $2 children 7–13, free for children 6 and under. Daily 8am–5pm. Closed Dec 25.

Yuma is one of the hottest places in the world, so it comes as no surprise the Arizona Territory chose this bleak spot for a prison (although there is a nice view of the confluence of the Gila and Colorado rivers from Prison Hill). The prison first housed convicts in 1876 but operated for only 33 years before being replaced by a larger prison. Despite the thick stone walls and iron bars, this prison was considered a model penal institution in its day. It even had its own generating plant for electricity and a ventilation system. The prison museum has some interesting displays, including photos of many of the 3,049 men and 29 women who were incarcerated at Yuma over the years. After the prison was shut down, the building served as a high school and as housing for the homeless during the Depression.

DOWNTOWN YUMA

Historic downtown Yuma isn't exactly a bustling place, and it doesn't abound in historical flavor, but the south-of-the-border atmosphere is well worth a visit. Huge well-shaped ficus trees provide deep shade, and at the center of the shopping district is a plaza similar to those found in towns all over Mexico. Funky and inexpensive crafts and antiques shops occupy an occasional storefront. An alleyway of shops off Main Street (at 224 Main St., across from Lutes Casino) has a potpourri of small tourist-oriented stores. Within just a couple of blocks of downtown, you can play in the sand or go for a stroll in Colorado River Crossing Beach Park, along the bank of the Colorado River. The park is at the north end of Madison Street.

DATES & DESERT TOURING

Date palms, that other symbol of the Middle East, also flourish here in the heat of the Arizona desert. Dates are among the most ancient of cultivated tree crops and were grown in the Middle East as far back as 3000 B.C. Right in Yuma, you'll find **Ehrlich's Date Garden,** 868 Ave. B (☎ **520/783-4778**), which sells nearly a dozen varieties of organically grown dates, as well as organic oranges. Prices are incredibly low, and the old-fashioned fruit stand is open daily 9am to 5pm 9 (but closed mid-May to August).

The Colorado River has been the lifeblood of the Southwestern desert for centuries, and today there's a wealth of history along its banks. **Yuma River Tours,** 1920 Arizona Ave. (☎ **520/783-4400**), operates narrated jet-boat tours from Yuma to the Imperial Wildlife Refuge (great bird watching) and an extended trip to Draper. Along the way, you'll learn about the homesteaders, boatmen, Native Americans, and miners who relied on the Colorado River. Tours, including lunch, cost $52 to $69. Alternatively, you can take a 3-hour paddle-wheel trip on the *Colorado King I* (☎ **520/ 782-2412**). Tours are $25 to $39 for adults and $15 to $20 for children 12 and under.

While the river was the reason for Yuma's existence, it was the railroad that finally forced the town to abandon its connection to the Colorado. Today you can ride the rails on the historic **Yuma Valley Railway** (☎ **520/783-3456**), which offers 34-mile excursions along the Colorado River between October and May. Along the way you may spot birds and other wildlife on the banks of the river, and you'll get views of Mexico across the river and rich agricultural lands on this side. Passengers ride in a 1922 Pullman coach pulled by a 1952 Davenport-Beshler diesel-electric engine. Fares are $11 for adults, $10 for seniors, and $6 for children ages 4 to 16. There are also picnic and steak runs.

If you're a bird watcher, an angler, or a canoeist, you'll want to spend some time along the Colorado River north of Yuma. Here you'll find the **Imperial and Cibola National Wildlife Refuges,** with their lakes and marshes. Plenty of bird species, good fishing and canoeing, and several campgrounds make it a popular area. For more information on this area, contact the Imperial Refuge (☎ **520/783-3371**) or the Cibola Refuge (☎ **520/857-3253**). One of the best ways to explore the Imperial National Wildlife Refuge is from a canoe. Boats can be rented from **Martinez Lake Resort** (☎ **520/783-9589**) for $32 a day plus shuttle and delivery charges. Both 1- and 2-day canoe trips are possible along this stretch of the lower Colorado, which features rugged, colorful mountains and quiet backwater areas.

Bird watchers will also want to head out to the **Betty's Kitchen Wildlife and Interpretive Area** and the adjacent **Mittry Lake.** To reach these areas, take exit 7E off I-8 and go north for 9 miles, at which point the road turns to gravel. Turn left in ¼ mile to reach Betty's Kitchen; continue straight on the gravel road to reach Mittry Lake. Fall and spring migration times are some of the best times of year for birding at these spots, but many waterfowl winter in the area.

GOLF

Golf courses cater to the snowbirds who descend on this area every winter. The **Mesa del Sol Golf Club,** 12213 Calle del Cid (☎ **520/342-1283**), off I-8 at the Fortuna Road exit, is the most challenging local course open to the public. On the other hand, the **Desert Hills Golf Course,** 1245 W. Desert Hills Dr. (☎ **520/344-GOLF**), has been rated the best municipal course in the state. Other area courses include the **Arroyo Dunes Golf Course,** 32nd Street and Avenue A (☎ **520/726-8350**), and the **Cocopah Bend RV Resort,** 6800 Strand Ave. (☎ **520/343-1663**). The 9-hole **Ironwood Public Golf Course,** 2945 W. Eighth St. (☎ **520/343-1466**), is worth a round if you're in the mood for only a quick nine holes.

WHERE TO STAY
MODERATE

Inn Suites Hotel Yuma Best Western. 1450 S. Castle Dome Ave., Yuma, AZ 85365-1732. ☎ **800/922-2034** or 520/783-8341. Fax 520/783-1349. 166 units. A/C TV TEL. $74–$109 double. Rates include continental breakfast. AE, DC, DISC, MC, V. Pets accepted.

If you've come to Yuma to escape the cold weather up north and want to enjoy some active sports, this hotel may be just what you're looking for. It has a pool, whirlpool, exercise room, and tennis courts, and there's a golf course nearby. The rooms are divided between studios and one- and two-bedroom suites, and all have microwave ovens, coffeemakers, refrigerators, and hair dryers. A poolside cafe serves breakfast, sandwiches, snacks, and cocktails. The hotel also offers complimentary afternoon cocktails.

La Fuente Inn & Suites. 1513 E. 16th St., Yuma, AZ 85365. ☎ **800/841-1814** or 520/329-1814. Fax 520/343-2671. www.lafuenteinn.com. 96 units. A/C TV TEL. $78–$88 double. Rates include continental breakfast. AE, DC, DISC, MC, V.

Conveniently located just off the interstate at 16th Street, this appealing hotel is done in Spanish-colonial style with red-tile roof, pink stucco walls, and a fountain out front.

The theme continues in the lobby with rustic furnishings and a tile floor. French doors open onto the pool terrace and a large courtyard, around which the guest rooms are arranged. Standard rooms feature modern motel furnishings, while the well-designed suites offer much more space. The hotel offers a complimentary evening happy hour, whirlpool, and fitness room (and use of a nearby fitness center).

Shilo Inn. 1550 S. Castle Dome Ave., Yuma, AZ 85365-1702. ☎ **800/222-2244** or 520/782-9511. Fax 520/783-1538. 134 units. A/C TV TEL. $89–$135 double; $129–$195 suite. Rates include full breakfast. AE, CB, DC, DISC, MC, V. Small supervised pets accepted ($10).

Located on the edge of town overlooking farmland and desert, the Shilo Inn is Yuma's most luxurious hotel, and the neatly manicured gardens provide an oasis of greenery in this dry landscape. The guest rooms have comfortable chairs, couches, and patios, as well as microwaves, refrigerators, and VCRs. In the bathrooms you'll find plenty of counter space and a hair dryer. The hotel's more expensive rooms are those with a view of the desert. For long-term stays, there are suites with kitchenettes. The hotel's casual dining room offers both indoor and terrace dining, and to one side of the dining room is a lounge that often has live music on weekends. The hotel offers room service, a large pool, a whirlpool, an exercise room, a sauna, and a steam room.

INEXPENSIVE

In addition to numerous older budget motels, Yuma has several newer budget chain motels, including two **Motel 6s** and a **Super 8.**

WHERE TO DINE

California Bakery Company. 284 S. Main St. ☎ **520/782-7335.** Reservations recommended. Lunch $5–$8; dinner main courses $10–$19. AE, MC, V. Mon–Sat 9am–3pm; Thurs–Sat 5–10pm. Closed during the summer. REGIONAL AMERICAN.

With decor more like what you'd find in Scottsdale or Santa Monica, this cavernous restaurant seems out of place in downtown Yuma, but the contemporary setting is quite welcome in this otherwise very traditional town. The owners seem to want to cover all the bases; within these walls you'll find a bakery (which opens at 9am), an espresso bar, a bar, and a restaurant (and there's live music on weekends). The menu isn't quite as contemporary as the interior decor, but you can get a tasty tortilla soup, blackened salmon Caesar salad, chicken cordon bleu, and lamb shanks braised in wine sauce. The smoked salmon rolls are a nibble-perfect appetizer. Definitely a step above burgers and fries.

✪ **The Garden Cafe.** 250 Madison Ave. ☎ **520/783-1491.** Main courses $5–$8.25. AE, MC, V. Tues–Fri 9am–2:30pm; Sat–Sun 8am–2:30pm. BREAKFAST/SANDWICHES/SALADS.

In back of the Century House Museum, you'll find Yuma's favorite breakfast and lunch cafe. Set amid quiet terraced gardens and large aviaries full of singing birds, The Garden Cafe provides a welcome respite from Yuma's heat. On the hottest days, misters spray the air with a gentle fog that keeps the gardens cool. There's also an indoor dining area. The menu consists of various delicious sandwiches, daily special quiches, salads, and rich desserts. Pancakes with lingonberry sauce are a breakfast specialty. On Sunday there's a brunch buffet. This place is a favorite of the ladies' lunch crowd and retirees.

✪ **Lutes Casino.** 221 S. Main St. ☎ **520/782-2192.** Main courses $3–$6. No credit cards. Mon–Fri 10am–8pm; Fri–Sat 10am–9pm; Sun 10am–6pm. Sometimes closes earlier. BURGERS/SANDWICHES.

You won't find any slot machines or poker tables at Lutes Casino anymore, just lots of very serious domino players (this is the state's only domino parlor). Today Lute's is a dark and cavernous pool hall, but it's better known as a family restaurant serving the best hamburgers in town. You don't need to see a menu—just walk in and ask for a special, or *especial* (this is a bilingual joint). What you'll get is a cheeseburger/hot dog combo. Then cover your special with Lute's own secret-recipe hot sauce to make it truly special.

Appendix: Arizona in Depth

Despite the searing summer temperatures, the desolate deserts, and the lack of water, people have been lured to Arizona for generations. In the 16th century, the Spanish came looking for gold—but settled for saving souls. In the 19th century, cattle ranchers came (despite frightful tales of spiny cactus forests) and found that a few corners of the state actually had lush grasslands. At the same time, sidetracked '49ers were scouring the hills for gold (and found more than the Spanish did). However, boomtowns—both cattle and mining—soon went bust. Despite occasional big strikes (such as the silver strike at Tombstone), mining didn't prove itself until the early 20th century, and even then, the mother lode was not gold or silver, but copper, which Arizona has in such abundance that it is called the Copper State.

In the 1920s and 1930s, Arizona struck a new vein of gold. The railroads made travel to Arizona easy, and the word of the mild winter climate spread to colder corners of the nation. Among the first "vacationers" were people suffering from tuberculosis. These "lungers," as they were known, rested and recuperated in the dry desert air. It didn't take long for the perfectly healthy to realize that they, too, could enjoy winter in Arizona, and wintering in the desert soon became fashionable with wealthy northerners.

Today it's still the golden sun that lures people to Arizona. Scottsdale, Phoenix, Tucson, and Sedona are home to some of the most luxurious and expensive resorts in the country, and more are under construction. The state has seen a massive influx of retirees, many of whom have found the few pockets of Arizona where the climate is absolutely perfect—not too hot, not too cold, and plenty of sunshine.

Although it's the Grand Canyon that attracts the most visitors to Arizona, the state has plenty of other natural wonders. The largest meteorite crater, the largest natural travertine bridge in the world, the spectacular red-rock country of Sedona, the sandstone buttes of Monument Valley, and "forests" of saguaro cacti are just a few of the state's other natural spectacles.

The human hand has also left its mark on Arizona. More than 1,000 years ago, the Anasazi, Sinagua, and Hohokam tribes built villages on mesas, in valleys, and in the steep cliff walls of deep canyons. In more recent years, much larger structures have risen in canyons across the state. The Hoover and Glen Canyon dams on the Colorado River are among the largest dams in the country and have created the nation's largest and most spectacular reservoirs, although at the expense of the rich riparian areas that once filled the now flooded desert canyons. Today these reservoirs are among the state's most popular destinations, especially with Arizonans, who flock to the water with an amazing variety of high-powered watercraft.

Just as compelling as its sunshine, resorts, and reservoirs are the tall tales of Arizona's fascinating history. This is the Wild West, the land of cowboys and Indians, of prospectors and ghost towns, coyotes and rattlesnakes. Scratch the glossy surface of modern, urbanized Arizona and you'll strike real gold—the story of the American West.

1 The Natural Environment

Although the very mention of Arizona may cause some people to turn the air conditioner on full blast, this state is much more than a searing landscape of cactus and creosote bush. From the baking shores of the lower Colorado River to the snowcapped heights of the San Francisco Peaks, Arizona encompasses virtually every North American climatic zone. Cactus flowers bloom in the spring, and mountain wildflowers have their turn in summer. In autumn the aspens color the White Mountains golden, and in winter snows blanket the higher elevations from the north rim of the Grand Canyon to the Mexican border.

But it's the Sonoran Desert, with its massive saguaro cacti, that most people associate with Arizona, and it is here in the desert that the state's two largest cities—Phoenix and Tucson—are to be found. The Sonoran Desert is among the world's most biologically diverse deserts. This is due in large part to the relatively plentiful rains in the region. In the Arizona desert, rain falls during both the winter and the late summer. This latter rainy season, when clamorous thunderstorms send flash floods surging down arroyos, is known as the monsoon season and is the most dramatic time of year in the desert. The sunsets are unforgettable, but then so, too, is the heat and humidity.

Before the coming of dams and deep wells, many Arizona rivers and streams flowed year-round and nurtured a surprising variety of plants and animals. Today, however, only a few rivers and creeks still flow unaltered through the desert. They include Sonoita and Aravaipa creeks and the San Pedro, Verde, and Hassayampa rivers. The green riparian areas along these watercourses are characterized by the rare cottonwood-willow forest and serve as magnets for wildlife, harboring rare birds as well as fish species unique to Arizona.

The saguaro cactus, which can stand 40 feet tall and weigh several tons, is the Sonoran Desert's most conspicuous native inhabitant. Massive and many-armed, these are the cacti of comic strips and Hollywood Westerns. However, this desert is home to many other lesser-known species of cactus, including organ pipe cactus (closely related to the saguaro), barrel cactus, and various species of prickly pears and chollas. Despite their spiny defenses, cacti are still a source of food and shelter for many species of desert animals. Bats sip the nectar from saguaro flowers, and in the process act as pollinators. Javelinas (collared peccaries), which are similar to wild pigs, chow down on the prickly pear fruit—spines and all. Gila woodpeckers nest in holes in saguaro trunks, while cactus wrens build their nests in the branches of the cholla cactus.

Just as cacti have adapted to the desert, so have the animals that live here. Many desert animals spend sweltering days in burrows and venture out only in the cool of the night. Under cover of darkness, rattlesnakes and great horned owls hunt kangaroo rats, coyotes howl, and javelinas root about for anything

Arizona: Hollywood Back Lot

Spectacular landscapes, rugged deserts, ghost towns, and the cowboy mystique have, over the years, made Arizona the location for hundreds of films. From obscure B Westerns starring long-forgotten singing cowboys to the seminal works of John Ford, Arizona has provided a stunning backdrop to stories of life in the Wild West. This state has become so associated with the Old West that Europeans, Asians, and Australians come from halfway around the world to walk where John Wayne once swaggered and where Clint Eastwood cultivated his outlaw image.

Over the years, Arizona has represented the past, the present, and the future, and the state's landscape is so varied that it has doubled for Texas, Kansas, Mexico, foreign planets, a postapocalyptic earth, and even New York. Production companies working on movies, television shows, and commercials have traveled to every corner of the state to find just the right setting for their productions.

In 1939, a movie set was built in Tucson for the filming of the movie *Arizona,* and when the shooting was done, the set was left to be used in other productions. Today this mock-Western town is known as Old Tucson Studios and is still used for film and video productions. Movies that have been filmed here include *Tombstone;* John Wayne's *Rio Lobo, Rio Bravo,* and *El Dorado;* Clint Eastwood's *The Outlaw Josey Wales;* Kirk Douglas's *Gunfight at the O.K. Corral;* and Paul Newman's *The Life and Times of Judge Roy Bean.*

Although John Ford was not the first to film at Monument Valley, he made this otherworldly landscape a trademark of his filmmaking, using the valley as the backdrop for such films as *Stagecoach, She Wore a Yellow Ribbon, My Darling Clementine, Rio Grande,* and *The Searchers.* Other Westerns filmed here have included *How the West Was Won, The Legend of the Lone Ranger,* and *Mackenna's Gold.* The valley has shown up in such non-Western films as *Back to the Future III, 2001: A Space Odyssey, Thelma and Louise,* and *Forrest Gump.* The red rocks of Sedona have attracted many filmmakers over the years. *Broken Arrow, 3:10 to Yuma, The Riders of the Purple Sage,* and *The Call of the Canyon* were all filmed in Sedona and the nearby Oak Creek Canyon.

The area around the small town of Patagonia, in southeastern Arizona, has served as a backdrop for quite a few films, including *Oklahoma!, Red River, McClintock, Broken Lance, David and Bathsheba,* and *A Star Is Born,* and television programs, including "Little House on the Prairie," "The Young Riders," and "Red Badge of Courage."

edible. Gila lizards, among the only poisonous lizards in the world, drag their ungainly bodies through the dust, while tarantulas tiptoe silently in search of unwary insects.

Outside the desert regions there is great diversity as well. In the southern part of the state, small mountain ranges rise abruptly from the desert floor, creating refuges for plants and animals that require cooler climates. It is these so-called sky islands that harbor the greatest varieties of bird species in the continental United States. Birds from both warm and cold climates find homes in such oases as Ramsey, Madera, and Cave Creek canyons.

Although rugged mountain ranges crisscross the state, only a few rise to such heights that they support actual forests. Among these are the Santa Catalinas outside Tucson, the White Mountains along the state's eastern border, and the San Francisco Peaks north of Flagstaff. However, it's atop the Mogollon Rim and the Kaibab Plateau that the ponderosa pine forests cover the greatest areas. The Mogollon Rim is a 2,000-foot-high escarpment that stretches from central Arizona all the way into New Mexico. The ponderosa pine forest here is the largest in the world and is dotted with lakes well known for their fishing. The Mogollon Rim area is also home to large herds of elk. At over 8,000 feet in elevation, the Kaibab Plateau is even higher than the Mogollon Rim, yet it is through this plateau that the Grand Canyon cuts.

This then is the natural environment of Arizona, a land of extremes where summer temperatures in the Sonoran Desert top 120°F while snow still lies atop the San Francisco Peaks. Life here has adapted to these extremes in fascinating ways still being deciphered by biologists throughout the state.

2 Arizona Today

Combining aspects of Native American, Hispanic, and European cultures, Arizona is one of the most culturally diverse states in the country. Here the Old West and the "New West" coexist. While the wealthy residents of Scottsdale raise Arabian horses as investments, the Navajos of the Four Corners region still raise sheep for sustenance and wool, herding their flocks from the backs of hard-working horses. Vacationers on Lake Powell water-ski through flooded canyons while cowboys in the southeast corner of the state still ride the range, mending fences and rounding up cattle.

Although Arizonans are today more likely to drive Hondas and Toyotas than to ride pintos and appaloosas, Western wear is still the preferred fashion of rich and poor alike. Cowboy boots, cowboy hats, blue jeans, and bolo ties are acceptable attire at almost any function in Arizona. Horses are still used on ranches around the state, but most are kept simply for recreational or investment purposes. In Scottsdale, one of the nation's centers of Arabian horse breeding, horse auctions attract a well-heeled (read lizard-skin–booted) crowd, and horses sell for tens of thousands of dollars. Even the state's dude ranches, which now call themselves "guest ranches," have changed their image, and many are as likely to offer tennis and swimming as horseback riding.

A long legacy of movies being filmed here has further blurred the line between the real West and the Hollywood West. More city slickers wander the streets of the Old Tucson movie set and videotape shoot-outs at the O.K. Corral than ever saddle up a palomino or ride herd on a cattle drive. Even dinner has been raised to a cowboy entertainment form at Arizona's many Wild West steakhouses, where families are entertained by cowboy bands, staged gunfights, hayrides, and sing-alongs, all in the name of reliving the glory days of "cowboys and Indians."

For Arizona's Indians, those were days of hardship and misery, and today the state's many tribes continue to strive for the sort of economic well-being enjoyed by the state's non-native population. Traditional ways are still alive, but tribes must struggle to preserve their unique cultures—their languages, religious beliefs and ceremonies, livelihoods, and architecture.

Arizona is home to the largest Indian reservation in the country—the Navajo nation—as well as nearly two dozen other smaller reservations. As elsewhere in the United States, poverty and alcoholism are major problems on Arizona reservations. However, several of the state's tribes have, through their arts and crafts, managed to both preserve some of their traditional culture and share it with non-natives. Among these tribes are the Navajo, known for their rugs and silver jewelry; the Hopi, known for their pottery and kachinas; the Zuni, known for their inlaid stone jewelry; and the Tohono O'odham, known for their baskets.

Lately, however, many non-natives have been visiting reservations not out of an interest in learning about another culture, but to gamble. Throughout the state, casinos have opened on reservation land, and despite the controversies surrounding such enterprises, many native peoples are finally seeing some income on their once-impoverished reservations.

Many of the people who visit these new casinos are retirees, who are among the fastest growing segment of Arizona's population. The state's mild winter climate has attracted tens of thousands of retirees to the state over the past few decades. Many of these winter residents, known as snowbirds, park their RVs outside such warm spots as Yuma and Quartzsite. Others, however, have come to stay and settled in retirement communities such as Sun City and Green Valley.

This graying of the population, combined with strong ranching and mining industries, has made Arizona one of the most conservative of states. Although by today's standards Barry Goldwater could almost be considered a liberal, his conservative politics were so much a part of the Arizona mindset that the state kept him in the Senate for 30 years.

Arizona's environmental politics have been somewhat contentious in recent years. Although many people think of the desert as a wasteland in need of transformation, others see it as a fragile ecosystem that has been endangered by the encroachment of civilization. Saguaro cacti throughout the state are protected by law, but the deserts they grow in are not. In Tucson, environmentalists have for several years been fighting (with limited success) to stop the suburban sprawl that's pushing farther and farther into saguaro country. The balance in this battle tipped in favor of preservation when rare ferruginous pygmy owls were found nesting in the Tucson area.

Way up at the north end of the state, remote Grand Canyon National Park is suffering from its own popularity. With more than five million visitors a year, the park now sees summer traffic jams and parking problems that have made a visit an exercise in patience. However, the national park is slowly implementing a plan to develop a combination light-rail and alternative-fuel bus system for transporting visitors to and around the South Rim and Grand Canyon Village. By having day-use visitors leave their cars outside the park and take the light rail to the South Rim, much of the park's traffic congestion should be alleviated. This new transportation system is not expected to be completed until 2004, but the new Canyon View Information Plaza, which will serve as the new visitor information center for the park, should be open to the public by the time you read this book.

In early 2000, President Clinton signed legislation creating two new national monuments in Arizona. The Grand Canyon–Parashant National Monument, in the northwest corner of the state adjacent to Grand Canyon National Park, preserves one of the most remote and inhospitable region's of the state. There are no paved roads within this monument and no visitor facilities. Although much more centrally located, the new Agua Fria National Monument, which preserves hundreds of Native American prehistoric sites, is only slightly less inaccessible. Once again, this national monument has no paved roads and no visitor facilities.

Efforts at preserving the state's environment make it clear that Arizonans value the outdoors, but a ski boat in every driveway doesn't mean the arts are ignored. Although it hasn't been too many years since evening entertainment in Arizona meant dance-hall girls or a harmonica by the campfire, Phoenix and Tucson have become centers for the visual and performing arts. The two cities share an opera company and a ballet company, and the Valley of the Sun is home to a number of symphony orchestras and theater companies. Early 1999 saw the opening of the Scottsdale Museum of Contemporary Art and a newly expanded Heard Museum. In Tucson, the Tucson Museum of Art has undergone a facelift and expansion.

Small towns around the state are supporting the arts. Whole communities such as Jerome, Tubac, and Bisbee, all nearly ghost towns at one time, have been reborn as arts communities. Where miners and outlaws once walked, artists now offer their creations for sale.

Tourism continues to boom in Arizona, and after a decade-long construction lull, new resorts are in the works in both the Valley of the Sun and Tucson. In particular, the north Scottsdale area, which has seen a residential building boom in recent years, is now seeing the construction of luxury resorts. Downtown Phoenix has now positioned itself as the state's sports and entertainment mecca, with Bank One Ballpark, the America West Arena, and numerous sports bars, nightclubs, and even a combination barbecue joint and sports bar operated by former rock star Alice Cooper. Scottsdale will soon be joining the sports scene with the construction of a new ice hockey arena for the NHL's Phoenix Coyotes. There is talk of a building a new football stadium for the Arizona Cardinals.

In Arizona today, the New West and the Old West are coming to grips with each other. Hopi perform their age-old dances atop their mesas. SUVs and convertible sports cars jockey for parking spaces at glitzy shopping centers in Phoenix and Tucson Grizzled wranglers lead vacationing Germans on horseback rides across open range. Ranchers find they have something in common with environmentalists—saving Arizona's ranch lands. What all these people have in common is a love of sunshine, which, of course, Arizona has in abundance.

3 History 101

Over the past 5 centuries, the land now known as Arizona has been Native American territory as well as part of New Spain, Mexico, and the United States. Early explorers and settlers saw little profit in the desert wasteland, but time proved them wrong: Mineral resources, cattle grazing, and cotton (after dams began providing irrigation water) all became important income sources. In this century, the economy has moved from the three Cs (copper, cattle, and cotton) to a service industries–based economy, with tourism as one of its major resources.

EARLY HISTORY Arizona is the site of North America's oldest cultures and one of the two longest continuously inhabited settlements in the United States (the Hopi village of

Dateline

- 9700 B.C. Paleo-Indians (the Clovis people) in southeastern Arizona are among the earliest recorded inhabitants of North America.
- A.D. 200 The Anasazi people move into Canyon de Chelly.
- 450 Hohokam peoples farm the Salt and Gila river valleys, eventually building 600 miles of irrigation canals.

continues

- **650** The Sinagua cultivate land northeast of present-day Flagstaff.
- **1100s** Hopi tribes build Oraibi village, the oldest continuously occupied village in the United States; the Anasazi build cliff dwellings in Canyon de Chelly; the Sinagua build Wupatki.
- **1250** The Sinagua abandon Wupatki and other pueblos.
- **1300** The Anasazi abandon cliff dwellings in Canyon de Chelly and Tsegi Canyon.
- **1350** The Hohokam build Casa Grande in the Gila River valley.
- **1400s** The Navajo people migrate south from Canada to northeastern Arizona.
- **1450** The Hohokam abandon lowland desert villages; the Sinagua abandon Verde Valley villages.
- **1539** Marcos de Niza ventures into present-day Arizona from Mexico (New Spain) in search of the Seven Cities of Cíbola.
- **1540s** Francisco Vásquez de Coronado leads an expedition to Arizona in search of gold.
- **1691** Jesuit Fr. Eusebio Kino begins converting Native Americans.
- **1751** The mission of Tumacacori and the presidio of Tubac, the first European settlement in Arizona, are established.
- **1776** A Spanish garrison is established in Tucson to protect the mission of San Xavier del Bac.
- **1821** Mexico gains independence from Spain and takes control of Arizona.
- **1848** Most of present-day Arizona is ceded to the United States following the Mexican-American War.
- **1853** In the Gadsden Purchase, the United States

continues

Oraibi). However, the region's human habitation dates back more than 11,000 years, to the time when Paleo-Indians known as the Clovis people inhabited southeastern Arizona. Stone tools and arrowheads of the type credited to the Clovis people have been found in southeastern Arizona, and a mammoth-kill site has become an important source of information about these people, some of the earliest inhabitants of North America.

Few records exist of the next 9,000 years of Arizona's history, but by about A.D. 200, wandering bands of hunter-gatherers began living in Canyon de Chelly in the north. These people would come to be known as the *Anasazi,* a Navajo word that means "the ancient ones." The earliest Anasazi period, from A.D. 200 to 700, is called the Basket Maker period because of the numbers of baskets that have been found in Anasazi ruins from this time. During this period the Anasazi gave up hunting and gathering and took up agriculture, growing corn, beans, squash, and cotton on the canyon floors in northeastern Arizona. In recent years, the term "Anasazi" has been replaced with "ancestral Puebloan," which is considered a more appropriate description of the people who built the many pueblos (villages) scattered across northern Arizona.

During the Pueblo period, between 700 and 1300, the Anasazi began building multistory pueblos and cliff dwellings. Despite decades of research, it is still unknown why the Anasazi began living in niches and caves high on the cliff walls of the region's canyons. It may have been to conserve farmland as their population grew and required larger harvests or for protection from flash floods or attacks by hostile neighbors. Whatever the reason, the Anasazi cliff dwellings were all abandoned by 1300. It's unknown why the villages were abandoned, but a study of tree rings indicates that the region experienced a severe drought between 1276 and 1299, which suggests the Anasazi left in search of more fertile farmland. Keet Seel and Betatakin, at Navajo National Monument, and the many ruins in Canyon de Chelly, are Arizona's best-preserved Anasazi ruins.

During the Anasazi Basket Maker period, another culture was beginning to develop in the fertile plateau northeast of present-day Flagstaff and southward into the Verde River valley. The *Sinagua,* a Spanish name that means "without water," built their stone pueblos primarily on hills and mesas such as those at Tuzigoot near Clarkdale and Wupatki near Flagstaff. They built cliff dwellings at places such as Walnut Canyon and Montezuma Castle. However, by the mid-13th century, Wupatki had been abandoned, and by the early 15th century Walnut Canyon and pueblos in the lower Verde Valley region had been abandoned.

By A.D. 450 the Hohokam culture, from whom the Sinagua learned irrigation, had begun to farm the Gila and Salt river valleys between Phoenix and Casa Grande. Over a period of 1,000 years, they constructed a 600-mile network of irrigation canals, some of which can still be seen today. Because the Hohokam built their homes of earth, few Hohokam ruins remain. However, one building, the Casa Grande ruin, has been well preserved, and throughout the desert the Hohokam left **petroglyphs** (rock carvings) as a lasting reminder that they once dwelt in this region. By the 1450s, the tribe had abandoned its villages and disappeared without a sign, hence the name *Hohokam*, a Tohono O'odham word meaning "all used up" or "the people who have gone." Archaeologists believe that the irrigation of desert soil for hundreds of years had left a thick crust of alkali on the surface, which made further farming impossible.

HISPANIC HERITAGE   The first Europeans to visit the region may have been a motley crew of shipwrecked Spaniards among whom was a black man named Estévan de Dorantes. This unfortunate group spent 8 years wandering from a beach in Florida to a Spanish village in Mexico. These wanderers arrived back in Spanish territory with a fantastic story of seven cities so rich in gold and jewels that the inhabitants even decorated their doorways with jewels. No one is sure whether they actually passed through Arizona, but their story convinced the viceroy of New Spain (Mexico) to send a small expedition, led by Fr. Marcos de Niza and Estévan de Dorantes, into the region. Father de Niza's report of finding the fabled Seven Cities of Cíbola inspired Don Francisco Vásquez de Coronado to set off in search of wealth. However, instead of fabulously wealthy cities, Coronado found only pueblos of stone and mud. A subordinate expedition led by Garcia Lopez de Cárdenas stumbled upon the Grand Canyon, while another group of Coronado's men, led by Don Pedro de Tovar, visited the Hopi mesas.

acquires the remainder of Arizona from Mexico.

- **1862** Arizona becomes the Confederate Territory of Arizona but is reclaimed by the Union later that same year.
- **1863** Arizona becomes a U.S. territory.
- **1869** Maj. John Wesley Powell explores the Grand Canyon by boat.
- **1880** Southern Pacific Railroad arrives in Tucson.
- **1881** Shoot-out at the O.K. Corral.
- **1886** Geronimo surrenders to the U.S. Army.
- **1911** Theodore Roosevelt Dam, on the Salt River, enables irrigation and development of the desert.
- **1912** Arizona becomes the 48th state.
- **1919** Grand Canyon National Park established.
- **1936** Hoover Dam completed.
- **1948** Arizona Indians receive the right to vote.
- **1981** Arizona judge Sandra Day O'Connor becomes the first woman appointed to the U.S. Supreme Court.
- **1991** A California jury finds Charles Keating guilty of defrauding Arizona investors who had deposited funds with Lincoln Savings and Loan.
- **1997** Gov. Fife Symington is convicted of bank fraud and resigns as governor.
- **1998** Bank One Ballpark, with retractable roof, opens in Phoenix.
- **2000** President Clinton creates two new national monuments in Arizona.

In the 150 years that followed, only a handful of Spaniards visited Arizona. In the 1580s and 1600s, Antonio de Espejo and Juan de Oñate explored northern and central Arizona and found indications that there were mineral riches in the region. In the 1670s, the Franciscans founded several missions among the Hopi pueblos, but the Pueblo Revolt of 1680 obliterated this small Spanish presence.

In 1687, Fr. Eusebio Francisco Kino, a German-educated Italian Jesuit, began establishing missions in the Sonoran Desert region of northern New Spain. In 1691, he visited the Pima village of Tumacacori. Father Kino taught the inhabitants European farming techniques, planted fruit trees, and gave the natives cattle, sheep, and goats to raise. However, it was not until 1751, in response to a Pima rebellion, that the permanent mission of Tumacacori and the presidio (military post) of Tubac were built. Together these two Spanish outposts became the first European settlements in Arizona.

In 1775, a group of settlers led by Juan Bautista de Anza set out from Tubac to find an overland route to California, and in 1776 this group founded the city of San Francisco. That same year the Tubac presidio was moved to Tucson. As early as 1692 Father Kino had visited the Tucson area and by 1700 had laid out the foundations for the first church at the mission of San Xavier del Bac. However, it was not until sometime around 1783 that construction of the present church, known as the White Dove of the Desert, began.

In 1821, Mexico won its independence from Spain, and Tucson, with only 65 inhabitants, became part of Mexico. Mexico at that time extended all the way to northern California, but in 1848 most of this land, except for a small section of southern Arizona that included Tucson, became U.S. territory in the wake of the Mexican-American War. Five years later, in 1853, Mexico sold the remainder of southern Arizona to the United States in a transaction known as the Gadsden Purchase.

INDIAN CONFLICTS At the time the Spanish arrived in Arizona, the tribes living in the southern lowland deserts were peaceful farmers, but in the mountains of the east lived the Apache, a hunting-and-gathering tribe that frequently raided neighboring tribes. In the north, the Navajo, relatively recent immigrants to the region, fought over land with the neighboring Ute and Hopi (who were also fighting among themselves).

Coronado's expedition through Arizona and into New Mexico and Kansas was to seek gold. To that end he attacked one pueblo, killed the inhabitants of another, and forced still others to abandon their villages. Spanish-Indian relations were never to improve, and the Spanish were forced to occupy their new lands with a strong military presence. Around 1600, 300 Spanish settlers moved into the Four Corners region, which at the time supported a large population of Navajo. The Spanish raided Navajo villages to take slaves, and angry Navajo responded by stealing Spanish horses and cattle.

For several decades in the mid-1600s, missionaries were tolerated in the Hopi pueblos, but the Pueblo tribes revolted in 1680, killing the missionaries and destroying the missions. Encroachment by farmers and miners moving into the Santa Cruz Valley in the south caused the Pima people to stage a similar uprising in 1751, attacking and burning the mission at Tubac. This revolt led to the establishment of the presidio at Tubac that same year. When the military garrison moved to Tucson, Tubac was quickly abandoned because of frequent raids by Apaches. In 1781, the Yuman tribe, whose land at the confluence of the Colorado and Gila rivers had become a Spanish settlement, staged a similar uprising that wiped out the settlement at Yuma.

By the time Arizona became part of the United States, it was the Navajo and the Apache who were proving most resistant to white settlers. In 1864 the U.S. Army, under the leadership of Col. Kit Carson, forced the Navajo to surrender by destroying their winter food supplies and then shipped the survivors to an internment camp in New Mexico. Within 5 years they were returned to their land, although they were forced to live on a reservation.

The Apache resisted white settlement 20 years longer than the Navajo did. Skillful guerrilla fighters, the Apache, under the leadership of Geronimo and Cochise, attacked settlers, forts, and towns despite the presence of U.S. Army troops sent to protect the white settlers. Geronimo and Cochise were the leaders of the last resistant bands of rebellious Apache. Cochise eventually died in his Chiricahua Mountains homeland, and Geronimo was finally forced to surrender in 1886. Geronimo and many of his followers were subsequently relocated to Florida by the U.S. government. Open conflicts between whites and Indians finally came to an end.

TERRITORIAL DAYS   In 1846, the United States went to war with Mexico, which at the time extended all the way to northern California and included parts of Colorado, Wyoming, and New Mexico. When the war ended, the United States claimed almost all the land extending from Texas to northern California. This newly acquired land, called the New Mexico Territory, had its capital at Santa Fe. The land south of the Gila River, which included Tucson, was still part of Mexico, but when surveys determined that this land was the best route for a railroad from southern Mississippi to southern California, the U.S. government negotiated the Gadsden Purchase. In 1853, this land purchase established the current Arizona-Mexico border.

When the California Gold Rush began in 1849, many hopeful miners crossed Arizona en route to the goldfields, and some stayed to seek mineral riches in Arizona. Despite the ever-increasing numbers of settlers, the U.S. Congress refused to create a separate Arizona Territory. When the Civil War broke out, Arizonans, angered by Congress's inaction on their request to become a separate territory, sided with the Confederacy; in 1862, Arizona was proclaimed the Confederate Territory of Arizona. Although Union troops easily defeated the Confederate troops who had occupied Tucson, this dissension convinced Congress, in 1863, to create the Arizona Territory.

The capital of the new territory was temporarily established at Fort Whipple near Prescott, but later the same year the capital was moved to Prescott, and in 1867 to Tucson. Ten years later Prescott again became the capital, which it remained for another 12 years before the seat of government moved finally to Phoenix, which is today the Arizona state capital.

During this period mining flourished, and although small amounts of gold and silver were discovered, copper became the source of Arizona's economic wealth. With each mineral strike, a new mining town would boom, and when the ore ran out, the town would be abandoned. These towns were infamous for their gambling halls, bordellos, saloons, and shoot-outs in the street. Tombstone and Bisbee became the largest towns in the state and were known as the wildest towns between New Orleans and San Francisco.

In 1867, farmers in the newly founded town of Phoenix began irrigating their fields using canals that had been dug centuries earlier by the Hohokam. In the 1870s, ranching became another important source of revenue in the territory, particularly in the southeastern and northwestern parts of the state. In the 1880s, the railroads finally arrived, and life in Arizona began to change drastically. Suddenly the mineral resources and cattle of the region were accessible to the East.

STATEHOOD & THE 20TH CENTURY   By the beginning of the 20th century, Arizonans were trying to convince Congress to make the territory a state. Congress balked at the requests, but finally in 1910 allowed the territorial government to draw up a state constitution. Territorial legislators were progressive thinkers, and the draft of Arizona's state constitution included clauses for the recall of elected officials. Pres. William Howard Taft vetoed the bill that would have made Arizona a state because he opposed the recall of judges. Arizona politicians removed the controversial clause, and on February 14, 1912, Arizona became the 48th state. One of the new state legislature's first acts was to reinstate the clause providing for the recall of judges.

Much of Washington's opposition to Arizona's statehood had been based on the belief that Arizona could never support economic development. This belief was changed in 1911 by one of the most important events in Arizona history—the completion of the Roosevelt Dam (later to be renamed the Theodore Roosevelt Dam) on the Salt River. The dam provided irrigation water to the Valley of the Sun and tamed the violent floods of the river. The introduction of water to the heart of Arizona's vast desert enabled large-scale agriculture and industry. Over the next decades more dams were built throughout Arizona. Completed in 1936, the Hoover Dam on the Colorado River became the largest concrete dam in the western hemisphere and formed the biggest manmade reservoir in North America. Arizona's dams would eventually provide not only water and electricity but recreation areas as well.

Despite labor problems, copper mining increased throughout the 1920s and 1930s, and with the onset of World War II the mines boomed as military munitions manufacturing increased the demand for copper. However, within a few years after the war, many mines were shut down. Arizona is still littered with old mining ghost towns that boomed and then went bust. A few towns, such as Jerome, Bisbee, and Chloride, managed to hang on after the mines shut down and were eventually rediscovered by artists, writers, and retirees. Bisbee and Jerome are now major tourist attractions known for their many art galleries.

World War II created demand for beef, leather, and cotton (which became the state's most important crop). During the war, clear desert skies proved ideal for training pilots, and several military bases were established in the state. Phoenix's population doubled during the war years, and after the war ended, many veterans returned with their families. However, it would take the invention of air-conditioning to truly open up the desert to major population growth.

During the postwar years, Arizona attracted a number of large manufacturing industries and slowly moved away from its agricultural economic base. Today, electronics manufacturing, aerospace engineering, and other high-tech industries provide employment for thousands of Arizonans. The largest segment of the economy, however, is now in the service industries, with tourism playing a crucial role.

Even by the 1920s, Arizona had become a winter destination for the wealthy, and the Grand Canyon, declared a national park in 1919, lured more and more visitors every year. The clear dry air attracted people suffering from allergies and lung ailments, and Arizona became known as a healthful place. Guest ranches of the 1930s eventually gave way to the resorts of the 1990s. Today Scottsdale and Phoenix boast the greatest concentration of resorts in the United States. In addition, tens of thousands of retirees from as far north as Canada make Arizona their winter home and play a crucial role in Arizona's economy.

Continued population growth throughout the 20th century created an ever greater demand for water. However, despite the damming of virtually all of Arizona's rivers, the state still suffered from insufficient water supplies in the south-central population centers of Phoenix and Tucson. It would take the construction of the controversial and expensive Central Arizona Project (CAP) aqueduct to carry water from the Colorado River over mountains and deserts and deliver it where it was wanted. Construction on the CAP began in 1974, and in 1985 water from the project finally began irrigating fields near Phoenix. In 1992, the CAP finally reached Tucson. However, with the populations of Phoenix, Tucson, and Las Vegas skyrocketing, the future of Colorado River water usage may again become a question for hot debate.

By the 1960s, Arizona had become an urban state with all the problems confronting other areas around the nation. The once-healthful air of Phoenix now rivals that of Los Angeles for the thickness of its smog. Allergy sufferers are plagued by pollen from the nondesert plants that have been planted to make this desert region look more lush and inviting. However, the state's economy is still growing. High-tech companies continue to locate within the state, and the continued influx of both retirees and Californians fleeing earthquakes and urban problems is giving the state new energy and new ideas.

4 A Look at Local Arts & Crafts

Although Santa Fe has for many years claimed the Southwest arts spotlight, Arizona, too, is a mecca for artists and art collectors. The Cowboy Artists of America, an organization of artists dedicated to capturing the lives and landscapes of the Old West, was formed in a tavern in Sedona in 1965 by Joe Beeler, George Phippen, Bob McLeod, Charlie Dye, John Hampton, and a few other local artists. Working primarily in oils and bronze, members of this organization depicted the lives of cowboys and Native Americans in their art, and today their work is sought after by collectors throughout the country.

As more and more artists and craftspeople headed for Arizona, the towns in which they congregated came to be known as artists' colonies, and galleries sprang up to serve a growing number of visitors. Although Sedona is probably the best known of these communities, others include the former mining towns of Jerome and Bisbee, and Tubac, the first Spanish settlement in Arizona. All three have numerous galleries and crafts shops. However, it is upscale Scottsdale that has the state's highest concentration of art galleries.

Red-rock canyons, pensive Indians, hardworking cowboys, desert wildflowers, majestic mesas, and stately saguaros have been the themes of this century's representational artists of Arizona. Although contemporary abstract art can be found in museums and galleries, the style pioneered by Frederic Remington and Charles M. Russell in the early 20th century still dominates the Arizona art scene. Remington, Russell, and those who followed in their footsteps romanticized the West, imbuing their depictions of cowboys, Indians, settlers, and soldiers with mythic proportions that would be taken up by Hollywood.

Further back, even before the first Spanish explorers arrived in Arizona, the ancient Anasazi were creating an artistic legacy in their intricately woven baskets, painted pottery, and cryptic petroglyphs and pictographs. In recent years both contemporary Native American and non-native artists have been drawing on Anasazi designs for their works. Today's Hopi, Navajo, and Zuni artisans have become well known for their jewelry, which is made of silver and semiprecious stones, primarily turquoise. The Hopi now carve images of their traditional kachinas for commercial distribution, and the Navajo continue to weave traditional patterns in their rugs. The Zuni, noted for their skill in carving stone, have focused on their traditional animal fetishes. However, since the founding of the Santa Fe Indian School in 1932, and later the Institute of American Indian Art, Indian artists have ventured into the realm of painting. Hopi artist Fred Kabotie and his son, Michael Kabotie, are among the best-known Native American painters.

Collectors, and those with a casual interest in Southwestern art, will find local arts and crafts available in every corner of the state. From exclusive Scottsdale galleries to roadside stands on the Navajo Reservation, Arizona arts and crafts are ubiquitous. The best places to look for Southwestern and cowboy (or Western) art are in Scottsdale, Tucson, Sedona, Tubac, and Jerome. Native American crafts can be found in these same towns, but it's somewhat more rewarding to visit trading posts and reservation studios and shops.

The best known of the trading posts are the Hubbell Trading Post in Ganado and the Cameron Trading Post in Cameron, but there are trading posts all over the state and many offer excellent selection and quality. Keep in mind that no matter where you shop for Native American arts and crafts, you'll find that prices are high.

The Indian tribes of Arizona tend to have one or two specialty crafts that they produce with consummate skill. Many of these crafts were disappearing when the first traders came to the reservations more than a century ago. Today most of the crafts are alive and well, but primarily as collectibles, not as items for everyday use. Prices are high because of the many hours that go into producing these items—what you're buying is handmade, using techniques that sometimes go back for generations.

Keep in mind when making purchases that you can avoid paying sales tax if you live outside Arizona and have your purchase shipped directly to your home. On a high-ticket item such as a Navajo rug, you could save quite a bit. Keep in mind that it's a good idea to make your jewelry purchases from reputable stores rather than from roadside stalls, of which there are many in the Four Corners region of the state. Many of these stalls sell cheap imitation Indian jewelry.

For a discussion of individual native crafts, see "A Native American Crafts Primer" in chapter 7, "The Four Corners Region: Land of the Hopi & Navajo."

5 Recommended Books

HISTORY Marshall Trimble's *Roadside History of Arizona* (Mountain Press Publishing, 1986) is an ideal book to take along on a driving tour of the state. The book goes road by road and discusses events that happened in the area. For a more thorough history of the state, pick up Thomas E. Sheridan's *Arizona: A History* (University of Arizona Press, 1995), an exploration of the state's past 11,000 years. *Arizona Memories* (University of Arizona, 1984), edited by Anne H. Morgan and Rennard Strickland, is an engaging collection of historical recollections by cowboys, miners, an Apache scout, a frontier doctor, a soldier's wife, and many other Arizonans.

THE GRAND CANYON/COLORADO RIVER John Wesley Powell's diary produced the first published account (1869) of traveling through the Grand Canyon. Today, his writings still provide a fascinating glimpse into the canyon and the first trip through it. *The Exploration of the Colorado River and Its Canyons* (Penguin, 1997), with an introduction by Wallace Stegner, is a recent republishing of Powell's writings. Stegner, with Bernard Devoto, writes about Powell in his *Beyond the Hundredth Meridian: John Wesley Powell and the Second Opening of the West* (Penguin USA, 1992). For an interesting account of the recent human history of the canyon, read Stephen J. Pyne's *How The Canyon Became Grand* (Viking Penguin, 1999), which focuses on the explorers, writers, and artists who have contributed to our current concept of the canyon. *The Man Who Walked Through Time* (Vintage Books, 1989), by Colin Fletcher, is a narrative of one man's hike through the rugged inner canyon. In *Down the River* (E.P. Dutton, 1991), Western environmentalist Edward Abbey chronicles many of his trips down the Colorado and other Southwest rivers. Among the essays here are descriptions of Glen Canyon before Lake Powell was created.

Water rights and human impact on the deserts of the Southwest have raised many controversies this century, none more heated than those centering on the Colorado River. *Cadillac Desert: The American West and Its Disappearing Water* (Penguin, 1993), by Marc Reisner, focuses on the West's insatiable need for water. *A River No More: The Colorado River and the West* (University of California Press, 1996), by Philip L. Fradkin, addresses the fate of the Colorado River.

NATURAL HISTORY/OUTDOORS   *Roadside Geology of Arizona* (Mountain Press Publishing, 1998), by Halka Chronic, is another handy book to keep in the car. If you're a hiker, you'll find Scott S. Warren's *100 Hikes in Arizona* (The Mountaineers, 1994) another invaluable traveling companion.

FICTION   Tony Hillerman is perhaps the best-known contemporary author whose books rely on Arizona settings. Hillerman's murder mysteries are almost all set on the Navajo Reservation in the Four Corners area and include many references to actual locations that can be seen by visitors to the area. Among Hillerman's Navajo mysteries are *Hunting Badger, The First Eagle, Sacred Clowns, Coyote Waits, Thief of Time, The Blessing Way, Listening Woman, The Ghostway,* and *The Fallen Man.*

Barbara Kingsolver, a biologist and social activist, has set several of her novels either partly or entirely in Arizona. *The Bean Trees, Pigs in Heaven,* and *Animal Dreams* are peopled by Anglo, Indian, and Hispanic characters, allowing for quirky, humorous narratives with social and political overtones that provide insights into Arizona's cultural mélange. Kingsolver's nonfiction works include *High Tide in Tucson* (HarperPerennial, 1996) and *Holding the Line: Women in the Great Arizona Mine Strike of 1983* (HarperPerennial, 1997). The former is a collection of essays, many of which focus on the author's life in Tucson, and the latter is an account of a copper-mine strike.

Edward Abbey's *The Monkey Wrench Gang* (Avon/Eos, 1997) and *Hayduke Lives!* (Little Brown & Co., 1991) are tales of an unlikely gang of "ecoterrorists" determined to preserve the wildernesses of the Southwest, including parts of northern Arizona. The former book helped inspire the founding of the radical Earth First! movement.

Zane Grey spent many years living in north-central Arizona and based many of his Western novels on life in this region of the state. Among his books are *Riders of the Purple Sage, The Vanishing American, Call of the Canyon, The Arizona Clan,* and *To the Last Man.*

TRAVEL   If you're particularly interested in Native American art and crafts, you may want to search out a copy of *Trading Post Guidebook* (Northland Publishing, 1995), by Patrick Eddington and Susan Makov, an invaluable guide to trading posts, artists' studios, galleries, and museums in the Four Corners region.

Index

See also Accommodations and Restaurant indexes, below.

General Index

ACCOMMODATIONS

RESTAURANTS

FROMMER'S® COMPLETE TRAVEL GUIDES

Alaska
Amsterdam
Arizona
Atlanta
Australia
Austria
Bahamas
Barcelona, Madrid &
  Seville
Beijing
Belgium, Holland &
  Luxembourg
Bermuda
Boston
British Columbia & the
  Canadian Rockies
Budapest & the Best of
  Hungary
California
Canada
Cancún, Cozumel &
  the Yucatán
Cape Cod, Nantucket &
  Martha's Vineyard
Caribbean
Caribbean Cruises & Ports
  of Call
Caribbean Ports of Call
Carolinas & Georgia
Chicago
China
Colorado
Costa Rica
Denmark
Denver, Boulder & Colorado
  Springs
England
Europe

European Cruises & Ports
  of Call
Florida
France
Germany
Greece
Greek Islands
Hawaii
Hong Kong
Honolulu, Waikiki &
  Oahu
Ireland
Israel
Italy
Jamaica
Japan
Las Vegas
London
Los Angeles
Maryland & Delaware
Maui
Mexico
Miami & the Keys
Montana & Wyoming
Montréal & Québec City
Munich & the Bavarian
  Alps
Nashville & Memphis
Nepal
New England
New Mexico
New Orleans
New York City
New Zealand
Nova Scotia, New Brunswick
  & Prince Edward Island
Oregon
Paris

Philadelphia & the
  Amish Country
Portugal
Prague & the Best of the
  Czech Republic
Provence & the Riviera
Puerto Rico
Rome
San Antonio & Austin
San Diego
San Francisco
Santa Fe, Taos & Albuquerque
Scandinavia
Scotland
Seattle & Portland
Singapore & Malaysia
South Africa
Southeast Asia
South Pacific
Spain
Sweden
Switzerland
Thailand
Tokyo
Toronto
Tuscany & Umbria
USA
Utah
Vancouver & Victoria
Vermont, New Hampshire
  & Maine
Vienna & the Danube Valley
Virgin Islands
Virginia
Walt Disney World &
  Orlando
Washington, D.C.
Washington State

FROMMER'S® DOLLAR-A-DAY GUIDES

Australia from $50 a Day
California from $60 a Day
Caribbean from $70 a Day
England from $70 a Day
Europe from $60 a Day

Florida from $60 a Day
Hawaii from $70 a Day
Ireland from $60 a Day
Italy from $70 a Day
London from $85 a Day

New York from $80 a Day
Paris from $85 a Day
San Francisco from $60 a Day
Washington, D.C.,
  from $60 a Day

FROMMER'S® PORTABLE GUIDES

Acapulco, Ixtapa &
  Zihuatanejo
Alaska Cruises & Ports of Call
Bahamas
Baja & Los Cabos
Berlin
California Wine Country
Charleston & Savannah
Chicago

Dublin
Hawaii: The Big Island
Las Vegas
London
Maine Coast
Maui
New Orleans
New York City
Paris

Puerto Vallarta, Manzanillo
  & Guadalajara
San Diego
San Francisco
Sydney
Tampa & St. Petersburg
Venice
Washington, D.C.

FROMMER'S® NATIONAL PARK GUIDES

Family Vacations in the National Parks
Grand Canyon

National Parks of the American West
Rocky Mountain

Yellowstone & Grand Teton
Yosemite & Sequoia/ Kings Canyon
Zion & Bryce Canyon

FROMMER'S® MEMORABLE WALKS

Chicago
London

New York
Paris

San Francisco
Washington, D.C.

FROMMER'S® GREAT OUTDOOR GUIDES

New England
Northern California

Southern California & Baja
Southern New England

Washington & Oregon

FROMMER'S® BORN TO SHOP GUIDES

Born to Shop: China
Born to Shop: France

Born to Shop: Italy
Born to Shop: London

Born to Shop: New York
Born to Shop: Paris

FROMMER'S® IRREVERENT GUIDES

Amsterdam
Boston
Chicago
Las Vegas

London
Los Angeles
Manhattan
New Orleans

Paris
San Francisco
Seattle & Portland
Vancouver

Walt Disney World
Washington, D.C.

FROMMER'S® BEST-LOVED DRIVING TOURS

America
Britain
California

Florida
France
Germany

Ireland
Italy
New England

Scotland
Spain
Western Europe

THE UNOFFICIAL GUIDES®

Bed & Breakfasts in California
Bed & Breakfasts in New England
Bed & Breakfasts in the Northwest
Beyond Disney
Branson, Missouri
California with Kids
Chicago

Cruises
Disneyland
Florida with Kids
Golf Vacations in the Eastern U.S.
The Great Smoky & Blue Ridge Mountains
Inside Disney

Hawaii
Las Vegas
London
Miami & the Keys
Mini Las Vegas
Mini-Mickey
New Orleans
New York City
Paris

Safaris
San Francisco
Skiing in the West
Walt Disney World
Walt Disney World for Grown-ups
Walt Disney World for Kids
Washington, D.C.

SPECIAL-INTEREST TITLES

Frommer's Britain's Best Bed & Breakfasts and Country Inns
Frommer's Britain's Best Bike Rides
The Civil War Trust's Official Guide to the Civil War Discovery Trail
Frommer's Caribbean Hideaways
Frommer's Food Lover's Companion to France
Frommer's Food Lover's Companion to Italy
Frommer's Gay & Lesbian Europe
Frommer's Exploring America by RV
Hanging Out in Europe
Israel Past & Present

Mad Monks' Guide to California
Mad Monks' Guide to New York City
Frommer's The Moon
Frommer's New York City with Kids
The New York Times' Unforgettable Weekends
Places Rated Almanac
Retirement Places Rated
Frommer's Road Atlas Britain
Frommer's Road Atlas Europe
Frommer's Washington, D.C., with Kids
Frommer's What the Airlines Never Tell You